KU-479-206

University of West London BSc (Hons) Nursing Pre-Registration Programme Course Reader

University of West London BSc (Hons) Nursing Pre-Registration Programme Course Reader

Edited by

Melanie Gasston-Hales
Victoria Allen
Phil Davey
Kay Mafuba
Deborah Taylor

Los Angeles | London | New Delhi
Singapore | Washington DC | Melbourne

Los Angeles | London | New Delhi
Singapore | Washington DC | Melbourne

SAGE Publications Ltd
1 Oliver's Yard
55 City Road
London EC1Y 1SP

SAGE Publications Inc.
2455 Teller Road
Thousand Oaks, California 91320

SAGE Publications India Pvt Ltd
B 1/I 1 Mohan Cooperative Industrial Area
Mathura Road
New Delhi 110 044

SAGE Publications Asia-Pacific Pte Ltd
3 Church Street
#10-04 Samsung Hub
Singapore 049483

Editorial arrangement © Melanie
    Gasston-Hales, Victoria Allen,
    Phil Davey, Kay Mafuba,
    Deborah Taylor, 2016

Introduction © Melanie
    Gasston-Hales, 2016
Chapter 1 © Dena Bain Taylor, 2013
Chapter 2 © Dena Bain Taylor, 2013
Chapter 3 © Alex Osmond, 2016
Chapter 4 © Catherine Delves-
    Yates, Karen Elcock, Carol
    Hall, Ruth Northway and Steve
    Trenoweth, 2015.
Chapter 5 © Catherine
    Delves-Yates, 2015.
Chapter 6 © Ruth Northway and
    Robert Jenkins, 2013
Chapter 7 © Ruth Northway and
    Robert Jenkins, 2013
Chapter 8 © Daryl Evans,
    Dina Koutsaftiki, C. Patricia
    Fathers, 2014
Chapter 9 © Jennifer Boore, Neal
    Cook and Andrea Shepherd, 2016
Chapter 10 © Janet Barker, Paul
    Linsley and Ros Kane, 2016

Chapter 11 © Martina O'Brien,
    Alison Spires and Kirsty
    Andrews, 2011
Chapter 12 © Janet Barker, Paul
    Linsley and Ros Kane, 2016
Chapter 13 © Pam Moule, 2015
Chapter 14 © Jackie Green, Keith
    Tones, Ruth Cross and James
    Woodall, 2015
Chapter 15 © Mike Thomas, 2014
Chapter 16 © Graham R. Williamson
    and Andrew Whittaker, 2014
Chapter 17 © Roger Gill, 2011
Chapter 18 © Peter Ellis and Shirley
    Bach, 2015
Chapter 19 © Jill Barr and Lesley
    Dowding 2016
Chapter 20 © Neil Gopee and Jo
    Galloway, 2014
Chapter 21 © David Oliver, 2015
Chapter 22 © Alistair Hewison, 2012
Chapter 23 © Matthew Aldridge, 2012
Chapter 24 © Bob Price and Anne
    Harrington 2016
Chapter 25 © Kath Sharples, 2011
Chapter 26 © Lioba Howatson-
    Jones and Mooi Standing, 2016

First published 2016
Reprinted 2017 (twice)

Apart from any fair dealing for the purposes of research or
private study, or criticism or review, as permitted under the Copyright,
Designs and Patents Act, 1988, this publication may be reproduced, stored
or transmitted in any form, or by any means, only with the prior permission
in writing of the publishers, or in the case of reprographic reproduction, in
accordance with the terms of licences issued by the Copyright Licensing
Agency. Enquiries concerning reproduction outside those terms should be
sent to the publishers.

British Library Cataloguing in Publication data

A catalogue record for this book is available from the British Library

Typeset by: C&M Digitals (P) Ltd, Chennai, India
Printed and bound by Henry Ling Limited, at the
Dorset Press, Dorchester DT1 1HD

ISBN 978-1-4739-9998-5

At SAGE we take sustainability seriously. We print most of our products in the UK. These are produced using FSC papers and boards.
We undertake an annual audit on materials used to ensure that we monitor our sustainability in what we are doing.
When we print overseas, we ensure that sustainable papers are used, as measured by the PREPS grading system.

Contents

Promoting Individual Health

Lifespan Development

Year 2

Nursing Practice and Decision Making 1

Principles of Pharmacology and Medicines Management

Becoming and Effective Professional Practicioner

Introduction to Public Health

Year 3

Research in Practice

Leading and Managing Care Services

Evaluating and Advancing Nursing Practice

Nursing Practice and Decision Making 2

Advanced Nursing Practice

Introduction to the UWL BSc Nursing Course Reader

Welcome to the University of West London, College of Nursing, Midwifery and Healthcare's Course Reader for the BSc (Hons) Nursing pre-registration programme.

The Course Reader is a book comprising a selection of key texts to introduce you to the module content. This provides you with a unique opportunity to prepare yourself in advance for each of your modules, each semester, each year of the course.

There are three sections; the first relating to academic writing skills, the second to the theory modules and finally the third section to practice learning.

Section 1 contains three introductory chapters to academic and professional writing. These chapters will complement what you learn in the Essential Skills for Higher Education module and will provide a quick reference guide for when you are writing your essays and preparing professional or clinical documentation.

Section 2 has been divided by year and by modules, to aid easy navigation of the book to the text you need. Each module has one or two book chapters or articles identified, which will provide an insight into a key theme of the module content. You will notice that for year 2 there is no allocated text for the Understanding Altered Physiology module, this is because a single chapter would not do the pathophysiology of the clinical conditions you will learn about justice.

Section 3 is made up of three chapters, selected to complement the preparation you will receive in advance of your clinical placements and the learning you will undertake when in practice.

I hope you find this book invaluable and wish you all the best in your studies.

Melanie Gasston-Hales
Senior Lecturer in Mental Health
Course Leader BSc (Hons) Mental Health Nursing

Introduction to the UWL BSc Nursing Course Reader

SECTION 1 Academic Writing Skills

Critical Reading and the Iterative Writing Process

Bain Taylor, D.

OVERVIEW

- First questions
  - What have I been asked to write?
  - Who is going to read this?
- The iterative writing process
  - Get ready
  - Analyze the assignment
  - Do the research
  - Active reading and brainstorming
  - Do an outline
  - Write the draft
  - Revise and edit
  - Proofreading

FIRST QUESTIONS

Professional writers make writing seem easy. Think about newspaper columnists or professional bloggers who publish a story every day, month after month, year after year. But any of them will tell you it's not so. Most famously, the American columnist Gene Fowler is widely quoted as saying, 'Writing is easy; all you do is sit staring at a blank sheet of paper until the drops of blood form on your forehead.'

In this chapter, we begin where any professional writer begins, with two questions: *What have I been asked to write?* and *who is going to read this?*

What have I been asked to write?

Broadly speaking, there are two kinds of writing: description and argument.

Within description, there are two main categories: description and narrative. Description paints a picture of something at a particular point in time and space. For example, clinical notes will describe a patient's presenting symptoms and diagnostic tests. Narrative tells a story across time, such as an experience caring for a patient or a midwife's engagement with a family.

'Argument' is a process in which we apply evidence to support an idea. The end goal of argument is to persuade the reader to accept an idea or act in a certain way. There are many methods by which arguments are developed, and you will find a guide to writing an argument in Chapter 5.

A famous American architect once said that 'Form follows function'. His idea was that an architect should base the design of a building on the purpose or function it is being built to accomplish. This is as true of writing as it is of buildings. Each form of writing, or 'genre', has its own conventions and guiding principles around structure and use of language, depending on the purpose of the genre. Ultimately, our professional, academic and research purposes shape our writing practices, which in turn improve our ability to achieve those purposes.

To sum up, the form for any particular document is determined according to our reason for writing it. If our goal is to report on research, we write in a genre called 'research reporting' using a conventional structure known as 'IMRAD' (more on that in Chapter 8). If our goal is to promote healthy behaviours in the community, we use the genre of 'health education' – materials such as brochures, posters, websites and social media (see Chapter 9). If our goal is to become reflective practitioners, we engage in a genre called 'reflective writing' (see Chapter 11).

Your course instructors will set a wide variety of assignments throughout your program, with several purposes in mind:

- to teach you the forms of writing that are most common in their particular field;
- to help you learn, by asking you to express in writing, the central ideas and facts taught by the course; in other words, your papers have an **evaluative function**; the instructor wants to judge 'how well is this person doing on my course?' and will express the answer as a grade;
- to teach you how to read beyond the course materials and to learn how to read these sources critically (more about that later) – that is, they have a **formative function**: by encouraging you to engage with what others have written, you learn to think more deeply about and engage with your professional community.

So you will be asked to undertake many types of writing that may be new to you, including but not limited to the following:

- literature reviews (such as an annotated bibliography, summary and critique, evidence-based report, or comprehensive review);
- clinical writing (such as clinical portfolios, practice guidelines and interventions, case history and pathophysiology);
- communication in practice settings (such as emails, memos and letters, briefing notes, applications and CVs or résumés);
- reflective writing (such as journals, narratives, personal statements);
- research papers (such as about the history, theory, and ethics of nursing);
- community health promotion and advocacy (such as brochures, websites, social media).

All of these genres are covered in later chapters.

Who is going to read this?

By 'audience', we mean the person or people who will be reading what you wrote. Writing is such a solitary endeavour that it is easy to forget there is a reader on the other end. But you are not writing in a vacuum – someone is out there who does not know what you know, and who will think or act on the basis of what you say. You mediate between the information and what your reader needs to know or be persuaded of. This means everything you write must be clear and persuasive to that audience. In other words, any piece of writing needs to be consciously directed toward its intended audience.

Your audience may be one individual or many. In your professional career, you will need to communicate persuasively with a wide variety of audiences, including your patients and the general public, your professional colleagues in your own and other health fields, health care managers and administrators, government and regulatory bodies, community agencies, and many others.

Based on who their audience is, writers make important choices about form, content, organization, and vocabulary. Here are some questions about audience to consider:

- How large is my audience? Is it an individual or a group (e.g., health team or organization) or the general public?
- What is my relation to the reader? (e.g., am I writing a paper to get a grade in a course? Am I explaining to teenagers why they shouldn't smoke cigarettes? Am I applying for a position? Am I asking a funding agency for a grant?)
- Am I speaking to my reader for myself or on behalf of a group or organization?
- Is my reader expecting this piece of writing? (e.g., is this a course instructor who's asked for this and is going to read it fully and carefully? Or is this a busy administrator or politician I've sent an unsolicited proposal to?)

- How important is my message to the reader? (i.e., how hard will I have to work to get and retain their attention?)
- What does my audience need or want to know?
- What does my audience already know? (i.e., how much do I have to explain to them?)
- What is the reader likely to do with what I've written? (i.e., will they use it as the basis for some decision, such as funding? Will they use it as the basis for some action, such as introducing a new intervention? Will it change their behaviours, such as adopting safe sexual practices?)
- What is the audience's level of general literacy (i.e., what level of vocabulary, tone and diction will the reader understand and respond to?)
- What is the reader's level of health literacy? (i.e., how much medical terminology can I use without defining or simplifying the language?)

THE ITERATIVE WRITING PROCESS

Broadly speaking, the writing process involves the following stages:

- defining the audience, purpose, and form;
- research and organizing/outlining;
- drafting;
- revising for accuracy and style;
- preparing the presentation copy.

Writing is an 'iterative' process; in other words, it involves multiple repetitions of the same process. Each repetition is called an 'iteration' and the end-point of one iteration serves as the start of the next. The iterative process repeats until the desired goal is reached. In writing, the individual iterations combine reading, thinking, writing, and revising. The early iterations consist largely of reading and thinking, with some writing; the latter stages involve some supplementary reading but consist primarily of writing and revising. All iterations involve a lot of intense thinking.

When we go through periods of intense thinking and cognitive activity such as higher education requires, our brains respond in physical ways. The brain is plastic, meaning that particular activities done intensely and/or repetitively will cause changes in the network of neurons. The connections (synapses) between neurons change – new connections are made, existing ones are strengthened or weakened (or broken altogether). In other words, links between ideas are made stronger or weaker such that thinking of one thing will be more or less likely to draw along the other connected idea. This is why, after years of study and writing, our ability to think analytically and efficiently is improved. However, it also means that after individual sessions of study and writing, we may feel tired. The brain needs time to accommodate itself to the new architecture it has constructed and to absorb all its new knowledge and ways of thinking.

Step 1: get ready

- Prepare your writing space. Clear away other projects and lay out the research materials you are starting with.
- For long or multi-section assignments, break the whole task down into stages and assign feasible deadlines for completing each stage.
- Decide on a writing schedule. The 'gold standard' of writing advice is to work on an assignment daily over a period of weeks. And it is true that it is more productive to work for an hour each day than to work for seven hours once a week. This is because long gaps between writing sessions interrupt the thinking process and you have to waste time getting back into it. It's what we all aspire to, and you will find variations of this in any guide to writing (including a number I myself have written). The reality, though, is that it's mainly professional writers and editors like the people who produce these guides who actually have the time to write every day and space assignments out over a period of weeks. Here's what one graduate student in the health professions had to say:

the wise advice of taking little nibbles daily seems never to apply for me. I tend to binge-write based on current academic, clinical, family, and work commitments. Then get really sick a few times and it's game-over. To my endless entertainment I have a book that describes how to manage research in the 'one bite at a time' fashion ... but I haven't read it through yet ... didn't find time!

Do try, though, to work out a schedule that allows you, if not to distribute your writing time widely, at least not to get sick from stress and overwork!

Step 2: analyze the assignment

- Carefully analyze the assignment. Underline or highlight key words and phrases.
- Ask yourself how this topic fits into the overall subject of the course. For example, does it require you to go into depth for a part of the material already covered in class? Does it ask you to apply a theory from the course to an example from your practice experience? An essay assignment expects you to use the concepts and ways of thinking that the course is trying to teach.
- How long is the assignment? Take careful note of the required length. Often instructors will not read anything beyond what they've asked for. (There is a reason for this: it's to prepare you for the professional world, where this is the norm.)

- What kind of paper is this? Does it ask you to integrate theory, research and/or practice? Does it ask you to pick an issue and write about it? Are you going to be interviewing anyone? Will you be incorporating your own life experience, either one in the past or from your current practice?
- Take note of any specific guidelines on how much research outside course readings the assignment asks for.
- Decide how you will focus the topic of the paper. For example, from the broad topic of 'diabetes' you could take any of these directions, depending on which is appropriate to the course:
  o epidemiology of diabetes;
  o the influence of social determinants of health on diabetes;
  o disease management;
  o the illness experience of the patient/family;
  o diabetes management in an acute vs. a home setting;
  o biophysical effects of drug therapy vs. quality-of-life effects of drug therapy.

Step 3: do the research

What kind of sources are you being asked to use? There are a number of types of 'literature' and you may be asked to draw on any or all of them. Most often, though, you will be asked to use articles from 'scholarly journals', also called 'peer-reviewed', 'refereed' or 'academic'. Peer-reviewed means the journal has a policy of having experts in the field evaluate an article before accepting it for publication. How do you know if that's the case? Most (but not all) peer-reviewed journals are listed, by title, in databases such as Ulrich's Periodicals Directory Online. If you don't find the journal listed in Ulrich's:

- Look at the editorial page, where you will find guidelines for authors wanting to submit an article – if the journal uses a peer-review process, it will say there.
- Look for information about the author on the first or last page of an article – he or she should be affiliated with a university or research organization. Be aware, though, that scholarly authors often write to inform the wider public about their research or ideas, so authorship doesn't always mean an article is scholarly.
- The length of the article is also a clue – longer articles (more than ten pages) are usually scholarly.
- Are there a lot of references in the article, at least ten? Some have as many as 100. As you become familiar with the names of scholarly journals and authors, are you seeing these names in the reference list?
- In many library catalogue systems, the initial search page includes a checkbox limiting the search to scholarly/peer reviewed

journals. If you check the box, search results will include only citations to scholarly articles.

- For your search, choose a database that is a major source of scholarly articles, such as MEDLINE or CINAHL or even Google Scholar. Google itself is *not* a reliable way to find scholarly articles. Neither is Wikipedia.

Table 3.1 breaks down the main types of literature and how you might be asked to use them.

For further reading

Cornell University Libraries, Olin & Kris Library. *Distinguishing scholarly journals from other periodicals.* Available at http://olinuris.library.cornell.edu/ref/research/skill20.html

Lederer, N. *Evaluation clues for articles found on the web or in library databases.* Colorado State University Libraries. Available at http://lib.colostate.edu/howto/evalclues.html

Lederer, N. *Popular magazines vs. trade magazines vs. scholarly journals.* Colorado State University Libraries. Available at http://lib.colostate.edu/howto/poplr.html

New York Academy of Medicine. *Grey literature page.* Available at: http://www.nyam.org/library/grey.shtml

Staines, G.M., Johnson, K. & Bonacci, M. (2008) 'Scholarly and popular literature: Making the comparison' in *Social Sciences Research: Research, Writing, and Presentation Strategies for Students* (2nd ed.). Lanham, MD: Scarecrow Press., p. 9.

Weintraub, I. (2006) *The role of grey literature in the sciences.* ACCESS: Brooklyn College Library and AIT E-zine, 10. Available at: http://library.brooklyn.cuny.edu.access/greyliter.htm

Finding the sources

Often it is very helpful to start with Wikipedia, just to get general information about your topic and some starting definitions. For example, for a paper on the history of nursing, you can find an overview of Florence Nightingale's life and times. You can also follow the links at the bottom to sources you can check to see if they are primary (e.g., her diaries) or more scholarly, which you can use for your paper.

Now you are ready to start the serious research. Start with the course readings, and use their reference lists and keywords (located below the title and author information in journal articles) to find more sources. Then use the reference list of each new article as a source to find other articles. Literature review articles and systematic reviews are a great source.

Take note of authors whose names keep turning up – they are likely to be the most important authors on the topic. You'll also see the names of major research institutions repeatedly, such as the Centers for Disease Control and Prevention (CDC).

The next step is to search electronic databases. Consult both general databases like Google Scholar and specialized databases such as Medline, PubMed, CINAHL, Ovid, or the Cochrane Library. The most useful professional index is likely to be MEDLINE (most comprehensive of the approximately 20 health-related databases of Medlar – Medical

Table 3.1 Types of literature

	Scholarly	Professional	Grey	Primary	Popular
Type of publication	Scholarly journals, articles, and books that are usually 'peer-reviewed' or 'refereed' (see below)	Trade and industry journals; professional college guidelines on standards of care, competencies, etc.	1. Reports, government documents, statistical reports, newsletters, bulletins, mission and policy statements; health promotion materials, fact sheets 2. The word 'grey' has nothing to do with quality or colour –it is a name originally given by librarians to reflect the challenge of cataloguing these materials	1. In social sciences and humanities, 'primary' refers to original source material that is closest to the person, period, or idea being studied. 'Secondary' refers to writings about the original sources. (NOTE: In sciences, 'primary' is used to mean peer-reviewed original research published in scientific and scholarly journals. 'Secondary' generally refers to review articles.)	1. Magazines, newspapers, general interest websites 2. Wikipedia and other 'wikis'
Published by	1. Academic institutions (e.g., a university) 2. Organizations that perform original research (e.g., WHO, CDC) 3. Commercial publishers (e.g., Sage)	1. Professional or occupational groups and organizations 2. Regulatory bodies (e.g., RNA, CNA, ANA)	1. Government agencies, research centres, universities, public institutions, non-profit organizations, and associations and societies 2. NOT commercial publishers	May or may not be a published item; can be an artifact, document, recording, video, etc. Health promotion posters and pamphlets would also be considered primary sources	1. Commercial publishers 2. Online community of contributors

(Continued)

Table 3.1 (Continued)

	Scholarly	Professional	Grey	Primary	Popular
Purpose	1. To disseminate scholarly knowledge and research 2. The major venue of communication for the science community to present results of current research to colleagues and students	To disseminate professional standards, news about the profession, professional trends, or editorial comment on the profession	1. To provide scholars, professionals and lay readers alike with research summaries, facts, statistics, codes and standards, and other data related to the expertise of the publishing organization 2. To disseminate current information to a wide audience		1. To entertain and inform the public or particular segments of the public 2. To make money for the publisher
Audience	Scholars, researchers, students	Professionals and practitioners within the field	Scholars, professionals and the general public	N/A	General public or a targeted demographic, e.g., golfers or pet owners
Subject matter	Narrow and specific topics related to research, theory or practice in the health and social sciences. Normally consist of an abstract, keywords, introduction, methods, results, discussion, acknowledgments and references	Specific topics relevant to the profession	A wide variety of topics	A wide variety of topics	A broad range of general interest topics intended to entertain and inform, to sell products, or promote a viewpoint

	Scholarly	Professional	Grey	Primary	Popular
Articles written by	Expert researchers with a) academic credentials (e.g., PhD) b) professional credentials (e.g., RN, MD) c) institutional affiliation (e.g., a university or research institute)	Experts on the topic with a) professional credentials such as RN b) institutional affiliation (e.g., a health centre, government, or professional body)	Experts within the organization	A person with direct knowledge of a situation, or a document, etc. created by such a person	1. Popular press: staff or free-lance writers. They may be experts on the topic, or have no prior knowledge at all. Articles often unsigned 2. Wikis (Wikipedia): Anyone. May or may not be an expert; entries can be incomplete or inaccurate
How articles are chosen	Usually go through a formal 'peer-review' process where experts in the field evaluate articles before they are accepted for publication	May be peer-reviewed or may be commissioned by the editor	May be peer-reviewed	N/A	1. Editor decides a topic is timely and assigns a writer OR a writer proposes a topic to an editor 2. Anyone can contribute but the best wikis (such as Wikipedia) enforce ethical and editorial guidelines and rank the accuracy and completeness of entries

(Continued)

Table 3.1 (Continued)

	Scholarly	Professional	Grey	Primary	Popular
Ratio of text to graphics	1. Heavily text-oriented. Articles can be long and dense. Graphic material usually confined to tables and figures 2. Journals usually have plain covers and paper	Heavily text-oriented with tables and graphs, but may also include photos, e.g., of professional events	Usually heavily text-oriented	Highly variable, from fully textual to fully graphic	1. Articles usually brief 2. Glossy paper and colour illustrations 3. Heavy use of creative visuals
Kind of language used	Highly technical and specific to the scholarly field; assumes the reader has the relevant technical background to understand, so there is little explanation of terms	Technical language of the field	Ranges from highly specialized to general	Highly variable	Geared to a wide audience; often no specialty or background knowledge is assumed; language can be very simple or may assume a certain level of education
Funded by	Academic or research institutions; government and other agency grants	1. Professional memberships 2. Advertising	Government or organizational funding	N/A	Sales and advertising revenues
Some important characteristics	1. They always cite sources (at least ten) 2. Reference lists cite other scholars 3. Affiliations of authors listed on the first or last page	1. May cite sources, but not usually as many as scholarly sources 2. Often contain advertising relevant to the occupation	1. Often lack the bibliographic control of scholarly sources, so basic information such as author, publication date or publishing body may not be provided 2. Little or no advertising	Often stored in archives, but may be digitized by the collection that holds the archive and available electronically	1. Do not cite original sources 2. Information may be second or third hand 3. Contain as much advertising as they can sell

	Scholarly	Professional	Grey	Primary	Popular
	4. Most don't include advertising, with some exceptions such as *Science* or *Nature* 5. many are listed in Ulrich's *Periodicals Directory*				
Examples	• *JAMA (Journal of the American Medical Association)* • *Journal of Maternal Child Nursing*	• *Nursing and Midwifery Council Code* • *Registered Nurse Journal*	Publications by • WHO or CDC • HMSO in UK • GPO in US • Queen's Printer in Canada • AGPS in Australia	Personal papers of historical persons such as Florence Nightingale	• *Today's Parent* • *Scientific American* • *Psychology Today*
Use for	1. Your main source for course papers 2. Important source for research and theory	Important for codes, guidelines and practice standards	1. Excellent for facts, statistics and other information or data to give a comprehensive view of the topic 2. As a supplement to scholarly journal literature	To give historical context	1. Only use in special circumstances such as a media analysis 2. Wikipedia is a great starting point for an overview of a topic or a definition. Use the reference list at the end of the entry to find some beginning research materials. But Wikipedia is NOT an acceptable source itself, just an entry point for research

Literature Analysis and Retrieval System). The other essential database for nursing students is CINAHL (Cumulative Index to Nursing and Allied Health Literature). Many college and university libraries offer workshops or online tutorials on how to search these.

Searches of electronic databases may produce a large number of results, even after you have narrowed your search with keywords and Boolean operators (such as 'and'/'or'). At this point, scanning the titles and reading abstracts will help you narrow further still until you get the number you need.

Not all sources are found in electronic databases, though. Some of your sources will be primary, such as the mission statements of your practice setting, or newspaper articles raising issues in health care.

Very important tip: Make up a bibliographic entry before reading a source. After reading, go back and add a few words to say what you might use it for. This saves time later when you are under stress to meet your deadline: 1. You will not forget you've read something and go find it again; 2. You will not have to spend time constructing your reference list because you can just copy-and-paste.

Step 4: active reading and brainstorming

There are two types of reading: **content** and **critical**. We read for content when we want to know how to assemble a piece of furniture, or what the statistics were on coronary disease in 1998. Content reading means reading for information. It employs what we call 'closed thinking'.

Critical reading means reading for idea and argument. We read critically when we want to make judgments about *how* a text is argued and what that argument is. It employs what we call 'open thinking'.

There is also a difference between **passive** reading and **active** reading. We read magazines or social media passively, sitting still as we absorb the content of one article or item and move on to the next. But when we read in order to write, the process becomes active. We physically engage with the material by writing on it and making notes about it. We integrate the activities of thinking and writing into the reading process. It is slower, of course, than passive reading but in fact, over the arc of writing the paper, we save time because we've been building written text right from the start.

The active reading process

- If there is an abstract, read it first to gain a good summary understanding of the article.
- Skim through the article, especially the introduction and conclusion, just to see the names of headings and get a sense of the article's structure. You'll also get a sense of which of the sections will be most relevant for your topic.
- Read the article right through once or twice passively, until you feel you have a good understanding of its contents. Never start copying sentences or passages that look useful without reading the article right through at least once. This is because writers will typically make the same point in a

variety of positions in the article, from different perspectives or in relation to different evidence. It's better to wait until you identify these different iterations of the point and can summarize or paraphrase them using words of your own, rather than just passively copying.

- Pick up a pen or highlighter. Go through the article carefully to underline, bracket or highlight key words, concepts, phrases or sentences. Engage with the material by making marginal notations or jotting down ideas/questions/points related to topic. Pay particular attention to the first sentences of sections and paragraphs – it is in these 'topic sentences' that writers state directly what point is about to be made.
- Read for understanding of their ideas and evidence, as well as to spark your own thoughts and questions about the article and your topic.
- A tip on reading research studies: if you have never taken a course on statistics or research design, skip over the 'Analysis' section that describes the statistical tests the researcher(s) performed to validate their results and establish that they are 'significant'. The significant results are then talked about in the Discussion section.

The second stage of active reading is 'brainstorming', which is a form of free associative writing in which you write down any and all thoughts that occur to you about your paper and the sources. Brainstorming can be done anywhere, even on public transit on the way to school or your practice setting. Don't worry about quality – go for quantity. You can't know whether an idea will turn out to be useful or not, so just get it all down. If you typically suffer from writer's block at the sight of a blank computer screen or paper, you'll find brainstorming especially helpful. No longer will you be starting your draft with that paralyzing blank screen or paper in front of you.

Very important tip: Reading articles in this way is time-consuming and therefore can create stress. Unfortunately, you need to spend extra time learning how to read articles when you are in the early stages of a program. Don't despair – you will get faster at it as you build your knowledge base.

Step 5: do an outline

Whether you are a 'linear' or an 'organic' writer (see Step 6 below), never be tempted to skip the outline stage and jump into writing the draft. The outline is the skeleton of your paper – it's not something you can build in retroactively. A linear writer might prefer a detailed outline, while an organic writer might prefer a sketch of the main points. Whatever kind of outline you prefer, take the time to organize your thoughts and write one.

- What does an outline do?
  - o keeps you on topic;
  - o helps you avoid repetition of ideas or evidence;

- ○ allows you to check the logic of your argument;
- ○ allows you to see if you've addressed all parts of the assignment;
- ○ it's an easy way to see if you've handled the topic adequately or need more points;
- ○ makes writing the draft much easier;
- ○ allows you to develop and refine your thesis (if there is one);
- ○ makes it easy to write your abstract or executive summary (if there is one);
- ○ allows a professor/colleague/friend to comment and advise you on your work-in-progress. Instructors rarely have time to look at drafts, but many will look at an outline.

Q. How many sections should my paper have?
A. It depends

You will always have an introduction and a conclusion, but the number of sections in the body of your paper will vary. Take a look at the assignment instructions: if the instructor lists specific sections she or he wants, that's how many sections you will have. In this case, you are likely to use section headings (see Chapter 6). Use the instructor's wording for the headings.

If it is an assignment that asks you to discuss a topic within any structure you choose, the answer depends on how many main points you have. There is no 'correct' number, but most people seem most comfortable with having three main points – perhaps it has to do with the primordial human desire for stories that have a beginning, a middle, and an end. You are less likely to use section headings for this kind of paper.

Q. How long should each section be?
A. Just as long as it needs to be

There's a common misconception that every section should be the same length. However, some main points take longer to cover than others. Perhaps there's more evidence to include, or it's a more complicated point, or it's the most important one.

Q. Do I always include a thesis statement? What is a thesis anyway?

'Thesis' is a word left over from the days when Classical Greek rhetoric was a standard part of education systems around the English-speaking world. It is just a way of saying that any piece of writing has to have a sentence (or two or three) that tells the reader what your topic is and what you've got to say about it. That is, it introduces a paper by giving a very brief summary of the content and central idea. I might say:

> Midwifery is the best health profession in the world.

That is not good enough, but it does the minimum – my topic is midwifery and I say it's a terrific profession. The problem is, it is not a provable statement. 'Best' is a relative term – what's best for a low-risk pregnancy is not what is best for a high-risk pregnancy, which would involve a team of health professionals. A good thesis makes a limited claim and also summarizes the main points that support it. For example:

> Midwifery is the best option for low-risk pregnancies because research has shown it results in lower maternity care costs, reduced mortality and morbidity related to caesarean and other interventions, lower intervention rates, and fewer recovery complications. (Schlenzka, 1999)

For further reading

Schlenzka, P. (1999). Safety of alternative approaches to childbirth (Doctoral dissertation). Department of Social Work and Sociology, Ferrum College. Cited at http://www.americanpregnancy.org/labornbirth/midwives.html

Sample outline 1: linear outline of an undergraduate nursing dissertation: linear structure

Thesis statement:

> This dissertation analyzes the care of a critically ill child integrating two modules: Caring for the Critically Ill Child (FC3D021) and Professional and Management Issues within Child Health (FC3D022). It will demonstrate an understanding of issues that arise during the care of a critically ill child and his family for Meningococcal Septicaemia (MS), along with management issues such as accountability and frameworks for assessment, and will relate theory and its research to practice.

Introduction:

a. Overview of the dissertation chapters

b. Overview of sources:

   –evidence-based research, theory, legislation, policies 1989–present

   –databases used: CINAHL, Cochrane, SIGN, NICE, DoH, NMC, HPA

Chapter 1: Meningococcal Septicaemia

a. Epidemiology

   –definition

   –prevalence

      –0.5–5 cases per 100,000 population per year worldwide (Milonovich, 2007)

      –higher during winter (SIGN, 2008)

      –25% have previous upper respiratory infection (Hart, 2006)

   –incidence

   –morbidity

   –mortality

b. Pathophysiology

   -Meningococci invade = endotoxin = binding protein = activation of macrophages

      -increased vascular permeability

      -pathological vasoconstriction and vasodilation

      -intravascular thrombosis

      -myocardial dysfunction (Pathan et al., 2003)

   -causes

      -absence of bactericidal antibodies

      -predisposing factors

   -clinical signs and symptoms

      -peticheal rash

      -compensated and uncompensated shock

      -leg pain, cold hands and feet

      -altered mental state, irritability, confusion

   -long term effects

      -circulatory failure and septic shock (Donovan, 2010)

      -organ damage, loss of limbs and skin necrosis (NICE, 2010)

      -emotional: nightmares, enuresis and temper tantrums

Chapter 2: Nursing care of the critically ill child

a. Assessment

   -ABCDE: Airways, Breathing, Circulation, Disability and Exposure

   -obtaining consent (NMC, 2008) (DoH, 2009) (WAG, 2010)

b. Stabilization

   -aggressive resuscitation and stabilization

   -monitoring for deterioration: PEWS

   -importance of close monitoring

c. Treatment

   -intravenous ceftriaxone (NICE, 2010)

   -blood cultures and meningococcal PCR (SIGN, 2008)

   -lumbar puncture if not contraindicated

d. Use of guidelines:

    –Paediatric Early Warning Tools (PEWS)

Chapter 3: Family-centred care (FCC)

a. Definition

    –in health/nursing policies (DoH, 2003) (Haines, 2005) (Moorey, 2010)

b. Continuum scale changes

    –five-part practice continuum tool (Coleman, 2003)

c. Advantages of family presence during invasive procedures

    –parental needs and empowerment

    –sense of closure/grieving process (Cottle et al., 2008)

    –study of nurse perspectives (Perry, 2009)

d. Disadvantages

    –health and safety/risk management

    –may prolong or impede procedures

    –stress for nurses

Chapter 4: The nursing role

a. Clinical governance

    –accountability

    –guidelines

    –competencies

b. Benchmarking

    –six generic skills in caring for the critically ill child

    –current lack of benchmarking

Conclusion

    –summary of dissertation

    –recommendations re

        –universal vaccinaton

        –health education

        –adoption of PEWS

        –role of FCC in critical care

        –adoption of benchmarking

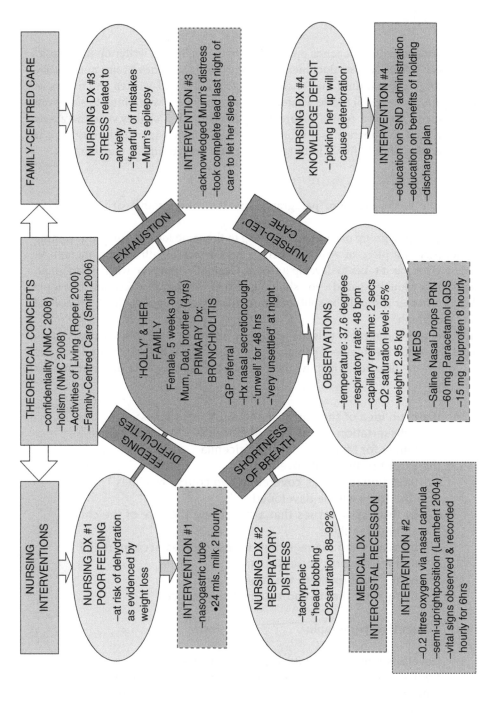

Figure 3.1 Sample outline 2: Concept map of an undergraduate nursing dissertation

Step 6: write the draft

How you write your draft depends on whether you are a 'linear' writer or an 'organic' writer. Linear writers write a document from start to finish. They prefer not to leave a sentence or paragraph until they're comfortable that it's well-written and makes its point. Organic writers will tackle whatever section they have something to say about at that moment. Maybe a course lecture has sparked an idea, or they've found a new article they want to integrate as a source. They build their paper until most of it is written; then they shift to linear writing to make sure everything fits together.

Crafting your paragraphs

If the outline is the skeleton, paragraphs are the muscles that drive the paper forward.

A paragraph is a group of sentences relating to the same idea or topic and forming a distinct part of a piece of writing. There is no 'correct' length for a paragraph. It should be as long as it takes to develop its topic. Generally, however, when a paragraph exceeds a page (double-spaced), you should question whether it covers only one topic or idea, or whether it should be split into more than one paragraph. There are several types of paragraph.

Introductory paragraph: tells the reader the following things. In the dissertation example above, the introductory paragraph functions as a thesis statement. Here, I've broken down its ideas to show how the paragraph introduces the dissertation as a whole:

- the main idea of the paper or section it introduces;
    o a dissertation on the care of a critically ill child and his family for Meningococcal Septicemia
- the extent or limits of coverage;
    o based on materials covered in two course modules
- how the topic will be developed;
    o by discussing issues that arise during the care of the child and his family
    o by discussing management issues such as accountability and frameworks for assessment
- the writer's approach to the topic;
    o by relating theory and research to practice.

Body (substantive) paragraph:

- Develops one idea and its supporting evidence.
- Contributes the substance of ideas and information. Most paragraphs are substantive: they develop the argument and deliver the evidence.
- There is no 'correct' length for substantive paragraphs but they are usually three sentences or more but less than a double-spaced page.

Transitional (non-substantive) paragraph:

- Provides a bridge from one section of a paper to another.
- May be as short as only one sentence.
- Ties together what the reader has read so far and what is to come.
- Can be positioned as the concluding paragraph of a section and offer a brief summary of the section.
- Can also be positioned as the introductory paragraph of a new section and offer a preview of its structure and argument.
- Does not contribute any substance to the argument, but functions to move the argument forward.

Concluding paragraph:

- Restates briefly the main ideas of the section or paper.
- Often moves the reader to consider upcoming sections, or may recommend future research or practice.

Types of sentences in paragraphs

Topic sentence:

- Usually the first sentence but may be the second.
- Announces the topic of the paragraph.

Supporting sentences:

- Present facts, reasons, examples, definitions, comparisons, or other evidence to support the central idea of the paragraph.

Concluding sentence:

- Usually the last sentence but may come second-last.
- Sums up the discussion, emphasizes the main point, restates key words of the topic sentence.

Transitional sentence:

- The first (or last) sentence of a paragraph may be a transitional sentence that creates a link to the previous (or next) paragraph.
- Moves the reader from the topic of one paragraph to the topic of the next.

A good paragraph will have **unity** (develops only one idea or point), **coherence** (moves smoothly and logically), and **emphasis** (sentences and words positioned for maximum clarity and impact).

Unity: Means that everything in the paragraph is included to advance one idea or point. Anything that doesn't advance the paragraph's topic should be cut out. The opening sentence (often call the 'topic sentence') tells the reader what the paragraph is about. The middle sentences expand and develop that idea, and the last sentence ties it all up. No extra ideas are introduced and every sentence contributes to the purpose of the paragraph.

Coherence: To be coherent, a paragraph must satisfy several criteria:

a)   relevance: every idea relates to the topic;
b)   effective order: ideas are arranged in a way that clarifies their logic and/or importance;
c)   inclusiveness: nothing vital to the reader's understanding is omitted.

Related to coherence is the stylistic principle of 'flow': the explicit linking words and similarities of grammatical pattern that link sentence to sentence (e.g., repeating key words, using parallel structures). Remember, no matter how clear the connections are to you as a writer, they will not be clear to the reader if they aren't expressed on the page.

Emphasis: This refers to the positioning of important ideas and words for maximum clarity and impact. Emphasis is discussed in detail in Chapter 4.

Step 7: revise and edit

To 'revise' means to 're-vision' – literally, to 're-see' at the **macro level** of overall content, organization, argument, and weight of supporting evidence.

To 'edit' means to sharpen or polish a document. Editing takes place systematically at the **micro level**. At the editing stage, you are attending to the details of language, format, and mechanics:

- **Use of language** refers to word choice, tone, point of view, and logical flow.
- **Format** refers to the physical appearance and arrangement of the document – for example, margin size, font and font size, page numbering, tables and figures, and headings.
- **Mechanics** refers to grammar, punctuation, syntax (sentence structure), spelling, and lack of typographical errors.

A checklist for revision and editing

Structure

- What is the organizing pattern (structure) of your document?
- Does your introduction clearly preview the organizing pattern of your document?
- Does your paper deal with all aspects outlined in the introduction?

- Is your paper broken down into manageable sections which are 'signposted' for your reader (by section headings or topic sentences)?
- Do all parts of your paper flow logically from one to the next with ideas in an appropriate sequence?
- Does the conclusion comprehensively summarize the main points of the paper? Does it offer an evaluation, interpretation, application, or sense of the relevance of your topic? If asked for, does the conclusion include recommendations? Or is it just a generalized statement (such as, 'and therefore midwifery is an important health profession')?

Content

- Reread your draft with your original purpose in mind and ask yourself whether your paper says what you intended it to say and includes all the information that a reader would need.
- Does your document establish common ground with the reader (i.e., explain to the readers why they should care about the problem or issue you've introduced)?
- Does your paper convey a thesis (main argument)?
- Does it identify a significant key issue or issues?
- Does it give a thorough analysis of the key issue's relevant aspects?
- Is your argument convincing because your ideas are fully explained and your arguments are proved by supporting evidence?
- Is there any evidence of unwarranted assumptions or bias that distorts your conclusion?
- Are all your conclusions supported and justified by the evidence?
- Does your argument avoid relying on opinion or generalization?
- Do you substantiate your argument with references to appropriate authorities in the literature?

Style

Check paragraph construction

- Are your paragraphs adequately developed to support your main ideas?
- Are there too many ideas in any paragraph?
- Is there a new paragraph each time there is a shift in topic?
- Are there adequate links/transitions between paragraphs?

Check sentence construction

- Can each sentence be understood on the first reading?
- Are any sentences too short or overly simple?
- Are any sentences too long and complex, with bits awkwardly tacked on or intrusively embedded?
- Is the order of words in any sentence inverted, with the result that the sentence is illogical or difficult to understand?
- Does every sentence coherently follow on from the one before?
- Have you avoided sentence fragments? Run-on sentences? Comma splices? (See the grammar tips in Chapter 4.)

Check the language

- Have you used concrete and specific words rather than abstractions whenever possible?
- Are all your words used correctly and unambiguously?
- Are technical words used appropriately and defined where necessary?
- Have you avoided 'elegant variation' and used terminology consistently so that your reader is never puzzled by varied terminology?
- Have you avoided clichés and language that is too informal?

Mechanics

- Are there any grammar or syntax (sentence structure) errors?
- Are there any punctuation errors?
- Are there any spelling errors? A note on spelling: computerized spell-checkers are a useful tool, but must be supplemented by a careful search of the document. Computerized checkers will not catch homophones (*there, their, they're*) or an incorrect spelling that results in a different but legitimate word (*from, form*).
- Are there any typographical errors?
- Are all reference citations correctly formatted?

When you are in the draft or revision stages, it's always helpful to get feedback from a reader:

- From your professor or marker – take advantage of office hours and extra tutorials.
- From the writing centre at your college or university – take advantage of these highly trained, very sympathetic, expert readers.
- From family and classmates – an objective eye is always helpful. If they don't understand your point, you aren't being clear enough.

Step 8: proofreading

Proofreading the final copy is an important part of the writing process. It requires a lot of concentration and should not be left for, say, 3 am when the assignment is due at 9 am.

To 'proofread' means to ensure that the final, submitted version is completely free of any minor formatting and mechanical errors. It also means ensuring consistency in formatting and mechanics. Especially in long documents (such as a dissertation), it is difficult for the writer to remember that on p. 3 a numbered list was formatted using (1), whereas the numbered list on p. 18 is formatted using 1.

Although some proofreading can be done on your electronic copy of the document, you will need to print out a hard copy to mark up, even if you will be submitting in electronic form.

The challenge in proofreading is maintaining a level of meticulous attention to detail, and keeping the mind focused on individual letters and marks rather than reading to follow the content. Here are some techniques that many writers find helpful:

- Each time you go through the document, read with a single purpose: spelling, punctuation, numbering, heading style, layout of tables and figures, or consistent use of key terms.
- Place a ruler beneath each line as you examine it to keep your eyes from wandering down the page.
- Move up the page from the bottom line to the top.
- Read the document from back to front.
- Read the document aloud to yourself or a colleague who is following a duplicate copy.
- Ask a colleague to proofread for you in exchange for proofreading something of theirs; proofread one final time when you get the paper back.
- Once you find an error or inconsistency in the hard copy, use the find-and-replace function of your electronic file to seek out all other instances of the error.

As someone once said, the only good paper is a done one. Congratulations – you are ready to submit!

An Introduction to Professional Writing

Bain Taylor, D.

ACADEMIC VERSUS PROFESSIONAL WRITING

In this chapter, we will look at a variety of important forms of professional writing. Before we do, let's clear up the differences (and similarities) between academic and professional writing:

Academic writing refers to the writing you do as part of a program of study. Programs in nursing, midwifery and other health professions ask students to engage, broadly speaking, in two forms of writing: writing that integrates theory, research and practice; and reflective writing.

Professional writing refers to the writing you do as a health professional in accordance with the standards of your profession's regulatory body.

Clinical or agency writing refers to the professional writing you do in the context of your practice setting.

A good question . . .

Why write the long, complicated documents of academic writing if I never use it in the workplace?

Academic writing develops transferable abilities:

- the ability to make decisions that are objective and informed;
- the ability to grasp and describe complex situations, analyze them, and clearly articulate conclusions and recommendations;
- the ability to describe and argue;
- the ability to achieve language 'correctness' and persuasiveness;
- the ability to use and document sources.

Academic writing also develops perspectives:

- on social issues;
- on self: becoming a reflective practitioner;
- on human behaviour and interaction.

Table 9.1   Comparison of academic and professional writing

	Academic writing	*Professional writing*
Who is the audience?	• Professors, often standing in for a professional audience • The academic community	• Colleagues in your own field • Multidisciplinary team • Agency administrators • Government and Regulatory bodies • Legal/Justice system • Clients • General public
What will your audience do with what you've written?	• Assess your understanding of the theory and research as applied to practice and assign a grade • Assess your development as a reflective practitioner and assign a grade	Make decisions and take action on, for example: • Treatment/intervention • Policy • Behaviour change • Funding • Replicating or carrying forward from what you did in practice

Table 9.1 (Continued)

	Academic writing	Professional writing
What is the purpose of writing?	• To demonstrate comprehensive knowledge of theory and research • To develop critical reading/thinking/writing skills • To appraise and conduct research • To become a reflective practitioner	• To report • To record • To recommend • To shape and evaluate policy • To propose and evaluate programs
What is the writing process?	• Iterative (reading, brainstorming, outlining, drafting, revising) • Idea-driven • Deadline-driven	• Often linear (e.g., forms, documentation, reports, requests) • Event-driven • Deadline-driven

But there are also similarities between academic and professional writing:

- both need an appropriate balance of description and argument;
- both use conventionalized/standardized structures that need to be learned; they force you to be adaptable to 'templates'
- both use conventional language, a 'technical discourse' that needs to be learned; they make you think about the tone and diction expectations of your audience;
- both require decisions about what to include in the space available;
- both require decisions about what to emphasize and how to use language to indicate emphasis;
- both must be both grammatically 'correct' and persuasive;
- both of them value clear, concise, logical writing;
- for both, the needs of the audience are always the first consideration:
  - o Who is my audience?
  - o What do they already know and what do I need to tell them?
  - o What will they do with what I've written?
  - o How much will/won't they read?

NURSING AND MIDWIFERY PORTFOLIOS

Andy Young (2007) defines a portfolio this way: 'A portfolio is a record of your clinical and professional nursing skills supported by a body of evidence. It also serves as a record of your clinical experience and journey from novice to expert'.

Professional colleges and regulatory bodies generally require health professionals, especially nurses and midwives, to maintain ongoing portfolios that are periodically reviewed. In the UK, for example, the National Health Service requires nurses to maintain a Knowledge and Skills Framework (KSF), a clinical portfolio that is reviewed annually by their employers within the NHS. Portfolios are also an important marketing tool if you wish to advance in your current position or move to a new one. CVs or résumés (described below) are an essential part of a job search, but a portfolio adds a whole new dimension by providing physical evidence of your skills and abilities. Likewise, they add a new dimension to your development as a person and a professional, because they actualize (make real) your goals, and allow you both to reflect back and plan for the future.

Oermann (2002) describes two types of professional portfolios: best-work and growth and development. **Best-work portfolios** are designed to be reviewed by others; they provide documented evidence of competencies and skills that are used by others to evaluate nurses for annual review, promotion and accreditation processes. 'Competencies' are specific and observable knowledge, skills and behaviours that are associated with effective functioning in a job. **Growth and development portfolios** allow nurses and midwives to monitor their own progress in meeting personal and professional learning goals; they are not intended for review by others, but materials from them are selected for inclusion in best-work portfolios.

Worldwide, portfolios are increasingly required as an assessment tool within nursing and midwifery programs. This is because a portfolio has the unique ability to capture learning over time in a way that tests or grades may not. It is a great advantage if you are required to build a portfolio during your student program, as that builds the skill and the habit of working on it, and gives you the opportunity for ongoing feedback. All you have to do, then, when you enter your post-registration career, is maintain the habit.

Guides on building and maintaining a portfolio often admonish people to work on theirs on a continuous basis, and to avoid the shoebox stuffed with documents and other artifacts. Or, as I call it (because I too am guilty of it), the archaeological system of filing. This 'system' can indeed work badly, as important documents have a habit of hiding themselves at exactly the moment you must put your hand on them. So, yes, it is always best to be proactive in maintaining your portfolio.

But life doesn't always allow us to be proactive, and as you enter your new career you will have an enormous lot of stuff thrown at you. As long as the 'shoebox' is actually an accordion folder that you have tabbed with the names of the parts of your portfolio, you'll be fine. It's easy to be proactive about tossing something into an accordion folder, and the work of seconds to jot down a few notes, on the front or back, about its relevance or meaning. The same is true for capturing reflective moments. Sometimes people will say they are too busy to be reflective, but in fact humans are by nature reflective beings. We think – sometimes obsess – over things that happen to us and what they mean to our lives. So when something about your day gets you thinking, and talking to your friends and family about it, why not also take a few minutes to write down what happened and what you are thinking/feeling right now? Into the folder (or your electronic portfolio folder) it goes, under 'reflective'. The more you put into your folder, the more material you have to work with. No need to decide now if something will be useful or not – just get it all in there. At this point, you are going for quantity. When you have a reason to fully update your portfolio – for accreditation or a new position – you are all set to sit down and work through the parts to update them using the folder materials. Your important materials won't have gone missing, and you'll have more than enough evidence to support them.

Although you are going for quantity, don't feel that because you've assembled a thick folder of evidence that you have to use it all. The folder is there as a resource to draw on as your portfolio changes over time.

Increasingly, both student and professional portfolios are created, maintained, and ultimately submitted online as e-portfolios. Much of what you collect, then, will already be in digital format, for example, photos, videos, scanned documents. The same principle as the physical accordion file holds true – whatever technology you use, maintain a portfolio folder on your central computer with files for the individual parts.

Formatting your portfolio

For a paper-based portfolio, use a three-ring binder. Use a tabbed divider for each section, even if there is only one sheet in the section. Each section gets a cover sheet listing the contents of the section (this is in addition to the listing in the portfolio's general Table of Contents). Include a cover sheet even if there is only one sheet in the section. Place each cover sheet and artifact into its own clear plastic page protector.

If you are building an e-portfolio, your program may provide an e-portfolio template, or there are numerous ones available online. Keep your e-portfolio backed up on a USB memory stick.

What to include in a portfolio

In general, every section of a portfolio should contain:

- descriptions of the relevant elements of your student and professional life;
- evidence, called 'artifacts', that support your descriptions;
- reflections on your artifacts and the personal/professional journey they represent.

An artifact is a physical record of an event – we might think of them as souvenirs of a trip. Like a souvenir photograph, a good artifact captures both the content and meaning of the event. For example, a care plan can be included not only to document your actions but also to allow you to reflect on how well you performed in a complex situation. An artifact may be a document such as a transcript of grades, a license, or a certificate. It may be a photograph. It may be job related, such as a job description, reference, list of previous employers, performance review forms, or record of committees you have belonged to. It may be a digital artifact such as a PowerPoint presentation or a poster. It may be creative work such as poetry, stories, or drawings that represent artistically the experience of you and/or your patients/families. In short, an artifact is almost anything that you think is relevant to your career and that will help you identify your achievements, skills and goals.

The names and content of the sections of your portfolio will vary depending on who is asking you for it:

- When it is a requirement within a nursing or midwifery program, it is to be hoped – but isn't always the case – that you are given a 'template' your instructors want you to follow. If you are given a template, it may be highly structured or it may allow considerable creativity on your part. You may be asked to maintain and submit your portfolio in traditional paper format, or you may be encouraged (even required) to submit it electronically.
- Institutions may require periodic submission of your portfolio in order to review your performance to date and potential for development. They often specify a particular format.
- Regulatory bodies may also require periodic submission of your portfolio for accreditation purposes, and often require a particular format, sometimes supplying electronic record sheets for you to follow.
- A job advertisement will ask for your CV or résumé as part of the application rather than your full portfolio. Even if not asked for, though, you may wish to bring your portfolio to the interview in case there is an opportunity to present it. When using a portfolio as part of an application for a job, make sure you include materials that demonstrate your skills are tailored to the needs of that particular organization. Similarly, include materials that demonstrate your abilities to fulfil the particular position you are applying for.

Whatever the format you use, it will include the following content sections or equivalents of them:

- a personal information sheet that lists your name and contact information, which should include your address, email address (if you have an institutional address, use that rather than your personal account), website (if you have one, but *not* your Facebook or other social media address), and telephone/ mobile/cellphone; when you have graduated and successfully passed your licensure examinations, you will add your registration number[s].
- an up-to-date copy of CV (curriculum vitae) or résumé – see below;
- personal history;
- educational achievements and goals;
- practice history and goals;
- work in the community, volunteer or charity work: highlight your specific role in the organization and the skills you developed;

- reflection: a crucial component of any portfolio, reflection should occur within each of your sections and then have its own section that both sums up and expands on your other reflections.

To help you gather the points you want to make, think about the following questions:

Who am I? To plan for our futures, we need to understand our past and our present, that is, what has brought us to this point and where are we now in the journey of becoming or being a nurse/midwife. These questions will help you reflect on your life and where you are on your nursing/midwifery journey, as well as what details about it you want to offer:

- If I were asked to write one paragraph to tell the story of my life, what would I include?
- How would I describe my personality? What are the best and worst aspects of my character? What have been the 'defining moments' (the real highs and hows) of my personal life? In what way[s] did they change my approach to life?
- What have been the defining moments of my nursing/ midwifery journey to date?
- Who are the people who have had the greatest impact (positive and/or negative) on my life? On my nursing/ midwifery journey to date?
- What are my strengths and weaknesses as a practitioner?
- What do I have to offer a multidisciplinary team?
- What do I believe to be the biggest problems faced by nursing or midwifery today? These could be problems related to broader government policies, the structure of the healthcare system, the nursing/midwifery role, nursing/midwifery practice, etc.

For a student portfolio, these are some types of supporting evidence you could use:

- autobiographical story and/or a few vignettes (i.e., a brief written 'snapshot' of a defining moment in your life and what it meant);
- a description of your philosophy of nursing;
- a personal coat of arms you design to represent your nursing/ midwifery values and career goals;
- photos;
- short video.

My education:

- What has my education given me in terms of clinical/practice knowledge?
- What critical and analytic skills has my education given me?

- In what ways has my education contributed to making me a competent and reflective practitioner?
- What detailed examples from my education can I highlight and include in my portfolio to support my answer to those questions? A student portfolio could include:
  o successful course assignments (perhaps with the marker's feedback);
  o evidence of interprofessional education;
  o self-evaluations;
  o preceptor evaluations;
  o academic achievements, honours, awards and scholarships;
  o professional documents such as proof of education, licenses, and certifications (including renewal dates and hours completed toward recertification);
  o continuing education and professional development;
  o in-service education;
  o presentations and/or education sessions to colleagues, groups of patients, multidisciplinary teams, the community.

My clinical/practice experience: This can be organized according to your competencies and your cases.

- What are some specific examples of times I've applied the nursing process to direct and indirect care of my patients and their families?
- Do I practise evidence-based care?
- What are some examples of my ability to care sensitively for patients/families of diverse backgrounds?
- What do I do that promotes a nursing model of patient/family-centred care or a midwifery model of partnership and support for women's right to self-determination in life processes?
- What feedback (positive and negative) have I received from my preceptor, manager, colleagues, patients/carers/families?
- What do I consider my areas of greatest strengths and greatest challenges?
- Possible types of evidence:
  o descriptions of relevant, significant clinical experiences;
  o proof of acquired skills;
  o clinical journals that include current evidence-based research and reflection to improve patient care;
  o a course paper that describes the nursing process from assessment, diagnosis and medical/nursing interventions to nursing care plan and discharge planning guide;
  o cultural assessments;

o   a concept map: a concept map is a way of graphically representing all dimensions of a patient's care, a concise web of information with a description of the patient at the centre; a concept map is a way of making sense, both in its details and its entirety, of all the patient information and the medical/nursing/midwifery process;

o   health promotion/education projects you designed and implemented in the practice setting or community.

My work in the community: This section can highlight and provide examples of:

- health promotion/education projects;
- needs assessments;
- activist and advocacy efforts;
- collaborative community efforts;
- volunteer and charity work.

For reflection: how can I make a difference?

- What are my career goals?
- What are my practice goals?
- Do I hope to make a difference in the field of policy and social advocacy? In clinical expertise? In research? In nursing/ midwifery care? In community health?
- What nursing and social theories are most relevant for me? How might I use them in my practice?
- What is my action plan for developing the skills and knowledge I will need?

For further reading

National Council for the Professional Development of Nursing and Midwifery. (2009, November). *Guidelines for portfolio development for nurses and midwives* (3rd ed.). Dublin: Author.

Oermann, M. H. (2002). Developing a professional portfolio in Nursing. *Orthopaedic Nursing, 21*(2), 73–78.

Young, Andy. (2007, January 1). Making your development portfolio work for you. *NursingTimes.net.* Retrieved from: http://www.nursingtimes.net/nursing-practice/ student-nurses/making-your-development-portfolio-work-for-you/201130.article

CVS AND JOB APPLICATIONS

The curriculum vitae vs. the résumé

A curriculum vitae (literally, course of life) or résumé is always part of a job application. The *Gage Canadian Dictionary* gives these two terms as synonyms:

Curriculum vitae, résumé = summary of one's life, qualifications, etc. Résumé is the general term; curriculum vitae is used mainly in academic and professional situations.

Source: Avis, W.S., Drysdale, P.D., Gregg, R.J., Neufeldt, V.E., & Scargill, M.H. (1983). *Gage Canadian Dictionary*. Toronto, Canada: Gage Educational Publishing.

As a nursing or midwifery student entering the profession in the UK, you will be asked for a CV. In the US, the term used is résumé, and in Canada you will find both terms used. I have used CV here, but the advice is the same regardless of which you are asked for.

What goes into a CV?

There are very few rules about what sections must be on a CV. There is also no 'right' length. In general, you can expect your CV to be just 1–2 pages at the beginning of your career, and to expand as your work experience grows. The key requirements are:

- name and contact details;
- education (post-secondary only, unless you are in years 1-2 of a post-secondary program);
- professional licensing or certification;
- previous work (or volunteer) experience: you may wish to divide this into sections such as 'relevant experience' and 'additional experience';
- professional memberships, presentations;
- awards and honours;
- references.

You may also wish to include

- Objective[s]: if you are applying to a job that is specifically described in the ad, these are a good way of highlighting how your qualifications fit the requirements. If the nature of the job is not clear, however, you run the risk of defining yourself in a way that doesn't match what they are looking for. It might be better in that case just to let the CV speak for itself – if you get an interview, it is common at that time for interviewers to ask about your current career objectives and long-term goals.
- Skills: a list of skills can be impressive as a way to highlight specific or uncommon skills, if you know they are relevant to the job.

The following advice on CVs and job applications was written by Dr Margaret Procter, Coordinator of Writing Support at the University of Toronto. It has been slightly adapted to reflect nursing and midwifery situations.

Application letters and CVs: some practical tips

- **Keep the reader's interest in mind.** Your message is 'you need me', not 'I want a job'. Know enough about the organization or agency to recognize what they want and need. Then the focus of your documents will be where you fit and what you can contribute. This principle will also determine your choice of emphasis and even your wording (not 'I have had four months of clinical placement' but 'My clinical placement experience will help me do X and Y').
- **Balance facts and claims.** Your documents will be boring and meaningless if they're just bare lists of facts. They will be empty and unbelievable if they are just grand claims about yourself. Use each of the two or three paragraphs in the body of your letter to make a few key interpretive statements ('I enjoy working collaboratively with the community to meet their identified needs'). Back up each one with some examples. Were you responsible for any innovations, changes or improvements? They could be big (e.g., 'achieved community consensus to open a harms reduction injection site in a residential neighbourhood of MyCity') or small ('initiated new sharps disposal procedure on my unit').
- **Write concisely.** There is no space available for word-spinning. At the beginning of your career, you may feel your CV looks a little thin – don't try to pad it with unnecessary words and details.

Specific points about application letters

- Write a letter for each application, tailored for the specific situation. Even if the ad calls only for a CV, send a letter anyway. The letter makes a first impression, and it can direct the reader to notice key points of the CV.
- Use standard letter format, with internal addresses (spell names correctly!) and salutations. Use specific names or at least position titles whenever possible (call the organization or check its website). Most application letters for entry-level jobs are one page in length – a substantial page rather than a skimpy one.
- Start strong and clear. For an advertised position, name the job and any reference numbers, and say where you saw the ad. For a speculative letter, name a specific function you can perform and relate it to something you know about the organization.
- Use paragraph structure to lead your reader from one interpretive point to another. Refer to specific information in

terms of examples for the points you're making, and mention that your CV gives further evidence.

- End simply by thanking the reader for their consideration, and/or that you hope to have the opportunity to speak with them in an interview.

Specific points about CVs

- Have more than one on hand, emphasizing different aspects of your qualifications or aims. Then you can update and revise them quickly when opportunities arise.
- Make them easy to read by using headings, point form, and lots of white space. Look at current books of advice or at online templates to see the range of page formats available. Create one that suits your situation rather than following a standard one rigidly.
- The basic choice is between the traditional chronological organization (with the main sections Education and Experience) and the functional one (where sections name types of experience or qualities of character). You can get some of the benefits of both by creating a one- or two-line introductory section called *Profile* or *Objective* to sum up your main unifying point. You may also use *Achievement* subsections to emphasize your most important qualifications. These may include a horizontal list of keywords in noun form to serve in electronic scanning for information.
- List facts in reverse chronological order, with the most recent ones first. Shorten some lists by combining related entries (e.g., part-time jobs). In general, omit details of high-school achievements. You also don't have to include personal details or full information for referees.

Finally, here are some pitfalls to avoid:

- ✗ unsupported claims;
- ✗ large empty spaces (in this case, it's better to condense the CV);
- ✗ font sizes of less than 12 point;
- ✗ crowded pages (use white space between sections, and make headings clearly visible);
- ✗ errors in spelling and grammar;
- ✗ elaborate fonts or formatting.

Sources

Freedman, L. (2011). *Résumés FAQ*. Toronto, Canada: Health Sciences Writing Centre, University of Toronto.

Procter, M. (1999). *Application letters and résumés: Some practical tips*. Toronto, Canada: University of Toronto.

CLINICAL AND AGENCY DOCUMENTATION

Every practice setting has its own process and requirements for documentation, as well as its own 'shorthand' and accepted abbreviations for describing common phenomena. When you start a clinical or agency placement, be prepared to have a lengthy orientation to various unit or agency writing protocols; there will also be legal documents to sign.

You can expect to be trained both formally through training sessions and informally through colleagues, preceptors or mentors. The formal means of training you and evaluating your progress are explained during orientation. Getting informal training and feedback 'on the ground', however, is less straightforward than attending training sessions. That's because the quantity and quality are dependent on the culture of the particular practice setting.

By 'culture' we mean two things: first, it's the collective behaviour of the people who are part of an organization. This behaviour is shaped by the organization's values and goals, its working language, and its norms of practice. Second, culture is the behaviours and assumptions that are taught, formally and informally, to new members of the organization (Shein, 1992). A simple way to express it is, an organization's culture is 'the way things get done around here' (Deal & Kennedy, 2000).

For further reading

Deal, T. E., & Kennedy, A. A. (2000). *Corporate cultures: The rites and rituals of corporate life*. Harmondsworth: Perseus/Penguin.
Shein, E. (1992). *Organizational culture and leadership: A dynamic view*. San Francisco, CA: Jossey-Bass.

This means you may experience a highly supportive preceptorship/mentorship relationship, and professional colleagues who are willing and able to devote time to answering questions and helping out. Or, this may not be so. Either way, during orientation, you might ask who the best person is to ask for help with documentation, recording and other writing. Experience in the setting will also quickly show you which colleagues you can most comfortably ask for help.

The effectiveness of your clinical or agency writing is often determined by how other health professionals read and use it. What you document should facilitate clinical reasoning, and it should communicate your patient's clinical issues to all members of the health care team. In modern interprofessional and multidisciplinary practices, your care may intersect with any or all of the following on a regular basis: physicians of numerous specialties, social workers, educators, administrators, nutritionists and dietitians, occupational therapists, physical therapists, pharmacists, and others.

What is captured in clinical/agency documentation?

The specifics of what is captured are determined by the following factors:

- the nature and setting of the work being done;
- the purpose of the patient contact you are recording;

- the information you judge is relevant to include;
- the electronic health record (EHR) management system in use in your setting.

The timing of clinical/agency record-keeping

- Documentation is ideally done when the event occurs or as soon as possible thereafter. This is made easier in hospital settings with bedside terminals.
- PDA technology can be indispensable for nursing/midwifery work both within organizations and in community practice.
- Further documentation is done at end-of-shift for handover.

Recording professionally

- Write concisely: less really is 'more'.
- Write precisely: what do you really mean to say? Recording is not literature where the reading audience interprets meaning.
- Do not use shortened terms that are unlikely to be known. Have you seen or heard others in your practice setting use the acronyms and abbreviations?
- Keep in mind that there is a legal dimension to professional record-keeping. Failure to document properly can be the basis of legal action such as a lawsuit.

How recording is done

Recording methods vary across a spectrum from notes written in pen on a paper form to complex computerized charting systems that are highly integrated with other hospital functions. In these systems, data are entered via a combination of keyboarding and choice of touchscreen options. Integration of voice technology is not far off. You will be trained in whatever system your practice setting uses.

What gets recorded

Problem-oriented records are organized according to the patient's health problems. All health professionals involved in the patient's care contribute to and use the same record, allowing coordination of care from initial contact to discharge and follow-up at home. Two widely used formats (SOAP and PIE) are given below, but all problem-oriented approaches follow the same basic structure:

Data base	Contains initial health information.
Problem list	Consists of a numerical list of the patient's health problems.
Plan of care	Identifies methods for solving each health problem.
Progress notes	Describe the patient's responses to what has been done and revisions to the original plan (Timby, 2009, p. 112).

For further reading

Power, R. (2011, 14 Sept.). *Writing styles: Academic, professional and agency writing: The practice* [PowerPoint presentation]. University of Toronto: Factor-Inwentash Faculty of Social Work.

Timby, B. K. (2009). *Fundamental nursing skills and concepts* (9th ed.). Philadelphia: Wolters Kluwer Health/Lippincott Williams & Wilkins.

SOAP note format

The purpose of SOAP notes is to document a patient's presenting signs, symptoms and other information, to create a nursing diagnosis, and to provide a plan for treatment and care. SOAP notes provide a record to evaluate the success of treatment and care, and they form part of the patient's medical and legal record. In a lawsuit, SOAP notes can be introduced in court to provide a record of the health care team's diagnosis and treatment. To maintain the integrity of that record, corrections must be done in a way that does not obliterate the original.

Depending on the protocols of your setting, SOAP notes may be written in pen in the patient's medical record and/or entered in a computerized documentation system. They begin with a record of the initial information required within the practice setting. Usually, this is the individual's name, case number, today's date, and any procedure coding that may be required. Your organization is likely to have a manual on policy and procedure for clinical abbreviations.

As Shannon Abbaterusso, RN and clinical instructor, advises:

> There is usually a list of attached abbreviations that are approved by individual institutions and it is important that they are noted as they can differ quite significantly. Clinicians need to be careful about using abbreviations that they learn from other staff members as there are usually many that are frequently used and not approved. Esp., as we see in the downtown hospitals there are many physicians and agency nurses that move from hospital to hospital and may not be aware of the specific hospital's expectations. (personal communication)

Correct coding and abbreviations are crucial to preventing medication errors. This includes knowing when not to use them, so you will also receive standards for what *not* to use. For example, .1mg can be misread as 1mg, resulting in a 10-fold medication dosage error (you should write 0.1mg), while 10µg (micrograms) can be misread as 10mg (milligrams), leading to a 1000-fold dosage error (you should write 10mcg). In general, it is dangerous to use abbreviations for drug names because multiple drugs may have similar abbreviations.

1   Sentences are direct and short, and often incomplete.
2   Language is clear, precise, and descriptive. It uses technical terminology and approved abbreviations, but not jargon (i.e., any health professional on your team can understand it).

The body of the note is broken up into the following four sections:

S = Subjective: what the patient said

- the reason for the visit;
- symptoms being experienced: the location, onset, severity, duration, and frequency;
- history of presenting condition;
- past medical and social history;
- current medications;
- other notes, e.g., appetite, diet.

O = Objective: what you did and observed as a result

- Record measurements and vital signs, such as weight and height, blood pressure, pulse, oxygen saturation.
- Clinical examinations of the patient's body systems.
- Avoid opinion and record only the facts observed. Do not make subjective assumptions about the patient, for example, 'Mum appeared angry.' She may appear so to you but be feeling some quite different emotion.
- Do not make a diagnosis in this section: for example, 'Baby C exhibited all the signs and symptoms of MS' suggests you have decided on a diagnosis before you collect and analyze all your data.

A = Assessment or Analysis: evaluate the information you have obtained

- This section analyzes the subjective and objective notes and synthesizes them to create one or more nursing diagnoses.
- To make a diagnosis, identify what the patient is at 'risk for', 'related to' what, as 'evidenced by' what.
- List ongoing and new problems along with current status (stable, progressing, improved, resolved).

P = Plan:

- recommendations for further tests and assessments;
- relief measures or actions that worsen the patient's symptoms;
- recommendations for treatment (type, frequency, duration);
- medication changes (started, discontinued, increased, decreased);
- expected outcomes, short-term goals, long-term goals;
- referrals;
- recommendations for patient education and home instructions;
- discharge notes.

Many hospitals and agencies split **Plan** into more precise categories to create *soapie* or *soapier* notes:

Implementation: Care provided

Evaluation: Outcome of treatment

Revision: Changes in treatment

Note: there has been a strong movement in hospital settings towards computer charting. This form of charting is called **charting by exception.** As Timby (2009) describes it:

> Charting by exception is a documentation method in which nurses chart only abnormal assessment findings or care that deviates from the standard. Proponents of this efficient method say that charting by exception provides quick access to abnormal findings because it does not describe normal and routine information. (p. 114)

PIE notes (problem, intervention, evaluation) assign a number to each of a patient/client's problems, and use the numbers subsequently as the notes progress through intervention and evaluation, for example, P#1, I#1, E#1, P#2, etc. There are a number of other variations, such as P-CARE (Patient, Clinician, Assessment, Results, Evaluation).

For further reading

Nursing and Midwifery Council. (2009). *Record-keeping: guidance for nurses and midwives.* London: NMC. Available at www.nmc-uk.org

Timby, B. K. (2009). *Fundamental nursing skills and concepts* (9th ed.). Philadelphia: Wolters Kluwer Health/Lippincott Williams & Wilkins.

WITNESS STATEMENTS

In the event of a lawsuit, a coroner's inquest, or for other reasons, nurses and midwives are sometimes required to make a statement or testify at a court hearing. It is important to be familiar with and understand the legal obligations and rights that are relevant to your jurisdiction. These can be found on the websites of your national and state/provincial regulatory bodies. These bodies also stand ready to guide you in dealing with legal matters arising out of your professional practice.

The prospect of giving testimony in the unfamiliar and somewhat daunting environment of court is a challenge if you are not experienced in it. Luckily, lawyers are no more likely to let a new nurse or midwife stand unprepared before a hearing than you are to hand over your stethoscope and point a lawyer toward your patient's bed. If you have kept high-quality notes and records, they will not be difficult to organize into a witness statement. The contents of a witness statement are described here by Alexandra Mayeski, a lawyer who specializes in health law:

> Witness statements should summarize the evidence that is to be given at the hearing. The evidence should be first hand. They should provide

some background of the person and why that person is giving evidence. The evidence of the witness at the hearing will usually be limited to that which is in the statement so you want to make sure everything is covered. (personal communication)

WRITING FOR HEALTH EDUCATION

My favourite example of the seemingly unbridgeable gap between science and the public is a 10-year-old analysis of the difficulty of scientific language. In this study a standard English-language newspaper was given a rating of zero. Anything above zero was more difficult; anything below easier. The highest rating was 55.5, assigned to a paper in the journal *Nature*. In fact nothing scientific rated less than 28.

But adult fiction came in at –19.3 and adult-to-adult conversations (casual) were –41.1. The only categories ranked lower were mothers talking to their 3-year-olds (–48.3) and farmers talking to dairy cows (–59.1).

From Jay Ingram, 'Why science stories bomb with readers', *The Toronto Star,* Sunday, December 30, 2001, p. F8

'Health education' is a broad term that refers to the process of educating people about health. The goal is to give people the knowledge and skills they need to make quality health decisions, and to behave in a way that promotes, maintains, or restores their health. Health education can be directed toward individuals, groups, or communities. Considering the findings of the study Mr Ingram describes, it goes without saying that the language you use in writing for health education needs to be crystal clear. But according to whose definition of 'clear' are you writing? The answer depends on which community is your target.

'Community' may be defined geographically (e.g., the catchment area of a hospital or agency); ethnically (e.g., Hmung, San) or racially (e.g., African American); by residence (e.g., a housing development or a neighbourhood); by stage in life cycle (e.g., infants, teens, older adults); by common health concern (e.g., stroke, homelessness); by use of a particular health or social service resource (e.g., community clinic); by adherence to a particular health belief system (e.g., users of herbal medicines); adherence to a particular health behaviour (e.g., smokers, drinkers) or by some combination of these or other characteristics. It's important to take careful account of these and other intersecting factors in understanding the population you are writing for.

According to Bell (1995, p. 300), effective health education materials . . .

- remove obstacles to learning and make the learning process easier;
- are free of confusing language and irrelevant content;
- encourage feelings of competency and self-worth;
- respect and value the past experience of the reader;

- are designed to integrate new learning into the past experience of the reader;
- indicate an achievable, observable goal, along with practical actions and behaviours to achieve it;
- are tested and refined in collaboration with individuals or groups who represent the intended audience.

In health education materials, then, it is important to clearly identify and understand the community, or population, and either conduct a needs assessment or in some way ascertain the message you want to deliver. And then you will need to tailor the language and design elements you use so they are the most easily understood, most engaging, and most persuasive for that population.

It is often advised that health education materials be written with the use of a readability formula, such as the SMOG Readability Formula or the Gunning Fog Index. These various formulas – none of which were designed for the health professions – count the number of letters in words and words in sentences, or use other simple mathematical methods, and then produce a score intended to predict what grade level of education is needed to understand the written material. Unfortunately, such scoring reduces the multiple influences on the complex process of reading to the single dimension of grade level. It doesn't account for the fact that even while we are still in school, we all read at different levels. Or that in the multicultural societies of today's world, not all individuals have gone through the same school system or learned the same forms of English. It doesn't take account of the multiple life experiences outside school that may encourage us to read and learn, or act as a barrier to further learning. Finally, it ignores the fact that it is possible to be very confusing and dull while using short words and sentences.

This is not to say that readability formulas have no value. Bell (1995, p. 303) reminds us that there are a great many members of society who are low-skilled readers, and these formulas do focus writers of health education materials on the need to write simply. Another appeal of a focus on educational level is the fact that individuals with less education tend to have more health problems, and therefore to be very important targets for health education materials. However, readability formulas should be used with caution, as a guide to locate areas where you may wish to revise, not as a guide to the actual revision. That needs to be based on your analysis of the target audience, and on the input that you gather from them as part of the development process.

Beyond the reader's past experience, the other important determinant of the language you use is **context**, that is, the circumstances under which they are reading. For example, when surgical patients are discharged and given instruction sheets for self-care, the sheets inevitably contain medical language they might normally not be familiar with. But having gone through the illness and surgical experience, they are likely to understand the medical terminology around it (and part of good discharge planning, of course, is probing whether they are indeed understanding), as long as everything around the terminology – the sentence structures and word choices – is clear, simple and direct. Bear in mind that people often receive health education materials when they and their families are in crisis.

To achieve maximum readability for a general audience, consider the following questions.

What exactly am I asking people to do?

- Can I express it in a few, simple words?
- Why exactly should they do it? Have I explained this?
- What will happen if they don't? Have I explained this?

How likely are they to do it?

- What will empower them to act?
- Can they incorporate my suggestions into their day-to-day life?

What are the barriers they face?

- Do I offer easy, practical suggestions to overcome them?
- Do the changes I suggest fit in with my readers' lifestyle?

Have I chosen a small number of key words I want my readers to remember?

- Do I repeat one or more in every section?

Am I blaming people or empowering them?

- No one appreciates being nagged or lectured. For example, which of these would make you more likely to act?
  - o No one likes the fat kid in the class. As a parent, it is up to you to keep your child from obesity.
  - o As a parent, you can not control what your children eat at school. But here are a few simple ways to help them choose healthy foods.

What is my layout like?

- Is there plenty of white space between my visual 'blocks' of text and illustration? This helps set them out for the reader.
- Do my illustrations/visuals send the right message clearly?
- Do I use bulleted lists as well as paragraphs?
- Do I make key messages larger or set them out or place them first?

What kind of language am I using?

- Do I use short paragraphs (1-4 sentences)?
- Do I use short sentences (generally not more than 10-12 words)?
- Do I use common words and mostly short ones?

- Do I address the reader directly as 'you'? Compare the impact of these two:
  - o Pain will be reduced within 24 hours.
  - o You will feel less pain within a day.
- Do I use catchy phrases that are easy to remember? Consider, for example, which of these you yourself would find easier to remember?
  - o You must seek treatment immediately or risk killing millions of brain cells.
  - o Time equals brain cells.

COMMUNICATING ONLINE

Professional email communication and email etiquette

From: 8432x@server.com

To: busyprof@university.edu

Subject: Re:

Yo prof!

Did i miss anything thursday? Cn U pls send me yr notes! ☺

Joey

Clearly 'Joey' didn't attend Thursday's class. But was it the course Busyprof taught in the morning or was it the night class? Is Joey's full name Joseph or Josephine, JoAnn, Jonghua or even Jasmine? The email address is no help because the student hasn't used an institutional email account. An email account given you by your college or university will always include your name. Next, a professor who has just been disrespectfully addressed as 'Yo prof' isn't inclined to waste much time trying to figure any of this out. Finally, notice that Joey clearly believes it doesn't matter if she or he attends classes. Professors find it frustrating when students think that everything of value in a class is covered in PowerPoint slides and handouts.

Your aim in an email is to communicate clearly and efficiently, presenting a professional identity to the recipient. Here is a summary of the good, practical advice most commonly given about professional email communication:

- Some general points about emails:
  - o One topic per email message – if you need to discuss two or more items, send two or more emails, with each topic identified in the subject line. Never leave the subject line blank, or write something meaningless like 'Hi.' If you are writing with a question about an assignment, say so: 'Question about MDW202 first assignment'.

- o   Keep your message short and to the point – unless you have a good reason for making it longer, your reader should be able to see the entire message on a single screen. This is to avoid a situation where a busy reader omits to scroll down and misses part of the message.
- o   Short paragraphs are easier to read than long ones.
- o   Be careful if you need to send sensitive information. Email is *not* a secure form of communication. If you need to include confidential or private information, make sure you encrypt the email. The simplest way to do this is to send the material in a password-protected attachment and to send the password in a separate email.
- o   Always proofread twice, slowly and carefully, before hitting 'send'.
- o   Never send an email when you are very upset about something to do with the recipient (e.g., a poor grade on a paper you worked hard on, or a colleague in your practice setting who failed to show up for a shift, making you work overtime). Wait at least a day. Write a draft if it makes you feel better, but keep your finger off that send button until you've revisited it and revised.
- Identify yourself properly:
  - o   Use your institutional email address, not a personal account. Personal accounts don't always include your name, but an institutional address will identify both your name and the organization where you study or work.
  - o   Always identify the key message of the email in the subject line, for example, 'Invitation to breastfeeding education session' or 'Questions re new intake process'.
  - o   Sign the message with your name and professional contact information. Don't add tag lines or quotes at the bottom. Don't include social media contacts such as a link to your Facebook account.
- Be courteous:
  - o   Unless you have a working relationship with the recipient, use formal modes of address (Prof., Dr., Mr., Ms, Sir/Madam). In North America, it is simply acceptable to use the person's full name (Dear JoAnn Kurtz).
  - o   Be patient if you don't receive an immediate reply – especially do not expect a fast reply to an email sent outside business hours.
- Respect confidentiality and privacy:
  - o   This cannot be overemphasized. In no area of your professional or personal life should you ever reveal identifying details of patients or clients.
  - o   Failure to respect confidentiality and privacy has both ethical and legal implications and may have serious consequences.

- Don't confuse social media with professional communication:
  - o Use full sentences, and check your spelling, grammar and punctuation.
  - o Don't type words or sentences in UPPERCASE – IT IS THE EQUIVALENT OF SHOUTING.
  - o Using all lowercase makes you seem lazy, as does omitting punctuation.
  - o Don't use emoticons such as smiley faces.
  - o Don't use abbreviations such as 'lol' or 'u' for 'you'.
  - o Don't include unsolicited, non-professional attachments, such as trip photos or YouTube videos.
- Replying to emails:
  - o Reply promptly, ideally the same day, even if it's only to acknowledge receipt and say that you will respond more fully later. However, if you receive a professional communication outside business hours or on the weekend, do not feel obliged to reply until regular working hours.
  - o Include the original message so the recipient has the context for your reply.
  - o If you have been asked a number of questions, make sure you clearly identify and answer them all.
  - o If others were copied on the original, make sure you are comfortable with everyone on the list reading your reply. If not, check and double-check to make sure your cursor is poised over 'reply' and not 'reply-all'.

Discussion boards, chatrooms, blogs, and other online forums

Increasingly, nursing programs are adapting social media for use within the course context, even assigning marks for (meaningful) participation in online forums. Learning to use social media is also excellent training if your goal is community practice as a nurse or midwife, when you may want to use email and social media to communicate with clients, or use websites for health promotion purposes. Currently, the most common online forums used in courses are discussion boards, chatrooms, and blogs.

Some cautions: within the course context, social media cease to be only a form of personal expression and assume a greater degree of formality. Be careful not to include opinions and details that you wouldn't mention in a face-to-face tutorial group. These include details about patients or healthcare settings that could identify them; sensitive or confidential information; negative 'venting' about instructors, courses or practice settings or preceptors.

An excellent source of guidance on using social media for nursing and midwifery is:

Fraser, R. (2011). *The nurse's social media advantage: How making connections and sharing ideas can enhance your nursing practice.* Indianapolis, IN: Sigma Theta Tau International Honor Society of Nursing.

Common Mistakes and How To Deal with Them

Osmond, A.

Learning outcomes

By the end of this chapter you should:

- be aware of, and recognise examples of, common mistakes that appear in academic writing
- understand how to avoid these mistakes.

This chapter deals with a variety of issues and mistakes that I have seen many times in essays. Some readers might recognise many of the issues here. Others might notice only a few areas for improvement in their own work.

Some of these issues are actual *mistakes*; sentences that contain them are grammatically wrong. Others, however, are not 'mistakes' in the sense of being incorrect; they might damage your writing in some other way.

Some of the issues have complex origins, some much simpler; some are easy to track down, while others are tougher to spot.

This chapter also includes some 'quick tips'. These are smaller bits of advice, dealing with easy-to-solve issues.

As you read through this section, remember that these issues are problematic because they hinder your writing's clarity, simplicity and effectiveness; and, therefore, your meaning. By now, you should realise how important these qualities are.

It is important to have an idea of context. If you've made one of the more minor mistakes, just once, you might not be penalised. However, if they appear throughout your work, or your essay includes a range of recurring mistakes, you are damaging your chances of getting the best marks. The more substantial issues might affect your mark in themselves.

I've identified these issues based on the experience I have had, and my colleagues have had, reading many kinds of assignments from a wide range of subjects. View these pages not as a warning, but as an opportunity.

You have the chance to learn where you can improve your writing, by avoiding the more common issues that appear in essays. Avoiding these will allow you to focus on developing your writing as a whole.

As you read, start to think about the nature of your own writing. Think about how likely it is that the issues discussed here are appearing in your essays. You might recognise some of them immediately.

Note that some of the mistakes identified here have already been mentioned in the book. Even so, I wanted all these common issues to appear together, to give you an idea of the kinds of things to start looking for as you write.

Additionally, I think I should repeat here the fact that this book does not stick to all the conventions of academic writing that I recommend. This might occasionally be noticeable in this chapter.

Mixed constructions

A 'mixed construction' will be grammatically incorrect. *How* it is incorrect will depend on the sentence itself. However, mixed constructions of various types appear commonly in essays.

Mixed constructions are sentences that are made up of various parts that do not connect properly grammatically. The different parts of the sentence might be linked by the same topic, or they might *almost* link in a grammatical way – but the result is a sentence that is incorrect, at best; at worst, mixed constructions can be potentially confusing to a reader.

If you follow the subject–verb–object rules discussed earlier, and ensure your verbs and pronouns agree, and construct sentences carefully, you shouldn't have too much of a problem with mixed constructions.

Most commonly, a mixed construction is a sentence that begins by saying one thing, and then shifts into a different kind of sentence. Let's look at some examples:

> ✗ Local government has had a variety of responsibilities in the UK however a successful result for the main political parties.
>
> ✗ In this experiment, quantities of several corrosive chemicals that are needed.
>
> ✗ Although the play's two main characters seem to be redeemed, but the outlook can be considered bleak.

Read the sentences aloud; they certainly *sound* wrong, somehow, don't they? I will examine them in order.

> ✗ Local government has had a variety of responsibilities in the UK however a successful result for the main political parties.

Here, the subject–verb–object arrangement operates correctly up to 'in the UK'. After that, there's a problem. The word 'however' does not properly connect the second part of the sentence with the first, which is, really, just a modified noun ('successful result' with some additional information). A verb of some kind is missing. 'However' does not seem to be the right conjunction in any case. Additionally, though, the problem with meaning is deeper here. It's not quite clear what the writer is actually saying. Determining this would be the first step in rectifying the problem. I will rewrite the sentence as if the point is that British local governments always have a certain set of responsibilities, regardless of the party in power in Parliament:

> ✓ Local government has a variety of responsibilities, which exist regardless of which political party is in power.

In the second example, from a chemistry essay, something is missing:

> ✗ In this experiment, quantities of several corrosive chemicals that are needed.

There is the sense that the sentence needs *more*. The reason for this is the word 'that' towards the end of the sentence. If the writer is simply pointing out the need for several corrosive chemicals, not much needs to be done: the sentence begins with a modifier, 'in this experiment'. A subject–verb agreement follows: the subject/noun is 'quantities of several corrosive chemicals'; the verb is 'are needed'. This is a rare sentence with no object. It is clear that the word 'that' performs no function. To solve this problem, I will remove 'that' and make the first part of the sentence the object:

> ✓ Quantities of several corrosive chemicals are needed in this experiment.

If the word 'that' appears because the writer wants to do *more* with the sentence, by suggesting perhaps that the need for corrosive chemicals leads to *something else*, then the sentence is more confusing. Again, the writer has to think through what they mean. Something like the following would be possible, of course:

> ✓ The quantities of corrosive chemicals that are needed in this experiment are substantial enough that specific certified laboratories can carry out this work.

Sometimes, as you can see, mixed constructions are mistakes that come from hurried writing. If you proofread carefully, you are likely to find them. Some of them, though, highlight a problem with unclear meaning. This, again, proves the importance of a common theme of this book – being sure of what you want to tell the reader.

The third, final example comes from a theatre studies essay:

> ✗ Although the play's two main characters seem to be redeemed, but the outlook can be considered bleak.

The problem here is that the word 'although' sets up the sentence's second half to provide a contradictory phrase – which it does – and the word 'but' has also been used. Using the two conjunctions has made the sentence confusing and incorrect. Removing either one solves the problem:

> ✓ Although the play's two main characters seem to be redeemed, the outlook can be considered bleak.
> ✓ The play's two main characters seem to be redeemed, but the outlook can be considered bleak.

There are, potentially, subtle differences of emphasis in the two different options, but ultimately, both sentences say the same thing.

Key point

Two of the three mixed constructions I've written are underlined in green by my word processor's spell-checking and grammar tool. The software can tell that the sentence is grammatically incorrect, but *it can't tell me why*. Additionally, the first mixed construction is not marked as incorrect at all. This highlights the limitations of technology; the next chapter will discuss this idea a little more.

Reading sentences aloud is a good way to find mixed constructions. They will sound wrong, even if you don't know why at first. In general, conjunctions and missing verbs are common causes of the problem. Think through what you want to say, and write it in a calm and unhurried way.

Dangling modifiers

As you become more confident in your writing, you'll naturally (and correctly) try to vary your sentence structure more. As you do so, of course, you need to take care to check your writing is still grammatically correct.

Dangling modifiers are a common problem. They occur in sentences that begin with a modifying phrase before the traditional subject–verb–object arrangement. Quite often these modifying phrases involve a verb ending in 'ing', or some other descriptive phrase made up of several words.

Here are two *correct* examples of this kind of sentence:

> ✓ Feeling pressurised by declining ratings, the executives changed the television network's advertising policy.
>
> ✓ Originally developed to enhance efficiency in local health authorities, the new database system played an important role in directly improving the experiences of service users.

These examples are correct, because the first modifying phrase modifies the subject of the next part of the sentence, which is the noun that appears *directly after the comma* (with the relevant articles, and in the second example, the adjective 'new').

Where, then, do people go wrong?

In a way, this issue is similar to the previously discussed 'mixed constructions': these sentences are problematic when the modifier does not clearly apply to the subject of the sentence. That is, the modifier 'dangles'. As with mixed constructions, it might be that parts of the sentence have been attached to each other, and all contribute to the same point, but do not work together grammatically.

The next two sentences are versions of the previous examples, rewritten incorrectly to demonstrate the 'dangling modifiers' problem:

> ✗ Feeling pressurised by declining ratings, the television network's advertising policy was adjusted by the executives.
>
> ✗ Originally developed to enhance efficiency in local health authorities, an important role emerged for the new database system, which would directly improve the experiences of the service users.

This issue can be quite difficult to detect. The two sentences above, if scanned (read quickly), might seem appropriate – particularly the second one.

As I've explained, when a sentence begins with a modifier, the modifier applies to the subject of the sentence, which will appear *at the beginning* of the second part of the sentence (after the comma). Applying this logic to the examples above reveals problems.

To test these sentences in your own work, take the first noun after the comma (the subject of the sentence), and place it *in front of* the modifier. Does your sentence make sense? Take a look at this step applied to the incorrect examples:

> ✗ **Feeling pressurised by declining ratings, the television network's advertising policy** was adjusted by the executives.
>
> ✗ The television network's advertising policy, feeling pressurised by declining ratings …

The bold text above includes the two parts I have reordered. Clearly, the 'advertising policy' cannot 'feel pressurised' by anything, given that it will be an inanimate text or legal document!

Doing the same exercise with the original, correct version of the sentence makes it clear that the *executives* (that is, people in charge of the television network) were 'feeling pressurised' – which makes perfect sense:

> ✓ **Feeling pressurised by declining ratings, the executives** changed the television network's advertising policy.
>
> ✓ The executives, feeling pressurised by declining ratings …

The second sentence, while longer, poses the same problem:

> ✗ **Originally developed to enhance efficiency in local health authorities, an important role** emerged for the new database system, which would directly improve the experiences of the service users.
>
> ✗ An important role, originally developed to enhance efficiency in local health authorities …

You can see that the *role* of the new database system cannot have been 'developed as a way to enhance efficiency'. That is what the new database system was developed for. Alternatively, the *role* of the database system might have been to enhance efficiency. It is very strange, however, to suggest that the role was developed to enhance efficiency.

The correct example makes things clearer:

> ✓ **Originally developed to enhance efficiency in local health authorities, the new database system** played an important role in directly improving the experiences of service users.
>
> ✓ The new database system, originally developed to enhance …

The key is to look out for any sentences you've written that begins with a modifier, separated from the main sentence by a comma. As you've seen, the modifier might contain a verb ending in 'ing', but not necessarily.

I'll show you one more incorrect example, and then a range of correct sentences written this way. This should give you a better idea of what they look like, and your skill in finding them will improve.

The following sentence, beginning with a dangling modifier, comes from an essay discussing the work and views of a historian:

> ✗ Writing about the later stages of the Cold War, the reader notices a more realist tone developing in Gottfried's analyses of, and conclusions surrounding, Western foreign policy.

Again, pair the modifying phrase with the *first noun* appearing in the second part of the sentence:

> ✓ The reader, writing about the later stages of the Cold War …

You can see here that a hurriedly written sentence, beginning with a dangling modifier, has ended up meaning something noticeably unusual. Read grammatically, the sentence suggests that Gottfried's *readers* have written about the Cold War. How can readers detect Gottfried's views in the text that they have, seemingly, written and *are reading*? The dangling modifier here has resulted in a sentence that defies logic!

To solve this problem, make sure that the point you need to make is clear to you. I know that in this example, *Gottfried* is doing the 'writing about the later stages of the Cold War'.

As such, I need to write a sentence that begins:

> ✓ Writing about the later stages of the Cold War, Gottfried …

Alternatively, I could change the modifier:

> ✓ Reading Gottfried's works on the later stages of the Cold War, the reader …

The problem with this second option is the repetition of 'read'; I could adjust further:

> ✓ Investigating Gottfried's conclusions about the later stages of the Cold War, the reader …

There are many possible options. For the sake of simplicity, I will complete a sentence based on the first solution: keeping 'Gottfried' as the subject of the sentence. Focusing on the historian I am writing about seems more appropriate than shifting my assignment's focus to the vague collection of 'readers'.

As always, when solving this problem, express your point simply and clearly. I might end up with something like this:

> ✓ Writing about the later stages of the Cold War, Gottfried develops a more realist tone as he analyses and draws conclusions from Western foreign policy.

In my improved example, I've made some changes beyond fixing the dangling modifier. I've emphasised verbs more than nouns to make the sentence seem more active: instead of the noun 'analysis', I've used the verb 'analyse'. Similarly, the noun 'conclusions surrounding' has become the verb 'draws conclusions from'.

Finally, rather than the 'realist tone' developing, I've used the more active formulation: 'Gottfried develops a more realist tone'. This keeps Gottfried as the subject, rather than the 'realist tone' itself, retaining the close focus on the historian I am analysing.

To conclude, here are several example sentences that *correctly* begin with modifiers:

✓ Having discussed the available treatment options, the physiotherapist and patient agreed upon a four-week regimen of various exercises.

✓ Subjected to increased academic interest over the past twenty years, project management, in its current range of forms, has been reinvigorated.

✓ Its script subsequently embellished by two co-authors, Cranston's fourth film marks a shift into less comedic territory.

Using 'It has been said that …'

As you've read in this book, and in the books on your reading lists, referencing appropriately and correctly, based on the research that you've done, is a *crucial* part of writing essays. In referencing, you have a system that enables you to incorporate the work of others into your own, and to do so in a way that is obvious and honest.

Because of this, if there is a point in your essay where your reader thinks you *could* or *should* have referenced, and you have not, you have a problem developing. Similarly, giving the vague impression that someone, at some point, *might* have written something that you're now going to use in your essay, is unacceptable. Referencing is clear, explicit and transparent.

The most common problematic phrases in this context aren't a problem in themselves. However, they pose a problem if they are not combined with adequate referencing, or if they are deliberately used to reinforce a point that is your own, and not anybody else's.

These common examples appear in sentences like the following:

✗ **It has been suggested that** the second episode of this popular television series represented the situation in Iraq.

✗ Although the stigma associated with AIDS sufferers has been considerably reduced, **it is said that** the illness still has negative connotations for many members of the public.

✗ Because the immediate practical benefits of high-cost, long-lasting physics research projects are often unclear, **the point has been raised that** substantial government investment in such projects might not have much support.

These sentences are grammatically correct, make clear points and are suitably academic in style. Yet, written as they are in an essay, they are going to cause huge problems.

Each one *immediately* raises a question in the reader's mind: '*Who* suggested that?'; '*Who* said that?'; '*Who* raised that point?'

There are several reasons for this mistake being made. One is that the author wants to make a point, but is (correctly) trying to avoid the first person in making it. To give it enough authority, a third-person statement like 'it has been suggested that' is chosen. Although the first person should be avoided, as you've learned, there is a deeper problem here: a problem with confidence. The next section of this chapter deals with this issue in particular.

The second reason, then, can be attributed to laziness or vagueness. As a student is frantically typing an essay mere hours from the deadline, they might remember a fantastic and important point from one of their lectures over the past year. Alternatively, they might think back to something that struck them from last night's pile of notes, journal articles, handouts and books.

In this scenario, the author *knows* that someone else has come up with an idea, or made a point (in the previous scenario, the author was making their own point), but can't remember who it is, or when it was made.

If this is the case, and you can't (or won't) find the information you need to reference a point, *you can't include it in your essay.* For some reason, sometimes people conclude that the phrase 'it has been suggested that …' is sufficient, and the reader will happily accept that a point has been made and has reinforcement behind it. This is not the case, however; that's exactly what referencing is for.

Another scenario involves the essay author trying, perhaps, to come up with some arguments that oppose the ones they have made in a previous section. They think of one, and then think something like, 'someone *must* have thought a similar thing at some point' and use the 'it has been said that …' or a similar phrase. In this situation, the writer knows they are making a point of their own, but is trying to give the impression it has been made by others.

There are two main options here: first, the student can include the point they are making, but as their own (again, the next section of this chapter is relevant here). They might decide, however, that this particular argument or point *needs* some reinforcement. They could, then, take a second approach: *deliberately* research the topic to see if this particular argument has been made.

Whether it has or not will affect what goes into the essay: if nobody has argued a particular point, the author could include it as their own. Alternatively, the author could include it as their own and detail why an argument might *not* have been made. If a point *has* been argued, the author has successfully carried out some deliberate, careful research that will probably have provided a range of material to write about. (Of course, if nobody has argued a particular point, the author may decide it is not worth making as a point of their own; this is fine, as long as the author thinks through the decision.)

Importantly, though, in either case, the author of the essay is using language, and using (or not using) referencing in an honest, clear way.

Key point

Another phrase commonly used in this manner is 'it has been argued that ...'.

In conclusion, then, do not use phrases like 'it has been suggested that' unless you can prove that they are true – that is, reference them. To clarify, the following sentence, reworked from one of the above examples, would be appropriate (providing the references are accurate, of course!):

> ✓ Although the stigma associated with AIDS sufferers has been considerably reduced, **it is said that** the illness still has negative connotations for many members of the public (Wilkins, 2002; Shapiro, 2008).

If you cannot prove that the phrase is true, you as the writer need to decide whether to research the point (and then decide how or whether to include it, based on what you discover), to discard it, or to *confidently make the point your own.*

Using 'I think/I feel ...'

Chapter 1 made clear the importance of being objective in academic writing. One convention that contributes to objectivity is avoiding the first person; academic writing should almost always be written in the third person.

Although following that convention will mean you're not in danger of making this mistake, I wanted to highlight it because it comes from a common problem with confidence in one's writing. A lack of confidence in our own work, especially as we are just starting our studies, is understandable. However, you don't want your writing to betray this.

Key point

Note that an earlier chapter discussed 'hedging'. 'Hedging' means deliberately writing to show that you cannot be sure of a particular conclusion; that is, being deliberately cautious. Effective hedging actually demonstrates confidence in how solid your arguments are. As such, do not confuse 'hedging' with writing that lacks confidence.

There is a tendency among students, in assignments that otherwise follow the main academic conventions, to occasionally write a sentence like the one in bold, below. The extract is from an essay on the ethical and medical issues surrounding human medicine trials.

> ✗ Crocker and Ryan's work was pivotal in revealing the problem of human medical testing (1998). Although the subject had previously been raised in fiction, often to create tension or horror (Crichton, 1969; Cook, 1990), Crocker and Ryan presented an accessible, scholarly paper that highlighted the number of problematic trials that had been conducted. When a medical trial ended in the high-profile, widely reported organ failure of the patients (*Daily Mail*, 2006; Ward, 2006), yet more popular attention was focused on the subject. **I believe that the Western public as a whole, having been exposed to these sources, is comfortable enough with the medical trial as a concept to engage with it in a transparent, scientific debate.**

The extract is well-written, clear, appropriately referenced and academically acceptable – *except for the sentence in bold.*

One problem, on the surface, is the fact that phrases like 'I believe that ...', 'I feel that ...', 'In my opinion ...' are not necessary in academic writing. Here is the same paragraph with the phrase removed:

> ✓ Crocker and Ryan's work was pivotal in revealing the problem of human medical testing (1998). Although the subject had previously been raised in fiction, often to create tension or horror (Crichton, 1969; Cook, 1990), Crocker and Ryan presented an accessible, scholarly paper that highlighted the number of problematic trials that had been conducted. When a medical trial ended in the high-profile, widely reported organ failure of the patients (*Daily Mail*, 2006; Ward, 2006), yet more popular attention was focused on the subject. **The Western public as a whole, having been exposed to these sources, is comfortable enough with the medical trial as a concept to engage with it in a transparent, scientific debate.**

Referencing has been used to demonstrate to the reader what has come from other sources. The last sentence, with no references, *must* be an argument that the author of the essay is making. The fact that it is clearly a conclusion drawing on the evidence in the previous sentences helps a great deal, but even if it were the first sentence in the paragraph, the reader would make the same assumption.

This idea came up in the referencing chapter: your work should always involve references that lead to your own conclusions and points. Unreferenced sentences will be read as your conclusions and points. There is no problem here.

Why, then, do these phrases ('I feel', 'I think', etc.) appear so often, even when students know not to use the first person 'I'?

The use of such phrases points to a lack of confidence.

This lack of confidence might be a *broad* one, very common when you are just starting out on a degree. This is often phrased as the question, 'Well, how can *I* include my own views among the points made by these *academics* and *experts*?' While it is understandable that you might have this worry, you need to get rid of it as quickly as you can. The reason that academic conventions, and referencing and critical thinking, are so important is that they allow you to present your evidence, come to your own conclusions and get involved in the academic debate around a subject by giving all this to the reader.

Remove these kinds of phrases and work at making your writing effective and your references appropriate and correct.

Alternatively, you might lack confidence *in this particular point*. If you have been happily writing your essay, and find that you have included one of these phrases – when you understand that you shouldn't – then actually examine the point you're making. Perhaps it does need a rethink.

Perhaps, instead, you need to 'hedge'; that is, be honest with the reader that your conclusion is tentative. This is *not* the same as telling the reader 'this point is my own; it doesn't belong to an expert, and you should be aware of that'. The reader knows this. Instead, you are saying, 'You're already aware that this point is mine, because it isn't referenced. I am making this point based on the evidence I have, which I've done my best to share with you, though I am being honest in that it *might be possible* to draw a different conclusion.'

Finally, then, here is the same example, but with some hedging language used instead of the 'I think' phrase:

✓ Crocker and Ryan's work was pivotal in revealing the problem of human medical testing (1998). Although the subject had previously been raised in fiction, often to create tension or horror (Crichton, 1969; Cook, 1990), Crocker and Ryan presented an accessible, scholarly paper that highlighted the number of problematic

(Continued)

(Continued)

trials that had been conducted. When a medical trial ended in the high-profile, widely reported organ failure of the patients (*Daily Mail*, 2006; Ward, 2006), yet more popular attention was focused on the subject. The Western public as a whole, having been exposed to these sources, **seems** comfortable enough with the medical trial as a *concept* to, **perhaps**, engage with it in a transparent, scientific debate.

The broad point here is that unreferenced points will (correctly) be read as your own work.

Do not feel that you cannot include your own points in your work. Ensure that you are comfortable enough with each point you make, and that you have presented the evidence that led you to make the point. Finally, 'hedge' where necessary.

Quick tip: affect or effect?

The words 'affect' and 'effect' are often confused. In general, 'affect' is used as a verb, while 'effect' is used as a noun. The following two sentences are correct:

✓ The treatment failed **to affect** the patient, whose condition worsened.

✓ The treatment had no **effect** on the patient, whose condition worsened.

Simply determine how you are using the word – whether it is an action (verb) or thing (noun). To remember this, remember that a verb is an action word. Action begins with 'a': 'affect' is the action.

Avoiding the word 'interesting'

This issue has nothing to do with grammar or academic conventions. Based on my experience looking at essays, the word 'interesting' should be avoided. It seems to cause potential problems, rather than lead to effective writing.

Try not to describe anything as 'interesting'. One problem is that if you call something interesting, your reader might suspect that you don't consider the rest of your work interesting! It is also quite a weak and overused word that does not actually mean much. (Remember, too, the advice in this book about excessive and unnecessary description in general.)

Plenty of alternative words exist. Below, I've demonstrated some sentences in which you might be tempted to include the word 'interesting', and then listed some other options:

> ✘ It is interesting that, in his final interview, Robertson did not mention the ongoing financial crisis, a topic that had permeated so powerfully into his latest poems.
>
> ✘ The two translations of this ancient Japanese text are almost identical, but the 1973 version, interestingly, uses the word 'right-mindedness' instead of 'righteousness'.

Alternatives include:

> ✓ It is worth noting … /It is worth pointing out …
>
> ✓ … notably …

Another different approach would be to shift the focus from pointing out that something is worth noting, to explaining *why* something is worth noting. You can link this to the larger point that you are making. In the box, you'll see one of the example sentences rewritten with this idea in mind:

> ✓ In his final interview, Robertson did not mention the ongoing financial crisis, a topic that had permeated so powerfully into his latest poems. This fact could support Willis' claim that the author was 'no longer so open about the intended meaning behind his work' (2010). The author himself once wrote that 'the reader plays the most important part of all' (Robertson, 2004). Alternatively, a more extreme conclusion, posited reluctantly by Browne (2010), suggests that Robertson's mental illnesses were, at this time, increasing in severity.

This seems rather a long extract – a whole paragraph now – when you consider that I only used it to replace calling something 'interesting'. However, if something is so noteworthy that you need to point it out, it probably is quite an important point to develop. In academic writing, you shouldn't point something out as being interesting in passing, or as a kind of 'add on'. Everything you write builds towards answering the essay question, or fulfilling the assignment brief. Logically, then, if you think you find something 'interesting', it is either interesting enough to merit full exploration, or not interesting enough to merit even a mention.

Quick tip: important ideas

The word 'interesting' appeared in my last sentence, which leads neatly on to this next tip. Using words such as 'interesting', 'crucial' or 'important' can cause a problem.
   Here is another example:

> ✗ It is crucial to understand the context of NASA at the time of the Cold War.

Don't label anything as 'important' or 'crucial' without explaining *why* it is so important. If you call a topic, idea, event or text important and don't tell the reader why, they will have certain worries and questions.
   They might think that you have gathered from your research, or vaguely remember from a lecture, that an idea is important; you haven't, though, grasped the topic enough to understand the importance of it.
   Alternatively, they might worry that they are missing out on key information, because you haven't explained the reasons that a topic is particularly important.

Poor presentation of tables and graphs

This issue really impacts on the impression an audience will have of your work, especially if it happens consistently throughout a longer piece of work (like a research project).

If you are going to include a graph or table which you have not produced, treat it like any other kind of reference (a quotation, a paraphrase, and so on). This means ensuring it is clear and readable, it is cited correctly in your text, and its relevance and importance is made obvious.

This last point means that not only do we use high-quality scans or images of the appropriate graphs (as opposed to poor-quality photocopies) and include not only a title (taken from the original source if possible), but also an appropriate and correct citation at the bottom right of the image (or footnote the title, if that's more consistent with your referencing style). Finally, make sure that you explain the diagram's presence in your text, in the same way that you'd expand on or develop a quotation.

Doing this might range from including phrases as short and simple as, 'As diagram A, above, shows, the corporation's profits increased during the first half of the year ...', to an entire paragraph explaining some of the key points or statistics visible in the diagram or graph. By doing this, you'll be showing that, as with your quoting and paraphrasing, you are using your research in a considered way, rather than just copying-and-pasting visual information and using that to make a point in, and by, itself.

Here is an example of a chart I have created, with the paragraph that follows it.

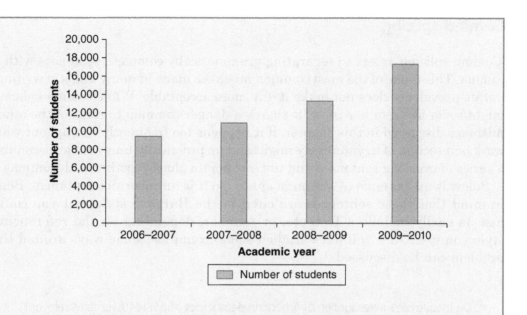

As the chart above shows, the number of students at Fordingham University has increased substantially each academic year since 2006. It is also apparent that the size of the increase has grown, particularly between academic years 2008–2009 and 2009–2010. This essay will examine the various factors that played a role in these increases.

Quick tip: practise or practice?

'Practise' and 'practice' are often confused or misused. 'Practise' is a *verb*, while 'practice' is the *noun*. Knowing what function the word fulfils in a sentence will determine which spelling to use. To recall this, I remember that 'ice' is a noun, so 'practice', ending with the noun, is also a noun.

As such, these two example sentences are appropriate:

✓ Most journal articles published in the field of occupational therapy are written by established professionals who **have been practising** for years.

✓ **The practice** of occupational therapy is inseparable from the theory behind it.

Cases like this demonstrate how important it is to have an understanding of basic English grammar – if you weren't aware of the difference between a noun and a verb, you might never get this right!

Comma splicing

'Comma splicing' refers to separating grammatically complete sentences with a comma. This is one of the most common mistakes made in many kinds of writing, but its prevalence does not make it any more acceptable! While comma splicing might seem like a minor issue, it shares a danger common to some of the other mistakes discussed in this chapter: if it happens too frequently throughout your work or a section of it, your essay might end up practically unreadable, becoming a series of overlong sentences and unclear points glued together with commas.

Below is an example of a comma splice (so it is an incorrect sentence). Bear in mind that these sentences are cited in the Harvard style, but you could just as easily include a footnote, or number, depending on the referencing style you use. Once you have studied some examples, some ways around the problem can be discussed.

> ✗ De Tocqueville's investigation of American democracy (1835/1840) remains relevant today, many politics courses still list it as core reading.

If we separate this example into two parts, using the comma as our point of division, we get these:

> De Tocqueville's investigation of American democracy (1835/1840) remains relevant today

and

> many politics courses still list it as core reading

Read these sentences aloud, separately, and it should be fairly obvious that they are complete. This means that we cannot separate them just by using a comma. Here is a similar sentence that is not an example of comma splicing:

> ✓ Although De Tocqueville's investigation of American democracy (1835/1840) is nearly as old as America itself, many politics courses still list it as core reading.

Separating this in the same way gives us:

> Although De Tocqueville's investigation of American democracy (1835/1840) is nearly as old as America itself

and

many politics courses still list it as core reading

The second part is identical, and it is still complete. The first part of the sentence, however, includes the conjunction 'although'. Read the first part of that sentence aloud and you will hear that something is quite obviously missing. That 'although' means that we need a second idea.

You may now have an idea about the rule to avoid comma splicing: at least one of the clauses, on either side of the comma, has to be incomplete when read by itself. This rule also applies to sentences made up of three or more clauses. Here is another comma splice:

> ✗ De Tocqueville investigated American democracy (1835/1840), his book is still widely considered relevant, the text is still listed as core reading on a wide range of politics courses.

This splits into three parts:

De Tocqueville investigated American democracy (1835/1840)

his book is still widely considered relevant

the text is still listed as core reading on a wide range of politics courses

Each of these, too, is complete; reading them aloud proves this immediately. We can ignore the citation, which might look different if another referencing style was being used. In any case, no referencing system would interfere with the grammatical sense of the sentence. Again, a slightly different example might not involve a comma splice:

> ✓ Nearly two hundred years after it was first published, De Tocqueville's (1835/1840) investigation of American democracy is still considered relevant, a fact emphasised by its inclusion as core reading in a wide range of politics courses.

Separating this into three parts gives us:

Nearly two hundred years after it was first published

De Tocqueville's (1835/1840) investigation of American democracy is still considered relevant

a fact emphasised by its inclusion as core reading on a wide range of politics courses

The second, or middle, clause is complete, and would work as a stand-alone sentence. The first, however, is a modifying clause that adds information (in this case, a rough date of publication) to another. As such, it does not make sense without the clause it is providing more detail about. As usual, reading this clause aloud will prove this point straight away. The same applies to the third clause. It is grammatically incomplete because it lacks a suitably formed verb, and if we wrote this as a sentence by itself, it might not be clear what 'a fact' refers to (here it is obvious because, again, the clause is modifying the previous one by telling us more about it).

This reaffirms the rule: at least one of the clauses in a sentence that separates clauses with commas must be grammatically incomplete – that is, unable to stand as a sentence on its own.

Your sentence might have six clauses, and this rule still applies; in fact, as I have already mentioned, comma splicing becomes a much more problematic issue when it is used to link clause after clause, resulting in confusing, breathless paragraphs. Reading your work aloud is a very simple way of tracking this down. If you have any doubt as to whether a sentence is comma spliced, separate it into its constituent clauses in a separate word processor document, or on a separate sheet of paper. Double-check that at least one could not stand by itself.

Take a look at this example paragraph:

> ✘ De Tocqueville investigated American democracy (1835/1840), his book is still widely considered relevant, the text is still listed as core reading on a wide range of politics courses. He wanted to see why republican representative democracy worked so well in the USA, he travelled round the states, he compared the American system to that of his native France, there are positive and negative aspects in what he found during this journey.

This paragraph 'sounds' very rushed and breathless, and it gives the impression that the author is stringing potentially valid, relevant points together without pausing to think about style or variety; the continued comma splicing actually makes the sentence very difficult to read. **This is important because** the presence of one paragraph like this in an essay means that there are likely to be others. As you can imagine, having to read whole sections of an essay written in this way would likely not have the best effect on your tutor's mood.

Identifying this very common problem is the first step; now we have to solve it.

Quite often the simple conjunctions 'and', 'but', 'then' and 'because' can be used, if they are appropriate.

For example, instead of the comma-spliced sentence:

> ✗ De Tocqueville's investigation of American democracy was published in two volumes in 1835 and 1840, it is still relevant today.

we could use:

> ✓ De Tocqueville's investigation of American democracy was published in two volumes in 1835 and 1840 but it is still relevant today.

Here, 'but' is actually providing another layer of meaning – it is surprising or striking that De Tocqueville's book is still relevant, while, perhaps, most other books written as long ago as the 1800s might not be considered useful now.

Sometimes we can use a semi-colon. There is often confusion as to what a semi-colon actually does; as mentioned in Chapter 3, this is its most common purpose. It is used to join grammatically complete statements where the writer feels the link is so important that using two separate sentences would damage it (my sentence at the bottom of the previous page, 'Identifying this very common problem …' is actually an example of this). When it comes to rectifying comma-spliced sentences, using semi-colons instead of separate sentences, occasionally, is a good way of varying our writing style. See the example below:

> ✓ De Tocqueville does detail many negative points inherent in the American system of representative democracy; he discusses at some length what he sees as a lack of intellectual freedom in the country (1835/1840).

Finally, we can use separate sentences. This is often the simplest option, and it is better to write a paragraph of short separate sentences that make your points and express your ideas clearly than to write one filled with overlong, convoluted sentences and comma splicing.

Here, the writer has separated a comma-spliced sentence into three separate ones:

> ✓ One of De Tocqueville's aims was to compare and contrast the American system with that of France. His book had a lasting impact on intellectuals in both countries. It is also striking that many of the predictions he made about the future of American democracy would come true.

As you learn to develop your writing, you'll find that using a combination of the different solutions (joining some sentences together, using some semi-colons, splitting some spliced sentences into separate ones) will make your writing more varied and thus more interesting for the reader.

Quick tip: beginning a sentence with a number

There are various rules around writing numbers. These can vary from subject to subject; as you can imagine, different subjects use numbers to different extents.

Here is one rule that is the same across subjects: if you start a sentence with a number, you *must* write it, not use digits.

The following sentence would not be acceptable:

> ✗ 2 of the patients in the control group recovered at the same pace as those taking the experimental drug treatment.

Note that this rule applies even with large numbers. So, if you have a very large number you don't want to write in full, for example:

> ✗ Ten thousand, six hundred and sixty-seven is the total number of deaths resulting from extreme weather in the country, according to figures released by the government.

rearrange your sentence so it does not appear at the beginning, like so:

> ✓ The government has released figures that estimate the number of deaths resulting from extreme weather in the country at 10,667.

Quick tip: conjunctions

Don't begin sentences with conjunctions (see Chapter 2 on basic grammar for a list, but the common ones are: 'and',' but' and 'or'). Sometimes doing this is acceptable in other forms of writing, but it should be avoided in assignments.

However, be careful not to confuse conjunctions with *prepositions* (a much longer list, including: 'with', 'to', 'under', 'above', and many more).

Using 'of' instead of 'have'

This mistake is common in speech as well as writing; it probably appears in essays because the writers of the essays make the mistake when they talk.

In Chapter 2, the verb as a grammatical device was defined and discussed. Chapter 3 examined the issue of verb 'tense'. Several tenses involve the word 'have' followed by an appropriate form of a particular verb.

The mistake being discussed here involves the word 'have' being incorrectly replaced by 'of'. 'Of' is not a verb, and as such, does not appropriately create a certain tense when it is paired with a verb. Here are some examples of correct usage:

> ✓ Although the legislation was only passed two years ago, its results, judging by rising grades in Indian primary schools, **have been** encouraging.
>
> ✓ Until the opening of the Soviet archives, commentators, politicians, historians and journalists could (and many did) warn about the expansionist nature of the Communist regime, but could **not have known** just how expansionist the empire was.
>
> ✓ Walker was approached by a major film studio interested in adapting his first novel, a full thirty years after the events of the novel are meant to **have taken place**. Walker turned the studio down because they insisted on updating the setting which would '**have been** disastrous' (Walker, 1986: 340).

The following versions of these sentences, then, would be incorrect (but this mistake is so common I would not be surprised if I saw them):

> ✗ Until the opening of the Soviet archives, commentators, politicians, historians and journalists could (and many did) warn about the expansionist nature of the Communist regime, but could **not of known** just how expansionist the empire was.
>
> ✗ Walker was approached by a major film studio interested in adapting his first novel, a full thirty years after the events of the novel are meant to **of taken place.** Walker turned the studio down because they insisted on updating the setting which would 'have been disastrous' (Walker, 1986: 340).

Note that in the final example, the second use of 'have been' is a *direct quote*, which the essay author could not change. In a way, this would act as a clue to the other mistake!

The most common formation of this mistake seems to be 'would have' and 'could have' (or the negative equivalents 'would not have' or 'could not have') being incorrectly written 'would of' and 'could of'.

'Of' is a preposition that labels a specific relationship between one noun and another; this relationship is often possessive, as it is in the following example:

> ✓ The effects **of** the excesses of Senators like Joe McCarthy and the House Un-American Activities Committee reverberated through American politics, massively straining public confidence in it, for decades. Additionally, as a consequence **of** the later Watergate scandal, faith in the federal government would drop even more.

As you can see, the phrase 'would of', for example, has nothing to do with the specific meaning of the word 'of', nor is it a correct verb form.

Use your word processor's 'find' tool to track down all your uses of the word 'of'. (There is another reason to do this, explained in a separate subsection.) Check that it has been used correctly, and is never connected to the verbs 'would', 'could', 'should' or 'will', in particular.

If you take care to write your verbs correctly, and think through the appropriate tenses for your sentences, as discussed in Chapter 3, you should not notice this problem at all.

Quick tip: overlong/convoluted sentences

This has already been mentioned, but is such a common mistake that I wanted to highlight it again in this section.

Briefly: if reading a sentence aloud leaves you breathless, it's too long! Simply break it down into manageable chunks, even if this occasionally leads to some repetition. Similarly, if you have difficulty checking that verbs (for example) agree with the appropriate nouns, because they are so far apart, you might have a problem.

The word 'of' and possessive replacements

The 'possessive', as well as the letter 's' and the apostrophe that goes with it, were discussed in Chapter 3.

Although this is not a mistake, as such, it's worth knowing that in *most* cases the word 'of' is used to represent the possessive. It can often, therefore, be replaced by the simpler possessive apostrophe and 's'.

Here are some examples that show this replacement in action:

The aim of the study was to investigate the effects of long-term steroid abuse by males between the ages of 19 and 27.

The study's aim was to investigate the effects of long-term steroid abuse by males between the ages of 19 and 27.

> One of the objectives **the designers of the game** set out to achieve, starting with **the style of the interface**, was creating a 'truly immersive experience' (Halshaw, 2006: 23).
>
> One of the objectives **the game's designers** set out to achieve, starting with **the interface style**, was creating a 'truly immersive experience' (Halshaw, 2006: 23).
>
> During the early stages of the primary campaign, it was clearly **the intention of Governor Clinton** to prove that he was **a different kind of Democrat**. **The structure of his campaign operation** allowed him to ensure this theme was reinforced at every level.
>
> During the early stages of the primary campaign, it was clearly **Governor Clinton's intention** to prove that he was **a different kind of Democrat**. **His campaign operation's structure** allowed him to ensure this theme was reinforced at every level.

In the last example, one use of the word 'of' ('a different kind of Democrat') has not been changed. The phrase 'a Democrat's different kind' does not make sense. This highlights the fact that it's always up to you as the author to choose whether to make this substitution. Sometimes, as in this example, the replacement doesn't make sense.

In other cases, using the possessive 's' might sound or read strangely; if in doubt, leave the original 'of' in the sentence.

Below are some phrases in which you need to keep the word 'of'. These are just some examples; again, using 'of' is not incorrect. The possessive can be simpler, but cannot always be used instead.

> part of the problem …
>
> several of the …
>
> many of the …
>
> some of the …
>
> one of the important facts from the …

Finally, I've included a sentence in which I *could* use the possessive, but would choose not to, because the resulting sentence seems a bit strange to me. Rather than change it to a sentence that bothers me in my essay, I've left it as it is.

> The shift of the focus in the play from the imprisoned criminals to their guards is a subtle one.

A version with the possessive replaced would look like this:

> The focus' shift in the play from the imprisoned criminals to their guards is a subtle one.

The phrase 'focus' shift' looks odd, and sounds odd when read aloud. It seems a bit forced and awkward. As such, replacing 'of' with the simple possessive should be seen as one potential technique available to you when writing. Sometimes it will help streamline your writing. At other times it should not be used.

'Putting things off'

An essay's introduction, or the introductory parts of chapters in a longer assignment, usually does a number of things. The introduction explains the context of a topic, outlines the reader's argument and, crucially, summarises what the essay is going to investigate.

The last of these, explaining the various steps an assignment will take, naturally involves sentences and paragraphs that tell the reader that something *will* be discussed, rather than actually discussing the particular something *now*.

This is appropriate, and readers will expect your introduction to do this. However, when the same phenomenon happens later in a piece of work, it can cause an unusual problem.

Sometimes, in essays, students give the impression of 'putting things off', by explaining what is going to appear in a piece of work, instead of just raising the topic.

Below, you'll see an example of this:

> ✗ Before discussing the present state of Marxist theory, a definition of Marxism is necessary.

While there is nothing grammatically wrong with this sentence, it is a waste of words that could be put to better use. The author should simply provide the 'necessary' definition, like so:

> ✓ Marxism can be defined as …

After a definition has been provided, the author can go on to discuss 'the present state of Marxist theory'.

The following example is similarly problematic:

> ✗ At this point, some information about the context of the NASA space programme at the time is needed.

The phrase 'at this point' means *now*. If some information is needed *now*, provide it now! The author could simply write a clear, simple paragraph detailing the context of the space programme:

> ✓ At the time, the NASA space programme was a complex set of projects, each with distinct aims, budgets and individuals who were involved.

This might strike you as a strange issue, but you'd be surprised how commonly it appears in assignments. After all, nobody *deliberately* decides to delay discussion unnecessarily.

This is just a theory of my own, but I think this happens because, to an author trying to make their work seem 'academic', highlighting the fact that you are about to provide an important definition can seem formal, somehow.

Take another look at the example about Marxism. I get the impression that a student, in writing this sentence, might think the sentence says something like this: 'I am discussing a very important and academic topic, and I understand that it's very important to define key terms in essays, so I am going to prove that I think this way by telling the reader I'm about to do so.'

The problem with this approach, of course, is that the student is forgetting that simply defining the 'important and academic topic' proves the same thing to the reader. In fact, it proves it in a simpler, more effective way.

Again, that is my tentative explanation for why this issue appears; remember, don't try to be any more formal than necessary. This applies to both the formality of writing style, as well as the over-formal approach of unnecessarily 'building up' to a grand topic, which actually just appears as if you are delaying the inevitable.

Bear in mind that if you *do* need to explain why a certain point needs to be made before another one, then it's appropriate to do so. That is, if you are aware that something needs to be delayed, and *can explain why*, then explain it. This, in fact, would be considered signposting. Consider this revised version of the previous example:

> ✓ In order to understand the part that the NASA space programme played in America's Cold War strategy, it is crucial to understand the context of NASA at the time.

If I were to take out the reason for delaying a discussion, I'd be left with a sentence more like the earlier, problematic ones:

> ✗ It is crucial to understand the context of NASA at the time of the Cold War.

The second version, and the earlier sentences, are examples of an unnecessary kind of signposting: 'I need to give you this important information now. Here is the important information.'

The first version of the NASA sentence, however, makes clear *why* the information is important: 'I need to give you this information *because it helps you understand* what comes next.'

To summarise: do not delay making a point, unless you can explain why you need to. If it is worth writing, it is worth writing now!

Further reading

Some of the books I've mentioned in other chapters deal excellently with what the authors have found to be common mistakes – I've covered the ones I see frequently, but there must be others! In particular, I would look at:

Godfrey, J. (2009) *How to Use Your Reading in Your Essays*. Basingstoke: Palgrave.

Peck, J. and Coyle, M. (2012) *The Student's Guide to Writing: Spelling, Punctuation and Grammar* (3rd edn). Basingstoke: Palgrave.

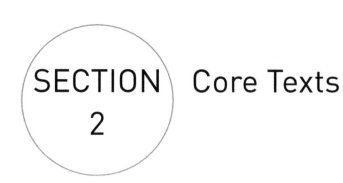

SECTION 2

Core Texts

Introduction to Nursing Theory

Hall, C.

Hi, my name is Celia, and I am a primary school teacher. I fell over in the sports hall this morning – silly really, I slipped on the floor. It was wet where the caretaker had washed it. He does it every morning and we are not meant to go in until it is dry, but it is a short-cut to the head's office and everyone does it all the time. My own fault, I suppose. Anyway, now I am in A&E and they tell me my wrist is broken in two places and it needs an operation to fix it. It certainly looks a funny shape at the moment. I don't know how I am going to cope. I'm a single mother with two kids, plus I have my job to think about; being busy with a class of 31 children, I am really worried about work and how I am going to pay the bills and the mortgage if I can't go to work. I don't get paid unless I work and my husband does not give us enough for the children as it is.

Celia, patient

At times, your job could involve not only looking after your patient but their families too. A placement I worked for children with LD required lots of work with the families – the families are entrusting you with their loved ones and need to know they can visit, approach with problems, ask what's happening and know their ideas, thoughts and feelings are being listened to as well.

Sarah Parkes, LD nursing student

THIS CHAPTER COVERS

- A toolbox for nursing
- Nursing theory – how models for nursing practice are constructed

- Using nursing philosophy in the care you deliver

CHAPTER 1

NMC
STANDARDS

ESSENTIAL SKILLS
CLUSTERS

INTRODUCTION

Celia's story demonstrates the complexity and challenge of the nursing care you will be delivering in your practice. Celia's is not an unusual case, and her story shows how one small slip can transform the life of a patient and their family, identifying many complexities for nurses who care in this situation.

Delivering the best nursing care is a priority for nursing as a profession and for those who work as nurses, wherever the care that they give is delivered. In order to be able to give the best care, we must recognize what the best care is, and what this means to different people.

At a basic level, this appears simple: those who are cared for should be safe and comfortable and, in essence, the nurse should 'do no harm', to quote Florence Nightingale (Wagner and Whaite, 2010). However, to be sure that this is actually the case, it is critical to look more deeply. This chapter will explore what the nature of nursing is, and the core concepts of nursing and the importance of being a skilled nurse. The chapter will draw on all fields of nursing to take examples, and will particularly consider application to two mini case studies. It would be useful to read Chapter 1 before this chapter, so you understand what nursing is.

A TOOLBOX FOR NURSING

Throughout this chapter, all of the models and processes of nursing we consider are simply part of the toolbox which enables you to ensure effective care as a nurse. As with any tool, the skill of the user and the capability of the tool within the **context** are important. What recent reports such as the *Mid Staffordshire NHS Foundation Trust Public Inquiry* (Francis Report, 2013), *Improving the Safety of Patients in England* (Berwick Report, 2013), the *Review into the Quality of Care and Treatment Provided by 14 Hospital Trusts in England* (Keogh Review, 2013) and the report on Winterbourne View Hospital (DH, 2013a) show us is that without such capabilities, no model, tool or **benchmark standard** can create excellent nursing. We will return to Celia later in the chapter, as her story raises many issues, but it is important to remember that despite the complexity of her needs, it is critical that nursing care is always holistic, individualized and person-centred.

Getting the basics right

Today, nursing is a profession which has had to determine the important patient care goals with a target-driven National Health Service (NHS), and this has led to criticism of nurses and those who assist them. Surely getting the basics right is most important, the newspapers shout in every article about yet more poor care identified in yet another 'poor' hospital. Francis (2013) identified that care given in the hospitals identified as 'poor' was not uniformly poor, but neither was care given in a 'good' hospital uniformly good, so no one has any room for complacency. The NHS as a whole service has taken these issues seriously, researching why some care is substandard and developing innovative ways to address the issues faced. The productive ward initiative with the aim to give staff more time to care, the six Cs (DH, 2012) and 'caring around the clock' (Hutchings, 2012) are but a few recent initiatives in which nurses have been encouraged to think about their patients and to ensure the comfort and safety of patients in hospital settings.

In community care, a greater focus upon basic care needs and on the individual's capacity to identify and 'whistleblow' on poor care is evident, with the scandals of Winterbourne View (2012) and Clwyd Mental Health Services raising the alarm about poor care.

While thinking about all of the problems and issues faced by nursing may not appear the best way to begin, there is also much to be celebrated in nursing today. By appreciating a little more of the philosophy and theory, you will be able to understand the actions taken to ensure that patients are safe and effectively cared for and to understand their personal and contextual needs. This will also help you to understand your future role.

NURSING THEORY – HOW MODELS FOR NURSING PRACTICE ARE CONSTRUCTED

To think effectively about nursing, it is important to explore a definition of the actions and those involved – the actors – within the nursing scenario. Like a good play, it is also important to consider the setting and the intended goal of the activity proposed. This takes you further than thinking about what nursing is and how its knowledge is constructed, and on to thinking about what being a nurse means within a wider context of caring for a patient in a given situation. In Chapter 1 you thought about the nurse as someone who is qualified, and also about yourself in terms of becoming a nurse. Now you need to be thinking about what it is that a nurse actually does and how they perform their role in practice. This will vary according to where nursing takes place. If, for example, you explore the role of the nurse in a community mental health setting, you may find that the core focus of the nurse's work with patients may be on empowering and enhancing the patient's self-esteem and improving their capacity to manage their own care and their life, while managing any potential risks. Alternatively, when looking after the needs of a patient in critically ill adult nursing or in a children's intensive care unit, you may see the nurse also acting as an authority, offering skills and expertise to deliver nursing and working in partnership to help ensure that families are informed when making decisions may be particularly difficult.

CHAPTER 1

Let's have a look at a real-life Case Study. This time the family are in a community care setting located at home.

CASE STUDY: SURINDERJIT (1)

Surinderjit is thirteen years old and his parents' only child. He presents with speech, language and communication needs, complex health needs and physical disabilities which means he must receive his food artificially. He is an expressive boy and tends to be hyperactive. He attends a school for children with special needs, where nurses enable him to be fed using a **percutaneous endogastric (PEG) tube**, but is at home in the morning and evening, and requires considerable attention. His father owns a business and works long hours, leaving much of the care to Surinderjit's mother. The family live in a terraced house on the outskirts of a large city known for its concentration of Sikh families. They live in the home of their extended family, although the only living relative is Surinderjit's paternal grandmother, Mrs Sukhdeep Kaur, who is seventy-nine. She speaks little English, although she has lived in England for many years and her sons were born here. The family are bilingual, speaking Punjabi and English. Her husband died some years ago. Mrs Kaur has until recently been physically fit and helped to care for her grandson, but was admitted to hospital four weeks ago following a stroke which resulted in right-sided **hemiplegia** and some difficulty with speaking. Mrs Kaur was discharged home two weeks ago with a supportive care package which includes social care morning and night to enable her to wash and dress, and nursing care to dress a small ulcer on her leg which resulted from damage when she fell. It is becoming clear, however, that the family are finding the pressure of caring for Mrs Kaur and Surinderjit challenging. The house is small and the amount of equipment needed to care for Mrs Kaur makes it very cramped. Mrs Kaur's daughter-in-law identifies that Mrs Kaur tried to get up to go to the toilet and fell again yesterday, and she is worried that Mrs Kaur will hurt herself. She is very stressed and says that Mrs Kaur had only just been to the toilet when it happened and surely did not need to go again. She says that Mrs Kaur seems disorientated and confused since she has returned home. Mrs Kaur's daughter-in-law doesn't think the family can continue like this.

• How would the nurse's role be different if they were looking after Mrs Kaur, as compared to looking after Celia?
• How would this differ again if you were looking after Surinderjit as a learning disability nurse working as a school nurse at his school?

Imagine Surinderjit is nineteen years old.

• How would this differ if you were looking after Surinderjit as a learning disability nurse working as the nurse at his college?

In thinking about the above scenario, it can be seen that there are differences to Celia's story at the start of the chapter. Celia will have an operation very soon, while Mrs Kaur will need daily care for a long time. You may have thought that Mrs Kaur's nurse is working in the community visiting people at home, while Celia's nurse is in a hospital and the nurse caring for Surinderjit is in a school. In each case the nursing care offered will be different because the individual patient and their context is different. The next question you may have could be: if the roles of those providing care are so different, how come they are all nurses? The answer to this lies in the ways in which these nursing roles are similar or common, rather than in their differences.

Core concepts of nursing

The practice of nursing is dependent on some key elements, and these are of critical importance when understanding nursing. The four core earliest and most commonly identified domains are those of Yura and Torres (1975), and for simplicity they have been adapted to:

- Nursing
- Patient
- Health
- Society.

For the purposes of this chapter, it is enough to identify that these core concepts are fundamental in defining any kind of nursing, and to then explore briefly what might be meant within each concept.

More expert theorists who have considered nursing models to try to explain how nursing and nurses function have examined in greater detail philosophical beliefs about these nursing concepts and the relationships between them. Doing this enables a blueprint for nursing practice to emerge. Hall and Ritchie (2013) explore this in more detail, and you are invited to consider how your own philosophy might contribute to the kind of care you feel is professionally **concordant** for you as a nurse.

These core concepts have been recognized within most **models of nursing** since an American Nursing Association Survey evidenced them formally. However, if you go back to models outlined as early as Nightingale's 1895 'Nursing, what it is and what it is not' (translated into modern nursing by Fitzpatrick, 1992), it is quite possible to see the **interplay** of these concepts in creating an environment for nursing to be delivered.

ACTIVITY 12.1 REFLECTIVE PRACTICE

Think about your nursing. How would you define the above concepts in **your** practice? And what would **you** say about the relationship between these? For example, would you **define** yourself as a nurse who works with your patients in an equal way? Do you negotiate care with them **or** do they lead in their care decisions? This is a consideration about the definition of the concepts of 'nurse' and 'patient' and the relationships between these two concepts. It is a starting point to think about the development of a theoretical stance for your nursing, and it is important, when you are giving care, for you to think about who and what may be in control and how this might be changed for better outcomes. It is important for leaders of nursing to be clear about how they want nursing to be delivered, too. A shared belief about nursing can help everyone to work in the same direction and towards the same vision. This discussion will now be considered further in respect of the case studies in this chapter.

Why have a blueprint or model for nursing practice?

As we have seen just by considering the differences in the care required by Celia, Mrs Kaur and Surinderjit, the various ways in which nursing is perceived can be quite different. Having an identified model or blueprint for care can be useful for nurses as it aids nursing thinking, planning of care and communication, plus it represents an **ideology** and expectations for all who work within a comparable area. While to some extent a **core mission statement** or philosophy (available in some placements) can do this, a model or framework adds detail by applying the ideas to nursing concepts. A model itself cannot actually deliver nursing care, but it can give clear ideas about how it is to be achieved. It may also cover all the care given and support the development of care pathways or the development of tools related to an aspect of care delivery. The skills and knowledge required for care delivery are the preserve of the nurse and you will need to develop these and use them appropriately, in combination with tools to deliver care. Common tools found in nursing today include **SBAR**, **APIE** and **SOAPIER**.

CHAPTER 15

USING NURSING PHILOSOPHY IN THE CARE YOU DELIVER

So, how are such tools, models and philosophies relevant to the everyday nursing care you deliver? Considering the theoretical aspects of the core concepts of nursing helps you to appreciate and communicate the care you are giving. Models address care and aid communication about what your role as a nurse is; how the patient may be viewed; what the context or environment of nursing might contribute; and what the intended outcome of care might look like. Tools must be used in addition to any theoretical model in order to enable the process to work in a practical situation. A model relies on concepts which have definitions, are culturally determined and change over time; models are, therefore, dynamic, and the ways in which they are used should change to meet contemporary needs.

Exploring the core theoretical concepts of a meta-paradigm of nursing

When considering a meta-paradigm of nursing, which essentially means taking a big view of what nursing is about, the first core concept of nursing is the nurse themselves, and their work. One of the most important considerations relates to what we know as nursing and what nursing knowledge is. Carper's **seminal work** (1978) defined nursing by the kinds of knowledge the nurse would need, including ethical, empirical, personal and aesthetic knowledge and consideration of the **praxis of nursing**. Within this, the importance of art and science, the need for critically evaluated best evidence and personal and ethical awareness are all clearly defined. Although dated, these ideas remain valid when considering contemporary nursing and its emphasis upon the values of those who deliver care.

The remaining three concepts (identified on the previous page) will now be investigated. After this we will look at how one model for nursing, that of Roper, Logan and Tierney (RLT) (1980, 2000), defined the four concepts and how this has been developed and changed to be used in practice today.

Patient

In order to nurse, it is important to have a patient to look after. While this may sound obvious, it is important to think of the role a patient and their family might play in receiving care. In times past, it was entirely acceptable for patients to be cared for by nurses until they were nursed back to health. Indeed, if you look at RLT's original descriptions of the patient and the role of their nurse, the expectation was that the nurse was primarily the doer, making the patient the one who was 'done unto'. Thus the patient was defined as being on a continuum of dependency to independence in their life activities, relying on the nurse to provide care where they were dependent. In recent years, though, a more contemporary view of the patient has developed. The more modern view has been that founded on the original work of theorists such as Dorothea Orem (1914–2007), an American theorist who identified a need for the patients to be empowered and their role of a normally self-caring individual who simply requires nursing to offer support in difficult times geared towards the idea that the self-caring person will re-emerge.

Clearly, when thinking about the patient in this way there are advantages, such as a greater emphasis on returning to independent living. This is also politically helpful in terms of the resources required to finance the NHS, as keeping people in their own homes and communities means a greater likelihood of them retaining their independence for longer, with greater reliance upon informal care and supportive nursing rather than hospital provision. The result of this change means a greater concentration of critically ill patients in the hospital or residential areas provided by the NHS and a changing role for nurses in these areas, moving towards more specialized roles. This takes us on to consider the role of the environment, or society, in care.

Society (or environment)

The society or environment in which nursing takes place influences how and what care may be and what the expectations are. There is even a school of theoretical thought which suggests that the role of the nurse can only ever be to influence the care environment and enable the patient to achieve the optimal situation in which to become healthy or maintain their health. Two theorists who have recognized this view include Florence Nightingale (1859, cited by Wagner and Whaite, 2010) and, more recently, Roy (1970). This may seem an odd priority for someone who is nursing patients, but if we relate it to the case studies in this chapter, providing a safe environment for Celia is going to be critical as she prepares for her operation and as she recovers. Much of the initial care given by the nurse will be focused upon monitoring and ensuring that Celia's post-operative environment has all the requirements (including provision of oxygen, suction, monitoring equipment and **analgesia**) to ensure she recovers safely.

The care environment approach is particularly critical where resources are limited and decisions may need to be made about who receives available treatment. We now return to the case of Surinderjit and consider some further information.

CASE STUDY: SURINDERJIT [2]

Surinderjit's family have explored many avenues for care and treatment. They know there is a facility in another country which treats young people with needs such as his, which could allow him greater independence. Surinderjit's family have been campaigning for support from the NHS to enable him to receive the treatment in the UK; however, the treatment required is expensive and provision of this resource would mean denying many other treatments for other NHS patients which could allow greater independence, such as hip and knee replacements. Many people across the world are like Surinderjit, because healthcare providers must make difficult choices about who should receive treatment and how much to invest in different care. In the UK this has been identified as the 'post code lottery', and there are many examples in the newspapers.

- What other environmental situations can you think of which may influence how and when nursing might be delivered, and to whom?

It is possible to think of situations where resources are very limited – in countries where there are insufficient life-saving resources, for example. Care decisions in these circumstances are influenced by what is not available and resources go to ensuring the fittest survive. Equally, the care setting may also be influenced by what is available and cultural expectations may vary as a result. When Mrs Kaur was admitted to hospital, she expected her family to visit and stay with her. Although Mrs Kaur and her family had lived in the UK for many years, Mrs Kaur's experience of hospitals related to caring for her own mother when she was hospitalized in India, during which time Mrs Kaur had stayed with her mother to care for her throughout her whole hospital stay. Thus she was quite confused when her family were asked to leave and did not stay to care for her. Mrs Kaur's cultural expectations were different from those of the prevailing culture within which she was being cared for.

The final consideration to explore is that of health.

I am very passionate about effective communication in nursing, talking to your patient, observing their body language and creating an environment where they feel able to talk to you about anything. Doing this will aid you in gauging whether your patients' needs are being met.

Charlie Clisby, NQN

Health

When considering definitions of health, the World Health Organization (1946) and Henderson (1966) offer perhaps the two most well known and sustained views in respect of a patient's health. Henderson proposed that an outcome of health may not necessarily be defined as a healthy life but that of a peaceful death, while the WHO record that health is not merely reflected in the absence of disease or disability, but implies that health lies in the individual's capacity to manage their circumstances in a healthy manner. These views are important and in the UK underpins the *NHS Constitution* (DH, 2013b). For Mrs Kaur and her family, a healthy future may involve establishing the ability to continue to work well with Surinderjit as he grows into adolescence, given the change in Mrs Kaur's physical circumstances and mental capacity. For Celia, her health outlook might be very different in the short and longer term: although it would be expected that her arm would heal within a few months, she may undergo serious mental stress as the result of being the sole earner in her family, and having a job which relies on her being available to work. Given Celia's history of depression following her divorce, ensuring a healthy outcome may mean giving consideration to her mental wellbeing and ensuring she has adequate social support as she works out how to support her family during the time she is unable to work. Without this Celia may need support from mental health services if her anxiety and depression return. She is a single mother and, as working will be difficult, this temporary physical disability will affect her financial commitments. There is evidence that poverty and lack of stability are far more common for individuals who have long-term disability issues or who support family members with disability than for others in society.

Changing care needs

In real-life situations theoretical frameworks are useful to aid the care that is given initially but this often needs to change as the setting the patient is cared for within changes. Thus theoretical frameworks need to be supplemented to ensure the patient receives the best nursing care throughout their whole experience. To demonstrate how this can be achieved, the template offered by Roper, Logan and Tierney's Twelve Activities of Living Model will now be explored.

Roper, Logan and Tierney

Roper, Logan and Tierney (RLT) first devised their model of nursing in the 1980s as a British model, one of many emerging at that time from the NHS. The model is situated within, or represents a time, of changes in how care was being provided. Care delivery was moving from the task-orientated approach strongly identifiable in the 1960s, where care focused upon nurses carrying out the same routinized task for all

I have used different elements of two models in practice so far, Soler and Surety, and it really helped me to develop a therapeutic relationship with a young boy who was admitted and could not speak English. I thought of the way and where I positioned myself, eye contact and spatial awareness.

Sian Hunter, child nursing student

patients in an area (for example, giving pressure area care or taking temperatures), to the prevalent theme of 1980s care delivery – promoting the benefits of individualized care. Models of care such as RLT enabled nurses to think about providing all the care needed by the individual patients for whom they were responsible. Today we see that this shift has been successful in enabling holistic care; however, task-based 'intentional rounding' has been implemented in areas where patients are largely independent but where some assistance may be required. This can be considered to be a hybrid approach, as it does continue to focus on individuals rather than the task-based whole-ward perspective.

Twelve Activities of Living

In the RLT model the patient is assessed according to a comparison between their normal activity and the current position. It was reasoned by RLT that, where a gap was identified, nursing would be required until the patient had resumed their usual independence or learned to manage their new circumstances, thus reaching a state of health. In later editions the twelve activities of daily living were amended to twelve activities of living (see Figure 12.1), since the activities were critiqued as not necessarily occurring on a daily basis.

The RLT model is part of the toolbox which enables you to ensure effective care. However, it is your ability which is important. Without a nurse who can 'knit' compassion, care, dignity, person-centred and value-based approaches into all they do, using a model alone does not deliver excellent nursing care.

- Maintaining a safe environment
- Communicating
- Breathing
- Eating and drinking
- Elimination
- Washing and dressing
- Controlling temperature
- Mobilization
- Working and playing
- Expressing sexuality
- Sleeping
- Death and dying

Figure 12.1 Activities of Living
Image © Robin Lupton

The focus of the nurse in later editions was also widened from that of 'doer' to one which enabled the patient, and a greater focus on social and psychological elements enhanced the original assessments. For many years this model formed the basis for documentation used in the assessment of patients, especially in care settings for adults' and children's health. Today you will see many recognizable elements in the care you offer if you are in the adult or child fields of nursing. In other areas, including mental health, a variety of models are used: Peplau's, Newman's and biopsychosocial models, for example. Increasingly, mental health trusts devise their own models, based upon mental, psychological, medical, behavioural, social, physical and forensic areas and encompassing risk.

Once again, the Going Further section of this chapter offers additional reading for you to increase your knowledge.

Returning to RLT, this remains a model for nursing which views the patient as a whole person who is nursed in respect of the activities undertaken in normal daily life. RLT is frequently used in the UK, especially in adult nursing. It assesses the patient's ability to undertake twelve activities of daily living (adapted from Henderson's 1966 US model). This was a small step from the medical systems approach which divided patients into their body systems.

Applying RLT to the care of Celia, it would be useful to consider her early needs in respect of her injury and the impact on her usual living activities. If she subsequently required mental health support, a different model or care pathway approach may be more useful in order to empower her. Suggestions might include the TIDAL Model (Buchanan-Barker, 2004) which focuses on empowering individuals.

ACTIVITY 12.2: REFLECTIVE PRACTICE

Reflect upon the care you were involved in delivering during a recent placement.

- What was the model of care used?
- How did it help you meet the patient's needs?

Assessment tools

While models such as RLT have value in assessment, in today's nursing, where interprofessional care pathways are well developed, assessment tools are now applied much more specifically than ever before and care is planned in light of evidence collated from these. Examples include the use of national early warning scores (NEWS) and assessment using Situation Background Assessment Recommendation (SBAR).

NEWS

These tools have the benefit of being multi-professional in use and enable physical care needs to be communicated rapidly. While original models of nursing are still in evidence, these have largely made way for care pathways where care is evidenced and written into core requirements used for all patients. The development of care plans for patients now applies a combination of individual assessment, skilled collation and use of the correct evidence-based tools and care pathways to enable the most effective delivery of the best nursing care.

CONCLUSION

Nursing theory and philosophy form an important basis for your everyday nursing practice. It is important to note that models and processes of nursing are simply part of the toolbox which enables you, as a nurse, to ensure effective care. Like any tool, though, it is the skill of the user and the capability of the tool within the context which are important. What the Francis, Berwick and Keogh reports (all 2013) teach us is that without a skilled nurse, no model, tool or benchmark standard has the capability to provide excellent nursing.

CHAPTER SUMMARY

- Delivering the best nursing care is a priority for nursing as a profession. In order to be able to give the best care, we must recognize what best care is, and what this means to different people.
- Considering the theoretical aspects of the core concepts of nursing helps you to appreciate and communicate the care you are giving.
- Nursing models address care and aid communication about what your role as a nurse is, how the patient may be viewed, what the context or environment for nursing might contribute and what the intended outcome of care might look like.

- Models and processes of nursing are simply part of the toolbox which enables you to ensure effective care as a nurse.
- Models and processes of nursing can be used within each field of nursing and will be useful to you in delivering patient care.
- There are four core concepts found in the meta-paradigm, or worldview, of nursing theory, and these are linked together in a model in order to enable you to provide holistic care.
- Nursing theories are developed while they are being used and intertwined with interprofessional theories to enrich the effectiveness of care delivery.

CRITICAL REFLECTION

Holistic care

This chapter has highlighted the importance of the use of a blueprint for models of care when determining an appropriate care pathway for your patient. Think about someone you have cared for recently and make a list of ways in which caring for them with an understanding of their personal situation can help meet their wider physical, emotional, social, economic and spiritual needs. Develop a comparison of the care you might plan for the different patients in this chapter. Now add your own patient, comparing the differences in respect of the definitions of their care. What model is your care based on and how is holistic care delivered?

Write your own reflection about your experience.

GO FURTHER

Books

Hall, C. (2013) 'Theory and practice – understanding the nature of nursing as a caring activity', in Hall, C. and Ritchie, D. (eds), *What is Nursing*, 3rd ed. Exeter: Learning Matters. pp.61-84.
This chapter develops the theoretical consideration of caring further and reviews some different models for each field of practice. The application of the theoretical considerations to different case situations means that this text is complementary to the chapter you have just read and will further extend your understanding and application of the conceptual elements of nursing theory.

Roper, N., Logan, W. and Tierney, A. (2000) *Activities of Living Model of Nursing*. Edinburgh: Churchill Livingstone.
Perhaps the best known British model of nursing care, but criticized for its perspective on the role of the nurse (as controlling care) and its medical and rather reductionist approach. This model developed dynamically through the 1990s and still forms the basis of many UK frameworks for nursing care today. It is most likely to be taught as a baseline for thinking about the practical application of a nursing philosophy.

Journal articles

Barker, P. (1998) 'Its time to turn the tide', *Nursing Times*, **94(46): 70-2.**
This short summary of the TIDAL model and its application in mental health nursing enables you to see how a model can benefit client care in the mental health setting.

Moulster, G., Ames, S. and Griffiths, T. (2012) 'A new learning disabilities framework', *Learning Disabilities Practice*, **15(6): 14-18.**
This summary of a learning disabilities framework enables you to see how a model can benefit client care in the learning disability setting.

Murphy, F., Williams, A. and Pridmore, J. (2010) 'Nursing models and contemporary nursing 1: their development, uses and limitations', *Nursing Times*, **106: 23.**
This paper continues a discussion about the use of models in nursing and the relative benefits and limitations.

Weblinks

Royal College of Nursing (2012) *Peter's Story*. **Available at: www.nursesday.rcn.org.uk/video/ entry/peters-story**
This weblink clearly demonstrates excellent care as reported by a user of the service and those who provided that service. You can use this link to apply your thinking about the philosophical approach being taken in the delivery of care to Peter. Think about how the nurses see their own role, the role of Peter, and the vision of health as a goal and the impact of society.

The TIDAL model
www.tidal-model.com/Theory.htm
This weblink will help you to learn more about the TIDAL model for mental health nursing and think about how this approach might be applied in your care.

Department of Health 6Cs, getting it right - an approach
www.england.nhs.uk/nursingvision
View this link and think about the underpinning philosophy of the 6Cs. What is being said about the nature of the nurse and the nature of the patient in particular? Also ask yourself - is it a good idea to have a strategic vision for a whole country? The 6Cs apply to the whole of England. What might the limitations of this approach be?

SBAR
www.institute.nhs.uk/safer_care/safer_care/Situation_Background_Assessment_ Recommendation.html
This weblink will help you learn more about a tool commonly used to apply the principles of nursing theory in practice through the use of assessment. Again, this is a national weblink. What are the possible advantages and limitations of a national tool for assessment?

Berwick, D. (2013) *A Promise to Learn - A Commitment to Act. Improving the Safety of Patients in England*. **National Advisory Group on the Safety of Patients in England. Available at: www.gov. uk/government/uploads/system/uploads/attachment_data/file/226703/Berwick_Report.pdf**
Look at section three of the summary of this report. This identifies the need for patient and public involvement in care. You can also see a vision or model for all professions including nursing, which clearly identifies putting the patient first and including them in decision-making. Think about how you could use these findings and recommendations in your nursing practice to make sure patients remain safe.

--- **REVISE** ---

Review what you have learned by visiting https://edge.sagepub.com/essentialnursing or your eBook

- Print out or download the chapter summaries for quick revision
- Test yourself with multiple-choice and short-answer questions

- Revise key terms with the interactive flash cards

CHAPTER 12

REFERENCES

Berwick, D. (2013) *A Promise to Learn – A Commitment to Act – Improving the Safety of Patients in England.* National Advisory Group on the Safety of Patients in England London: Department of Health. Available at: www.gov.uk/government/uploads/system/uploads/attachment_data/file/226703/Berwick_Report.pdf (accessed 28 March 2013).

Carper, B. A. (1978) 'Fundamental patterns of knowing in nursing', *Advances in Nursing Science,* 1(1): 13–24.

Department of Health (2012) *Compassion in Practice.* London: DH.

Department of Health (2013a) *Winterbourne View Hospital: Department of Health Review and Response.* London: TSO. Available at: www.gov.uk/government/uploads/system/uploads/attachment_data/file/213215/final-report.pdf (accessed 18 February 2015).

Department of Health (2103b) *The NHS Constitution: The NHS Belongs to US All.* Available at: www.gov.uk/government/uploads/system/uploads/attachment_data/file/170656/NHS_Constitution.pdf (accessed 18 February 2015).

Egan, G. (1994) *The Skilled Helper: A Problem Management Approach to Helping.* Hampshire: Brooks/Cole.

Fitzpatrick, J. (1992) 'Reflections on Nightingale's perspective of nursing'. In F. Nightingale, *Notes on Nursing: What it Is, and What it Is Not.* Philadelphia: Lippincott. pp. 18–22.

Francis, R. (2013) *Report of the Mid Staffordshire NHS Foundation Trust Public Inquiry* (The Francis Report). London: The Stationery Office. Available at: www.midstaffspublicinquiry.com/sites/default/files/report/Executive%20summary.pdf (accessed 28 March 2013).

Hall, C. and Ritchie, D. (2013) *What is Nursing,* 3rd ed. Exeter: Learning Matters.

Henderson, V. (1966) *The Nature of Nursing: A Definition and its Implications for Practice, Research and Education.* New York: Macmillan.

Hutchings, M. (2012) 'Caring around the clock: Rounding in practice', *Nursing Times,* 108(49): 12–14.

Keogh, Sir B. (2013) *Review into the Quality of Care and Treatment Provided by 14 Hospital Trusts in England* (Keogh Review). London: NHS England.

Moulster, G., Ames, S. and Griffiths, T. (2012) 'A new learning disabilities framework', *Learning Disabilities Practice* 15(6): 14–18.

Roper, N., Logan, W.W. and Tierney, A.J. (1980) *The Elements of Nursing.* Edinburgh: Churchill Livingstone.

Roper, N., Logan, W. and Tierney, A. (2000) *Activities of Living Model of Nursing.* Edinburgh: Churchill Livingstone.

Roy, C. (1970) 'Adaptation: a conceptual framework for nursing', *Nursing Outlook,* 18(3): 43–45.

The Productive Series: Releasing Time to Care. Leeds: Virtual College Group/NHS Institute for Innovation and Improvement. Available at: www.theproductives.com (accessed 28 March 2013).

Wagner, D. and Whaite, B. (2010) 'An exploration of the nature of caring relationships in the writings of Florence Nightingale', *Journal of Holistic Nursing,* 28 (4): 225–34.

World Health Organization (1946) 'Preamble to the constitution of the World Health Organization as adopted by the International Health Conference, New York, 19–22 June 1946: signed on 22 June 1946 by the representatives of 612 states (Official Records of the World Health Organization No 2, p. 100) and entered into force on 7 April 1948'.

Yura, H. and Torres, G. (1975) 'Today's conceptual frameworks with the Baccalaureate nursing programs', *National League for Nursing Publication,* 15(1558): 17–75.

Value-Based, Person-Centred Care

Delves-Yates, C.

> The NHS belongs to the people ... It touches our lives at times of basic human need, when care and compassion are what matter most.
>
> *The NHS Constitution (DH, 2013)*

When I look back over my ninety-four years of life I have done many things – being part of the Fire Service during World War II; spending many years in Africa with my young family, who now have families of their own; welcoming both my mother and mother-in-law into my home to care for them when they couldn't care for themselves and deciding at the age of seventy-four I was still young enough to be a blushing bride for the second time.

Having moved from my own home to my son's when I came to be in need of extra help, and now relying on the care of others for many of my needs, what makes that care easier to accept is if it comes from those who don't just see me as an elderly lady but are able to appreciate me as a person. I am not just someone who needs help with a bath!

Joan Earley, patient

In my experience as a nurse, care, compassion and dignity are vital. These values help create a safe environment and reduce fear and anxiety at one of the most vulnerable times of a person's life.

Delivering the nursing care I provide with compassion and dignity makes all the difference between working with humanity in partnership with patients and just completing a series of tasks.

Trish Mayes, adult nurse

THIS CHAPTER COVERS

- What is value-based, person-centred care?
- Compassion
- Caring
- Dignity

- Person-centred care
- Spirituality
- What to do if care is not value-based or person-centred

NMC
STANDARDS

ESSENTIAL SKILLS
CLUSTERS

INTRODUCTION

As identified by Joan, it is fundamentally important to deliver care with that special extra ingredient which makes it easily acceptable. That special extra ingredient is being compassionate and caring, delivering dignified care which is person-centred and value-based. However, as we discuss in this chapter, it can be difficult to define exactly what we mean by these terms, and this is made even more complex by the fact that every patient you will nurse is an individual with unique needs and expectations regarding how they want those values to be expressed. It is very much easier to identify when compassion, care and dignity are missing, and it is to our professional shame that there have historically been many instances when we have failed those who depend upon us.

Trish clearly highlights the importance of care, compassion and dignity in making patients feel safe at times at which they are most vulnerable. As she explains, the essence of nursing is not in completing a series of tasks, but in delivering care with humanity.

This chapter will discuss fundamentally important values in nursing practice. We will consider what compassion, caring, dignity, person-centred care and value-based nursing practice are; how you can ensure your care upholds and promotes these values; and what to do if you observe care in which they are missing. We will also address the topic of spiritual care, deliberating its importance in holistic care and how you can deliver care designed to meet all of your patient's needs.

WHAT IS VALUE-BASED, PERSON-CENTRED CARE?

ACTIVITY 13.1 REFLECTIVE PRACTICE

If you were asked, 'What is value-based, person-centred care and why is this important in nursing?' what would you say?

ACTIVITY 13.1

Compassion, caring and dignity are the most important things in nursing because it helps the patient to feel valued as a person. I always treat patients with compassion, care and dignity because I would expect that if I was ill and in hospital. I was doing the observations on placement and a lady asked me if it would be ok if she could have a shower before she went home. I said that it was fine and went to help her. She said that I treated her so well and she felt loved. This made me realise that it only takes a small amount of time to treat patients with compassion and respect and it makes all the difference to them.

Hannah Boyd, adult nursing student

When people are in hospital, they are more vulnerable than when they are well at home due to being in an unfamiliar environment and being with unfamiliar people. It is therefore important that nurses show compassion to their patients to make them feel at ease and promote

As you may have found in Activity 13.1, explaining value-based, person-centred care is a monumental task. This is made more difficult because not only will nurses have differing views on what it is, but so will patients. It could be that we are setting ourselves an impossible task not only in trying to define this, but also in trying to deliver care based upon these values. However, if we review our Code (NMC, 2015) and the guidance on professional conduct for nursing and midwifery students (NMC, 2009), the fundamental role which values hold in all aspects of nursing care becomes clearly evident.

So, our quest not only to define them, but also to find ways to ensure we deliver them as an everyday part of our nursing practice, continues.

The second part of Activity 13.1 – why is it important – is actually much simpler. As Joan tells us at the very start of the chapter, a patient is not just someone who needs, for example, a bath; they have life histories and experiences that have made them unique individuals, which, in order to provide the care they find acceptable, we need to take into account. While pinning down exactly what the 'slippery' concepts of compassion, caring, and dignity entail may be difficult, understanding their fundamental importance in every aspect of nursing care is not.

Just like the balls of wool used for knitting, the fundamental values of compassion, caring, dignity, person-centred and values-based care are all strands of nursing care which need to be intertwined. However, as nurses, the end result we desire is not a jumper, but effective care that meets all of a patient's unique needs.

recovery. It is also vital to observe someone's dignity; nurses may require patients to unveil more of themselves than they would usually feel comfortable with, especially to a stranger. Nurses need to understand patients' preferences regarding personal hygiene so they know how best to respect people's privacy.

Michelle Hill, NQ RNLD

COMPASSION, CARING, DIGNITY

ACTIVITY 13.2 REFLECTIVE PRACTICE

Undertake a search of the news headlines, either from your local area or from the national news. Find two news reports highlighting instances where patients were delivered nursing care that was not compassionate, caring, dignified, person-centred or value-based.

- Read the reports and reflect upon the details.
- What do you think was the cause of the fundamental lapse in care?
- What would you have done if you had seen this inadequate care being delivered?

Image © Robin Lupton

Just as we would all choose different colours of wool and different knitting patterns to suit not only a patient's needs but also our knitting ability, all of these values will be woven into the care that you deliver in a unique manner. As was identified in the news headlines you found in Activity 13.2, it is often easier to realize what you *haven't* got – it is far more noticeable when a stitch is missing or a knitting pattern is incorrect than when all is perfect. However, as patients have the right to expect the care they receive to be of the highest standard, delivered by professionals (DH, 2013), our professional 'knitting' can only ever be perfect.

To enable us to understand what is meant by the terms compassion, caring, dignity, person-centred care and value-based nursing practice, and how we can ensure they are promoted in our everyday nursing practice, we will now consider each term individually, starting with compassion.

COMPASSION

THE FRANCIS
REPORT

COMPASSION

Compassion has been a value central to nursing since the profession was established, but it seems to be the one thing that the profession has been charged with losing, diluting and undervaluing as other priorities take its place.

As you will see discussed in many other chapters, the Francis Report (2013) and a number of other reports, such as that of Heslop et al. (2013), consider occasions when patients were not treated with the compassion they deserved, along with a number of other serious failings.

Although the reports of Francis (2013) and Heslop et al. (2013) are the most recent examples of such failings, numerous other reports have repeatedly demonstrated similar inadequacies, ever since the poor conditions experienced by elderly patients in the 1960s were reported by Robb (1967). Learning from such appalling evidence is crucial. Promises that nothing like this will happen again are made repeatedly, but conscious effort is required to guarantee change. We must ensure this is the case.

Compassion, in a similar manner to caring, is directly derived from the ethical principle of benefi-cence. Beneficence is the ethical principle which requires that we seek to do or produce good for others. While the role of the nurse is diverse and multi-faceted, all nursing practice shares the same ultimate aim to improve the lives of those receiving care.

Let us consider a nursing activity – assisting a patient with a bath, for example, as Joan mentioned at the start of the chapter. The good done through this act is not just that of the direct effect of the patient being clean; it also depends upon how the bath is given.

CASE STUDY: HECTOR

Hector is nine years old and while playing in the garden, tripped and fell through a pane of glass in his grandfather's greenhouse. Luckily for Hector he sustained only minor injuries, but he did need four sutures in a deep wound in his hand. When Hector was at his local hospital having the wound sutured he was very scared and crying, because 'it hurt' and he 'didn't like seeing the blood'. The nurse sutur-ing Hector's hand told him to 'stop being a baby' and as he was a 'big boy now he was not to cry', and said that 'the more he cried, the longer it would take, so the more it would hurt'.

Hector has arrived for an appointment to have his wound dressed at his GP's surgery, where you are on placement. The receptionist comes to find you and your **mentor** to tell you that Hector, your next patient, has arrived, but he is hiding behind a chair in the waiting room, because he doesn't want to come and see 'the nasty nurses who hurt'.

1. What do you think might be the reason why Hector associates nurses with things that hurt?
2. How are you and you mentor going to deliver effective and compassionate care to Hector in order to help him realize that not all nurses are nasty and hurt?

CASE STUDY:
HECTOR

Hector's experience with the nurse at the hospital is a clear demonstration that effective nursing involves far more than just carrying out tasks. The nurse sutured Hector's cut, so she successfully completed the task, but did so in a way that made a bad situation worse. She most certainly failed in her duty to make Hector's life better. Having a wound sutured in a compassionate or a non-compassionate manner can result in two very different experiences. Even if the amount of pain and discomfort for Hector had been the same, if the nurse had acted in a compassionate manner she would have done Hector's 'inner being' far more good, showing him that nurses help when things are bad. She would also have gained Hector's trust, and so his experience of healthcare, including having his wound re-dressed by you and your mentor, would have been far less stressful.

Having gained an understanding of the importance of compassion in nursing practice and ways to ensure you promote this value, we shall now consider caring.

In my ward placement I worked with patients that had had a stroke; some of these patients had temporarily lost the use of their voice and their ability to complete tasks of daily living. I had to try to understand what they needed and were trying to say as these patients were relying on me for their care. I could only try to understand how frustrating it must be to be unable to communicate their needs to me and others, and when they got irritated I accepted that and tried to make things better.

Sarah Parkes, LD nursing student

WHAT'S THE EVIDENCE?

Reification and compassion in medicine: A tale of two systems

An article by Smajdor (2013) asks if compassion has disappeared in healthcare, and, if so, what is emerging to fill its place?

- Reflect upon your experiences of nursing.
- To what extent do you think you have witnessed nursing care being delivered compassionately?
- Now read the article and consider if the view expressed can be applied to your experience.

REIFICATION
AND
COMPASSION
IN MEDICINE

CARING

Caring is frequently described as being at the heart of nursing, but perceptions of what exactly that means appear to differ between nurses. Some nurses focus upon attaining the skills which enable them to deliver care based on a range of specialist technical interventions, as they feel this is the most important aspect of care; others feel that caring means their ability to relate to their patients and 'be there for them'. Thus there is disagreement between nurses as to which 'type' of caring is effective, which raises an interesting further question – who should be the judge of what is important about care? Patients, relatives and carers may have a very different perception. Baughan and Smith (2008: 53) highlight behaviours that are indicators of care, which can be integrated into your actions. These are:

1 Simple acts of kindness
2 Promoting dignity
3 Using and developing skills of empathy by 'tuning in' to the patient
4 Ability to move our gaze from the body (as an object of intervention) to the person (living a life)
5 Developing trust
6 Giving effective reassurance by giving the other person confidence in our ability to listen and to help them

7 Being proactive – asking patients what they need – not waiting to be asked
8 Recognizing the limitations of one's own skills
9 Entering into a partnership with patients and their families to gain knowledge and share the 'power'
10 Engaging in anti-discriminatory practice by respecting another human being, irrespective of their age, gender, cultural origins, class, status or the condition from which they suffer

As we have identified caring behaviours, we will now move to considering dignity, the last of the three values, which must always be evident in the care you deliver.

ACTIVITY 13.3 REFLECTIVE PRACTICE

Reflect upon an experience when you have been involved in delivering care.

- Can you identify any of the 'caring indicators' in the list on p. 173 in your experience?
- Which of the 'caring indicators' do you think you need to develop further?

DIGNITY

When people are in hospital, they are more vulnerable than when they are well at home due to being in an unfamiliar environment and being with unfamiliar people. It is therefore important that nurses show compassion to their patients to make them feel at ease and promote recovery. It is also vital to observe someone's dignity; nurses may require patients to unveil more of themselves than they would usually feel comfortable with, especially to a stranger. Nurses need to understand patients' preferences regarding personal hygiene so they know how best to respect people's privacy.

Michelle Hill, NQ LD

DIGNITY

Dignity has been identified as important by patients in a wide range of settings, with patients who perceived their care as respectful and dignified reporting the highest levels of satisfaction. Further to this, healthcare professionals worldwide agree that promoting patient dignity is a fundamental element of their practice (Matiti, 2011). It is possible to conclude, therefore, that there is a shared view between not only nurses but also all healthcare professionals and their patients that dignity is important, with such a view enshrined in both **legislation** and professional guidance (see Table 13.1).

Table 13.1 Professional guidance and legislation identifying the importance of dignity

The Code: Professional Standards of Practice and Behaviour for Nurses and Midwives (NMC, 2015)
Guidance on Professional Conduct for Nursing and Midwifery Students (NMC, 2009)
The International Council of Nurses' Code of Ethics for Nurses (2006)
Article 3 of the UK Human Rights Act (1998)
Article 1 of the United Nations International Bill of Rights (1996)
Amsterdam Declaration on the Promotion of Patient's Rights (WHO, 1994)
The European Regions of the World Confederation for Physical Therapy (2003)
General Medical Council Guidance (GMC, 2006)
General Pharmaceutical Council Standards of Conduct, Ethics and Performance (2010)

Despite this agreement, however, the practicalities of promoting dignity within healthcare settings remain problematic, and it is not always achieved (Francis, 2013; Heslop et al., 2013). Potential reasons suggested for this is that the 'notion' of dignity is not clearly understood (Matiti, 2011) and there is a need to aid healthcare professionals to identify practical ways of promoting patient dignity.

ACTIVITY 13.4 REFLECTIVE PRACTICE

Look up dignity in three different dictionaries – either online or hard copy.

- Can you relate these definitions to the care you deliver to patients?

It is frequently stated that the word dignity comes from two Latin roots – *dignus* and *dignitas*. Both of these Latin roots have very similar meanings: *dignus* means 'worth' and *dignitas* means 'merit'. Hereby we meet our first problem. It is possible that when looking for definitions of dignity, the words you find need explanation themselves, and may not necessarily translate easily to the care you deliver to patients.

Matiti (2011: 21) helpfully outlines the meaning of dignity:

- Everyone has a unique and dynamic concept of dignity
- Although there is no universal definition of dignity, there are commonly identified attributes of dignity through which it is maintained and promoted.

- Each individual perceives these attributes differently, depending on how they perceive the influencing factors.
- Perceptions of dignity are influenced by experiences in healthcare; the care environment procedures and healthcare workers' behaviour can all affect perceptions of dignity.

Matti shows that not only can dignity often mean different things to different people, but it can vary depending on the context. Although this increases our understanding of the numerous aspects of practice where dignity is important, and of its **subjectivity**, we still do not have a concrete understanding of exactly what dignity is, or ways in which we can translate it to our care. If a **concept** – such as dignity – proves difficult to define, pointers to its meaning can be gained from considering the other theoretical concepts often used to describe its meaning (Ganter and Willie, 1998). In this way it is possible for us to find the attributes (Chinn and Jacobs, 1983) of dignity (see Table 13.2), which we can then ensure feature in the care we deliver.

Table 13.2 The attributes of dignity

General attributes nurses must attain	Attributes felt by patients to be important
Respect	Self-respect and **self-esteem**
Effective communication	Independence
Autonomy	Personal standards are appreciated
Privacy	Control over surroundings and how others treat them
Worth	Able to make choices
Empowerment	Self-confidence and self-identity

So while we have to accept that it is difficult to define exactly what is meant by dignity, it is possible, by focusing upon its attributes and turning these into practical actions, to understand the fundamental importance of dignity and ensure it is evident in our everyday nursing. In addition to focusing on the attributes, further assistance is offered by Matiti and Baillie (2011: 13), who develop the earlier work of Haddock (1996) by producing a definition of dignity that can be applied to nursing practice:

... feeling and being treated as being important and valuable when in situations that are considered threatening.

If we expand this definition to cover not only situations that are considered threatening, but also everyday activities, it is possible to demystify the concept of dignity and find a way to ensure it is always promoted in our care.

I always try to involve patients in their own care, especially with elderly patients. I feel it can be quite undignified having someone making assumptions and doing everything for you – if that patient wants a shower rather then a wash by the bed, why not? And if they want to get dressed into their normal clothes rather then a hospital gown (circumstances permitting), surely that is a lot more dignified.

Charlie Clisby, NQN

ACTIVITY 13.5: REFLECTIVE PRACTICE

Reflect upon your most recent experience of patient care.

- How many of the attributes of dignity in Table 13.2 were present in the care you were involved in delivering?
- Would the patients whose care you were involved in say that they were 'feeling and being treated as being important and valuable when in situations that are considered threatening' and in everyday activities?

Effective nursing practice, although based upon fundamental values, requires further structuring in order to ensure it can meet all of a patient's needs. To consider the structures within which we deliver care, we will now consider person-centred care and value-based nursing practice to identify the guiding features.

PERSON-CENTRED CARE

CHAPTER 11

The 'person' is a frequently used foundation of many nursing theories and models. Person-centred care is an approach based on the work of Tom Kitwood (1937–1998), an English **gerontologist**, which respects and values the uniqueness of every individual and seeks to maintain their **personhood**. This is done by creating an environment in which personal worth, individuality, respect, independence and hope are all evident. The term 'person-centred care' is frequently used interchangeably with 'patient-centred care'; however, if this change in terminology is unaccompanied by an understanding of the foundations of person-centred care, there is a danger of misunderstanding its true importance. Person-centred care was devised as an approach that moved the provision of care away from a position in which personhood did not factor.

The features of person-centred care are:

- Knowing the patient as a person
- Enabling them to make decisions based on informed choices about what is available
- Shared decision making rather than exerting control over the patient
- Providing information that meets the individual needs of patients
- Supporting the person to express their choices
- Ongoing evaluation to ensure that care remains appropriate for the individual.

Value-based practice

We all hold values and beliefs, which have been formed by our individual experiences throughout our lives so far. Our values and beliefs shape our attitudes, and so the ways that we think, feel and behave. As nurses, the values and beliefs we hold can have an impact upon the care we deliver.

ACTIVITY 13.6: REFLECTIVE PRACTICE

Reflect upon what you have read so far in this chapter.

- What do you think is the relationship between the fundamental values of compassion, care and dignity and person-centred care?

CASE STUDY: VALERY

Valery is fifty-two and has a long history of intravenous drug and alcohol dependency. She has 'lived' in a bus shelter for the past three weeks because she was asked to leave the hostel where she was staying after punching another resident and causing £1,584 of damage because she was in a 'rage'. Valery often has mood swings, one moment appearing to be calm and the next becoming angry, provocative and rude for no reason. She is frequently late or completely misses appointments. Today she walks into your clinic, shouting, three hours late.

When you see Valery she is very dishevelled; her hygiene is poor and she smells overpoweringly of stale body odour and cigarettes. When she greets you her speech is slurred, but you can just make out that she is saying: 'You! I have been waiting ages for you. There you are – wasting my time again. Just give me my drugs, you idiot, and get out of my way.'

1. As you read the case story of Valery and imagined yourself as the nurse who she had come to see, what were your thoughts?
2. Would your thoughts alter if you were to learn that Valery had been clean from drugs and alcohol for six months, the reason for this visit was to collect antibiotics for a recurrent chest infection and her slurred speech, forgetfulness, mood swings and poor hygiene were all due to pre-senile dementia?

CASE STUDY:
VALERY

There are no right or wrong answers in this Case Study. The values you hold are your values, and make you the person you are. However, you must remember that your values may not be the same as the patient's. Inflicting your values upon a patient may be seen by them as judgemental and unprofessional (NMC, 2015), resulting in a negative effect upon the care they receive from you.

As has been outlined so far in this chapter, the provision of healthcare is inseparable from values such as compassion, care and dignity. Considering the patient's values within this also plays a crucial role. At times this can be challenging, as values can be complex and conflicting. This is particularly so when a patient's values seem to be at odds with the evidence-based practice we wish to provide or the ethical principles most people uphold, or if a nurse's personal values have the potential to compromise the care delivered.

ACTIVITY 13.7 REFLECTIVE PRACTICE

Watch the following video case study on values and difficult personal choices.

- Reflect on how this enables you to better understand how to support patients who need to make tough personal choices which may bring their values into question.

VALUES AND
DIFFICULT
PERSONAL
CHOICES

Value-based practice, a framework developed originally in mental health care, identifies the values we hold as being **pervasive** and powerful influencers of the decisions made relating to care, and highlights that their impact is often underestimated (Petrova et al., 2006). Value-based practice suggests that some approaches to care enable us to ignore important displays of values because unless there is evidence of conflicting values, we presume they are shared. Value-based practice is an approach to supporting care that provides practical skills and tools for discovering an individual's values and negotiating ways in which these can be upheld in care delivery. It aims to introduce a wide range of views and enable the recognition of specific values that may be held by certain cultures, small groups, or those held only by certain individuals.

As we have previously discussed, in person-centred care, it is the values of the patient that dominate. However, one of the features of value-based practice is that the focus on the patient's values is supplemented with paying attention to a wider range of values, including those of the family, carers, healthcare professionals and society, as well as the values embedded in research, the organization of services and policy documents. Awareness of such a range of values is important, as they all have the potential to hinder effective patient care. While we may like to think it is possible to 'hold back' our personal values, this is far from simple. Recognition of our own values is a necessary step in understanding the patient's. The more aware we are of our own values and personal beliefs, the more likely it becomes that the values that enhance effective relationships will be strengthened (Trenoweth et al., 2011).

Throughout the chapter so far we have considered fundamental nursing values, how we can promote them in practice and the wider frameworks or structures of care that enable us to provide patients with effective nursing care. We will now move on to the topic of spirituality: an aspect of care that we need to deliver in order to work holistically with our patients, but one which is frequently overlooked.

SPIRITUALITY

Oldnall (1996) found that nurses are aware that patients have spiritual needs; however, they are unable to deliver spiritual care for two reasons: first, due to a lack of spiritual education within nursing education; second, due to the idea that spiritual care is an area dealt with by chaplains and other religious groups.

ACTIVITY 13.8 REFLECTIVE PRACTICE

Reflect upon your most recent experience of caring for someone. Can you identify any care you delivered that could be described as spiritual?

It is possible that your reaction after reading Activity 13.8 could be 'Spiritual care? Is that really up to me?', or even 'Spiritual care – what exactly is that?'

First, let's answer the question as to whether spiritual care is a feature of nursing care. Throughout the whole of this book, a **holistic** approach has been emphasized and has been described as an important aspect of nursing care. In many chapters it has been highlighted that

- no matter where or with whom they practise, nurses always work in a holistic way;
- when it is said that nurses deliver holistic care, this means that they consider the individual's

physical, psychological, social, emotional, intellectual and spiritual needs.

SPIRITUALITY

From this we can see that spiritual care is an important aspect of a holistic approach, making this an area that, as a nursing student and then a registered nurse, you will need to incorporate within your care.

Second, we must actually answer the question of what spiritual care is – this is necessary before being able to consider the importance of spirituality in nursing care any further! If you asked many people what they understand by the word 'spirituality', they may well tell you that it 'relates to connecting with God', or is 'a search for the sacred' or 'religiousness'. But is this a **contemporary** understanding of the meaning?

ACTIVITY 13.9: REFLECTIVE PRACTICE

Reflect upon what the word 'spirituality' means to you. Do you see it as having a religious association or is your understanding more secular? Does spirituality have any links to other aspects of your
everyday life?

- Make a note of your thoughts and compare them with the information presented in the rest
  of the chapter.

You may have found, in the thoughts you had when undertaking Activity 13.9, that the concept of spirituality is both broad and subjective, and maybe that you could write a very long piece explaining what
spirituality means to you. This may be true for some people; others may have given it very little previous
thought. Despite this, it is possible to identify common features of most individuals' answers when they
are asked the same question, such as:

- Hope
- Meaning and purpose
- Forgiveness
- Beliefs and values
- Spiritual care

- Relationships
- Belief in God or deity
- Morality
- Creativity and self-expression (McSherry, 2008).

When we consider these features, it becomes clear that spirituality can be seen to be associated with more
than just religion. Spirituality can be viewed as an integral aspect of everyday life which can be relevant to
all individuals – although we must take care to always remember that each individual will have their own
unique view of spirituality, just as you noted down when you completed Activity 13.9. It also becomes evident that a formal association with religion may or may not be a feature in an individual's personal description of spirituality. An illness or crisis of any sort may be the catalyst that leads an individual to consider or
re-evaluate their spirituality.

So, although we have to conclude that each individual's understanding of spirituality is complex,
subjective and highly personal, we can view spirituality as relating to all activities that bring value and
meaning to our everyday life and relationships. In addition to this, spirituality can be seen as a constant
feature within our past, present and future. Thus, as nurses who care for patients while they experience
a range of challenging situations, spirituality clearly becomes a fundamentally important aspect of the
nursing care we provide.

How can I deliver spiritual care?

ACTIVITY 13.10: CRITICAL THINKING

Imagine the scene. You are at a wedding reception and have been seated at a table between two
people you don't know. The conversation is becoming very stilted, so in an attempt to get everyone
talking you say, 'Well, what shall we talk about - religion or politics?'

- What do you think their responses will be?
- Is your attempt to enliven the conversation likely to be successful?

ACTIVITY 13.10

As we have already mentioned, spirituality is complex, subjective and highly personal. In the same way
that you are unlikely to ask people about sensitive or intimate issues until you know them very well, if
spirituality is mentioned – which many people often view as being linked to religion – it is possible that

people will either stop talking or will feel they are being called to account for their personal views and become argumentative. So how can you manage to avoid reactions such as these and incorporate the spiritual dimension within the care you deliver?

If you study the figure below, what do you see hidden in the middle of the word 'spirituality'?

Figure 13.1 Spirituality contains ... (McSherry, 2008)

While it also has other meanings, ritual can be considered to relate to 'often repeated actions' which are concerned with the ordinary events and routines of everyday life. You may well have experienced some rituals during your experiences of caring for patients – actions that have been undertaken without consideration as to whether they are truly necessary, such as temperature, pulse and blood pressure being recorded at certain times of the day. Although the necessity of ritualistic nursing actions should be questioned, the structure and security provided by rituals can be positive. So, when considering the delivery of spiritual care, it can be very helpful to view it as an integral aspect of the rituals involved in ordinary events and routines of everyday life.

If we take such an approach, it is not necessary to apply any specific additional models to enable us to deliver spiritual care. We can integrate it into the areas we already consider within the nursing process to assist us in delivering individualized, holistic, patient-centred, evidence-based care.

Spiritual care is sometimes considered to be the same as psychological support. It is true that the two share many similarities, as psychological and spiritual wellbeing are intertwined – but spiritual care differs from counselling, for example. In fact, it is not possible for spiritual care to be described as any particular activity; it is far more complex, and actually is more about 'being' than doing.

CHAPTER 16

In effect it is about being caring, genuine and open in your communication with patients, offering them the opportunity to discuss any issues they feel are relevant and responding appropriately.

Rieg et al. (2006) suggest the very practical approach of asking a patient questions:

1. Ask open questions, focusing on how the patient is feeling. Good questions to get the conversation started can be:
'What do you find to be the most difficult part of your current situation?'
'What hurts or angers you most at the moment?'

2. Then find out what the patient believes would be helpful, by asking them:
'What has helped you the most when you have felt like this before?'
'Do your friends, family or faith help you?'
(based on Rieg et al., 2006).

Such an approach will give an adult patient an opportunity to express a need for spiritual support. When caring for children or individuals with a learning disability, for example, you may need to modify the language; possibly, with a child, you may need to ask the questions of their favourite teddy bear. In this way it becomes clear that the questions you are asking relating to spiritual care are just the same as those you will ask relating to their physical or psychological comfort.

Thus, as seen earlier, asking a patient about their spirituality can be seen as an 'often repeated action' or ritual. Once you have discovered what the patient's needs are, just as with any other aspect of care, you can plan, implement and assess a range of actions to achieve the goal desired.

WHAT TO DO IF CARE IS NOT VALUE-BASED OR PERSON-CENTRED

Throughout your nursing programme you will see a wide range of care in a variety of settings. Your placements will ensure you gain the experience of being involved in delivering care in acute areas, such as general hospitals or specialist ones, and community environments, such as GP surgeries, patients' homes or residential care homes. The care you are involved in delivering will be emergency, long-term and short-term, and you will become an expert at assessing, planning, implementing and evaluating the care your patient needs. You will work with many nurses and be supported by a number of mentors.

This experience is designed to ensure that when you become a registered nurse, you are capable of working without supervision to deliver competent care to the patients for whom you are responsible. While a nursing student you will find some of the nurses and mentors you work with to be inspirational. They will become your **role-models**, whose standards and abilities you will aim to imitate throughout the rest of you career.

While you experience the delivery of care in this wide range of settings, you will observe nurses approaching the same tasks differently. Just because your current mentor undertakes a nursing procedure in a different way from your previous mentor, it doesn't necessarily make it wrong – it is just different. However, there may be times when you experience care that does not seem 'right' to you. As has been outlined throughout this chapter, and as you were asked to consider in Activity 13.2, not all care delivered to patients is good. Your role is to ensure that if at any time you feel the care you have seen is not 'right', not upholding the values of compassion, caring and dignity for example, you speak out.

The NMC (2009) offers clear guidance upon this, outlining that you should:

- Seek help and advice from a mentor or tutor when there is a need to protect people from harm.
- Seek help immediately from an appropriately qualified professional if someone for whom you are providing care has suffered harm for any reason.
- Seek help from your mentor or tutor if people indicate that they are unhappy about their care or treatment.

CHAPTER 22

As nurses we come into contact with vulnerable patients on a daily basis. Their protection is central to your role. Care which does not uphold the fundamental nursing values outlined in this chapter is never acceptable.

CONCLUSION

Compassion, care and dignity are fundamental nursing values which must be upheld in all aspects of our practice. Their exact meaning may be difficult to define, especially as they can be subjective, thus differing depending upon the situation and patient. However, it is possible to define certain features of nursing care which promote these values, and we must ensure they are evident in the care we deliver.

Person-centred care and value-based nursing practice enable the nursing care we deliver to meet the unique needs of patients while setting care within the wider values of contemporary society. In order to understand a patient's values, we need to be able to recognize our own.

Spirituality plays an important role in the delivery of holistic care; thus, we need to be able to discuss spiritual needs with patients and provide care to meet these. If we consider spirituality as an element of everyday ritual, it can provide structure and security, and we can address it in the same manner as any other aspect of care.

Throughout your nursing career your primary role is, at all times, to protect those in your care. Any care that does not uphold the nursing values we consider to be fundamental can never be accepted.

CHAPTER SUMMARY

- Promoting compassion, care and dignity is fundamentally important in every aspect of nursing care.
- A number of serious failings of care can be identified within the history of nursing since the 1960s.
- Numerous nursing theories and models are based upon person-centred care, creating an environment where the uniqueness of each individual is recognized. While the terms 'person-centred care' and 'patient-centred care' are frequently used interchangeably, it should be remembered that person-centred care was devised as an approach that moved care provision away from a position in which personhood did not factor.

- We all hold values and beliefs which, because they shape the ways in which we think, feel and behave, can impact upon the care we deliver.
- The more aware we are of our values and beliefs, the more likely it becomes that the values enhancing effective relationships with patients will be strengthened.
- Spirituality is both an integral aspect of daily life and a necessary consideration when delivering holistic nursing care. If it is considered as an everyday ritual, which provides security and structure, it can be incorporated into the areas of care that we already consider within the nursing process.
- As a nurse, your primary function is to protect those in your care. Care which does not uphold and promote fundamental nursing values is never acceptable.

CRITICAL REFLECTION

Holistic care

This chapter has highlighted the importance of compassion, caring, dignity, spirituality, a person-centred approach and value-based practice when providing holistic care for a patient. Review the chapter and note down all the instances in which you think delivering compassionate, caring, dignified, spiritual, person-centred and value-based nursing care will help meet the patient's physical, psychological, social, economic and spiritual needs. Think of a variety of different patients across the fields, not just those within your own field. You may find it helpful to make a list and refer back to it next time you are in practice, and then write your own reflection after your practice experience.

GO FURTHER

Books

Clarke, J. (2013) *Spiritual Care in Everyday Nursing Practice*. Basingstoke: Palgrave Macmillan.
An interesting and informative text considering the spiritual needs of individuals in an everyday context.
Woodbridge, K. and Fulford, K. W. M. (2004) *Whose Values? A Workbook for Values Based Practice in Mental Healthcare*. London: The Sainsbury Centre for Mental Health.
An excellent workbook which will help you to understand how diverse values relate, interact and impact on experiences, actions and relationships. While the workbook was designed specifically for mental health care, it is relevant to nursing care in all fields.

Journal articles

Gustafsson, L., Wigerblad, A. and Lindwall, L. (2014) 'Undignified care: Violation of patient dignity in involuntary psychiatric hospital care from a nurse's perspective', *Nursing Ethics*, 21: 176–86, http://nej.sagepub.com/content/21/2/176
An interesting article identifying seven themes which describe nurses' experiences of violation of patient dignity.

Holloway, M. (2006) 'Death the great leveller? Towards a transcultural spirituality of dying and bereavement', *Journal of Clinical Nursing*, 15(7): 833–9.
A very readable article which outlines four beliefs that overwhelmingly gave comfort to people who reported no religious affiliation at all.

Rieg, L. S., Mason, C. H. and Preston, K. (2006) 'Spiritual care: Practical guidelines for rehabilitation nurses', *Rehabilitation Nursing*, 31(6): 249–55.
An informative article outlining practical guidelines for nurses when assisting patients to meet their spiritual needs.

Weblinks

The Kairos Forum
www.thekairosforum.com
A Forum for People with Intellectual or Cognitive Disabilities (KFICD) seeks to highlight and respond to the spiritual and religious needs of people with disabilities.

http://allnurses.com/nursing-and-spirituality/religion-culture-nursing-517282.html
A discussion board where views on spirituality and nursing are shared.

www.dignityincare.org.uk
Website of the Dignity in Care network, which is led by the National Dignity Council. The website offers resources, support and a network of Dignity Champions: over 40,000 individuals and organizations who work to put dignity and respect at the heart of UK care services to enable a positive experience of care.

www.nursetogether.com/compassion-and-respect-in-nursing-care
A website for nurses offering, amongst other things, interesting articles and stimulating discussion.

www.gov.uk/government/publications/the-nhs-constitution-for-england
The NHS Constitution, establishing the principles and values of the NHS in England.

www.show.scot.nhs.uk
NHS Scotland, highlighting the principles and values of the NHS in Scotland.

www.wales.nhs.uk
NHS Wales, highlighting the principles and values of the NHS in Wales.

http://online.hscni.net
The official gateway for Health and Social Care in Northern Ireland, highlighting its principles and values.

 **REVISE**

Review what you have learned by visiting https://edge.sagepub.com/essentialnursing or your eBook

- Print out or download the chapter summaries for quick revision
- Test yourself with multiple-choice and short-answer questions

- Revise key terms with the interactive flash cards

 CHAPTER 13

REFERENCES

Baughan, J. and Smith, A. (2008) *Caring in Nursing Practice*. Dorchester: Pearson Education.
Chinn, P. and Jacobs, M. (1983) *Theory and Nursing*. St Louis: Mosby.
Department of Health (2013) *The NHS Constitution*. London: Department of Health.
Francis, R. (2013) *Report of the Mid Staffordshire NHS Foundation Trust Public Inquiry*. London: The Stationery Office.

Ganter, B. and Willie, R. (1998) *Formal Concept Analysis: Mathematical Foundations*, trans. C. Franzke. Berlin: Springer-Verlag.

Haddock, J. (1996) 'Towards a further clarification of the concept "dignity"', *Journal of Advanced Nursing*, 24(5): 924–931.

Heslop, P., Blair, P., Fleming, P., Hoghton, M., Marriott, A. and Russ, L. (2013) *Confidential Inquiry into Premature Deaths of People with Learning Disabilities (CIPOLD)*. Bristol: Nora Fry Research Centre. Available at: www.bris.ac.uk/cipold (accessed 18 February 2015).

Matiti, M.R. (2011) 'The importance of dignity in healthcare'. In M.R. Matiti and L. Baillie (eds), *Dignity in Healthcare*. London: Radcliffe Publishing. pp.3–8.

Matiti, M.R. and Baillie, L. (2011) *Dignity in Healthcare*. London: Radcliffe Publishing.

McSherry, W. (2008) *Making Sense of Spirituality in Nursing and Health Care Practice*, 2nd ed. London: Jessica Kingsley Publishers.

Nursing and Midwifery Council (NMC) (2009) *Guidance on Professional Conduct for Nursing and Midwifery Students*. London: NMC.

Nursing and Midwifery Council (NMC) (2015) *The Code: Professional Standards of Practice and Behaviour for Nurses and Midwives*. London: NMC.

Oldnall, A. (1996) 'A critical analysis of nursing: Meeting the spiritual needs of patients', *Journal of Advanced Nursing*, 138–44.

Petrova, M., Dale, J. and Fulford, B. (2006) 'Values-based practice in primary care: Easing the tensions between individual values, ethical principles and best evidence', *British Journal of General Practice*, 56(530): 703–9.

Rieg, L. S., Mason, C. H. and Preston, K. (2006) 'Spiritual care: Practical guidelines for rehabilitation nurses', *Rehabilitation Nursing*, 31(6): 249–55.

Robb, B. (1967) *Sans Everything: A Case to Answer*. London: Nelson.

Smajdor, A. (2013) 'Reification and compassion in medicine: A tales of two systems', *Journal of Clinical Ethics*, 8(4): 111–118.

Trenoweth, S., Docherty, T., Franks, J. and Pearce, R. (2011) *Nursing and Mental Health Care: An Introduction for All Fields of Practice*. Exeter: Learning Matters.

The Meaning of Vulnerability

6

Northway, R. and Jenkins, R.

NMC Standards for Pre-registration Nursing Education

This chapter will address the following competencies:

Domain 1: Professional values

3. All nurses must support and promote the health, wellbeing, rights and dignity of people, groups, communities and populations. These include people whose lives are affected by ill health, disability, ageing, death and dying.
4. All nurses must work in partnership with services users, carers, families, groups, communities and organizations. They must manage risk, and promote health and wellbeing while aiming to empower choices that promote self-care and safety.

Domain 3: Nursing practice and decision-making

9. All nurses must be able to recognise when a person is at risk and in need of extra support and protection and take reasonable steps to protect them from abuse.

NMC Essential Skills Clusters

This chapter will address the following ESCs:

Cluster: Organisational aspects of care

11. People can trust the newly registered graduate nurse to safeguard children and adults from vulnerable situations and support and protect them from harm.

By entry to the register:

v. Recognises and responds when people are in vulnerable situations and at risk, or in need of support and protection.
viii. Works collaboratively with other agencies to develop, implement and monitor strategies to safeguard and protect individuals and groups who are in vulnerable situations.

18. People can trust a newly registered graduate nurse to enhance the safety of service users and identify and actively manage risk and uncertainty in relation to people, the environment, self and others.

> ### Chapter aims
>
> By the end of this chapter you will be able to:
>
> - discuss the different ways in which 'vulnerable' and 'vulnerability' have been defined;
> - identify the factors that can contribute to vulnerability and also those that can reduce vulnerability;
> - recognise the implications for nursing practice.

Introduction

In health and social care settings the terms 'vulnerable' and 'vulnerability' are commonly used. For example, reference is made to the 'protection of vulnerable adults' and some service users are referred to as being 'vulnerable'. In the context of research mention is often made of 'vulnerable subjects' (see Chapter 10) and, as noted above, the NMC Essential Skills Clusters refer to 'vulnerable situations'. It can therefore be seen that 'vulnerable' is a term that is used to describe someone or something, while vulnerability is the state of being vulnerable. Hoffmaster (2006) highlights how there seems to be an assumption that we all know what vulnerability means, and that we all understand it in the same way. Indeed, it is probably one of those terms that we use every day without really stopping to think what it means. We assume that we understand its meaning(s), and that others hold the same views and perspectives. However, Scanlon and Lee (2007) suggest that there is vagueness and a lack of **consensus** in the literature as to the meaning of vulnerability, implying both a lack of clarity and the presence of differing views and opinions. This chapter will help you to explore some different meanings of vulnerability and encourage you to think about the implications for practice. Before reading further take some time to complete Activity 2.1.

Activity 2.1   *Critical thinking*

Read through the following brief pen pictures of individuals and decide whom you think is vulnerable. Why do you feel they are vulnerable?

Jenny Atkins is 35 years old and works as a freelance illustrator. When she was in her early twenties she was diagnosed as having **bipolar disorder**. Most of the time this is fully controlled by regular medication but sometimes she does experience periods of severe depression, when she finds it difficult to do anything, and also periods of mania, when she rarely sleeps and works non-stop.

George Lewis is 85 years old and lives in a sheltered housing complex where he has his own flat. His mobility is poor as is his eyesight, but generally his health is good. He has all of his shopping delivered, someone comes in to assist him with bathing and someone calls in each day to check that he is OK.

continued . . .

James Brookes is 21 years old. Two years ago he had a motorcycle accident, which has left him unable to use his legs. He has an electric wheelchair and an adapted car, and both his home and workplace have been adapted such that he is largely independent. However, as a result of his injuries he does continue to experience some pain that is poorly controlled.

Adele Jones is 19 years old and has **Down's syndrome**. She loves the same things as most 19 year olds and takes great pride in her appearance. She lives at home with her family but has a wide circle of friends and enjoys going out and meeting new people. She has just left school and is in the process of moving to college.

When you have completed this activity turn to the end of the chapter where you will find some suggested areas you may not have considered.

Defining vulnerability

Defining and understanding vulnerability is not just an academic exercise, since if we cannot clearly define a problem then our ability to address it is severely reduced. In particular, if we want to improve practice and develop policies to facilitate this, we need to understand both the nature of the problem and the factors that cause it. Also, we need to acknowledge that, as individuals, we may hold different understandings of vulnerability and what it means to be vulnerable, and this may have particular implications when we as nurses seek to support individuals, fam̲i̲l̲i̲e̲s̲ ̲a̲n̲d̲ communities.

Policy definitions

The Department of Health (2010a) suggest that there is no formal definition of vulnerability in healthcare. However, as noted above it is important that understandings of the term are explored in order that appropriate practice is developed. This means that the broader literature needs to be considered.

Within the *No Secrets* policy guidance, which sets out the framework for protecting adults from abuse, a 'vulnerable adult' is defined as being someone:

> *who is or may be in need of community care services by reason of mental or other disability, age or illness; and who is unable to take care of him or herself or is unable to protect him or herself against significant harm or exploitation.*
> (DH, 2000a, pp8–9)

A number of aspects of this definition are worth considering further. It indicates that an individual must either be receiving, or may need to receive, community care services. However, it could be the case that an individual may not receive or require such services but may still be vulnerable. For example, an older person may cope independently but still be vulnerable to financial abuse by family members; or consider the situation of Jenny in Activity 2.1, who may cope without any support from services, but who may nonetheless be vulnerable to abuse and ridicule from other people when she is going through a manic stage of her illness. The definition also suggests that the reason someone may require services is due to the presence of particular personal characteristics/circumstances such as age, disability or illness, which seems to locate the origin of the vulnerability within the person. This use of terminology has been criticised, since people do not like being labelled as being 'vulnerable', and the need for a new statutory definition has been highlighted (Magill et al., 2010). The Department of Health (2000a) definition does go on to identify additional criteria, namely the inability to care for or protect oneself from harm, but even this seems to locate the problem as being an individual deficit. An alternative view might be that someone is vulnerable due to being subjected to significant harm or exploitation by someone, or something. This would lead us to consider what it is that people are vulnerable to.

In fairness, the Department of Health definition is set out for a specific purpose, that is, to identify who is, and who is not, covered by the policies and procedures set up to protect vulnerable adults from abuse (the implications of which are discussed in Chapter 6). As such, it is an official means of setting inclusion and exclusion criteria rather than a broader definition of vulnerability. However, it does highlight some potential difficulties, such as the danger of regarding all members of particular groups as being vulnerable. For example, not all older people are vulnerable, not all disabled people are vulnerable, and there are some people to whom such labels are not applied who are or may be vulnerable. Look back at Activity 2.1: did you consider Adele to be vulnerable just because she has Down's syndrome? Did you consider other aspects of her life and how she might feel about them? As the Department of Health (2011a, p10) highlights, *A person's disability or age does not of itself make the person vulnerable* and Martin (2007) argues that it is something outside the individual that creates vulnerability.

The view expressed by Martin might also be challenged on the grounds that it seems to ignore factors internal to the individual, and if vulnerability is solely created by external factors, a given experience would lead everyone to be vulnerable in the same way, and yet this does not seem to offer sufficient explanation. For example, while everyone admitted to a hospital may, to some degree, be vulnerable, the nature and extent of that vulnerability will differ from one individual to another. Other factors also need to be considered if the complex nature of vulnerability is to be understood.

Vulnerability: a multidimensional concept

Scanlon and Lee (2007) suggest that, in the wider literature, three forms of vulnerability are identified: social, psychological and physical. Table 2.1 sets out some examples of these different forms.

While each of these three areas is presented separately here, they can interact and overlap. For example, illness can be both caused by and made worse by poverty, and our ability to protect ourselves from harm can be affected by our age. Scanlon and Lee (2007), however, do not view vulnerability as a fixed or inevitable state: not all older people are vulnerable and many people with mental health problems cope well on a day-to-day basis. The personal **capacity** of individuals can mediate the effects of vulnerability, which means that increasing personal capacity can be an effective way of reducing vulnerability.

Form of vulnerability	Examples
Social	• Age • Poverty • Cultural issues
Physical	• Physiological imbalances • Impaired resistance to harm • Illness
Psychological	• Low self-esteem • Mental ill health • Fear

Table 2.1 Forms of vulnerability (adapted from Scanlon and Lee, 2007)

The analysis provided by Scanlon and Lee (2007) moves us beyond just looking at individual characteristics such as illness and disability, and introduces additional factors such as social factors and personal resources. For example, two people may have similar levels of depression but one is socially isolated, has limited finances and receives poor support from his general practitioner. In contrast, the other has a small but close circle of friends, good family support and a general practitioner who puts her in touch with a counsellor and an exercise class. The first person is likely to be more vulnerable than the second due to the resources each has access to. Similarly, one person with learning disabilities living in a residential home may be at greater risk of abuse than another, because the latter has relatives who regularly visit and who encourage the person to be assertive, but the former does not have personal visits and after years of living in group settings finds it difficult to speak up.

Vulnerability has many dimensions. Another useful framework is offered by the Department of Health (2011a), which argues that vulnerability is affected by three key factors:

- **personal circumstances** – this will include (but is not limited to) disability or ill health;
- **risks from the environment** – this will include factors such as the level of social contact, a lack of adaptations to meet individual needs and the quality of care received;
- **resilience factors** – this will include support networks, personal strengths and coping mechanisms.

Vulnerability is therefore an interaction between internal and external circumstances and resources that promote resilience. This means that the same circumstances will affect individuals differently and also that identical circumstances may have an impact on an individual in different ways at different times. For example, there are some circumstances that we cope with adequately when we are well but find difficult at times of illness. A person who is visually impaired may cope well within the home as he or she knows where everything is in that environment. However, should the person have to visit a GP surgery, managing the unfamiliar environment could prove difficult and thus the person's vulnerability is increased. Individual vulnerabilities may therefore differ over time (Sellman, 2011) and are also affected by both the physical and psychological environment. Context is therefore an important dimension when considering the appropriateness or otherwise of definitions of vulnerability (Scanlon and Lee, 2007) and, in addition to time and location, culture is an important dimension of context. Different cultures have different beliefs concerning dementia, with some not recognising it as a specific condition but rather as a normal part of the ageing process. In such a situation an older person with dementia may not be seen by his or her family as more vulnerable than other older people. Nurses, however, may find themselves torn between their professional responsibility to promote the safety and well-being of their patients and their desire to respect cultural beliefs. Dilemmas such as this are discussed further in Chapter 3.

Scanlon and Lee (2007) distinguish between actual vulnerability (known factors that cause an individual to be susceptible) and potential vulnerability (circumstances that may cause an individual to be susceptible). This suggests that, if risk factors are known, there is the potential to either eliminate them or to predict and manage them, although Scanlon and Lee do note that, while some factors may be preventable or amenable to adjustment, others (such as social status) may be more complex and difficult to change. De Santis (2008), however, proposes that the concept of vulnerability lacks consistency because it is often used interchangeably with the concept of risk. He maintains that the two concepts are different in that *Vulnerability is the relationship between the person and their environment. Vulnerability is the level at which the culmination of risk factors results in harm for the client* (p282). Thus, one risk factor alone may not have an adverse impact, two may not cause harm, but when others are added an individual becomes vulnerable.

It must also be remembered that the risks associated with vulnerability are not equally distributed throughout society (Delor and Hubert, 2000), hence it is important to remember that some combinations of risks affect some people more than others and also that some people may face greater risks than others. In the situation of a natural disaster such as a flood, where everyone in a given area may be at risk, disabled people may face increased risk due to the difficulties they may face in getting themselves to safety. Flaskerud and Winslow (2010) note how people who have personal resources such as money, power and access to healthcare are able to use these resources to reduce their risk of vulnerability, whereas those who lack such resources are exposed to greater risk and consequently experience poorer health status. The potential for this situation to become a downward spiral is evident, whereby poorer health status exposes people to additional risks, which further diminish their resources and thus increase their vulnerability.

As has been highlighted, vulnerability has been defined in different ways, but for the purpose of this chapter the following definition is offered (see also Figure 2.1):

> *Vulnerability is not an inevitable consequence of particular personal characteristics but rather the complex interaction between the physical and psychological characteristics of an individual and their physical, social, psychological and economic environment. Since it is not inevitable, vulnerability may be reduced and potentially eliminated where it is deemed to be harmful.*

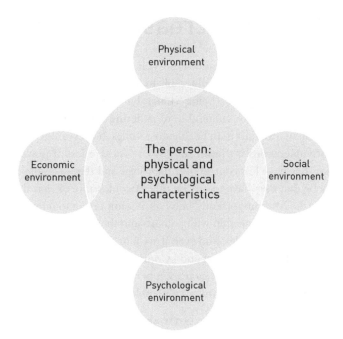

Figure 2.1 A model of vulnerability

Using the framework in Figure 2.1 to assist you, undertake Activity 2.2.

Activity 2.2   *Reflection*

Think about some of the patients and clients with whom you have worked. Can you identify any factors that protected them from or reduced their vulnerability?

Some suggested areas for consideration are given at the end of the chapter.

Activity 2.2 asked you to try to identify some factors that can protect people from vulnerability. This is important within nursing practice as there is a danger that sometimes we focus just on the areas of difficulty or deficit rather than on the strengths that individuals, families and communities possess. By identifying strengths we can support people in recognising their personal strengths and/or in identifying ways they can increase their strengths rather than just applying the label of 'vulnerable adult'. Such an approach is also more likely to have longer-term benefits: as people recognise their personal capacity, their confidence in addressing potential areas of vulnerability increases. It does not deny the existence of vulnerability, but rather encourages an active rather than passive approach.

Factors that can increase vulnerability

It is important that, when seeking to understand vulnerability, we question what it is that an individual, family or community may be vulnerable to. In the context of healthcare, for example, we often talk about individuals or groups being 'vulnerable to' certain illnesses or conditions. Each winter people who are particularly vulnerable to suffering severe effects of the flu virus are encouraged to get vaccinated against it. In healthcare settings, however, one of the factors that can give rise to feelings of vulnerability is a feeling of powerlessness or loss of power. Illness may make some people feel that they have lost control over their lives and that decisions are being taken by other people. It may be that they have to rely on other people more or that they are restricted in terms of what they can do. Most importantly, however, it is important to remember that, no matter how much we aim to work in partnership with patients and their families, there is still a great deal of power attached to professional roles, and even if we aim to work in empowering ways we may still be perceived both by those we support and by others as being more powerful. Simply taking on the role of patient or client may thus increase a person's vulnerability and, in the context of safeguarding, this may make him or her more vulnerable to abuse and neglect.

Take some time to complete Activity 2.3 before reading on.

Activity 2.3   *Critical thinking*

Think about the following settings and consider the factors that may give rise to abuse or neglect:

- an individual's family home;
- a nursing home;
- a hospital ward.

Some outline answers are given at the end of the chapter.

In undertaking Activity 2.3 you will probably have seen that abuse and neglect may occur in a range of settings. Sometimes, however, the factors that cause an individual to be vulnerable can vary and, when considering safeguarding, it is particularly important to identify such factors so that, wherever possible, abuse may be prevented. Particular combinations of factors may lead to individual vulnerability being increased. For example, the Department of Health (2011a) refers to the presence of recurring themes in inquiries concerning failures in care including:

- a lack of patient empowerment particularly in relation to choices concerning their care;
- patients' voices not being heard;
- a lack of preventative and early warning systems, giving rise to abuse and neglect;
- health staff not recognising abuse and neglect;
- safeguarding being viewed as the responsibility of others.

To this list could be added factors such as a lack of staff development, poor recruitment procedures, or isolated staff teams (see also Chapter 1). In developing nursing practice it is therefore important to consider the factors that may give rise to vulnerability, those that may be used to reduce or prevent it, and the significance of time and context. Practice implications will be explored later in this chapter, but first it is important to explore who might (actually or potentially) be vulnerable in healthcare settings.

Who is vulnerable?

The short answer to this question is 'everyone': we all have the potential to be vulnerable whether on a short-term basis or permanently (CARNA, 2005). However, as Sellman (2011) observes, this position does not help us in understanding why particular individuals or groups may require particular consideration in relation to their vulnerability. For this reason he suggests that we should distinguish between ordinary vulnerability (by virtue of being human) and situations where someone is 'more-than-ordinarily' vulnerable. He further adds that, when individuals require the input of health services, they are often 'more-than-ordinarily' vulnerable, hence the importance of nurses being able to recognise and respond appropriately to vulnerability.

As has already been seen, some definitions, such as that offered by the Department of Health (2000a), set clear criteria as to who should be considered vulnerable in specific contexts. In addition, society sometimes assumes that certain groups of people are inevitably vulnerable. For example, some people hold the view that all people with learning disabilities need to be 'looked after' as they are not capable of independent living. Similarly, older people are often thought of as being frail and as having impaired thinking simply by virtue of being a certain age. Clearly, this is not always the case and such views can both stigmatise and, ironically, increase vulnerability through a lack of opportunity to develop or maintain independence. So, while certain people may be at increased risk of vulnerability and harm, labelling entire groups in this manner fails to take account of individual variations and capacities, which (as has already been noted) have an impact upon actual and potential vulnerabilities. Read the case study below and consider whether you feel Mr James is vulnerable and how you have arrived at your assessment of his situation.

Case study: An incorrect assumption of frailty

Albert James is 76 years old and recently he slipped on the ice and fell, breaking his femur. He has been in hospital but is now ready to be discharged. However, as he lives on this own and has no family support close at hand, it has been decided that he should transfer to a local nursing home for a few weeks to enable his physiotherapy to continue and to provide him with additional support. When he arrives at the nursing home he is made welcome, he has a comfortable room and the food is good. From what he can see of the other residents they appear to be very frail and he doesn't really have anyone to interact with except for the staff. While the staff are very pleasant, he does get irritated when they try to do things for him that he is able to do independently. He is also unclear as to why they keep asking when his family will be visiting as they have some things they need to discuss with them. He has asked what these things are, but they say it is nothing for him to worry about. The following weekend, when his son visits, the staff ask him if it is all right for them to wash his father's clothes and to take his photograph for their records. Most worryingly, they ask what should be put on his father's file concerning whether to resuscitate or not should the situation arise.

In the case study above it can be seen that staff had looked at Mr James's age and the fact that he had been admitted to the nursing home and assumed that he was both mentally and physically frail. They had possibly made this assumption based on their knowledge of the clients with whom they usually worked. However, by making this assumption and by seeking to overprotect him, they had increased his vulnerability. In particular, they had made him vulnerable to loss of **autonomy** (see Chapter 3, pages 47–9) and control over his own life. While this case study illustrates how the assumptions of care staff led to them 'taking over' and limiting his control, it is also important to remember that assumptions can lead to healthcare staff overestimating individuals' capacity for self-care and leaving them without assistance. Examples of such 'care' are unfortunately all too common as, for example, we hear of people unable to feed themselves being left to cope alone and their food then being taken away on the assumption that they were not hungry as they hadn't touched it. Such a situation constitutes neglect of the person's nutritional needs and hence is a form of abuse. However, as can be seen, it is not an inevitable consequence of having particular support needs, but rather that an individual is made vulnerable due to an inaccurate assessment of those needs and the failure to provide appropriate support.

The case study also shows how an individual may view themselves as being independent while others view that person as being vulnerable and seek to limit his or her opportunities or to protect him or her. Alternatively, it is possible for an individual to feel very vulnerable, but for others not to recognise this or to ignore it, encouraging him or her instead to take risks. For example, an older person who has had a fall may feel vulnerable and thus is reluctant to mobilise, but the staff view this as important if future vulnerability is to be avoided.

This difference between subjective and objective dimensions of vulnerability can also be seen in relation to situations where there have been allegations of abuse. For example, an adult with learning disabilities who has been giving away most of his or her money to 'friends' may not consider themselves to be vulnerable or abused, yet policy frameworks would identify such behaviour on the part of the 'friends' as financial abuse. Similarly, a young woman with severe depression as a result of experiencing sexual abuse as a child may feel that she has done something wrong to make her abuser act in that way and that she rather than the abuser is to blame.

The interaction between objective and subjective dimensions of vulnerability is complex (Sellman, 2011). Sellman refers to the work of Clarke and Driever (1983), who argue that vulnerability is internal and subjective while risk is external and objective. First, Sellman challenges this position, arguing that with some people (for example, those with a severe learning disability) it may be difficult to determine whether they (subjectively) view themselves as vulnerable, yet most people observing them (objectively) would recognise their vulnerability. Second, he points to the practice of seeking to reduce subjective feelings of vulnerability as an integral part of therapeutic practice. Where the feelings of vulnerability are based on false beliefs, challenging such beliefs may be helpful. For example, where someone with **epilepsy** is reluctant to go out socially, even though he or she has not had a daytime seizure for many years, it may be appropriate to challenge the person's perceptions about his or her vulnerability in social situations, and to encourage the person to try going out more.

However, where the feelings of vulnerability are an accurate reflection of reality, seeking to reduce them may give rise to feelings of invulnerability and invincibility, which themselves can lead to unwise risk taking and increased vulnerability. For example, if a young person suffers extreme anxiety in social situations, fearing everyone wants to harm him or her, it might be helpful to work with that person to alter his or her beliefs and increase his or her self-confidence. However, if the person is led to develop the belief that he or she will not be harmed in any social situation, the person may place themselves in situations of unwise risk. Similarly, if there is a strong possibility of the young person being confronted with harmful situations, it would not be appropriate to encourage him or her to increase social activity without also enabling the person to develop personal safety measures or different social activities.

Of course, the situation can become even more complex when, for example, a young woman with learning disabilities wishes to go out with her sister and friends to a night club and does not understand why she may be more vulnerable in such an environment. Her parents refuse to let her go, to which she responds by becoming very angry, accusing them of treating her like a child. Why is her sister allowed to go and yet they stop her? While the individual's desire to take part in social activities can be understood (and many parents would worry at their teenagers going to clubs), increased parental concerns about personal safety can also be understood. Our own assessment of our vulnerability and the assessment of others may be very different. Similarly, professional assessments of vulnerability may be very different from the views of the individuals with whom such professionals work. Take some time to work through Activity 2.4.

Activity 2.4   *Critical thinking*

- Think about the nature of vulnerability and try to list as many factors as you can that may make people feel vulnerable.
- Try also to think about situations in which you feel vulnerable. What is it that makes you feel this way?

There are some comments regarding this activity at the end of the chapter.

Recognising our own vulnerability

If everyone is vulnerable, it follows that we as nurses are also vulnerable. This is true in our everyday lives, but particularly so in relation to our professional lives. In Activity 2.4 some of the situations you identified in which you feel vulnerable may have related to your personal life while others relate to your work. For example, in our work we bear witness to some very difficult and harrowing situations: we can be subjected to physical or verbal abuse, we may undertake physically demanding work that places us at risk of injury and we may be bullied by colleagues. Often, however, as nurses we are expected not to show our vulnerability, which can mean that we do not recognise our own vulnerability. Activity 2.5 asks you to think about this issue and how it might be addressed.

Activity 2.5   *Critical thinking*

Think of the settings in which nurses work and the types of work they undertake.

- Which factors might increase their vulnerability?
- How might their vulnerability be reduced?

Some outline answers are given at the end of the chapter.

In Activity 2.5 you may have managed to identify both factors that give rise to vulnerability and some actions that could be taken to reduce such vulnerability. You may also have been able to think about some of the situations in which you have found yourself and perhaps how you might handle such situations differently in the future. Malone (2000) argues that, while choosing to be a nurse can be a way of increasing control over the uncertainties of life, it also brings people face to face with their fears concerning these uncertainties. Despite the fact that nurses might be viewed as being at greater risk of harm than other occupational groups, Sellman (2011) argues that they are not 'more-than-ordinarily' vulnerable, as usually they have the capacity for self-protection. He argues that they are at risk of exposure to occupational hazards and that they are witness to the 'more-than-ordinary' vulnerability of others on a regular basis within their work. It may be possible to reduce or remove any occupational hazards. Witnessing the vulnerability of other people, however, is a common feature of nursing that highlights the importance of us developing effective coping mechanisms. If you are a student nurse this may be a particular challenge, as you may not have had much experience of such situations or opportunities to develop your coping mechanisms. You may, therefore, feel particularly vulnerable but feel that you should be able to cope. Being willing to recognise our own vulnerability rather than being ashamed of it is, however, an important first step in being able to develop appropriate coping strategies. As Hoffmaster (2006) argues, *none of us is invincible.*

Case study: Recognising our own vulnerability

Luke Samuels is a second-year student nurse. He is 34 years old, is married and has two young children. Just before his placement with the district nursing team his father died from pancreatic cancer and, although Luke had been with him when he died, the time between diagnosis and death had been quick and so the family had not had long to adjust to what was happening. When he started the placement he didn't want to appear difficult or weak and so didn't mention his recent bereavement to his mentor. However, one of the patients they visited was a young man of a similar age to him who also had two young children and who had returned home from hospital as he wished to die at home. Luke finds this situation very difficult and tries to cope, but this results in him becoming quite withdrawn and uncommunicative. Noticing this, his mentor challenges him, and asks if there is anything wrong. Initially he says that everything is fine, but then breaks down and talks about his experience and his feelings. They discuss this and make arrangements for him to receive some additional support. As a result, Luke feels better able to work with the patient and takes pride in trying to make his final days as comfortable as possible.

Working to support people who are vulnerable can be very stressful and over time this can lead to burnout. However, as Sellman (2011) observes, there does not seem to be any evidence that nurses working within **palliative care** settings have higher levels of burnout than those working elsewhere, and yet the very nature of their work means that they work on a daily basis with people who are at the end of their lives. Some emergency nurses in Malone's (2000) study used strategies such as distancing themselves from situations as a means of coping, whereas others actively engaged with their patients and their suffering. While distancing may afford a degree of protection to nurses it can, unfortunately, also lead to dehumanisation of patients and neglect of their care. Malone thus refers to the 'paradox' of vulnerability whereby *it can be either bond or barrier between nurse and patient* (p9). Effective coping thus requires that nurses recognise their own vulnerability and Hoffmaster (2006) argues that to be able to truly care for others requires that we recognise our common humanity and common vulnerability. Vulnerability in this context thus becomes a strength rather than a sign of weakness since it allows us to develop **empathy** and understanding. Supportive strategies such as debriefing after particularly stressful clinical events, clinical supervision, use of a personal tutorial system and the use of support services such as counselling can all be useful ways of recognising our vulnerability and addressing it in a constructive way.

> **Research summary: Meanings of vulnerability**
>
> Stenbock-Hunt and Sarvimaki (2011) report a study of 16 nurses in Finland who were experienced in working with older people. The study sought to explore participants' meanings of vulnerability. Interviews were recorded, transcribed and then analysed using a **qualitative** interpretative approach. One core theme (vulnerability as being human and having feelings) and six sub-themes (having feelings, experiencing moral indignation, being harmed, having courage, protecting oneself, and maturing and developing) emerged. Vulnerability was viewed not only as a burden being associated with negative feelings, but also as a resource both for improving care and for personal development. While the limitations of the study are noted, it concluded that *Only if nurses are able to deal with their own vulnerability will they be able to develop an existential and ethical attitude and encounter older persons' vulnerability* (p40).

Implications for practice

If we accept that everyone is vulnerable, it follows that in considering the implications for practice we have to determine the implications for the individuals, families and communities with whom we work, and whom we seek to support. However, we also need to consider the implications for how we support colleagues, and seek and accept support for ourselves: if we as nurses are vulnerable ourselves, this will affect (either positively or negatively) the care and support we are able to provide to others. Take some time to work through Activity 2.6.

> **Activity 2.6**   *Decision making and communication*
>
> - How would you assess someone's vulnerability?
> - What factors would you consider and which sources of information would you use?
>
> *Some outline answers are given at the end of the chapter.*

In practice we need to be able to *recognise* factors that may increase vulnerability. Think back to Figure 2.1 and consider how personal characteristics (both physical and psychological) might interact with social, physical, economic and psychological environments to give rise to vulnerability. Indeed, such a framework might usefully form the basis of an assessment. Having identified such factors we also need to recognise their significance within the particular context in which we are working. For example, we need to understand that over-reliance on complex written information may make people with learning disabilities more vulnerable or that loud, busy environments may increase the agitation and confusion of people with dementia. We need to understand that a person who has recently suffered a traumatic event may be vulnerable to adverse psychological consequences even if they are not apparent at present. We also need to understand that our perception of vulnerability may differ from that of others and that an apparently similar combination of circumstances may affect people very differently.

Accurate, comprehensive and timely assessment is therefore required in order that actual vulnerability can be identified and situations of potential vulnerability are, wherever possible, predicted and averted. In relation to looking after ourselves and supporting our colleagues we need to recognise factors that may make us feel vulnerable, and where the circumstances cannot be altered or avoided (for example, being confronted by people in distress) we need to identify commonly occurring situations and work proactively with others to develop our coping mechanisms.

We need to be able to *respond* appropriately when we encounter people in vulnerable situations or who feel themselves to be vulnerable. For example, continuing the examples previously discussed, we need to make sure that we have easy-to-read information available for people with learning disabilities when they attend health clinics, we need to make sure that there are quiet waiting areas for people with dementia when they attend Accident and Emergency (A&E) departments and we need to make sure that people suffering the effects of trauma are provided with appropriate specialist help. We also need to be able to respond at an emotional level, recognising others' distress and responding in a valuing and supportive manner and offering opportunities for individuals to talk about and explore their feelings.

We also need to be able to regularly *review* situations to determine levels of vulnerability in dynamic and changing situations. For example, someone who has a terminal illness may be vulnerable to infection at one stage due to the effects of **chemotherapy**, at another time may be vulnerable to depression as he or she tries to adjust to the situation, and at another time may be vulnerable to extreme levels of pain. This means that the person's situation needs constantly reassessing, as what reduces vulnerability at one stage may not be effective at another.

This book is about safeguarding and so the importance of recognising, responding and reviewing needs to be carefully considered in this context. The issues will be expanded upon elsewhere in the book, but here it is relevant to note the importance of being alert to signs of abuse and neglect, being aware of the appropriate responses and being alert to the need to review both situations and actions taken on a regular basis (see Figure 2.2).

It is also important to consider whether a certain degree of vulnerability can be helpful in some situations (for example, it is suggested in the previous section that recognising our own vulnerability can be important in the development of an empathetic and caring attitude). This needs to be countered by recognising that feelings of invincibility can also be problematic since they may lead individuals to take unwarranted and unnecessary risks. Clearly, however, most people would want to avoid situations in which they are 'more-than-ordinarily' vulnerable. Where factors that may give rise to vulnerability can be predicted, it may therefore be important to work with clients in order to increase their resilience. This could, for example, include actions such as ensuring that they have appropriately trained support at key times, providing them with communication aids so that they can make their views known to others or reducing their anxiety levels through desensitisation programmes. Increasing resilience to abuse is particularly important and could include strategies such as assertiveness training, provision of information concerning rights or increasing awareness of what constitutes abuse. It may also include working to strengthen people's support networks.

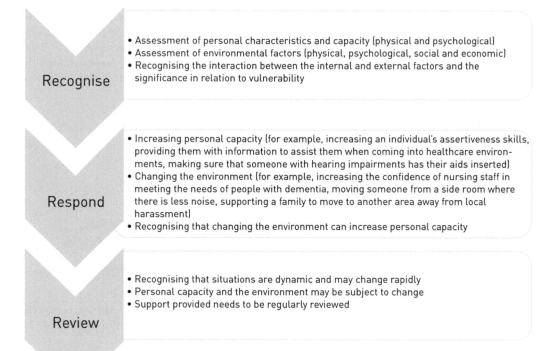

Figure 2.2 Addressing vulnerability in practice

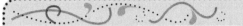

> ## Chapter summary
>
> This chapter has explored a number of different definitions of vulnerability and has challenged the assumption that we all understand vulnerability in the same way. It has been argued that vulnerability is a complex concept, that everyone is vulnerable, and that vulnerability is influenced by the interaction of internal and external factors. Since vulnerability may be reduced or eliminated, nurses, who work regularly with people who are particularly vulnerable, have a key role to play in recognising, responding to and reviewing vulnerability. Also, since nurses themselves may be vulnerable, they have a responsibility to recognise and respond to their own vulnerability and that of their colleagues.

Activities: Brief outline answers

Activity 2.1 Critical thinking, pages 26–7

In undertaking this activity you may have looked at the brief outlines provided and concluded that all of the individuals are vulnerable by virtue of their age, disability or health needs. However, a closer look reveals that, while the individuals concerned may be potentially vulnerable, a number of measures are in place to reduce their vulnerability, such as the provision of personal support, services, aids and adaptations. It might also be important to consider whether, if asked, the individuals concerned feel vulnerable. Nonetheless, it is important to note that there is the potential for vulnerability. For example, what if Jenny experiences a period of severe depression, feels unable to go out and has no friends or family to support her? What if James has to go into hospital for assessment of his pain and is told that he cannot take his electric wheelchair with him? He would then be dependent upon staff to meet his needs and his vulnerability may increase. Vulnerability is therefore a complex issue.

Activity 2.2 Reflection, page 31

A number of factors may protect individuals from vulnerability or reduce the impact of vulnerability. Some you may have identified include:

- good support networks of family and/or friends;
- financial resources;
- well-planned packages of care that meet individual needs;
- personal coping mechanisms such as assertiveness, good self-esteem and self-awareness;
- legal provisions such as the Mental Health Act 1983 and the Mental Capacity Act 2005 (see Chapter 6 for further details).

Activity 2.3 Critical thinking, page 32

Some factors that may lead to abuse and neglect may be common to all settings, while others may differ between informal (home) and formal (nursing home and hospital) care. Some factors you may have identified include:

- differences in power whereby the abuser is in a powerful position relative to the person for whom he or she is caring;
- carers lacking the appropriate value base and/or the necessary skills;
- carers and those for whom they care lacking awareness as to what constitutes abuse and neglect;

- a lack of monitoring;
- stress;
- people who require support lacking a voice or, even if they do speak up, not being believed;
- low self-esteem and self-worth.

Activity 2.4 Critical thinking, page 35

To some extent what makes us feel vulnerable will inevitably be individual. However, there are some situations and experiences that commonly give rise to feelings of vulnerability. These include:

- having an illness that interferes with our usual day-to-day functioning;
- being admitted to hospital – even the process of changing into nightclothes and going to bed may make us feel more vulnerable;
- being in a situation where nothing is being explained to us even though we know it affects us;
- loss and bereavement;
- being in new situations;
- feeling that we lack the knowledge and skills needed for a situation.

Activity 2.5 Critical thinking, page 36

In thinking about the ways in which nurses might be vulnerable, some of the things you may have considered might include:

- not feeling adequately prepared for a situation;
- dealing with patients and relatives who become verbally or physically abusive;
- levels of responsibility and/or dealing with very complex situations;
- low staffing levels;
- lone working in a community setting;
- witnessing the vulnerability of other people and sometimes not being able to do anything to reduce it;
- having to cope with difficulties and challenges in our own lives while supporting others going through difficult situations that may sometimes be similar to our own circumstances.

Activity 2.6 Decision making and communication, page 38

In assessing people's vulnerability you could use the framework offered by the Department of Health (2011a) as discussed earlier in the chapter. You would therefore try to determine the following.

- What are their personal circumstances? This could include consideration of factors such as the presence of any disability, illness and/or personal support needs. It might also include factors such as their normal living circumstances and their personal views, beliefs and wishes.
- What risks can be determined in their environment? This might include aspects such as the frequency and nature of social contacts (not all may be positive and some may be abusive), physical barriers within the environment that have a negative impact on mobility and self-care, and environments that may have a negative impact on the psychological vulnerability of an individual.
- What factors are present that may reduce vulnerability? This may include aspects such as personal strengths, social networks and financial resources.
- In seeking to gather this information it would be important to speak with the individual concerned, any relevant family or carers and other professionals who regularly support that person. In addition, it would be important to use good observational skills. Any differences in perception should be noted.

Further reading

Abley, C, Bond, J and Robinson, L (2011) Improving inter-professional practice for vulnerable older people: gaining a better understanding of vulnerability, *Journal of Inter-professional Care*, 25(5): 359–65.

Fyffe, DC, Botticello, AL and Myaskovsky, L (2011) Vulnerable groups living with spinal cord injury, *Topics in Spinal Cord Injury Rehabilitation*, 17(2): 1–9.

Parley, F (2011) What does vulnerability mean? *British Journal of Learning Disabilities*, 39(4): 266–76.

Useful websites

http://patients-association.com

The Patients Association campaigns for improvements in patient care and has published a number of reports highlighting the vulnerability of patients.

www.mencap.org.uk

Mencap campaigns for better support for people with learning disabilities and for recognition of their rights. A key area of campaigning has focused on highlighting their vulnerability to poor healthcare provision.

Safeguarding

Northway, R. and Jenkins, R.

> ### NMC Standards for Pre-registration Nursing Education
>
> This chapter will address the following competencies:
>
> **Domain 1: Professional values**
>
> All nurses must act first and foremost to care for and safeguard the public.
>
> 2. All nurses must practice in a holistic, non-judgmental, caring and sensitive manner that avoids assumptions; supports social inclusion; recognises and respects individual choice; and acknowledges diversity. Where necessary, they must challenge inequality, discrimination and exclusion from access to care.
>
> 3. All nurses must support and promote the health, wellbeing, rights and dignity of people, groups, communities and populations. These include people whose lives are affected by ill health, disability, ageing, death and dying. Nurses must understand how these activities influence public health.
>
> 4. All nurses must work in partnership with service users, carers, families, groups, communities and organisations. They must manage risk, and promote health and wellbeing while aiming to empower choices that promote self-care and safety.
>
> **Domain 3: Nursing practice and decision-making**
>
> 9. All nurses must be able to recognise when a person is at risk and in need of extra support and protection and take reasonable steps to protect them from abuse.
>
> **Domain 4: Leadership, management and team working**
>
> 2. All nurses must systematically evaluate care and ensure that they and others use the findings to help improve people's experience and care outcomes and to shape future services.
>
> 3. All nurses must be able to identify priorities and manage time and resources effectively to ensure the quality of care is maintained or enhanced.

NMC Essential Skills Clusters

This chapter will address the following ESCs:

Cluster: Organisational aspects of care

11. People can trust the newly registered graduate nurse to safeguard children and adults from vulnerable situations and support and protect them from harm.
17. People can trust the newly registered graduate nurse to work safely under pressure and maintain the safety of service users at all times.
18. People can trust a newly registered graduate nurse to enhance the safety of service users and identify and actively manage risk and uncertainty in relation to people, the environment, self and others.
19. People can trust the newly registered graduate nurse to work to prevent and resolve conflict and maintain a safe environment.

Chapter aims

After reading this chapter, you will be able to:

- discuss a 'protection of vulnerable adults' approach to policy and practice;
- explain how a 'safeguarding' approach differs from the 'protection of vulnerable adults';
- identify the key components of a safeguarding approach;
- discuss the implications of safeguarding for the delivery of nursing practice.

Introduction

The number of competencies and essential skills linked to this chapter (see above) should give you an indication of how important safeguarding is to the delivery of professional nursing care: it is a responsibility of every nurse. This chapter will, therefore, introduce you to the concept of safeguarding, and explore its implications for nursing practice. Before you read on, however, take time to complete Activity 5.1 and keep your answer to this activity to hand as you read through the rest of the chapter.

| Activity 5.1 | *Reflection* |

Think about a healthcare setting with which you are familiar and imagine that you are a patient/client using that service.

- What would you want to see put in place to ensure your safety and well-being in that setting?
- What would need to happen for your rights to be upheld?

Try to think about policies, practices and the environment of care.

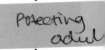

Some ideas are given at the end of the chapter.

The protection of vulnerable adults

Within the UK we have a relatively long history of having a legal framework to protect children from abuse and neglect. However, it was not until 2000 that England and Wales developed a framework of policy guidance designed to protect adults from abuse. Even then, what was published was 'policy guidance' rather than a clear legal framework, which meant that the guidance was open to local interpretation and implementation (see Chapter 6 for further discussion). Inevitably, policy interpretation and guidance has varied and this has an impact on the extent to which people are protected from abuse or, where abuse occurs, an appropriate, effective and timely response is forthcoming; it is implementation of policy that protects people (Northway et al., 2007). The Commission for Social Care Inspection (2008) examined how effective adult protection policies had been within England. It found uneven progress in the development of effective services, variability in the quality of support provided and variability in terms of action to prevent abuse and achieve better outcomes. The presence of strong leadership, development of strategic partnerships, and a correlation between councils who were performing well and the quality of the care provision within regulated services, were also observed.

The recent consultation document concerning the Social Services (Wales) Bill 2012 thus recognises concerns that adult protection has not had the same attention as child protection, where there is a 'very well-developed and understood legal framework' (Welsh Government, 2012). Relevant legislation will be discussed in Chapter 6, but here we need to consider the term 'protection of vulnerable adults', and how this has developed to the more recent terminology of 'safeguarding'. First take a few minutes to complete Activity 5.2.

Activity 5.2   *Critical thinking*

Think about the phrase 'protection of vulnerable adults'.

- What does the word 'protection' suggest to you?
- What do you think vulnerable adults might need 'protecting' from?
- How would you feel if you were considered to be a 'vulnerable adult' who was in need of 'protection'?

An outline answer is given at the end of the chapter.

Chapter 2 examined different meanings and understandings of vulnerability. These include it being viewed as a characteristic of an individual, and the idea that individuals may be vulnerable to harm from a range of internal and external factors. In the context of the policy guidance, individuals had to meet the specified criteria, that is, to have certain personal characteristics and to be in receipt of community care services (DH, 2000a; NAfW, 2000). The definition of vulnerable adults as set out in this guidance was, however, challenged on the grounds that it appeared to exclude those who may be vulnerable even though they do not receive community care services (House of Commons Health Committee, 2007).

The term 'vulnerable adult' has become commonly used within health and social care services. It has different meanings in policy guidance, **common law** and **statutes** (Magill et al., 2010). Also, those who are referred to in this manner are not always happy with the terminology (Magill et al., 2010). Support for change was also found in the review of *No Secrets* (DH, 2009b), where 90 per cent of respondents were in favour of changing the definition, and many preferred adoption of the term 'adult at risk' rather than 'vulnerable adult'. In Scotland the Adult Support and Protection (Scotland) Act 2007 does refer to adults 'at risk of harm', and currently within Wales proposals to move to use of similar terminology are being consulted upon (Welsh Government, 2012). Within the Welsh proposals people would be deemed to be at risk if they belong to particular groups (such as people with mental health problems, older people and people with learning disabilities) *and* they are the victim (or potentially the victim) of one or more of the identified forms of harm or abuse. It can been seen that this moves away from the idea that simply by being identified as belonging to a particular group you are inevitably vulnerable: actual or potential harm must also be present.

Safeguarding

The previous section noted that, in relation to children, a legal and policy framework was established in the UK long before any developments took place relating to adults. In terms of supporting children a change in terminology took place and 'child protection' was largely replaced with 'safeguarding'. A similar change has taken place in relation to adults, although the rationale for change may have had a slightly different emphasis. Before exploring this change further take some time to work through Activity 5.3. As you do this try to think of arguments both for and against the issues you identify.

Activity 5.3   *Critical thinking*

- Why do you feel the UK has had a relatively long history of putting measures in place to prevent and respond to the abuse of children, but has only recently started to develop similar measures to protect adults at risk of harm?
- Do you feel it is appropriate to change the terminology to 'safeguarding' in relation to adults as has been the case concerning children?

An outline answer is given at the end of the chapter.

Sometimes a change in terminology is just that: the words change but practice does not. In this context the change is, in part, a response to criticisms that the phrase 'protection of vulnerable adults' was perceived as negative, and as portraying adults as being passive. In addition, policy guidance was often interpreted as addressing abuse and neglect once it has occurred, rather than preventing it from occurring in the first place. In 2005 the Association of Directors of Social Services (ADSS) indicated that the previous terminology would be replaced by 'safeguarding' and this meant:

> *all work which enables an adult 'who is or may be eligible for community care services' to retain independence, wellbeing and choice, **and** to access their human right to live a life that is free from abuse and neglect.*
> (ADSS, 2005, p5)

The NHS has also adopted the terminology of 'safeguarding', arguing that it is concerned with promoting the safety and well-being of all patients while recognising that those least able to protect themselves from harm may require additional support (DH, 2011a). The Department of Health (2011a) also identifies that safeguarding encompasses a wide range of activities, ranging from prevention of harm and abuse to multi-agency responses when abuse and harm occur. It can thus be seen that it is a rights-based approach that is both proactive and reactive.

Another definition of safeguarding has been proposed by the British Medical Association (BMA):

> *Safeguarding is about keeping vulnerable adults safe from harm. It involves identifying adults who may be vulnerable, assessing their needs and working with them and with other agencies in order to protect them from avoidable harms.*
> (2011, p11)

Some might criticise this definition for continuing to refer to 'vulnerable adults', but it does introduce two important elements. First, it stresses that safeguarding involves working *with* people who may be vulnerable to harm; it is not about them taking a passive role while others do something to them. Second, it draws attention to the need to be proactive by noting that, in some instances, it is possible to identify the risk of harm and to intervene to prevent it from occurring.

The breadth of the activities involved in safeguarding, and the range of agencies and people who may be involved, are highlighted by the Northern Ireland Office and the Department of Health, Social Services and Public Safety (DHSSPS) (2010). They suggest that, while health, social care and criminal justice agencies have a leading role to play, the involvement of other organisations and agencies across statutory, voluntary, community, private and faith sectors is also required. Safer communities, public transport policies, public health, education and adult learning opportunities are also identified as important elements of successful safeguarding, along with the input of families, carers and good neighbours. It is not the responsibility of one or two statutory agencies – every citizen has a role to play.

Case study: Josh Walsh

Josh is 20 years old and is in his second year at university. During the summer holidays at the end of his first year, his best friend at home was killed in a motorcycle accident. At the time, Josh seemed to be coping reasonably well and went back to university as usual in October. Within a few weeks, however, it became obvious that he was having difficulties. He didn't want to worry his family, who were 150 miles away, and he didn't want to worry his friends at university so he kept things to himself. His results had been good all through his first year but they started to dip, and then he started not handing in work. No matter how hard he tried he just couldn't concentrate, he wasn't eating and he wasn't sleeping; most of his time was spent alone in his room. When he did see other people he tried to behave as though everything was all right; no one noticed that things were wrong. One day another student noticed that he hadn't seen Josh for a few days. He knocked on his door, but there was no answer, so he fetched a member of staff who went with him into Josh's room where they found him in bed, unable to communicate with them. After assessment by the GP Josh was diagnosed as suffering from severe depression, and was admitted to a local mental health unit; he has been there for four weeks. Initially he was withdrawn, but when his mood started to lift he began to express ideas of self-harm and had to be monitored very closely. This now appears to have passed and discussions are taking place in preparation for his discharge. Josh is adamant that he wants to return to university and to get things back to normal.

Activity 5.4   *Critical thinking*

Think about the situation of Josh in the case study above.

* What do you feel needs to be in place to safeguard him from harm when he is discharged?

An outline answer is given at the end of the chapter.

Another important element of safeguarding identified by the Department of Health (2011a) is that of learning from practice, and using this learning to inform future interventions (see Figure 5.1). This is essential in the context of seeking to protect people who may be at risk of harm, since harm will not always be prevented and it is essential that we learn from these situations in order to try to prevent similar situations from occurring in the future. Unfortunately, however, as was seen in Chapter 1, we do not always seem to learn the lessons from inquiries into abuse and poor standards of care, even though the reports of such inquiries note similar findings.

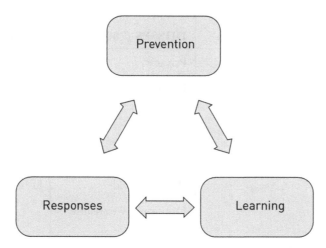

Figure 5.1 Key elements of safeguarding identified by the Department of Health (2011a)

To relate this to your personal practice, take a few minutes to complete Activity 5.5.

Activity 5.5   *Reflection*

Think about a care situation in which you have been involved where a patient or client has come to some harm.

- How was the situation managed?
- What did you learn from the situation?
- Did you learn anything that you could use in your practice to try to prevent a similar situation from occurring in the future?

Some guidance is included at the end of the chapter, but try to address the questions yourself first.

The principles of safeguarding

Most discussions concerning safeguarding make reference to principles or values that underpin the approach and some examples of these are set out in Table 5.1. Looking at the table you will see some principles that were discussed in Chapter 3, where we explored ethical issues; the relationship between ethics and safeguarding should be clear. In Table 5.1 it can be seen that some principles appear in more than one list, for example empowerment and rights. Others are clearly linked, such as justice and legal protection. Some are self-explanatory but others perhaps require some further discussion.

Some of these principles, such as legal protection and rights, will be explored later in this book (see Chapter 6) and the relevance of key legislation to safeguarding will also be discussed there. Other principles will be discussed here before considering their implications for care planning and delivery.

Department of Health (2011a)	DHSSPS (2006)	Reece (2010)
Empowerment	Privacy	Protection
Protection	Respect and dignity	Promotion of well-being
Prevention	Choice	Empowerment
Proportionality	Legal protection	Rights
Partnerships	Rights upheld	Justice
Accountability	Opportunity to realise potential	

Table 5.1 Principles underpinning safeguarding

Protection and the promotion of well-being

Having previously identified that the word 'protection' can be problematic, it also needs to be acknowledged that there are clearly situations where some adults are at risk of harm or abuse. In such circumstances they may need protection from others, themselves or particular situations, and therefore it needs to be included as a principle that informs safeguarding. However, placing protection alongside other important elements recognises that it is an essential part of the overall approach, but that other elements are also required. Protection suggests that a preventative approach is required, as well as a response where abuse has occurred, so as to prevent further harm. The inclusion of 'promotion of well-being' also suggests a wider-ranging approach. Rather than just preventing harm it requires that a positive approach to enhancing well-being is taken. If you refer back to Chapter 3 it can be seen that beneficence and not just non-maleficence is required.

Empowerment

Within healthcare situations patients can often be (or feel they are) less powerful than the health professionals who are working with them. Professionals may be seen as knowledgeable experts and patients are expected to take on a passive role in complying with the professional advice given to them. We have all probably heard people with whom we are working say 'whatever you think is best'. However, this situation makes people vulnerable to loss of control over their own lives, over decisions that are made, and sometimes subject to treatment that they find abusive or harmful. Clearly, there are some situations where people lack the capacity to take control or to express their views and wishes. In such circumstances legal safeguards are required and these will be discussed in Chapter 6. At other times it is important to safeguard against the potential for a lack of control and power by working in an empowering way; empowerment is a key principle underpinning a safeguarding approach.

Empowerment has been defined in a number of ways, but one helpful definition in this context is that provided by Slettebo (2006), who suggests that it is *a process of equipping a person to be in charge of his or her own life* (p115). This shows how it is a developmental process that seeks to increase people's capacity to take control and this in turn gives rise to two points that are important in relation to safeguarding. First, it suggests that, where people appear to be at risk of harm, we can support them to increase their personal capacity and hopefully reduce the risk of harm occurring: their current abilities can be enhanced. Second, where abuse or harm has occurred an empowering approach can be used to reduce feelings of powerlessness that can arise from abuse and also assist people to feel better able to anticipate and manage future risks.

Accountability

It is important to note that the Department of Health (2011a) identifies the need for accountability in relation to safeguarding. Outcome 7 of the Care Quality Commission standards relates specifically to safeguarding from abuse those people who use care services. It states that *People should be protected from abuse, or the risk of abuse, and their human rights are respected and upheld* (CQC, 2010, p93). Unfortunately, however, major concerns have been expressed regarding non-achievement of this standard in some services for people with learning disabilities (CQC, 2012) and moderate concerns have also been identified in acute hospital settings (see the CQC website for up-to-date information at www.cqc.org.uk). Some of the issues to emerge in these reports were a lack of staff training regarding safeguarding, patients feeling at risk from other patients, and a failure to protect patients. Establishments assessed as failing to achieve the necessary standards are given a specified period to respond and to say how they intend to improve the situation.

Proportionality

In some circumstances where harm occurs it is reasonably clear as to what the response should be. For example, if a law has been broken prosecution may be necessary, and if guilt is proven an appropriate sentence is handed down based on official guidelines for the specific offence. However, in other circumstances the required response may be less clear and it is important to know whether to respond, how to respond and what sanctions should be applied. Think about a situation in which a family member comes into a ward and takes £20 of her elderly mother's money without her knowledge or consent. Then think about another situation in which you observe that an elderly lady you have been visiting in the community seems to have little food in the house, her house is cold and she seems to have a lot of unpaid bills. When you discuss this with her you eventually find out that a neighbour who comes to visit her has been collecting your patient's pension, saying that she would pay the bills and get the shopping and take a little bit of money to pay her for her time. Your patient says that she knows this means she doesn't have any money, but she is worried that, without her neighbour helping her, she wouldn't be able to cope. Both of these situations could constitute financial abuse, but should they be dealt with in the same way?

The Department of Health (2011a) identifies 'proportionality' as a key principle underpinning safeguarding, arguing that responses to abuse and harm should be in keeping with the nature and seriousness of the concern. It also stresses that responses should be those that place least restriction on the rights of the individual who has been harmed, taking account of factors such as his or her age, culture, wishes, lifestyle and beliefs. Finally, the Department suggests that proportionality also means that concerns must be addressed in the most effective and efficient manner.

Essence of Care benchmarks

Many of these principles can be seen in other policies that inform the provision of healthcare and this highlights how safeguarding is (or should be) an integral part of healthcare provision. For example, great emphasis has been placed on promoting and monitoring the fundamentals or essence of care. In 2010 the Department of Health published *Essence of Care 2010* (DH, 2010b), which sets out standards for and indicators of quality care. A general principle stated throughout the document relates to safeguarding: *robust, integrated systems are in place to identify and respond to abuse, harm and neglect*. Some of the specific areas discussed link directly to the principles underpinning safeguarding set out in Table 5.1, such as 'Benchmarks for Respect and Dignity' and 'Benchmarks for Promoting Health and Well-Being'. Examples of indicators in each of these areas are set out in Table 5.2.

It should be noted that Table 5.2 includes only examples of some of the many outcomes, factors and indicators of best practice identified by the Department of Health (2010b), and you may wish to look at the relevant document and consider some of the other areas addressed. The examples given do, however, demonstrate a few important points. First, it can be seen that in all areas reference is made to 'people' rather than 'patients', 'service users' or other terms that are frequently used within healthcare settings. This careful choice of words reflects the importance of valuing and respecting all people because they are just that, people. Second, if you read the examples of best practice carefully you will see that the emphasis is on supporting people to take as much control as possible over what happens to them and on the importance of creating environments in which this can happen. People are not viewed as being passive recipients of services that are controlled by healthcare professionals. Instead, they are active partners in the process of healthcare planning and delivery.

Each of the principles set out in this section has implications for the delivery of nursing care and these will be discussed further in the next section. Before you read on, however, take some time to complete Activity 5.6.

Activity 5.6   *Leadership and management*

- Imagine you have just been appointed to manage a clinical area or community team. Take one of the principles set out above and identify how you would ensure that it is upheld within the area you are managing.
- How do you feel that it would help to promote the safeguarding of people who might otherwise be at risk of harm, abuse or neglect?

An outline answer is given at the end of the chapter.

Outcome	Factor	Best practice
People experience care that is focused upon respect	Attitudes and behaviour	People and carers feel that they matter all of the time
	Personal boundaries and space	People's personal space is protected by staff
	Privacy, modesty and dignity	People's care ensures their privacy and dignity and protects their modesty
	Privacy – private area	People and carers can access an area that safely provides privacy
People will be supported to make healthier choices for themselves and others	Assessment	People, carers and communities are enabled to identify their health and well-being promotion needs
	Environment	People, carers, communities and agencies influence and create environments that promote people's health and well-being
	Outcomes of promoting health and well-being	People, carers and communities have an improved, sustainable and good-quality health and well-being

Table 5.2 Essence of Care *benchmarks (DH, 2010b)*

Safeguarding in practice

As has already been seen in this chapter there are a number of levels at which different responsibilities for safeguarding can be seen to operate. These are set out in Figure 5.2.

Individual level

As nurses we are all responsible and accountable for our practice, and for ensuring that we are fit for practice. Our *Code* (NMC, 2008a, pp3–7) identifies a number of areas that are related to our safeguarding responsibilities, such as the following.

- You must disclose information if you believe someone may be at risk of harm, in line with the law of the country in which you are practising.
- You must respect and support people's rights to accept or decline treatment and care.
- You must be able to demonstrate that you have acted in someone's best interests if you have provided care in an emergency.
- You must act immediately to put matters right if someone in your care has suffered harm for any reason.
- You must act without delay if you believe that you, a colleague or anyone else may be putting someone at risk.
- You must inform someone in authority if you experience problems that prevent you working within this code or other nationally agreed standards.
- You must report your concerns in writing if problems in the environment of care are putting people at risk.

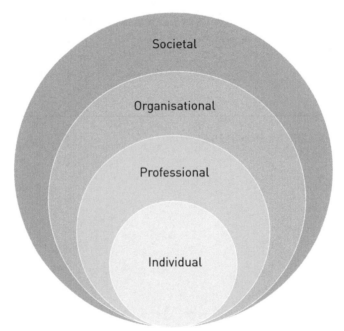

Figure 5.2 Levels of responsibility for safeguarding

However, despite these clear links between our *Code* and our safeguarding responsibilities, it has been suggested that nurses remain unclear as to their responsibilities in relation to safeguarding (Draper et al., 2009; Straughair, 2011). The Department of Health (2011a) has therefore developed guidance that focuses on the role of health service practitioners. Within this document it identifies themes that have recurred in recent 'high-profile' inquiries into failures of care (see Chapter 2).

If such situations are to be prevented we all, as individual practitioners, have responsibilities. For example, we need to accept that we all have a responsibility for safeguarding adults who are in our care or whom we support. Our employers, other agencies and other professionals do have a role, but this does not excuse us from accepting responsibility for our own contribution. If we are to work in empowering ways we need to enable patients and clients to exercise as much control over their lives as possible, recognising that, at times, their health status may limit the extent to which this is possible and that, at times, there may be legal restrictions (see Chapter 6). At a practical level this might include making sure that they have access to accurate and timely information made available in a format, and at a pace, that enables them to understand. Using simple, clear language, providing audio and not just written formats, using Braille, translation into other languages, and using pictures rather than words, may all be required to meet individual information needs. Empowerment might also involve working with patients and clients to develop their confidence in managing their health, to enhance their assertiveness skills or to recognise threats to their health and well-being.

It is important to note that the themes identified by the Department of Health (2011a) include recognition that patients' voices are not always heard. This highlights how an empowering approach to safeguarding requires that we, as individual practitioners, also need to examine (and if necessary change) our behaviour. For example, are there examples of situations where we have taken away someone's power by not really listening to him or her? It may be that the person has been trying to take control over a situation by telling us something he or she feels is important but, while we have heard what the person says, we have not really listened. The person's power has been reduced because we have not really understood what he or she has been trying to tell us and therefore have not acted on it. We also need to remember that people can 'tell' us things in other ways; it is not just what they say. Body language, mood and facial expressions can all be powerful ways of communicating, but we need to be alert to these and seek to understand their significance, thus increasing the control that patients have over what happens to them.

The Department of Health (2011a) suggests that neglect and abuse are not always recognised by healthcare staff. However, if we accept that we all have a responsibility for safeguarding adults, it follows that we need to understand exactly what constitutes abuse and neglect. Also, if inquiries into failures of care highlight a lack of transparency in relation to investigations, it also follows that as individuals we have a duty to ensure that we are aware of our responsibilities for identifying and reporting suspected abuse and neglect in line with agreed procedures. Furthermore, it is important that we make ourselves aware *before* we encounter such incidents as this will increase both our confidence and competence in what can be a difficult situation.

It is also important to recognise that we have a duty in preventing abuse and neglect; we have a proactive as well as a reactive role. The Department of Health (2011a) suggests that there are two main areas we need to consider here. First, we need to work with the patients and clients we are supporting to help them recognise and reduce risks to their health and well-being. This might include working with patients and their families to understand how they perceive risk. It also requires that both the benefits and the possible disadvantages of taking risks are considered (DH, 2011a). The second area we need to focus on is preventing neglect, harm and abuse within healthcare settings (DH, 2011a). This requires that, at all times, we treat individuals with dignity and respect and that we are prepared to challenge and report poor practice if we observe it or its effects.

Professional level

The nursing profession within the UK is regulated by the Nursing and Midwifery Council (NMC). The key aim of this organisation is *to safeguard the health and well-being of the public* (NMC, 2010a). This is achieved via a range of activities, including setting and monitoring standards of professional education, maintaining the professional register, setting professional standards for practice and providing guidance, and investigating and hearing cases of professional misconduct. Each of these areas has significance in relation to safeguarding.

In setting the standards for professional education, the NMC (2010c) has outlined explicit standards relating to safeguarding and others that have relevance to safeguarding, as can be seen at the beginning of each of the chapters in this book. All universities providing nursing education thus have to ensure that the curriculum they deliver includes appropriate theoretical and practical experience to ensure that students are able to meet the required standards in these and other areas.

All registered nurses are required to renew their registration every three years and, in doing so, they are required not only to pay a registration fee but also to declare that they have undergone required periods of professional updating. This register can be checked online, meaning that employers and even members of the public are able to check the registration status of individual practitioners.

The *Code* (NMC, 2008a) sets out the key standards against which nursing practice is assessed and identifies the responsibilities of all nurses. Some of these relate specifically to safeguarding, while others relate to other areas of nursing practice. Some identify how a nurse's personal practice must be safe, competent and delivered in a professional manner so as to protect the health and well-being of patients and clients. However, it is also stressed that, where the environment of care means that nurses cannot practise in this manner, they must inform relevant persons in authority and put their concerns in writing. Also, if they or another person places a person at risk, they should then act without delay. Although a professional requirement, raising such concerns can be very difficult and the NMC has subsequently issued further guidance on *Raising and Escalating Concerns* (NMC, 2010b). Within this document it is stressed that practitioners raising a genuine concern will be viewed as upholding professional responsibilities. A failure to report concerns is 'unacceptable': such a failure to act could bring into question the nurse's continued fitness to practise and place his or her registration at risk.

Where professional misconduct is suspected, nurses are reported to the NMC, which has a duty to investigate and to hold a hearing. Outcomes of such hearings can include the nurse being removed or suspended from the register.

Organisational level

Although safeguarding has now become a more widely integrated part of NHS provision, it has been suggested that as an organisation the NHS has demonstrated a lack of ownership of safeguarding (DH et al., 2009). Some of the healthcare organisations responding to the consultation concerning a review of *No Secrets* indicated that there was a widely held perception that care provided by health professionals is 'safe', although the report also cites examples indicating that this is not always the case (DH et al., 2009). The Department of Health (2011a) subsequently notes that individual practitioners cannot effectively manage concerns relating to safeguarding adults without the support of their service. It is important that healthcare organisations develop and maintain systems, structures and a culture in which safeguarding is recognised as a central concern. Some of these features will be explored in more detail in Chapters 8 and 9. In this chapter we do, however, need to look at some of these issues.

Healthcare organisations are often large and complex, employing many staff. While we are concerned here primarily with nurses, it is important to remember that *all* staff have responsibilities in relation to safeguarding. It is therefore important that organisations do all they can to make sure that the staff they recruit have the personal and professional characteristics required. This involves ensuring that references are taken up and that checks are made to confirm that references are genuine. Pre-employment checks in relation to criminal records need to be undertaken. Where professional registration is a requirement of a post, checks need to be made to ensure that such registration is current and has not lapsed. Interview procedures need to be carefully structured so as to make certain that key requirements of the post are tested while observing the demands of relevant legislation (for example, relating to equalities).

Clearly, duties relating to employees do not end once someone is in post, and organisations need to ensure that appropriate training is provided relating to safeguarding responsibilities and that such training is provided on a regular basis. This training needs to include issues such as the nature of abuse and neglect, the principles of safeguarding, and individual responsibilities in relation to responding to and reporting abuse. Clear policies and standards need to be in place and monitoring of such standards needs to occur. Where poor practice does occur, mechanisms need to be in place to ensure that it does not recur (Morgan, 2010).

Should harm, neglect or abuse take place, it is essential that lessons are learnt so that potential areas for change can be identified, thus reducing future risks. Clinical supervision can be one way of facilitating reflection on such incidents (Morgan, 2010) and this can be a helpful basis for both individual and organisational learning. Organisations therefore need to ensure that clinical supervision is an integral part of their staff support systems.

As noted above, organisations need to have policies in place that clearly set out the steps to be taken should harm, abuse or neglect be suspected. Each area will have its own such policy and it is essential that you take time to acquaint yourself with this policy and to seek clarification if any aspects are unclear. However, in setting out the broad responsibilities of organisations, the Department of Health (2011a) advocates a 'stepped' approach. Such an approach and its practice implications are set out in Figure 5.3.

Identify
- Actual and potential risks – these may be to self, to others, within the environment, preventable or possibly to reduce their impact
- Patients and clients who may be vulnerable
- Strategies that may be used to reduce or prevent risk

Make decisions
- Refer to the principles of safeguarding
- Refer to local/organisational policies
- Refer to relevant legislation
- Decide when to refer on

Multi-agency responses
- Refer to multi-agency policies and procedures
- Be clear as to who is responsible for which actions
- What outcomes are sought by the patient and other key people?
- Assessment and investigation
- Protection plan?

Outcomes and learning
- Were the patient's outcomes met?
- How effectively was the incident managed?
- Are there any wider themes/trends that need to be addessed?
- Is there a need for a case review?
- How should future practice be changed?

Figure 5.3 A stepped approach to safeguarding (adapted from DH, 2011a)

It can be seen in Figure 5.3 that individual, professional and organisational responsibilities all come together in a stepped approach to safeguarding. To apply this to practice, take some time to read through the case study of Emily Saunders and then complete Activity 5.7.

Case study: Emily Saunders

Emily is 25 years old and lives with two other people of a similar age. She likes loud music, enjoys going to the cinema and loves ice cream. She has an infectious laugh and often finds things funny. Emily has severe learning and physical disabilities; she cannot communicate verbally and needs to use a wheelchair if she goes out. She also has epilepsy. As she and her housemates need assistance with most aspects of daily living, there are usually two staff supporting them at all times.

continued . . .

*Yesterday Emily came into the hospital's A&E department supported by a member of staff. Her support staff had noticed that she had been very withdrawn and irritable, that she seemed to be experiencing some abdominal pain, and that she had some blood in her stools. When she arrived at A&E the staff member who came with her said that she would need to return to the house as she had left the other member of staff alone. She gave the nurse Emily's **hospital passport** and said that this document would provide the staff with the information they needed to look after Emily. She apologised, however, that Emily's medication had recently been changed and that the passport had not been updated to reflect this. She wrote the name of the new medication on a piece of paper and said that it was important to give Emily her tablets in the right order – the big tablet first and then the small tablet. Having been assessed in A&E, it was decided that Emily should be admitted for observation and investigations. When she was transferred to the ward the staff were informed of Emily's hospital passport and the admitting nurse read it before slipping it into the case file. It was her intention to use the information in the passport to develop Emily's care plan, but as she was going off duty a colleague said that she would do the care plan. Unfortunately, the first nurse forgot to tell her colleague about the hospital passport and so this information was not used to develop a plan that reflected her needs. At teatime a meal was put in front of Emily, but the staff did not initially realise that she needed assistance with eating. When they finally went to assist her the food was cold; also, it was cottage pie and carrots: Emily hates carrots and pushed the staff and the food away. Information about her support needs and likes and dislikes was in her hospital passport. She was not offered any drink and the nurse who assisted her thought it wouldn't be a problem as someone else would help her to have a drink later. This didn't happen. When she was given her medication she refused to take it as the tablets were given together in a medication cup.*

During the evening Emily became very distressed and the staff tried without success to calm her. In fact, Emily needed to go to the toilet and her shouting had been her usual way of telling other people about her need. When she was incontinent she became even more distressed, particularly when the nurse told her she should have asked to go to the toilet. Also, she was in pain and she was trying to tell the staff this by rocking and screaming. Again, this information was in the hospital passport. Overnight Emily became increasingly more distressed; the nursing staff believed that this was due to her learning disability. In the morning the nurse in charge telephoned the house staff to say that Emily was being discharged as they had been unable to find a cause for her current problems. The support staff have arrived on the ward to find Emily in an extremely agitated and distressed state and they are still concerned that she is unwell.

Activity 5.7   *Communication and decision making*

Read through Emily Saunders' case study.

- Were Emily's health and well-being safeguarded?
- How did breakdowns in communication contribute to a breakdown in care?
- To what extent did poor communication lead to poor decision making?
- Go through the various stages in this case study and suggest ways in which communication could have been improved and more effective care could have been provided.

Some discussion is included at the end of the chapter to assist you.

Societal level

Harm, abuse and neglect occur within the context of society and, while individuals, professionals and organisations such as the health service have responsibilities in relation to safeguarding adults, communities and wider society also have a key role to play. For example, the Department of Health (2011b) suggests a focus on community empowerment and localism. This involves communities making decisions as to what their priorities are, including how adults at risk of harm may best be protected. The Northern Ireland Office and the Department of Health, Social Services and Public Safety (DHSSPS, 2010) also see an important role for local communities, noting that all citizens have a responsibility to safeguard vulnerable adults through being aware of danger signs, and also acting on their concerns should they suspect abuse or neglect. They view a range of community-based agencies such as housing, public transport and adult education as having a key role to play, as well as members of the public supporting individuals and families through acts of good neighbourliness and citizenship.

For the wider public to be aware of their potential role in relation to safeguarding requires, however, that they are provided with information concerning both the nature of abuse and neglect, and the potential role they can play. The health service and healthcare practitioners, including nurses, have a key role to play in raising general awareness about neglect and abuse along with providing information about how to raise concerns.

Chapter summary

This chapter has examined the protection of vulnerable adults and the reasons for moving towards a safeguarding approach. The broader nature of safeguarding has been explored, stressing that it encompasses both a proactive and reactive approach to harm, abuse and neglect. The principles that underpin safeguarding have been examined and some implications of a safeguarding approach for the development of practice considered. A 'stepped' approach is advocated with action required at individual, professional, organisational and societal levels. Responsibilities at each of these levels and the interaction between the levels have been explored.

Activities: Brief outline answers

Activity 5.1 Reflection, page 87

Your answer to this activity will inevitably depend on the particular area you decided to focus on and your particular needs. However, following are some of the things you might have identified.

- **Policies** – You might want to know that there are agreed policies in place for things such as seeking consent, dealing with confidential information, reporting any adverse incidents, checking the professional status of staff, and record keeping.
- **Practices** – You might want assurance that staff are competent to carry out the interventions required; you might want to know that the care you receive is considered 'best practice'; and you might expect your care to be carried out in a way that protects your dignity, is respectful and recognises your individuality.

- **The environment of care** – You might want to ensure that any equipment used is safe, that you can be afforded privacy, that you are not subjected to undue noise, that there is good communication, that your nutritional and hydration needs will be met, that infection risks are minimised and that you are not at risk of harm.

Activity 5.2 Critical thinking, page 88

In Chapter 2 we examined some different ways of understanding 'vulnerability' and it was seen that, while some may view vulnerability as an inevitable part of belonging to certain groups, others view it as something that can be prevented or minimised. In this context, however, the phrase 'protection of vulnerable adults' has been criticised for portraying a passive view of those to whom the label is applied. Being in need of protection can be viewed as a weakness and it can be stigmatising. While we may use this terminology to refer to people we support, we might perhaps feel uncomfortable at the thought of the label being applied to us. It is important to recognise this and to increase our understanding of why some people we support find it difficult to accept some of the labels that are applied to them by services.

Activity 5.3 Critical thinking, page 89

Concerns are often expressed about drawing too many parallels between addressing abuse, harm and neglect that occurs to adults and that which occurs to children. Legally, there are differences (see Chapter 6) but also it is generally felt important to recognise that adults (generally) have greater autonomy and that they are often better able to protect themselves from harm. Nonetheless, the term 'safeguarding' describes an approach that is broader than just responding to abuse, neglect and harm when it occurs: a proactive approach is also included with an emphasis on prevention. Safeguarding has therefore gained wider acceptance in relation to supporting adults at risk of harm, since it is felt to be less stigmatising and it includes prevention.

Activity 5.4 Critical thinking, page 90

It is important to undertake an assessment of Josh's current mental health state and his risk of self-harm. Before his discharge from hospital it will also be important to work with Josh to ensure that a plan is in place to provide support. This may include the support of community nurses, psychologists or regular contact with therapeutic services such as counselling. It will also be important to work with him to identify any triggers for his recent illness and any signs that, with hindsight, were an indication that things were wrong. This information can then be used to try to avoid triggers or manage them more effectively, and the signs can be documented in a relapse plan that Josh (and others who support him) can use to recognise if his health is deteriorating again. It will be important to ensure that he has people to support him and that he and his supporters know who to contact if problems arise.

Activity 5.5 Reflection, page 91

Obviously we do not want harm, abuse or neglect to occur, but unfortunately sometimes such incidents do happen. What is important is that we learn from these incidents and use that learning to avoid future problems. When you thought of the incident in this activity, were you aware of a procedure that was followed and any forms that had to be completed? What happened to any forms? Were they looked at to identify learning points and was this information fed back to the clinical area? For example, if an elderly patient with dementia has had a fall as a result of wandering from the ward, can we learn anything about how best to observe patients with dementia? If a disabled patient fails to receive adequate hydration as a consequence of not being able to reach a glass of water, can we learn anything about the positioning of the glass and other equipment and the importance of checking with the patient how he or she would like things placed to best meet his or her needs? If a patient with mental health problems is abused by another patient, what can we learn about better risk assessment and staff support?

Activity 5.6 Leadership and management, page 94

Again, your answer will depend on which principle you decided to focus on. However, if we take empowerment as an example, you might promote this in a clinical setting in a variety of ways, including:

- making sure that information is available for patients and families in formats that are accessible to them;
- taking time to explain things to patients and families;
- not assuming that you know best and instead working in partnership with patients and their families to plan and deliver care;
- supporting patients to remain self-caring wherever possible to avoid loss of skills;
- making sure that patients who need them have access to their glasses, hearing aids and wheelchairs;
- ensuring that new staff are inducted into this approach to care;
- challenging staff if they do not work in an empowering way;
- making sure that patients and families know how to raise concerns about care and that they feel able to do so without fear of it adversely affecting their care.

Activity 5.7 Communication and decision making, page 101

This case study highlights how one breakdown in communication can be compounded by subsequent errors that have a cumulative effect on patient care. Individual mistakes can easily occur and in isolation may not have a major impact. However, when taken together they can have severe effects.

The house staff had been proactive in developing a hospital passport for Emily and this should have assisted the hospital staff, but it had not been updated to reflect recent changes. The staff member was unable to remain with Emily and thus the only source of information the hospital had was the passport. But this was never used and most staff were unaware of its existence. As a result, Emily did not receive care that met her needs and her behaviour deteriorated. This was seen as a consequence of her learning disability, rather than as the result of a failure to understand her ways of communicating her needs and a failure to address her pain. Her needs were neglected and she was sent home without any resolution regarding her health problems.

You might wish to rewrite this case study showing how good communication could lead to a positive outcome for Emily.

Further reading

British Medical Association (BMA) (2011) *Safeguarding Vulnerable Adults: A toolkit for general practitioners.* Available online at www.bma.org.uk/ethics/doctor_relationships/safeguardvulnerableadults.jsp.

This document explores definitions, practice implications and legal issues.

Department of Health (DH) (2011) *Safeguarding Adults: The role of health service practitioners.* Available online at www.dh.gov.uk/publications.

This document expands on many of the points discussed in this chapter.

Pritchard, J (2008) *Good Practice in Safeguarding Adults: Working effectively in adult protection.* London: Jessica Kingsley.

This book is a good overview of adult safeguarding.

Reece, A (2010) Leading the change from adult protection to safeguarding adults: more than just semantics. *Journal of Adult Protection,* 12(3): 30–4.

This paper explores the change in terminology discussed in this chapter.

Useful websites

www.cqc.org.uk

On the Care Quality Commission website you can review the outcomes of the various inspections undertaken. One standard relates specifically to safeguarding.

www.nmc-uk.org

The NMC website provides information regarding professional standards and regulation.

Thinking Health Promotion

Evans, D., Coutsaftiki, D., and Fathers, C. Patricia

NMC Standards for Pre-registration Nursing Education

This chapter will address the following competencies:

Domain 1: Professional values

2. All nurses must practise in a holistic, non-judgemental, caring and sensitive manner that avoids assumptions, supports social inclusion, recognises and respects individual choice and acknowledges diversity. Where necessary, they must challenge inequality, discrimination and exclusion from access to care.

3. All nurses must support and promote the health, wellbeing, rights and dignity of people, groups, communities and populations. These include people whose lives are affected by ill health, disability, ageing, death and dying. Nurses must understand how these activities influence public health.

7. All nurses must appreciate the value of evidence in practice, be able to understand and appraise research, apply relevant theory and research findings to their work, and identify areas for further investigation.

Domain 3: Nursing practice and decision-making

5. All nurses must understand public health principles, priorities and practice in order to recognise and respond to the major causes and social determinants of health, illness and health inequalities. They must use a range of information and data to assess the needs of people, groups, communities and populations and work to improve health, wellbeing and experiences of healthcare; secure equal access to health screening, health promotion and healthcare; and promote social inclusion.

NMC Essential Skills Clusters

This chapter will address the following ESC:

Cluster: Organisational aspects of care

9. People can trust the newly registered graduate nurse to treat them as partners and work with them to make a holistic and systematic assessment of their needs; to develop a personalised plan that is based on mutual understanding and respect for their individual

continued ... •••

situation promoting health and well-being, minimising risk of harm and promoting their safety at all times.

By the second progression point:

3. Understands the concept of public health and the benefits of healthy lifestyles and the potential risks involved with various lifestyles or behaviours, for example substance misuse, smoking, obesity.

4. Recognises indicators of unhealthy lifestyles.

By the third progression point:

18. Discusses sensitive issues in relation to public health and provides appropriate advice and guidance to individuals, communities and populations, for example contraception, substance misuse, smoking, obesity.

Chapter aims

By the end of this chapter you will be able to:

*   define health and health promotion;
*   discuss the contribution of the World Health Organization (WHO) to the development and practice of health promotion;
*   appreciate the contribution of health promotion strategies to the promotion of good health and well-being;
*   understand and integrate theories and models of health promotion into nursing practice.

Introduction

This chapter will encourage you to think about health promotion in relation to your nursing practice. Thinking like a health-promoting nurse will enable you to integrate the principles and practice of health promotion into your nursing care. How do you think like a health promoter? To do so, you need to view patients beyond their presenting diagnosis or condition and be mindful that you can contribute and support patients to improve their health by adopting an **empowering** approach while delivering care related to recovery from illness.

The chapter explores the concept of health and how this informs your health promotion practice. It enables you to develop your knowledge and understanding of the health promotion concept and its contribution to improving the health and quality of life of the individual and the population at large. The chapter explores the origin of health promotion and discusses international and national health strategies and their contribution to the development of your health promotion practice. Theories and models of health are examined in order to enable you to structure your health promotion practice.

What does it mean to be healthy?

Case study: What does it mean to be healthy?

Abdul, a 52-year-old school teacher, underwent pancreatectomy and chemotherapy following a diagnosis of an advanced pancreatic cancer. As a result of removing his pancreas he is on insulin injections. He says:

'I have accepted my diagnosis and now I want to live a normal life. I am confident and competent in self-injecting the prescribed insulin. Shahita, my partner, is my rock. We are able to set realistic and achievable daily goals. Since my illness we have adopted a healthy lifestyle. Our diet, including the diet of Leon (our dog), is much healthier and also we are more physically active. I take Leon for a walk in the nearby park daily. I enjoy the fresh air and meeting the regular dog walkers.

I am back to full-time work. I enjoy teaching and I get a lot of personal satisfaction knowing that I contribute to my pupils' learning and development. I value the daily structure and social interaction offered by my work. I receive encouragement and support from my colleagues. We are able to have a laugh. However, I am aware that some colleagues feel that I am too ill to be working. They all know that my expected survival time is 18 months.

I have accepted that I do not have long to live; however, 18 months is still a long time. I still have inspirations and dreams. I want the remainder of my life to be lived in full. Shahita and I decided to get married and to have a huge wedding in three months' time. I feel that I am doing the things I always wanted to do but somehow I never got around to doing. I have made a will: I want to put my financial and private affairs into order before the inevitable happens.

Shahita and I talk a lot about death. I am not afraid of dying but I am afraid of how I will die. Will I be in pain? I am very lucky to live next door to Helen, a retired midwife and health visitor. I have known her all my life. She actually delivered me! I have frequent conversations with Helen, updating her with my medical progress, and I am able to seek her advice. She is able to explain things to me. I find her a great emotional support. I have very open and confidential conversations with Helen. I can shed a tear in front of Helen without feeling embarrassed or less of a man.

In the evenings I feel quite tired. I tend to spend most evenings reading the Qur'an or watching television. Some evenings my siblings will come to visit. I enjoy reminiscing with them about the past and the good old days. Overall I have good and bad days like everybody else.'

The case study illustrates that different people have different views of what it means to be healthy. For example, some of Abdul's working colleagues view health as being free from disease. Abdul, on the other hand, is in remission and views health as personal fulfilment.

Exploring the concept of health

You need to develop a comprehensive understanding of the health concept because it informs and shapes your health promotion practice. One important point to bear in mind is that an individual's health status is not static. It is constantly changing throughout the day and is evolving throughout a lifetime. Have you noticed how you feel different at different times of the day – for example, in the morning you may have felt very energetic and by midday you may feel exhausted – or how your mood fluctuates during the day?

Health encompasses the following different dimensions.

- **Physical**: this is quite obvious as it relates to the functions of your body, e.g. 'I am not well because I have a headache.'
- **Emotional**: this can relate to how you cope with feelings, such as anxiety and depression, or your ability to recognise your own emotions, such as fear and joy.
- **Intellectual**: this means that you have the ability to think clearly and coherently.
- **Sexual**: this means that you have the ability and freedom to establish intimate, loving relationships as well as the choice and ability to procreate.
- **Social**: this means that you have the ability to make and maintain relationships with other people, e.g. having friends.
- **Spiritual**: this means that you are able to achieve peace of mind or are able to be at peace with your own self. As a nurse you must recognise that this is not only associated with religion. People who do not have a religion can achieve spiritual health by adopting principles of behaviour that lead to spirituality.

Activity 1.1 is designed to enable you to develop a clear understanding of the above health dimensions.

Activity 1.1	*Critical thinking*

Review Abdul's case study above and discuss either with your peers or with a member of your family the following questions regarding Abdul's health.

- Is he physically healthy?
- Is he emotionally healthy?
- Is he intellectually healthy?
- Is he sexually healthy?
- Is he socially healthy?
- Is he spiritually healthy?

Were there any differences of opinion? Were all of you able to support your argument?

An outline answer is provided at the end of the chapter.

Activity 1.1 has demonstrated to you that health is a very difficult concept to define. When you discussed Abdul's health dimensions, what personal factors influenced your own assessment?

The meaning of health can be influenced by a multitude of factors, such as family and cultural background, religion, educational level, gender, ethnicity and **social class**. Outside influences include the effects of the media, social environment and government policies. In addition, the individual's personal life experience will influence his or her views of health.

These influences apply equally to **lay** people and health professionals. For example, if you reflect back from the start of your nursing course up to the present time, you may realise that your past and current views about health are different. This can be attributed to the influence of your professional socialisation in the clinical practice and the nursing knowledge you have gained. As a result your health views have been reshaped as you have been exposed to a new professional culture and have developed new expertise.

Lay perceptions of health

As a nurse you are working in **partnership** with patients and their families, aiming to establish an interactive therapeutic relationship that encourages patients and families to participate in their care and to take responsibility for their health. Therefore, you need to give 'voice' and 'choice' to patients (DH, 2006a). To facilitate this process you have to seek out their health views. Knowing their health views enables you to design and implement health promotion programmes relevant to patients and communities.

Lay people's perspectives of health have been researched extensively over the last 40 years. Some people may view health:

- *in terms of not being ill* – 'I am well today because I do not have a cold or a headache';
- *in the context of physical fitness* – taking regular exercise and being fit;
- *in terms of control and risk* – binge drinking is seen as a health risk while being able to drink 'normal' amounts of alcohol is seen as being in control and having the ability to manage health;
- *in terms of not having a health problem that interferes with daily life* – an elderly person may consider being healthy as being able to walk or cook or going out to visit friends;
- *in the context of social relationships* – having friends and family around for social support and interaction;
- *as psychosocial well-being* – emotional well-being is being happy and undertaking recreational activities such as going on holidays.

As you can see, lay people's concept of health is diverse, ranging from the functional and medical perspective to the psychosocial perspective. The different views are associated with social class issues, for example working-class people may see health from the functional perspective while the higher **socio-economic status** groups may see health from the psychosocial perspective. Age and gender are contributing factors; young men may view health from the physical activity perspective, while women may emphasise the social perspective of having friends and family around them. You need to address these influences when you plan your health promotion practice (Chapters 4 and 7), aiming to deliver a personalised health promotion practice that empowers patients to improve their health status.

How do health professionals view the concept of health? Are there any differences between lay and professional views?

Professional perceptions of health

Health professionals view the concept in relation to the following health models. Understanding the different models of health will enable you to understand how the different health professionals with whom you work interpret health and working in partnership (see Chapter 7) to develop a health promotion practice with common goals and objectives to improve patients' health.

Medical model

Under the medical model of health your practice has a disease orientation instead of a positive health orientation. You view patients only in terms of their presenting illnesses, therefore you focus on the physical dimension of health without taking into consideration the other dimensions previously discussed in this chapter. This means that you view each patient as a body (which includes brain function) in terms of possible defective parts and your aim is to repair the parts. It means that you medically manage the diagnosis of patients. Your health promotion will focus on teaching, coaching and information giving regarding treatment and understanding the pathophysiology of the medical condition or disease concerned. You will be involved, for example, in teaching and demonstrating to patients such things as how to use their inhalers to improve their breathing without considering other factors that may influence recovery, such as personal circumstances and health inequalities.

The medical model of health can be criticised for having an authoritarian approach to patient care. The patient is seen as a passive participant. All decisions are made by the professionals 'who know best'. It encourages patients' dependency on doctors and nurses. However, you need to recognise the valuable and significant contribution of biomedical factors to health improvement in the arena of public health.

In summary, from the health promotion and public health perspective (Chapter 6) the main focus in the medical model is on treatment and cure. It provides the basis for encouraging patients' **concordance** with current treatment and also enables you to use this as a building-block when you are considering self-management strategies (Chapter 5).

Holistic model

A well-documented and widely used definition of health by many health professionals is that of the World Health Organization (WHO, 1948): *Health is a state of complete physical, mental and social wellbeing and not merely the absence of disease.* The combination of physical, social and mental well-being is known as the 'health triangle'.

The model expands on the medical model of health by embracing the concept of well-being. However, the definition implies a utopian view of achievement of health. It is therefore, arguably, idealistic in that it is impossible to attain a 'complete state' of health. One may also argue that it excludes people such as Abdul (who has a terminal illness), or people with chronic diseases (e.g. schizophrenia, Parkinson's) or a disability (e.g. visual impairment or learning disabilities), or people who, due to circumstances beyond their control, such as poverty, are unable to achieve optimum health.

In health promotion terms the **holistic** approach emphasises the need to integrate health education and prevention activities that constitute evidence-based practice. Your practice has to be informed not only by the medical aspects of health but also by local and national health strategies. The model encourages a reorientation of NHS provision from the acute health **sector** to primary care (community health sector).

Wellness model

The WHO, moving with social trends and political ideologies, furthered the concept of health by developing a wellness model, which is built on the principles of the holistic model.

The Ottawa Charter for health promotion considered health to be not just a 'state', but a *resource for everyday life, not the objective of living. It is a positive concept emphasising social and personal resources, as well as physical capabilities* (WHO, 1986). This definition is relevant to current health promotion practice, which strives to improve quality of life of all people regardless of their health status. It includes healthy people, people with disabilities, people with mental health issues, people with learning disabilities and people with long-term conditions. It highlights the need for the individual to be resilient by adapting to life changes such as illnesses and changes in socio-economic circumstances.

The model encourages health professionals to promote **anti-discriminatory** practice. For example, you as a health promoter, through the application of an empowering approach to your practice (Chapter 5), will support people with physical impairment, such as wheelchair users, to secure employment and lead independent lives. You will act as an enabler to facilitate them to adapt positively to life's changes and to strive for personal growth and fulfilment by developing problem-solving skills and increasing their **self-esteem**. The model encourages patients' active participation in the decision-making process by encouraging them to value their own expertise and experience.

Thinking about the complexities of health through the different perspectives of the three models discussed above could be confusing. We suggest that you consider the WHO (1948) definition of health in combination with its 1986 definition as a resource.

In this way nurses can act in partnership with other healthcare professionals, patients and their families, to devise an eclectic model of health incorporating the three components of body (physical), mind (mental) and community (social) aspects of health, as well as the ability of people to gain control of their own health (adapting and growing).

To assist you we will be looking in future chapters at:

- enabling patients to change their health behaviours (Chapter 2);
- empowering them to understand their illnesses (Chapter 4);
- supporting them to 'self-manage' their illnesses (Chapter 5).

However, before you develop your nursing practice to integrate health promotion principles, you need to have a deeper understanding of the health promotion concept.

Defining health promotion

Health promotion is about improving the health status of individuals and the population as a whole. Key to the term 'health promotion' is the word 'promotion'. This means placing the notion of the absence of disease and well-being at the forefront of your nursing practice. This shift in emphasis will help you think about improving, advancing, encouraging and supporting your patients to achieve optimum health. These activities are all part of a health-promoting perspective.

Today health promotion is an important focus of UK public policy in all sectors, with an emphasis on the social and environmental aspects as much as the physical and mental. Therefore, nurses have to view health promotion from both a holistic and a wellness model of health. It is helpful to understand the major socio-economic determinants of health. Very often these are outside the control of the individual, but they can have an enormous effect on the individual's health; for example, employment redundancy may lead to poverty and may affect the individual's physical health and mental health, such as increased smoking or depression.

The fundamental aim of health promotion is to empower an individual or a community to take control of aspects of their lives that have a detrimental effect on their health. The WHO (1986) defines health promotion as *a process of enabling people to increase control over, and to improve, their health*. This definition implies that you need to act as an enabler by strengthening knowledge, attitudes, skills and capabilities of your patients to overcome negative health. Additionally, governments are urged by the WHO to formulate health strategies to facilitate this enabling process.

Activity 1.2 aims to encourage you to explore the scope of health promotion by considering a selection of possible health-promoting activities.

Activity 1.2   *Critical thinking*

Which of the following activities do you consider to be health-promoting by enabling or empowering?

- A TV advertisement around the Christmas period that encourages the public 'not to drink and drive'.
- A radio message on your local radio encouraging young people to ring a helpline if they feel that they are victims of abuse.
- Practice nurses delivering a smoking cessation programme.

continued . . .

- Nurses teaching carers how to feed their loved one at home via a PEG (percutaneous endoscopic gastrostomy) feeding tube.
- Legislation on the compulsory use of car seat belts.
- The Alcohol Health Alliance, representing all major medical and nursing organisations, **lobbying** the government to increase the minimum price for alcoholic drinks.
- Local authorities organising park walks for young mothers.
- Health agencies such as Age UK giving information during winter on how to keep warm.
- Environmental health officers inspecting restaurants and cafés to monitor hygiene standards.
- Restaurants providing food information on their menus such as the fat content of their lamb moussaka.
- Practice nurses immunising older people against the flu virus.
- Nurses washing their hands.
- Student nurses receiving training on moving and handling.
- Supporting people with learning disabilities to use public transport.

An outline answer is provided at the end of the chapter.

A very broad range of activities can be considered to be part of health promotion. If the broader views of health are accepted (holistic and wellness), then health promotion matches that breadth. Acting on socio-environmental, as well as physical, influences on health enables us to accept that many people, professionals, organisations and government work to promote health in all sorts of ways, as you can see in Activity 1.2 and in the next section. This modern view of the potential for improving health began in the 1980s with an international shift in emphasis to give this broader range.

The origin of health promotion

Health promotion gained momentum in the global **health agenda** in the latter part of the twentieth century. This took place against a backdrop of discontent and frustration in international political and public opinion with the status quo of the medically dominated healthcare systems. Those systems were failing to combat ill health and to meet the health needs of the populations they were serving, despite a constant increase in financial investment.

Health promotion emerged as a process to shift healthcare provision away from a hospital setting centred on the medicalisation of health towards a community setting informed by the principles of public health (Chapter 6). This transition was facilitated as the holistic and wellness models of health started to gain momentum and the dominant medical model started to be eroded.

The WHO has been instrumental in the development of health promotion. Its commitment to using health promotion to improve global health is seen in a number of international charters and declarations. The most significant are the Ottawa Charter, the Adelaide Conference and the Bangkok Charter.

Concept summary: The Ottawa Charter

This charter (WHO, 1986) created the following principles for health promotion action, which are still relevant today.

Build healthy public policy

Health promotion goes beyond healthcare. **Policy** makers across all government sectors must consider health consequences and accept responsibility for health. This means that, when considering transport, housing or employment policies at local or national level, they should be asking about their health implications. In addition, policy decisions should be made to improve health from central government, such as the smoking ban and wearing car seatbelts.

The key issue in achieving a successful health promotion policy is joint action between the different sectors at a national level and interprofessional working at a local level. All of the diverse parties involved in policy making have to ensure that these policies enable all people to make healthier choices.

Create supportive environments

The environment we live in affects our health; for example, changing patterns of life, work and leisure and our natural environment have a significant impact on our health. Therefore, health promotion has to influence the generation of living and working conditions that are safe, stimulating, satisfying and enjoyable (Chapter 7).

Strengthen community action

Health promotion works through concrete and effective community action in setting priorities, making decisions, and planning and implementing them to achieve better health. At the heart of this process is community empowerment (Chapter 7).

Develop personal skills

Health promotion supports personal and social development through the provision of information, education or health-enhancing **life skills**. It has to enable people to learn, throughout life, to prepare themselves for all their health-related problems and to cope with long-term conditions and injuries (Chapters 4 and 5).

Reorient health services

The role of the health sector must move beyond its traditional responsibility for providing curative and clinical health. In the UK the NHS should focus more on the prevention of illness and the promotion of positive wellness.

Reorientation also involves changes being made to professional education in order to meet the health needs of the population. This can be seen in the current changes taking place in nurse education, which has moved to a graduate level – a change that aims to prepare nurses to be appropriately qualified and equipped to meet and serve the health needs of people in the twenty-first century.

The Ottawa Charter remains one of the most influential charters within the field of health promotion and public health. It is based on a **strategy** of enabling people to control health, advocating that health must be prioritised in all sectors and mediating between possible partners to improve health.

Following on from Ottawa, the Adelaide Conference (WHO, 1988) brought health promotion practice to new levels with health being viewed as a 'human right'. Health was no longer to be seen as a mere commodity. The conference introduced the concept of **equity**, highlighting that all people and patients have to be treated the same.

Later, the Bangkok Charter (WHO, 2005) urged all global governments to integrate effective health promotion interventions into their domestic and foreign policies. They are asked to implement interventions that have been proven to contribute to positive health and well-being into everything they do, whether it is town planning, road expansion or financial cutbacks. Policies, not only in times of peace but also in times of war and conflict, need to be 'healthy', so, for example, nurses who are currently working in the armed forces in the war zone of Afghanistan have to use a repertoire of evidence-based health interventions to promote a sense of well-being to the soldiers.

The WHO, in addition to international charters and declarations, has placed health promotion at the heart of its current global health agenda by its *Health for All Policy for the Twenty-first Century* (World Health Assembly, 1998), by continuing the previous vision of the *Health for All by the Year 2000* strategy (WHO, 1981).

Concept summary: WHO *Health for All Policy for the Twenty-first Century*

The *Health for All* (HFA) policy calls for social justice, which means that each person should be treated fairly and equitably. It lists ten global health targets set out in three domains, reflecting the most prevalent health problems in the world.

Improving health outcomes

- Health equity: this will be assessed by measuring a child's growth, i.e. height and weight levels for age (children under five years).
- Survival: to improve maternal mortality rates, child mortality rates (under five years) and life expectancy.
- Reverse global trends of five major pandemics (TB, malaria, HIV/AIDS, tobacco-related diseases and violence/trauma) by implementing disease control programmes.
- Eradicate and eliminate certain diseases (measles, leprosy and vitamin A and iodine deficiencies).

Determinants of health

- Improve access to water, sanitation, food and shelter.
- Measures to enhance healthy lifestyles and weaken damaging ones.

Health policies

- Develop, implement and monitor national HFA policies.
- Improve access to comprehensive, essential quality healthcare.
- Implement global and national health information and surveillance systems.
- Support research for health.

Each region of the WHO (Africa, Americas, Southeast Asia, Europe, Eastern Mediterranean and Western Pacific) and subsequently individual countries have modified and incorporated this strategy into their own plans to meet the health needs of the populations they serve. The WHO (1998a) developed a strategy for Europe known as Health 21.

The following case study outlines the different global health challenges.

Case study: Different global health challenges

Mrs Shah, a registered nurse, has returned to England after spending two years working as a volunteer nurse in one of Africa's underdeveloped countries. She gives a seminar to her work colleagues, aiming to share her working experience in Africa.

Her account supports the need for a global health strategy and highlights the importance of gaining the political commitment of international organisations, as well as national governments, to implement the WHO's strategy. In summary, Nurse Shah highlighted the following issues:

'Every day, people of all ages in sub-Saharan Africa die unnecessarily. The main cause is infectious diseases such as malaria, tuberculosis, HIV/AIDS and diarrhoea. One of the biggest challenges healthcare providers face is the delivery of adequate healthcare for people living with chronic lifestyle conditions. People in rural areas have to walk many miles to access care. Many die in transit.

Another frustrating thing for me was the fact that healthcare professionals work in isolation, particularly those working in rural settings, and could not keep abreast with the latest information on epidemics. This also precludes them from sharing their information with the global health community. Nurses in the region are increasingly faced with the burden of providing healthcare to rural populations, much more than the doctors. Enhancing health professionals', especially nurses', access to relevant accurate and up-to-date clinical information is vital to improving healthcare.'

Recognising aspects of the international view of health promotion will help you to understand the global background to what is happening in the UK, strategically and politically. As a member state of WHO (European Region) the UK is instrumental in helping to formulate the international strategies, and in turn to an extent follows those strategies.

UK national strategic policies for public health and health promotion

In the UK the concept of health promotion can be dated as far back as the nineteenth century, forming part of the public health movement for sanitary reforms to improve the ill health of people living in overcrowded industrial towns. Florence Nightingale embraced the principles of public health to inform nursing practice (Nightingale, 1859).

The first ever public health strategy published in the UK was *The Health of the Nation* (DH, 1992) by the then Conservative government. It has to be commended for responding to the call of 'health for all by the year 2000' by the World Health Organization (WHO, 1981). It provides an example of an effort being made at a policy level to improve health by encompassing both prevention and health promotion. However, it could be criticised for adopting a medical approach (that is, by aiming to prevent premature death due to ill health) to the detriment of addressing the broader economic and social factors that influence health.

This was superseded by the strategies of the new Labour government in *Saving Lives: Our healthier nation* (DH, 1999) and, later, *Choosing Health: Making healthier choices easier* (DH, 2004b). The former set targets to be achieved by 2010, continuing the theme set by its predecessor to tackle ill health. It also took into consideration health inequalities (Acheson, 1998) by addressing **social exclusion.** The strategy embraced a social model of health by promoting collaboration between health and local authorities. The latter strategy goes further by recognising the social, environmental, economic and cultural impacts on health. However, there was an absence of national policies (social and economic) to tackle the fundamental causes of inequality. The focus was on lifestyle issues aiming to change individual behaviour, thus introducing the notion of **victim blaming**. Scotland, Wales and Northern Ireland had their own similar strategies.

All these health strategies use health promotion to facilitate the achievement of **health improvement** and to encourage people to 'make healthy choices easier', political jargon originated by the WHO and used to achieve **health gain**. The policies aim to improve the health of the individual and the population by addressing the wider issues that affect health, such as health inequalities and environmental issues.

The current UK coalition government has produced its own strategy, *Healthy Lives, Healthy People: Our strategy for public health in England* (DH, 2010c). It focuses on behaviour-change strategies by encouraging individuals to engage in healthy behaviour and to take more control and responsibility for their own health, thereby moving away from the notion of the 'nanny state', whereby people expect the state to take care of their own health (Chapters 2 and 6). Scotland, Wales and Northern Ireland constructed their own strategies based on that of England.

As the various successive governments endeavour to improve people's health and to promote positive health, healthcare professionals have witnessed the establishment of the following.

- **NHS Direct**: launched in 1998 as a nurse-led telephone helpline and internet service providing information and advice on health to the public. The current coalition government is phasing out NHS Direct. In April 2013, the NHS 111 free-of-charge service was launched. It is intended to operate 365 days a year, aiming to improve access to the NHS when patients are in need of medical help or advice, but in circumstances where the need is not urgent enough to justify making a 999 call. It is staffed by fully trained advisers supported by nurses and paramedics. It is driven by the ideology to manage patients in a more cost-effective and integrated way. Its launch has already been controversial. Healthcare professionals and patients have criticised the system as being a 'cut price' replacement of NHS Direct nurses, with telephone advisers lacking professional training in healthcare, thereby leading to delays in treatment and putting patients' lives at risk.

- **NICE (National Institute for Health and Care Excellence)**: responsible for providing national guidance on promoting good health, and preventing and treating ill health.
- **Public health observatories**: established in 2000 in each NHS region. Their role is to ensure that health and social care systems are equipped with health intelligence to improve health and reduce inequalities, to promote research and to set up disease registers.
- **Health Protection Agency (HPA)**: set up in 2003 to protect the public from infectious diseases and environmental hazards. The HPA is one of a number of quangos (quasi-autonomous non-governmental organisations) that the current government is abolishing as from 1 April 2013. This protection function will be transferred to central NHS control.
- **Patient Advice and Liaison Services (PALS)**: designed to bring citizens more closely into decision-making processes.
- **Expert Patients Programme (EPP)**: to help people manage their own illnesses (see Chapter 5, pages 95–6).
- **NHS walk-in centres**: launched in 1999, aiming to provide the general public with more convenient access to NHS services matching modern living patterns, and managed by local community health organisations to deal with minor illnesses and injuries. They are predominantly nurse led. As from April 2013 such centres will be financed by the area's Clinical Commissioning Groups.
- **Polyclinics** (more recently called multi-centres): established on the recommendations of Lord Darzi (a parliamentary undersecretary in the House of Lords), they are a network of GPs in multi-purpose health centres, which provide some hospital services, such as X-rays, minor surgery and outpatients' treatment.

As well as these strategic innovations, we have seen a focus on addressing **inequalities in health**, which has been informed by WHO's work (see Chapter 6 for a fuller explanation).

We now go on to look at health promotion theories and models to guide your work. We previously looked at theories of health; however, theory is also important in 'thinking health promotion', as without it we may act randomly and without the evidence to support practice. Theoretical structures are based on ideas from philosophical or organisational constructs and, more recently, are deduced from practice itself. You will find health promotion theories used throughout this book; here we give an overview of the most important ones. A model, as compared to a theory, is a framework that derives from theory and attempts to represent reality, rather like a model of a building representing the building's parts and functions. Models provide a systematic, well-researched approach to health promotion practice.

Theories informing health promotion

As with nursing, there are a number of theories that underpin the practice of health promotion. These are informed by a multitude of academic disciplines such as **epidemiology** and **demography**, ethics and law, health psychology and politics.

Epidemiology and demography

These disciplines provide information about a population's health status. The information focuses on the severity, range, frequency and duration of diseases, the associated social disability and mortality .They also inform you about the relationship between ill-health and socio-demographic variables such as age, culture, economic status, educational attainment, employment status and ethnicity, including the geographical variable (north–south divide).They enable you to identify priorities, set targets (Chapters 4 and 7), plan and implement health promotion interventions suitable for a target group based on an assessment of its health needs, and finally to evaluate their efficacy. For example, if the locality where you are working has a large older population with a high incidence of falls at home, you need to deliver health promotion programmes that enable them to avoid falls at home. Another example is organising child immunisation programmes if the locality has many families with young children.

Within the field of mental health, epidemiology and demography will enable you to ascertain the complexities of mental health and to deliver appropriate services to improve the health and social function of individuals suffering with mental illness. This can be achieved by providing local services for early detection, care, treatment and rehabilitation. Engagement in community health education programmes, in order to tackle the social stigma, myths and misconceptions surrounding mental health, is setting the ground for resettling people with mental illness back into the community, thereby safeguarding their human rights and dignity.

Modern epidemiology is shifting from a population level (traditional epidemiology), which was informed by a public health model taking into consideration the cultural and historical perspective of diseases, to an individual level informed by a model of science (tissues, cells, and anatomy and physiology). This has implications for health promotion policy as the focus will be on targeting solely the **pathophysiology** of disease to the exclusion of addressing and tackling the social determinants and their impact on health. Prevention will focus on behaviour change with the inherent notion of victim blaming.

In summary, epidemiology and demography together provide you with a scientific basis to determine the distribution and determinants of health and disease of the population you serve, and to determine the scope for health promotion practice.

Ethics and law

Ethics and law are concerned with making a series of value judgements about what health means to the individual or to the community and about whether, when and how to intervene. A central ethical question for you is what is acceptable or unacceptable. Ethics and law enable you to consider principles such autonomy, respect for the individual, freedom to make decisions without coercion, voluntary participation, confidentiality, informed consent, social justice, equity and the mental capacity of patients. These principles inform you how to develop a non-discriminatory and **non-judgemental** practice. You need to ensure that the patient is changing behaviour on a voluntary basis and by exercising free will. For example, if a smoker decides to continue smoking, after receiving health education on the risks of smoking and the accessibility and availability of smoking cessation programmes, you have to accept that he or she is exercising free will and choice without being blamed for failure to conform, known as victim blaming.

Your practice can be informed by the principles of *beneficence* and *non-maleficence*. These mean that your health promotion interventions promote good and also prevent, remove and avoid harm to your patients. These principles place the common (majority) good before individual considerations. An example is fluoridisation of drinking water supplies to promote dental health. This is beneficial to the majority even though it may not further benefit a minority.

You will be engaging in a diversity of health promotion practices across the different fields of nursing (Adult, Mental Health, Child and Learning Disabilities). Each field imposes a variety of ethical dilemmas. You will need to address these by using a collaborative approach (involving patients, families, doctors and other health professionals) and critically appraising your health promotion interventions using available evidence to consider the following questions.

- Does this health promotion practice impinge on the freedom or autonomy of the patients, for example implementation of a 'non-smoking policy' in a long-stay mental health unit?
- Is this health promotion intervention a source of collective good or benefit for patients, for example the provision of immunisation services for young children, bearing in mind the well-publicised controversy over MMR (measles, mumps and rubella) immunisation and its current health implications, or the screening for Down's syndrome during pregnancy?
- Does this health promotion practice encourage victim blaming and stigmatisation, for example health education focusing on lifestyle?
- Are the benefits of this health promotion provision equally distributed among all the people living in the area, for example access to health services for screening by people with learning disabilities, available resources in different languages, and policy setting that acknowledges different rules of faith?
- Does this health promotion practice safeguard confidentiality, dignity and mental capacity, for example in the cases of contraception and teenagers, or contraception and people with learning disabilities?

In summary, ethics and law inform your health promotion practice by ensuring that people should be free to achieve well-being. They must have real opportunities to live and act in accordance to their values and capabilities, and their participation must be voluntary.

Health psychology

Health psychology is a subdivision of psychology that seeks to explain how people behave in relation to their health. In promoting health we are interested in how people change to healthy behaviours. There are many individual theories to explain this, briefly explained below.

Theories of reasoned action and planned behaviour

These theories (Ajzen and Fishbein, 1980) increase understanding of the factors that influence people's intention to behave in a certain way, which in turn enables you to develop interventions that meet individuals' needs, for example the use of **peer education**. These theories do not explain the impact that emotions and religious beliefs have on behaviour, for example religious beliefs may contribute to stigmatisation of certain diseases such as HIV/AIDS.

The health belief model

This model (Becker, 1974) demonstrates that behaviour change is dependent upon the individual's belief about his or her susceptibility to a disease, severity of the illness, and the cost and benefit analysis involved in any change of behaviour. Becker's health belief model enables you to understand and predict why individuals will or will not participate in different prevention activities such as health screening programmes. Therefore, the model is useful in planning preventative services. However, it has very limited value in planning health promotion interventions to tackle addictive behaviours such as drug addiction because there is a lack of information on how to modify complex health beliefs associated with long-term and socially determined behaviours.

The health locus of control theory

This theory (Rotter, 1966) explains the extent to which people feel that they have control over events and how their personalities are shaped as a result of these beliefs. The theory suggests that people who feel in control of their lives (**internal locus of control**) are more likely to change their behaviour than people who feel powerless (**external locus of control**). This theory contributes to our understanding of people's engagement in the process of behaviour change. However, it lacks reliability as it is very difficult to predict behaviour on the grounds of attitude alone without taking into account the interaction between people and their environment.

The social cognitive theory

This theory (Bandura, 1977) provides a framework for understanding, predicting and changing behaviour. Bandura explored the concept of **self-efficacy**, or the belief an individual has in her or his ability to change or overcome difficulties. He claimed that human behaviour change is governed by the following principles:

- **self-efficacy**: an individual's confidence to carry out a certain behaviour;
- **expectancy**: the belief that a certain action will result in the desired outcome;
- **incentives**: where behaviour is guided by the value the individual places on the perceived outcome.

This will vary with different situations; for example, a smoker may be confident that he or she can resist smoking when other people smoke at work, but may be less confident that he or she can do this when in the pub socialising with smoker friends. This theory provides a powerful link between the individual, the environment and behaviour. However, the challenge is around the development of self-efficacy skills.

Overall, health psychology theories provide you with a sound understanding of human behaviour based on attitudes, beliefs, values, power and control, which can be used to help people change from risky behaviour and to adopt healthy behaviour by making healthier choices. However, reliance solely on behaviour change is restrictive and has been criticised as 'victim blaming' for placing the onus of change solely on the individual.

All these theories from other disciplines inform health promotion theory construction, just as theories from psychology, sociology, ethics and medicine all inform nursing theory. The next section looks at two models developed for planning health promotion initiatives: the first is a strategic planning model for community health promotion and the second is a model for encouraging behaviour change in individuals and groups.

Health promotion models

There is a variety of models that are informed by different theoretical perspectives such as health psychology; most acknowledge the need to improve health through education, prevention of illness, and promotion of positive wellness. Some models emphasise one aspect or another, but most can be adapted to incorporate thinking about the broader aspects of health improvement and address the Ottawa Charter principles and inequalities in health (Marmot, 2010).

Tannahill's (1985) model gives an overview of the three main organisational aspects of health promotion (see Chapter 2 for further explanation). It presupposes that health education has existed for many years, in schools for children, and for adults mainly through health professionals and the media. It acknowledges the historical and current importance of preventive services in public health, such as immunisation and screening. In addition, following the WHO imperative to generate healthy policies, the model incorporates policy making as its third part. The whole can be seen as a very useful planning, implementing and evaluating device for health promotion practice – educating about smoking, screening for smoking-related diseases and setting no-smoking policies. You can use this model as a thinking tool to imagine the whole of what you can set up as you plan health promotion for one patient, for groups of patients or for communities.

Disease prevention traditionally can be categorised into three different levels. This is useful for thinking of the scope of preventive services and strategies.

*   **Primary prevention**: targets healthy people and aims to empower them to continue their healthy status, for example by the uptake of flu vaccination.
*   **Secondary prevention**: targets people who are at risk of developing ill health, aiming to persuade them to seek screening, i.e. cervical screening.
*   **Tertiary prevention**: targets unhealthy people, aiming to empower them through **self-management** of their illnesses, for example by complying with medication.

In summary, Tannahill's model provides a structured approach for organising, delivering and evaluating health promotion. Nurses can draw on practical experience to distil the model as health education, prevention and health policy form an integral part of nursing practice. It does not, however, inform you about what motivates individuals to change behaviour or how to sustain this change. It could be argued that it has a paternalistic approach to health promotion practice.

Prochaska and DiClemente's (1982) model is one that incorporates many aspects of health psychology (see Chapter 2 for further explanation). This model was developed to explain how individuals move towards adopting behaviour that will maintain good health. It uses stages of change as its core construct and integrates processes and principles of change derived from different theories, hence it is called 'transtheoretical'. The model presumes the individual will go through stages of changing health behaviour that are cyclical and shows that, having completed one change, the person may well go on to feel that she or he can make another. Its main focus is on the individual's readiness to change or attempt to change towards a healthy behaviour. The key concepts of this model are: pre-contemplation, contemplation, decision and determination, action and maintenance.

- At first the individual does not think of making a change – 'I'm OK as I am' – perhaps influenced by health belief and attribution theory.
- Then something may happen to make her or him consider a change – 'Maybe I should do something about it.' The influence here could be what others say (social cognitive theory).
- Having made a tentative decision, the individual then wonders how to make the change – 'I'll look into it.' The internal locus of control is becoming stronger.
- The individual engages in a new behaviour, trying it out.
- Sustaining the change over time takes inner strength. Social support and self-efficacy help with this stage.
- At any time in the cycle, the individual may revert to unhealthy behaviour, known as a 'relapse stage'. It is important to acknowledge the individual's effort and achievements so far and instil in her or him a sense of self-worth for accomplished achievement during the process of change.

Many practitioners within the field of health promotion have supported the Prochaska and DiClemente (1982) model as it allows the practitioner to tailor interventions according to individuals' specific needs. However, you need to be aware that implementation of these interventions may be time-consuming, expensive and complicated. Therefore, the model's use may not be suitable in a very busy acute clinical setting, where patients stay for a short period of time and require rapid treatment, unless the aim of the encounter is refocused on just moving the patient from one stage to another. It will be appropriate for use in clinical areas such as mental health or in a community setting where rapid behaviour change is not necessary.

In summary, this model is useful from a programme planning perspective, as it enables you to plan health promotion activities that will influence behaviour change according to patients' stage of change and motivation to change. Examples will be the use of written material, use of media, organisation of health and/or social support events, providing personal counselling and follow-up consultations, aiming to raise awareness of a behaviour's risk and benefits, and providing support to facilitate change. Health psychology and health promotion models may explain some aspects of behaviour, but do not expect them to solve the problem! You have to be discerning with regard to your choice of model by being eclectic and flexible in your mode of approach, by being able to move from a bottom-up to a top-down approach according to the situation and problem.

There are other models and theories of health promotion and public health to be found in the literature. We have chosen to focus on these two examples, but encourage you to read around the subject and to think about which model or theory is being used when you read about health promotion initiatives (see Further reading at the end of this chapter).

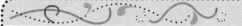

Chapter summary

This chapter has enabled you to develop an understanding of the health promotion concept, its origin and development in the UK up to the present day. It has explained how the perceived concept of health by patients and health professionals can influence health outcomes. The WHO views health promotion as instrumental in achieving global health and has identified nurses as key players who, working in partnership with others, can have a positive impact on health improvement. The WHO states that nurses can achieve this by acting as patients' advocates, mediators and enablers.

The promotion of positive health is the mutual responsibility of the individual, who has to take responsibility for his or her own health by adopting healthy behaviour, and of the state, which also has responsibility through the development and implementation of national and local health policies to address the wider determinants of health in order to improve the health status of the nation.

The chapter has examined different health promotion theories and models that enable you, as a nurse, to plan and implement health promotion within your nursing practice in order to empower patients to achieve optimum health.

Activities: brief outline answers

Activity 1.1: Critical thinking (page 8)

- **Physical**: No, Abdul is not physically healthy as he has cancer and diabetes. However, according to Abdul he is physically healthy as he feels well and he is in remission. He is able to walk and go to work.
- **Emotional**: Yes, he has the ability to recognise his emotions, i.e. fear of death.
- **Intellectual**: Yes, he is healthy as he has the capacity to think clearly and coherently. He can make decisions about his personal affairs and he can do his work.
- **Sexual**: Yes, he has an intimate and loving relationship with his partner.
- **Social**: Yes, he is healthy as he has a strong friendship circle.
- **Spiritual**: Yes, he reads the Qur'an and he has a religious faith, and considers himself spiritually healthy, a view shared by his family and colleagues.

Overall, then, although his health professionals and his work colleagues may say he is not, Abdul considers himself to be healthy.

Activity 1.2: Critical thinking (pages 12–13)

All of them are health promotion activities. Consider the range of people involved and types of activity – education, prevention measures and policies. All will educate for health, prevent disease or protect the public.

Further reading

Naidoo, J and Wills, J (2010) *Developing Practice for Public Health and Health Promotion* (3rd edn). Oxford: Elsevier.

This is a good overview of health promotion, which also explains a range of health promotion models.

Ogden, J (2007) *Health Psychology: A textbook* (4th edn). Milton Keynes: Open University Press.

This is a good review of health psychology theory and research.

Homeostasis in Person-Centered Practice

Boore, J., Cook, N., and Shepherd, A.

───────── **UNDERSTAND: KEY CONCEPTS** ─────────

Before working through this chapter, you might find it useful to do some reading around person-centred practice.

The weblinks for these reading suggestions can be easily accessed via the companion website https://edge.sagepub.com/essentialaandp.

PERSON-CENTERED
CARE MADE
SIMPLE

PRIORITISING
PERSON-CENTERED
CARE

───────── **LEARNING OUTCOMES** ─────────

When you have finished studying this chapter you will be able to:

1. Understand the key principles of person-centred practice
2. Understand what is meant by homeostasis
3. Explain briefly why understanding homeostasis is an essential aspect of person-centred practice
4. Identify the major functions of the body in contributing to the overall functioning of the human body

INTRODUCTION

The Person-Centred Practice (PCP) Framework (McCormack and McCance, 2016) is an integrated approach to people who need healthcare. It emphasises the importance of focusing on the unique characteristics of the individual in assessing need and planning and providing care. It is based on the primary concept of personhood which emphasises the importance of the individual with their own characteristics, values, beliefs and attitudes, their own life story and future plans. Person-centred practice necessitates knowledge and understanding of the individuality of the person.

Biological characteristics also vary between individuals and understanding how the human body functions is equally essential for providing high-quality care. However, the approach used within the PCP Framework tends to be seen as focusing primarily on individuals' unique psychological, social, spiritual and environmental characteristics. In providing person-centred care it is essential to integrate and coordinate all the different components of care for the person. The biological functioning of an individual influences psychological, social and spiritual responses and vice versa.

The core concept in relation to physiological aspects of the individual is homeostasis and all the biological systems of the body contribute to this. So what is meant by homeostasis? In brief, homeostasis is the property of maintaining equilibrium – a stable (or nearly stable) condition of the different properties in the body (for example, body temperature, blood glucose level) through the action of the different bodily systems.

APPENDIX 3

In this chapter we are going to explore these two major concepts in some detail as an introduction to the book as a whole. In addition, please note that as all biological works use the same terms to describe the position and orientation of different components of the body, these are presented in the Appendix section and can be used for reference.

Context

THE BODIE
FAMILY

Among our Bodie family, there are people of four generations with different health needs and varying abilities to maintain homeostasis. Danielle, the baby, is only two months old and at this age her homeostatic mechanisms are limited in ability. She requires appropriate interaction, nutrition and care to ensure that her body systems maintain homeostasis as she grows into a healthy child, mature adult and healthy older woman. The adults of working age have to balance meaningful work, family life, social activities and physical exercise in aiming to maintain homeostasis demonstrated through health and well-being. The great-grandparents' abilities to maintain homeostasis will be declining and good nutrition (not too much salt or sugar), physical exercise and mental activity are necessary to maintain optimum health and, at least as important, to reduce the risk of developing cognitive impairment. During illness or following accidents, the care provided aims to support physiological function and maintain homeostasis to promote recovery and healing. The PCP Framework (McCormack and McCance, 2016) provides guidance on all the different components of healthy living – psychological, social, environmental and physiological – and is applicable to all generations of this family.

UNDERSTANDING PERSON-CENTRED PRACTICE

McCormack and McCance (2016) describe the PCP Framework and Figure 1.1 shows the key elements within this model starting from the outside layer and working inwards.

Macro context

The macro context considers the strategic, political, social, educational and professional drivers that directly and indirectly impact on all other components of the PCP Framework. For example, health and social care policy is one of the identified macro components that will influence the culture and direction

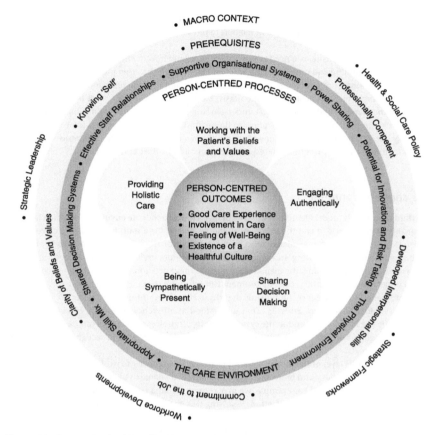

Figure 1.1 Person-Centred Practice Framework

McCormack and McCance (2016) *Person-centred Practice in Nursing and Health Care: Theory and Practice.*
Wiley Blackwell. © John Wiley & Sons 2016.

of person-centred care in practice as it sets the strategic direction for the provision of care and development of the profession – regionally, nationally and internationally. Policy is largely driven by influential and strategic leadership, and this leadership must first recognise the value of person-centredness in order to thread it through any frameworks that structure policy and healthcare drivers, particularly in the development of the existing and future workforce. This clearly would also include the strategic alliances between these social policies, the underpinning frameworks and higher education. Unless the macro context has a synergy with person-centredness, it can inhibit the realisation of person-centred practice.

Prerequisites

The prerequisites are those attributes of the nurse that are required before being able to provide high-quality person-centred care and are shown in the second circle of Figure 1.1. Four of the attributes identified are central for interaction, professional behaviour and role performance while the Professionally

Competent prerequisite has been defined as 'the knowledge and skills of the nurse to make decisions and prioritize care, and includes competence in relation to physical or technical aspects of care' (McCormack and McCance, 2006: 475).

To achieve this prerequisite, you need to learn and understand how the human body works and be able to apply this in planning and providing care, in combination with the other prerequisites identified. For example, professional competence requires nurses to understand that the signs and symptoms of illness represent an impairment in achieving homeostasis. More specifically, nurses must be able to pinpoint where that imbalance is and recognise that understanding how the body maintains homeostasis usually is the key to interventions to assist the return to homeostasis. How we achieve that knowledge, retain it and apply it to practice will be underpinned by our self-awareness, dedication to compassionate care, and our ability to work with others through respectful cognisance of values and beliefs.

The care environment

The third layer in this model identifies a number of factors within the care environment which influence the quality of care provided and the experiences and reactions of the staff, persons being cared for and visitors. Many of these factors are determined by the organisational structure and the model of the team working within the clinical setting. In a practice team which prides itself on a person-centred approach to care and effective team working, the members are likely to make decisions based on the research evidence and an understanding that the social environment can minimise stress.

To comprehend the evidence supporting the physical care environment requires an understanding of the biological sciences. Stress is often understood as a psychological state of being distressed (regulated by the nervous and endocrine systems) but its physiological changes can have a deleterious effect on an individual's physical health status. It is important to be able to recognise and minimise these effects.

In considering this layer of the model, we must recognise that in order to work effectively with others, we must develop therapeutic and professional relationships that enable us to draw on the strength of others to find effective solutions. For example, we may recognise that a person's immunity is compromised and that they are showing signs of infection. Resolving this challenge requires nurses to work effectively with doctors and pharmacists, at the very least, in order to utilise their expertise for the common good of the person in their care. However, they all must also respect that the person being cared for has choice in deciding whether to have the infection treated or not – their particular life circumstances may result in them deciding that treating the infection is detrimental to their health in other ways (e.g. risk to a foetus for a pregnant woman). In this way, a sharing of power is vital. Each member of the care team does not oppress the other, including the person being cared for. This leads neatly into the next level of the model, processes – in person-centred processes.

Person-centred processes

The processes in PCP are identified in the five 'petals' of the Framework (Figure 1.1). These all interact and are essential in the provision of care but, in the context of this book, providing holistic care includes the care required to support physiological function. However, psychological and spiritual aspects of care interact with physiologically based care in achieving effective care outcomes.

In the previous layer of the model we gave the example of someone with an infection. Person-centred care processes recognise the need to be authentic in the way we engage with people, showing compassion and understanding of their perspective on their health in a wider, holistic context, and working with their beliefs in a shared decision-making process. Taking the example on a different track, this could mean arranging for someone to receive the antibiotic therapy at home as they feel a need to be cared for in their own personal space. This could include recognising that their immune response to the antibiotics could be monitored effectively through blood samples taken by the community nurse, enabling the wider context of the person's health to be taken into consideration.

Person-centred outcomes

The person-centred outcomes are shown in the centre of the Framework (Figure 1.1) and incorporate all aspects of well-being. The physiological parameters that nurses measure may relate to the physical care but are equally applicable to the range of care processes and person-centred outcomes. For example, a raised heart and respiratory rate may indicate a person being in a state of anxiety or pain: understanding how the human body works will enable you to understand the implications of these measurements. In working with the example used earlier regarding caring for a person with an infection, if we have followed through the model, the person may feel their care experience was positive as they managed to have the care needed in their own home, they were involved in that decision, and this led to an overall feeling of personal well-being that was achieved, in part, by restoring a state of physiological and psychological homeostasis.

The importance of this model of care is its focus on the uniqueness of the individual. It emphasises the importance of integrating all aspects of the person in ensuring high quality of care for the individual person and their family.

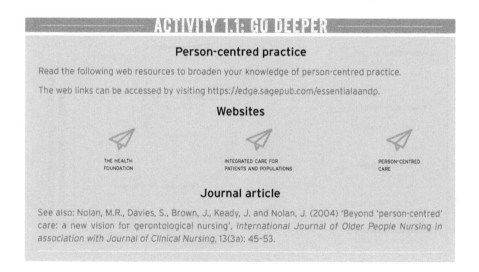

ACTIVITY 1.1: GO DEEPER

Person-centred practice

Read the following web resources to broaden your knowledge of person-centred practice.

The web links can be accessed by visiting https://edge.sagepub.com/essentialaandp.

Websites

THE HEALTH FOUNDATION

INTEGRATED CARE FOR PATIENTS AND POPULATIONS

PERSON-CENTRED CARE

Journal article

See also: Nolan, M.R., Davies, S., Brown, J., Keady, J. and Nolan, J. (2004) 'Beyond 'person-centred' care: a new vision for gerontological nursing', *International Journal of Older People Nursing in association with Journal of Clinical Nursing*, 13(3a): 45–53.

THE HUMAN BODY AND HOMEOSTASIS

Within the context of person-centred practice, we need to consider how the human body is composed and how it works. Starting at the beginning, all living things are composed of cells. Some are single-celled (unicellular) (Chapter 4) others, including human beings, are multicellular consisting of millions of cells

CHAPTER 4

(considered in more detail in Chapter 2). In all such organisms every cell of the body performs a range of functions to maintain its own existence and also contributes to homeostasis of the whole through its special contribution as part of tissues, organs and systems of the body.

UNDERSTAND

An organism is an individual living thing that responds to stimuli, grows and maintains homeostasis, and reproduces. It can be plant or animal, uni- or multicellular.

The human body consists of a number of body systems which contribute to the maintenance of homeostasis through interacting to undertake the functions above. A good understanding of the body, its functions and organisation will enable you to provide appropriate care and to help people to maintain their own health. Figure 1.2 identifies the different body systems and their contributions to homeostasis and continuation of the species which are outlined in Table 1.1. In later chapters you will learn about the different systems in greater detail.

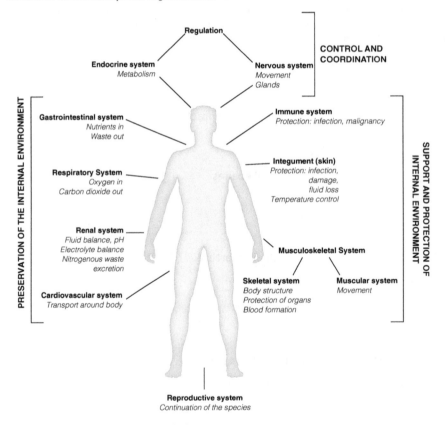

Figure 1.2   Body systems in homeostasis

Table 1.1 Contributions to homeostasis and species continuation

Chapters	Notes
Part 2: Control and Coordination	
5. The Nervous System: Control of Body Function	Rapid regulation of bodily activities through speedy nerve impulses carried through central and peripheral nervous systems (PNS): Central Nervous System (CNS) is brain and spinal cord; PNS is all of the nervous system outside the CNS

6. Special and General Senses: Responding to the Environment	Sensory division carries information to CNS from special and general sense organs and information is interpreted in the CNS
	• Motor division controls glandular secretions and muscular movements:
	  ○ somatic (voluntary) actions
	  ○ autonomic (involuntary) activities:
	    □ sympathetic division: fight, flight, fright response increases nutrient supply
	    □ parasympathetic division: reduced activity, but increased availability of nutrients

7. The Endocrine System: Control of Internal Functions	Slower regulation of bodily activity through action of numerous endocrine glands which regulate metabolism, and thus level of activity, of many organs of body through secretion of hormones (chemical messengers) carried in body fluids to target cells
8. The Digestive System: Nutrient Supply and Waste Elimination	Consists of gastrointestinal tract (GIT) and accessory organs. Enables food to enter body and be used for body function GIT: essentially external to internal body environment, hollow tube runs from mouth (where food enters) to anus (where waste exits)
9. Metabolism and Liver Function	Accessory organs: liver, gallbladder and pancreas contribute to digestion and storage of nutrients. Liver has major role in metabolism
Part 3: Preservation of the Internal Environment	
10. The Respiratory System: Gaseous Exchange	The respiratory system in combination with the cardiovascular system (see below): enables oxygen (O_2) to reach body cells, eliminates carbon dioxide (CO_2)
11. The Renal System: Fluid, Electrolyte and Acid–Base Balance	The renal system is crucial in homeostasis through maintaining chemical composition of body fluids and eliminating waste products
Appendix 1: Introductory Science	CO_2 from cell activity dissolves in water to form carbonic acid which, in excess, decreases pH (acid-base balance), i.e. increases the acidity of body fluids. Maintaining pH within its normal range (7.35–7.45) is undertaken by renal and respiratory systems combined
12. Internal Transport: The Cardiovascular and Lymphatic Systems	Cardiovascular system: heart pumps blood with requirements for cell function through blood vessels around the body Contains: erythrocytes (red blood cells), carry oxygen; lymphocytes (white blood cells), involved in immunity; thrombocytes (platelets), control bleeding The circulation has two main parts: • Systemic: carries blood around upper body, including head and arms, and lower body containing major organs and legs • Pulmonary: carries blood between heart and lungs, permits exchange of blood gases The lymphatic system is functionally part of cardiovascular and immune systems; considered in relation to the immune system

(Continued)

Table 1.1 (Continued)

Chapters	Notes
13. The Immune System: Internal Protection	Immune system consists of the lymphatic system, lymph nodes, parts of GI tract, bone marrow, thymus gland, spleen It defends the body against disease-causing microorganisms and abnormal cells (e.g. cancer cells) through: • Innate immunity (non-specific defence mechanisms); common to all, activated by any foreign bodies. Reduces entry of microorganisms and other foreign bodies • Adaptive immunity: highly specific response to particular foreign body dealing with infective (pathogenic) organisms (used in immunisations) The foreign body is an antigen: different types of white blood cells (leucocytes) create antibodies Antigen–antibody reaction neutralises antigen effect. The immune response takes time to achieve full level of activity
14. Skin and Temperature Regulation	The skin, or integument, provides protection in different ways: • Flexible waterproof tissue prevents loss of fluid, nutrients and electrolytes from body, prevents damage from minor trauma and is physical barrier to pathogenic microorganisms • Sensory receptors enable the skin to send information about heat, trauma, etc. and CNS initiates evasive action • Prevents the body getting too hot, protects against UV light, production of vitamin D for bone formation Temperature regulated by hypothalamus, skin plays an important role
15. The Musculoskeletal System: Support and Movement	Consists of skeleton and muscular system Skeleton: • provides framework and, with muscular system, permits movement • provides protection for major organs within skull, chest (thorax), pelvis Bone marrow has major role in formation of blood cells Muscles have power of contraction. Three groups shown in Table 1.2
16. Reproductive System	Male and female reproductive systems together enable continuation of the species through creation of the embryo which develops in the female. The mother's physiology adapts to safely carry baby through pregnancy and to nurture infant through breast-feeding
17. Development through the Lifespan	Body systems develop through the stages of life including foetal development, childhood, puberty, maturity and aging. Functional ability also alters through these stages. Understanding these enhances the quality of person-centred care

Part 4: Support and Protection of the Internal Environment

Part 5: The Next Generation

Table 1.2 Types of muscle

Skeletal muscle (voluntary, striated or striped)	Responsible for voluntary movement of the body thus providing protection by enabling movement away from danger; controlled by somatic (voluntary) nervous system	Chapter 15
Smooth muscle (involuntary or non-striated)	Different in appearance from skeletal muscle, controlled largely by autonomic nervous system. Examples: gastrointestinal tract and contraction of the blood vessels	Chapter 8
Cardiac muscle	Forms the heart and beats regularly throughout life, controlled by autonomic nervous system	Chapter 12

Regulation through feedback

In order to understand how the body functions to maintain homeostasis it is necessary to comprehend feedback and how it balances the levels of the different parameters so important for life (see Figures 1.3a and b).

There are three parts to any feedback system identified in the figures:

- Sensory receptors which monitor the level of the parameter being regulated;
- The control centre which receives information about changes and sends orders to effectors;
- Effectors: muscles, glands, etc. which alter the parameter in whichever direction is needed.

The control centre is often the Central Nervous System (CNS) or the hypothalamus and/or pituitary gland (part of the CNS and also of the endocrine system) but in some situations the sensory receptor, control centre and the effector organs are all in the same cell. An example of this is in the control of blood glucose levels, which is managed completely by the specialist cells of the islets of Langerhans (in the pancreas).

For each parameter controlled though feedback, there are set points of upper and lower levels between which the blood constituent (e.g. blood glucose, different electrolytes or blood oxygen concentration) or physical measurement (e.g. blood pressure or ventilation rate) varies. At the bottom of the two figures the way in which the parameter varies is illustrated.

There are two types of feedback:

- Negative feedback is the most common type of feedback system (Figure 1.3a). This aims to maintain the particular parameter (e.g. body temperature) within normal limits. If the particular characteristic being controlled moves away from normal, this is sensed and information interpreted by the control system. This then initiates changes to return the parameter back towards its original level.

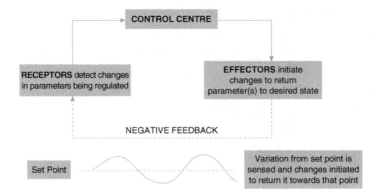

Figure 1.3a Negative feedback

- Positive feedback works to increase the change occurring (Figure 1.3b). For example, the initial changes which occur in blood clotting stimulate other reactions which increase blood clotting to prevent loss of blood.

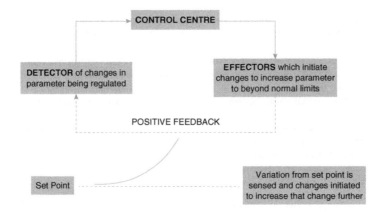

Figure 1.3b Positive feedback

Integration of function

The major point to emphasise here is the importance of the integration of functions of all the different systems of the body. The nervous and endocrine systems carry out the main functions of control and coordination and are studied early in this book (Chapters 5, 6 and 7). These two systems are closely linked both anatomically and functionally.

The brain is the main controlling point of the nervous system sending nervous impulses rapidly along nerves transmitting information to and from different parts of the body and dealing with both voluntary and involuntary activity. The hypothalamus and pituitary gland are the main control centres for the endocrine system of numerous endocrine glands, but they are also part of the brain.

--------------------------------- **UNDERSTAND** ---------------------------------

Endocrine glands release hormones directly into the blood stream and are thus known as ductless glands.

Exocrine glands release secretions (e.g. sweat, digestive enzymes) through ducts to the surface of an organ (e.g. the skin) or into a cavity (such as the digestive tract) and are ducted glands.

As we will see in studying the other systems of the body, the nervous and endocrine systems have links to organs and systems to control and integrate their functions. All the other systems also have links with each other's functions. Various bodily systems ensure that nutrients are provided, waste products removed, chemical composition of the blood maintained, the body protected and moved and other activities performed. All these systems are supplied with the necessary oxygen and nutrients, and waste products removed, by the cardiovascular system. What is clear is that all systems work together for full body function.

In delivering person-centred care, it is also important to understand the changes that take place in the human body through foetal development, maturation, adult life and ageing. As these changes occur, the ability of each person to care for themselves and have normal social interactions and behaviour all adjust to cope with these changes.

HOMEOSTASIS AND THE PERSON

Now that you have some understanding of how the body maintains homeostasis through the collective work of all the systems, where does this fit with person-centred practice? Holism is a concept central to person-centred practice. It refers to all of the concepts that make up personhood, for example, the biological, psychological, sociological and spiritual aspects of a person. So let's make some links.

A person's state of mind, for example, fundamentally originates in their nervous system where experiences and learning integrate with emotion. The strength of someone's muscles and bones, including how they are coordinated by the nervous system, are central to the ability of a person to undertake their particular job, for example, a builder would be dependent on strength and coordination. In some cultures, someone's career may also be an important part of their identity, how they provide for themselves and their family, and in turn how this enables them to pursue activities that maintain well-being as well as to afford food that supports optimal health.

It is essential as a nurse to consider the social context of a person's health and well-being. While you will explore the anatomy and physiology of the human body in this text, it is necessary to apply this within the context of people living in society. For example, we know that excessive alcohol consumption inhibits the function of phagocytes (a type of white blood cell) and also suppresses the development of T-cells that form part of the immune response (Williamson and Williamson, 2010). Understanding how this inhibits homeostasis provides the nurse with the opportunity to engage in health education and promotion activities to prevent people from becoming immunocompromised through excessive alcohol use. However, the person-centred nurse must consider the social factors that influence such behaviours – it is not merely a case of educating people to drink alcohol sensibly, it is about considering what has caused the excessive alcohol intake and addressing those factors. For example, this could be low stress tolerance, low self-esteem, addiction, or a coping mechanism for poverty. Considering that alcohol consumption is highest in those living in low socio-economic circumstances (WHO, 2011), the challenge for nurses and healthcare services is to truly examine those relationships in order to access the real potential to improve health and well-being.

When you think of all of these issues, they map directly into the PCP Framework – central to the person-centred outcomes are: a good care experience, involvement with care, feeling of well-being and existence of a healthful culture. Identifying a good care experience will be influenced by how holistic care is – this relates to the person's experiences (think of the nervous system and its control of emotions, experiences and learning) and how they are able to fulfil their social roles (such as their job, providing for their family, engaging in rewarding activities that are healthy). The latter also contributes to their sense of well-being. A nurse should focus on facilitating empowerment to support the return to optimal health whereby all of this is possible, thus working within the context of person-centred practice.

ACTIVITIES: APPLY

1. Working in a small group or alone, undertake some vigorous activity such as running up and down a flight of stairs or round the block. Identify the changes you can observe and others that you know about. Your results should relate to virtually all systems of the body.
2. Think about how someone responds to being in an accident, having pain or being startled. How do these compare with the findings of the previous activity?

Again in small groups, or alone using a mirror, flash a torch into one eye and observe the changes that occur and compare them with the other eye. Explain what is happening to cause these changes.

CONCLUSION

You should now have an understanding of homeostasis and how all of the body systems work in harmony to maintain it. Additionally, you should also now understand the components of the PCP Framework and how the function of the human body relates to it. While this chapter has provided an overview of these concepts, we will explore each system and other biological concepts in more detail later in the book to enhance your understanding and the relevance to practice. However, before that, in the next chapter we will examine the individual building blocks of the human body, the cells.

Key points

- Homeostasis is essential for maintaining the function of individual cells, bodily systems and the human body as a whole. The body responds to the internal and external environments to maintain health and safety.
- The function of all body systems is integrated and regulated by the two regulatory systems – the nervous and endocrine systems.
- Specific terms are used in describing the human body to enable everyone to understand it in the same way.
- Homeostasis is a key component of personhood. Personhood is the focus of person-centred practice.

GO DEEPER

Further reading

McCormack, B. and McCance, T. (2016) *Person-centred Practice in Nursing and Health Care: Theory and Practice*. Chichester: Wiley-Blackwell.

Ross, H., Tod, A.M. and Clarke, A. (2015) 'Understanding and achieving person-centred care: the nurse perspective', *Journal of Clinical Nursing*, 24(9/10): 1223-33.

Manley, K., Hills, V. and Marriot, S. (2011) 'Person-centred care: principle of Nursing Practice D', *Nursing Standard*, 25(31): 35-7.

REVISE

Having studied this chapter you should appreciate the importance of understanding homeostasis and its application in person-centred practice. Homeostasis can only occur when all the different systems of the body are functioning normally.

In order to help you revise, consider the following questions, answers for which can be found by visiting https://edge.sagepub.com/essentialaandp. Test yourself by revising the chapter first, and then answer these questions without looking at the book. Afterwards compare your answers with the text and with the notes you made. Did you miss anything in your notes? Here are the questions:

CHAPTER 1

Having read this chapter, you should be able to:

1. Write a paragraph about how an understanding of the human body contributes to person-centred practice.
2. Briefly describe what is meant by homeostasis.
3. Explain briefly why understanding homeostasis is an essential aspect of delivering person-centred practice.

For additional revision resources visit the companion website at: https://edge.sagepub.com/essential aandp.

- Revise key terms with interactive flashcards
- Test yourself with multiple-choice questions
- Access the glossary with audio to hear how complex terms are pronounced
- Print out or download the key points from the chapter for quick revision
- Explore recommended websites suitable for revision.

CHAPTER 1

REFERENCES

McCormack, B. and McCance, T.V. (2006) 'Development of a framework for person-centred nursing', *Journal of Advanced Nursing*, 56(5): 472–9.

McCormack, B. and McCance, T. (2016) *Person-centred Practice in Nursing and Health Care: Theory and Practice*. Chichester: Wiley-Blackwell.

Nolan, M.R., Davies, S., Brown, J., Keady, J. and Nolan, J. (2004) 'Beyond 'person-centred' care: a new vision for gerontological nursing', *International Journal of Older People Nursing in association with Journal of Clinical Nursing*, 13(3a): 45–53.

Williamson, J. and Williamson, R. (2010) 'Alcohol and the pancreas', *British Journal of Hospital Medicine*, 71(10): 556–61.

WHO (World Health Organization) (2011) *Environmental Burden of Disease Associated with Inadequate Housing*. Copenhagen: WHO.

10

Clinical Judgement and Decision Making

Barker, J., Linsley, P., and Trueman, I.

Learning Outcomes

By the end of the chapter you will be able to:

- discuss the nature of clinical judgement and decision making;
- recognise the processes involved in clinical judgement and decision making;
- identify and use appropriate decision-making frameworks.

INTRODUCTION

Evidence, Based, Practice

Portney (2004) suggested that EBP should more correctly be called evidence-based decision making, as it requires practitioners to draw on a range of information and make a decision as to what is actually required. This is a view supported by Tiffen et al. (2014) who acknowledge that clinical decision making is the fundamental role of the nurse. Melnyk and Fineout-Overholt (2005) have stated it is useful to think of EBP as requiring clinicians to be involved in two essential activities – critically appraising evidence (discussed in Chapter 6) and using clinical judgement to consider how applicable the evidence is to their own area of practice.

It has been identified that prior to the advent of EBP most health professionals based clinical decision making on 'their vast educational knowledge coupled with intelligent guesswork, hunches and experience' (Pape, 2003: 155). Reliance on such approaches is no longer seen as appropriate due to a number of factors, particularly over confidence (Thompson et al., 2013). Clinical judgement and decision making are identified as central to clinical competence. Nursing not only involves knowing the how and why of delivering a certain type of care but also the ability to give sound rationales and justifications for clinical judgements and decisions taken. The NMC (2010) made decision making one of the four competency domains which must be acquired before registration, emphasising its importance in delivering professional care.

However decision making is not a straightforward activity. Clinical decisions are often characterised by situations of uncertainty where not all the information needed to make them is, or can be, known. It is also recognised that nurses have become data inputters and not users of data and that there is an over reliance on protocol rather than thinking through the situation at hand. The increasing complexity of the care needs of individuals, care interventions and care delivery settings requires finely honed clinical judgement skills to ensure clinical decision making is of the highest standard. Lamb and Sevdalis (2011) have identified that clinical judgement and decision-making skills take practitioners beyond purely technical or knowledge-based skills, proposing these to be 'key non-technical' skills essential for the safe delivery of care. Therefore these concepts will be explored here and the relationship between scientific knowledge and practice experience debated.

Activity 4.1

Before reading any more of this chapter, answer the following questions: How do you put what you have read into practice? How does this affect the way in which you make clinical decisions?

WHAT IS CLINICAL JUDGEMENT?

As identified above clinical judgement is an essential skill for all health professionals and one that separates them from undertaking a purely technical role. Various terms are used in relation to this activity (clinical reasoning, problem solving and critical thinking) but all are related to the ability to consider the various issues at hand, make a judgement in relation to the impact of the various elements and come up with a decision as to what appropriate action to take. Levett-Jones et al. (2010) suggested there are five 'rights' in relation to this concept – right cues, right patient, right action, right time for the right reason.

Tanner (2006: 204) defined clinical judgement as 'an interpretation or conclusion about a patient's needs … and/or the decision to take action' and suggests that there are various factors that impact on this process:

- nurses' experiences and perspectives/values – a 'knowing what to do' (these have a greater impact on clinical judgement than scientific evidence);
- a knowledge of the patient and their preferences – 'knowing the patient';
- the context and culture of the care environment – 'knowing their own environment where specific care will be delivered'.

There is a need to consider how the evidence relates to the practice context – is it transferable; are there identifiable risks and/or benefits to using the evidence in practice? There also needs to be an evaluation of the options with an acceptance that decisions made may vary from patient to patient in the same situations. For example research evidence may suggest a certain course of action is appropriate in women aged between 50 and 60 with leg ulcers or that a particular drug is the treatment of choice for depression in adolescents. However in reality such interventions may not be appropriate for particular individuals whilst for others these are the treatment of choice.

Decisions will have implications for patient outcomes and as such must deserve serious consideration. The number and type of decisions that nurses and other healthcare professionals face are determined to some extent by their understanding and perception of their work, operational autonomy, and the degree to which they see themselves as active and influential decision makers. Thompson et al. (2001) identified that nurses made clinical decisions in six key areas:

1. Intervention/effectiveness: choosing between intervention X and intervention Y.
2. Targeting: these decisions relate to 'choosing which patient will benefit the most from this intervention'.
3. Timing: these commonly take the form of choosing the best time to deploy particular interventions.
4. Communication: these decisions focus on choices relating to ways of delivering and receiving information to and from patients, families and colleagues. Most often these decisions relate to the communication of risks and benefits of different interventions or prognostic categories.
5. Service organisation, delivery and management: decisions concerning the configuration or processes of service delivery.
6. Experimental, understanding or hermeneutic: these decisions relate to the interpretation of cues in the process of care. The choices involved might include deciding on the ways in which a patient may be experiencing a particular situation and are intuitive to some extent.

Decision making is influenced not only by the available evidence but also by individual values, client choice, theories, ethics, legislation, regulation and healthcare resources (DiCenso et al., 2005). No decision however should ever be made without an accompanying judgement as to the appropriateness of that decision.

Reflect on a recent practice experience where a particular intervention appeared more appropriate for some patients than others. What factors impacted on the suitability of specific interventions for different individuals?

Activity 4.2

Activity 4.3

Can you identify any decisions that you made recently where you may not have been aware of why you made the decision? Reflect on why you made this decision and what influenced you.

It is proposed that practitioners consider evidence in terms of its relevance and weight; however this is an individual assessment so what might be considered relevant and given greater weight by one clinician may not be considered in the same way by another (Lasater, 2011). In any two clinical situations the context and individual nurse's experience/knowledge will impact on the judgements and decisions made. All clinical judgements have ethical considerations, with the health professional weighing up the potential benefits and risks involved in any decision made. Frequently there are a number of options available, each of which carries its own risks and benefits. This adds another dimension to the decision-making process and often it is the patient's preferences that indicate which is the best choice (see Chapter 3). Therefore reflection is central to clinical judgement as it requires health professionals to consider and make links between the evidence, their own knowledge, skills and experience and that of other team members as well as patient preferences, beliefs and values. However for this to be effective in aiding clinical judgement it must be undertaken in a clear and structured way rather than simply 'thinking about' the issues. Reflection is explored further in Chapter 11; however it is useful to consider the issues specific to clinical decision making here.

It has been identified that appropriate reflection and particularly reflective writing encourage the transfer of knowledge from one situation to another and help in knowledge transformation – consideration of the relevance current experiences may have for future activities (Nielsen et al., 2007). It is also proposed that this promotes the development of critical thinking – a central component of clinical judgement. Nielsen et al. (2007) have provided a guide for reflection aimed at developing clinical judgement skills.

Activity 4.4

Locate the following article: Nielsen, A., Stragnell, S. and Jester, P. (2007) 'Guide for reflection using the Clinical Judgment Model', *Journal of Nursing Education*, 46(11): 513–516. Using Nielsen et al.'s guide, reflect on a recent incident from your own area of practice.

The reasoning processes used in clinical judgement tend to be described as involving either analytical or intuitive activities (Tanner, 2006). The former involves the breaking down of a problem into its constituent parts, considering these, and weighing up the alternative approaches available in solving the problem. Usually this involves the processing of scientific data. Intuitive processes are seen as drawing on inherent knowledge, skills and experiences to find the answer to the problem. These two options are often seen as the opposite poles of a continuum. However, the idea of a 'cognitive continuum' is possibly more helpful in understanding the processes involved as these two activities are not 'mutually exclusive' (Standing, 2008: 127). Different approaches can be used in different situations depending on the complexity, ambiguity and presentation of the issue and both may be necessary when dealing with uncertain situations. The more complex, familiar or urgent the issue the more likely you are to rely on intuition. Any combination of these three elements will result in the use of differing levels of analysis and/or intuition.

Identify and record:

- a situation where you have made a clinical decision on an emotional or biased basis;
- your actions as a result of this;
- the resulting care that followed.

Activity 4.5

Standing (2008) provided a cognitive continuum of clinical judgement in nursing based on identifying nine cognitive modes used by nurses in practice (see Table 4.1). No one mode is seen as more important than another; these simply reflected the types of knowledge drawn on in the clinical judgement and decision–making processes of nurses and the sort of activities

Table 4.1   Cognitive modes of nursing practice

Judgement process	Description
Intuitive	Drawing on tacit knowledge and arriving at a judgement without being aware of the process by which it was reached. Usually occurs in face-to-face care delivery situation.
Reflective	Incorporates both reflection in and on care delivery actions.
Patient and peer assisted	Encompasses seeking patient preferences and/or the expertise of other healthcare professionals.
System assisted	Involves the use of guidelines, problem-solving frameworks and decision aids.
Critical review of evidence (experience and research)	Identification of relevant information and application of this to the current situation.
Action research and audit	Gathering information through implementing and evaluating changes to care delivery systems.
Qualitative research	Seeking to understand the patient's experience and inform future practice by undertaking qualitative research.
Survey research	Answering questions related to future care delivery by collecting data via surveys.
Experimental research	Testing the effectiveness of intervention through the use of experimental research designs such as RCTs.

nurses are likely to engage in. The intuitive mode is seen most frequently in face-to-face encounters with patients, whereas the experimental research mode is related to establishing effectiveness of intervention and is more distant from day-to-day care activities.

It has been proposed that an over-reliance on intuition may give rise to problems associated with bias – an under- or over-estimation of the importance of certain factors or information. Bias in the form of stereotyping, prejudice or selective memory can influence how you perceive and respond to information and individual patients. Equally, basing judgements and decisions purely on personal experience and knowledge result in important research evidence being ignored or undervalued. Hammond (2007) identified that where analytical approaches to decision making are used errors occur infrequently but when they do they are often on a large scale; whereas errors resulting from intuition-based approaches occur frequently but tend to be small in nature. It is therefore essential that nurses can defend judgements and justify how they reached these and the decisions made.

WHAT IS CLINICAL DECISION MAKING?

Thompson and Stapley (2011) proposed that clinical judgement and clinical decision making are closely linked but separate concepts. The former is about an evaluation of a situation, and the latter is concerned with whether or not to take action and what type of action to take if necessary. For example one might consider that a particular patient's diet is poor (judgement) and choose to provide them with an education package related to healthy eating (decision). Benner et al. (1996: 2) suggested that clinical judgement relates to

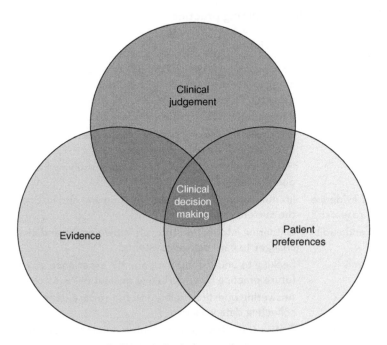

Figure 4.1   Components of clinical decision making

'the ways in which nurses come to understand the problems, issues, or concerns of clients/ patients, to attend to salient information and to respond in concerned and involved ways'. In this way decision making is seen as an interaction between three things – the patient's preferences (discussed in Chapter 3); the evidence available on which to base practice; and the clinical judgement of the nurse involved based on personal experience and knowledge. These three components come together to produce a clinical decision as to what action should be taken – see Figure 4.1.

The core skills relating to good decision making have been identified as:

- Pattern recognition: learning from experience.
- Critical thinking: removing emotion from our reasoning, being 'sceptical', questioning and not taking things at face value, examining assumptions, being open-minded and respective to change, and lastly being able to evaluate the evidence.
- Communication skills: active listening – listening to the patient, what they say, and what they don't say; adopting and pursuing a patient-centred approach – the ability to provide information in a comprehensive way to allow patients, their carers and family to be involved in the decision-making process.
- Team work: using the gathered evidence to enlist the help, support and advice from colleagues and the wider multidisciplinary team.
- Sharing: learning and getting feedback from colleagues on your decision making.
- Reflection: using feedback from others, and the outcomes of the decisions to reflect on the decisions that were taken in order to enhance practice delivery in the future. (Adapted NHS Scotland, 2015)

> Consider the last clinical decision you made. How did you arrive at the decision? Were you aware of analysing the various aspects of the issue or was it reached more intuitively? Did you make the judgement and decision objectively, using all the data and evidence to hand? Did your personal attitudes or biases have a part to play in the decision? Did you involve the patient in the decision-making process – from the initial information gathering to agreeing a course of action? Examine your own decision-making patterns.
>
> **Activity 4.6**

The nursing process of assess, plan, implement and evaluate requires quality decision making. For example, during the assessment phase of the cycle, increased knowledge on the part of the nurse leads to greater clinical currency and judgement. The more experienced nurse knows what to look for based upon clinical knowledge and personal experience and can use this information alongside the available evidence, policy and procedure to inform the care that they give. Evaluation ensures that decisions are reviewed and lessons are learnt. A good decision from an evidence-based perspective is one that successfully integrates four elements:

- professional expertise ('know-how knowledge');
- the available resources;

- the patient's (informed) values;
- the research knowledge ('know-what' knowledge).

Poor decision making in nursing usually happens when nurses use the wrong type of information to inform their decisions or place too much emphasis on a particular form of information (Dowding and Thompson, 2004). Therefore it is crucial to ensure that when making decisions the appropriate sources of information are accessed. When studying decision making in nurses, Rycroft-Malone et al. (2009) found that nurses used a range of strategies, drawing on informal protocols – local ways of working – interactions with co-workers and patients, instinct and formal protocols. However the primary approach used was interactions with others: here nurses discussed decisions made with colleagues and preferred to approach more senior colleagues for information rather than turning to protocols. Protocol-based care has generally been advocated as helping health professionals reach the 'best' decision in relation to the situation they seek to facilitate. It is said these simplify and aid decision making, promoting standardised practice based on best available evidence in the form of care pathways, guidelines and/or algorithms. Rycroft-Malone et al. (2009) found that less experienced staff tended to use protocols more frequently but as individuals become more experienced there was a tendency to rely on memory and past experiences. Although nurses recognised that protocols should be used more frequently, time constraints were said to reduce ability to refer to these. Protocols were often referred to after delivering care to see if decisions made fell within stated guidelines. Nurses expressed a belief that protocols encouraged standardisation, which it was felt did not necessarily equate to best practice as it was seen as being impersonal and therefore challenged individualisation of care.

There are many different types of clinical decisions which nurses are called upon to make. Thompson et al. (2004) identified 11 different forms of decisions made in everyday practice (see Box 4.1).

Box 4.1   Forms of decisions made in practice

Intervention	Targeting	Timing	Prevention
Referral	Communication	Assessment	Diagnosis
Information	Experience	Service delivery	

Activity 4.7

Reflect on one recent day in clinical practice and consider if, when and how you were involved in the 11 types of decisions identified in Box 4.1. Identify how these decisions were made and whether you felt you had the appropriate evidence on which to base those decisions.

There are various conceptual models available to explain the factors involved in making a clinical decision. Tanner (2006) proposed that it is a four-stage process involving noticing, interpreting, responding and reflecting. Lasater (2006) identifies that each of these stages has specific components:

1. Noticing – observing, noticing change and collecting information.
2. Interpreting – making sense of the information and prioritising.
3. Responding – planning intervention, using clear communication and appropriate skills.
4. Reflecting – evaluating the incident and looking for ways to improve performance.

Standing (2011) suggested that clinical decision-making skills have 12 facets (see Box 4.2).

Box 4.2   Clinical decision-making skills

Collaboration	Experience and intuition	Confidence	Prevention
Systematic	Prioritising	Observation	Diagnosis
Standardisation	Reflectivity	Ethical sensitivity	
Accountability			

Identify one patient whose care you were recently involved with. Consider each of Standing's decision-making skills and identify whether or not you used these in making care delivery decisions.

Activity 4.8

In making a clinical decision, it is proposed that a nurse's judgement is helped if the most up-to-date evidence is available and the needs of the service user are clearly identified. However, simply providing nurses with appropriate evidence will not in itself enhance the decision-making processes. Thompson (2003) put forward the notion of 'clinical uncertainty' in relation to decision making; that is, the idea that the practice of nursing takes place in the face of ever-changing demands. A patient's needs and status will change over time, thus resulting in complex and often competing demands.

If decision making is to be effective then health professionals need to be aware of such changes and factor them into any decisions to be made. Therefore it is necessary to consider the implications of a decision over time, what Melnyk and Fineout-Overholt (2005) describe as 'clinical forethought'. This has four components – future think, forethought about specific populations, anticipation of risks and the unexpected (see Table 4.2 for an overview). Issues that may have an impact on, and implications for, care delivery should be identified and considered. Clinical judgement is used in managing these uncertainties and arriving at a decision as to how to proceed – many see this as the 'art' of nursing – and is central to clinical expertise.

Table 4.2 Clinical forethought

Type	Description
Future think	<ul><li>Considering the immediate future and anticipating issues that might arise</li><li>Identifying immediate resources needed</li><li>Considering future responses</li><li>Evaluating judgement and making adjustments as necessary</li></ul>
Specific patients	<ul><li>Considering general trends in patient experiences and responses to intervention</li><li>Identifying local resources available to deal with potential issues</li></ul>
Risks	<ul><li>Anticipating particular issues that may impact on a specific individual – such as anxiety, distress</li></ul>
The unexpected	<ul><li>Expecting the unexpected</li><li>Anticipating the need to respond to new situations and resources – yours and organisational – if difficulties arise</li></ul>

Activity 4.9

Imagine you are about to administer a new form of medication to a patient for the first time. What 'clinical forethought' issues can you identify?

As identified above, nurses' personal knowledge and experience have the greatest impact on these decision-making activities, moulding how the nurse interprets the situation and deals with the uncertainties. The greater the knowledge/experience, the larger the number of perspectives and possibilities that are likely to be identified. As discussed in Chapter 2, Benner (1984) proposed that the 'expert' nurse draws on knowledge in an intuitive way and reaches conclusions without being able to verbalise the process by which those decisions were reached (see Chapter 2 in relation to tacit knowledge). However Fitzpatrick (2007) suggested an expert nurse in relation to EBP needs to be able to make clear and reasoned links between theory and practice with the ability to integrate patient perspectives into this 'mix'.

Nursing expertise is defined by Titchen and Higgs (2001: 274) as the 'professional artistry and practice wisdom inherent in professional practice'. Clinical expertise is viewed by Manley et al. (2005) as having a number of components (see Box 4.3). The development of these aspects of clinical expertise are said to be linked to 'enabling factors' – the ability to reflect; to organise practice giving consideration to overarching influences; to work autonomously; to develop good interpersonal relationships; and to promote respect.

> ### Box 4.3   Nursing expertise
>
> 1. Holistic practice knowledge – integrating various forms of knowledge, academic and experiential, into their delivery of care.
> 2. Knowing the patient – respecting the patient's views/perspectives, encouraging patient decision making and promoting independence.
> 3. Moral agency promoting respect, dignity and self-efficacy in others whilst maintaining own professional integrity.
> 4. Saliency – observing and picking up on cues from patients, recognising the needs of patients and others.
> 5. Skilled know-how – problem solving, responding to changing environment of care and adapting to needs as appropriate.
> 6. Change catalyst – promoting appropriate change.
> 7. Risk taker – weighing the risks and taking appropriate decisions, to achieve best patient outcomes.

APPROACHES TO DECISION MAKING

There are a number of frameworks that can be used to help with decision making.

Facione (2007) offered a six-step approach to effective thinking and problem solving which he proposed involves five 'whats' and a 'why':

1. What is the question facing you?
2. What are the circumstances that surround the problem?
3. What are the most reasonable top three or four options?
4. What is the best course of action?
5. Why are you choosing this particular option?
6. What did you miss?

> Consider an area of concern in your area of practice. Using Facione's framework identify how best to address the issues of concern.
>
> **Activity 4.10**

Hoffman et al. (2010) proposed a clinical reasoning cycle, based on research concerning expert nurses' thought and decision-making processes. It was suggested that this cycle can be used to promote the development of practice-specific knowledge and clinical reasoning skills in students and novice practitioners. There are eight steps in the cycle:

1. Describe the patient and the context of their care situation.
2. Consider all the information currently available (notes, charts, history) and gather any further information needed. Apply the theoretical knowledge you already have to the patient's illness/presentation and the situation.
3. Review all the data you have to get a full picture of the patient and their context. Identify what is and is not relevant, and any patterns and relationships between the various pieces of information. Compare the current situation to your past experiences and suggest possible outcomes.
4. Evaluate the information to clarify the nature of the problem to be addressed.
5. Set your goals and time frame within which these will be achieved.
6. Implement your plan of action.
7. Evaluate outcomes.
8. Reflect on the experience and identify learning needs.

Activity 4.11

When in your own area of practice use Hoffman et al.'s framework in relation to a specific patient problem.

Carroll and Johnson (1990) suggest an alternative seven-stage model of decision making, which does not follow a linear pattern but can be repeated or returned to as necessary:

1. Recognition of the situation.
2. Formulation of explanation.
3. Alternative generation of other explanations.
4. Information search to clarify choices and available evidence.
5. Judgement or choice.
6. Action.
7. Feedback.

Activity 4.12

Think about the above three frameworks and decide which one reflects your decision-making process in clinical practice.

EBP calls for a more analytical approach to making clinical decisions, and it is anticipated there will be a conscious weighing up of the options and consideration of the various issues.

The McMaster's EBM group caution against the use of clinical experience and intuition in the absence of evidence based on systematic observation in making clinical judgements (Eraut, 2000). However it should not underestimate how much interpretation may be needed in deciding how evidence should be used – EBP cannot always provide concrete evidence on which to base practice. A possible model for this process is given in Figure 4.2.

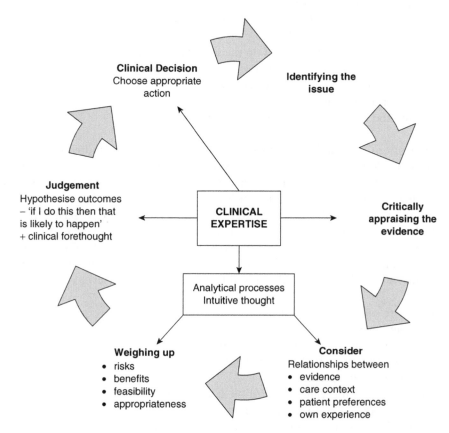

Clinical Decision
Choose appropriate action

Identifying the issue

Judgement
Hypothesise outcomes – 'if I do this then that is likely to happen' + clinical forethought

CLINICAL EXPERTISE

Critically appraising the evidence

Analytical processes
Intuitive thought

Weighing up
- risks
- benefits
- feasibility
- appropriateness

Consider
Relationships between
- evidence
- care context
- patient preferences
- own experience

Figure 4.2   Model for clinical decision making

GROUP DECISION MAKING

Healthcare does not take place in a vacuum but is delivered by a team of professionals and ancillary staff. Many of the decisions made in clinical practice are taken collectively. This brings both advantages and disadvantages. By definition, group decisions are participatory and subject to social influence. Perhaps the greatest advantage is that group members tend to be from different specialties and as such provide more information and knowledge. Implementation of the decision is more effective since the people who are putting the decision into practice have contributed to its formulation and feel an investment in it. The participative nature of group decision making means that it can act as a training ground for junior members of staff to develop the skills of questioning and objective analysis and for senior members of staff to act as role-models. The seven-step model presented below offers a structured approach to group decision making.

1. Identify the decision to be made.
2. Examine the data. Perhaps most importantly ask what additional information is needed.
3. Establish criteria. Identify the criteria or conditions that would determine whether a chosen solution is successful.
4. Discuss potential solutions based on the available evidence.
5. Evaluate options and select the best one. Remember not everyone will necessarily agree; however whatever decision is reached should be based on the best evidence at the time.
6. Implement the solution.
7. Monitor and evaluate the outcome. (Adapted from University of Waterloo (2015))

Group decisions can also be less efficient that those made by an individual. Group decisions can take longer to reach and there may be conflict between group members as to what to do and what is the best evidence to support a particular approach. One of the biggest disadvantages to such decision making is the phenomenon known as Groupthink. Groupthink was a term first put forward by Irving Jarvis (1972) to describe the situation in which a group makes faulty decisions because group pressures lead to a deterioration of 'mental efficiency, reality testing and moral judgement' (1972: 9). Groupthink occurs when individuals in a group feel under pressure to conform to what seems to be the dominant view of the group and can lead to the following barriers:

- incomplete survey of alternatives;
- incomplete survey of objectives;
- failure to examine risks of preferred choice;
- failure to reappraise initially rejected alternatives;
- poor information search;
- selective bias in processing information at hand;
- failure to work out contingency plans;
- low probability of successful outcome.

Activity 4.13

Ferguson and Day (2007) proposed that novice nurses lack confidence in their own clinical judgement and decision-making processes. Complete a SWOT analysis (see Appendix 1) in relation to your own skills in this area and identify your future learning needs.

Summary

- The complexity of care requires finely honed clinical judgement skills to ensure clinical decision making is of the highest standard.
- Nurses' experiences and perspectives/values have a greater impact on their clinical judgement than scientific evidence.
- Clinical judgement and clinical decision making are closely linked but separate concepts.
- Involvement of service users in the decisions and sound clinical decision making are central to EBP.
- Clinical judgement is seen as the 'art' of nursing and central to clinical expertise, and involves the weighing up of options and reaching a decision as to appropriate action.
- Both analytical process and intuitive thinking are central to clinical judgement.

FURTHER READING

Standing, M. (2011) *Clinical Judgement and Decision Making for Nursing Students*. Exeter: Learning Matters. This book provides an in-depth exploration of decision-making processes.

Thompson, C. and Dowding, D. (2009) *Essential Decision Making and Clinical Judgement for Nurses*. Amsterdam: Elsevier. This provides an in-depth exploration of issues related to clinical judgement and decision making.

E-RESOURCES

NHS National Prescribing Centre: has a series of short videos related to EBP and decision making, including individual decision making. www.npc.nhs.uk/evidence/making_decisions_better/making_decisions_better.php

The Principles of Pharmacology

Spires, A., and O'Brien, M.

NMC Standards for Pre-registration Nursing Education

This chapter will address the following competencies:

Domain 1: Professional values

4. All nurses must work in partnership with service users, carers, families, groups, communities and organisations. They must manage risk, and promote health and wellbeing while aiming to empower choices that promote self-care and safety.

Domain 3: Nursing practice and decision-making

2. All nurses must possess a broad knowledge of the structure and functions of the human body, and other relevant knowledge from the life, behavioural and social sciences as applied to health, ill health, disability, ageing and death. They must have an in-depth knowledge of common physical and mental health problems and treatments in their own field of practice, including co-morbidity and physiological and psychological vulnerability.

3. All nurses must carry out comprehensive, systematic nursing assessments that take account of relevant physical, social, cultural, psychological, spiritual, genetic and environmental factors, in partnership with service users and others through interaction, observation and measurement.

4. All nurses must ascertain and respond to the physical, social and psychological needs of people, groups and communities. They must then plan, deliver and evaluate safe, competent, person-centred care in partnership with them, paying special attention to changing health needs during different life stages, including progressive illness and death, loss and bereavement.

NMC Essential Skills Clusters

This chapter will address the following ESCs:

Cluster: Organisational aspects of care

17. People can trust the newly registered graduate nurse to work safely under pressure and maintain the safety of service users at all times.

continued overleaf . . .

continued . . . .

Cluster: Medicines management

36. People can trust the newly registered graduate nurse to ensure safe and effective practice in medicines management through comprehensive knowledge of medicines, their actions, risks and benefits.

By the second progression point:

1. Uses knowledge of commonly administered medicines in order to act promptly in cases where side effects and adverse reactions occur.

Chapter aims

By the end of this chapter, you should be able to:

*   understand the principles of pharmacodynamics and pharmacokinetics;
*   discuss factors affecting the pharmacodynamics and pharmacokinetics of medicines.

Introduction

Case study

Mary Santini is a 70-year-old lady. She was admitted to the Accident and Emergency Department after being found on the floor at home by her neighbour. She has sustained a fracture to the neck of her left femur and bruising to her temple. Mary's neighbour has brought her medication into the department. She is taking lithium for her bipolar disorder. Mary is in pain, but since she has bruising to her temple, the doctors need to rule out a possible head injury. They are reluctant to prescribe her morphine, due to its sedative properties, which may mask any signs or symptoms of a head injury, and have decided to prescribe diclofenac instead. Two weeks later Mary has recovered from the surgery to her fractured neck of femur. She is well enough to go home and has been discharged with a supply of her lithium medicine and diclofenac for pain relief. Three weeks later Mary dies.

Had the doctors and nurses understood that patients receiving lithium can accumulate toxic levels of lithium in the bloodstream when taking diclofenac, they would not have prescribed or administered diclofenac in this case. Mary might still be alive. While this is a fictitious scenario, such cases do too often occur, and they could so easily be avoided if doctors and nurses understood the basic principles of pharmacology and medicine interactions.

This chapter will enable you to understand how medicines work in the body (**pharmaco-dynamics**) and how medicines are **absorbed**, **distributed**, **metabolised** and **excreted** (**pharmacokinetics**) from the body. It is important that you learn the principles of pharma-cokinetics and pharmacodynamics to enable you to understand how medicines work and therefore be aware of any possible **adverse reactions** to medicines. This will enable you to take appropriate action should your patient suffer any such effects. It is also necessary to understand the various factors that affect the pharmacodynamics and pharmacokinetics of medicines for your particular patient group, for example the route of administration and the age, sex, nutri-tional status, illness, body weight, genetics and ethnicity of the patient.

You may feel quite daunted when it comes to trying to understand pharmacological principles and how they apply to specific medicines and relate to your nursing practice. It is neither necessary nor possible to know the name and function of every single medicine that is available. You should concentrate on becoming familiar with the processes involved in the **pharmacology** of medicines and then be able to apply them to common groups of medicines that you will encounter in your nursing practice.

As a foundation-year student the NMC (2010a, b) requires you to ensure that your practice is safe and effective. You can demonstrate this through comprehensive knowledge of medicines and their actions, risks and benefits. In order to pass through the second progression point in your programme you must be able to prove that you have acquired the necessary knowledge of com-monly administered medicines in order to act promptly in cases where side effects and adverse reactions occur.

Pharmacology

What medicines are

Medicines are made up of drugs, which are chemical compounds that are taken into the body to initiate a reaction in order to cause some sort of change to, or effect on, the body. The term 'medicines' and 'drugs' are often used interchangeably. However, it is important to note that a medicine may contain more than one drug or chemical compound, so a medicine can contain two or more drugs. These chemical compounds are made up of both natural and synthetic substances. Natural substances can come from a variety of sources, such as plants. Digoxin, a medicine used to treat **atrial fibrillation**, is extracted from the leaves of the digitalis plant. There is a whole host of herbal medicines available that are sourced from plants. Animal products are also used in medicines. Insulin obtained from the pancreas of pigs and cows is an example that, until fairly recently, was used in the treatment of **diabetes**. Now insulin is manufactured synthetically. Other natural sources used in medicines are derived from minerals and salts. Chloride and potassium are examples of such medicines. Synthetic medicines are those that are manufactured from man-made materials, mostly petrochemicals.

Typically, at least three names are applied to the same medicine. This is because medicines can be referred to by either their **chemical**, **generic** or **trade** (also referred to as **brand** or **proprietary**) **name**. The chemical name describes the molecular structure of the medicine. It is often only used during the developmental stages of the medicine. The generic name is a shorter version of the chemical name and the trade name refers to the title that the pharmaceutical company, who manufactured the medicine, gives it. The generic name is often the preferred method for prescribing medicines. This is because it more clearly indicates the class of the medicine and generic names are generally recognised internationally. The generic name tends to be more readily recognised by practitioners. For example, ibuprofen is a generic name for a **non-steroidal anti-inflammatory medicine (NSAID)** to treat pain associated with inflammation. Nurofen is an example of a popular NSAID. Nurofen is a brand name, but if you look at the ingredients that make up this medicine you will notice that ibuprofen is the main drug.

Medicines are also grouped into **classes** according to either their use or if they share similar characteristics. So, for example, paroxetine is the generic name given to a class of medicine that is termed a selective serotonin uptake inhibitor. Its chemical name is (3S, 4R)-3-(1, 3-benzodioxol-5-yloxymethyl)-4-(fluorophenyl) piperidine and its chemical structure is: $C_{19}H_{20}FNO_3$. Clearly, trying to recall the chemical compounds that make up this medicine would be very difficult. Imagine if you had to do this for all medicines! One of the main reasons why patients are prescribed this medicine is to treat the symptoms of depression. Seroxat is an example of one of the trade names of this medicine.

The use of medicines

Medicines are used to either treat or prevent a disease. When they are used for **therapeutic** (treatment) reasons, their purpose is to cure a disease, to reduce or improve the unpleasant symptoms a patient may be experiencing as a result of their disease, or to control the progression of a disease. For example, **antibiotics** may be administered to a patient who has a wound infection. The antibiotics will destroy or deactivate the bacteria present in the wound, thereby curing the wound infection. NSAIDs may be administered to a patient with **osteoarthritis** and will help to reduce inflammation and pain associated with this disease, thereby decreasing the amount of pain a patient will experience. Cytotoxic medicines may be administered to a patient with cancer to slow down the progression of the disease. They work by interfering with how cells are replicated, thus reducing the number of cancerous cells left in the body.

Medicines are also used for **prophylactic** reasons. When administered for this purpose the aim is to prevent a disease or a dangerous or unpleasant symptom of a disease from occurring. **Statins**, for example, are used to reduce **cholesterol** levels. High levels of cholesterol play a major role in the development of **heart disease** and **strokes**. It is thought that giving patients statins will reduce the development of such diseases. **Vaccines** are another example of medicines that are commonly given to prevent the development of diseases, such as mumps, measles or swine flu.

Medicines can also be used for diagnostic purposes. For example, **mydriatics** may be administered into the eye to facilitate the examination of the eye.

Activity 3.1   *Evidence-based practice and research*

Answer the following scenarios to test your understanding of medicines use. For each scenario decide what the medicine is used for, a reason why the patient may have been prescribed it and whether it has been prescribed for therapeutic or prophylactic reasons. You may wish to provide your answers in a table. You could use the following headings in your table: medicine, its use, why it is prescribed, prophylactic or therapeutic.

(a) Tia Hamilton is a nine-year-old girl who has recently emigrated from South Africa. She has been prescribed Bacillus Calmette-Guerin (BCG) vaccine.

(b) Rory Winters is a 45-year-old man. He has been prescribed paracetamol 1g as a once-only prescription.

(c) Jordan Black is a 28-year-old woman. She has been prescribed citalopram 20mg, to be administered once a day.

(d) Jacob Rogers is a 65-year-old man. He has been admitted to the ward for a left total knee replacement. He has been prescribed cefuroxime 1.5g IV for one dose and then 750mg for a further two doses only.

An outline answer is provided at the end of the chapter.

Pharmacokinetics

Pharmacokinetics is the study of what the body does to a medicine. It derives from the Greek words *pharmakon* (drug) and *kinetikos* (motion). It looks at how medicines are absorbed, distributed, metabolised and excreted from the body.

Absorption

The route of administration is the way the medicine enters your patient's body. The way that medicines are absorbed in the body initially depends on the route of administration. The most common route for administering medicines is by the oral route and most medicines that are taken orally are absorbed from the stomach, into the small intestine and then into the bloodstream. Due to the relatively fast emptying time of the stomach, many medicines will initially pass through the stomach before they are absorbed. It is in the small intestine that most absorption of oral medicines occurs.

Medicines can also be administered by the intravenous route (directly into a vein), intramuscularly (into a muscle), subcutaneously (under the skin), transdermally or topically (through the skin). With these routes the medicine enters the bloodstream directly from the site of administration.

Other routes include sublingual (under the tongue), **buccal** (in the cheek) and **nasal** (via the nasal passages). With these routes the medicine is absorbed through the **oral mucosa** and **mucous membranes** that line the nasal passages.

Your patients may also take their medicines via inhalation (directly into the lungs), or the **aural** route (into the ears) and the **ocular** route (into the eyes). Medicines may also be given **rectally** (directly into the rectum), **vaginally** (into the vagina), **intrathecally** (directly into the central nervous system) and **intravesically** (directly into the bladder).

Activity 3.2   *Evidence-based practice and research*

Consider the patients you will be predominantly caring for during your nursing pro-gramme. Identify the advantages and disadvantages to your patients of receiving their medicines by the various routes available. You could do this in the form of a table.

An outline answer is provided at the end of the chapter.

The absorption process begins when the medicine is introduced into the body. It ends when the medicine reaches the circulatory system. In order to reach the circulatory system the medicine first needs to dissolve to enable it to cross a **cell membrane**. How a medicine dissolves once it enters the body depends on its route of administration and also the chemical compounds that make up that particular medicine. Cell membranes are able to absorb medicines by various processes:

*   **passive diffusion**;
*   **facilitated diffusion** (also known as **facilitated transport**);
*   **active transport**.

Before you continue reading this chapter, you may find it useful to refresh your understanding of **cell physiology**, to which the processes involved in absorption relate. Medicines that can **ionise** in solution will be unable easily to cross the cell membrane. Un-ionised medicines will find it far easier to cross the cell membrane. The process of ionisation will be explained in more detail later in the chapter.

Passive diffusion

Passive diffusion occurs when the concentration of the medicine on one side of the cell mem-brane is greater than that on the other side of the cell membrane. The medicine will move along a **concentration gradient** through the cell membrane to the area where there is less concentration of the medicine. This process does not require any energy; it is purely driven by the concentration gradient. (Imagine you parked your car on the top of a steep slope and took the handbrake off. The car would roll down the slope, even with the engine switched off.) This process will occur more quickly if the medicine molecules are small, soluble in water and are **lipids**.

Facilitated diffusion

Facilitated diffusion requires **carrier proteins** to move a medicine molecule across a cell membrane. The process still involves a medicine moving along a concentration gradient, to enable a higher concentration of the medicine to cross the cell membrane to the lower concentration. The carrier protein **binds** with the medicine molecule to move it across the cell membrane. (Imagine you needed to get the car back up the hill. The car would need to be filled with petrol in order for you to be able to turn on the ignition and drive it back up.)

Active transport

Active transport requires energy to move a medicine molecule across a cell membrane. With this process medicine molecules are pumped across the cell membrane, against a concentration gradient. The energy required is in the form of **adenosine triphosphate (ATP)**. This form of absorption will occur in cases where medicine molecules are too large to cross the cell membrane or they are moving against a concentration gradient. (Imagine you had to push the car back up the steep hill. You would need a lot of energy in the form of physical strength to enable you to do this.)

Ionisation of medicines

As already discussed, some medicine molecules require a form of energy in order to cross a cell membrane and enter the cell. We have discussed the forms of energy required for facilitated diffusion (carrier proteins) and active transport (such as ATP to pump the medicine molecules into the cell). The environment inside a cell is more acidic than outside, with the exception of cells lining the stomach. Referring to basic cell physiology, we know that molecules comprise two or more **atoms**. Atoms are electrically neutral, whereby they comprise negatively charged **electrons** and positively charged **protons**. When atoms lose or gain an electrical charge they become **ions**. Ions carry an electrical charge that enables them to move across cell membranes. There are factors that affect this process. For example, a very acidic environment such as the stomach (where medicines are absorbed when given via the oral route) will suppress the electrical charge of a medicine with a weak acid base such as aspirin (acetic acid). In this case the atoms that make up the medicine molecule will cross the cell membrane and enter the cell. Therefore a medicine with similar properties to aspirin will be absorbed mainly in the stomach. Many medicines have weak acid bases and thus, if administered via the oral route, will be absorbed largely in the stomach and small intestine.

Activity 3.3   *Evidence-based practice and research*

For each route of administration, list one commonly used medicine.

An outline answer is provided at the end of the chapter.

Distribution

Once a medicine has crossed the cell membrane and entered the circulatory system, it is distributed to the body tissues. Ideally, we would only want the medicine to target a specific tissue. For example, if a patient was administered gliclazide, to regulate their blood glucose levels, we would want it to selectively target the pancreas, which is the organ responsible for insulin production, which assists in regulating blood glucose levels. However, once a medicine enters the circulatory system it will travel to all parts of the body. Where it travels is dependent on whether it is a water-soluble or fat-soluble medicine. Medicines that are water soluble will stay in the circulating blood and also in the fluid surrounding the cells (**interstitial space**). Medicines that are fat soluble will target fatty tissues. This may offer an explanation as to why side effects are common with many medicines. Body tissues that are highly vascularised will receive the medicine before less well-vascularised areas. Like absorption, there are several factors that affect how a medicine is distributed.

Blood–brain barrier

Many medicines are unable to enter the brain due to a barrier between the brain and the circulatory system. This is commonly known as the blood–brain barrier. The barrier is comprised of a membrane that separates the circulating blood and **cerebrospinal fluid** (**CSF**). It was discovered about a hundred years ago during an experiment where staining was carried out. Dye was injected into animals and was taken up in all body tissues except the brain. A further study a few years later, where dye was injected into the cerebrospinal fluids of animals, showed the uptake of dye in the cerebrospinal fluid only. The blood–brain barrier was later confirmed in the 1960s with the introduction of the scanning electron microscope. Its mechanism is primarily to protect the brain from harmful substances such as bacteria and from hormones and neurotransmitters that are found elsewhere in the body. Only some medicines, made up of very small molecules, are able to cross this barrier. Consequently, this could prove problematic when trying to administer medicines that need to be delivered to the brain.

Metabolism

Metabolism is a process whereby the medicine is converted from one chemical compound into another. This is enabled by enzymatic activity. The processes involved will convert the medicine into a water-soluble form to make it easier to be excreted from the body. The main organ in the body where metabolism takes place is the liver. Metabolism has an effect on the **bioavailability** of a medicine. Bioavailability refers to the amount of the medicine that is left unchanged that is able to reach the circulatory system. It is important to know this, since medicine dosages will be prescribed according to the bioavailability of the medicine. The amount of medicine left unchanged can be influenced by a process called the **first pass effect** or first pass metabolism.

First pass effect

The first pass effect, also known as first pass metabolism, begins during the absorption process of a medicine, but it also influences the distribution of the medicine. All medicines that are absorbed from the gastrointestinal tract pass into the **portal blood system**. This part of the circulatory system transports the absorbed molecules of the medicine via the portal vein to the liver before the medicine is distributed to various parts of the body. The liver metabolises a large proportion of the medicine into **metabolites**. With some medicines so many metabolites are lost or **deactivated** during this process that only a small amount of the active medicine remains, which can then pass into the blood circulation and on to the rest of the body. This is known as the first pass effect. This explains why many medicines that are absorbed via the gastrointestinal system are administered to patients in higher doses than those given via alternative routes.

Activity 3.4   *Evidence-based practice and research*

Medicines administered by the intravenous route have 100 per cent bioavailability.

(a) What does this mean?
(b) Why does this happen?

An outline answer is provided at the end of the chapter.

Plasma protein binding

Most medicines bind to proteins as they flow through the body. The binding (or the bound medicine) does not produce any physiological effect. Only the unbound or free medicine is available to the tissues to exert a therapeutic effect. Certain medicines are more highly bound to proteins than others. These medicines need to be administered in higher doses to bring about a therapeutic effect. This is because there is less of the free medicine available in the circulatory system to reach the tissues, and also highly bound medicines are released more slowly into the circulatory system. Aspirin is an example of a medicine highly bound to the protein albumin. Several factors impact on the binding process. Aspirin and warfarin bind to the same protein, since both medicines have **anticoagulant** properties; it is often the case that the same or similar classes of medicines will compete for the same protein. If both medicines are administered at the same time, warfarin will be displaced. There will be higher levels of warfarin in the circulatory system. A reduction in plasma protein levels seen in malnourished patients and older adults will also have an effect on the action of a highly bound medicine.

Excretion

Excretion is the final process involved in pharmacokinetics and is the process involved in removing the medicine or its residue from the body. Medicines are excreted via several routes, the most common being via the kidneys (excreted in urine). Other routes of excretion include the gastrointestinal tract (excreted in faeces), the skin (excreted in sweat) and the lungs (excreted during exhalation of breath).

The rate of excretion is important as it determines the duration of action of the medication. Medicines that have been made water soluble by metabolism in the liver are easily excreted via the kidneys by a process known as **glomerular filtration**. Some medicines are reabsorbed through the **renal tubules** of the kidney by active transport (see the section on absorption on pp71–2).

Half-life (*t* 1/2)

The half-life of a medicine refers to the length of time it takes for the medicine to leave the body and leave one half of it remaining in the circulatory system. The half-life of a medicine is measured by the amount of medicine remaining in plasma. It is based on the plasma levels of a healthy individual. How quickly a medicine is eliminated from the body depends on several factors. For example, it can be excreted from the body, or moved to another body compartment such as intracellular fluid. The medicine can also be destroyed in the blood. Plasma protein binding, as discussed earlier, also has an effect on the half-life of a medicine. For example, highly bound medicines have a longer half-life than unbound medicines. This is because they remain in the body longer and release their active ingredient more slowly. The symbol *t* 1/2 is used to refer to the plasma half-life of a medicine.

To measure the half-life of a medicine, a dose is given to a patient (usually in a clinical trial). Blood samples are then taken at intervals and the results of the samples are plotted on a graph. Initially, the concentration levels of the medicine in the blood will be high and will gradually decline as the medicine is absorbed from its site of entry, distributed to its site of action, metabolised in the liver and finally excreted from the body. Figure 3.1 shows how the plasma levels of a medicine administered by the intravenous route (where rapid absorption into the circulatory system occurs) may look if the blood levels were plotted on a graph.

It is important to know the half-life since this will determine how much of a medicine should be given and also how frequently it should be administered. It is important to remember that various factors will affect the half-life of a medicine. For example, poor renal function in an older adult may result in the medicine taking longer to be excreted from the body. The half-life of a medicine is usually calculated during the trial or testing stages of a new medicine. This will be done before the medicine is made available for use on patients.

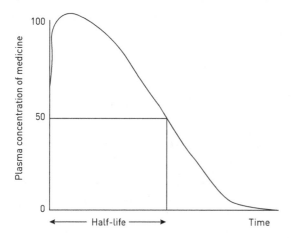

Figure 3.1: Plasma concentration levels and half-life of a medicine after a single dose administered via intravenous injection

---

Activity 3.5   *Evidence-based practice and research*

Tom Reynolds is a 46-year-old man. He has recently been diagnosed with schizophrenia. He has commenced treatment for his condition and has been prescribed flupentixol 12mg daily, which is an antipsychotic medicine. It has a half-life of approximately 20 hours.

Approximately how much of the medicine would remain in Tom's circulatory system after 20 hours?

Answers are provided at the end of the chapter.

Therapeutic range

In order to ensure a medicine is present in a sufficient concentration to have a desirable effect, without side effects, ideally the medicine should be present at a therapeutic level. Too much of a medicine will produce undesirable effects and too little will produce little therapeutic effect. Sometimes it is necessary to administer a **loading dose** of the medicine in order for it to be effective and to quickly bring the medicine into the therapeutic range. Smaller, regular maintenance doses are then administered to ensure the medicine stays within the therapeutic range in the blood.

Figure 3.2 demonstrates the concept of a therapeutic range. In this diagram you can see that a loading dose of a medicine has been administered. It quickly reaches and surpasses the ideal range for the medicine to be at its most effective. At this stage the patient may experience some unpleasant or even toxic effects of the medicine. The plasma concentration of the medicine then falls and it is at this stage that the medicine is unlikely to be effective. Subsequent doses of the medicine are given (we can see this from the peaks in the lines). These doses are called maintenance doses and are usually smaller than the initial loading dose. Once again we can see the peaks and troughs in the plasma concentration levels of the medicine. Ideally, we would want a medicine to stay in the therapeutic range for as long as possible as here it will give the patient the

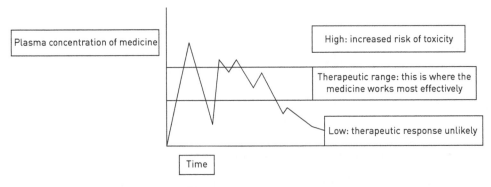

Figure 3.2: The therapeutic range of a medicine

most benefit and least side or toxic effects. This will be dependent on factors such as the strength of the dose given, the route of administration and the timing of the doses. Some medicines have very narrow therapeutic ranges and hence the patient needs close and regular monitoring of their plasma levels. Warfarin is one such example. Patients who are prescribed this medicine initially have their plasma concentration levels checked on a daily or alternate-day basis to determine the dose of warfarin they should be administered.

Factors affecting the pharmacokinetics of medicines

Routes of administration

As discussed earlier, there are several routes in which a medicine can be administered. The method by which a medicine enters the body plays a major role in the absorption process. For example, when taken via the oral route medicines are subjected to an acidic environment in the stomach that breaks down the chemical compound of the medicine. With many medicines taken via this route, much of the active ingredient is deactivated by this acidity and subsequently lost to the circulatory system. If food is present, stomach acidity is higher and it takes longer for the stomach to empty. Consequently, any medicines ingested will be subjected to a higher acidic environment for longer. This can be further exacerbated by the presence of certain foods in the stomach that can increase stomach acidity. Examples include protein products and alcohol. Some medicines will also affect the rate at which the stomach empties. For example, metoclopramide, a medicine commonly used to treat nausea and vomiting, increases the rate at which the stomach empties. This in turn will increase the rate of absorption. If several medicines are taken at the same time, some may be absorbed more quickly or more slowly than intended. Other routes that also result in a medicine entering the stomach include **enteral** routes such as via **nasogastric** or **gastrostomy** tubes.

The intravenous route for administration results in all of the medicine reaching the circulatory system. This is because medicines administered via this route are not absorbed in the stomach and are not subjected to the stage of first pass effect (see pp74–5), where much of a medicine is deactivated in the liver. This is why intravenous doses of a medicine are usually lower than when given via the oral route.

The rate of absorption of a medicine given via the intramuscular route is dependent on which muscle the medicine is injected into. Blood flow to the muscle will also be a factor in how much of the medicine is absorbed into the muscle. If the muscle is cold, the blood vessels will **vasoconstrict**, thus decreasing absorption. If the muscle is warm (for example, through exercise), then blood vessels will **vasodilate** and the absorption rate will be increased. Similar to the intravenous route, medicines administered in this way will bypass the stomach and the first pass effect in the liver.

The subcutaneous route for injecting medicines is another common route to use. The medicine is injected under the top two layers of skin. The absorption rate is considerably slower when compared to the intravenous or intramuscular route because the medicine has to pass through the fatty layers under the skin and then be absorbed into the circulatory system. Once again, the stomach and first pass effect are bypassed. Like muscle, the skin is affected by heat and cold, which in turn will affect the absorption rate of the medicine.

Medicines administered rectally or vaginally are usually in the form of **suppositories**, **pessaries**, liquids or creams. They are absorbed into the lining of the rectum or vagina and are then absorbed into the bloodstream. This method also bypasses the stomach and liver.

Sublingual or buccal administration results in the medicine being absorbed through the mucous membranes under the tongue or in the cheek. Similarly, if the nasal route is used, the medicine can be absorbed directly through the mucous membranes that line the nose. Some medicines will also be absorbed from the nasal mucosa and into the CSF (see the section on the blood–brain barrier on p74), thus exerting an effect on the brain. Absorption is often quicker than with the oral route since the medicine is able to directly enter the circulatory system. Only the **enzymes** present in saliva may deactivate some of the medicine, but these effects are much less when compared to those of the first pass effect.

The transdermal or topical route enables a medicine to be absorbed into the skin. As with the subcutaneous injection, this method is slow and the absorption rate is affected by heat or cold, due to the effects of vasoconstriction or vasodilation of the capillaries.

The ocular route enables a medicine to be absorbed through the cornea and conjunctiva of the eye to produce a local effect, while the aural route is used where a local effect of the medicine is required in the ear. Ointments, for example, would be administered directly into the ear.

Inhalation routes are used when a medicine needs to go directly into the lungs or other parts of the respiratory system. Smaller molecules of a medicine will be able to diffuse into the lungs and into the **alveoli**. Larger molecules of medicine may only be absorbed and diffused into the **bronchioles**.

Using the intravesical route enables a medicine to be administered directly into the bladder. Absorption of the medicine will have a local effect, that is, directly at the intended site. Superficial bladder tumours are commonly treated via intravesical medicines. There is a risk, however, that some of the medicine will be absorbed into the circulatory system and subsequently may have a systemic effect.

The intrathecal route enables a medicine to be administered directly into the intrathecal space surrounding the spinal cord. The medicine is injected into CSF to enable it to work on the central nervous system (CNS). This route will bypass the blood–brain barrier.

Age

Children's bodies are fundamentally different from those of adults, so there will be several differences to how their bodies deal with medicines. For example, children have less fat and muscle mass, so medicines delivered by the topical or subcutaneous route may have faster absorption rates. In the early stages of life the liver is less effective at metabolising medicines. The kidneys are also less able to excrete medicines in the first six weeks or so of life. The ageing process itself does not have an effect on the absorption of medicines. However, older adults may have underlying health conditions that impact on absorption rates. For example, if they have a gastrointestinal disease this may affect how the medicine is absorbed in the stomach. Older adults may also be taking several medicines at a time, some of which may interfere with the absorption of other medicines. Older adults have less **albumin** (a protein) in their blood. Therefore, less of the medicine undergoes protein binding and so more of the medicine is in the circulating blood and tissues. As a higher concentration of the medicine is present, this will produce an increased pharmacological effect. Enzymatic activity in the liver lessens with advancing age and this can lead to medicines not being metabolised, which again will cause increased levels of the medicine in the body. These increased levels could be dangerous to the patient. Medicines may also accumulate in the body due to a decrease in renal function, where medicines are not able to be fully excreted in the urine.

Size and body weight

Patients who are heavier may need larger doses of a medicine to bring about the desired effect. This is because they have more body tissue to absorb the medicine. Depending on the route of administration, this will also impact on the absorption of the medicine. For example, a medicine administered via the subcutaneous route will be absorbed much more slowly in a patient with excess adipose fat.

Gender

Physical differences between men and women will also affect absorption of medicines. For example, women have more fat cells than men and for medicines that deposit in fat the absorption rate will be slower.

Ethnicity/genetics

It is also known that genetic factors play a role in how a medicine works. For example, Herceptin, a medicine used in the treatment of breast cancer, is only effective for patients who have a particular **receptor** called human epidermal growth factor receptor 2 (HER2) in their genetic make-up. Some ethnicities are found to have higher rates of enzymatic activity in the liver than others and are therefore able to metabolise medicines more quickly. Those who have faster rates are known as fast **acetylators** and those with slower rates are called slow acetylators.

Nutritional status

Malnutrition (which includes anorexia and obesity) can affect how a medicine is absorbed. Anorexic patients have less body mass, which leads to less fat and muscle and fewer proteins. Medicine molecules need to bind with proteins to assist in the delivery of the medicine to its site of action. Obese patients have larger fat deposits and this may affect how some medicines are absorbed.

Medical conditions

There are numerous medical conditions that will impact on the absorption rate of medicines. These conditions are largely focused on the gastrointestinal system. For example, if a patient has diarrhoea, the absorption process will be speeded up as bowel motility is increased. Similarly, if a patient has undergone a bowel resection, part of the bowel used for absorption is no longer there. This may result in some or even all of the medicine not being absorbed.

Medicine product

Some medicines are designed to be absorbed more slowly than others. To stop them from being absorbed too quickly, they will be manufactured with an **enteric coated shell**, which is a protective cover that is able to resist breakdown by the stomach enzymes. The cover is designed to start disintegrating once the medicine enters the small intestine, which is less acidic than the stomach.

Psychological factors

How a patient feels about their medicine may also impact on how it actually works. If a patient believes that their medicine is beneficial to them, it is more likely to be effective. This is known as the **placebo** effect – *placebo* is Latin for 'I will please'. It is thought that physiological processes occur in the body that bring about a desired effect when the medicine is taken. For example, if morphine is given to a patient, the brain will release its own **endogenous** substances (natural pain killers) and the effect of the morphine in relieving the patient's pain may be greater than if the patient believed it would not help to reduce their pain. The use of placebos will be discussed in more detail in Chapter 4.

Pharmacodynamics

Pharmacodynamics is concerned with the effects a medicine has on the body. Ideally, we would want a medicine to act just enough to produce the desired effect. Unfortunately, side effects are often seen with many medicines. This is partly due to the chemical structure of the medicine and how the body is able to deal with it. The premise of pharmacodynamics is that a medicine is only able to work provided it stimulates a reaction with a living organism. The action of a particular medicine is dependent on proteins. These are present in the body in the form of receptors, enzymes and **ion channels**.

Receptors

It is thought that medicines may act at specific areas either on the cell membrane or within the cell. These specific areas are termed as receptors, which are proteins. These receptors react with certain chemicals in the body such as **hormones** and **neurotransmitters** to influence cell activity. Medicines that target receptors are called **agonists** or **antagonists**. Medicines bind with such receptors to either stimulate or prevent a response. Medicines that stimulate a response are termed as agonists and those that prevent a response are termed antagonists. Any chemical that binds to a protein receptor is termed a **ligand**. Receptors also have two properties – **specificity** and **affinity** (see below) – and medicines are designed to fit a receptor that can recognise it. Receptors are three-dimensional structures that will only allow a medicine that fits it exactly to attach (a bit like a key in a lock). The actions of a medicine are largely affected by how much of the medicine reaches a receptor and whether there is affinity (attraction) between the medicine and the receptor on the cell wall.

Agonists

Agonist medicines bind to receptors to bring about a physiological response. An example is insulin. If a patient is administered this medicine it will bind to specific insulin receptors to change the **permeability** of the cell membrane. This will enable glucose to move into the cell. Insulin is the hormone responsible for controlling the levels of glucose in the blood. As the dose of the agonist increases, the number of receptors activated also increases, thereby increasing the amount of insulin and the consequential effects on blood glucose levels. The amount of medicine administered will eventually reach a threshold where all the relevant receptors will be activated and there will be no more effect from the medicine. This is the reason why medicines are prescribed in a specific range of doses.

Antagonists

Antagonist medicines bind to receptors to prevent a physiological response. An example is diphenhydramine, which is an antihistamine used in the treatment of allergies. This medicine will bind to a histamine receptor to block the production of histamine. Therefore, physiological reactions associated with allergic reactions such as swelling or even anaphylaxis (see Chapter 5) will subside or be prevented from occurring. Like agonists, once a dose threshold has been reached there will be no more receptors to block. If increased doses of histamine are given, side effects will occur such as increased drowsiness.

Partial agonists

Partial agonists are medicines that are able to both stimulate and block a physiological response. How they work depends on the dosage of the medicine or the duration of its action. Its effects are less than those of agonists.

Affinity and specificity

Receptors are able to recognise specific chemical compounds present in the body, food and medicines. They will bind to these chemicals selectively. They also have the ability to bind tightly to certain chemicals they recognise. This means that the receptor has a high attraction or affinity to the chemical (in this case the medicine). The higher the affinity, the greater is the efficacy of the medicine and the lower the dose required to bring about a desired effect. Specificity means that some drugs can be designed specifically to bind with particular receptors.

Enzymes

Medicines can also exert their effect by disturbing the way in which enzymes act as catalysts for a variety of chemical reactions. Some medicines are termed **enzyme inhibitors** because they will bind to enzymes to decrease or stop the activity of a particular enzyme. For example, **ACE (angiotensin converting enzyme) inhibitors** such as enalapril, used to treat **hypertension**, work by inhibiting the conversion of angiotensin 1 to angiotensin 2. This prevents vasoconstriction of the blood vessels. It also inhibits the release of aldosterone, which subsequently causes less retention of sodium with a resultant fall in a patient's blood pressure. Other medicines work on enzymes to increase their activity. **Enzyme activators** are not as common as enzyme inhibitors.

Ion channels

Ions experience difficulty crossing cell membranes and entering cells. They therefore enter or leave cells via small pores created by ion channels. Ion channels can open or close in response to a stimulus, such as a medicine. Examples of medicines that will close an ion channel are **calcium channel blockers**, such as verapamil, which is used to slow down the heart rate.

Activity 3.6   *Evidence-based practice and research*

Refer back to the start of the chapter, where we met Mary Santini, the patient admitted to A & E after sustaining a fractured left neck of femur. Using the knowledge you have acquired, consider the pharmacodynamic and pharmacokinetic factors that may have contributed to Mary's death.

An outline answer is provided at the end of the chapter.

Chapter summary

This chapter has covered the basic principles of pharmacology. You should now understand how medicines affect the body (pharmacodynamics) and how medicines are absorbed, distributed, metabolised and excreted from the body (pharmacokinetics). Factors influencing these processes have also been discussed. Using this knowledge will enable you to have a better understanding of how the medicines you administer to your patients work. It should also help you to explain to your patients why they may experience some side effects with their medicines. Knowing your patients and understanding why medicines have to be taken as per instructed will ensure that side effects and adverse reactions are recognised, minimised and dealt with promptly. Completion of the activities will assist you in achieving the necessary proficiency for entry into your field of practice programme.

Activities: brief outline answers

Activity 3.1 Use of medicines (page 71)

Medicine	Its use	Why it is prescribed	Prophylactic or therapeutic?
BCG vaccine	Prevent development of tuberculosis (TB).	Mia has immigrated from a country where TB is prevalent.	Prophylactic
Paracetamol	Treatment of mild to moderate pain. Can also be used to reduce a high body temperature.	Rory may have a high temperature or he may have experienced pain.	Therapeutic
Citalopram	Treatment of depression or panic disorders.	The dose Jordan has been prescribed indicates that she is suffering from either depression or panic attacks.	Therapeutic
Cefuroxime	This is an antibiotic used in the treatment of, or to prevent, infection.	Jacob has been prescribed it to reduce the risk of him developing an infection post-operatively. If he was to develop an infection, this could impact on the viability of his artificial knee. The first dose is usually administered at the time of his anaesthetic, with the second dose administered 8 hours later and the third dose after 16 hours.	Prophylactic

Activity 3.2 Routes of administration (page 72)

Route	Advantages	Disadvantages
Intravenous	Quick administration; direct entry into circulation; rapid onset of action; no needles.	Requires peripheral cannula; risk of bloodstream infection.
Intramuscular	Quick administration; rapid onset of action.	Painful; needle phobias.
Subcutaneous	Quick administration.	Painful; needle phobias; slow onset of action.
Intrathecal	Quick administration; rapid onset of action; direct access to brain and nerves.	Painful; patient needs to keep very still during administration stage.
Intravesical	Local site of action; less likely to be unpleasant side effects associated with systemic action.	Urethral catheter required; invasive procedure; risk of urinary tract infections.
Transdermal/topical	Easy; self-application.	Messy; slow onset of action.

Rectal	Useful for those patients who are nil-by-mouth or suffering with nausea.	Slow onset of action; invasive procedure; may be uncomfortable.
Vagina	Local site of action; less likely to experience unpleasant side effects associated with systemic action.	Invasive procedure; may be uncomfortable; slow onset of action.
Oral	Easy; self-administration; medicine can be taken in a variety of different forms, e.g. tablets, liquids.	Tablets hard to swallow; unpleasant taste; difficulties with nausea and vomiting.
Sublingual/buccal	Easy; self-administration.	Unpleasant taste; patient needs education regarding not swallowing medicine.
Nasal	Easy; self-administration.	Irritant to nasal passages; unpleasant taste.
Inhalation	Easy; self-administration.	May leave unpleasant taste; good technique required.
Aural/ocular	Local site of action only.	Precision required for application of medicine.

Activity 3.3 Medicines for different routes (page 73)

There is a whole host of medicines that are administered by the various routes. The table below lists only a few. Please refer to a BNF for your particular patient group.

Route	**Medicine**
Intravenous	Benzylpenicillin
Intramuscular	Haloperidol
Subcutaneous	Heparin
Intrathecal	Bupivacaine
Intravesical	Doxorubicin
Transdermal/topical	Hydrocortisone
Rectal	Diclofenac
Vagina	Clotrimazole
Oral	Paracetamol
Sublingual/buccal	Glyceryl Trinitrate
Nasal	Ephedrine Hydrochloride
Inhalation	Salbutamol
Aural	Neomycin Sulphate
Ocular	Pilocarpine

Activity 3.4 Bioavailability (page 75)

(a) This means that all of a medicine that is given by the intravenous route remains active when it enters the circulatory system.

(b) This happens because the absorption process is bypassed as the medicine enters directly into the bloodstream and does not go through the process of first pass effect or metabolism.

Activity 3.5 Half-life of medicines (page 77)

6mg

Activity 3.6 Pharmacodynamic and pharmacokinetic factors (page 83)

Mary may have had impaired renal function, due to her age and dehydration. This would impact on the kidneys' ability to excrete both the diclofenac and the lithium effectively. Lithium has a relatively long half-life of about 22 hours. Lithium is mainly absorbed in the gastrointestinal tract and only very small amounts of lithium are metabolised. Therefore, most of it is freely circulating in the blood. This half-life would be extended if Mary had renal impairment. Most lithium is excreted via the kidneys. Non-steroidal anti inflammatory medicines such as diclofenac slow down the excretion of lithium. This causes an increase of lithium levels in the blood. Toxicity of lithium can lead to relatively mild symptoms such as diarrhoea and vomiting, and to life-threatening conditions such as renal failure, coma and even death.

Knowledge review

Now that you've worked through the chapter, how would you rate your knowledge of the following topics?

	Good	Adequate	Poor
1. Principles of pharmacokinetics. 2. Principles of pharmacodynamics. 3. Factors affecting pharmacokinetics. 4. Reducing adverse reactions.			

Where you're not confident in your knowledge of a topic, what will you do next?

Further reading

Clancy, J and McVicar, A (2009) *Physiology and Anatomy for Nurses and Healthcare Practitioners: A homeostatic approach*, 3rd edition. London: Hodder Arnold.

This is a useful accompaniment to pharmacology. Section 2 of this book provides a comprehensive overview of cell physiology and cell metabolism, both of which play vital roles in the pharmacology of medicines.

Greenstein, B and Gould, D (2004) *Trounce's Clinical Pharmacology for Nurses*, 17th edition. Oxford: Elsevier.

This is an easy-to-read book focusing on the principles of pharmacology. It also explores the use of medicines in relation to body systems and classes of medicines.

Karch, AM (2008) *Focus on Nursing Pharmacology*, 4th edition. Philadelphia, PA: Lippincott Williams and Wilkins.

This is a comprehensive textbook featuring an introduction to pharmacology. It also discusses medicines in relation to body systems.

Useful websites

www.bnf.org/bnf

This is home to the online *British National Formulary* where information on clinical conditions, medicines and their preparations can be reviewed. Please note, user registration is required, although this is free of charge.

www.bnfc.org/bnfc

This provides access to the online *British National Formulary for Children* where information on clinical conditions, medicines and their preparations can be reviewed. Please note, user registration is required, although this is free of charge.

www.merck.com/mmhe

This site gives access to The Merck Manuals online medical library. It provides a very useful and easy-to-navigate resource covering material on pharmacodynamics and pharmacokinetics in depth. No registration or subscription is required.

What is Evidence-Based Practice?

Barker, J., and Linsley, P.

Learning Outcomes

By the end of the chapter you will be able to:

- define evidence-based practice;
- understand how evidence-based practice came into being;
- discuss the pros and cons of evidence-based practice;
- identify the components of evidence-based practice and the skills associated with it;
- consider why your practice needs to be evidence-based.

INTRODUCTION

Evidence-based practice (EBP) is now a well-established but not necessarily understood concept in health and social care. Many terms are used in relation to EBP – evidence-based nursing, evidence-based nursing practice, evidence-based medicine, evidence-based decision making and evidence-based healthcare. Essentially, they are the same thing, just different terminology being applied to different professions and settings. Whilst the term continues to be developed and refined there are a number of definitions of EBP to help guide the clinician (Porter and O'Halloran, 2012). Perhaps the best known and accepted of these is that by Sackett et al. (1996) who defined EBP as:

> The conscientious, explicit, and judicious use of current best practice in making decisions about the care of individual patients. The practice of evidence based medicine means integrating individual clinical experience with best available external clinical evidence from systematic research. (Sackett et al., 1996: 71)

This definition, whilst proving popular, has been criticised, as it seemingly ignores the contribution that patients play in the decision-making process. Muir Gray (1997) sought to address this short fall in thinking by building on the work of Sackett and his team and put forward this definition of EBP in response:

> Evidence based practice is an approach to decision making in which the clinician uses the best evidence available, in consultation with the patient, to decide upon the option which suits the patient best (Muir Gray, 1997: 3)

The above definition highlights the need to consult with the patient and involve them in decisions about their own health and wellbeing. It also takes into account patients' preferences, including their wish to avoid risks associated with interventions. Indeed Sackett and his team (2000: 1) reviewed and developed a simpler but more telling definition of EBP in response to Gray's work, and defined EBP as:

> The integration of the best research evidence with clinical expertise and patient values.

This notion of patient involvement is echoed in more contemporary definitions of EBP, for instance:

> Evidence based practice entails making decisions about how to promote health or provide care by integrating the best available evidence with practitioner expertise and other resources, and with the characteristics, state, needs, values and preferences of those who will be affected. (Peile, 2004: 103)

EBP is more than using findings from research. It is the integration of this **evidence** and knowledge to current clinical practice, for use at a local level, ensuring that patients receive the best quality care available. Implicit in such discussions is the message that healthcare, wherever it is delivered, must be based on good, sound, evidence. In days gone by, when asked why something was done in a particular way, a nurse's mantra was 'Sister says so' or 'We've always done it this way'. It has been suggested that historically clinical issues have been based on a form of craft-based knowledge or 'habit, intuition and sometimes plain old guessing' (Gawande, 2003: 7). This is no longer sufficient and there is an expectation that strong evidence must underpin nurses' practice. Conceptually, EBP promotes the value of utilising knowledge from many sources and, through critical evaluation of the data from these sources, making an informed decision (in conjunction with the patient) on the most effective course of treatment/intervention (Gambrill, 2007).

Activity 1.1

Reflect on the evidence that underpins your clinical practice. Where does this come from? How do you keep up-to-date with current developments and changes in practice? How easy is it to make changes to your practice using new evidence?

Whilst the importance of research in the delivery of nursing care has always been emphasised, the idea of evidence-based practice is seen as focusing the minds of those involved in care delivery on the use of appropriate evidence. Nurses need to be certain that their practice is current and up-to-date and that they are doing the best for those that they look after. EBP provides healthcare professionals with the means by which to explore practice and address any shortfall in the care that they give. The question then becomes one of how can the evidence be located? With the advent of the internet, busy healthcare professionals can no longer hope to keep up-to-date with all the possible sources of evidence, nor can they read and critically appraise all of the articles relevant to their practice. This is why an evidence-based approach to practice is needed. EBP provides a systematic framework for reviewing the evidence to underpin practice. There is a range of such evidence that can inform practice – personal experience and reflection literature, research, policy, guidelines, clinical expertise and audit (Dale, 2005) – all of which have their place within EBP and will be explored further in the various chapters of this book.

WHERE DID THE IDEA OF EBP COME FROM?

Professor Archie Cochrane, a British epidemiologist, is most frequently credited with starting the EBP movement. In his book *Effectiveness and Efficiency: Random Reflections on the Health Service* (Cochrane, 1972) he criticised the medical profession for not using appropriate evidence to guide and direct medical practice and challenged medicine to produce an evidence base. He argued there was a need to ensure treatment was delivered in the most effective manner and to ensure that available evidence was used in a consistent way.

When Cochrane talked of evidence, he meant randomised control trials (RCTs), which he viewed as providing the most reliable evidence on which to base medical care. RCTs are a form of research which uses experimental designs to identify the effectiveness of interventions. The use of systematic reviews, which summarise the findings of a number of RCTs looking at similar areas of interest, was suggested as the 'gold standard' of the scientific evidence on which to base medical interventions.

The medical profession responded to Cochrane's challenge by creating the Cochrane Centre for systematic reviews, which opened in 1992 in Oxford. The Cochrane Collaboration was founded in 1993, consisting of international review groups (currently encompassing more than 28,000 people in over 100 countries) covering a range of clinical areas and producing systematic reviews. These reviews are published electronically, updated regularly and there are now over 4600 available.

Visit the Cochrane Collaboration website (www.cochrane.org). How easy is the site to navigate? What sort of evidence does the site provide? How useful is the evidence? Could you readily relate/make use of this evidence as part of your clinical practice?

Activity 1.2

Whilst the underpinning principles of evidence-based medicine (EBM) were hotly debated, the medical profession in general began to accept the idea, and 1995 saw the first issue of the journal *Evidence-Based Medicine for Primary Care and Internal Medicine*, published by the British Medical Journal Group. In 2007 EBM was identified as one of 15 major milestones in the development of medical practice since 1840 (*BMJ*, 2007). Nursing, emulating its medical counterpart, began to explore the notion of basing its practice on reliable sources of evidence, which resulted in the journal *Evidence-Based Nursing* first published in 1998.

SOCIAL AND POLITICAL DRIVERS OF EBP

Scott and McSherry (2008) suggested a number of social and political factors facilitated the emergence of the emphasis on evidence at this time. The availability of 'knowledge' via the internet and other sources brought into being 'expert patients' – well-educated and informed individuals who accessed information relating to health and illness. Expectations of these expert patients were that healthcare professions would be aware of and use up-to-date information/research in their delivery of care and treatment. There was no longer a willingness simply to accept treatment or care purely on the advice of a doctor or nurse.

The concept of EBP was also seen as attractive by governments and health service administrators because of its potential to provide cost-effective and clinically effective care (McSherry et al., 2006). In the mid-1990s the UK government of the day identified that quality assurance was to be placed at the forefront of the NHS modernisation agenda. Two White Papers – *The New NHS: Modern and Dependable* (Department of Health [DH], 1997) and *A First Class Service: Quality in the New NHS* (DH, 1998) – outlined the plans for promoting **clinical effectiveness** and introducing **clinical governance**. These promoted systems to ensure quality improvement mechanisms were adopted at all levels of healthcare provision. Central to clinical governance were concepts of risk management and promoting clinical excellence. (See Figure 1.1 for an outline of the clinical governance framework.)

Clinical effectiveness was defined by the NHS Executive (1996) as 'the extent to which specific clinical interventions when deployed in the field for a particular patient or population, do what they are intended to do, that is maintain and improve health and secure the greatest possible health gain'. This definition continues to underpin the current Department of Health approach to clinical effectiveness (DH, 2007a), with the various stages of the process being identified as:

- the development of best practice guidelines;
- the transfer of knowledge into practice through education, audit and practice development;
- the evaluation of the impact of guidelines through audit and patient feedback.

Put simply, clinical effectiveness can be seen as identifying appropriate evidence in the form of research, clinical guidelines, systematic reviews and national standards; changing

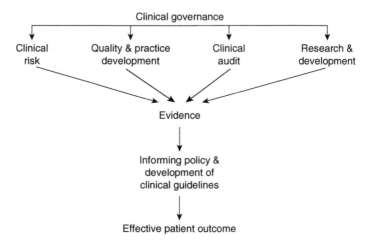

Figure 1.1   Representation of the elements of clinical governance

practice to include this evidence; and evaluating the impact of any change and making the necessary adjustments through the use of clinical audit and patient feedback/service evaluation. Reading and understanding research, being aware of current policies and procedures, and knowing about the recommendations and standards in practice are all part of the nurse's role (Royal College of Nursing, 2007). Table 1.1 provides an overview of the key aspects of research, **clinical audit** and **service evaluation**.

Two organisations were created aimed at promoting an evidence-based approach to healthcare, which are known today as the National Institute for Health and Care Excellence (NICE) and the Care Quality Commission (CQC). These bodies provided guidance for healthcare managers and practitioners and were charged with ensuring this guidance was followed in England and Wales. In Scotland the Health Technology Board fulfilled a similar purpose. Clinical governance was introduced to ensure health-care was both efficient and effective; healthcare professionals were expected to show EBP supported all aspects of care delivery and service developments. It was hoped that the introduction of these measures would result in a shift in organisational culture from one that was reactive, responding as issues arise, to one with a proactive ethos, where the healthcare offered was known to be effective and therefore avoided unforeseen outcomes.

NICE and the now CQC have continued to develop strategies to promote clinical effectiveness; the former through initiatives such as 'How to...' guides, quality standards and supporting a resource known as 'NHS Evidence'. The NHS Evidence site provides access to various forms of evidence which may be of use in clinical practice and provides examples of best practice. The CQC was charged with ensuring the safety and quality of care through inspection and assessment of all healthcare provision. The NHS Institute for Innovation and Improvement was set up in 2006 with a remit to support the implementation of service improvement initiatives within the NHS (although this was subsequently disolved).

Table 1.1   Research, audit and service evaluation

Research	Service evaluations*	Clinical audit
The attempt to derive generalisable new knowledge including studies that aim to generate hypotheses as well as studies that aim to test them	Designed and conducted solely to define or judge current care	Designed and conducted to produce information to inform delivery of best care
Quantitative research – designed to test a hypothesis. Qualitative research – identifies/explores themes following established methodologies	Designed to answer: 'What standard does this service achieve?'	Designed to answer: 'Does this service reach a predetermined standard?'
Addresses clearly defined questions, aims and objectives	Measures a current service without reference to a standard	Measures against a standard
Quantitative research – may involve evaluating or comparing interventions, particularly new ones Qualitative research – usually involves studying how intervention and relationships are experienced	Involves an intervention in use only. The choice of treatment is that of the clinician and patient according to guidance, professional standards and/or patient preferences	Involves an intervention in use only. The choice of treatment is that of the clinician and patient according to guidance, professional standards and/or patient preferences
Usually involves collecting data that are additional to those for routine care but may include data collected routinely. May involve treatments, samples or investigations additional to routine care	Usually involves analysis of existing data but may include administration of interview or questionnaire	Usually involves analysis of existing data but may include administration of interview or questionnaire
Quantitative research – study design may involve allocating patients to intervention groups Qualitative research – uses a clearly defined sampling framework underpinned by conceptual or theoretical justifications	No allocation to intervention: the health professional and patient have chosen intervention before service evaluation	No allocation to intervention: the health professional and patient have chosen intervention before audit
May involve randomisation	No randomisation	No randomisation
Normally requires Research Ethics Committees (REC) review	Does not require REC review	Does not require REC review

*Service development and quality improvement may fall into this category

Source: Defining Research (Health Research Authority, 2009).

Identify one condition/disease you have come across recently in clinical practice. Visit the NICE website (www.nice.org.uk) and locate the NICE guidance and NHS evidence available in relation to your chosen condition/disease. Now ask the same questions you did of the Cochrane database: How easy is the site to navigate? What sort of evidence does the site provide? How useful is the evidence? Could you readily relate/make use of this evidence as part of your clinical practice?

Activity 1.3

WHY DOES YOUR PRACTICE NEED TO BE EVIDENCE BASED?

The need for frontline staff to be empowered to deliver a quality service is a major aspect of contemporary healthcare policy. As Craig and Pearson (2007) have already identified, few would disagree with the ideas underpinning EBP – namely, that care should be of the highest standard and delivered in the most effective way. Indeed practising without any 'evidence' to guide actions amounts to little more than providing care that is based on trial and error, which would not be advocated. However, as identified above, care is not always based on the best evidence, with Greenhalgh (2006) suggesting that many of the decisions made in healthcare are based on four main sources of information:

1. *Anecdotal information.* Here it is considered that 'it worked in situation X so it must be appropriate to (the similar) situation Y'. However, as Greenhalgh points out, while situations may seem very similar, patient responses are often very different.
2. *Press cuttings information.* Here changes are made to practice in response to reading one article or editorial, without critically appraising and considering the applicability of those results to the specific setting.
3. *Consensus statements.* Here a group of 'experts' will identify the best approaches based on their experiences/beliefs. Whilst clinical expertise does have a place in EBP, it does not operate without some problems. For example, clinical wisdom once held (and to a certain extent still does hold) that bed rest was the most appropriate form of treatment for acute lower back pain. However, research in 1986 demonstrated that this is potentially harmful.
4. *Cost minimisation.* Here the limited resources available within a healthcare setting will often result in choosing the cheapest option in an effort to spread resources as widely as possible. However, EBP can ensure the most effective use of limited and pressurised resources. Whilst certain types of care may appear more expensive on the surface, if these prove more effective, they may turn out to be cheaper in the long run.

Despite widespread recognition of the need for nursing practice to be based on sound evidence, frontline staff experience considerable challenges to implementing evidence-based care at an individual and organisational level. In particular, frontline nurses have difficulty interpreting research findings and although willing to use research they often lack the skills to do so. Perhaps part of the problem related to nursing developing an EBP ethos is that nursing is often considered as more of an art than a science and as such certain types of evidence are valued above others, such as expert opinion and practice experience. However, Polit and Beck (2008: 4) identified that any nursing action must be 'clinically appropriate, cost effective and result in a positive outcome for clients'. The complexities of healthcare, and the uncertainty of people's responses to and experiences of different types of interventions, require that full consideration is given to all available evidence.

Patients are likely to know a great deal about their own health needs and to expect health professionals to base care decisions on the most up-to-date and clinically relevant information. There is also an expectation that professionals will be able to comment in an informed way on any research reported in the media and identify its relevance to an individual's health needs. Miller and Forrest (2001) proposed that the ability to ensure that a professional's knowledge and skills remain current increases their professional credibility; allows them to be an important source of information to those in their care as well as colleagues; and enables all professionals involved in care delivery to make well-informed decisions. It has also been suggested that EBP can foster a lifelong learning approach – an essential requirement in the health professions if staff are to remain effective in rapidly changing healthcare environments (see Figure 1.2 below).

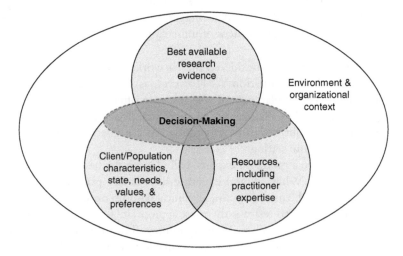

Figure 1.2   The integrated elements of EBP

Source: Council for Training in Evidence-Based Behavioral Practice (2008).

CONCERNS ABOUT EBP

Evidence-based approaches are not without their problems. As Davies et al. (2007: 26) identified, it has both 'enthusiastic supporters and vociferous detractors'. Melnyk and

Fineout-Overholt (2005) suggested that EBP is viewed by many as simply another term for research utilisation. It has also been argued elsewhere that the value of research has been over-emphasised to the detriment of clinical judgement and person-centred approaches, while others point to a lack of evidence to support the notion that EBP improves health outcomes.

Kitson (2002) has pointed to an inherent tension between EBP and person-centred approaches. She has argued that clinical expertise is vital in ensuring that patients' experiences and needs are not sidelined in the pursuit of 'best evidence' in the form of research findings and the development of generalised clinical guidelines. Some individuals have suggested that such broad general principles are not applicable to certain aspects of care. Davies et al. (2007) suggested that practitioners often feel that an over-emphasis on EBP inhibits their ability to provide individualised care. Melnyk and Fineout-Overholt (2005) have identified this as a 'cookbook' approach, where a general recipe is followed with no consideration for the specific needs or preferences of individuals. There are concerns also around the ability to have a consensus in relation to the various interpretations available when translating evidence into guidelines and the relevance of these for individual areas of practice. There are also issues related to the updating of evidence and the ability to ensure that the information gathered is current. However, DiCenso et al. (2008) argue that as clinical expertise and decision-making processes are central to EBP, in considering the use of general guidelines both of these processes must be used in the same way with any form of evidence including guidance.

Brady and Lewin (2007) argue that whilst the idea of clinical expertise is readily accepted by most experienced nurses, the majority of those same nurses are often unaware of the latest research in their area of practice. Nurses are generally presented as relying on intuition, tradition and local policies/procedures to guide their practice. There is also a perceived lack of enthusiasm in relation to the implementation of nursing research. Stevens (2004) proposed that healthcare providers frequently do not use current knowledge for a number of reasons, not least of these being the rapidly growing and changing body of research, some of which is difficult to apply to practice directly. As the aim of EBP is to deliver high quality care, nurses need to have an understanding of what the exact elements of EBP are and to then develop the necessary skills and knowledge to enable them to carry this out. Glasziou and Haynes (2005) proposed that some research, essential to the delivery of quality care, will go unrecognised for years and suggested the major barriers to using evidence are time, effort and the skills involved in accessing information from the myriad of data available.

Ingersoll (2000) also argued that focusing EBP on care delivery reflects the differences between it and research. Research concentrates on knowledge discovery whereas in EBP the application of knowledge is central. In addition she has suggested that whilst this emphasis on EBP is a welcome initiative, the wholesale 'lifting' of approaches and methodologies from another discipline such as medicine is not. Nurses need to make sure that the evidence used is relevant to the practice of nursing. There is a traditional view that evidence-based practice should be informed solely through quantitative research. However, Ellis (2010) advocates that it is more about using various forms of information, not just research, to guide and develop practice. Ellis (2010) goes on to note that there is little agreement between professionals as to what constitutes 'good evidence'. While nurses may be motivated to approach practice from an evidence-based perspective, the literature actually suggests that evidence-based practice is rigid and prescriptive, and diminishes any professional autonomy. French (1999) went further to suggest that as EBP is so closely linked with evidence-based medicine (EBM) and its preference for certain types of evidence, there is a danger that this promotes the use of medical knowledge over other forms and therefore leads to a medicalisation of healthcare environments to the detriment of other disciplines. Best evidence in the medical context is often taken to mean quantitative research findings in the form of RCTs. Some have questioned its compatibility with nursing and the other health professions, suggesting instead the use of a more open approach. Dale (2005) proposed that this issue has the potential to create interprofessional conflict, as that which nursing may count as appropriate evidence on which to base practice may be somewhat different from that of the medical profession.

Perhaps the biggest concern with EBP is that healthcare professionals may not have the necessary level of skill to interpret and make use of the evidence that they find. Advances in technology and scientific research possibilities and approaches further compound this. In addition, it is anticipated that there is little time allocated for learning these skills due to the busy and stressful nature of the profession. Healthcare professionals need both the knowledge and skills to make use of the available evidence that is both timely and worthwhile.

WHAT SKILLS ARE NEEDED?

Whilst the idea for evidence-based medicine (EBM) grew out of Cochrane's work, McMaster Medical School in Canada is credited with coining the term in 1980 to describe a particular learning approach used in the school. This approach had four steps (Peile, 2004) and these are as follows:

1. Ask an answerable question.
2. Find the appropriate evidence.
3. Critically appraise that evidence.
4. Apply the evidence to the patient, giving consideration to the individual needs, presentation and context.

In addition to this, Aas and Alexanderson (2011) suggested a 'Five A' step process (see Figure 1.3). For the purposes of this book the authors have added an additional sixth stage, that of assess; this sits at the start of the cycle whereby the clinician identifies a problem and the need for further information and action. EBP should be all about doing – tackling real problems in clinical practice.

The most important element of the cycle is the asking of the question. The question should focus on the problem, the intervention and the outcome. Herbert et al. (2005: 12) expanded the notion of the clinical question to include:

- effects of the intervention;
- patients' experiences;
- the course of the condition, or life-course (prognosis);
- the accuracy of diagnostic test or assessments.

Evidence-based questions are usually articulated in terms of: What is the evidence for the effectiveness of x (the intervention) for y (the outcome) in a patient with z (the problem or diagnosis)?

Figure 1.3   A 'Five A' plus one step approach to EBP

Taking the above together, there is a need to develop particular skills and knowledge related to:

- the ability to identify what counts as appropriate evidence;
- forming a question to enable you to find evidence for consideration;
- developing a search strategy;
- finding the evidence;
- critically appraising the evidence;
- drawing on clinical expertise;
- issues concerned with patient preference;
- application to the context of care delivery;
- putting the evidence into practice.

Consider the list of skills identified above as associated with EBP. Choose three areas that you feel you have most difficulty with and undertake a SWOT analysis in relation to each one using the grid in Appendix 1.

Activity 1.4

Summary

- EBP is a global phenomenon which promotes the idea of best practice, clinical effectiveness and quality care and involves an integration of evidence, clinical expertise, patient preferences and the clinical context of care delivery to inform clinical decision making.
- EBP focuses on critically appraising evidence to support care delivery rather than on research to discover new knowledge.
- The emergence of the expert patient has given rise to the need for health professionals to ensure they are up to date and their care is based on best evidence available.
- Government initiatives have promoted EBP as a way of providing both clinically effective and cost-effective healthcare.
- Various steps are associated with the EBP process – forming a question; finding evidence; critically appraising the evidence; integration of evidence into practice.
- The knowledge and skills associated with EBP are an essential component of nursing practice.

FURTHER READING

Cranston, M. (2002) 'Clinical effectiveness and evidence-based practice', *Nursing Standard*, 16(24): 39–43. This article provides a concise account of the meaning of clinical governance, the place of clinical effectiveness within this concept and the drive towards EBP.

Greenhalgh, T. (2014) *How to Read a Paper: The Basics of Evidence-Based Medicine* (5th edn). Oxford: Wiley-Blackwell/BMJ Books.

Rycroft-Malone, J., Seers, K., Titchen, A., Harvey, G., Kitson, A. and McCormack, B. (2004) 'What counts as evidence in evidence-based practice?', *Journal of Advanced Nursing*, 47(1): 81–90. This article gives a clear overview of the evidence-based movement and issues related to the nature of evidence.

Spruce, L. (2015) 'Back to basics: implementing evidence-based practice' *Jan*, 101(1): 106–12.

E-RESOURCES

Cochrane Collaboration: promotes, supports and prepares systematic reviews, mainly in relation to effectiveness. www.cochrane.org/

Joanna Briggs Institute: promotes evidence-based healthcare through systematic reviews and a range of resources aimed at promoting evidence synthesis, transfer and utilisation. www.joanna briggs.org

National Institute for Health and Care Excellence: provides guidance and other products to enable and support health professionals deliver evidence-based care. www.nice.org.uk

13 Critical Appraisal of Health and Social Care Research

Moule, P.

LEARNING OUTCOMES

On completion of this chapter the reader should be able to:

- appreciate the need to critically appraise research and evidence
- identify the strengths and weaknesses of qualitative and quantitative research
- critically appraise a research journal article.

KEY CONCEPTS

- critical appraisal
- critiquing framework

INTRODUCTION

Individuals working in a health and social care setting need to be able to critically appraise research for many different reasons. In Chapter 1 the term 'research literate' was used as a basis for discussion. This discussion centred on the need to be able to appreciate the skills and knowledge required to understand and use research to provide a high-quality service. A result of having these skills and knowledge is the ability to be able to read and critically appraise the many research articles in journals.

Evaluative and critical skills are used in our everyday life. Every time a decision is made in the supermarket regarding the brand of toothpaste or shampoo we buy, we are influenced by sources, such as marketing, the media, our experiences, family tradition, the cost, and so on. So these skills are not new but they do need to be developed to be applied to the world of research.

Before critically appraising research it is important to recognise that this does not necessarily mean being negative. Critical appraisal, sometimes referred to as critiquing, is more about looking for strengths and weaknesses in a study and making a balanced judgment about what has been presented in the publication. Moule and Goodman (2014) suggest that research studies are not perfect and that all should be critically appraised. Being critical involves making informed judgments about the merit of a piece of research, appraising the good and bad points of research. The process should be objective and balanced and consider the significance of the research to the field.

Developing critical appraisal skills has become crucial to all professionals and students regardless of their working background. Many courses ask for a research critique or demonstration of critical appraisal skills within their assessment schemes. Some institutions of higher education include a **literature review** in their dissertation assessment which will require critically appraising many pieces of research in trying to answer a **research question**. Acquiring the skills needed to critically appraise published research depends on practice and thoughtful reading of research articles and reports. At first the language can appear alien, and sometimes the results appear to be written in a format requiring high levels of statistical knowledge to interpret. This may leave the reader feeling bewildered.

A worthwhile introduction to reading research and developing critical appraisal skills is to read several research articles which all address the same (or similar) topic. This topic should be one in which the reader is particularly interested either for an assignment or because the articles relate to a specific subject. It is surprising how an interest in a specific subject helps overcome some of the immediate challenges of reading research. The other point to recognise is that not all parts of the research paper need be understood in the first couple of readings. However, gradually, as knowledge is increased, more and more will be understood. One approach is described by Maslin-Prothero (2010) that suggests there are three levels of reading: scanning, in-depth reading and inferring. An initial skim read to decide on the section of the paper to concentrate on, is followed by in-depth reading of these sections, inferring by thinking about context and questioning the material. Appendix 2 includes the stages of critical appraisal.

In the final stages of reading a research article various questions can be asked at each stage of the research process. This helps identify both strengths and weaknesses of the study; it also breaks down the task into 'manageable chunks'. The rest of this chapter looks at various parts of the research process and identifies areas that the reader could question. A critical appraisal framework is found in Appendix 3. More detailed frameworks can be found in Moule and Goodman (2014) and on the website: www.casp-uk.net.

SETTING THE RESEARCH SCENE

In the first part of the article the author should identify the purpose of the study and why the research needs to be completed. This might be because a problem was identified or the researcher had a question they wanted to answer. Whatever the reason, all research should contribute to knowledge, either by identifying more questions to ask or by adding findings to the current body of knowledge. There needs to be some reassurance from the research that the study will fulfil this requirement and that the researcher is appropriately prepared to be conducting the study. There should be a clear purpose for the research, with a researchable problem.

Unless the researcher is using **grounded theory** and is purposely not looking at the related literature until later in the study, the literature review should provide a background to the study. In the literature review there should be a comparing and contrasting of the literature, and a critique of it rather than simply a description. The strengths and weaknesses of previous studies should be identified and the dates of the studies should be noted. Although the literature review should include any seminal work on the topic, regardless of its age, there should be an attempt to embrace the most recent work as well.

Developing from the background and literature review, the researcher should establish a focus for the study. In a quantitative study this should be a defined focus often in the form of a **hypothesis** but it might also be a question or an aim (see Chapter 7). If there is a hypothesis it should be seen to emerge from the literature and it must be relevant to the topic being studied. The wording of the hypothesis should be clear and at least two variables identified. It should also be obvious whether the researcher is looking for a relationship between two or more variables or for differences between groups. When appraising a quantitative report where a null hypothesis is tested, the reader should check to see whether a null hypothesis has been used and if the statistical analysis includes a two-tailed test of significance.

In qualitative studies there should be a focus for the study in the form of aims, questions or objectives. These can be scrutinised for their relevance to the research approach and the literature review. In both qualitative and quantitative studies the hypothesis, aims or objectives should be examined to see if they link the previous work completed in this topic area with the research about to be undertaken. By keeping this as a central focus when appraising a study the reader can often discover inconsistencies either with the literature and the approach or with the literature and the design. In order to do this the reader must be familiar with the purpose of research aims, hypotheses and questions.

PRACTICE EXAMPLE

Bobillier Chaumon et al. (2014) considered whether information and communication technology (ICT) could improve the quality of life of elderly adults living in residential home care units. The introduction to the article presents literature that supports the issues, which include the desire and benefits of remaining in one's own home, but the need for residential living by those with dependency issues. The possibilities that ICT might offer to support the elderly living in institutions is proposed and research supporting the impact on quality of life is presented. It is also made clear that there is limited research assessing the psycho-social impacts of ICT on elderly adults living in residential units. The paper then presents three hypotheses supported by the literature presented. These suggest that positive relationships are expected from the implementation and use of technologies in terms of: (1) self-esteem; (2) social integration; and (3) social practices.

When applying the critical appraisal framework (see Appendix 3) the purpose of the study is included in the introduction. Existing knowledge is presented and the rationale for the study is articulated. The three research hypotheses are developed directly from the problem and propose that there will be positive impacts from the implementation of ICT on self-esteem, social integration and social practices such as being more engaged in organised activities. The literature search includes a range of literature, pertinent to the topic area. The review includes up-to-date publications, but also some earlier work from the late 1990s, all tending to support the need for and use of ICT.

The literature search strategy is not included, though this is often the case in a research paper. The review underpins the research hypotheses, and there is evidence to suggest that ICT can impact on the psychosocial wellbeing of the elderly.

COLLECTING THE DATA AND SAMPLE SELECTION

One of the ways the researcher can demonstrate their creativity is in the design of their study. There should be some indication of how they decided on their eventual research design – the influences and the constraints. The researcher should be able to demonstrate that the chosen design is appropriate to the study. For example, Eriksson et al. (2010) used observations to study the interplay between critically ill patients and their next of kin. An alternative might have been to interview relatives and ask them how they interacted with their relatives when visiting them in an intensive care environment. However, the researcher recognised that there might be a difference between what people say they do and how they actually behave. Therefore, interviewing respondents could be seen as an inappropriate research design in this instance, even though it would have been less time consuming and expensive.

The heart of critical appraisal lies in an analysis of the way in which data were collected to solve the research problem. Therefore, in any research critique there should be an examination of alternative strategies to the one presented. Once the design has been examined the data collection methods and the **sample** used need careful scrutiny. The appropriate size of the sample will differ depending on the research approach used. In qualitative studies a small sample is used to gain in-depth information. Even with a small sample, the researcher should justify the selection of individuals. In qualitative studies the researcher might focus on particular respondents because of a specific interest. Particularly in a grounded theory approach the researcher will look at the early data received and use that to guide where they go for subsequent data. This should be explained and rationalised in the study.

When critically appraising **quantitative research** the reader should examine the sample selection very carefully. The whole thrust of studies which attempt to test a theory using a **quantitative data collection** method is the transfer of the results from the sample to the research population. In an attempt to eradicate **bias** the researcher should strive to use a random sample in which everyone in the research population has an equal chance of being included. As most research studies have constraints on them in terms of cost, a totally randomised sample is rarely seen in health and social care research. However, the implications of how the sample was selected should be included and allowed for in any discussion of the results and attempts at generalising the results. The sample should also mimic the research population in terms of its constitution. A quick look at a research study to see how the sample and research population match up in their constituent parts will give the reader an insight into the research. A researcher can only generalise to a research population that matches the sample group. When examining how the sample was selected, it is also important to examine how the participants were recruited and how they gave **informed consent**. There may have been a difference in the participants who participated and those who declined to participate or were not selected.

The data collection method should be described as well as rationalised. There may be an example of the data collection tool in the article and this allows for an examination of the **questionnaire** or interview schedule. Any measuring tool should also be included along with a discussion on how it was tested for **reliability** and validity and how the individuals collecting the data were trained in its use. At this point in the study there might be a description of the pilot study. This should indicate any changes made to the data collection tool and identify any problems the researcher found with the research design. It can take some honesty for the research to identify such problems. If results of the pilot study are not given, the reader is left unsure of what was found and somewhat insecure concerning the data collection methods used.

When evaluating a questionnaire, there needs to be an examination of the types of questions used and their relevance to the approach taken. A qualitative approach will require the interviewer to use open questions, which allow the respondent to explain exactly how they feel/think. The closed questions and measuring scales found in quantitative studies should be examined for their ease of use, their clarity and the clarity of the instructions given for their use. All questions should give respondents an opportunity to add any other thoughts they might have on the subject. In observational studies there should be some indication of the role of the observer and whether it was covert or overt observation and whether the researcher included the effect of researcher presence on any results. The researcher should also detail how the field notes were recorded and when full notes were written up.

PRACTICE EXAMPLE

Yee Chin et al. (2014) undertook a longitudinal survey in Hong Kong, which aimed to detect levels of depression in adults and explore their management. A primary care setting was used. Community doctors were invited to join a research network set up by the study. Doctors were recruited to the network using a postal list of family physicians. Patients were recruited through each doctor's practice using random selection. Each doctor was allocated recruitment days randomly and patients were invited to take part in the study on these days if they met the selection criteria (aged over 18 years, consulting the doctor, had not previously completed the study and were able to understand either English, Cantonese or Mandarin). A coded anonymous survey was completed. This included a Patient Health Questionnaire for self-reported depression, validated for use in primary care; personal data questions adapted from previous studies; and data from the standard data collection tool used by each doctor. A sample calculation was undertaken suggesting 1,540 participants were required. Ethical approval was provided by a number of hospital ethical review boards.

When applying the critical review questions (see Appendix 3), the study had sought and received appropriate ethical review. Patient consent was not discussed in the paper, though in completing and returning the questionnaires the patients were giving implied consent. The method of recruiting the doctors, through invitation to join a network interested in depression, led to a restricted sample. A random sampling process was used to recruit the patients to the study. The sample size had been determined by a sample size calculation. In total, over 10,000 patients were recruited. This equated to a response rate of 81%, as 19% of patients approached to take part declined. The data collection tools used had been previously validated and provided a resource-effective way of capturing data to answer the research questions, from the sample.

There were some limitations of the study design. As stated earlier there was a bias in sampling towards doctors with an interest in mental health, as the sample was taken from network members who had an interest in this area. In addition, whilst a random sampling strategy

(Continued)

(Continued)

was employed, the final sample included a high proportion of patients recruited from Hong Kong island, the least populated area in the region. The screening for depression was based on self-reported measures (the completion of the questionnaire by patients), rather than a clinical diagnosis of depression, which is likely to be more accurate. It is possible that involving doctors with an interest in mental health issues could have affected the results of the study; for example, there may have been improved detection rates and treatments.

RESULTS AND DATA ANALYSIS

Possibly the one aspect that many individuals feel least able to critically appraise is the result and analysis section of a research study. The first area that needs to be examined is the relevance of the results to the research approach taken. If a qualitative approach was taken the results section should demonstrate the emergence of themes from the data. Results should not necessarily offer an explanation but may simply give the reader the findings. In such research reports the researcher should indicate how the results were authenticated. This might involve **triangulation** when two methods could be used to collect the same information, for example, in-depth **interviews** and **observations** of behaviour, or the data may be returned to participants. In the search for themes from qualitative data a colleague might be asked to identify themes from a sample of the responses to see if there is agreement or participants might be involved in validating any emerging themes. The steps that have been taken to demonstrate the **trustworthiness** of the data in a qualitative study should be clear.

If a quantitative approach was taken in which the variables were measured, the results section should give the full range of responses. The beginning of the section should also identify the response rate from any questionnaires used. A description of the results might include pictorial representation, such as pie or bar charts, tables or graphs. These can help the reader get an overview of the results. However, all sections of any diagrams need to be accurately labeled otherwise the reader is left trying to guess what is being referred to. The diagrams should also be clear and able to 'stand alone'. If they require text to explain them they are usually inadequate.

In quantitative analysis the researcher should justify the use of specific statistical tests. The reader should be able to see a clear link between the research approach, the level of measurement gained from the data collection tool and the statistical tests used. The level of significance produced by the statistical testing should also be examined to ensure it is above the 5% ($p<0.05$) level. In health and social care research if there is a greater than 5% probability that the results occurred by chance they are usually deemed non-significant (see Chapter 10).

PRACTICE EXAMPLE

Whiting (2014) wanted to explore parents' experiences of caring for a child with complex health needs. A series of semi-structured individual interviews were completed with 33 families of children with life-limiting conditions, a disability or technology dependence. The interviews were recorded and transcribed to allow verbatim analysis. The findings are presented as key themes with sub-themes relating to each of these. The themes are supported by verbatim quotes from the participants.

The themes emerged from an analysis of the interview transcripts. The interviews had been guided by a very open question, asking what it meant to be the parent of a disabled child. The parents provided their perspectives on this and a process of analysis identified the key themes. Some papers may provide more detail than offered here on aspects such as: the framework for analysis; how this was undertaken; and whether there has been any process of verification or independent review of the analysis.

CONCLUSIONS AND DISCUSSION OF RESULTS

One of the dangers in any research report is that the researcher will attribute more meaning to the results than the analysis will support. In moving from the data analysis section to the interpretation and conclusions the reader should be able to follow a logical progression. Any generalisation made by the researcher should be examined in the light of the results section and (if it is a qualitative study) the sample used. One of the most frequently seen problems with research is that of a small sample used in a quantitative study. For example, following statistical testing and finding significant results the researcher 'ignores' the size and constitution of the sample. The researcher need not be criticised for using a small sample but can be challenged for generalising the results from the sample to the research population without acknowledging the limitations of the study.

If the research has a hypothesis, the interpretation of the results should be examined in the light of it. The hypothesis should be accepted or rejected. The data may or may not support the hypothesis. Remember nothing in research is ever proven (see Chapter 7) as there is always an element of chance in the results, or there may be an error in the data collection methods.

Health and social care research should always address any implications for practice and policy. Ultimately research is about adding to a body of knowledge and that might be about, for example, the individuals who decide to be social workers or it may be about patients' perceptions of the physiotherapy treatment they receive. There should always be an identifiable link between the research undertaken and its practical application.

KEY POINTS

- It is essential that all health and social care workers develop critical appraisal skills.
- In order to understand research papers it is necessary to read them several times.
- All readers of research should use a systematic framework to appraise research papers.

FURTHER READING

Aveyard, H. (2010). *Doing a literature review in health and social care* (2nd edn). Berkshire: Open University Press

Aveyard, H. and Sharp, P. (2013). *A beginner's guide to evidence based practice in health and social care* (2nd edn). Berkshire: Open University Press.

Cottrell, S. (2011). *Critical thinking skills: Developing effective analysis and argument.* Basingstoke: Palgrave Macmillan.

Hart, C. (1998). *Doing a literature review.* London: Sage

WEBSITES

Critical Appraisal Skills Programme (CASP): www.casp-uk.net
NICE Evidence Search: www.evidence.nhs.uk

Assessing Health and Its Determinants

Green, J., Tones, K., Cross, R.
and Woodall, J.

In questions of science, the authority of a thousand is not worth the humble reasoning of a single individual.

Galileo Galilei (1564–1642)

Overview

This chapter considers approaches to assessing the health of communities and identifying the range of factors which impact on health and health inequalities. It will:

- identify the contribution of epidemiology to understanding health and its determinants
- establish the need for alternative perspectives including the lay perspective
- consider salutogenic as opposed to pathogenic explanations of health and ill health
- consider lifestyle and environment as determinants of health
- focus on inequality, social capital and social exclusion, with particular reference to issues of definition and measurement
- examine asset based approaches to assessing health needs.

INTRODUCTION

Green and Kreuter (1991, 2005) trace their initial motivation to develop a planning model for health education to their observation that, in practice, they could frequently discern no apparent reason for choosing the health issue to be addressed, nor the target population to be reached. Furthermore, the intervention strategy selected was also often simply a preferred method of working rather than the most strategic option to achieve defined outcomes. They assert that 'the systematic and critical analysis of priorities and presumed cause–effect relationships can start the planner on the right foot in health promotion today' (1991: 25). What is required, therefore, is:

1. an analysis of health issues/problems
2. prioritization
3. analysis of the determinants.

We are said to be living in an increasingly target-driven culture. It is paramount, therefore, that we remain critically aware of how targets are defined and, indeed, given our earlier discussion of ideology, whether they are appropriate. Health promotion, as noted in Chapter 1, is characterized by its multisectoral nature and the involvement of a variety of different professional groups. Furthermore, a central tenet of health promotion is the importance of involving individuals and communities. The differing ideological positions and values among various professional and lay groups will inevitably influence the way in which the determinants of health and causal factors are defined, the evidence that is accepted to support their existence and the ways in which priorities are identified and framed. We will begin by looking at epidemiological perspectives before considering alternative or complementary approaches.

EPIDEMIOLOGICAL PERSPECTIVES

Epidemiology has been viewed as a 'primary feeder discipline' for health promotion by virtue of its contribution to setting the agenda and its role in driving the system (Tannahill, 1992; Macdonald and Bunton, 2002). As we shall see, there is considerable criticism of over-reliance on epidemiological perspectives, which are often equated with a biomedical interpretation of health. However, for now, we will confine discussion to consideration of its scope and potential contribution.

Epidemiology has typically been defined as 'the study of the distribution and determinants of disease in human populations' (Barker and Rose, 1984: v). While this draws attention to the focus of epidemiology on populations rather than individuals, it will be immediately apparent that this interpretation conforms to a negative model of health. More recent definitions signal some move towards including a positive dimension – for example, 'the study of the distribution and determinants of health-related states or events in specified populations, and the application of this study to control of health problems' (Last, 1988, in Bonita et al., 2006: 2). This particular example also emphasizes the action-orientated role of epidemiology.

Unwin et al. (1997) identify three categories of information needed as a basis for planning interventions to improve the health of populations and communities:

- basic demographic information
- the health status of communities
- determinants of health in the community.

Kroeger (1997) further lists nine key epidemiological questions that can inform the planning process. These can be organized under four headings, as shown in the box.

Nine epidemiological questions

Identification

1. What are the main health problems?

Magnitude and distribution

2. How common are they?
3. When do they generally occur?
4. Where do they occur?
5. Who is affected?

Analysis

6. Why does the problem occur?

Action and evaluation

7. What measures could be (were) taken to deal with the problem?
8. What results were anticipated (achieved)?
9. What else could be done?

Source: Derived from Kroeger (1997)

Descriptive epidemiology

As we demonstrated in Chapter 1, health is both a contested concept and a subjective state. It is not without difficulty, then, that epidemiology seeks to measure health objectively. Basch (1990) asserts that some composite indicator of health status is desirable but, ultimately, unattainable and a best estimate is therefore obtained by looking at levels of ill health. Descriptive epidemiology is essentially concerned with charting the disease burden of communities, together with the patterns of distribution of diseases – classically in relation to time, place and persons. There is frequently a heavy reliance on the use of routinely collected official health data, such as mortality and morbidity statistics, together with basic population data.

Mortality rates

The collection of data on vital events has its origins in the civil registration of births, marriages and deaths. By way of illustration, registration in England and Wales began in 1837, subsequent to the Births and Deaths Registration Act of 1836. Prior to this, the only records were in parish registers. In other contexts records began only relatively recently.

Because of the legal requirement to register deaths, mortality data are regarded as providing a complete representation. Deaths are recorded by underlying cause – confirmed either by a medical practitioner or an inquest. The death certificate requires identification of the immediate cause of death together with any underlying cause, defined as 'the disease or injury which initiated the train of events leading to death' (Unwin et al., 1997: 12). Other significant conditions contributing to death can also be recorded. The production of mortality statistics is based on coding of the underlying cause of death according to the *International Classification of Disease* (ICD). Since 1948, the World Health Organization has been responsible for ten-year revisions of the ICD, which is now undergoing its eleventh revision since its inception (WHO, 2013a). Distinguishing between the immediate cause of death and underlying cause can be a source of error. Death rates are expressed in a number of different ways, as summarized in the box.

Mortality rates

Actual rates	
Crude mortality rate	Number of deaths per 1000 people
Age-specific mortality rate	Number of deaths per 1000 people in a specific age group
Infant mortality rate	Number of deaths in the first year of life per 1000 live births.
Under-five mortality rate	Number of deaths in the first five years of life per 1000 live births
Sex-specific rates	Number of deaths per 1000 women/men
Cause-specific rates	Numbers of deaths from a specific cause per 1000 people
Constructed rates	
Age-standardized mortality rates	The death rate that would exist in a population if it had the same age structure as a standard population (e.g., national population, European standard population, Segi World Population, WHO World Standard Population; Ahmad et al., 2001) A direct method of standardization
Standardized mortality ratio (SMR)	The ratio of the actual number of deaths in a population to the number of deaths that would be expected if that population had the same levels of mortality as a reference population. The ratio is multiplied by 100. An SMR greater than 100 indicates a level of mortality higher than the reference population. An indirect method of standardization.

Clearly, each of the various mortality rates will create a different overall picture. The actual rates provide insight into the burden of mortality, but, given that the level of mortality is influenced by the age structure of the population, they are of little use when comparing populations with different age structures. The standardized rates, although artificial constructs, compensate for variations in age structure and can be used for comparative purposes. It is important, therefore, that appropriate rates are selected according to the intended purpose.

Morbidity rates

An important distinction in morbidity rates – and indeed health-related behaviour – is between incidence and prevalence. *Incidence* represents the number of new cases within a particular time period. *Prevalence*, in contrast, includes all the cases – either at a point in time (point prevalence) or over a defined period in time (period prevalence). Prevalence is often depicted as a pool, its overall magnitude being determined by the balance between factors filling and emptying the pool, as shown in Figure 2.1.

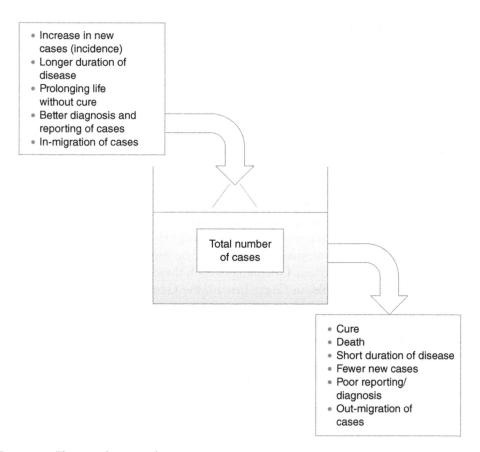

- Increase in new cases (incidence)
- Longer duration of disease
- Prolonging life without cure
- Better diagnosis and reporting of cases
- In-migration of cases

Total number of cases

- Cure
- Death
- Short duration of disease
- Fewer new cases
- Poor reporting/ diagnosis
- Out-migration of cases

Figure 2.1   The prevalence pool

Morbidity data, unlike mortality data, are not complete in the sense that only those who come into contact with the health services will be routinely recorded. They are regarded as representing the tip of the clinical iceberg (Last, 1963) and below the surface are those who are self-medicating, using alternative therapy, with subclinical symptoms or just putting up with their symptoms. Last (1963) estimated that as much as 94 per cent of ill health remained 'undetected' by professionals. This still rings true in 2015. For example, in most contexts, known cases of AIDS will only signify a small proportion of HIV infections in the wider population. The volume under the surface is likely to be greater the less serious – and *ipso facto* the more common – the condition. It will also be influenced by the availability of services and cultural factors associated with their usage. The main sources of routinely collected morbidity data in the UK are summarized in the box.

Routine morbidity data in the UK

- Hospital activity data
- General practice data
- Cancer registrations
- Notification of infectious disease
- Sexually transmitted diseases
- HIV/AIDS
- Congenital anomalies.

Countries such as India and China, for example, use sample registration systems that rely on lay reports of causes of death. Given that the majority of day-to-day illnesses never bring people into contact with formal healthcare systems, they will go unreported or underreported. The 'iceberg' concept is helpful here. As Donaldson and Scally (2009: 19) assert, the number of people who actually make contact with formal healthcare services is 'often referred to as the tip of the iceberg'. Figure 2.2 applies the notion of the clinical iceberg to the availability of data and their completeness in what might be referred to as a 'data iceberg'.

Relatively little routine information is available on minor illnesses, states of wellbeing or health-related behaviour. Obtaining data on these is, therefore, usually dependent on surveys. For example, in Great Britain, the General Household Survey, for example, used to ask each year about:

- long-standing illness, disability or infirmity and the extent to which this limits activities
- acute sickness or restricted activity during the preceding two weeks
- use of health services
- general health during the preceding year.

It also included questions about health-related behaviour such as smoking and drinking and other issues on a more occasional basis (see Office for National Statistics

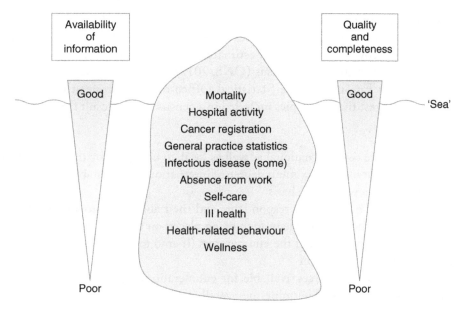

Figure 2.2   The data iceberg

(ONS), 2005). The General Household Survey has now been subsumed under the Integrated Household Survey (IHS). One of the key themes within the IHS is 'Health and Disability'.

Population data

Bonita et al. (2006) note that the central tool of epidemiology is the comparison of rates:

> Rate = number of events in a population (numerator) ÷ size of the population (denominator)

In order to calculate rates, it is essential to know the size of the population and, for comparative purposes, the characteristics of that population. Such information is typically obtained by a census, which has been defined as 'a complete count or enumeration of a population conducted under the auspices of some governmental authority' (Ginn et al., 1995: 293). The United Nations Statistics Division also notes that national population and housing censuses provide valuable information on vulnerable groups, such as those affected by gender issues, children, youth, the elderly, those with impairment or disability, and the homeless and migrant populations (United Nations Statistics Division, 2002).

The first complete modern census was carried out in Sweden in 1749 (Ginn et al., 1995). The UK census dates back to 1801 and has been conducted every ten years since then, with the exception of 1941. The nature of a census is such that it attempts to count the entire population. It therefore provides the denominator information required for the calculation of rates. The census also provides the opportunity to collect additional information on a range of demographic and socioeconomic factors – those selected tend to vary over time and between countries. Despite attempting to obtain complete coverage, it has been estimated that there was, in fact, only 90.4 per cent coverage in the 2011 UK Census (ONS, 2012). The United Nations Economic Commission for Europe and the Statistical Office of the European Communities (undated: 7) suggest that the topics included in a census should result from a balanced consideration of:

- the needs of the country, national as well as local, to be served by the census data
- the achievement of the maximum degree of international comparability, both within regions and on a worldwide basis
- acceptability of questions to respondents and their ability to provide the required information without an undue burden being placed on them
- the technical competence of the enumerators (if any) to obtain information on the topics by direct observation
- the total national resources available for enumeration, processing, tabulation and publication, which will determine the overall feasible scope of the census.

The UN provides a list of recommended areas and topics to be included in a country's census. A list of the areas included in Jamaica's 2011 census is provided in the box.

Areas included in Jamaica's 2011 Census

Topics included based on UN recommendations:

- Geographical and Internal Migration Characteristics
- International Migration Characteristics
- Household and Family Characteristics
- Demographic and Social Characteristics (sex, age, marital status, religion, ethnicity)
- Fertility and Mortality (number of living children, household deaths, etc.)
- Educational Characteristics
- Economic Characteristics (occupation, time worked, income, etc.)
- Disability Characteristics

Additional topics included:

- Usual mode of Transportation
- Individual Use of Information and Communication Technology Devices
- Social Welfare Benefits
- Union Status – Consensual (Non-legal) Unions

Source: Adapted from Nam (2013)

Kerrison and Macfarlane (2000) draw attention to two potential limitations of health data obtained by census processes. First, the precise wording of the questions is important in relation to the response elicited. Second, it relies on the accuracy of self-reporting, which will be subject to a whole range of potentially contaminating or distorting factors. In relation to using census data to estimate homelessness the Australian Bureau of Statistics (2012) point to two key limitations. First, under/over estimation – whereby 'people are enumerated in the Census but the data collected about them is not sufficient to be certain about whether or not they were homeless on Census night'; second, under-enumeration – 'people who were not enumerated in the Census' (ABS, 2012, no page number).

Life expectancy, HALE, DALYs and QALYs

Life expectancy is frequently used as a general indicator of a population's health status. It is the average number of years that individuals of different ages can be expected to live if current mortality rates apply (Bonita et al., 2006). It is included as a measure in the Health Profile for England – life expectancy at birth for England and Wales was 79 years for boys and 82.8 years for girls born during 2010–12 (as at October 2013, see ONS, 2013). However, not all those years are likely to be lived in full health (Department of Health, 2007). The notion of healthy life expectancy or health-adjusted life expectancy (HALE) makes allowance for this. It is the: 'average number of years that a person can expect to live in "full health" taking into account years lived in less than full health due to disease and/or injury' (WHO, 2013b). HALE therefore 'summarises mortality and non-fatal outcomes in a single measure

Table 2.1   Comparison of life expectancies and early mortality in selected countries

Indicator	Value (year) Sierra Leone	Value (year) Japan	Value (year) Guyana
Life expectancy at birth (years) both sexes	45.0 (2011)	83.0 (2011)	63.3 (2011)
Life expectancy at birth (years) males	45.0 (2011)	79.0 (2011)	60.0 (2011)
Life expectancy at birth (years) females	45.0 (2011)	86.0 (2011)	67.0 (2011)
Healthy life expectancy (HALE) at birth (years) males	34.0 (2007)	73.0 (2007)	52.0 (2007)
Healthy life expectancy (HALE) at birth (years) females	37.0 (2007)	78.0 (2007)	55.0 (2007)
Probability of dying (per 1000 live births) under 5 years of age (under-5 mortality rate)	185.0 (2011)	3.0 (2011)	36.0 (2011)
Infant mortality rate (per 1000 live births)	119.0 (2011)	2.0 (2011)	34.0 (2011)

Sources: Derived from WHO (2013c); World Bank (2013); UNICEF, undated (a); and UNICEF, undated (b)

of average population health' (Salomon et al., 2012). A systematic review by Salomon et al. (2012: 628) examining HALE in 187 countries over two decades concluded that HALE 'differs substantially between countries' and that 'as life expectancy has increased, the number of healthy years lost to disability has also increased in most countries'. Table 2.1 provides a comparison of life expectancy, healthy life expectancy and early life mortality rates in three countries – the country with the lowest, Sierra Leone, the country with the highest, Japan and the country with the lowest life expectancy in South America, Guyana.

Mortality can be considered premature if individuals do not survive to an expected age and this shortfall can be regarded as years of life lost. The total number of premature years of life lost (PYLL) due to different causes of mortality can be calculated. The use of PYLL as a measure of disease burden and for comparative purposes clearly attaches more weight to deaths occurring in younger age groups.

The concept of PYLL is extended and refined by the notion of disability adjusted life years (DALY), which, in addition to premature loss of life, includes loss of healthy life, broadly referred to as disability:

> One DALY can be thought of as one lost year of 'healthy life'. The sum of these DALYs across the population, or the burden of disease, can be thought of as a measurement of the gap between current health status and an ideal health situation where the entire population lives to an advanced age, free of disease and disability. (WHO, 2013d)

The severity of the disability is graded on a scale from 0 (perfect health) to 1 (dead).

DALY = YLL + YLD

The DALY was introduced in the World Development Report 1993 (World Bank, 1993) as a means of measuring the global burden of disease. Effectively, it is a measure of the health gap between the current situation and the ideal in which everyone lives to an old age in full health. In most countries, disability becomes more significant as death rates go down (Institute for Health Metrics and Evaluation, 2013). Whereas assessing disease burden had formerly been overly reliant on mortality statistics, the DALY provided a broader view of disease burden by including conditions that affect health status. The use of DALYs, for example, has revealed the magnitude of the contribution of neuropsychiatric conditions to the global disease burden – an issue that had been overlooked by analyses of mortality statistics (WHO, 1999). By way of example, the Global Burden of Diseases, Injuries and Risk Factors Study 2010 found that mental and substance use disorders accounted for 7.4 per cent of all DALYs globally and 22.9 per cent of overall years lived with disability (YLDs) (Whiteford et al., 2013). 'Mental and substances use disorders were the leading cause of YLD worldwide' (Whiteford et al., 2013: 1575). On a global scale, there has been a significant change during the past 25 years in terms of the risk factors associated with different diseases (Lim et al., 2012) – see Table 2.2. We are now seeing a shift towards non-communicable diseases in adults from communicable diseases in

Table 2.2   Leading risk factors 2010

Leading risk factors in 2010	% DALYs	Leading risk factors in 1990	% DALYs
High blood pressure	7.0	Childhood underweight	7.9
Tobacco-smoking, including secondhand smoke	6.3	Household air pollution from solid fuels	6.8
Household air pollution from solid fuels	4.3	Tobacco-smoking, including secondhand smoke	6.1

Source: Lim et al. (2012)

children. However, as Lim et al. (2012) point out, this shift does vary across different regions and, 'in much of sub-saharan Africa, the leading risks are still associated with poverty and those that affect children' (p. 2224).

Table 2.3 shows how the leading causes of DALYs have changed in the twenty years since 1990 to 2010.

Table 2.3   Leading causes of DALYs

Ranking	2010	1990
1	Ischaemic Heart Disease	Ranked 4
2	Lower respiratory tract infections	Ranked 1
3	Stroke	Ranked 5
4	Diarrhoeal diseases	Ranked 2
5	HIV/AIDS	Ranked 33
10	Road injury	Ranked 12
11	Major Depressive Disorder	Ranked 15

Note: There are substantial differences in rankings of leading causes in different global regions.

Source: Murray et al. (2012)

The well-known health promotion maxim of adding life to years not just years to life draws attention to the issue of *quality* of life. Although, in principle, quality of life embraces 'emotional, social and physical well-being, and ability to function in the ordinary tasks of living' (Donald, 2001), quality of life measures tend to focus on disease states. The notion of quality adjusted life year (QALY) was developed as a means of assessing the benefits of interventions in terms of the number and quality of years gained. The QALY was primarily developed to provide a utility rating to compare the health benefits of different interventions. It is a way of assigning a numerical value to a health state, based on the premise that, if a year of good-quality life expectancy is given the value of one, then a year of poor-quality or unhealthy life must be worth less than one. It therefore combines the length and quality of life into a single index (Bowling, 1997a).

Quality in this context is generally taken to be the absence of negative health states (that is to say, disease and disability) rather than positive well-being, which we discuss below. The EuroQol Group has developed the EQ-5D as a standardized instrument for measuring health outcome (EuroQol, undated). It uses five dimensions of health (mobility, self-care, usual activities, pain/discomfort, anxiety/depression), and each dimension comprises three levels (some, moderate or extreme problems). Given the subjective nature of quality of life and the various philosophical interpretations of health and well-being referred to in Chapter 1, it will come as no surprise that there is considerable debate about attempts to measure these factors objectively.

This use of QALYs has been much criticized. The criticisms are both technical, on account of their method of construction, and ethical (for a full analysis, see Edgar et al., 1998). Reed Johnson (2009) points out that, although the simplicity of the QALY has led to its widespread use, there are several limitations including empirical and conceptual ones. The use of QALYs as a means of prioritization of healthcare has been viewed as unjust because it is essentially ageist – systematically favouring interventions that improve the health status of the young by virtue of their longer life expectancy. It also arbitrates on the basis of capacity to benefit rather than on the basis of actual need – a point that we will return to in Chapter 5. However, arguments in defence of QALYs refer to the need for a single index of health with which to compare the outcomes of different interventions in order to deploy limited resources to achieve maximum benefits for the community (Williams and Kind, 1992). Kelly (2006: 183) confirmed that evidence about cost-effectiveness based on cost per QALY will form an 'integral part' of the development of National Institute for Health and Clinical Excellence (NICE) guidance about public health. The Wanless Report (2002), for example, compared the cost-effectiveness of smoking cessation estimated between £212 and £873 per QALY with £4000 to £8000 per QALY for statins (drugs that reduce cholesterol). The second Wanless Report (2004) used Type 2 diabetes as a case study and identified a number of interventions below £20,000 per quality adjusted life year, the level at which NICE criteria used for making judgements about cost-effectiveness become more stringent (see box).

Interventions for Type 2 diabetes that are cost-effective using a threshold of £20,000 per QALY

- tight control of blood glucose and blood pressure for all diabetics
- ACE inhibitors for diabetics with one other risk factor not otherwise quantified (e.g., for tight control of blood pressure)
- retinopathy screening for all diabetics
- foot screening for those at high risk
- screening obese for impaired glucose tolerance (IGT) and relevant treatment
- multiple risk factor management
- self-care including patient education
- reduction of obesity and physical inactivity in high risk groups.

Source: Wanless (2004: 144)

The allocation of resources based on DALYs is surrounded by similar arguments to those about QALYs. In addition, the greater value attached to adult life as opposed to that of children or the elderly in the construction of DALYS, attracts particular criticism (Abbasi, 1999).

Positive health

Much of the foregoing has focused on mortality and morbidity. The application of this information to the assessment of health is predicated on the assumption that the absence of disease is indicative of health. Yet, we noted in Chapter 1 that health is more than just the absence of disease. Catford's (1983) early attempt to identify positive health indicators provides examples of individual behaviour and health knowledge, socioeconomic conditions and aspects of the physical environment. However, the analysis is still located within a disease causation continuum. The factors identified can only be deemed healthy by virtue of their contribution to prevention of disease and do not, of themselves, constitute positive well-being. Surveys such as the Health Survey for England collect data about the nation's health and exposure to selected risk factors (Department of Health, 2007a). The survey was established in 1991 to monitor trends and progress towards national health targets (Mimas, 2001). It includes a questionnaire as well as objective measures such as physical measurements and the analysis of blood samples. The survey has a 'core' that is repeated annually (blood pressure, height and weight, smoking, drinking and general health), plus additional modules on topics of special interest such as cardiovascular disease and accidents. In 2011, a 'Well-Being Module' was added that asked participants to rate their well-being on a scale of 0–10 (0 being low and 10 being high).

Kemm (1993) notes the relative ease of defining negative rather than positive health states and the greater success of epidemiology in handling the former rather than the latter. Bowling (1997a: 5) suggests that positive health:

> implies 'completeness' and 'full functioning' or 'efficiency' of mind and body and social adjustment. Beyond this there is no one accepted definition. Positive health could be described as the ability to cope with stressful situations, the maintenance of a strong social support system, integration in the community, high morale and life satisfaction, psychological well-being, and even levels of physical fitness as well as physical health.

Both authors are in agreement that the components of well-being require both precise definition and the formulation of criteria. A key issue is whether positive and negative states are opposite ends of the same dimension with some neutral midpoint or, as argued by Downie et al. (1996), they occupy different dimensions. These alternative conceptualizations are shown in Figure 2.3. Kemm (1993) asserts that there is little evidence to support positive health being viewed as a distinct dimension, although there may be theoretical reasons for doing so. Furthermore, positive and negative health may occupy the same dimension for some aspects, such as objective physical health, but different dimensions for subjective health.

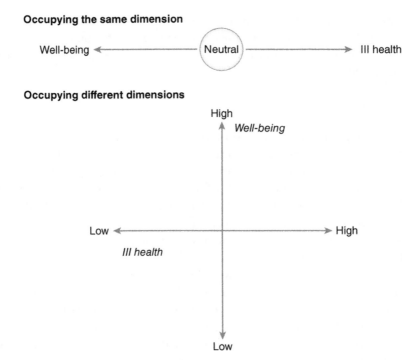

Figure 2.3   Dimensions of well-being and ill health (derived from Kemm, 1993; and Downie et al., 1996)

A number of devices and scales exist for assessing aspects of quality of life and well-being. These include:

- SF-36
- Health Assessment Questionnaire
- Sickness Impact Profile
- Missoula-VITAS Quality of Life Index
- European KIDSCREEN

There is considerable variation in the conceptual underpinnings of the various instruments and their validity and reliability. (For a more detailed discussion, see Bowling, 1997a, 1997b; Edgar et al., 1998; and Donald, 2001.) Some of these scales derive from professional perspectives; some have incorporated lay views in their development.

Health and happiness

A number of measures have been developed in order to measure happiness. For many, happiness is inextricably linked to health. As Borghesi and Vercelli (2010) point out, the causal relationship between health and happiness is well documented.

When asked about happiness, people often refer to their current health status; conversely, health status impacts on perceived levels of happiness. There have been several attempts, at an international level, to develop measures of happiness (Dixey et al., 2013a). Happiness can be measured using subjective (that is to say, self-reporting) or objective (that is to say, observing physiological states) means. A number of factors are assumed to impact on levels of personal happiness such as income. However, the relationship between health and happiness is not straightforward. For example, people have an amazing capacity to adapt to very difficult life circumstances, including significant challenges to health. For further, more detailed discussion on some of the paradoxes in the relationship between health and happiness, see Borghesi and Vercelli (2010).

Analytic epidemiology

While the patterns of distribution of disease revealed by descriptive epidemiology may generate tentative hypotheses about causation, analytic epidemiology focuses specifically on exploring cause-and-effect relationships. One of the best known early examples is the work of John Snow, who, by meticulously mapping cholera outbreaks in London during 1848–49 and 1853–54, was able to demonstrate that the disease was spread by contaminated water (Chave, 1958). Although derided by the miasmatists, who favoured the view that such diseases were caused by the miasma emanating from filth and putrefying material, and well in advance of Koch's discovery of the micro-organism that causes cholera in 1884, Snow's work provided evidence to support the general introduction of public health measures, such as improved water and sanitation – over and above the renowned removal of the handle of the Broad Street water pump to halt an outbreak of cholera in the vicinity.

The evidence for causality is subject to epistemological debate. Furthermore, many contemporary health problems are not the product of simple cause-and-effect relationships. Analysis is often concerned with multiple causes and, in some instances, multiple effects. Frequently, therefore, the focus is on complex multifactorial webs. Moon and Gould (2000) identify three main conditions that must be present if observed associations are to be judged as causally linked. First, do the levels of exposure and disease vary in the same way – that is, co-variation? Second, does cause precede the effect – that is, temporal precedence? Third, have other possible explanations and confounding factors been eliminated?

A number of different types of epidemiological studies are used to explore causality. These range from observational studies, such as ecological and cross-sectional studies, which are regarded as relatively weak in their capacity to demonstrate causality, to the more robust case control and cohort studies. Intervention or experimental studies are more able to control for confounding variables and may take the form of randomized controlled, field or community trials. Bonita et al. (2006) provide a useful set of guidelines for assessing causality and these are listed in the box.

Guidelines for causality

Temporal relation	Does the cause precede the effect?
Plausibility	Does it make sense in the light of existing knowledge and mechanisms of action?
Consistency	Do other studies produce similar findings?
Strength	Is there a strong association?
Dose–response relationship	Does increase in exposure produce increased effect?
Reversibility	Does the risk decrease when the possible cause is removed?
Study design	Is the evidence robust and derived from strong studies?
Judging the evidence	How many lines of evidence lead to the conclusion?

Source: Derived from Bonita et al. (2006: 90)

We will give further consideration to the complexity of causal relationships in health promotion programmes when we discuss evaluation in Chapter 11. However, returning to the subject of disease causation, Bonita et al. (2006: 83) define the cause of a disease or injury as:

> an event, condition, characteristic or a combination of these factors which plays an important role in producing the health outcome. Logically a cause must precede an outcome. A cause is termed *sufficient* when it inevitably produces or initiates an outcome and is termed *necessary* if an outcome cannot develop in its absence. [Emphasis in the original]

It therefore follows that, in many instances, well-recognized causal factors are neither necessary nor sufficient. Take smoking, for example. Some people who have never smoked will develop lung cancer, so smoking cannot be seen as necessary, and some people who smoke do not develop lung cancer, hence smoking is not sufficient. There is, however, indisputable evidence that smoking is an important causal factor that increases the probability of developing lung cancer and, conversely, that this will be reduced by the cessation of smoking. Thus, it becomes important to think in terms of probability and risk. The term 'risk factor' is applied to those factors that are associated with the development of a disease, but not sufficient in themselves to cause it – often with the underlying intent of identifying factors that can be modified to prevent disease occurring. 'Relative risk' is the ratio of the rate of the disease in those exposed to a particular factor to the rate in those not exposed (see the box on risk). It indicates the number of times that it is *more likely* that an individual exposed to the factor will develop the disease. It is useful in establishing the strength of the association and also in graphically encapsulating the levels of additional risk incurred by individuals.

In contrast, the notion of 'attributable risk' acknowledges the fact that many diseases develop independently of exposure to risk factors. In order to assess the amount of disease that is actually attributable to exposure, the rate in those not exposed to the risk factor (that is, those who would have developed the disease regardless of exposure) is subtracted from the rate in those exposed (see box for formula).

A related concept is the 'population attributable risk' (see box). This indicates the amount of disease that would be avoided in a population if exposure to the risk factor was completely eliminated.

Assessment of risk

Relative risk (×)	= rate of the disease in those exposed to the risk factor ÷ rate of the disease in those not exposed
Attributable risk (rate)	= rate of the disease in those exposed to the risk factor − rate of the disease in those not exposed
Population attributable risk	= attributable risk × proportion of the population exposed to the risk factor

Establishing the potential and feasibility for prevention rests on the capacity to identify modifiable risk factors. Conventionally, different levels of prevention are distinguished:

- **primary prevention** is concerned with preventing the development of disease by reducing exposure to risk factors – environmental and behavioural
- **secondary prevention** in contrast, focuses on early diagnosis – for example, by screening – to improve the prospects of treatment
- **tertiary prevention** includes measures to reduce the consequences of illness and is often seen as integral to a rehabilitation programme.

A fourth level of prevention has also been recognized (Bonita et al., 2006):

- **primordial prevention** aims to prevent the emergence of social, economic and cultural patterns known to be associated with disease in cultures that already have healthy traditional ways of life.

More recently recognition is also given to an additional level of prevention:

- **quaternary prevention** which aims to mitigate or avoid the results of unnecessary or excessive interventions (Cook, 2012) or over-medicalisation (Starfield et al., 2008).

A further issue is whether it is preferable to target preventive interventions at the population in general or high-risk groups (Rose, 1992). Arguments in favour of the high-risk approach include its greater cost-effectiveness and the fact that people who are known to be at high risk may be more motivated to change. However, it presupposes that it is both possible to identify those at risk and that the disease will not occur in those who do not fall within this category. Nor would such an approach contribute to changing general norms, so it might be more difficult for individuals to make changes. Furthermore, health and health behaviour are influenced by a broad range of social and environmental factors that can only be tackled at the population level. Even when focusing on specific behaviour, the whole population approach has the capacity to achieve a significant reduction in disease. Although major change may be achieved at the population level, it requires many individuals to make changes and relatively few of them will gain any personal benefit – referred to by Rose (1992) as the 'prevention paradox'. Charlton (1995) notes that a population-wide approach potentially labels the whole population as being at-risk. It also creates the new category of the 'worried-well'. As Illich (1976: 97) cautioned, this can also lead to undue dependence on the medical profession and the medicalization of life – so-called social iatrogenesis:

> The concept of morbidity has been enlarged to cover prognosticated risks … People are turned into patients without being sick. The medicalization of prevention thus becomes another major symptom of social iatrogenesis.

THE NEED FOR ALTERNATIVE PERSPECTIVES

Two key questions are often asked when assessing the utility of health information:

- Is it necessary?
- Is it sufficient?

Both are pertinent to the selection of information to identify priority health issues and assess health needs. Furthermore, the answers to both will be influenced by issues of ideology, epistemology (concerned with the nature of knowledge and how it is acquired) and, not least, practicality.

Fundamentally, much epidemiology is about association rather than cause (Smith, 2001). Epidemiological approaches to assessing health status and identifying the determinants of health are consistent with a modernist emphasis on rationality and faith in the scientific method. De Kadt (1982) suggests that perspectives on health are informed by the dominant conceptions of medicine. Of particular relevance are its mechanistic nature, together with its focus on micro-causality. As a consequence, attention is directed towards individuals who become sick and, by inference, their unhealthy lifestyles rather than the social, economic and environmental factors that are responsible for these lifestyles. Krieger (2001) states that the early epidemiology and public health of the mid to late nineteenth century clearly recognized that population health is shaped by both social and biological processes. However, increased interest in personal preventive measures in the late nineteenth and early twentieth centuries signalled a shift in emphasis for mainstream modern epidemiology. Criticism of this shift has come from within epidemiology itself as well as from other fields, such as sociology and anthropology. Moon and Gould (2000: 143) draw on an editorial in *The Lancet* (Anonymous, 1994) to suggest that:

> the discipline's focus is now so far 'downstream' that it has lost sight of what is going on up river. The result is an exclusion of the *contexts* in which disease happens unless they are immediately measurable and the *voices* of those people whose social conditions threaten their health …

They are critical of the way in which modern epidemiology is consistent with, and upholds, dominant value systems. Furthermore, they challenge the methodological assumptions associated with its positivist methodological position – particularly its reductionist principles and the lack of attention to context. While accepting that there is some value in identifying causal factors, they assert that they reveal little about the structural factors that influence people's lives.

The emergence of 'social epidemiology' in the 1950s was distinguished by its explicit focus on the *social* determinants of health – a position reflected in the 'new public health' movement. 'Critical epidemiology', furthermore, 'places an emphasis on the social and power relations that shape disease definition and disease causation' (Moon and Gould, 2000: 7).

Issues of micro-causality are undoubtedly relevant to understanding the factors that impact on health status, such as is the case with exposure to the *tubercle bacillus* and the development of tuberculosis. However, they are not sufficient. They need to be understood in the context of the social and environmental factors – such as overcrowding, social class, poverty and urbanization – that are also associated with the development of the disease. Furthermore, Kelly and Charlton (1995) caution against reification of the social system and a simple deterministic view of the relationship between social factors and ill health, which merely replicates the type of thinking integral to a biomedical approach – albeit further upstream. They note the tension in health promotion discourse between free will and determinism – that is, between *agency* and *structure* – and call for an understanding of the reciprocal relationship between the two.

The application of science and rationality to the analysis of the determinants of ill health, or even positive health states, assumes that there is an objective reality. A postmodern understanding, in contrast, views reality as both contextual and contingent. Rather than one objective reality, there are multiple perspectives and interpretations of reality. Graham's work on smoking provides a useful example. Smoking is strongly linked to social disadvantage. An 'outsider's' view of mothers in low-income households sees smoking as irrational by virtue of the cost and health risks incurred. However, an 'inside view' is that, for the mothers themselves, smoking can be part of their coping strategy. Graham's (1987) study revealed that, from the mothers' perspective, smoking was associated with breaks from their caring role, which enabled them to recharge, and was also a means of coping when things got too much. Looking at the issue from the perspective of the mothers transforms apparently irrational behaviour into a rational response to their situation. Similarly, young women's risky health practices such as binge-drinking are often viewed as problematic by health professionals, yet young women tend to frame such practices in more positive, agentic ways (Cross et al., 2011; Cross, 2013a, 2013b).

Furthermore, contrary to the customary view that science and the scientific method are concerned with the objective pursuit of truth, in fact, science itself is socially constructed – both in its focus and its methods. The breadth of scientific enquiry is restricted by the limits of current paradigms (Kuhn, 1970). The construction of problems – the ways in which they are framed and the determinants explored – are all socially shaped (Peterson and Lupton, 1996; Lupton, 2006). How far upstream will, or should, the quest for determinants go? What risk factors are regarded as legitimate areas of enquiry? What evidence will be accepted?

Official statistics form the basis of much epidemiological and, indeed, sociological enquiry. It is appropriate at this point to consider the nature of official data.

Official health data – reality or myth?

The characteristics of official health statistics are that they generally include large data sets that have been collected regularly by official agencies over long periods of time. It is a truism that data do not exist in their own right, but are constructed. There are clearly issues concerning the technicalities of data collection, its representativeness and completeness. As we have already noted, official health data will only include those who have come into contact with services, registered vital events or been included in official surveys. Consulting a doctor or taking time off work will inevitably be influenced by a range of social and cultural factors. The collection of some official data – such as mortality and census data – attempts to include all cases, whereas surveys will only involve a sample.

The way in which data are classified and categorized is also socially constructed. For example, in relation to certification of death, 'old age', which featured prominently as a cause of death in the late nineteenth century, becomes an inadequate descriptor in our more biomedically enlightened times – more specific causal explanations are required. There is a well-known tendency towards under-reporting of emotionally charged issues, such as suicide and AIDS. Furthermore, at what point in the temporal sequence of causality do we identify a single cause? For a child dying in one of the least developed parts of the world, is it measles, malnutrition or poverty? For a man dying prematurely in a rundown inner-city area, is it lung cancer or smoking or unemployment? Interestingly, the tenth revision of the *International Classification of Disease* introduced a set of codes for factors that influence health status and contact with health services. When even ostensibly objective issues such as mortality and morbidity can be seen to be socially constructed, assessing 'quality of life' becomes even more problematic. Classifying people by gender, ethnic group and socioeconomic status provides further evidence of social construction.

Official data, then, are not facts in their own right, but are constructed. The ways in which they are constructed will be influenced by both technical and ideological issues. There are several questions to consider when assessing the quality of official health data (see the box for examples – this is by no means an exhaustive list).

Key issues and questions that should be considered for any data set providing information on population health

- Accuracy – to what extent is the data correct?
- Precision – have appropriate measures of uncertainty been included?
- Completeness – how much of the data is missing?
- Timeliness – what period does the data refer to? Is it relevant to the current position?
- Coverage – is the whole population of interest represented?
- Accessibility – who has access to the data?
- Confidentiality/suppression/disclosure control – what restrictions/regulations are being followed?
- What was the original purpose of collection/collation of the data? (May be a source of bias.)
- Who undertook the data collection? – This may not be available.
- How was the data collected? – This may not be available
- Whether what is included in the data set is the actual requirement, or whether it will have to act as a proxy for the real item.
- Is the data set comparative, what are the comparators and are they appropriate?
- If the dataset presents rates or ratios, have appropriate techniques been used to control for differing population structures?

Source: Adapted from Goodyear and Malhotra (2007)

Goodyear and Malhotra (2007) have listed a number of issues and questions worth applying to any information data set on public health. Their list is by no means exhaustive, and arguably not necessarily specific to public health data, but it does raise a number of important considerations with which to interrogate such information.

May (1993) identifies three schools of thought in relation to official statistics:

- **realist** considers official statistics to be objective indicators of phenomena
- **institutionalist** sees official statistics as artificial constructs revealing more about an institution's priorities in collecting data than the phenomena they purport to represent
- **radical** extends the institutionalist view to include discretionary practices embedded within and replicating the power structure and dynamics of society.

By way of example, let us take the use of waiting lists for hip replacement surgery as an indicator of prevalence and need. A realist interpretation would presuppose that individuals have equal access to general practitioners, who would refer them to hospital for treatment and the length of the waiting lists would simply be the product of the number of individuals requiring treatment and the period required for throughput. An institutionalist view would question the way in which the hospital constructed the waiting list for treatment. For example, have treatment waiting lists been kept short by having a long waiting period prior to consultation? A radical view would locate this last question within the context of any national imperative to reduce waiting lists and political pressure to demonstrate more efficient services. Changes in these contextual factors would inevitably influence the comparability of data over time.

Conspiracy theorists would subscribe to the view that statistics are deliberately manipulated to suit an agenda rather than being the unconsciously biased products of systems and practices. Huff's delightfully subversive *How to Lie with Statistics* (1979) identifies a number of tactics. These include:

- using a sample with an in-built bias, such as self-selected respondents
- choosing the 'right' average – if a distribution is skewed, the median will be less affected than the mean, so, for example, a few high-earners would raise the mean earnings but not the median
- using very small samples
- manipulating graphs:
  - numbered axes
  - plotting means to obscure highs and lows
  - changing the vertical scale or cutting off the bottom of graphs to exaggerate trends
  - using pictorial representation
- tacitly implying associations when none have been proven
- assumptions about causality.

The danger in seeing official data merely as social constructs is that it can lead us to reject them as having no inherent value. We then have a limited capacity to assess health status and identify problem issues. The evidence that initially exposed, and continues to document, the effects of social inequality, for example, drew substantially on official health data. Without this insight, it would have been difficult to mount an argument in favour of tackling social inequality. What is needed is the *critical* use of health data that takes full account of the ways in which they have been constructed. This is aptly summed up by Roberts (1990: 13):

> An over-reverent approach to figures supports the empiricist fallacy that figures are merely given objective facts, a proper understanding of which compels one conclusion and one only. An over-sceptical approach sustains the equally erroneous belief that statistics are mere mystification, a way of obscuring truth and legitimizing error, that they are born in deception and formed of quantified ideology.

The lay perspective

The lay perspective introduces a completely different dimension. Lay knowledge is rooted in the direct and vicarious experience of individuals and communities and their cultural understandings. It is interpreted within the context of people's real lives and day-to-day experiences. The earlier reference to the 'clinical iceberg' would indicate that most of our individual and collective experiences of ill health and health occur below the surface. There, it is effectively hidden from the reaches of routine data-collection systems and, hence, does not feature in most official accounts of health.

Faith in the value of lay knowledge about health and ill health has been central to the development of the self-help movement – a movement that challenged medical, and, indeed, expert hegemony. Furthermore, community activists have used their own insights, derived by means of what has been termed popular or lay epidemiology, to mount campaigns to tackle what they perceive to be the cause of local health problems. Williams and Popay (1994) provide a number of high-profile examples, such as tackling the problems of toxic waste and environmental pollution but, equally, lay epidemiology can support the case for local measures, such as improved housing and traffic-calming measures.

Allmark and Tod (2006) assert that lay epidemiology is a term 'used to describe the processes through which lay individual understand and interpret health risks' (p. 460). Moon and Gould (2000: 7) note that, although critics have challenged this approach as being 'anecdotal, uninformed and even dangerous', it provides direct insight into the ways in which health and ill health are commonly experienced, understood and managed. In an exploration of lay epidemiology and cancer, possible causes were attributed to behavioural, environmental, biological and psychological factors, however, the participants also emphasized the 'randomness' of cancer (Macdonald, 2011). Clearly, as Allmark and Tod (2006) argue, an appreciation of lay epidemiology is relevant for planning preventive (and more effective) health promotion interventions. Likewise, establishing the meaning that certain so-called risky health practices hold for people is important in designing health communication messages aimed at reducing risk (Cross, 2013b). A further example is provided by United Nations Children's Fund (UNICEF) (2007) report on the views of young people who have experienced conflict (see box).

The voice of young people living in conflict zones

We all have one thing in common: Our lives have been affected by armed conflict. That is why, even though we come from different places and our problems are not always the same, we speak with one voice.

We have not given up all hope yet. We still want to go to school and play with our friends. We want to help build peace in our societies and make this world a better place. We still have big dreams.

For some of us, getting together for the sake of this report gave us a rare opportunity to sit with our friends and share our stories. It has also been an opportunity to finally tell you what we feel and think.

But talking is not enough. Will we see any change after you meet to talk about us? Will you hear our voices and act on what we tell you?

Source: UNICEF (2007)

Lay interpretations of health are complex and multidimensional. Far from being trivial, they demonstrate coherent and sophisticated understandings. A number of major studies have explored these understandings (for example, Herzlich, 1973; Blaxter and Patterson, 1982; Williams, 1983; Cornwell, 1984; and Stainton Rogers, 1991). Blaxter (2007) identifies five categories of responses given when people are asked about what health is as follows:

- Health as not ill
- Health as physical fitness, vitality
- Health as social relationships
- Health as function
- Health as psychosocial well-being

Lay recognition of the absence of disease, illness and pain as integral to health is note-worthy as the professional discourse on well-being does not always explicitly address this issue.

There is some interplay between professional and lay accounts of health, though. Lay perspectives often encompass knowledge and understandings developed within expert paradigms (Shaw, 2002). For example, the germ theory is fully integrated into most Western lay interpretations of disease. It is interesting to note, however, that lay accounts might include such reductionist explanations, but they also go further, address-ing issues associated with meaning, such as 'Why me?' and 'Why now?' (Williams and Popay, 1994). A full understanding of health and ill health will necessarily seek to incor-porate these hitherto often private accounts.

The premise underpinning our earlier discussion of risk was that, from an epide-miological perspective, it can be measured objectively. In the same way that health and illness are not simple biological states, but are socially constructed, lay inter-pretations and perceptions of risk are also complex. As we will explore more fully in Chapter 3, they derive from the interplay of a plethora of psychosocial and cultural factors.

Frankel et al. (1991) note that lay perceptions of risk are often in tune with main-stream epidemiological analyses. For example, with regard to coronary heart disease, there is lay understanding of an association with both hereditary factors and adverse social circumstances – issues that rarely feature in health education campaigns. Frankel et al. raise the interesting question as to why there was a rapid and dramatic reduction in egg consumption in the UK in the late 1980s in response to concerns about salmonella infection when years of warning about the harmful effects of the cholesterol content of eggs brought about little change. They propose that there are different lay concep-tualizations of risk. At one end of the spectrum, the risk is both immediate and easily imagined and therefore to be avoided – encapsulated as 'bad/poisonous behaviour'. At the other end of the spectrum, risks are perceived to be less immediate and less specific. Some behaviours associated with this type of risk, such as smoking, are acknowledged to be harmful, but may also have desirable aspects – hence, they are termed 'bad/desirable behaviour'. They suggest that the advertising industry attempts to keep behaviour away from the bad/poisonous end of the spectrum by emphasizing the desirable elements. Individuals may also use humour to the same effect – for example, 'naughty but nice' and 'what's your poison?'

The biomedical model has often been criticized because of its expert-led, top-down orientation. However, even interpretive approaches – which purport to provide greater insight into the experiences of lay people – may still remain an essentially expert-led analysis of that experience. A true commitment to including the lay perspective involves going beyond seeing people merely as research subjects. It requires an egalitarian approach to seeking their active involvement at all stages of the research process – not least in formulating the priority issues to address.

Pathogenesis or salutogenesis

Regardless of whether or not they conform to a reductionist, biomedical or more interpretive position, the majority of studies of the determinants of health and ill health are located within a pathogenic paradigm. As Kelly and Charlton (1995: 82) note:

> The social model of health is, in this regard, no different to the medical model. In the medical model the pathogens are microbes, viruses or malfunctioning cellular reproduction. In the social model they are poor housing, unemployment and powerlessness. The discourse may be different but the epistemology is the same. The social model is not, in our view, an alternative to the discredited medical model. It is a partner in crime and a very close modernist relative.

Antonovsky (1984) asserts that the fundamental assumption of this paradigm is that individuals are in a state of balance or homeostasis and that when this state is challenged by microbial, physical or chemical factors or psychosocial stressors, regulatory mechanisms come into play to restore homeostasis. He identifies a number of consequences of this thinking:

- the tendency to think dichotomously about people, classifying them as healthy or diseased
- a focus on disease states or risk factors
- the search for cause or multifactorial causes
- the assumption that stressors are bad
- mounting wars against specific diseases
- ignoring the factors associated with wellness.

In proposing a salutogenic paradigm, Antonovsky advocates a radical change in perspective concerning what is involved in staying healthy. This shifts the focus away from specific diseases and towards those general factors involved in health, and in moving along what he terms the 'health-ease/dis-ease continuum' (Antonovsky, 1984: 117). He does not, however, totally abandon the pathogenic paradigm, but offers salutogenesis as an *additional* perspective.

I am not proposing that the pathogenic paradigm be abandoned, theoretically or institutionally. It has immense achievement and power for good to its credit. I have attempted to point to its limitations, to the blinders involved in any paradigm.

Salutogenesis focuses on the factors associated with successful coping, which are envisaged as buffers mitigating the effects of stressors. While there are numerous individual coping variables, Antonovsky (1987: 19) proposes the 'sense of coherence' (SOC) as an overarching explanatory variable.

The sense of coherence is a global orientation that expresses the extent to which one has a pervasive, enduring, although dynamic feeling of confidence that:

1. the stimuli deriving from one's internal and external environments in the course of living are structured, predictable and explicable
2. the resources are available to one to meet the demands posed by these stimuli and
3. these demands are challenges, worthy of investment and engagement.

These three components of the SOC are called comprehensibility, manageability and meaningfulness.

In considering how a strong SOC helps people to cope with stressors, Antonovsky (1987) attempts to identify generalized and specific resistance resources. The features that such resistance resources have in common are:

- **consistency** – the greater the consistency of life experiences, the more they will be comprehensible and predictable
- **underload–overload balance** – demand is appropriate to capability
- **participation in decision-making** – the emphasis here is on active participation rather than control.

Early formulations of the SOC suggested that it was the product of early life experiences and that, by adulthood, it was more or less a fixed part of a person's makeup. Such a view offers little to those seeking to improve health. However, Antonovsky subsequently accepted that movement along the SOC can occur even in adulthood, albeit within fairly narrow limits. While he still subscribes to the view that macrosocial change is the only way to achieve substantial change in SOC for most people, he accepts that changes in everyday life can make some difference (Antonovsky, 1984). Antonovksy (1996) argued for the importance of a salutogenic orientation in health promotion and, more recently, a number of Scandinavian scholars have taken up this concept (Eriksson and Lindström, 2008, 2012; Lindström and Eriksson, 2006). Lindström and Eriksson (2009) have also used a salutogenic approach to guide healthy public policy.

Whose voice counts?

The validity of different accounts of health is the subject of debate, caught up in epistemological questions concerning ways of knowing and what constitutes truth.

Beattie (1993) provides a useful analysis of 'different ways of knowing' based on modes of thought and the focus of attention. Modes of thought are seen as ranging from 'hard' mechanistic approaches consistent with the natural sciences to 'soft' humanistic approaches associated with sociological enquiry. Similarly, lay perspectives are often regarded as prerational and trivial in contrast to the rational, and therefore supposedly serious, view of the so-called experts. The focus of attention ranges from individuals to collectives. Figure 2.4 provides an overview of the relationship between these and identifies four models.

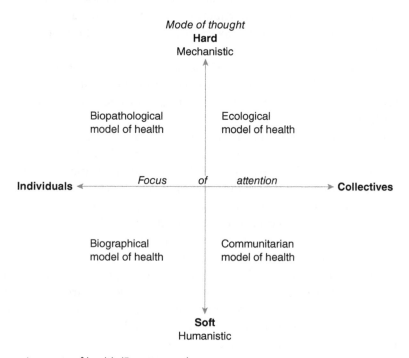

Figure 2.4   Accounts of health (Beattie, 1993)

Beattie equates each model with different sociopolitical philosophies and attempts to identify cultural bias within the various accounts of health as summarized in Table 2.4.

Table 2.4   Accounts of health – sociopolitical philosophies and cultural bias

Account of health	Sociopolitical philosophy	Cultural bias
Biopathological	Conservative	Subordination
Biographical	Libertarian	Individualism
Ecological	Reformist	Control
Communitarian	Radical pluralist	Cooperation

Source: Beattie (1993)

One of the characteristic features of health promotion is its concern with holism – a view of health that includes positive well-being in addition to the absence of disease, a broad conceptualization of the determinants of health and an emphasis on participation. Its information needs, therefore, are necessarily broad and include a range of different professional interpretations deriving from different disciplinary bases and including the lay perspective.

Much of the literature on lay perspectives draws on a discourse of conflict, couched in such terms as 'mounting a challenge' to biomedical interpretations and 'struggle over meaning'. Sociological accounts are also frequently expressed in this vein. Debate about the relative merits of the contributions of different research disciplines and perspectives is helpful in so far as it exposes the strengths and limitations of the various approaches and their respective utility – particularly when this results in positive attempts to redress shortcomings by seeking complementary approaches. It becomes damaging when it is merely a contest between different epistemological positions and methodologies in laying claims to the truth and different accounts of health are afforded different status.

A narrow and partial analysis of health problems cannot provide a secure basis for identifying priority issues and their determinants. Green and Kreuter (1991: 50) suggest that priorities are 'generally based on an analysis of data indicating the pervasiveness of the problems and their human and economic cost'. Mainstream epidemiological diagnoses, as we have noted, are concerned with objectively assessing the magnitude and distribution of diseases and health states together with the factors that contribute to them. Green and Kreuter strongly argue that a wider view is needed and problems should be defined from the outset in broad social terms. They offer two main reasons for this. Involving communities helps to ensure that their priority social and quality of life concerns are addressed and so avoids missing the mark in relation to social targets. It also contributes to encouraging community participation. They see the relationship between social and epidemiological diagnoses as complementary, operating in what they term either a 'reductionist' or an 'expansionist' way. Starting with an analysis of social problems, a reductionist approach would analyse the health and non-health factors that contribute to, or cause, the problem. The expansionist approach, in contrast, starts with an epidemiologically defined issue and works towards identifying the way this 'fits' into the larger social context. Green and Kreuter suggest that this avoids any tendency towards oversimplification.

While recognizing its contribution, Tannahill (1992) also cautions against an overemphasis on epidemiology as a driver in health promotion programme planning. He suggests that it neglects methodological issues by focusing on 'what to' rather than 'how to', creates an incomplete view of health, takes a narrow view of outcomes and leads to unsound programme planning. Of particular concern is the translation of single-issue problems into single-issue programmes, which ignores, on the one hand, the broader determinants and, on the other, that there may be factors common to a number of different conditions. For example, tobacco would be a common issue in relation to coronary heart disease, cancers and addiction, and all three are influenced by socioeconomic status. Programmes that address single issues in isolation – so-called 'vertical programmes' – therefore risk duplication of messages and inefficiency. Our position is that we need multiple complementary perspectives to identify priority health issues and their determinants.

DETERMINANTS OF HEALTH

Major improvements in health in the latter part of the nineteenth century have been attributed to improvements in the environment and general living and working conditions. The development of the germ theory and the improved possibility for immunization towards the end of the nineteenth century shifted the emphasis towards personal preventive services. The introduction of insulin and sulphonamide drugs in the 1930s heralded the dawn of the therapeutic era (Ashton and Seymour, 1988). The numerous subsequent technological developments in the biomedical field and faith in their capacity to improve health led to the rise of high-tech medicine. An increasingly technological view of health resulted in a shift in emphasis away from public health and community-based services and towards hospitals – so-called 'disease palaces'. Green (1996) noted that, in North America, towards the end of the twentieth century, over 90 per cent of expenditure on health was on medical care and less than 10 per cent on promoting healthy behaviour, lifestyles and environments, even though these accounted for between 50 and 71 per cent of all preventable premature mortality before the age of 75.

The Lalonde Report (Lalonde, 1974) is frequently cited as the seminal document challenging the narrow, technically focused emphasis on disease and advocating a broader, social model. It recognized the need for a simple conceptual framework to bring order to the many and various factors influencing health:

> to organize the thousands of pieces into an orderly pattern that was both intellectually acceptable and sufficiently simple to permit a quick location, in the pattern, of almost any idea, problem or activity related to health; a sort of map of the health territory. (Lalonde, 1974: 31)

This was achieved using the 'health field concept', which identified four main elements – human biology, environment, lifestyle and healthcare organization (see the box).

Elements of the 'Health Field Concept'

- Human biology includes all those aspects of health, both physical and mental, which are developed within the human body as a consequence of the basic biology of man [sic] and the organic makeup of the individual.
- The environment includes all those matters related to health which are external to the human body and over which the individual has little or no control.

(Continued)

> *(Continued)*
>
> - Lifestyle consists of the aggregation of decisions by individuals which affect their health and over which they more or less have control.
> - Healthcare organization consists of the quantity, quality, arrangement, nature and relationships of people and resources in the provision of healthcare.
>
> *Source*: Lalonde (1974: 31–2)

The health field concept therefore marked a radical break from the increasing emphasis on high-tech medicine, elevating the other three categories to equal standing. The concept itself is both simple and comprehensive. It was designed to provide insight into the factors associated with sickness and death and identify courses of action to improve health. The health field concept was also expected to encourage an analysis of any health problem in relation to all four categories. It could therefore be used to identify areas for research and guide policy and planning.

Some fifteen years after the publication of the health field concept, Raeburn and Rootman (1989) noted that the development of health promotion within this framework had focused particularly on lifestyle with insufficient attention being given to the influence of the environment, a concern echoed by others such as Morgan (2006). They also suggested that it was implicitly concerned with reduction of morbidity and mortality. To address these limitations, they proposed an expanded model that includes both inputs and explicit outputs (see Figure 2.5). The output side moves beyond morbidity and mortality to include functional capacity, positive health indicators and subjective perceptions. The input side is derived from the five action areas of the Ottawa Charter. With the exception of human biology, the other elements of the original health field concept are present. The reasons offered for its omission are that it is both a 'given' and an issue that falls under the aegis of health services rather than within the wider domain of policy, planning and research to promote overall health and well-being.

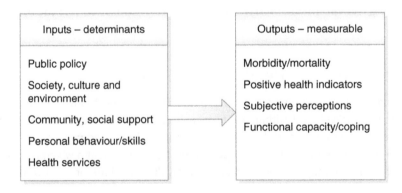

Figure 2.5   The expanded health field concept (derived from Raeburn and Rootman, 1989)

Lifestyle and environment

The relative importance of lifestyle and environment as determinants of health has been the subject of much debate – a debate that has contributed to defining health promotion as a discipline.

Lifestyle

The recognition of chronic diseases as the major cause of death in the more highly developed parts of the world in the mid twentieth century – against a backdrop of escalating healthcare costs – brought renewed interest in the role of prevention. Lifestyle is identified as a key factor in improving health status. Non-communicable diseases (NCDs) (cardiovascular diseases, cancers, respiratory diseases and diabetes) account for over 36 million deaths per year (WHO, 2013c). These NCDs share four 'lifestyle' risk factors: tobacco use, physical inactivity, alcohol misuse and unhealthy diet (WHO, 2013c).

Despite widespread recognition of the importance of lifestyle factors, there is little agreement about the meaning of the term. The concept of lifestyle generally refers to behavioural practices and ways of living (Fugelli, 2006; Korp, 2008) and to the behaviour/s that people engage in as they go about their daily lives (Ioannou, 2005).

The way in which the construct has become blurred over the years is succinctly encapsulated by Sobel (1981: 1, in O'Brien, 1995: 197): 'If the 1970s are an indication of things to come, the word lifestyle will soon include everything and mean nothing, all at the same time.' O'Brien's analysis of the appropriation of 'lifestyle' identifies three major influences:

- new systems of product marketing that segment the population into groups on the basis of lifestyle characteristics and consumption patterns (see the box for examples)
- counterculture movements and alternative lifestyles as markers of ideological commitments
- critiques of modernization and a reemphasis on self-determination.

Green and Kreuter (1991: 12) draw on anthropological, sociological and psychological interpretations to define lifestyle as:

> patterns of behaviour that have an enduring consistency and are based in some combination of cultural heritage, social relationships, geographic and socio-economic circumstances, and personality.

They are critical of the widespread and erroneous use of the word 'lifestyle' for any kind of behaviour and note that it has even been applied to temporary behaviour or single acts. A cursory glance at the literature reveals a plethora of papers about lifestyle factors and various risks of disease and ill health. More recently we have seen a focus on the clustering of unhealthy behaviours or 'multiple lifestyle risk' (Buck and Frosini, 2012: 4). Although many adults in the UK have improved their health behaviours, research reveals that nearly 70 per cent of the adult population continue to engage in two or more unhealthy behaviours (drinking excess alcohol, poor consumption of fruit and vegetables, little physical activity and smoking) (Buck and Frosini, 2012).

One example of an attempt to classify different categories of lifestyle is provided in the box.

Examples of lifestyle categories

Superprofiles use census and other data to distinguish ten lifestyles. The categorization was principally developed for marketing purposes but has also been used within the context of health inequality:

- affluent achievers
- thriving greys
- settled suburbans
- nest-builders
- urban venturers
- country life
- senior citizens
- producers
- hard-pressed families
- have-nots
- unclassified.

See: Local Government Data Unit – Wales (2003); Carr-Hill and Chalmers-Dixon (2005)

Green and Kreuter (1991: 13) suggest that the term 'lifestyle' should be used only to describe 'a complex of related practices and behavioural patterns, in a person or group, that are maintained with some consistency over time'. They argue that greater precision in the distinction between behaviour and lifestyle supports a more holistic and comprehensive approach to promoting health. If behaviour is understood within the context of the complex web that makes up a lifestyle, it immediately becomes evident that attempts to change that behaviour will need to have regard for the social, environmental and cultural circumstances that sustain that lifestyle. Furthermore, it demands sensitivity to possible knock-on effects for other aspects of the lifestyle. They also suggest that the use of the terms 'behaviour', 'action' or 'practice' to describe targets signals greater realism than the more aspirational term 'lifestyle', which is notoriously difficult to influence independently of the wider environmental context. This raises the issue of the relationship between lifestyle and environment, which we will explore more fully along with a consideration of environmental factors.

Much of the literature on lifestyle is located within a pathogenic paradigm and focuses on the association between risk behaviours and disease (Antonovsky, 1996).

In contrast, the focus within a salutogenic paradigm would be on the identification of those aspects of lifestyle that actively promote health – so-called 'salutary factors' – rather than the absence of risk factors. The recent interest in 'social capital' makes some move towards incorporating this salutogenic perspective.

Environment

The health field concept's interpretation of 'environment' placed considerable emphasis on the *physical* aspects of the environment with only passing reference being made to the *social* environment. Its central defining criteria for environmental factors are that they are external to the body and outside our immediate control. More recently, there has been much greater emphasis on social, cultural and economic aspects, particularly in the context of inequality.

Environmental factors can influence health either directly or indirectly. Simple examples of direct effects include exposure to toxic materials, shortage of food, lack of safe drinking water and overcrowding. Others factors will operate in a more indirect way. For example, lack of facilities for exercise in the environment will be associated with lower levels of physical activity and poorer heart health, while poor access to health services will be associated with low levels of uptake and so on.

Environmental factors may also interact – in some instances creating vicious circle effects. Poverty is associated with poor housing, diet, education and healthcare for example, leading to fewer life chances overall. Even ostensibly random occurrences, such as natural disasters, disproportionately affect poorer communities. It is estimated that, of the 80,000 deaths that occur each year because of natural disasters, 95 per cent occur in poorer countries (WHO, 2001). Equally, global warming – itself the product of atmospheric pollution – is predicted to affect water supplies and food production, resulting in population displacement as well as causing changes in some disease patterns. Again, the major effects are anticipated to be felt to the greatest extent by the world's most vulnerable populations. WHO predicts that over and above natural disasters, climate warming will increase vector-borne disease such as malaria and dengue fever along with food and water-borne diarrhoeal diseases. Climate change disproportionally affects the world's poorest countries (Intergovernmental Panel on Climate Change (IPCC), 2013).

Our earlier discussion of the term 'lifestyle' indicated that it is heavily influenced by the environment. The Lalonde Report discusses the validity of using free choice as the basis for distinguishing between lifestyle and environmental factors in the health field concept. The premise is that individuals can make choices about their lifestyle, but can do little about the environment. The Lalonde Report (Lalonde, 1974: 36), while accepting that the environment does affect lifestyle, concludes that: 'the deterministic view must be put aside in favour of faith in the power of free will, hobbled as this power may be at times by environment and addiction'. However, there has been increasing doubt about whether or not behaviour can legitimately be seen to be under autonomous control. Green and Kreuter (1991: 12) see it as 'socially conditioned, culturally embedded and economically constrained'.

O'Brien (1995: 192) draws on earlier sociological interpretations of lifestyle to identify two main elements in its construction – political, economic and cultural resources
and the psychosocial characteristics of the individual or groups – that is, a combination
of environmental and personal factors, with the former having the major influence:
'"Lifestyle" implied "choice" within a constrained context and the contexts were held to
be more important than the choices.'

There is clearly tension between recognizing humans as autonomous free agents
and taking a deterministic view of environmental factors. This tension between agency
and structure is also evident in decisions about the relative merits of environmental or
lifestyle approaches to health promotion. Clearly, the two are inextricably linked. The
PRECEDE planning model (Green and Kreuter, 1991, 2005) (see Chapter 4) recog-
nizes the interrelationship between behaviours and environment. It identifies factors
in the environment and conditions of living that facilitate actions by individuals or
organizations – 'enabling factors'.

Diagrammatic representation of the health field concept – which has typically
shown the four elements of lifestyle, environment, human biology and healthcare
organization as discrete entities – has perhaps reinforced the tendency to see them as
independent variables. Nesting the main determinants within each other, as depicted
by Dahlgren and Whitehead (1991), is more indicative of their broad interrelationships
and the respective positioning of macro and micro determinants, as shown in Figure 2.6.

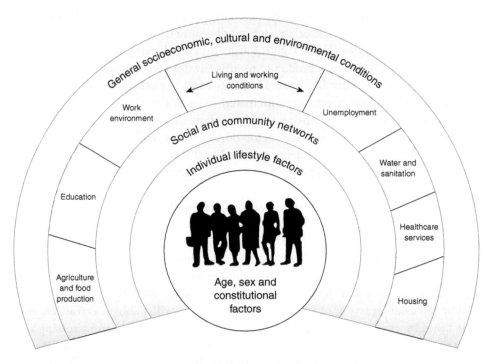

Figure 2.6   The main determinants of health (Dahlgren and Whitehead, 1991)

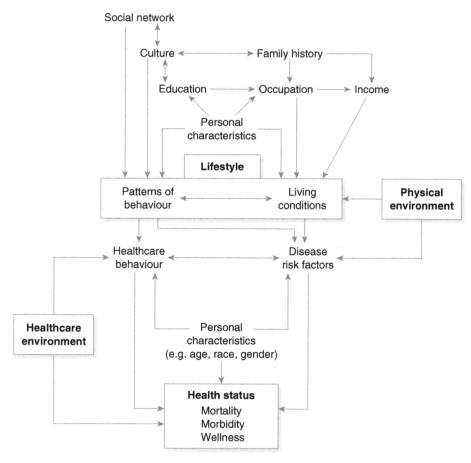

Figure 2.7   Some interrelationships in the complex system of lifestyle, environment and health status (Green et al., 1997)

Green et al. (1997) provide a more detailed analysis of the complex interrelationships, as shown in Figure 2.7.

An alternative approach acknowledges the relative importance of the various major determinants of health at different stages of the lifespan – for example, the powerful early influence of primary socialization. This conceptualization is central to the notion of the 'health career', which charts individuals' progress through the lifespan and the ways in which different factors come into play over time (Tones and Tilford, 2001). The focus is on individuals and their cumulative experience rather than a more general overview of determinants. Figure 2.8 represents the health career as a coaxial cable, with the central core being made up of an individual's values, attitudes and beliefs. The health career analysis can assist in ascertaining the key influences on individuals at different stages in their life and also in identifying opportunities for intervention.

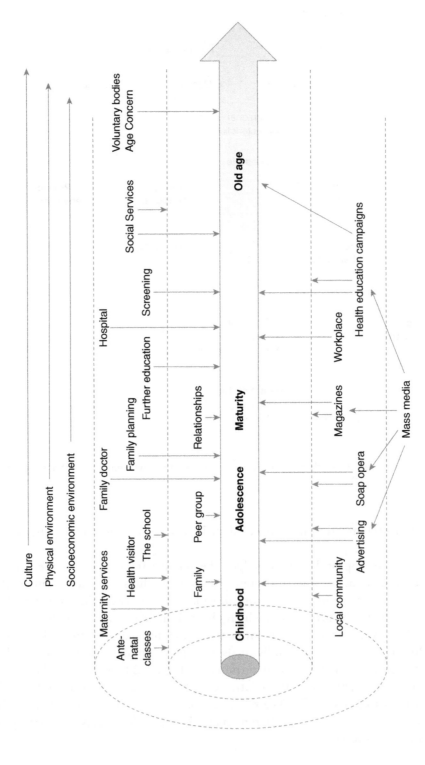

Figure 2.8 The health career

Social capital

There is an increasing body of evidence suggesting that social relationships and social support are protective against ill health, while social isolation and exclusion are associated with higher levels of ill health. For example, Thoits (2010) points out that one of the five major findings of a huge body of sociological research is that the negative impacts of stressors on health and well-being are reduced when people have social support. Similarly, a meta-analytic review by Holt-Lunstad et al. (2010) examined the findings of 148 studies from North America, Europe, Asia and Australia and found a 50 per cent increased likelihood of survival for people who had stronger social relationships.

Stansfield (1999) makes the important distinction between social networks and the functional aspects of support. A measure of social networks would include the number and frequency of contacts – taking account of the closeness of the contacts – and the density of the network. The quality of the support would include positive emotional and practical support and also any negative, undermining aspects of close relationships. Over and above offering direct support and encouraging health-enhancing behaviour, social connectedness, in itself, has been shown to have a positive effect on health status, possibly by acting as a buffer for stressors.

Mittelmark (1999a: 447) suggests that the anticipated benefits of strengthening social ties are 'better-functioning individuals, families, neighbourhoods and work groups, and improved physical and mental health'. He also summarizes the various pathways that have been proposed to explain how social ties affect health. These include:

- sources of information to help avoid high-risk or stressful situations
- positive role models
- increased feelings of self-esteem, self-identity and control over the environment
- social regulation, social control and normative influences
- sources of tangible support
- sources of emotional support
- perceptions that support is available
- buffering actions of others during times of stress.

The conceptual model developed by Berkman et al. (2000) locates social networks within the upstream social and cultural context that shapes them. It then identifies four primary pathways through which social networks operate downstream at the behavioural level:

1. provision of social support
2. social influence
3. social engagement and attachment
4. access to resources and material goods.

While the emphasis in the literature is on the health-enhancing consequences of social ties, Mittelmark draws attention to the emerging evidence (spearheaded by fields such as gerontology) that they may also be a source of social strain. Such strain would derive from actions by persons in an individual's social network, such as excessive demands, criticism, invasion of privacy and meddling, that, 'intended [or] unintended, cause a person to experience adverse psychological or physiological reactions' (Mittelmark, 1999a: 448). There is evidence to suggest that membership of certain social networks may actually be detrimental to health. For example, research in North America by Christakis and Fowler (2007) shows that obesity seems to spread through social networks.

Furthermore, Mittelmark contends that social support and social strain are not opposite ends of the same continuum – and so not mutually exclusive – but separate constructs. It follows, then, that there can be four permutations – high support/high strain, high support/low strain and so on.

The notion of 'social capital' has been applied to the social resources within a community and is currently enjoying a good deal of popularity. As Campbell (2011) argues, there is increased attention being given to social capital as a determinant of health. The concept was first explored by Bourdieu (1980) and further developed by other authors such as Coleman (1988, 1990) and Fukuyama (1999). However, the term is particularly associated with Putnam and his early work on local government in Italy (Putnam, 1993). For Putnam (1995: 67), social capital:

> refers to features of social organization such as networks, norms and social trust that facilitate coordination and cooperation for mutual benefit ... life is easier in communities blessed with a substantial stock of social capital ... networks of civic engagement foster sturdy norms of generalized reciprocity and encourage the emergence of social trust. [They] facilitate coordination and communication ... and allow dilemmas of collective action to be resolved. Finally, dense networks of interaction probably broaden the participants' sense of self, developing the 'I' into the 'we' ...

This interpretation encompasses more than just the existence of community networks and the resources available. It also includes the social norms of trust and reciprocity, a sense of belonging and willingness to engage in civic activity. While the density of networks is of general relevance to social capital, the notion has been extended to include different forms based on the characteristics of networks:

- **Bonding social capital** – refers to the ties between people in closely linked similar situations such as families or closely knit neighbourhoods
- **Bridging social capital** – refers to looser connections between people which may cross-cut boundaries, for example workmates and wider friendships
- **Linking social capital** – refers to links between people occupying different hierarchical and power positions, i.e. those who are not on an equal footing. (Woolcock, 2001; National Statistics, 2003; Performance and Innovation Unit, 2002)

Fukuyama (1999), writing from the perspective of an economist, provides an interesting interpretation of social capital. He notes that the usual definitions of social capital actually refer to *manifestations* of social capital rather than to its basic constructs. Thus, his (1999: 1–2) definition is as follows:

social capital is an instantiated informal norm that promotes cooperation between two or more individuals. The norms that constitute social capital can range from a norm of reciprocity between two friends, all the way up to complex and elaborately articulated doctrines like Christianity or Confucianism. They must be instantiated in an actual human relationship: the norm of reciprocity exists *in potentia* in my dealings with all people, but is actualized only in my dealings with *my* friends. By this definition, trust, networks, civil society, and the like which have been associated with social capital are all epiphenomenal, arising as a result of social capital but not constituting social capital itself.

According to Fukuyama (1999: 2), the norms that constitute social capital are 'related to traditional virtues like honesty, the keeping of commitments, reliable performance of duties, reciprocity, and the like'. Notwithstanding the potential for cooperation, which can extend beyond the immediate group, social capital can have negative effects (just as 'physical capital can take the form of assault rifles or tasteless entertainment, human capital can be used to devise new ways of torturing people'). Moreover, a group's internal cohesion may be achieved by treating outsiders with suspicion, hostility or even hatred. According to the author, organizations such as the Ku Klux Klan and the Mafia, because they have shared norms and cooperate, actually have social capital, but they produce 'abundant negative externalities for the larger society'. 'Good' social capital results in 'positive externalities' – that is, it will be beneficial to external individuals and groups. Furthermore, if a group's social capital produces positive externalities, the 'radius of trust' will extend beyond the group itself. Fukuyama sees modern society as a series of overlapping radii of trust – from friends, family and cliques up to large organizations and religious groups. Small radii of trust and within-group solidarity reduce the capacity for cooperation with outsiders and may be typical of more traditional social groupings. As Campbell (2011) argues, 'different forms of social capital may serve to advance or exclude different social groups' (p. 5965).

The large variety of overlapping social groups in modern societies may make it easier to transmit information, have greater resources and be readier to innovate than was the case in the past. Fukuyama asserts that social capital is an important feature of modern economies and underpins modern liberal democracy.

There has been considerable recent interest in the notion of social capital as a means of improving health prospects and particularly as a response to the adverse effects of social exclusion, which we will discuss below. A recent study examined data from the European Social Survey from 14 European countries in order to establish the causal impact of social capital on health (Rocco and Suhrcke, 2012). The authors found a strong causal relationship between social capital and individual health. A large-scale systematic review by McPherson et al. (2013) on the role and impact of social capital on the health and well-being of children and adolescents concluded that there is 'solid evidence to demonstrate that family and community social capital are associated with differences in children's and adolescents' experiences of health and wellbeing' (p. 37). The reviewers do point out, however, that understanding exactly *how* social capital impacts on health and well-being is less clear. As Eriksson (2011) and Campbell

(2011) argue, the links between social relationships and health are numerous, highly complex and not straightforward. In addition, social capital is hard to research for many different reasons as will now be discussed.

Assessing levels of social capital is challenging because of the nebulous nature of the concept and its cultural sensitivity (Babb, 2005). Eriksson (2011) also asserts that social capital is highly context-specific; as are the potential health impacts. Campbell et al. (1999) describe an exploratory qualitative study in the UK to assess the applicability of Putnam's conceptualization of social capital to the UK context as well as the variations in social capital between different communities with comparable socioeconomic status but different health experiences. They conclude that:

- the social capital constructs of trust and civic engagement may be particularly relevant to health status
- sources of social capital may cross the geographically defined boundaries of communities
- some network types (diverse and geographically dispersed) might be more health-enhancing than others
- Putnam's typology of social networks needs to be expanded to include informal networks
- the provision of community facilities does not constitute social capital – the processes by which such facilities are established and run require consideration
- Putnam's notion of community cohesion should be reconsidered in the light of the high levels of mobility and plural nature of contemporary communities
- there are major differences within communities in the ways in which social capital is created, sustained and accessed.

Commonly used measures of social capital are the levels of civic participation and social trust (Cooper et al., 1999). For example, Kawachi (1997) reports high levels of trust being associated with both lower mortality rates and higher levels of reported good health in the United States. Furthermore, bowling league membership (used by Putnam (1995) as indicative of levels of social participation) also correlates with lower mortality rates.

Fukuyama (1999) distinguishes two broad approaches to measuring social capital:

- a census of the groups and group membership in a given society
- a survey of levels of trust and civic engagement.

Putnam, for example, draws on group membership (derived from the number of groups, bowling leagues, sports clubs, political groups and the membership of groups) as an indicator of the level of civic engagement and social capital in society. He is sceptical about the contribution of 'mailing list' organizations to social connectedness on the grounds that the members do not actually meet and their ties are to a common ideology rather than to each other (Putnam, 1996), and he is cautious about the impact of the Internet:

I think strong social capital has to have a physical reality – a purely virtual tie is a pretty thin reed on which to build anything; it's highly vulnerable to anonymity and spoofing and very difficult to build trust. (Putnam interviewed by Bunting, 2007)

Nonetheless, the increased role of virtual communities in contemporary society is beginning to receive attention (see Chapter 9 for further discussion).

Fukuyama identifies a number of additional relevant variables:

- the internal cohesion of groups
- the radius of trust and the extent to which this encompasses the whole group plus or minus outsiders
- group affiliation and the extent to which this engenders distrust of outsiders.

Coulthard et al. (2002: 1) suggest that the main indicators of social capital are:

- social relationships and social support
- formal and informal social networks
- group memberships
- community and civic engagement
- norms and values
- reciprocal activities, such as childcare arrangements
- levels of trust in others.

Within the UK, there has been considerable interest in developing a harmonized approach to measuring social capital in official surveys. For this purpose, the definition adopted by National Statistics was: 'networks together with shared norms, values and understandings that facilitate cooperation within or among groups' (Cote and Healy, 2001, cited by Babb, 2005). The following five key constructs were identified and modules of questions developed for each:

- civic participation
- social networks and support
- social participation
- reciprocity and trust
- views about the local area.

However, it is acknowledged that cultural specificity and national characteristics may limit its use for international comparison (Babb, 2005). Furthermore, the way in which social capital has been conceptualized may fail fully or adequately to address the experience of specific groups such as young people who tend to have more informal social networks and less involvement in political and civic activity (Deviren and Babb, 2005). Harpham et al. (2002) point out that there are several important issues when measuring social capital such as establishing a measure of social capital that captures the latest theoretical developments and at what level measurement should take place (individual, community, and so on).

INEQUALITY AND SOCIAL EXCLUSION

Exposure to a plethora of different determinants throughout the course of life will inevitably result in some variations in health experience. A central concern of health promotion – one that is driven by a vision of health as a basic human right, together with a commitment to the fundamental value of social justice – has been to reduce inequality in health, both within and between nations (see box for examples). There is a vast body of literature on inequality that addresses the key issues of social class, gender, ethnicity, age, disability and unemployment – many of which are interrelated and mediated through poverty and social exclusion. However, we will confine ourselves here to key definitional issues.

Selected key facts on health inequalities in Scotland (Derived from Audit Scotland, 2012)

	Least deprived areas	Most deprived areas
Average life expectancy	84.2 years (women) 76.8 years (men)	81 years (women) 70.1 years (men)
Exclusive breastfeeding at 6–8 weeks	40%	15%
Alcohol-related hospital admissions per 100,000 population	214	1,621
Percentage of adults who smoke	11%	40%
GP consultations for anxiety (per 1000 patients)	28	62

While some variation in health experience is unavoidable, much of it can be attributed to unequal opportunities – that is, social inequality. The use of the term 'equity' introduces greater precision here. The World Health Organization (2011) defines health inequities as:

> differences in health status or in the distribution of health resources between different population groups, arising from the social conditions in which people are born, grow, live, work and age. Health inequities are unfair and could be reduced by the right mix of government policies.

The important point to note here, therefore, is that health inequities are amenable to change. The box below provides a simple checklist for assessing which differences in health are inequitable. However, in many industrialized countries, the term 'inequalities in health' is often taken to be synonymous with inequity (Leon et al., 2001).

Which health differences are inequitable?

Determinant of differentials	Potentially avoidable?	Commonly viewed as unacceptable?
Natural biological variation	No	No
Health-damaging behaviour if freely chosen	Yes	No
Transient health advantage of groups who take up health-promoting behaviour first (if other groups can easily catch up)	Yes	No
Health-damaging behaviour where choice of lifestyle is restricted by socioeconomic factors	Yes	Yes
Exposure to excessive health hazards in the physical and social environment	Yes	Yes
Restricted access to essential healthcare	Yes	Yes
Health-related downward social mobility (sick people move down social scale)	Low income – yes	Low income – yes

Source: Whitehead (1992: 4)

There is considerable evidence that social class is a key determinant of health status. For example, Erikson and Torssander (2008) analysed mortality data in Sweden in relation to social class and found that the risk of dying for any cause of death was double for men in the unskilled working class as compared with men in the higher professional and managerial occupations. As seen in this study, social class has typically been measured as occupational class. In Erikson and Torssander's (2008) they used the following classifications:

Social Class

I   Higher managerial and professional occupations

II   Lower managerial and professional occupations

IIIa Intermediate occupations

VI   Lower supervisory and skilled manual occupations

IIIb Routine non-manual occupations

VII   Unskilled manual occupations

IVcd Employers and own account workers in agriculture

IVab Employers and own account workers not in agriculture

(Note: 'the roman numerals correspond to the categories in the class schema suggested by Erikson and Goldthorpe' (p. 474).)

In the UK, the main government classification system – the social class based on occupation (Registrar General's Social Class) – was based on grouping occupations according to the levels of skill involved. Using this system, the population could be divided into six classes, as shown in the box below. This broad pattern of categorization was introduced in 1921 and, apart from subdividing class III into manual and non-manual in 1971, has remained substantially unchanged.

    A new social classification system was introduced in 2001 to reflect the changing patterns of work – the National Statistics Socio-economic Classification (NS-SEC) – see the box on page 99. Although still based on occupation, it focuses on employment conditions and, particularly, the amount of control that people have over their own and other people's work rather than on skill. It also includes a category for the long-term unemployed and those who have never had paid work.

Socioeconomic classifications

Social class based on occupation

I Professional occupations
II Managerial and technical occupations
III Skilled occupations:

    (N) non-manual
    (M) manual

IV Partly skilled occupations
V Unskilled occupations

National Statistics Socio-economic Classification (NS-SEC)

1	Higher managerial and professional occupations	Professional and managerial
1.1	Large employers and higher managerial occupations	
1.2	Higher professional occupations	
2	Lower managerial and professional occupations	
3	Intermediate occupations	Intermediate
4	Small employers and own account workers	
5	Lower supervisory and technical occupations	Routine and manual
6	Semi-routine occupations	
7	Routine occupations	
8	Never worked and long-term unemployed	

Source: Derived from National Statistics (2007); and Babb et al. (2004)

Much of the evidence on health inequality is based on occupational class. However, there has been some debate about its relevance for groups such as women, the unemployed, the elderly and children, and concern that occupational class may not fully reflect their circumstances. For example, married women have often been classified by their husband's occupation. This conceals their own employment status and may fail to fully recognize the effects of paid employment and working conditions on women's health. Sacker et al. (2000) note that, using the NS-SEC, occupational class emerged as the most important influence on mortality for men, but was less sensitive to variation in mortality for women, even when allocated by their own occupation.

A further issue concerns what occupational class actually measures. Family members are usually classed according to the occupation of the head of the household and, although they may not be directly exposed to occupation-linked factors, share the variation in health associated with social class – for example, children from lower social classes are at greater risk of injury through road traffic accidents and dying in a house fire (Errington and Towner, 2005). Occupational class, therefore, clearly encompasses a whole constellation of factors over and above different occupational conditions. These would include levels of income, housing, area of residence, education and lifestyle. In the UK, the landmark Black Report analysed possible explanations for variation in health status with social class and concluded that, although genetic and cultural factors might make some contribution, the major underlying factor was material inequality and deprivation (Department of Health and Social Security, 1980). This has been picked up by the work of others such as Sir Michael Marmot.

The increasing emphasis on health and social inequalities has resulted in critiques of existing measures of social class that have traditionally been biased towards categories of employed men to the exclusion of many minority groups. More recently, Savage et al. (2013) have proposed a new model for social class. Based on data from a large-scale survey carried out by the BBC in the UK in 2011, Savage et al. have devised an alternative seven-category classification system that does not solely rely on occupational status. This is a much more nuanced model that, the authors argue, better reflects a multidimensional picture, recognizing 'social polarisation in British society and class fragmentation in its middle layers … and the interplay between economic, social and cultural capital' (Savage et al., 2013: 219). See Table 2.5 for details.

Table 2.5   Summary of social classes

Social class	Description	Average household income (£)	Average number of social contacts*
Elite	Very high economic capital (especially savings), high social capital, very high highbrow cultural capital	89,082	16.2
Established middle class	High economic capital, high status of mean contact, high highbrow and emerging cultural capital	47,184	17.0
Technical middle class	High economic capital, very high mean social contacts, but relatively few contacts reported, moderate cultural capital	37,428	3.6
New affluent workers	Moderately good economic capital, moderately poor mean score of social contacts, although high range, moderate highbrow but good emerging cultural capital	29,252	16.9
Traditional working class	Moderately poor economic capital, although with reasonable house price, few social contacts, low highbrow and emerging cultural capital	13,305	9.8
Emergent service workers	Moderately poor economic capital, although with reasonable household income, moderate social contacts, high emerging (but low highbrow) cultural capital	21,048	14.8
Precariat	Poor economic capital and the lowest scores on every other criterion	8,253	6.7

Note: * Average number of social contacts refers to a number derived from a possible 34 types. For further information, see Savage et al. (2013)

The average number of social contacts is selected here as an indicator of social capital. Interestingly, the precariat does not have the worst mean for this indicator; it is second lowest to the 'technical middle class'. The average household income has also been included here as an indicator of economic capital. The differences (inequalities) between the classes are striking. Out of interest, the average income in the UK at the time of editing this chapter (early 2014) was £26,000.

Income has frequently been identified as a key determinant of social variation in mortality. Dorling et al. (2007) distinguish different levels of income (see box). They note that over the last 15 years there have been more poor households in Britain, but fewer that are very poor and there has been an increased polarization between different areas – wealthy areas have become wealthier and poor areas poorer.

Levels of income

- *Core poor:* people who are income poor, materially deprived and subjectively poor.
- *Breadline poor:* people living below a relative poverty line, and as such excluded from participating in the norms of society.
- *Non-poor, non-wealthy:* the remainder of the population classified as neither poor nor wealthy.
- *Asset-wealthy:* estimated using the relationship between housing wealth and the contemporary Inheritance Tax threshold.
- *Exclusive wealthy:* people with sufficient wealth to exclude themselves from the norms of society.

Source: Dorling et al. (2007)

Wilkinson and Pickett (2009) note that societies with a smaller gap between the least well-off and the most well-off fare better on a range of health-related indicators than societies with larger gaps. Notably, it is not just the people at the lower end of the scale who fare badly in more unequal societies but everyone along the social gradient.

Absolute and relative poverty

Poverty influences physical health as it limits access to good-quality nutrition and housing, but also has an effect on mental health (Shaw et al., 1999). The Marmot Review Team (2011) highlighted this again more recently. Yet, against a backdrop of overall improvement in general prosperity and health status, differentials seem to be widening – a pattern not untypical of industrialized nations, as established in Wilkinson and Pickett's (2009) work. A key factor would seem to be income inequality (Davey Smith, 1996). Indeed, Wilkinson (1994) states that life expectancy has increased most in industrialized nations where income differences have narrowed and mortality is more closely related to income inequality *within* countries than absolute differences in income *between* countries (Wilkinson, 1997).

This raises the issue of absolute and relative poverty. *Absolute* poverty exists when insufficient resources are available to provide the basic essentials of life, such as food and shelter. The World Bank, for example, has used the notional US$1 per day as an absolute minimum survival budget. However, this measure of extreme poverty has little meaning in the context of advanced industrialized societies. Some countries, such as the United States, have defined an official poverty line based on the cost of a basic food basket. The Canadian Council on Social Development (2001) provides an analysis of different ways of defining poverty and notes the debate over which items should be regarded as necessities. A key issue concerns whether a poverty line should be set in relation to a basic survival budget or a level of income that would enable people to participate in society.

Relative poverty, in contrast, is defined by the European Commission (2004) as follows:

> People are said to be living in poverty if their income and resources are so inadequate as to preclude them from having a standard of living considered acceptable in the society in which they live. Because of their poverty they may experience multiple disadvantage through unemployment, low income, poor housing, inadequate health care and barriers to lifelong learning, culture, sport and recreation. They are often excluded and marginalised from participating in activities (economic, social and cultural) that are the norm for other people and their access to fundamental rights may be restricted.

An article by Frank (2000) in the *New York Times Magazine* drew attention to the importance of relative poverty/affluence in people's lives:

> Consider a choice between the two scenarios:

> - World A: You earn $110,000 per year and others earn $200,000.
> - World B: You earn $100,000 per year and others earn $85,000.

> The figures for income represent real purchasing power. Although in absolute terms individuals would be better off in Scenario A, a majority of Americans chose Scenario B.

There are several different ways of establishing relative poverty levels – for example, the proportion of income needed to cover the basic necessities of life, the proportional relationship to the median income and measures based on 'market baskets', which would include items in line with community norms.

A national survey of poverty and social exclusion in Britain published by the Joseph Rowntree Foundation (Gordon et al., 2000) used a variety of measures of poverty. These included not being able to afford what are generally perceived to be 'necessities'. The box gives a list of items that over 75 per cent of the adult population regard as necessities. It is clear that the interpretation of what constitutes a necessity goes beyond the basic survival needs of subsistence diet, shelter, clothing and fuel to include participating in social customs, fulfilling obligations and taking part in activities.

Items perceived as necessities

Item	% considering item 'necessary'
Beds and bedding for everyone	95
Heating to warm living areas of the home	94
Damp-free home	93
Visiting friends or family in hospital	92
Two meals a day	91
Medicines prescribed by doctor	90
Refrigerator	89
Fresh fruit and vegetables daily	86
Warm, waterproof coat	85
Replace or repair broken electrical goods	85
Visits to friends or family	84
Celebrations on special occasions such as Christmas	83
Money to keep home in decent state of decoration	82
Visits to school, such as sports day	81
Attending weddings, funerals	80
Meat, fish or vegetarian equivalent every other day	79
Insurance of contents of dwelling	79
Hobby or leisure activity	78
Washing machine	76
Collecting children from school	75

Source: Derived from Joseph Rowntree Foundation (2000)

The Joseph Rowntree Foundation has attempted to develop a Minimum Income Standard for Britain. This goes further than thresholds based on relative income, measures of deprivation or budget standards calculated on baskets of goods and services to establish a level of income which is sufficient to support 'having what you need in order to have the opportunities and choices necessary to participate in society' (2008: 1).

The United Nations Development Programme (UNDP), recognizing the complex relationship between economic indicators such as per capita income and human well-being, uses the Human Development Index (HDI) for international comparison. The HDI measures life expectancy, educational attainment and income and combines these to create a single statistic by which social and economic development are measured and compared across countries (UNDP, 2013). In 2012, Norway was ranked highest and Niger and the Democratic Republic of Congo were ranked lowest. (For further information see: hdr.undp.org/en/statistics/hdi)

Whereas absolute poverty is a central issue in the developing world, poverty in urban, industrialized countries has been defined (Supplementary Benefits Commission, 1979, cited in Dahlgren and Whitehead, 1991) as:

> a standard of living so low that it excludes and isolates people from the rest of the community. To keep out of poverty they must have an income which enables them to participate in the life of the community.

This definition focuses attention on social exclusion, which is currently receiving considerable attention. Although social exclusion is defined in a number of different ways common components are 'disadvantage in relation to certain norms of social, economic or political activity pertaining to individuals, households, spatial areas of population groups: the social economic and institutional processes through which disadvantage comes about: and the outcomes or consequences for individuals, groups or communities' (Percy-Smith, 2000: 4). Therefore, this disadvantage is not solely restricted to economic factors, but would also include other forms of cultural and social discrimination. Major groups of socially excluded people are the unemployed, ethnic minorities, refugees, the elderly, lone parents and their children and those, especially children, with disability.

Clearly, social exclusion exerts a powerful psychosocial influence and there are obvious links with the notion of social capital. Kawachi (1997) demonstrates lower levels of social trust in states with a higher 'Robin Hood Index' – a measure of income inequality based on the proportion of aggregate income that would have to be redistributed to level up earnings. Similar findings are obtained for participation in voluntary associations. However, Lynch et al.'s (2000) analysis of income inequality and mortality cautions against an exclusive emphasis on psychosocial effects and the lack of social cohesion, which, they allege, is akin to victim-blaming at the community level. They propose that the main causes of health inequality are material – including access to both private and social resources, such as education, healthcare, social welfare and work. Raphael's (2001a: 30) analysis of social inequality and heart disease in Canada provides a concise summary of the interaction between these various elements:

> Social exclusion is a process by which people are denied the opportunity to participate in civil society; denied an acceptable supply of goods or services; are unable to contribute to society, and are unable to acquire the normal commodities expected of citizens. All of these elements occur in tandem with material deprivation, excessive psycho-social stress, and adoption of health-threatening behaviours shown to be related to the onset of, and death from, cardiovascular disease.

Composite indicators of deprivation

The concept of deprivation can apply both to individuals and areas and includes material and social elements (Krieger, 2001). There is some evidence that, independently of an individual's level of deprivation, living in a deprived area has an adverse effect on health (Shaw et al., 1999).

There are composite indicators of deprivation that can be used to assess the overall levels of deprivation within different areas. The Jarman and Townsend indices have been used widely in the UK and draw on census data (see the box). The Jarman index has been much criticized – both on account of its method of construction and also because it is biased towards classifying areas in London as being deprived rather than those in the North (Talbot, 1991). This has been attributed to the skewed distribution of single-parent families and highly mobile populations, for example, which tend to be more concentrated in the inner London area.

The Jarman and Townsend Indices of Deprivation
Jarman underprivileged area score (UPA)

Derived from GPs' views about factors that influence their workload.

- Percentage of children under five
- Percentage of unemployment
- Percentage of ethnic minorities
- Percentage of single-parent households
- Percentage of elderly living alone
- Overcrowding factor
- Percentage of lower social classes
- Percentage of highly mobile people
- Percentage of unmarried couple families
- Poor housing factor

The above ten items were originally included in the Jarman UPA score, but the last two are omitted from the Jarman UPA8 score.

Townsend combined deprivation indicator

- Percentage of economically active residents aged 16–59/64 who are unemployed
- Percentage of private households that do not possess a car
- Percentage of private households that are not owner occupied
- Percentage of private households with more than one person per room

Source: Derived from Whitehead (1987)

Attempts to measure levels of deprivation on a large geographic scale often obscure smaller pockets of deprivation. There is considerable interest, therefore, in small area analysis. In the UK, the government uses seven dimensions of deprivation as follows:

- Income deprivation
- Employment deprivation
- Health deprivation and disability
- Education deprivation
- Crime deprivation
- Barriers to housing and services deprivation
- Living environment deprivation. (English Indices of Deprivation, 2010)

Carr-Hill and Chalmers-Dixon (2002) emphasize that these various indices are artificial constructs and only partial or proxy measures of phenomena such as deprivation. They caution against reification, which can occur when operational constructs used as approximate measures become substituted for the actual meaning of the concepts they purport to measure. While their argument focuses on the measurement of deprivation, it would apply equally to other indicators of health status.

Childhood poverty

Childhood poverty, particularly when persistent over a number of years, is of concern not only because of its immediate effects on this vulnerable group but also because of longer-term effects and its contribution to sustaining cycles of deprivation. Within the UK, an estimated 4 million children live in poverty despite the previous two governments' pledges to eradicate it. International comparison clearly presents challenges in terms of selection and comparability of indicators. UNICEF's (2010) comparison of children's material well-being among 24 industrialized nations ranked Switzerland the highest and Slovakia the lowest, with the UK in 19th place. For educational well-being, Finland was ranked highest and Belgium lowest (UK was 13); for health well-being, the Netherlands was ranked highest and Hungary lowest (UK was 11). There is a great deal of evidence that investing in childhood has huge repercussions for adult life. It is clear that early intervention at this stage of the life course is an important health and social investment that has the potential to impact on health and social inequalities. The highest priority policy recommendation in the Strategic Review of Health Inequalities in England Post-2010 *Fair Society, Healthy Lives*, was that every child is given the best start in life (Marmot, 2010).

Strategies to reduce childhood poverty have therefore become a central plank in attempts to address inequalities in several countries. In the UK, for example, the Child Poverty Act of 2010 outlined a cross-party governmental commitment to tackling this issue. The aim is to eradicate child poverty by the year 2020. This was reinforced in the child poverty strategy of 2011. As a result of an analysis of international examples of effective approaches in reducing child poverty, the National Children's Bureau (NCB) produced a set of guidelines that included increasing free early years education and reducing childcare costs. Specifically, the NCB recommended that the following be embedded in any strategy designed to tackle child poverty:

- Having a robust mechanism for taking forward a cross-government child poverty strategy holding all government departments to account

- Introducing a package of measures to promote maternal employment
- Supplementing families' incomes for engaging in activities that promote child well-being
- Taking forward evaluated neighbourhood-based approaches to tackling child poverty and promoting health well-being. (Fauth et al., 2013: 4)

Tackling inequality

Measuring inequality within and between nations is not an abstract exercise, but serves to expose social injustice and highlight the need for action (see, for example, Acheson, 1998). Marmot (2005: 1099) drew attention to the inequitable 'spread of life expectancy of 48 years among countries and 20 years or more within countries' in his call for political action to address inequality. The need to measure and understand the problem was recognized in the priorities for action set out in the final report of the Commission on Social Determinants of Health (CSDH) (2008) – see box.

Principles of action for closing the health gap

1. Improve the conditions of daily life – the circumstances in which people are born, grow, live, work and age.
2. Tackle the inequitable distribution of power, money and resources – the structural drivers of those conditions of daily life – globally, nationally and locally.
3. Measure the problem, evaluate action, expand the knowledge base, develop a workforce that is trained in the social determinants of health, and raise public awareness about the social determinants of health.

Source: CSDH (2008: 2)

The central arguments in this section point to the importance of policy-level interventions in tackling the determinants of health. Health public policy is discussed in detail in Chapter 5. An effective policy response clearly depends on tackling the cause of inequality. Only at a policy level is it possible to tackle the conditions that give rise to certain sets of behaviours. While the extreme effect of poverty and deprivation may be self-evident, Marmot emphasizes the importance of understanding the social determinants of health inequalities – which he refers to as the 'causes of the causes'. The CSDH report (2008) notes the need to tackle the unequal distribution of power, money and resources.

Looking at inequality within countries, Wilkinson and Marmot (2003) identified the following key areas:

- the social gradient
- stress
- early life

- social exclusion
- work
- unemployment
- social support
- addiction
- food
- transport.

Further work led by Sir Michael Marmot highlights how health inequalities are linked to a person's social position – for example, where they live and the type of employment they are engaged in (Marmot, 2010). The Marmot Review concluded that we needed to focus more on inequalities in well-being rather than health; that examining the 'causes of the causes' is of paramount importance; that mental health is extremely important in determining physical health and life chances; and, finally, that there should be a focus on resilience (personal and community). The notion of resilience is receiving increasing attention and it links to more salutogenic approaches to understanding health.

Graham and Kelly (2004: 1) also recognize a 'number of axes of social differentiation' over and above social class. These include ethnicity, gender, sexuality, age, area, community and religion that are mediated by dimensions such as socioeconomic disadvantage and discrimination. They propose *social position* as the lynchpin in the causal chain of factors affecting health status through its influence on access to societal resources as well as exposure to risk. They emphasize the distinction between the determinants of health and determinants of health inequality.

The fact that the overall health status is improving in industrialized countries such as the UK yet inequalities persist – or even increase – raises fundamental questions about the relationship between efforts to improve health and efforts to tackle health inequality. There are two broad options for tackling inequality (Graham and Kelly, 2004):

- focusing on the poorest and most socially excluded who experience poorest health
- recognizing the whole social gradient, including those who could not be regarded as socially excluded, yet are still disadvantaged in health terms because of their social position.

Clearly, to be effective, any efforts must be based on an understanding of the *unequal distribution* of the determinants of health.

Asset-based approaches

More recently, particularly in Scotland for example, there has been a move towards more asset(s)-based approaches to health promotion and public health and the use of these in addressing health inequalities. Asset-based approaches counter deficit-based approaches to assessing health promotion need (Morgan and Ziglio, 2007: 17). They focus more on the positive aspects of health and what makes us healthy rather than on what makes us sick (Foot, 2012). Assets are defined as 'the collective resources which individuals and communities have at their disposal, which protect against negative health outcomes and promote health status' (Glasgow Centre for Population Health, 2011: 2). To adopt an assets-based approach is to recognize the experience, skills, strengths, knowledge and potential that already exist in a group or community and how these (may) contribute to the support of health and well-being. There is an obvious connection here to salutogenic and resilience-building approaches and, in fact, Morgan and Ziglio (2007: 17) set out the case for using 'salutogenic indicators' in a key paper on asset-based approaches. Asset-based approaches are becoming an important part of mainstream approaches to promoting health (Glasgow Centre for Population Health, 2011). There are clear links here to capacity and issues such as social capital.

There are a number of challenges in using and developing asset-based approaches, such as how assets are measured, establishing the relationship between assets and well-being and issues to do with how we measure and assess positive health and well-being in a culture that has been more concerned with measuring ill health and disease (Glasgow Centre for Population Health, 2012). However, the focus on empowerment and on health gain is key and there is, therefore, a central place for asset-based approaches in tackling health inequalities despite the challenges faced. Nevertheless, Friedli (2012) adopts a more cautionary approach and is more critical of such approaches, arguing that they focus attention away from economic, material and structural issues onto psychosocial factors. Notwithstanding such critiques, asset-based approaches are forming an important part of Joint Strategic Asset Assessments (JSAA). JSAAs are a refocusing of Joint Strategic Needs Assessment and promote an asset-based approach to needs assessment (Tobi, 2013). Such approaches are being more commonly drawn on in UK-wide efforts to promote public health. For further discussion of Joint Strategic Needs Assessment, see Chapter 6.

THE CONTRIBUTION TO PROGRAMME PLANNING

It is axiomatic that planning interventions to promote health requires understanding of the current health status of populations and the factors that influence it. We have considered different approaches to assessing health and its determinants.

Rather than engage in sterile debate about the relative superiority of biomedical or interpretivist approaches, we would contend that they offer complementary insights. Tension arises from the unequal power positions of those subscribing to different methodologies and the dominance of biomedicine. This has been challenged from both professional and lay quarters. In that health is essentially a subjective experience, the lay perspective is particularly relevant. Furthermore, understanding a complex multidimensional concept such as health necessarily needs to draw on multiple perspectives – including salutogenic as well as pathogenic perspectives.

The emergence of health promotion as a discipline placed an emphasis on environmental influences on health – both directly and in terms of shaping behaviour and lifestyle. Notwithstanding the debate about the primacy of agency or structure, it is clear that there is a reciprocal relationship between the two elements. The complexity of the interrelationship has become more evident as our conceptualization of the environment has broadened. While the contribution of social and socioeconomic aspects of the environment has been recognized for some time, the recent resurgence in interest in social capital focuses attention on social connectedness and opportunities for civic engagement.

The measurement of health and quality of life and their determinants is undoubtedly challenging. To conclude this chapter, we should note that the capacity to assess the health of communities and identify key determinants underpins rational planning processes. Clearly, the way in which such an assessment is approached should reflect the ideology and values of health promotion and pay particular attention to factors associated with health inequalities.

Key Points

- Measuring health and its determinants is of fundamental importance to efforts to improve health.
- Epidemiological measures contribute to our understanding of health and its determinants – particularly in relation to mortality and morbidity.
- Multiple perspectives, including the lay perspective, are needed for a more complete understanding of health, including positive well-being.
- Salutogenic as well as pathogenic explanations of health should be considered.
- Both environment and lifestyle factors influence health and are themselves interrelated.
- Social aspects of the environment, including social connectedness and social capital, have an impact on health status.
- Poverty and material deprivation are major causes of health inequality.
- Understanding the wider social determinants of health inequality and social exclusion are of central importance in developing initiatives to tackle inequality.

On the companion website

- Morgan, A. and Ziglio, E. (2007) 'Revitalising the evidence base for public health: an assets model', *Promotion & Education*, 14: 17–23.
- Savage, M., Devine, F., Cunningham, N., Taylor, M., Li, Y., Hjellbrekke, J., Le Roux, B., Friedman, S. and Miles, A. (2013) 'A new model of social class? Findings from the BBC's Great British Class Survey Experiment', *Sociology*, 47: 219–50.
- Thoits, P. (2010) 'Stress and health: major findings and policy implications', *Journal of Health and Social Behaviour*, 51: doi: 10.1177/0022146510383499.

The following case studies on the companion website are relevant to the content of this chapter:

- *Tobacco Control*– Soroya Julian (Jamaica)
- *Community-Based Health Planning and Services Initiative* – Grace Kafui Annan and Ebenezer Owusu-Addo (Ghana)

- *Integration of Research Evidence into Local Public Health Decision-Making* – Maja Larsen and Arja R Aro (Denmark)
- *Healthy Homes* – R. Egan, K. Hicks and M. Dalziel (New Zealand)
- *Traditional Beliefs and Elephantitis* – Mustapha Sonnie (Sierra Leone)
- *Lay Community Health Workers* – Modou Njai (The Gambia)
- *Knowledge-Based Strategies for Action* – Monica Lillefjell and Ruca Maass (Norway)
- *Friendly Schools, Friendly Families* – Sharyn Burns, Gemma Crawford, Donna Cross and Jude Comfort (Australia)

Paradigms and Philosophies

Thomas, M.

DEFINITION

'Epistemology', in philosophy, is the theory of knowledge, especially the analysis of its methods, validity and scope. It concerns itself with both the acquisition and limits of human knowledge and explores elements of science, such as evidence and methods of enquiry, as well as cognitive processes that make sense of knowledge, such as perception, sensory input, memory, beliefs and cultural contexts.

Knowledge is generally held to be based on three points Plato set out in his writings:

- a person has knowledge if there is a belief in the knowledge (for example, I am hungry)
- the knowledge is true (I have not eaten for several hours)
- there are good grounds for having belief in the truthfulness of the knowledge, it can be justified (this experience has occurred before).

This approach is open to challenge and many philosophers have grappled with variations on knowledge and truth. Russell (1967) argued that there are different types of knowledge and, while some may be based on personal beliefs (internalised knowledge of sensory input, for example), some are proposed to us by others (propositional knowledge) and, therefore, require different perceptions of trust and evidence. Another view is that knowing *about* something is different from knowing *how* to do something.

In the late seventeenth century, Locke (1961) took an empiricist view that knowledge is derived from a mental perception of the senses and experiences. Rationalists such as Descartes (Cottingham, 1997) counter-proposed that knowledge based on perception may be erroneous and argued that a heightened sense of reason and rationality is needed to demonstrate the evidence-base of knowledge. This debate continues to the present day as new technology, techniques and methods of inquiry suggest that many suppositions and assumptions underpinning what we know are erroneous. This means that epistemology, of necessity, seeks to understand the concept of truth and the beliefs out of which the emphasis on scientific methodologies has grown and the consequential quest for reliability, validity, repeatability and the ability to generalise.

Such a rationalist and sceptical approach provides the basis for scientific paradigms and is the drive behind wanting to find the 'theory of everything', but it is not without its detractors. The phenomenological approach to science suggests that we can never truly know everything and all we have is a contextual truth, based on the time and place of existence.

The term 'paradigm' was popularised by Kuhn's (1970) work on scientific structures when he used it to describe types of thinking specific to particular assumptions and approaches used in different research methods. It is applied to the research approaches used by different schools to explore phenomena. For example, researchers appear to prefer positivist, naturalistic or constructivist paradigms, each with their own rules and expectations with regard to research activities. Paradigmatic thinking helped science to understand that there are different methodical approaches to scientific endeavours that support epistemology.

KEY POINTS

- Epistemology is the study of knowledge itself – how it is structured and demonstrated and how beliefs and cognitive processes work to support trust in knowledge
- Paradigms are different approaches to scientific inquiry each with their own beliefs, assumptions and methodical techniques

DISCUSSION

Epistemology is often confused and used interchangeably with ontology, but they are different branches of the philosophy of knowledge. 'Ontology' can be summarised as the study of the *characteristics* of reality, or being, while epistemology studies *how* we know about reality (Gomm, 2004). To make matters worse, some branches of existential and phenomenological philosophy use the term ontology to refer to the study of essence or existence.

Irrespective of philosophical concerns, what is important is to have a 'purpose', sometimes referred to as a 'justification', for a study (Clough and Nutbrown, 2007); in other words, is the phenomenon to be studied real? If so, then there will be assumptions made about the researcher's own approach. For example, if a researcher wishes to study nursing in the community, there are three options for how this can be done:

- by going out with district nurses and working alongside them – a 'naturalistic' approach
- by measuring pre- and post-intervention scores and outcomes data – a 'positivist/empirical' approach
- by exploring nursing via the experiences and thoughts of the district nurses – a 'phenomenological' approach.

Researchers have their own views about which is the best approach, often based on their assumptions, beliefs and knowledge about the area to be studied. They may believe that there needs to be strict control of the variables to be measured and the potential for intervention and influence on the experimental process need to be minimised. Alternatively, they may believe that reality is a social or personal construct, a subjective experience and only by interacting with the subjects themselves can patterns emerge.

Understanding your own paradigm approach is an important first step in research design as beliefs and assumptions about gathering data will determine which research method will be appropriate. The main two categories are 'quantitative' and 'qualitative'. These each have various methodological approaches that can be used, such as, for quantitative methods, deduction, experimental design and statistical analysis, and, in qualitative methods, induction, interpretation and flexible designs.

The terms 'positivism' and 'empiricism' are used to describe a scientific approach that rejects ideas not necessarily based on fact in favour of a pragmatic approach using valid measurements to collect evidence. It is the most dominant paradigm in the field of scientific inquiry because of its emphasis on description, explanation and empirical facts.

Originally, positivism/empiricism was accepted as an approach that was applicable in both the physical *and* social sciences, but the growth of the logical positivism movement (also known as logical empiricism) in the mid-twentieth century, with its stress on rationality using mathematical analysis, means that, today, it is almost exclusively used to describe quantitative empirical approaches. It is still used in economics and public health where there is an emphasis on epidemiology and statistical analysis.

Interestingly, 'post-positivism' somewhat undermines the positivists' assumption by using qualitative in addition to quantitative analysis, to double-check the results of experiments (Blaxter et al., 2006). Post-positivists believe that research gives only a partial glimpse of reality, but, nevertheless, they prefer the more detached, mathematical assumptions of positivism, with qualitative methodologies used as comparators for numerical results rather than being the primary methodology.

'Naturalistic' paradigms have some links with positivism, but assume that our reality is only a part of nature, time and space. The preferred approach is to study phenomena in a natural setting. Naturalism begins to separate from the positivist paradigm in its acceptance that some areas of study may initially appear to be outside mathematical formulae (for example, societal culture or attitudes), but they are still rational as every study gives a *glimpse* of reality, never the full picture.

This assumption can be confused with 'phenomenology' as some use the term to denote naturalistic approaches (Polit et al., 2001). It differs from the phenomenological method of the same name, however, which studies how individuals make sense of their own reality via individual experiences.

Naturalistic paradigms gather evidence to produce theory that can later be tested as technologies and techniques develop and are primarily used in the fields of psychology, sociology, biological and environmental sciences.

'Constructive' or 'interpretative' paradigms reject the positivist assumption of there being one objective reality that can be measured. Constructivism is an approach that accepts knowledge as not something acquired as if from nowhere, but a product of effort and cognitive processing. Constructivists understand reality via the assumptions we make that build on existing knowledge, which may be erroneous or eventually become extinct. Different observers invent their own explanations about the same phenomena and it is their scientific inquiry into these that produces tools to support their theories. Methodologies are invented to reinforce existing knowledge rather than discover completely new knowledge, as knowledge is constantly based on previous studies and findings.

The constructivist paradigm can be observed when researchers defend theories that cannot yet be tested or demonstrated via traditional positivist or naturalist approaches. Constructivists, therefore, reject metaphysical ideas but do accept that reality is socially constructed and there are as many realities as there are people to interpret them (Robson, 2011). Constructivism/interpretivism can be seen in research carried out in areas such as quantum physics, economics, psychology, learning theory and theory construction.

CASE STUDY

Elisabeth is a nurse who is undertaking a Masters degree at a local university. She has to choose a project for her research dissertation and wants to study what patients think about the care given on her ward.

Elisabeth was perfectly clear about her study topic until she started to read around research and all the different terms and definitions, often used interchangeably, and became confused about her research approach. She went to see her supervisor, who suggested they started from the beginning and asked why

Elisabeth wanted to carry out her study – whether it was for policy purposes, quality purposes or to involve patients in the operational aspects of care? Elisabeth decided that she wanted to find out if the patients liked the care and so her study would be centred on quality issues.

With her supervisor, Elisabeth began to explore what type of evidence would answer her question: what do patients think about the care given on the ward? There was currently a focus on care, compassion and patient dignity, so Elisabeth knew she could get existing questionnaires and interview schedules. Her supervisor then asked Elisabeth to explain in detail what she wanted to explore: was it a focus on causative factors, identifying areas that cause positive or negative reactions (noises at night, for example), or was her study trying to find out what could be done to improve future care? Elisabeth decided on the latter and went on to discuss the ethical and organisational regulations to be addressed before her study could commence (Mason, 2002). The session ended with a summary of the above stages and contextualising them within an epistemological framework.

Elisabeth left the supervisory session much clearer about the approach for her dissertation. In epistemological terms, she was taking a constructivist/interpretative paradigm because she was interested in, and believed (assumed), that the patients made sense of their own realities and would have different perceptions of their care. Elisabeth believed strongly in the individualisation of care, so this paradigm fitted in with her worldview and beliefs.

Within her interpretative paradigm she planned to use a qualitative method and utilise both questionnaires and focus group interviews to gather data. These are validated tools, used with existing measuring instruments (questionnaire/interviews), so would give her study both reliability and validity and allow her to plan and implement an enhanced patient care programme.

CONCLUSION

Although it is not imperative that healthcare staff become deeply immersed in philosophical discussions about the nature of reality and existence (ontology) or how we know what we know (epistemology), an understanding of how knowledge is gained and the methods for gaining that knowledge (paradigms) is important in clinical care. By understanding the pre-study assumptions and beliefs about scientific approaches made by researchers, the reader of a published study is better able to critique the method, data collection, analysis and conclusions and judge whether the findings are relevant to their care environment or not. It also allows for a higher level of understanding regarding the reliability and validity of the findings.

Equally important, by exploring their own beliefs and assumptions about how knowledge is gained, healthcare professionals can develop an understanding of research paradigms, methods and the methodologies regarding their topics of study that they could use and best suit their worldviews.

FURTHER READING

Clough, P. and Nutbrown, C. (2007) *A Student's Guide to Methodology* (2nd edn). London: Sage.
Robson, C. (2011) *Real World Research* (3rd edn). Oxford: Wiley-Blackwell.

16 Planning and Undertaking a Literature Review or Documentary Analysis

Williamson, G., and Whittaker, A.

Chapter aims

After reading this chapter, you should be able to:

- understand what a literature review is;
- feel confident about undertaking a literature search;
- understand what a documentary analysis is;
- feel confident about undertaking a documentary analysis;
- be able to source high-quality material in your topic area.

Introduction

You will have had some thoughts about your research topic and be starting to formulate your research question. The next stage is to undertake a literature review in order to establish what is already known about your research topics, and we will begin with this. We will then discuss documentary analysis, which is quite different from a literature review because it is a form of primary research in its own right. This chapter aims to guide you through that process, using case studies and activities to illustrate the different stages. This is a distinct process from conducting a systematic review and meta-analysis, which is a literature review undertaken using a strict, explicit and transparent set of formal protocols that seek to minimise the chances of systematic bias and error (Macdonald, 2003). We devote Chapter 8 to an introduction to systematic reviews and meta-analyses.

It is important to see your literature review as an ongoing process that would start in the early stages of planning your proposal, and would continue throughout the life of your project, if you were actually undertaking one. This would not be just about updating your literature review as new material becomes available: if you were undertaking data collection, these data would be likely to suggest new ways of looking at your research topic. Consequently, developing your literature review would be a continual process, in which you re-engaged with the literature as your project developed.

This chapter will begin by defining what is meant by a literature review and exploring its roles and functions. The process of undertaking a *literature search* will be reviewed, focusing on the challenge of finding high-quality material in your topic area. Chapter 9 looks at how a literature review and documentary analysis can be written up.

The procedures for undertaking a literature search and making effective notes will be examined. You will be asked to consider what it means to analyse critically the literature that you find and clear guidelines will be discussed. The process of writing up your literature review will be considered and some of the problems frequently encountered by students will be examined.

What is a literature review?

A literature review is a comprehensive summary and critical appraisal of the literature that is relevant to your research topic. It presents the reader with what is already known in this field and identifies traditional and current controversies as well as weaknesses and gaps in the field.

The terms *literature search* and *literature review* are sometimes treated as if they were synonymous, but a literature search refers to a systematic process of identifying material that is appropriate whereas a literature review refers to a critical evaluation of that material.

In a traditional dissertation (or a research article), you will discuss what you found in the body of literature at two stages. First, you will present it in your literature review to demonstrate your understanding of what has already been written in your field. This will be used to inform your study design. You then revisit it after your findings to discuss any similarities and differences between what you found and what previous researchers have found. In a proposal, you will only use the literature to create an introductory argument or give background to the study, which will also inform the study design.

Hart (2001) identifies two key areas when you begin a research project or write a proposal: the literature relevant to your research topic and the literature on research *methodology* (i.e. how to plan and conduct research). This is an important distinction because you are likely to have only searched for the former during your previous academic study. Reading this book is an excellent start to developing your knowledge of the latter and each chapter contains recommended texts for further reading.

There are many reasons for undertaking a literature review. It is an essential part of your project planning (and would form a necessary part of any project you might actually undertake). A systematic review and meta-analysis might also be acceptable for Master's qualification instead of an empirical research project (i.e. where you collect your own data), and might form part of a dissertation or extended study project in third-year undergraduate nursing programmes. It enables you to gain an understanding of what has already been written about your topic, including reviewing which research designs have been used and the key issues that have been identified. Consequently, it is an essential part of developing expertise in your field, both in the topic area and in research methodology, and will inform your project plan.

Conducting your literature search

A literature search is the first stage in your literature review and is an organised investigation for material relevant to your topic across a range of sources. In your previous studies, you may have concentrated on using textbooks to inform your coursework. The purpose of textbooks is to provide students with an overview of what is generally agreed in a particular field. Although textbooks may report the results of research studies, they may not be sufficiently current or detailed for the purposes of your literature review. You need to expand the range of literature that you utilise and this should include reading the original research studies themselves to be able to appraise them critically.

Types of literature

The main types of literature that will be relevant are described below.

Journal articles in printed and electronic form

These are generally regarded as being of the highest quality because most journals are peer-reviewed. This means that articles submitted to the journals will be anonymised and sent out to reviewers with expertise in the field. These reviewers will evaluate the potential article and will submit detailed feedback that the author must address before it is of a publishable standard. This does not guarantee that everything in an article is correct, but it is relatively stringent. Whilst articles from non-refereed journals may be of a similar standard, they have not been through this process. Journals will state that they are peer-reviewed if this is the case and many search engines allow you to search for refereed journals only.

Books in printed and electronic form

There are good-quality control mechanisms built into book publishing, but they are not regarded as being as stringent as for peer-reviewed journals. You may be used to reading textbooks that provide you with a good overview of an area, but the research studies that they describe are likely to be classic studies rather than the most recent material.

Official and legal publications

These include legislation, policy and discussion documents as well as research studies and summaries of research findings in specific subject areas, such as hospital discharge or child protection. As well as governmental bodies, this includes material from other public organisations (e.g. Joseph Rowntree Foundation, NSPCC).

Systematic reviews and meta-analysis, clinical guidelines, National Service Frameworks

Systematic reviews and *meta-analyses* are exceptionally influential in medical, nursing and healthcare research as they inform decision making and treatment options on a daily basis, and provide an evidence base for the national recommendations for standards of treatment and care produced by the National Institute of Health and Care Excellence (NICE) and other bodies, such as the Scottish Intercollegiate Guidelines Network (SIGN). The most important and influential body funding systematic reviews and meta-analyses is the Cochrane Collaboration, but such reviews are also often published in journals.

Clinical guidelines can be extremely authoritative if published by influential bodies such as NICE and SIGN, and have gone through extensive processes of literature search and review before conclusions relating to effectiveness and cost-effectiveness of new treatments are given. Many NHS Trusts develop their own guidelines, which go through clinical governance approval, but that does not necessarily mean that they are completely authoritative. National Service Frameworks (NSFs) also contain authoritative reviews of evidence and are important in signposting standards of care for particular groups. For example, the NSF for Older People (Department of Health, 2001) contains 369 references, weighted so that greater importance is given to systematic reviews and meta-analyses than expert opinion, and this contributes a great deal to the overall recommendations produced.

Grey literature

This is material that is not published through traditional commercial sources but is available through specialised sources (e.g. research reports from local public or voluntary organisations). It is often unclear what quality control systems have been used, but they may contain some very useful and relevant information. University libraries will have copies of PhD and MSc theses submitted at their institutions, and conference abstracts may be useful in identifying 'cutting-edge' work. Whether to include them in your literature review depends upon what other material you have found. If you have found similar material from more conventional sources, you may not need to include them. But such material can be very valuable as long as you recognise the relative authority and its strengths and weaknesses.

How do I start my literature search?

The focal point of your literature search will be a systematic examination of a number of electronic bibliographic databases, which will enable you to search effectively across a large number of journals. These are available through your university library and are often available to access remotely through your home computer.

Most databases have 'basic' and 'advanced' search engines, so try using the latter for more specific and detailed searches and combine your key words to find more relevant results. When you search using an electronic database, you will be provided with an abstract that summarises the study. If your university has a subscription to that journal, you will also be able to get access to the full text version. The content of most electronic databases consists of journal articles, but some may include references to other material, such as books, reports and websites. Since no bibliographic database contains every journal available, you will need to search a number of databases to ensure that you identify all of the material available. Google Scholar is also useful and recommended, although it is likely to throw up thousands of hits, of which only a few will be relevant. You should also search the Cochrane Collaboration website and the NHS Evidence website.

It is tempting to start searching immediately, but you should first put together a search profile. This will direct your search and should consist of the following:

- Your research question: this guides every aspect of your project. For example: 'What are the reasons for delays in hospital discharge for older people?' Make sure you express the research question as a full sentence with a question mark at the end.

- Key words: these are the main terms that relate to your research question, which you will use as search terms. They should include alternative terms that may be used in the literature; for example, using 'older people' but also alternative (and often out-of-date) terms such as 'elderly' or 'geriatric'.
- Parameters: these are any restrictions that will narrow down your search, such as a particular time period or country of research or factors related to the population studied (e.g. age, gender and ethnicity); for example, deciding that you want literature on hospital discharge delay from the UK and relating to older people rather than other age groups.
- PICO: The mnemonic PICO (Sackett et al., 1997) is a useful means of structuring a search. PICO stands for:

  o population (or illness or condition);
  o intervention (treatment or service);
  o control (or comparison);
  o outcome.

- Using PICO to write down for yourself exactly what you are searching for allows you to structure your search very clearly and make sure you don't go off track. You will always have a population (or illness or condition) in your search; you may not always have an intervention in the sense of a treatment option but this could also relate to service delivery; you may not have a control (comparison) unless experimental designs are involved and the outcomes may not be clearly articulated at the search stage. Even so, PICO can help plan your literature search. Another useful mnemonic is SPIDER (Cooke et al., 2012). This stands for:

  o sample;
  o phenomenon of interest;
  o design;
  o evaluation;
  o research type.

Case study: Developing key words

Joan decided that the research question that she is most interested in discovering literature on is identifying best practice in diabetic foot care. For her literature search, her first task is to develop a list of key words that she is going to use.

Activity 2.1   *Critical thinking*

What will Joan include in her search profile? What will she include in her research question, key words and parameters? What will she include in her PICO assessment?

There is a brief summary of answers at the end of the chapter.

It can be confusing and frustrating at first to use some electronic search engines because they use *Boolean operators*. This sounds technical, but it is a relatively simple system to enable you to narrow your search and find the most relevant resources. These are built into the advanced search functions and it is worth understanding how they work. Although each database uses them in slightly different ways, the general principles apply.

The three most commonly used Boolean operators are 'AND', 'OR' and 'NOT'. If you insert the word 'AND' between search terms (e.g. 'elderly' AND 'discharge') you will narrow your search to texts that contain both terms. If you insert the term OR between search terms, you will broaden your search to include texts that contain either term. These can usefully be combined; for example, 'elderly AND discharge OR hospital' will identify resources that discuss the elderly in the context of either discharge or hospital settings. If you insert the term 'NOT' this will exclude any resources containing the second search term. This is useful when it has more than one meaning and you wish to restrict it. For example, if your search term is 'counselling' and you want to exclude careers counselling, you would use 'counselling NOT careers counselling'. Another useful function is the truncation symbol (* ! #), which lets you type in the first part of a word and then the search engine will find alternative endings; for example, adolesc* will find adolescent, adolescents, adolescence, and so on.

It is important to be systematic about your searches to ensure that you have identified all the relevant literature. Having all of your material in one place means that you will not have to search through different notebooks or diaries to find a reference. This should include all the searches that you undertake, including the date, bibliographic database and search terms used. A popular format is an electronic word-processing document with dated entries that enable you to track the progress of your research and to search for specific words. If you prefer to work on physical copies, consider having a folder of A4 sheets that can be taken out and placed into a ring binder as you go along. Whichever format you choose, you should maintain regular electronic or photocopied back-ups to ensure that the material is not lost.

Make a record of when you undertake a search, including the key words you used and date. You will need to use more than one database because every database has a limited coverage. More importantly, make a references list as you go along so that you avoid having to search for a reference at the last minute. There are a number of reference manager software packages, such as Mendeley, EndNote, ProCite and RefWorks; these will allow you to get the citation style exactly correct. Your university is likely to have adopted one and it is worth becoming familiar with it because it will create a central database of references that can be adapted into different citation systems, meaning, for example, that if you were planning to publish your work in an article, you could automatically adjust all the references to the style of that journal if it was different from that used by your university. Some software, such as Mendeley, allows you to store your articles in PDF format ('portable document format': articles which look exactly as if you have printed them from a journal) and can automatically input details of the articles, though it is important to check these for accuracy.

An additional search method that can be productive (but far less systematic) is to review the references section of material that you have already obtained. This can be particularly helpful when you have found an article that directly responds to your research question, because the references section is likely to include relevant material. As you gather more articles and books, you may find the same texts being referred to. This usually indicates that these are central texts for your topic and should be included in your literature review. This form of searching can be quite fruitful, but rather haphazard and biased because the writers may not be familiar with all of the literature and may not have included material that they want to distance themselves from. Hence, it should be regarded as a supplement rather than a replacement for a full literature search using electronic databases. You can try this trick with authors' names, so you search for everything that a particular author has written, then try the same thing with all the co-authors on their papers. You can usually do this in the electronic databases you'll be using by clicking on the relevant buttons. Although not systematic, it does give you a feel for who is publishing what in a particular field.

Effective reading and note taking

Having identified suitable material, it is important that you are able to use effective reading and note-taking skills to make the most of the time that you have. Rather than printing everything and working your way through a large pile of material, use active reading skills to identify which material is most relevant and take appropriate notes. As you should be able to get electronic full-text PDFs, often it is not necessary to print the articles you find on paper if you are comfortable reading them on screen.

A classic technique (Robinson, 1970) for achieving this is known as the SQ3R reading strategy, which comprises the following five stages:

1. Survey (or skim): conduct a preliminary scan of the material to get a general sense of what the material is about. This may simply consist of reading the abstract if it is a journal article. Does it look relevant? If not, discard at this stage.
2. Question: actively ask yourself what the article or chapter is about and what questions it might answer in order to decide whether the text is worth reading more carefully.
3. Read the text more carefully if it has passed the above tests. Read actively, questioning the author's arguments, and make appropriate notes.
4. Recall (or recite) the main points when you have finished reading, using your own words.
5. Review: test yourself to see what you can recall. If there are sections that you cannot remember, you may need to reread the material.

One of the most useful tips for saving time and reducing stress is to make sure that you keep a note of the full reference for the material that you are reading. While this may seem like a nuisance at the time, it will be preferable to hunting around for it at the last minute, long after you originally read it. It is particularly important to keep the reference list of your proposal or project report up to date as you go along (unless you are using a reference manager software package such as Mendeley or EndNote, which will help you).

When you are reading and taking notes, try to make links with other material that you have read. When you read your first article, it is difficult to have a framework to judge it against. When you have read a number of articles, you will have a greater understanding of the literature and will find it easier to evaluate a particular article or book.

> ### Case study: Recording searches
>
> *Susan developed a system for recording her literature searches and the material that she found. Using her research journal she recorded every search. She also noted the numbers of search hits and how she reduced large numbers of hits to those of more relevance to her interests, as these details are frequently needed in assignments and proposals, so that it can be shown that a search is systematic and inclusive rather than biased in some way.*
>
> *Susan read the abstract of every article in order to gain a sense of what it contained. She decided to use a traffic light system to organise the material into three groups (red, amber and green lights). For some articles, reading the abstract was enough for her to realise that the article was not relevant to her research and was discarded at that stage (red light). Other articles looked very promising and highly relevant to her research topic so were grouped together (green light). A third group were articles that were potentially relevant, depending upon how her research developed (amber light). She decided to devote most of her attention to the 'green light' group in order to develop a good knowledge of her specific research topic but to keep material from the 'amber light' group in case her research changed as it developed.*

If, like Susan, you used a traffic light system, you could mark all the printed papers and keep them together in a folder, or you could simply keep the PDFs in separate folders in your computer's memory. Using Endnote will allow you to catalogue very efficiently and insert citations directly into the text and reference list.

What if I find too much or too little material?

In literature searching it is highly unusual to get exactly what you want, in the quantity that you want it, first time around. Usually you will need to repeat searches in different databases, refine your search terms and search again and again. As you start your literature search, you may find yourself confronted with either too much or too little material. It is more common to find that your literature search has identified too much material. The development of digital technology has seen a revolution in the information that is available for your research compared to 10 or 15 years ago. The disadvantage of this is that it is easy to become overwhelmed by the sheer volume of information that is available. If you have identified too much material, your search is too broad and needs to be narrowed down. This can be done in a number of ways. First, you could be more specific about your topic. Second, you can be more specific about your parameters (e.g. choosing a specific time period or restricting your search to UK materials).

If you have identified too little material, you need to think about your search terms. Whereas some areas really do have very little written about them, it is more likely that your search terms are not finetuned enough to pick them up. If you have identified a small amount of material, read it to find out the terminology that is used in your research field. Think of alternative terms and enlist the help of your supervisor and/or fellow students in this task. If you still cannot identify any literature in your research field, it may be necessary to consider adjusting your research topic to ensure you have sufficient material to discuss in your literature review. If you genuinely cannot find anything on a subject area you will need to look at related subject areas for justification, rationale and methodological ideas concerning how you write your proposal.

Critically analysing the literature

In order to be worth including in your literature search, a text needs to be both relevant and of sufficient quality. Avoid the pitfall of reading material that is interesting, but not directly relevant to your research. This can take up a considerable amount of your time and the material is unlikely to feature in your final dissertation.

When you are evaluating a research study, there are a number of questions that you should ask yourself:

- Research design: does the study provide a clear rationale for the choice of research design? Research questions can usually be approached using a variety of research designs so a good study will provide a clear and robust rationale for its choices, including a discussion of why it did not use alternative designs.
- Data collection methods: does the study provide a clear rationale for the choice of data collection methods? For example, a study may have chosen interviews rather than questionnaires or focus groups. Is a coherent account given for this choice? Were known weaknesses addressed and did the data collection methods work in practice?
- Sampling: how well do the sampling procedures match the research question? Sampling is particularly important in quantitative research because this limits the extent to which the findings can be generalised. Were known weaknesses addressed and did the sampling procedures work in practice?
- Data analysis: how robust is the data analysis? A good study will give a clear account of how the data were analysed, whether quantitative or qualitative. Does the data analysis follow the model described? If it is a quantitative study using statistical analysis, are the tests used appropriate? Please see the end of the chapter for recommended texts on quantitative data analysis and www.socialresearchmethods.net to provide a useful guide to appropriate statistical tests. If it is a qualitative study, does the analysis provide sufficient context for the material to be understandable? Does it account for the diversity of participants' views?
- Credibility of the findings: how credible are the findings? You need to consider whether the conclusions are supported by sufficient evidence and whether they have a consistent logic. It is important to be rigorous about this, because we tend to view findings that we agree with as more credible.
- Generalisability of the findings: to what extent can the findings be generalised to other settings? For quantitative studies, statistical generalisation is important and this is linked to sampling procedures. For qualitative research, generalisation is not viewed in the same way and the important issue is whether the concepts that are generated are meaningful in other settings. Is the study clear about the extent to which its findings can be generalised to other settings? If so, does this seem reasonable given the limitations of the study?

- Research ethics: how does the study address ethical issues? This should include ethical procedures followed and address issues such as informed consent, ethical data management and how potential risks were avoided. It can also include discussion of the values that underpin the study.

Not all of the literature you identify will be research studies. They may be opinion pieces in which the authors put forward a particular argument or viewpoint based upon their experience or on previous literature. However, many of the same criteria are relevant. Is the argument plausible? What evidence do the authors provide to substantiate their claims? Sometimes you may find an article that provides a literature review of your topic area. This may be useful for understanding the key issues and authors. However, do not assume that the authors are coming from an impartial perspective. They may have an allegiance to a particular point of view or position and, consequently, they may place less emphasis on, or even ignore, literature that does not support their stance.

A number of frameworks for critiquing literature of all kinds, including empirical research studies, clinical guidelines and systematic reviews and meta-analyses, are available. Some useful websites are suggested at the end of this chapter.

Documentary analysis

This section discusses documentary analysis, which is one of the lesser known and used social research methods; it appears similar to a literature search but is quite different.

Documentary analysis is likely to become more popular in the future because the increasing availability of online documents means that significantly more data are readily available. Indeed, digital archives could revolutionise some research forms such as historical studies in a way equalled only by the invention of printing (McCulloch, 2004, page 41).

This section introduces you to a process of undertaking a documentary analysis, using the example of a case study to illustrate the process. Issues in choosing documentary analysis as a method for proposals will be discussed in this chapter, and issues in analysis will be discussed in Chapter 5.

First of all, what do we mean by a 'document'? The question of what constitutes a document is interpreted in an increasingly wide variety of ways; for example, not just paper documents, but visual data such as photographs and television programmes. Consequently, the term 'text' rather than document has been used to include a wider variety of material (O'Leary, 2004).

The significant growth in online material has provided rich new sources of data. Subject-based discussion groups or bulletin boards provide interesting material but raise new ethical dilemmas. For example, service users and carers use bulletin boards anonymously as a way of accessing support and sharing experiences. Although the information is public and usually anonymous, the individuals cannot be considered to have consented to have their information used for research purposes. These ethical dilemmas are likely to become more acute as more online material becomes available.

Documents are central to the everyday realities of working in the healthcare field and serve many purposes. Legislative and policy statements issued by governmental departments set out the principles and priorities of the current administration and their development is recorded through the parliamentary process. Inquiry reports investigate individual cases where things have gone seriously wrong and make recommendations for the future. Media documents in print, online and audiovisual forms record events that can shape public opinions about health and social care issues. Governance documents, such as committee minutes, record key discussions and decisions made about resource allocation and other key decisions. Individual case records document events and processes and record decision making by different professionals, including nurses. All of these are legitimate sources for documentary analysis.

Documents not only passively record events, but can have a profound influence on the ways that we understand and structure those events. When you go out to conduct a patient assessment, it is likely that the documentation that you complete will influence how you see the service user, your role and the function of your service. This too is a legitimate focus for research and can identify implicit beliefs and assumptions contained within documents.

Scott (1990) outlines four criteria for judging documents for research purposes. The first criterion is authenticity, which focuses on issues of soundness and authorship. We need to establish the authenticity of the document and the identity of the author. For example, government documents and inquiry reports may be published under the name of a minister or chairperson but may be the work of a team of people (Scott, 1990).

The second criterion is credibility, which focuses on sincerity and accuracy. We must consider the extent to which a document is likely to be an undistorted account. No account will be entirely undistorted, because decisions have been made about what to include or what to leave out as well as how the material will be presented. The task is to establish the extent to which the author had a clear interest in presenting material in a certain light. For example, both government policy documents and nursing reports share the dual functions of informing readers and also persuading them about the wisdom of the course of action proposed.

The third criterion is representativeness, which focuses on the extent to which the documents available are representative of all documents (whether the document is typical of its kind). For historical documents, this can include asking whether some documents survived while others did not. It can also raise issues of power; for example, when a service user goes to see a psychiatrist, it will usually be the psychiatrist who documents the encounter. Similarly, meetings can involve considerable debate, but the version that is presented in the minutes would usually have precedence.

The final criterion is meaning, which focuses on whether the evidence is clear and comprehensible. It is also important to establish whether the meanings contained within a document are literal or whether they are latent (Scott, 1990). Literal meanings are explicit and straightforward, whilst latent meanings are implicit and require further interpretation.

The research question and approach will influence how you approach your documents. If it is a traditional, positivist approach, documents may be seen as providing straightforward evidence for social phenomena. For example, newspaper articles may provide evidence of the frequency and severity of attacks by people diagnosed with schizophrenia on members of the public. If your research approach is interpretative, documents may be interpreted as reflecting how social phenomena have been constructed. The same newspaper articles would be viewed, but the interpretation and analysis are different.

Common pitfalls

The relatively infrequent use of documentary analysis is at least partly due to the confusion about how to complete a documentary analysis. One of the most common problems that students experience is confusing a documentary analysis with a literature review. Sometimes students think that they are doing a documentary analysis because they are reviewing the previous academic and practitioner research on their chosen topic. In fact, they are completing a literature review, which is required in every traditional research proposal and dissertation. This confusion is understandable because students will be analysing documents. However, although superficially similar, documentary analysis is used in a more restricted sense.

A literature review is a critical summary of what other researchers have found (i.e. their analysis of their data). So a literature review reports what other people have found. A documentary analysis is an analysis of data which reports findings from an investigation.

The key to understanding how a documentary analysis differs from a literature review lies in the distinction between primary and secondary sources. A *primary source* is raw data collected to analyse for a research topic whilst a *secondary source* is someone else's analysed data that would form part of your literature review. An analogy would be the study of gender in the paintings of Picasso – the paintings themselves would be primary sources to be analysed, whilst the writings of other commentators would be secondary sources to be discussed in a literature review.

Case study: Documentary analysis

Sarah is a student on a mental health placement. She is aware of how people with mental health problems can experience considerable stigma and discrimination (Green et al., 2002, 2003). She is interested in how the media portrays women with a diagnosis of schizophrenia and has decided to use documentary analysis for her research project within a feminist paradigm.

Sarah has decided to use documentary analysis for several reasons. First, it has lower ethical risks than other methods and usually does not require ethical approval if using publicly available data. Second, it does not require her to gain access to participants. Third, it is easy to collect data, especially if using online sources. This enables more data to be collected and more time for analysis. Finally, the data already exist and are not biased by the researcher in the same way as can happen in interviews and focus groups.

Activity 2.2   *Critical thinking*

Sarah has the documents listed below. Which document is included in the literature review and which document is going to be studied in the documentary analysis?

1. An article from the *Times Online* about a young man with a diagnosis of schizophrenia who was involved in a dispute with a neighbour.
2. A book that describes research into how people with mental health problems are portrayed in the media.

There is a brief outline answer at the end of the chapter.

The distinction between primary and secondary data can occasionally become blurred because it is not only what type of documents are used, but the way in which they are used. For example, a research project about how drug users and their health are portrayed in government policy would be analysing government policy documents as primary sources but also discussing them in a literature review. However, the main secondary sources are likely to be commentators who present their own analyses of how drug users and their health are viewed within society.

The process of conducting a documentary analysis has three stages:

1. deciding on a research question and designing a plan;
2. deciding which documents to analyse and what to include in the sample;
3. collecting and analysing your data.

The first two stages will be discussed in this chapter, and stage three in Chapter 5.

Stage 1: Research question and study design

Most research methods are located within a particular tradition; for example, surveys and questionnaires within the quantitative tradition, interviews within the qualitative tradition. Documentary analysis is unusually versatile in that both quantitative and qualitative research designs can be used.

Research summary

One of the research studies that Sarah found for her literature review was a study about how people with mental health problems are represented in the media.

The Glasgow Media Group produced a classic study into media portrayals of people with mental health problems (Philo, 1996). In order to identify the dominant messages which are being given out about mental illness across a variety of media, the study included all media content for a period of one month. The sample included television news and press reporting, popular magazines, children's literature, soap operas, films and dramas.

(Continued)

(Continued)

The study yielded a total of 562 items whose content fell into five main categories:

1. violence to others;
2. harm to self;
3. prescriptive/advice;
4. criticism of accepted definitions of mental illness;
5. 'comic' images.

The authors found that the category of 'violence to others' was by far the most common, outweighing the next most common ('advice') by a ratio of almost four to one. They also found that items linking mental illness and violence tended to receive 'headline' treatment, while more sympathetic items were largely 'back page' in their profile, such as problem page letters or health columns. For an excellent update on media representations of mental health, see Clements and Foster (2008).

Having read the Glasgow study, Sarah has decided that *content analysis* would be a suitable method for her research. Content analysis is a way of analysing documents and texts by measuring the frequency and prominence of specific words or phrases.

Advantages and disadvantages of documentary analysis

Documentary analysis has a number of advantages and disadvantages as a research method. One of the main advantages is that the data already exist so it is a matter of gaining access rather than collecting data. It is an attractive research method because it avoids the time-consuming process of negotiating access to participants and arranging interviews or focus groups. This makes it economical to collect data, in both cost and time. This is particularly true if using documents in electronic form because text organisation is easier and search engines enable quick location of items of interest. Since the documents already exist independently, they cannot be biased by the researcher in the same way as interviews and focus groups.

As with all research designs, consideration needs to be given to ethical concerns and documentary analysis should not be considered an ethically neutral process (McCulloch, 2004). However, it presents lower ethical risks than other methods because it does not directly involve participants. Consequently, ethical approval is often not required if you are using publicly available data. The highest risks relate to the use of sensitive information, such as client information, but issues around copyright, freedom of information and data protection need to be addressed by all research projects.

The availability of data means that it is easy to become overwhelmed by the amount of information and to find it difficult to decide what to leave out. Since an analysis of data occurs outside the original context in which the document was produced, the framework that was used to create the original document may be significantly different from the framework that would be used to analyse it. Whilst this may produce valuable insights, it can be challenging.

Documents available may be limited both in scope and in quality, or may not focus solely on the issue you are interested in. The quality of the documents may be variable and, if they are in different formats, they may be difficult to compare and may require considerable preparation before they can be analysed. For example, if you were comparing a child death inquiry report from the 1970s with a modern inquiry report, the quality, detail and format of the documents are likely to be quite different (Parton, 2004). There may be omissions and inaccuracies in the original documents and some documents may be more likely to survive than others. Although bias cannot be introduced into what is contained within the documents, personal biases may influence which types of records are used and their interpretation. These issues do not preclude using documentary analysis, but would require discussing in your proposal or dissertation.

Stage 2: Deciding which documents to analyse and what to include in a sample

Applying sampling concepts to documentary analysis requires the development of clear rules about what should be included in the sample, known as inclusion criteria. These criteria identify what is a suitable document and exclude documents that fall outside a study, and should be acknowledged in proposals and dissertations.

Activity 2.3   *Critical thinking*

In the case study, Sarah is interested in how newspapers have portrayed women with a diagnosis of schizophrenia. What inclusion criteria should Sarah use for her study?

There is a brief outline answer at the end of the chapter.

One of the most common questions is 'what is an acceptable sample size?' Documentary analysis is one of the research methods that has the greatest variability in sample size because the documents themselves are so variable. Government policy documents or inquiry reports can be several hundred pages long and the sample size will be different compared to analysing short newspaper articles. Consequently, this issue needs to be discussed with supervisors and outlined in proposals.

What if there are too many or too few documents?

A common difficulty is having too many or too few documents to choose from. To some extent, this can be controlled through inclusion criteria, either by narrowing the criteria to reduce the number of documents or by widening the criteria to increase the number of documents included in the sample. In the case study, Sarah could reduce or increase the number of documents by looking for a shorter or longer time period or she could change other criteria, such as including feature articles as well as news items.

However, this approach can distort the sample. For example, Sarah could pick a short time period and this could coincide with a major news story about a person diagnosed with schizophrenia, which would present a significantly different picture to another time period. A commonly used alternative approach when you have too many documents is to use random sampling, which is particularly appropriate for content analysis. Random sampling involves making a selection of cases (the sample) from the whole group of possible cases (the population) on the basis of chance. In random sampling, each case has an equal chance of being selected.

In Sarah's case, she completed an electronic search and found that there were 600 news articles involving people diagnosed with schizophrenia during 2013. Since this is too large a number to analyse, she decided to select a 10% sample randomly, namely 60 articles. She could do this through a random number table or through an online random number generator (such as www.randomizer.org). Having obtained 60 random numbers between 1 and 600, she would select the articles from her search that corresponded with these numbers.

If there are too few documents, a more qualitative analysis may be appropriate, depending on the research question. In Chapter 5, qualitative approaches to data analysis such as thematic analysis will be outlined and these may be more appropriate. Documents in electronic format are much easier to analyse.

Case study: Preliminary searches

Sarah decided to use ProQuest, a national electronic database of newspaper articles from a range of national tabloid and broadsheet newspapers. The ProQuest database includes the Daily Mail, Daily Telegraph, Guardian, Times *and* Independent *newspapers. This was available through her university library and enabled her to undertake a preliminary search to establish how much material is available.*

In order to undertake her preliminary search, she must decide which search terms to use. Since she is searching for articles that refer to individuals diagnosed with schizophrenia, she used the search term 'schizo*'. The Boolean operator '*' is a wildcard, which means that all phrases that include the word stem 'schizo' (e.g. schizophrenia, schizophrenic), will be included. She considered using wider terms such as 'mental health', but a preliminary search retrieved a very large number of articles that rarely related specifically to schizophrenia.

She found that there are approximately 50 articles per month that refer to individuals diagnosed with schizophrenia, spread evenly over the year. Looking at a one-year time period, the search returned 600 articles spread evenly throughout the year. Sarah randomly chose a 10% sample (60 articles) over the year. If it were a topic that was likely to show variations throughout the year, e.g., news coverage of sunburn, then an alternative would be systematic sampling focusing upon specific time periods.

The articles that Sarah identified took two days to code, working on the basis of approximately 10–15 minutes per article. Once Sarah had identified a suitable article, she was able to store it ready for analysis, making sure that she kept details of the source and date of the article.

Chapter summary

This chapter began by defining what is meant by a literature review and exploring its roles and functions. The process of undertaking a literature search was reviewed, focusing on the challenge of finding high-quality material in your topic area.

The procedures for undertaking a literature search and making effective notes were examined. You were asked to consider what it means to analyse critically the literature that you find and clear guidelines have been discussed.

We then examined how to undertake a documentary analysis, making the point that, although superficially similar, there are key differences between a documentary analysis and a literature review.

Activity answers

Activity 2.1: Critical thinking (literature searches) (page 33)

Joan is already clear about her research question, namely, 'What is best practice in caring for diabetic leg ulcers?' For her, the key words 'diabetic feet' and 'diabetic leg ulcer care' were relevant; she realised that 'diabetes' alone would be unmanageably large. She added 'treatment' and 'research' to limit the search to these areas only. She wanted to include literature from outside the UK but was aware that she would need to restrict it to material in English, as this was her only language. Her PICO was as follows:

- population: diabetics;
- intervention: leg ulcer care;
- control (comparison): dressing types;
- outcome: healing rates.

Activity 2.2: Critical thinking (documentary analysis) (page 41)

1. The article is a primary source – raw data about how the media portrays people with mental health problems.
2. The book is a secondary source – a developed analysis based upon the author's own research, which Sarah needs to discuss in her literature review.

Activity 2.3: Critical thinking (inclusion criteria) (page 43)

In the case study, the inclusion criteria would be that the articles are news articles, rather than other forms of articles, such as features. The articles must relate to an individual diagnosed with schizophrenia, which must be used in a clinical sense, not a colloquial or metaphorical sense (e.g. not 'his performance on the football pitch was schizophrenic'). Sarah has decided that she will use only articles from the latest full year.

Further reading

Literature reviews

Aveyard, H (2014) *Doing a Literature Review in Health and Social Care: A Practical Guide*, 3rd edition. Berkshire: Open University Press.
A useful and rigorous account of conducting a literature review.

Cullum, N, Ciliska, D, Haynes, B and Marks, S (2007) *Evidence-Based Nursing: An Introduction*. Oxford: WileyBlackwells.
A useful and interesting guide to understanding evidence-based practice in nursing.

Ellis, P (2013) *Evidence-Based Practice in Nursing*, 2nd edition. London: Sage/Learning Matters.
More detailed information about evidence-based practice in nursing.

Fink, A (2005) *Conducting Research Literature Reviews: From the Internet to Paper*, 2nd edition. London: Sage.
A useful guide which focuses on evaluating quantitative research and provides an outline of appropriate statistical tests when appraising research evidence.

Greenhalgh, T (2010) *How to Read a Paper*, 3rd edition. London: BMJ Publishing.
A book-length guide to appraising research papers from both quantitative and qualitative traditions.

Greenhalgh, T and Taylor, R (1997) How to read a paper: papers that go beyond numbers (qualitative research). *British Medical Journal*, 315: 740–743.
A classic article that provides a clear account of evaluating qualitative research studies.

Hart, C (1998) *Doing a Literature Review: Releasing the Social Science Research Imagination*. London: Sage.
A classic introduction to compiling your literature review that gives detailed guidance on structure and evaluating arguments.

Documentary analysis

Atkinson, P and Coffey, A (2004) Analysing documentary realities, in Silverman, D (ed.) *Qualitative Research: Theory, Method and Practice*, 2nd edition. London: Sage.
Interesting and useful discussion about documentary analysis from a qualitative perspective.

Epstein, I (2010) *Clinical Data-Mining: Integrating Practice and Research*. Oxford: Oxford University Press.
An excellent and interesting account of a new approach to documentary analysis, including practical examples of previous clinical data-mining studies. An insightful and entertaining read, likely to become a classic.

Prior, L (2003) *Using Documents in Social Research*. London: Sage.
Detailed account of documentary analysis from a qualitative perspective. Interesting discussion of the philosophical basis for documentary analysis.

Scott, J (1990) *A Matter of Record: Documentary Sources in Social Research*. Cambridge: Polity Press.
A classic text in documentary analysis, concentrating mainly on historical documents.

Useful websites

http://ethos.bl.uk/Home.do
British Library search engine for searching for PhD theses.

www.casp-uk.net
The Critical Appraisal Skills Programme (CASP) has developed the following tools to help with the process of critically appraising articles:

- systematic reviews;
- randomised controlled trials (RCTs);
- qualitative research;
- economic evaluation studies;
- cohort studies;
- case-control studies;
- diagnostic test studies;
- clinical prediction rules.

www.evidence.nhs.uk/default.aspx
NHS Evidence provides a database of publications for health and social care practitioners.

www.jrf.org.uk
The Joseph Rowntree Foundation is a national research and development charity that funds a range of research into social policy.

www.socialresearchmethods.net
The Web Center for Social Research Methods is a USA-based resource that provides useful material, including content on choosing appropriate statistical tests and concept mapping.

www.vts.intute.ac.uk
Intute Virtual Training Suite is based at Bristol University and provides online training to enable you to make the most effective use of online resources for nursing courses.

Introduction: The nature and importance of Leadership

Gill, R.

Everyone says there's a lack of leadership in the world these days. I think we should all be thankful, because the only reason for leadership is to convince people to do things that are either dangerous (like invading another country) or stupid ([like] working extra hard without extra pay).

Obviously you don't need any leadership to lead you to, for example, eat a warm cookie. But you need a lot of leadership to convince you to march through a desert and shoot strangers. Generally speaking, whenever there is leadership, there's lots of hollering and very few warm cookies. Let's enjoy the lack of leadership while we have it.

Scott Adams, *Don't Step in the Leadership*[1]

OVERVIEW

- In recent times the notion of leadership has increasingly met with cynicism and become a 'hot topic' for debate. Despite a burgeoning but fragmented literature, there is no agreed paradigm so far for the study and practice of leadership.
- This lack of consensus on what leadership is together with a spate of high-profile failures due to poor or absent 'leadership' have proven to be contributory factors towards the cynicism that has since developed.
- Yet 'good' leadership – that is both effective and moral – has nevertheless been long recognized as crucial to human achievement and well-being.
- This chapter considers the multiplicity of definitions of leadership and proposes an integrative and over-arching definition: *leadership is showing the way and helping or inducing others to pursue it.*
- Leadership is characterized by six core themes and their associated practices: envisioning a desirable future, promoting a clear purpose or mission, supportive values, intelligent strategies, and empowering and engaging all those concerned.
- Leadership effectiveness can be evaluated either in terms of behaviour – the extent to which a leader helps or induces others to pursue a given way and purpose or mission – or in terms of outcomes – the extent to which a given desired future becomes a reality as a result of a leader's behaviour. This means that there are many different possible measures of leadership according to the nature of the envisioned future, purpose and context in which leadership takes place.

(Continued)

(Continued)

- One fruitful approach to understanding leadership is to study followership: what followers expect of leaders and how leaders can satisfy these expectations.
- The chapter compares and contrasts concepts of management and leadership: we manage things and processes, but we lead people.
- Leadership is about showing the way – from where we are now to a desired place or state. Leadership, therefore, is about change and so we must explore the leadership of change.
- The past emphasis on individual leadership and command-and-control has been superseded by an emphasis today on shared and distributed leadership and collective leadership capacity. An organization's collective leadership capacity is the basis for a distinctive leadership 'brand' and its ability to change.

What is Leadership?[2]

Every week, probably even every day, we can read a fresh new article or book that says: 'Effective leadership is the key to success' – defined in terms of organizational and managerial effectiveness, financial results, or people's morale and happiness, or all of these. When I entered 'leadership' into Google on 24 February 2011, I was presented with 'about 176,000,000' entries. I then focused my curiosity and entered 'definition of leadership'. In 0.4 of a second I was presented with a mere 59,100,000 suggestions.

Now I cannot claim that this introductory section in Chapter 1 is a comprehensive summary of the extant literature on the question 'What is leadership?' But without reviewing all of it (to say the least), this is my humble attempt. After all, according to one Malaysian writer, theorizing about leadership is 'great fun, hugely indulgent and largely useless' (doing it instead, he says, is much more worthwhile).[3] Nevertheless, my aim in the first part of this chapter is unapologetically to indulge in what hopefully is an interesting – if not fun – account of how concepts and definitions of leadership agree and differ and the problems associated with this lack of consensus. I then attempt a synthesis that reflects the essence of the etymology of the term that I hope will be defensible to scholars and useful to practitioners.

How Concepts and Definitions of Leadership Agree and Differ: A Problem that Needs Resolving

Walter Friedman describes some of the earliest references to leadership in American newspapers and books. He says, 'The term "business leadership" appeared in U.S. newspapers only occasionally during [Andrew] Carnegie's heyday'[4] (b.1835, d.1919). Popular books on leadership started to appear from 1912 onwards. The British Academy of Management says: 'The subject of leadership has created a plethora of publications, research and debate and has become a key issue in both the public and private sectors'.[5] Today, leadership is a hot topic for debate.

The burgeoning leadership literature ranges from highly cerebral academic research studies and scholarly treatises that few if any actual leaders will read to idiosyncratic personal prescriptions by self-acclaimed paragons of virtuous leadership of how to be an outstanding leader at the 'popular' end of the spectrum. Some of the contributions to the leadership literature are both fictional and speculative:

> ... [divining] the dubious leadership acumen of either long-dead military leaders [e.g. Attila the Hun] of questionable reputation or fictional characters [such as Winnie the Pooh and Captain Picard of Star Trek] in order to proffer it to the masses as pearls of wisdom.[6]

John Roulet, a management consultant in the United States, feels that there is a surfeit of books, articles and discussion about leadership, with 'much competing and confusing information in the public domain' and that 'today's leaders seem to be getting worse instead of better'.[7] And Joel Kurtzman says that '... a consensus has so far failed to emerge with respect to what leadership is, how leaders develop, and – perhaps most important – how to become a more effective leader'.[8]

One of the problems with leadership studies, Robert Terry says, is that the subject has 'suffered from a lack of a common language'.[9] Victor Vroom of Yale University states, '... like many popular terms, [leadership] has been used in many different ways'.[10] Perhaps 'leadership' is a 'Humpty Dumpty' word:

> When I use a word, Humpty Dumpty said, in a rather scornful tone, it means just what I choose it to mean – neither more nor less. The question is, said Alice, whether you can make words mean so many different things. The question is, said Humpty Dumpty, which is to be master – that's all.[11]

Bruce Winston and Kathleen Patterson, addressing the problem of the lack of consensus on what leadership is, suggest, as I do, that the problem arises from studying the parts of leadership rather than the whole.[12] This is what I mean when I suggest that those theories which are well known to academics and practitioners alike – such as action-centred leadership, the managerial (leadership) grid, situational leadership and transformational/transactional leadership (which we discuss in Chapter 3 on leadership theories) – are each individual pieces in the jigsaw puzzle that is leadership. Winston and his team at Regent University carried out an extensive review of the leadership literature and produced 92 categories made up of over 1,000 constructs or statements relating to leadership. They distilled these into the following 'integrative definition of leadership':

> A leader is one or more people who selects, equips, trains, and influences one or more follower(s) who have diverse gifts, abilities, and skills and focuses the follower(s) to the organization's mission and objectives causing the follower(s) to willingly and enthusiastically expend spiritual, emotional, and physical energy in a concerted coordinated effort to achieve the organizational mission and objectives.

The definition then proceeds to describe *how* leaders do this. However this definition, while a heroic effort, is contentious in several ways. It has a top-down, directive tone that might be appropriate in some organizational and national cultures (see our discussion of culture in Chapter 6 on leadership and values), but not as a universal definition. For example, a leader might well 'focus' a follower – or somebody else who may not be a 'follower' as such – but the intention might be to *help* that person to identify, clarify, pursue or fulfil his or her personal 'mission' or objectives.

The definition also refers to 'gifts, abilities, and skills' – a confusing admixture. Elaborated in a later explanation, with a Christian biblical reference to Chapter 12 in *Romans*, it is still not made clear what these (seven) 'gifts' – 'driving characteristics of the individual' – are and how they are different from, and perhaps supplementary or complementary to, abilities or skills. Indeed their 'natural abilities', what people can do easily and well, that people are born with and which mature 'enough to be defined and measured' by the age of 14 years, and skills – 'function-related knowledge and physical skills that contribute to the success and efficiency in completing tasks' – are ill-defined, confusing and highly contentious.

How can one scientifically investigate something that is beset by its multiplicity of definitions? Indeed the very existence of 'leadership' as an observable phenomenon in daily life in organizations has been questioned by some scholars, such as Mats Alvesson and Stefan Sveningsson.[13] They say: 'Our general impression is that it is difficult to say anything of the possible existence of leadership in the great majority of organizations and management situations.' For example, they found the accounts that managers in a research-and-development company gave of leadership to be ambiguous, incoherent and often contradictory.

Simon Kelly, correctly in my opinion, questions whether the problem that Alvesson and Sveningsson see is 'a consequence of the research methods being used to make leadership visible and researchable in the first place'.[14] And one problem here is interpretation: the 'meaning of a word [in our case "leadership"]', Louis Pondy says, 'is the set of ways in which it is used'.[15] This requires further discussion that is beyond the scope of this book but which Kelly's article might assist.

Even the UK's Investors-in-People institution (IIP) does not explicitly define leadership. It says: 'Leadership and management are almost impossible to define because they mean different things to every organisation.'[16] Manfred Kets de Vries of INSEAD puts it more strongly:

> When we plunge into the organisational literature on leadership, we quickly become lost in a labyrinth: there are endless definitions, countless articles and never-ending polemics. As far as leadership studies go, it seems that more and more has been studied about less and less, to end up ironically with a group of researchers who studies everything about nothing. It prompted one wit to say recently that reading the current world literature on leadership is rather like going through the Parisian telephone directory while trying to read it in Chinese![17]

Warren Bennis, noted writer and leadership scholar, observes that: 'Leadership is what the French call a portmanteau field – a field with many different variables.'[18] He says there is no agreed paradigm for leadership or framework for studying it:

> Researchers have so far failed to come up with a widely accepted framework for thinking about leadership. There is no equivalent of Competitive Strategy, Michael Porter's 1980 classic, accorded near-biblical reverence by strategy experts ... I don't think [leadership] is yet a 'field' in the pure sense. There are something like 276 definitions of leadership. You can't say that there is a paradigm, any agreed-upon set of factors, that is generally accepted.

Gary Yukl criticizes the unhelpful way such variables have been classified:

> Sometimes different terms have been used to refer to the same type of behaviour. At other times, the same term has been defined differently by various theorists. What is treated as a general behaviour category by one theorist is viewed as two or three distinct categories by another theorist. What is a key concept in one taxonomy is absent from another. Different taxonomies have emerged from different research disciplines, and it is difficult to translate from one set of concepts to another.[19]

Keith Grint of Warwick Business School in the UK in his 'constitutive approach' questions whether we can be objective at all in defining the context of leadership and the leadership required. He suggests that when we do this we are merely constructing our own view of leadership behaviour and the situation in which it takes place:

> We may never know ... the true essence of an identity, a leader, or a situation ... and must often base our actions and beliefs on the accounts of others from whom we can (re)constitute our version of events ... Leadership is an invention ... [it] is primarily rooted in, and a product of, the imagination.[20]

This view is misleading and unhelpful. Leadership may be 'created' or 'designed', for example as a process or a relationship, but it is hardly imagined, an invention – a 'fabricated story', 'made up, especially so as to deceive'.[21] In the 'real' world (whatever that is, Grint may say), we all experience and recognize leadership, 'good', 'bad' and inconsequential.

More reasonably David Collinson and Keith Grint do point out that, while there was still (in 2005) 'little consensus on what counts as leadership, whether it can be taught, or even how effective it might be', the recent plethora of publications of all kinds on leadership '[extols] the need for excellence in management and leadership ... in part fuelled by a breakdown in confidence in leadership'.[22] Our Scott Adams quotation on page 1 captures the confusion and cynicism that have grown rapidly around the idea of leadership since he wrote those words in 1999. This cynicism perhaps is a consequence of the unacceptable face of leadership in recent times that has so deeply pervaded politics, business and sport.

Top-level leaders are frequently criticized for being out of touch with employees in their organizations. And this appears to have grown in recent years. In reporting research findings in January 2011 from Roffey Park, the management development institute in the UK, Carly Chynoweth notes that 'Many board directors seem to be living in a rose-tinted bubble ... They feel more positive about everything ... than their counterparts in executive management' as well as middle and junior managers.[23] This includes optimism about the future, the organization's sense of collective purpose, leadership in the organization, perceptions of the respect with which the organization is held by outsiders, and the extent to which leaders behave ethically towards stakeholders.

Almost as jaded a view of leadership as Scott Adams's, and perhaps reflecting the times,[24] is that from novelist and former journalist Robert Harris:

What [is] leadership, after all, but the blind choice of one route over another and the confident pretence that the decision [is] based on reason?[25]

'The main goal of ... leadership', according to Donald Krause, 'is to accomplish useful and desirable things that benefit the people being led'.[26] This is arguable. It certainly may be argued as desirable or ideal and may be part of a definition of good leadership. But on the other hand it may be argued as unrealistic. In reality many people are led by those who lead them not for their benefit but for the benefit of others elsewhere. Leaders in the business world may argue reasonably that in meeting shareholders' expectations, or even customers' needs and expectations, they are providing a benefit to employees – for example, employment and income. But this benefit is not necessarily their *raison d'être*. And, of course, some leaders will 'lead' (use) others to further their own interests.

Leadership has been variously defined in terms of traits, process, skill(s), competency, a relationship, and a construct. Sociologists frame leadership in terms of relationships among people rather than in terms of individual traits or characteristics, often focusing on power and dominance.[27] James MacGregor Burns argues that 'to understand the nature of leadership requires understanding of the nature of power'.[28] The two essentials of power, Burns states, are motives and resources. He explains that leadership is not just a top-down phenomenon with clear unidirectional causality between leaders' and followers' behaviour but also a series of complex, reciprocal relationships involving a use of power and the control of resources.

According to a 1920s' definition, leadership is 'the ability to impress the will of the leader on those led and induce obedience, respect, loyalty, and cooperation'.[29] By current standards this is a remarkably authoritarian viewpoint that has little currency today (at least in democratic countries and enlightened organizations). Donald Krause, drawing on the writings of Sun Tzu and Confucius, suggests that leadership comprises:

... the will to control events, the understanding to chart a course, and the power to get a job done, cooperatively using the skills and abilities of other people.[30]

There are various levels at which one can define leadership. Jay Lorsch defines a leader straightforwardly and simply as 'an individual who influences others to follow him or her'.[31] Lorsch argues that leaders use influence gained from various sources of power (discussed in the chapter on leadership and engagement) such as charisma and knowledge (personal power) or the right to insist on action and the right to dispense rewards and punishments (position power or authority). He also argues that the definition applies equally to a senior executive and a first-level supervisor: both must get others to do their bidding. Lorsch's definition is appealing in its simplicity. But its brevity sacrifices clarity, scope and depth and begs many questions. For example, follow *where* (to what?) and *why*? And use influence *how*? It is also not true to the etymology of the word 'leader', namely 'one who shows the way'.

Underlying the leadership development programmes at the Leadership Trust is the following concept of leadership:

> **Leadership is using our personal power to win the hearts and minds of people to achieve a common purpose; the minds ... by giving people a clear understanding of what they have to do, why, and how it might be done; the hearts ... by generating feelings of challenge, involvement, ownership, commitment and excitement.**[32]

This otherwise useful working definition implies a directive style of leadership rather than a contextually more variable one. But it also implies three important principles of leadership:

1. There must be a common, shared mission or purpose, or at least one that a leader gets commitment to, and clear strategies for pursuing it.
2. Hearts and minds have to be won in the sense that the vision, mission and strategies must make sense intellectually and must also appeal to, or create, positive emotions, engagement and motivation or inspiration as a result.
3. The use of position power (authority) is abrogated in favour of gaining commitment through using one's personal power.

James MacGregor Burns defines leadership as a mobilization process undertaken by individuals who are using the power they draw from motives, values and access to resources in a context of competition and conflict in their pursuit of goals.[33] Another political scientist, Joseph S. Nye, Jr – former Dean of Harvard Kennedy School (the John F. Kennedy School of Government) – defines leadership as '[helping] a group create and achieve shared goals'.[34] Nannerl Keohane, a former president of both Wellesley College and Duke University and also a political scientist, says that leaders 'determine or clarify goals for a group of individuals and bring together the energies of members of that group to accomplish those goals'.[35] And an appealing definition of leadership comes from Charles Handy: 'To combine the aspirations and needs of the individuals with the purposes of the larger community to which they all belong.'[36]

Leadership is recognized in the well-known Business Excellence model promoted by the European Foundation for Quality Management (EFQM) and the British Quality Foundation (BQF). This model includes 'leadership' as an underpinning enabler in attaining key performance results. Leadership is defined as how:

> **... leaders develop and facilitate the achievement of the mission and vision, develop values required for long-term success and implement these via appropriate actions and behaviours ... [for example, strategies, management systems and operational plans].**[37]

Leadership is evaluated in the EFQM/BQF Excellence Model according to several sub-criteria:

* Leaders develop the mission, vision and values and are role models of a culture of excellence.
* Leaders are personally involved in ensuring the organization's management system is developed, implemented and continuously improved.
* Leaders are involved with customers, partners and representatives of society.
* Leaders motivate, support and recognize the organization's people.

In this model, leadership also includes:

* Stimulating and encouraging empowerment, innovation and creativity.
* Aligning organizational structure to support the delivery of policy and strategy.
* Supporting and engaging in activities that aim to improve the environment and the organization's contribution to society.
* Personally communicating the organization's mission, vision, values, policy and strategy, plans, objectives and targets to people.

This model identifies key themes or concepts in leadership: vision, mission, values, strategy, empowerment and motivation, but not all of these in a formal, composite way. We deal with this in later chapters as the basis for a formal model of leadership. The model also links leadership to management, implying rightly that both are necessary for organizational effectiveness.

All of these definitions share a common theme – the idea of facilitating the accomplishment of shared goals. Most definitions (the EFQM's excepted) say little or nothing about *how* this is done. Many are prescriptive (like the Leadership Trust's and the EFQM's) or aspirational (like Charles Handy's) rather than descriptive of the reality (like Nannerl Keohane's). And most stray from the etymological essence of the term 'leadership'. So how can we make sense of the multiplicity of definitions that exist for leadership?

Towards a General Definition of Leadership

I propose that one useful thing to do when exploring the meaning of leadership is to consult the etymology of the word and see how its meaning has developed.

The word 'lead' comes from the Old English *lædan*, corresponding to the Old Saxon *ledian* and Old High German *leiten*, meaning to 'take with one', to 'show the way'.[38] *Ledere* was the term for a person who shows other people the path to take and guides them safely along the journey.[39] The Old Icelandic derivative *leidha* means 'the person in front', referring to the person who guided ships through the pack-ice in spring. The word 'leader' appeared in the English language in the thirteenth century, but 'leadership' appeared only in the early nineteenth century. The terms *leadership* and *leader* are used today in ways that stray from their etymology and original meaning, which we will now discuss.

Showing the way is the essence of leadership. My definition of leadership, which underpins the model of the six core themes discussed in the following chapters, is this:

Leadership is showing the way and helping or inducing others to pursue it. This entails envisioning a desirable future, promoting a clear purpose or mission, supportive values and intelligent strategies, and empowering and engaging all those concerned.

The word 'induce' is used in preference to 'influence' because it has a wider meaning: 'to succeed in persuading or leading (someone) to do something',[40] 'prevail upon', 'bring about', 'cause' or 'attract' in addition to 'influence'. 'Influence' on the other hand has a more restricted meaning: 'to have an effect on the character or behaviour of someone'.[41] The wider meaning of 'induce' embraces leadership behaviour that employs position power or authority, such as directing or insisting on (even enforcing) particular actions by others in appropriate situations, as well as personal power – influence or persuasion – in more usual situations. This definition allows for the possibility of leading not only in the sense of 'being followed' but also in the sense of getting others to follow the way shown by the leader. It does not prescribe whether or not the leader should actually participate personally in that activity or whether or not others must necessarily (though desirably) be voluntarily willing.

'Showing the way' presupposes knowing, or at least believing in, that way. And 'the way' implies the route to a destination: a vision of a desirable future position – *what* we want to be or *where* we want to be. This may be a state of being or a position or place, even more specifically a goal, an objective or a target. Knowing or believing in the way also presupposes the desirability of this known or believed-in destination.

Desirability relates to *why* one wishes to promote and pursue a particular vision. One reason is that this vision relates to our purpose or mission. A purpose or mission is what we do and why we do it; a vision is a mental image of what the future will (or could) be like, based on imagination or wisdom,[42] which we discuss in Chapter 4 and Chapter 5 respectively. A related reason is that the vision relates to what we believe in, what we feel is meaningful, valuable and worthwhile in our work, and perhaps in our life in general. This spiritual dimension concerns our values and beliefs. So leadership is about promoting and pursuing a vision and a mission or purpose that reflect particular values. Effective leadership includes the creation and sustaining of a *shared* vision, mission or purpose and values.

But *how* do leaders and followers effectively pursue a vision, mission and values? They do so through *strategies* – 'ways and means' that involve the use of resources (as Burns says). Hence we have financial strategies, marketing strategies, product strategies, IT strategies, people strategies, and so on. Because leaders, like managers and indeed all of us, get things done with, by and through other people, we need to consider that special resource – people. What does it take for human beings to get things done? The answer is the ability (power) to do so and the desire to do so; in other words empowerment and motivation. Leadership therefore is about empowering people to be *able to* do what needs to be done and influencing, motivating or inspiring people to *want to do* what needs to be done. Influence, motivation and inspiration constitute what is now popularly known as *engagement*.

This definition provides the model of six themes and associated practices of leadership that this book proposes. This model is a synthesis of the extant themes, models and theories in the leadership literature. It prescribes the *practices* of effective leadership – *what effective leaders do*. The outcome of *effective leadership* is the achievement of what was intended – both the results (vision, goals, etc.) *and* appropriate behaviour – by a led person or group of people. We speak of effective leadership at a variety of levels: oneself, one-to-one (as in coaching or counselling, for example), team or group, organization-wide, national, regional or global. *'Good' leadership*, however, is defined by intentions (purpose, vision, goals), achievement (of what was intended) and behaviour (in achieving it) that are judged by those involved or affected to be ethical or moral (on the basis of their personal and shared values).

Good versus Bad Leadership

What is 'good' leadership as distinct from non-leadership and 'bad' leadership? Joanne Ciulla makes the point that 'good' has two senses that need to be interrelated: good in the moral sense and good in the sense of being effective (even if also morally 'bad').[43] Barbara Kellerman developed this distinction in her book *Bad Leadership*, with a model (Figure 1.1) and many case examples, acknowledging the 'dark side' of human nature and how this affects leaders and followers alike.[44] She identifies seven major forms of bad leadership: incompetent, rigid, intemperate, callous, corrupt, insular and evil. Her argument is that, if bad leadership is to be avoided, leadership must reflect a shared responsibility between leaders and followers. Birgit Schyns and Tiffany Hansbrough explain that leaders, followers and situational factors can make leadership go awry.[45]

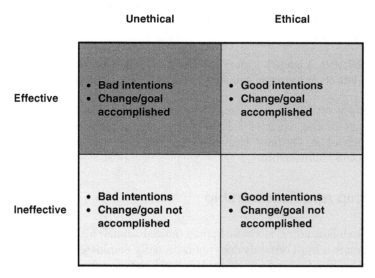

Figure 1.1 'Good' and 'Bad' Leadership (based on Barbara Kellerman, 2004, *Bad Leadership: What It Is, How It Happens, Why It Matters*. Boston, MA: Harvard Business School Press, 32–37)

So what is *good* leadership? Barbara Kellerman observes:

> Scholars should remind us that leadership is not a moral concept. Leaders are like the rest
> of us: trustworthy and deceitful, cowardly and brave, greedy and generous. To assume that
> all leaders are good people is to be wilfully blind to the reality of the human condition, and
> it severely limits our scope for becoming more effective at leadership.[46]

Most leadership textbooks – and indeed most leadership books for practising
executives – constantly provide case studies or case examples of brilliant leadership.
These are about what we might call 'heroic leaders', those people who turned around
failing organizations apparently single-handedly (and inadvertently took the credit
for doing so, which is why they would have agreed to the case study or example).
There are occasional books on bad leadership, like Barbara Kellerman's. One notable
case of bad leadership in 2010 illustrated Tony Hayward's rise and demise as a 'leader';
until that date he had been the CEO of BP. As Rosabeth Moss Kanter says, 'The case
of Tony Hayward and the Gulf oil spill will be fodder for business school discussions
for years to come, as a how-not-to-do-it guide for leadership when disaster strikes.'[47]

In an insightful psychological analysis, Jean Lipman-Blumen explains how 'toxic'
leaders first charm and then manipulate, mistreat, weaken and eventually devastate
their followers.[48] She explains how human beings are psychologically susceptible to
toxic leadership and how we can reduce our dependency on 'strong' leadership, identify 'reluctant leaders' and nurture leadership within ourselves. Michael Maccoby
believes this dependency is the result of what Sigmund Freud called 'transference' –
the tendency to relate to a leader as some important person from the past, such as a
father or mother, a brother or sister, or even a nanny.[49]

Those who suffer toxic leadership are, of course, primarily subordinates or followers. Leaders do not exist, of course, without followers. Leadership implies followership
(oneself in the case of 'self-leadership'). As Manfred Kets de Vries and Elizabeth
Laurent-Treacy say:

> Without followers, a leader's journey is solitary and unproductive. If the conductor of an
> orchestra lifts his or her baton and none of the musicians responds, there is no music.[50]

Followership is attracting increasing attention. For example, reflecting the trend, the
term appears in the name of a leadership centre established in 2010 in Durham
Business School at Durham University in the UK: the International Centre for
Leadership and Followership.

Leadership and Followership

The desire to follow others is a basic human (indeed animal) instinct, Robert Ardrey suggests,[51] although it most certainly does not necessarily dominate human behaviour. While
most theories of leadership focus on leaders, Stephen Covey suggests that: 'A more fruitful approach is to look at followers, rather than leaders, and to assess leadership by asking
why followers follow.'[52] This question can be addressed by looking at the needs and aspirations that people have and how leaders use power in helping people to satisfy them.

Sometimes we will lead – in domains where we have expertise, for example – and sometimes we will follow, when we need direction or lack expertise. 'Followers also have the power to resist and to lead', says Joseph S. Nye, Jr, former Dean of the Kennedy School (the John F. Kennedy School of Government) at Harvard University.[53] As Stephen Fineman says, we talk a lot about our leaders – our bosses and politicians – and we also criticize them freely:[54] we can make intelligent judgements for ourselves. But our desire to follow has deep emotional roots, and interestingly the Bible emphasizes followership more than leadership.

While many writers have identified a 'crisis' in leadership, there is perhaps also a crisis in followership that has lasted some 20 years so far. Robert Kelley reports one study that indicated dissatisfaction among followers with their leaders:

* Forty per cent questioned their ability to lead.
* A minority (14 per cent) of leaders were regarded as role models.
* Fewer than half were trusted.
* Forty per cent were regarded as having ego problems: they were perceived to be threatened by talented subordinates, needing to act in a 'superior' way, and not sharing recognition.[55]

James MacGregor Burns points out that:

> One talent all leaders must possess [is] the capacity to perceive needs of followers in relationship to their own, to help followers move toward fuller self-realization and self-actualization along with the leaders themselves.[56]

This is about empowerment. Followership, according to one leadership development practitioner, results from being empowered – through delegation, creating team values, coaching and mentoring, and building a high-performance team.[57]

In the political world, leaders appear to have fewer and fewer 'followers'. In democratic nations they are elected, but by whom? The 2001 general election in the UK was one example of a growing crisis in followership, where the lowest turnout for 80 years gave a large majority to the ruling Labour Party. Even so, only a small minority of the electorate actively supported the nation's political leadership – in effect they were 'followers'. And even within the Labour Party, there was some dissension from the policies the government was following, for example by the trade unions that supported it. Nor was the Conservative Party immune from dissension, which was part of the reason for its downfall from government in 1997 and its several subsequent leadership crises. And the proportion of the US electorate that 'followed' president George W. Bush was 51 per cent, according to the 2004 election.

The British government's report on *Strengthening Leadership* includes an interesting analysis of followership:

> ... the most successful organisations appear to be those where the errors which the leaders inevitably make are compensated for by their followers: responsible followers prevent irresponsible leaders. But where followers are unable or unwilling to constrain their leaders

the organisation itself may well suffer. This 'compensatory followership' operates right across the organisational and political spectrum such that, for example, the obsequient behaviour of most of Hitler's entourage (fortunately) failed to prevent him from making catastrophic strategic errors in the latter half of the Second World War.[58]

The report also gives a more contemporary example. In many hospitals, consultants are 'treated as "gods" and junior staff [are] afraid of "telling tales"'. While making mistakes is essential to learning and progress, examples of unnecessary tragic mistakes as a result of this culture in hospitals appear all too frequently. Institutionalizing the role of devil's advocate is one way of preventing leaders from making such mistakes.[59] Followers take turns to express dissent from the group's decisions with the purpose of focusing the attention of the group and the leader on potential problems.

Jonathan Swift, in *Gulliver's Travels*, provided a graphic account of how leaders may reflect the characteristics of their followers in an extreme way and how they may have a 'favourite' who is hated by everybody else:

> ... in most Herds there was a Sort of ruling Yahoo, (as among us there is generally some leading or principal Stag in a Park) who was always more *deformed* in Body, and *mischievous in Disposition*, than any of the rest. That, this *Leader* had usually a Favourite as *like himself* as he could get, whose Employment was to *lick his Master's Feet and Posteriors, and drive the Female* Yahoos *to his Kennel*; for which he was now and then rewarded with a Piece of Ass's Flesh. This *Favourite* is hated by the whole Herd; and therefore to protect himself, keeps always *near the Person of his Leader*. He usually continues in Office till a worse can be found; but the very Moment he is discarded, his Successor, at the Head of all *Yahoos* in that District, Young and Old, Male and Female, come in a Body, and discharge their Excrements upon him from Head to Foot. But how far this might be applicable to our *Courts* and *Favourites*, and *Ministers of State*, my Master said I could best determine.[60]

Whether Swift's analysis can be applied to business and political leadership today is self-evident. Political journalist and broadcaster Jeremy Paxman, describing former British prime minister Tony Blair's attempts to act 'normal', says: 'The successful leader would like to be as like his followers as possible.'[61] He quotes the political reporter, James Margach, who likens political parties, in the way they turn on their discarded leaders, to crabs, which devour their sick, wounded and dying.[62] Paxman describes how vulnerable political leaders are: cabinet ministers in particular, once discarded, will usually simply vanish from public view.[63] For prime ministers, losing an election or being sacked by their party, he says, can bring castigation and public humiliation – they become the 'excrement' of Jonathan Swift's yahoos. This is also true for prime ministers who resign over-tardily.

Added to this Paxman describes how power in (British) politics has come to be concentrated less in parliament and more in the prime minister, perhaps in a very small number of ministers (but not the Cabinet as a whole), and even in a coterie of special advisers who, controversially, will sometimes be given executive powers over the Civil Service. The media are quick to report the discarding of such special advisers – Swift's 'favourites' – and they usually suffer the same insalubrious fate.

Paxman suggests that loyalty, a characteristic of voluntary followership, is vacuous in politics: he comments, 'There is no room for either friendship or gratitude at the top.'[64] Witness the frequent Cabinet reshufflings, acrimonious ministerial sackings and resignations in government, and the subsequent sniping at the prime minister by those who are sacked. Add to this what Paxman says is an increasing tendency by prime ministers not only to make decisions without the consensus of, or even without consulting, their Cabinet but also to direct their ministers what to do, and we must call into question how effective prime ministers really are as *leaders*.

Followership in the literal sense has been evolving into collaboration and partnership. Even Admiral Lord Nelson, for example, saw his captains as a 'band of brothers'. And former US Secretary of State Colin Powell says that 'Leadership does not emerge from blind obedience to anyone.'[65] Leaders provide followers with protection and meaning. Followers identify with charismatic leaders, for better or worse, with pleasure and pride.

According to the respondents in Kelley's study of followership, the best followers are those who think for themselves, give constructive criticism, are 'their own person', and are innovative and creative.[66] Kelley's review of follower characteristics revealed an additional dimension, namely active engagement in the task: the best followers will take the initiative, participate actively, be self-starters, and do more than what is required.

Michael Maccoby, a noted psychologist, says that the definition of a leader is simple: 'A leader is someone whom people follow.'[67] And why do people follow leaders? Maccoby suggests one reason for this is fear, and he cites the example of people living in Iraq under the rule of Saddam Hussein. Another reason, he says, particularly in respect of religious leaders, is love, devotion or respect. However, this can be dangerous, and indeed sometimes lethal, as was the case for cult leader Jim Jones's 909 followers. And in addition, as Kurtzman says, 'followership is no excuse for wrongdoing, even when following the will of an elected leader', a principle established at the Nuremberg trials at the end of the Second Word War.[68]

Followership is dangerous when it entails surrendering one's judgement or one's will to a leader: being aligned to a common purpose does not entail surrendering the right to express an opinion, oppose a decision or withdraw from the group. Effective organizations and leaders respect dissidence. Followership also occurs, however, when one works with a leader whose purpose one shares, says Maccoby.[69] We discuss the place of purpose in leadership in Chapter 5.

Followers exert their influence on leaders in many ways. In democracies, Nanerl Keohane says, they hold the ultimate authority, and leaders are both formally and informally accountable to them.[70] A special report on global leaders by *The Economist* in January 2011 endorses this view:

> Elections force politicians to take the public's wishes into account every few years. Competitive markets force business leaders to heed their customers' demands all the time. And the law applied to rich and poor alike ... in liberal democracies the powerful get on by pleasing others. In short, they work for us.[71]

For a further discussion of followership, *The Art of Followership* by Ronald Riggio and colleagues is recommended.[72]

Leadership versus Management

The relationship between the concepts of management and leadership is the subject of continuing discussion among academics and consultants. For example, Marcus Buckingham, well known for his work on emphasizing strengths, writing in *Harvard Business Review*, says:

> [Great managers] discover what is unique about each person and then capitalize on it ... This is the exact opposite of what great leaders do. Great leaders discover what is universal and capitalize on it.[73]

This view is highly questionable: what Buckingham says is management is in fact equally a key aspect of effective leadership, posited specifically in one particular theory of transformational leadership that we discuss in the next chapter. If there is a real difference between what managers do and what leaders do, it is not this. Robert House and R.N. Aditya suggest that:

> Scholars of the traditional management and leadership literatures seldom take advantage of each other's contributions and, consequently, these two literatures are not adequately integrated.[74]

The term 'management' derives from *manus*, the Latin word for 'hand'. The term had to do with handling things, and it gained currency in its modern sense during the Industrial Revolution in the nineteenth century. The archaic French *ménager* meant to 'use sparingly'.

In the oft-quoted words of Warren Bennis and Bert Nanus, 'Managers are people who do things right; leaders are people who do the right things.'[75] For example, leaders ask the right questions about strategy and make sure the right answers are implemented.[76] And David Wills, training manager for the Motherwell Bridge Group in Scotland, says:

> Leadership is ... about vision and having the courage to do the right thing – different from management, which is all about doing the thing right – even if there is a risk.[77]

But this distinction is epistemologically unsound, according to Peter Gronn:

> ... it is an attempt to resurrect the traditional distinction between facts and values. Thus, 'things right' reduces to a competence or technical mastery [management], whereas 'the right thing' [leadership] implies desirable ends, purposes or values.[78]

The Work Foundation (formerly The Industrial Society) in the UK defines the differences between management and leadership simply. Managers plan, allocate resources, administer and control, whereas leaders innovate, communicate and motivate.[79] Vision is one of the key differences between a manager and a leader, according to Stanley Deetz and colleagues.[80] General Sir William Slim, the inspiring Second World War leader, saw the difference in the same way. In a speech in Adelaide as Governor-General of Australia in 1957, he said:

> ... we do not in the Army talk of 'management' but of leadership'. This is significant. There is a difference between leaders and management. [Leadership represents] one of the oldest, most natural and most effective of all human relationships. [Management is] a later product, with neither so romantic nor so inspiring a history. Leadership is of the spirit, compounded of personality and vision; its practice is an art. Management is of the mind, more a matter of accurate calculation of statistics, of methods, time tables, and routine; its practice is a science. Managers are necessary; leaders are essential.[81]

Amin Rajan contrasts management and leadership thus:

- Management is about path following; leadership is path finding.
- Management is about doing things right; leadership is about doing the right things.
- Management is about planning and budgeting; leadership is about establishing direction.
- Management is about controlling and problem solving; leadership is about motivating and inspiring.[82]

Warren Bennis suggests that the differences between leadership and management can be summed up as 'the differences between those who master the context and those who surrender to it' respectively.[83] These differences are detailed in Table 1.1 below.

John Kotter says that management produces orderly results that keep something working efficiently, whereas leadership creates useful change; neither is necessarily better or a replacement for the other; both are needed if organizations and nations are

Table 1.1 Differences between Managers and Leaders

The manager	The leader
Administers	Innovates
Is a 'copy'	Is an 'original'
Maintains	Develops
Focuses on systems and structure	Focuses on people
Focuses on control	Inspires trust
Takes a short-range view	Has a long-range perspective
Asks how and when	Asks what and why
Imitates	Originates
Accepts the *status quo*	Challenges the *status quo*
Is a classic 'good soldier'	Is his or her own person
Does things right	Does the right thing

to prosper.[84] A more useful suggestion is that we do not need both managers and leaders (i.e. people in separate roles) but managers who are leaders and leaders who are managers – people who can 'do the right thing right'? As Mitch McCrimmon says, 'It is vastly more empowering to define management as a type of activity than as a role.'[85] And with regard to organizational change, which is for some the preserve of a 'leader', he says:

> Leadership sells tickets for the journey and, if resistance emerges en route, the tickets can be resold, but the bulk of the journey is a project requiring good management skills.[86]

Warner Burke also agrees that both management and leadership are needed: 'For clarity of goals and direction, managers need leaders. For indispensable help in reaching goals, leaders need managers.'[87] We 'manage from the left, lead from the right', Stephen Covey says.[88] In terms of brain dominance theory, the manager's role is mainly left-brain dominated, whereas the leader's role is right-brain based. The left hemisphere of the brain deals more with words, specific elements, logic, analysis, sequential thinking and time. The right hemisphere deals more with emotions, aesthetics, pictures, relationships among elements and the *gestalt*, synthesis, and intuitive, simultaneous, holistic thinking, free of time constraints. An Eastern view is that leading involves the *yin* and managing involves the *yang*.

Managers may be good at *managing* and nominally regarded as leaders, but the most effective managers exercise *effective leadership*. John Nicholls says:

> When we say that an organisation lacks leadership we mean that its managers are neglecting their leadership responsibility. It is leadership that is missing, not leaders. If every manager understood and fulfilled his or her leadership responsibilities, there would be no shortage of leadership. It is attention to their managerial leadership responsibilities that converts competent administrators into effective managers.[89]

And Bernard Bass says:

> Management is not only leadership, nor is leadership only management; however, those appointed to a position of responsibility as managers need to appreciate what leadership is expected of them.[90]

People in management positions who have people reporting to them and avoid the leadership role may be perceived merely as administrators.[91] But while leadership is about innovation and change, Kouzes and Posner argue that it is not necessarily about entrepreneurship:

> Leaders must be change agents and innovators. But they need not be entrepreneurs, if by that term we mean those who actually initiate and assume the risk for a new enterprise. Neither must they be 'intrapreneurs' – entrepreneurs within a corporation. In fact, we maintain that the majority of leadership in this world is neither entrepreneurial nor intrapreneurial.[92]

United Technologies Corporation (UTC), the aerospace and defence company, published an arresting notice in the *Wall Street Journal* and several other newspapers and magazines in 1984:

People don't want to be managed.
They want to be led.
Whoever heard of a 'world manager'?
World leader, yes.
Educational leader.
Political leader.
Religious leader.
Scout leader.
Community leader.
Business leader.
They lead.
They don't manage.
The carrot always wins over the stick.
Ask your horse.
You can lead your horse to water, but you can't manage him to drink.
If you want to manage somebody, manage yourself.
Do that well and you'll be ready to stop managing.
And start leading.[93]

Eighteen years later, in 2002, UTC was ranked the world's most admired company in the aerospace and defence sector.[94] And in 2007 UTC was one of America's best-performing conglomerates and a darling of Wall Street, with shareholder returns that outstripped even GE's.[95] The point is that many of us over-manage people and under-lead them. The company's philosophy – and its practice – have evidently paid off, perhaps because its executives manage *things* and *processes* but *lead* people.

And this is the key point. Looking at the putative 'differences' between managers and leaders, nobody would ever want to be a manager, says psychologist Adrian Furnham: managers are dull; leaders 'fizz with electric creativity'.[96] Furnham also holds that neither stereotype exists: it is a 'false dichotomy'. But it is a helpful conceptual distinction if it is related to context. Good managers may be leaders too – they have to exercise leadership (with other people) in carrying out their managerial functions (with things and processes). And good leaders are poor managers. As Furnham says:

The greatest of leaders are often forceful organisers as well as visionaries ... people who manage their own businesses know the importance of processes and procedures. A business with leaders and no managers would surely fail much faster than one full of managers and without leaders.[97]

Some companies have forsaken the title 'manager' for 'leader', for example W.L. Gore & Associates, one of the UK's best companies to work for (see Chapter 6). However, this may be symptomatic of what Julian Birkinshaw suggests is the demeaning of management over the past few decades in favour of leadership.[98] He says we need a fuller understanding of what management is really about, but unfortunately he muddies the water by defining it as 'the act of getting people together to accomplish desired goals'.

So far we have discussed the concept of leadership – in essence, showing the way; how leaders have followers; and how leadership relates to management. These discussions have brought up the issue of change. If leadership is about anything, it is about change. Leadership is showing the way from here to there, a way that may be unfamiliar or even unknown, to a place or state imagined but never before sought or reached. It is about a change from the present to a desired future.

Leadership and Change[99]

All things change, nothing is extinguished. There is nothing in the whole world which is permanent. Everything flows onward; all things are brought into being with a changing nature; the ages themselves glide by in constant movement.

So wrote the Roman poet Ovid, in *Metamorphoses*.[100] And in the graphic words of an African proverb, it is a journey that takes place every day:

Each morning a gazelle wakes up knowing that it must outrun the fastest lion or be eaten. And every morning the lion wakes up knowing that it must outrun the slowest gazelle or starve. Gazelle or lion, every morning you must run. That's what change is all about.[101]

The early 1980s saw a marked growth in interest in the leadership of change. Rosabeth Moss Kanter's concept of the 'change master' focused on entrepreneurship and innovation in organizations.[102] Bernard Bass's Full-Range Leadership model, which we discuss in Chapter 3, explained how leaders changed how people feel about themselves and could be inspired to achieve performance beyond their previous expectations – the concept of transformational leadership.[103]

The challenges ahead, more than ever before, require organizations, industries and societies to change and to keep changing. Change may be planned, proactive and about creating the future. Or it may be unplanned, reactive and about adaptation. In Warren Bennis's view, 'Leaders have to … create an environment that embraces change, not as a threat but as an opportunity.'[104] The change imperative itself has changed. The challenge used to be to respond positively to the need for change. Now it is the need to actively *create* change. This was expressed forcefully by the former chairman of British Leyland, Chloride and Dunlop, Sir Michael Edwardes:

And they [the new breed of top executives] have a particular drive, a desire to bring order out of chaos, or if something is too cosy, to create chaos in order to bring change.[105]

Change may be imposed, from a position of authority, or participative, generating ownership, commitment and creativity. Philip Sadler distinguishes between incremental and transformational change, in which incremental change concerns activities within a given culture and the latter changes the culture.[106] The most negative reaction that people display at work is not concerned with money, but with change. People will resist change for many reasons. Milan Kubr identified the following:

* A lack of conviction that change is needed.
* A dislike of *imposed* change.
* A dislike of surprises.
* A fear of the unknown.
* A reluctance to deal with unpopular issues.
* A fear of inadequacy and failure: a lack of know-how.
* Disturbed practices, habits and relationships: 'We've always done it this way.' Moving people from their 'comfort zone' means moving from the familiar, secure and controllable to the unfamiliar, insecure and uncontrollable.
* A lack of respect for and trust in the person promoting change.[107]

James O'Toole says that:

> ... to be effective, leaders must [set] aside that 'natural' instinct to lead by push, particularly when times are tough. Leaders must instead adopt the unnatural behavior of *always* leading by the pull of inspiring values.[108]

He says that any reversion to paternalistic behaviour will break trust with followers: the ultimate lack of respect for others is 'to impose one's will on them without regard for what they want or need and without consulting them'.[109] In fact, O'Toole in his analysis concludes: 'the major source of resistance to change is ... having the will of others imposed on us'.[110]

In addition, self-interest and shifts in power and influence will hinder change efforts. A loss or change of role is one example here. That change is difficult has been long recognized, for example by Machiavelli:

> ... there is no more delicate matter to take in hand, nor more dangerous to conduct, nor more doubtful in its success, than to set up as a leader in the introduction of changes. For he who innovates will have for his enemies all those who are well off under the existing order of things, and only lukewarm supporters in those who might be better off under the new.[111]

Andrew Mayo says, 'Our organisations are littered with the debris ... of yesterday's [change] initiatives.'[112] One reason for this may be the consequences of the tendency to introduce change when meeting any new situation. As Charlton Ogburn says:

> ... we tend to meet any new situation by reorganizing; and a wonderful method it can be for creating the illusion of progress while producing confusion, inefficiency, and demoralization.[113]

The ghosts of changes past can often return to haunt us. What effect does the history of change in an organization have on shaping employees' attitudes and behaviour, especially regarding change itself? With respect to change, 'once bitten, twice shy', one might imagine. But what exactly happens? And what leadership lessons can we learn from research into change?

Recent research investigated this question in two studies in the Philippines, one in a property development firm that was merging with another and the other in an educational institution that was undergoing extensive restructuring.[114] Based on theory deriving from previous research, cause-and-effect chains were hypothesized (see Figure 1.2).

In a questionnaire survey of 155 employees in the property development firm (a sample of just under 50 per cent of the total number), eight items measured aspects of poor change management (e.g. 'In my experience, past change initiatives have failed to achieve their intended purpose'). Trust was measured using seven items and cynicism was measured using eight items taken from previously validated questionnaires.[115] Inept change management was found to be inversely related to trust and directly related to cynicism, as had been predicted.

In the educational institution, the same procedure was followed with a sample of 124 employees (a response rate of 62 per cent), but with two additional aspects investigated. In the implementation of previous changes, staff had not been consulted and management had acted in an autocratic manner, leading to lawsuits being brought by some disaffected staff. Job satisfaction was measured using three items, turnover intentions were measured by four items and openness to change was measured using four items, again taken from validated instruments.[116] Data on employee turnover were collected two years later. The results for trust and cynicism were the same as in the first study. In addition, trust was found to be positively related to job satisfaction and inversely related to turnover intentions. And cynicism was found to be inversely related to openness to change. Actual employee turnover was predicted only marginally by intention to leave.

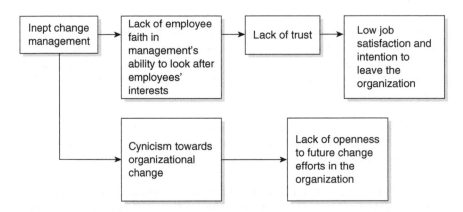

Figure 1.2 Cause and Effect in Organizational Change

Ineptly managed change clearly has dysfunctional consequences. It causes negative attitudes towards both change in general and the organization itself. A vicious cycle then results whereby employees will avoid participating in change initiatives, consequently prejudicing future changes and thereby reinforcing negative attitudes and behaviour.

In the words of Clarence Darrow, the American lawyer in the famous 'Scopes Monkey Trial' in 1925 defending the teaching of Darwinism by high school teacher John Scopes, 'It is not the strongest species that survive, nor the most intelligent, but rather the one most adaptable to change.'[117] There are many reasons why change efforts fail:

* A lack of communication or inconsistent messages.
* A lack of commitment to change due to a lack of compelling evidence for the benefits of change – and based on unrealistic expectations of the change effort. This lack of commitment shows itself in objections, an unwillingness to consider options or look at process issues and the use of 'hidden agendas' or delaying tactics.
* A lack of commitment by top-level management.
* A lack of dedicated effort.
* A lack of expertise in the organization.
* Poor planning and coordination.
* A lack of necessary resources, including training.
* Inconsistent human resource policies or systems, such as performance criteria used in performance appraisal and the way people are rewarded for their performance.
* Conflict between functional areas.
* An imposition of 'intellectual' solutions on emotional problems: a lack of emotional intelligence.
* A history of failed change initiatives leading to a 'culture' of change failures.

Traumatic change brings with it some well-known reactions: first, a denial that it has happened; then anger about its having happened, bargaining over what to do, depression, and finally acceptance.[118] John Mulligan and Paul Barber speak of the *yin* and *yang* of change: the social and emotional considerations and the technical aspects respectively.[119] The model of response to change used in leadership development programmes at the Leadership Trust has immobilization first (a non-response or 'freezing') and then minimization ('This doesn't concern or affect us'); after this come self-doubt and depression, the low point at which change either fails or its reality is accepted (in which case change is tested in a search for its meaning and benefits), followed up by internalization. Perhaps the simplest model of change is that of Kurt Lewin:[120]

* Unfreezing – creating anxiety or dissatisfaction about the *status quo* or a problem and stimulating a desire for change.
* Changing – new behaviour and activity which people identify with and internalize.
* Refreezing – positively reinforcing the initial change successes.

While the challenge of change requires effective management, even more does it require outstanding leadership. The challenges are to find new and better ways of motivating people, especially to make effective change happen, satisfy people's needs and expectations, and win their hearts and minds:[121]

* Responding positively to the need for change.
* Actively creating change.
* Making people comfortable with change.

John Kotter provides a model for creating effective change:[122]

1. Create a sense of urgency and importance to change
   Examine the market in which the organization operates and the competitive realities.
2. Create the guiding coalition
   Put together a group with enough power to lead the change and get it to work together as an effective team.
3. Develop a vision and strategy
   Create a vision for a desired future state as a basis for directing the change effort. Develop strategies for achieving the vision.
4. Communicate the change
   Use every method possible to constantly communicate and explain the new vision and strategy and ensure the guiding coalition models the behaviour expected of employees.
5. Empower people for action
   Get rid of obstacles to change, change systems or structures that undermine the vision, and encourage risk taking and new ideas and innovative activities.
6. Generate short-term wins
   Plan and create visible improvements in performance, or 'wins'. Visibly recognize and reward people who made the wins possible.
7. Consolidate gains and continue the change effort
   Use increased credibility to change all systems, structures and policies that do not fit together and do not fit the vision. Recruit, promote and develop people who can implement the change vision. Reinvigorate the change process with new projects, themes and change agents.
8. Embed the new approaches in the culture.
   Create better performance through customer-oriented and productivity-oriented behaviour and more effective management and leadership.

Kotter's model of change is criticized by Chris Argyris.[123] He says that it reflects 'Model 1' behaviour (command-and-control) that is aimed at getting compliance from people rather than Model 2 behaviour that is genuinely people-centred. Moreover, he questions whether creating a new sense of urgency would lead to desired outcomes and whether people in these circumstances would fully understand what they have to do and produce new ideas for overcoming obstacles.

Moreover, unrealistic expectations associated with a sense of urgency are very frequently dashed, with consequent demoralization and embarrassment. Leo Apotheker, who was appointed CEO of the Hewlett-Packard Company in November 2010, was asked by the *Wall Street Journal* why he wanted organizational change to happen so fast. He answered:

> **There was a debate in the Swedish parliament in the 1960s about whether they should move from driving on the left side of the road to the right side of the road. True story. One member said jokingly we could do it gradually: on Monday the trucks, on Tuesday the bicycles, and Wednesday the cars. If a change has to happen why wait and do it gradually?**[124]

Malcolm Higgs and Deborah Rowland report a study in seven organizations that found emergent change was more successful than master change or directive change.[125] The most effective change leadership behaviour was framing change rather than shaping behaviour or creating capacity. In fact a leader-centric shaping of behaviour impaired the implementation of change.

During strategic change a consensus appears to develop, but less through gaining strength and more through increasing scope, according to Livia Markoczy.[126] A consensus during the early stages of successful strategic change tends to appear mainly not in the top management team but in the key interest groups, such as product development or marketing.

Today change that is continuous or discontinuous and not stability is the order of the day. Alvin Toffler, in his disturbing and challenging book *Future Shock*, says: 'Change is essential to man ... Change is life itself' and that 'a strategy for capturing control of change' is essential to avoiding future trauma and to the future well-being of the human race.[127] As Warren Bennis says, 'Change is the only constant.'[128]

Change must be well managed. This entails planning; organization in terms of roles and responsibilities, procedures and adequate resources and know-how, monitoring and control; and compatible and supportive corporate policies, systems and practices. Raymond Caldwell, using a Delphi process with change agents, found that managing and leading changes were two distinct but complementary processes.[129] Effective leadership is necessary for change to be successfully introduced and sustained. Rosabeth Moss Kanter notes how there has been a shift of emphasis from managing change to leading change.[130]

Change requires not only good management but also good leadership.[131] What is our vision for change: what or where do we want to be? Why do we want or need to change anyway? What is important to us in the change process: what values and ethical principles will guide us? How are we going to change: what are our strategies for change? How will we empower people to *be able to do* what needs to be done? And how will we influence, motivate and even inspire them to *want to do* what needs to be done?

For the chief executive this means 'developing a vision of the future, crafting strategies to bring that vision into reality [and ensuring] that everybody in the organisation is mobilising their energies towards the same goals … the process we call "emotional alignment"', say Alan Hooper and John Potter.[132] Their model of leadership proposes seven competencies: setting the direction, making decisions, communicating effectively, creating alignment, setting an example, getting the best out of people, and acting as a change agent.[133] It can be argued that the most difficult challenges facing leaders today are making sure that people in the organization can adapt to change and that leaders can envisage where the organization is currently placed in the market and where it should be in the future.[134] Change is now driven by a global orientation and customer needs and demands. It requires, Manfred Kets de Vries says, an 'authoritative (or respect-based) leadership rather than authoritarian (position-based) leadership'.[135] Peter Drucker says:

> To survive and succeed, every organization will have to turn itself into a change agent. The most effective way to manage change successfully is to create it. But experience has shown that grafting innovation on to a traditional enterprise does not work. The enterprise has to become a change agent. This requires the organized abandonment of things that have been shown to be unsuccessful, and the organized and continuous improvement of every product, service, and process within the enterprise (which the Japanese call *kaizen*). It requires the exploitation of successes, especially unexpected and unplanned-for ones, and it requires systematic innovation. The point of becoming a change agent is that it changes the mind-set of the entire organization. Instead of seeing change as a threat, its people will come to consider it as an opportunity.[136]

The most frequently mentioned key to successful change, according to an American Management Association survey of 259 senior executives in *Fortune 500* companies in the United States, is leadership (see Table 1.2).[137]

Table 1.2 Keys to Successful Change

	% mentioning this as important
Leadership	92
Corporate values	84
Communication	75
Teambuilding	69
Education and training	64

Leadership for change requires competencies that can span the cognitive, emotional, cultural, spiritual, moral and behavioural domains of our being. And in the end, to change anything, perhaps we have to change ourselves in the process. In the words of an African proverb:

> When I was a young man, I thought I would change the world.
> When I was middle-aged, I thought I would change my village.
> Now that I am an old man, I think I will change myself.[138]

The Impact and Importance of Leadership

The rulers of ancient China studied leadership at great length. They were preoccupied with change and its associated chaos and uncertainty, as indeed we still are today. The writings on leadership of the general Sun Tzu in *The Art of War* and the philosopher Confucius in *The Analects* have endured over some two and a half millennia and are still quoted far and wide today. One lesson from Sun Tzu is that even the most brilliant strategy requires effective leadership to be successful.[139] This is a lesson that receives scant attention from strategy theorists and eludes many business school texts on business strategy, or is at best treated *en passant*. The importance of strategy to leadership is discussed in chapter 7.

Leadership is the crucial issue, Rosabeth Moss Kanter says, when a company is failing and its survival is at stake.[140] It matters most in respect of an openness and honesty in dialogue, mutual respect, collaborative problem solving, and the encouragement of initiative. She says that withholding information from employees and the public compounds a financial or strategic mess: the cover-up can be worse than the mistake. 'Leadership is the ultimate advantage', says Nikos Mourkogiannis. 'When it's present, it makes all other advantages possible. And poor leadership can turn even the best advantage into a disaster.'[141]

Mutual respect is not gained by punishing those responsible for mistakes. It is gained through recognizing what people have to offer and involving them in problem solving and decision making, for example in strategy formulation. And problem solving and a commitment to solutions in turnaround situations require collaboration across organizational boundaries. Moss Kanter quotes as an example how Greg Dyke, on taking over as Director-General of the BBC in 1999, used this approach in his 'One BBC: Making It Happen' strategy to rehabilitate a demoralized organization. Initiative can be encouraged by empowering employees to take action, again something that had been missing at the BBC and which Dyke introduced. Creating such a culture is key for leaders in turnaround situations. In the words of Moss Kanter: '... this is the true test of leadership: whether those being led out of the defeatism of decline gain the confidence that produces victories'.[142]

The Industrial Revolution, starting in the UK, shifted the emphasis from political and military leadership to business and economic leadership – building industrial enterprises, opening up markets, and innovation.[143] Such leadership, however, was ascribed to the relatively few ('born' leaders?) who were usually autocrats. As Douglas McGregor stated in his seminal book *The Human Side of Enterprise*:

> **Traditionally, leadership has tended to be equated with autocratic command and there are still many who see leadership mainly in terms of the issuing of orders which are eagerly obeyed by followers whose loyalty is largely determined by the charisma of the leader.[144]**

Over half a century later, this is still true.

Research by the Council for Excellence in Management and Leadership, set up by the British government in April 2000, revealed a need to 'increase the commitment of organisations of all sizes, in both the private and public sector, to develop better managers and leaders'.[145] The Council acknowledged a 'direct link between leadership capability and sustained high performance'.[146] Its research findings included the following:

* There are still shortages in the quality and quantity of people with leadership skills. Yet the need for those with leadership skills is increasing all the time. There need to be some 400,000 new entrants to management and leadership positions each year.
* Larger organizations prefer customized leadership development programmes.
* Few professional associations require any management learning prior to membership and Continuing Professional Development (CPD) requirements, despite a recognition by professionals of the importance of leadership development.
* There is a lack of data on leadership development for benchmarking purposes.

The CEML research was the basis for proposals and an agenda for action on leadership development. However, according to research carried out in 2010 by the Kenexa Research Institute, an American talent management consultancy, surveying some 29,000 employees in 21 countries, the UK was ranked 17th on a leadership effectiveness index.[147] The UK lagged behind the United States and Germany and also behind China and India, who ranked joint first, but was ahead of bottom-ranked Japan. Kenexa identified two key priorities for leadership development in the UK:

1. *Building trust by employees in their leaders.* Jack Wiley, executive director of the Institute, says:

    The abilities to inspire trust [in leaders] and to remain trustworthy are essential qualities for any leader ... We found that certain actions and behaviours are important for developing leadership trust. These include working ethically and with integrity, supporting whistle-blowers, 'walking the talk' and giving credit where it is due.

2. *Engaging in open, honest, two-way communication.* Wiley says:

    There's also a need to communicate openly, to listen and to remain approachable. Direct reports need to feel safe enough to tell their leader the truth.

We discuss the values underlying leadership in Chapter 6 and leadership development in Chapter 11.

The importance of leadership is commonly judged in terms of its impact on the *effectiveness* of an entity that is led. 'The ultimate measure of effectiveness for leaders', according to Bill George, 'is the ability to sustain superior results over an extended period of time'.[148] However, leadership is a more widely pervasive phenomenon than this. Its primary significance, according to some scholars, is not economic, rather it is its importance in stemming the loss of meaning associated with 'modernity', for example the moral collapse of firms.[149] Richard Hackman also believes that the leadership role is best seen not in terms of its economic impact but in terms of its shaping of the organizational context, such as goals, membership, incentives and culture.[150]

In addition Nitin Nohria and Rakesh Khurana argue that its scope and importance need to be addressed not only in terms of their impact on performance effectiveness but also, and more importantly, in terms of their influence on organizational life – such as meaning, morality and culture.[151] They also argue convincingly that these require urgent attention with respect to leadership education and development in institutions of higher education – and, I would add, in business school MBA programmes especially.

Leadership throughout the Hierarchy: Individual, Shared and Distributed Leadership

Until recently many of the texts on leadership had assumed that leadership was 'a solo act – a one-person undertaking – regardless of whether the organization being led ... [was] a nation, a global corporation or a scout troop'.[152] The conventional view of leadership is that individual leaders make a significant and even crucial impact on the performance of their organizations, though research findings are inconsistent.

For example, Alan Berkeley Thomas in a study of large retail firms in the UK found that individual CEOs *do* make a difference.[153] More recently Noam Wasserman and colleagues also found in their study that, while industry structure and company history may explain a greater variance in company performance over time, the influence of CEO leadership is also substantial, although it may vary across industries.[154] However, Bruce Pasternack and colleagues claim there is little correlation between CEO leadership behaviour and organizational performance.[155] And Richard Wellins and Patterson Weaver Jr quote a study of 83 leadership successions in 1997 and 1998 by Margaret Wiersma that showed little relationship between the loss of a CEO and company performance.[156]

The 'heroic' model of solo leadership that attributes greatness, charisma and near-infallibility to a single leader is flawed: 'both dangerous and dangerously naïve' according to Keith Grint.[157] Totalitarian regimes 'led' by a single leader – whether in countries or companies – are testimony to this view. What CEOs who are effective leaders themselves do is to create a 'leadership culture' that is characterized by collective or distributed leadership and therefore a multitude of leaders throughout the organization. In the words of Henry Kissinger, former US Secretary of State, 'A leader becomes great if he institutionalizes a system, if it doesn't become totally dependent on one person.'[158] British supermarket chain Tesco's long-serving chief executive Sir Terry Leahy's announcement in June 2010 that he was to retire in nine months' time led to a significant fall in the share price, suggesting just such a dependency.

This dependency has been reinforced by executive education and leadership development programmes that emphasize the individual leader:

> The parsing of leadership styles has become de rigeur in American business schools. Professors teach students to adopt the right leadership style for themselves, using '360-degree feedback' to make them aware of how they are perceived by others – and how to manage those perceptions. A growth industry called executive coaching caters to the leadership-impaired.[159]

Dennis Tourish and colleagues studied transformational leadership education in 21 leading business schools and found a confusing conflict between the widely posited purposes of leadership and an undue emphasis on the individual 'heroic' leader.[160] This conflict concerns the 'unresolved tension between two ... ideas': the purpose of a collective interest and common purpose that characterizes transformational leadership and the purpose of self-interest (derived from agency theory) in which transformational leaders exert a top-down influence over the activities of others in pursuit of their visions, missions and objectives. Each purpose or aim undercuts the other. And Tourish and colleagues say: 'Business school educators tend ... to uncritically exaggerate the contribution [individual] leaders make to business success' and 'use stories which chronicle how powerful and charismatic leaders routinely rescue organizations from the precipice of failure'.

New 'post-heroic' ideas, however, have emphasized the value of more collaborative and less hierarchical practices that are enacted through fluid, multi-directional interactions, networks and partnerships.[161] While these ideas about 'shared', 'distributed', 'collaborative' and 'networked' leadership are not necessarily interchangeable, they all imply a more collaborative and shared notion of power and authority.

Individual Leadership

Solo leadership is not necessary, not desirable, and probably impossible in today's organizations, according to James O'Toole and Bruce Pasternack and colleagues.[162] The new view of leadership is that the traditional role of a single leader who 'leads' by command-and-control can no longer work because the challenges and problems facing organizations today are too complex and difficult for one person or even a small group of executives to handle on their own.[163] 'Contextualists' argue that many situational factors constrain solo leaders.[164] What is needed, Wilfred H. Drath says, is a 'relational dialogue ... people making sense and meaning of their work together... [creating] a world in which it makes sense to have shared goals or shared knowledge'.[165]

The 'heroic' model of leadership attributes greatness and infallibility to individual leaders, according to Keith Grint, which, to repeat, is 'both dangerous and dangerously naïve'.[166] Business leadership that depends on one all-powerful leader, Pasternack and colleagues say, is 'unstable in the long run'.[167] The examples they give are the disintegration of the ITT Corporation after CEO Harold Geneen's retirement and the way in which General Motors after Alfred Sloan, Polaroid after Edwin Land, and Coca-Cola after Roberto Goizueta seemed to lose their way.

There are many examples of once-lauded heroes falling out of favour: *The Economist* quotes Bernie Ebbers of WorldCom, Diana Brooks of Sotheby's, Jean-Marie Messier of Vivendi Universal, Percy Barnevik of ABB, Kenneth Lay and Jeffrey Skilling of Enron, and even the iconic Jack Welch of General Electric.[168] Stefan Stern cites Tony Hayward, former CEO of BP, whose star waned over the disastrous Gulf oil spill in 2010 owing to his inflexibility and lack of dynamism, his appearance as 'a rabbit in the headlights of a car' and, above all, his ill-considered and clumsy public statements.[169] Stern says that Hayward's 'pleasing self-effacing' style when he took over from Lord Browne in 2007 'didn't cut it at the height of the crisis of 2010 ... A reminder that the best leaders do not simply adopt one fixed (heroic) [style], but are able to adapt to suit the circumstances' (as we will see in Chapter 2 when we discuss situational leadership).[170] Tony Blair, as a former UK prime minister, is another example of a heroic leader eventually falling out of favour.

One problem is the celebrity status that is accorded to solo leaders which feeds their egos and reinforces their ambitions. The result is that:

> Nearly all CEOs think of themselves as the sort of all-knowing, tough, take-charge leader whose photo appears on the cover of *Forbes*, and they find irresistible the temptation to centralize authority in their offices, making all important ... decisions themselves.[171]

This phenomenon is not limited to 'heroes' in the business world of capitalism. It is apparent in communist cultures too. For example, personality cults developed around communist leaders like Jiang Zemin and Zhu Ronji in the People's Republic of China. Says Susan V. Lawrence of the Beijing Bureau of the *Far Eastern Economic Review*, 'China's state media [are] increasingly given over to paeans to Jiang', and he has engaged in adorning public buildings with his calligraphic inscriptions 'with enthusiasm'.[172]

Individual leadership, nevertheless, still has a place. It is necessary in small and start-up companies and in organizations where inspiration is needed to bring about transformational change, say Pasternack and colleagues.[173] But they also add:

> CEOs of large companies should ... see that it is more productive and satisfying to become a leader of leaders than to go it alone.[174]

Shared and Distributed Leadership

Various references in the literature have been made to leadership that is shared, distributed, distributive, dispersed, collective, or (not a pre-possessing term) institutional. *For clarity's sake, distributed leadership may be regarded as the (hierarchically) vertical dispersal of authority and responsibility and shared leadership as the 'horizontal' aspects of these phenomena.* House and Aditja say:

> The process of leadership cannot be described simply in terms of the behavior of an individual: rather, leadership involves collaborative relationships that lead to collective action grounded in the shared values of people who work together to effect positive change.[175]

Burdening the lexicon, they distinguish among 'delegated leadership', 'co-leadership' and 'peer leadership'. And co-leadership itself is interpreted in different ways, for example in terms of one co-leader 'playing second fiddle' to another[176] or as two leaders working side by side with equal managerial responsibility.[177] Others use the term to mean the same as leadership that is shared among many individuals. Shared leadership is nothing new, having been recorded in ancient times:

> Republican Rome had a successful system of co-leadership that lasted for over four centuries. This structure of co-leadership was so effective that it extended from the lower levels of the Roman magistracy to the very top position, that of consul.[178]

A survey by the Manufacturing Foundation found that leadership in successful middle-market manufacturing firms in the UK tended not to reside in one person at the top but existed as a shared role among the top management team.[179] Shared leadership reflects a shared ownership of problems; an emphasis on learning and development (empowerment) to enable sharing, understanding and contribution; and a culture of openness, mutual respect and trust. Michael Kocolowski suggests that healthcare and education (in the United States), where most studies have been conducted, are two sectors that are especially open to shared leadership.[180] The successful recovery of British supermarket Asda as part of Walmart in the 1990s was overseen by co-leaders Archie Norman and Allan Leighton.

Michael Useem found that 'The best projects [by MBA students] come from the teams that learn to act together and exercise shared leadership.'[181] Shared leadership is characterized by:

- The quality of interactions among people rather than their position in a hierarchy.
- The effectiveness with which people work together in solving a problem rather than a solo performance by one leader.
- Conversations rather than instructions.
- Shared values and beliefs.
- Honesty and a desire for the common good rather than self-interest, secrecy and spin.

In 2001 Bruce Pasternack and colleagues, in collaboration with the World Economic Forum and the University of Southern California, surveyed over 4,000 people in leadership roles in 12 large organizations on three continents and interviewed 20 to 40 in each one. They found that many successful companies – such as the Intel Corporation, Motorola, and the Hyundai Electronics Industries Company in South Korea – were developing an institutional leadership capacity rather than depending on a charismatic CEO: 'Rather than an aria, leadership can be a chorus of diverse voices singing in unison.'[182] The measure they developed is known as the Leadership Quotient (LQ). Leadership, James O'Toole says, is an 'organizational trait'.[183]

However, O'Toole and colleagues reported on the indifferent reception these findings had at the 2000 World Economic Forum in Davos, Switzerland, despite evidence being provided of a sufficient number of cases of shared leadership that could attest to its success:

... this resistance to the notion of shared leadership stems from thousands of years of cultural conditioning [starting perhaps with Plato's views]. We are dealing with a near-universal myth: in the popular mind, leadership is always singular.[184]

Marianne Döös and Lena Wilhelmson reported on a study showing that two-thirds of Swedish managers had a positive attitude towards shared leadership (or co-leadership).[185] They studied four pairs of leaders in four Swedish organizations that were concerned with product development, management consulting, communications and soccer. Their common characteristics included shared values, mutual confidence, shared approaches to planning and visualizing, capitalizing on differences and a receptivity to new ideas, and a joint recognition of setbacks and successes. The Amana Corporation's CEO Paul Staman commented:

> [Shared leadership] allows more time for leaders to spend in the field; it creates an internal dynamic in which the leaders constantly challenge each other to higher levels of performance; it encourages a shared leadership mindset at all levels of the company; it prevents the trauma of transition that occurs in organizations when a strong CEO suddenly leaves. [What makes this work is] a shared set of guiding principles, and a team in which each member is able to set aside ego and 'what's in it for me' thinking.[186]

Jay Carson and colleagues, studying 59 consulting teams, found that shared leadership predicted team performance as rated by clients.[187] They also found that external coaching and the internal team environment, consisting of a shared purpose, social support and a voice, were associated with the emergence of shared leadership.

Leadership involving two people can, however, prove very dysfunctional despite its lasting many years. For example, during the period 1997–2007 in the UK the relationship between the then prime minister Tony Blair and his Chancellor of the Exchequer (finance minister) Gordon Brown was, *The Times* said, seriously flawed, with a consequential 'terrible, wasteful cost in allowing governance to play second fiddle to psychodrama'.[188]

The idea of distributed leadership (also known as institutional or dispersed leadership) takes shared leadership further. It was first described by Philip Selznick in 1957.[189] Jeff Gold and Alma Harris highlighted a study of distributed leadership in two schools and how it occurred through 'mediation in the form of [dialogue] and representational symbols' with the aim of identifying actions for improvement and monitoring any subsequent progress.[190]

Peter Gronn, in his meta-analysis of empirical studies in 20 organizations with distributed leadership, observes that this often begins spontaneously but eventually becomes institutionalized.[191] He identifies two features of distributed leadership: interdependence and coordination. Interdependence is characterized by an overlapping of leaders' responsibilities and the complementarity of responsibilities. Coordination and alignment among co-leaders are key to success, but not only at the top.

O'Toole found that 'many of the key tasks and responsibilities of leadership [are] institutionalized in the systems, practices, and cultures of the organization'.[192] Institutionalized leadership is characterized by an empowerment to act like owners and entrepreneurs rather than 'hired hands'; to take the initiative and accept accountability; and to create and adhere to agreed systems and procedures. O'Toole and colleagues suggest that the reason for the continued success of companies under the successive tenure of several CEOs – and for the failure of previously successful CEOs in new companies – is to do with organizational variables like systems, structures and policies, 'factors that are not included in research based on a solo leadership model'.[193]

Flexible distributive leadership is required to cope with the increasing volatility, complexity and variety of organizations' external environments, according to Michael Brown and Denny Goia.[194] And distributive leadership, in Peter Gronn's view, has emerged as a result of the development of new organizational forms – such as flatter structures that are more organic and virtual organization – that require greater interdependence and coordination.[195] The current interest in institutional leadership reflects a post-industrial division of labour that is characterized by distributed workplaces, which include such phenomena as 'hot-desking' and working from home. This kind of working has been made possible by developments in IT. But Keith Grint warns that, 'In attempting to escape from the clutches of heroic leadership we now seem enthralled by its apparent opposite – distributed leadership: in this post-heroic era we will all be leaders so that none are.'[196]

Yet a study of 12 universities in the UK by George Petrov of the University of Exeter's Centre for Leadership Studies found that distributed leadership was being used as 'a cloak to hide an increasing lack of consultation with staff ... used by those in positions of real power to disguise power differentials, offering the illusion of consultation and participation while obscuring the mechanisms by which decisions are reached and resources distributed'.[197] Petrov sees distributed leadership not as a successor to individual leadership but as a parallel process.

Bruce Pasternack and colleagues suggest that whether (and how) a CEO builds institutional leadership, as did Jack Welch at General Electric and Yotaro 'Tony' Kobayashi at Fuji Xerox, can make a difference to organizational performance.[198] Pasternack says:

> Too much is being written about the CEO as the great leader and not enough about organizations that demonstrate leadership capacity throughout the organization ... Really good leaders take their skill and abilities and build into their organizations the capacity for leadership all the way down the line.[199]

And Mary Curnock Cook, chief executive of UCAS, the UK's university and college student admissions service, sees distributed leadership as the organization's DNA:

> Leadership can and should take place at all levels in an organisation. It's not something that comes only from the top. I like to think of leadership being the DNA of a company.[200]

Hierarchical Level and Leadership

If distributed leadership is important, then it would be interesting as well as useful to explore the similarities and differences in leadership behaviour and effectiveness across the various levels of an organization's hierarchy. Most early empirical research studies of leadership focused on first-line or middle-level managers owing to the availability of access and large enough sample sizes.[201] However, in line with the growing acceptance of qualitative research, in more recent times we have seen many more studies of CEOs that have been based on interviews with them – indeed there has been a plethora of such studies.

Organizational hierarchy is associated with 'command-and-control' leadership. On the one hand, Robert Fuller says, authority and hierarchy are associated with inflexibility, slow decision making and a lack of responsiveness towards customers, and, on the other hand, if 'rank matches with experience, expertise and judgement ... [these] ensure that the person who is best qualified to make the decision is the one with the authority to make it'.[202] Fuller makes the point that 'the problem is not hierarchy *per se*, but the abuse thereof', such as self-aggrandizement and self-preservation.[203] Frances Hesselbein says 'when people move into a circular system, enormous energy is released'.[204] But many organizations will probably always have hierarchies, and leadership in relation to organizational level is therefore a worthwhile consideration.

Leadership has been traditionally conceived as a top-down, hierarchical and formal role.[205] Clearly there are many people with formal leadership titles throughout hierarchical organizations – not just CEOs – who are effective leaders, however we would choose to define what 'effective' means here. Nevertheless, Scott DeRue and Susan Ashford correctly question why some people in formal leadership positions are not seen as leaders and why some people are seen as leaders even though they do not hold formal leadership positions.[206] Leadership theory has come to encompass more than formal, traditional leadership, namely a broader relationship of mutual influence 'composed of reciprocal and mutually reinforcing identities as leaders and followers [that] is [dynamic and] endorsed and reinforced within a broader organizational context'.[207] In other words, according to several scholars, leadership is a socially constructed and reciprocal relationship between leaders and followers.[208]

However, traditional, hierarchical and formal organizations with leadership of one kind or another in evidence do still exist today, and they do so in abundance. For example, leadership for Scott Goodwin, CEO of Voxclever, an IT and telecoms company founded in 2008, is 'to provide a clear framework for the business and make it abundantly clear to my managers what their roles and responsibilities are'.[209] And in such organizations we can indeed find effective leaders – and effective and happy 'subordinates' who may or may not be 'followers' in the currently fashionable sense. Are work situations commonplace where 'individuals "claim" an identity and others affirm or "grant" that identity as the underlying process by which leader and follower identities become socially constructed and form the basis of leader-follower relationships'?[210] I have yet to witness any CEOs or indeed any managers throughout an organizational hierarchy 'claiming' their leadership role and their staff 'granting' it. In formally *leaderless* groups, where leaders may emerge because of their value, contribution and esteem in a group, as described by Bernard Bass in his classic 1954 article,[211] what DeRue and Ashford describe certainly makes sense.

But such democracy in commonplace conventional organizations is still a long way off for many if not most corporate cultures and national cultures. Indeed in some cultures 'democracy' is a deception, an illusion, wishful thinking, or is even regarded as subversive. And yet the uprisings in many Arab countries in early 2011 would seem to signal an accelerated change in this unhappy state of affairs towards a more truly democratic, inclusive and participative form of leadership that resonates with the self-actualization of humanity.

Any comprehensive theory of leadership therefore would need to encompass leadership – its nature, occurrence and development – both in formal organizations and in informal groups. Moreover, such a theory must not lose sight of what the word 'leadership' means – 'showing the way and drawing people with you' – and eschew fanciful and impertinent constructions of what one or another academic *wants* it to mean. This is the approach that this book takes.

Likely hierarchical differences in leadership behaviour were pointed out long ago by Philip Selznick.[212] According to Robert Lord and Karen Maher, 'the perceptual processes that operate with respect to leaders are very likely to involve quite different considerations at upper versus lower hierarchical levels'.[213] Top-level leaders are responsible for the vision and mission of the organization – where it is heading, the development of appropriate strategies and strategic goals, and creating and promoting shared values throughout the organization. Lower-level leaders are responsible for formulating plans to implement strategies, accomplishing routine tasks and encouraging individual involvement and team working. Amatai Etzioni sees top management as being concerned with ends rather than means, middle management with means rather than ends, and first-level management with daily operations.[214] At all levels, however, there are two needs: to empower people – to *enable* people to do what needs to be done – and to engage them – to get them to *want* to do what needs to be done.

Richard Wellins and Patterson Weaver Jr argue that first-level and middle managers are:

> ... the leaders who really make or break a company, and who offer the greatest return on a development investment ... Working daily on the front lines, these people *see* problems, opportunities, and challenges. They are the most visible level of leadership to employees and customers. They bear the brunt of the responsibility for engaging the workers, building morale, and retaining key players ... [They] are the lynchpin between the strategy set at the top and the execution of that strategy through the ranks.[215]

At lower organizational levels, Daniel Katz and Robert Kahn, however, suggest little leadership as such is required, as the focus is on administrating to maintain effective operations.[216] This is contentious: leadership is needed wherever there are subordinates or followers. And administrative tasks are a means by which objectives and performance standards are achieved: plans have to be formulated to carry out tasks and achieve objectives. Katz and Kahn say that, at middle levels, administrative procedures are developed and implemented, and human relations skills are important. At the top level of an organization these administrative procedures are initiated to reflect new policy. Executives with overall responsibility for an organization will practise *strategic leadership*,[217] which we discuss in the chapter on leadership and strategy.

However, any division, department or section in a company can have a vision of where or what it needs to be. It can, and ought to, have the strategies to pursue this. And, while it may – and hopefully does – share the core corporate values, it can also define additional values, for example the performance standards that are particularly important to that part of the company and guide its members' behaviour. Examples are external or internal customer service, production quality and data accuracy. Conversely, CEOs must also be concerned with individual involvement and team working among their board members and senior management. Stephen Zaccaro and Richard Klimoski argue that a leader's position in the organizational hierarchy determines the choices available to him or her, the impact of those choices, and the requirements of the leader.[218]

In addition to a critical review of the major theories and models of leadership, we explore in Chapter 3 how transformational and transactional leadership – an important and useful current model of leadership – is distributed throughout organizational hierarchies.

The collective leadership capacity of an organization is the sum total of distributed leadership at all hierarchical levels. And, as Peter Drucker says, this is the basis for its survival and success: it provides an organization's ability to act as its *own* change agent.[219] When the collective leadership capacity of an organization is strong, we may say that that organization has a strong *leadership brand*. Dave Ulrich and colleagues state:

> **Leadership brand occurs when leaders at every level are clear about which results are most important, develop a consistent approach to delivering these results, and build attributes that support [their] achievement ...[220]**

Creating and sustaining a leadership brand[221] is a way to build employee engagement and commitment to the company,[222] just as a product or service brand is a way to build client or customer loyalty. Brand loyalty, in the case of leadership, requires employee engagement and commitment.

 ## Further Reading

John Adair (1989), *Great Leaders.* Guildford: The Talbot Adair Press.

John Antonakis, Anna T. Ciancolo and Robert J. Sternberg, Editors (2004), *The Nature of Leadership.* Thousand Oaks, CA: SAGE Publications.

Bernard M. Bass (2008), *The Bass Handbook of Leadership: Theory, Research, and Managerial Applications,* Fourth Edition. New York, NY: Free Press.

Warren Bennis, G.M. Spreitzer and T.G. Cummings, Editors (2001), *The Future of Leadership.* San Francisco, CA: Jossey-Bass.

Alan Bryman, David Collinson, Keith Grint, Mary Uhl-Bien and Brad Jackson (2011), *The SAGE Handbook of Leadership.* London: SAGE Publications.

James MacGregor Burns (1978), *Leadership.* New York, NY: Harper and Row.

Roger Gill, Editor (2005), *Leadership under the Microscope.* Ross-on-Wye: The Leadership Trust Foundation.

Keith Grint (2005), *Leadership: Limits and Possibilities.* Basingstoke: Palgrave Macmillan.

Keith Grint (2010), *Leadership: A Very Short Introduction.* Oxford: Oxford University Press.

Brad Jackson and Ken Parry (2008), *A Very Short, Fairly Interesting and Reasonably Cheap Book about Studying Leadership.* London: SAGE Publications.

Barbara Kellerman (2008), *Followership: How Followers Are Creating Change and Changing Leaders.* Boston, MA: Harvard Business Press.

Donald G. Krause (1997), *The Way of the Leader.* London: Nicholas Brealey.

Antonio Marturano and Jonathan Gosling (2008), *Leadership: The Key Concepts.* Abingdon: Routledge.

Joseph Masciulli, Mikhail A. Molchanov and W. Andy Knight, Editors (2009), *The Ashgate Research Companion to Political Leadership.* Farnham, Surrey: Ashgate.

Nitin Nohria and Rakesh Kumar, Editors (2010), *Handbook of Leadership Theory and Practice*. Boston, MA: Harvard Business Press.

Peter G. Northouse (2010), *Leadership: Theory and Practice*, Fifth Edition. Thousand Oaks, CA: SAGE Publications.

John L. Pierce and John W. Newstrom (2008), *Leaders and the Leadership Process*. New York: McGraw-Hill.

Ronald E. Riggio, Ira Chaleff and Jean Lipman-Blumen, Editors (2008), *The Art of Followership*. San Francisco, CA: Jossey-Bass.

Birgit Schyns and Tiffany Hansbrough, Editors (2010), *When Leadership Goes Wrong: Destructive Leadership, Mistakes, and Ethical Failures*. Charlotte, NC: Information Age Publishing.

Simon Western (2008), *Leadership: A Critical Text*. London: SAGE Publications.

Gary Yukl (2009), *Leadership in Organizations*, seventh Edition. Upper Saddle River, NJ: Prentice Hall.

Stephen J. Zaccaro and Richard J. Klimoski, Editors (2001), *The Nature of Organizational Leadership: Understanding the Performance Imperatives Confronting Today's Leaders*. San Francisco, CA: Jossey-Bass.

 ## Discussion Questions

1. Why is there no agreed paradigm for leadership?
2. 'Leadership is showing the way and helping or inducing others to pursue it'. Discuss.
3. What is 'good' leadership?
4. 'Leaders are people who do the right thing; managers are people who do things right' (Warren Bennis). Discuss.
5. 'And when we think we lead, we are most led' (Lord Byron). Discuss.
6. Why is the study of followership useful to understanding leadership?
7. Change management or change leadership? Which is more important?
8. Do leaders behave differently across hierarchical levels in organizations?
9. Is the day of the individual, 'heroic' leader giving way to the age of collective leadership?
10. How might collective organizational leadership enable an organization to be its own 'change agent'?

Experience of Management and Leadership

18

Ellis, P. and Bach, S.

NMC Standards for Pre-registration Nursing Education

This chapter will address the following competencies:

Domain 1: Professional values

2. All nurses must practise in a holistic, non-judgmental, caring and sensitive manner that avoids assumptions, supports social inclusion; recognises and respects individual choice; and acknowledges diversity. Where necessary, they must challenge inequality, discrimination and exclusion from access to care.

5. All nurses must fully understand the nurse's various roles, responsibilities and functions, and adapt their practice to meet the changing needs of people, groups, communities and populations.

Domain 4: Leadership, management and team working

4. All nurses must be self-aware and recognise how their own values, principles and assumptions may affect their practice. They must maintain their own personal and professional development, learning from experience, through supervision, feedback, reflection and evaluation.

Essential Skills Clusters

This chapter will address the following ESCs:

Cluster: Organisational aspects of care

12. People can trust the newly registered graduate nurse to respond to their feedback and a wide range of other sources to learn, develop and improve services.

14. People can trust the newly registered graduate nurse to be an autonomous and confident member of the multi-disciplinary or multi-agency team and to inspire confidence in others.

> ### Chapter aims
>
> After reading this chapter, you will be able to:
>
> - identify some of the values which underpin nurse leadership and management;
> - understand how the experience of being led affects the ways in which we choose to lead and manage in nursing;
> - comment on why leadership and management in nursing are important;
> - begin to create a coherent picture of what leadership and management structures in nursing look like.

Introduction

The purpose of this chapter is to increase your awareness of the personal and professional values that influence the ways in which managers and leaders should behave. The chapter will both challenge and reinforce some of the assumptions you hold about the ways in which leaders and managers function.

Our **values** and assumptions about leadership and management are to a great extent derived from our experiences of leading and managing, and of being led and managed. This means they will reflect our personal interpretation of what happened during the process. It is important that, at the start of any quest to understand leadership and management, we should first understand ourselves and our motivations. Only in this way can we hope to understand the context of leadership and management and the behaviours and motivations of those we seek to lead.

As well as exploring the context of values in relation to leadership and management, this chapter will explore some of the characteristics of leaders and managers. These descriptions will reflect the characteristics leadership and management theorists believe good managers and leaders should portray, including their personality traits. After examining these characteristics, you will be encouraged to formulate a picture of how you believe good leaders or managers should behave, and the essential qualities you believe they should exhibit within the nursing context.

(For more detailed discussion of theories and frameworks for leadership and management, and how they can be adopted and adapted by you to help meet the challenges of nurse leadership in the twenty-first century, see Chapter 6.)

A further important theme of this chapter is why leadership and management are important in nursing practice now and in the future, as well as how an understanding of them can contribute to your personal and professional development. We will examine this issue at least in part by discussing the some of the findings of the Francis report (2013), which examined serious failures in care.

Towards the end of the chapter, some of the reasons for the existence of different leadership and management roles in nursing are introduced and discussed. You are invited to collect some data on the nursing structures where you work and how these impact on the work you and your colleagues do.

Understanding context and values

Our ideas and opinions about good leadership and management are coloured to a great extent by our personal experiences of leadership and management, whether we are managers, leaders or team members. The assumptions we have about management and leadership styles and behaviours are also affected by our understanding of what is going on and the motivations behind the management and leadership styles we adopt or see adopted. The inability to understand why a certain approach to management or leadership has been adopted can lead to misconceptions and misunderstandings; this is something an understanding of the context of nurse leadership and management allows us to see beyond. Sometimes this context is better developed as we gain more experience as nurses and reflect thoughtfully on what these experiences actually mean.

Activity 1.1   *Reflection*

When you first came into nursing and went into practice for the first time, how did you feel about the efforts made by the staff to get frail, elderly patients to engage in self-care, for example, encouraging elderly patients to get out of bed in the morning and to get washed and dressed? Now you understand a bit more about the purpose and nature of nursing, have you changed your view? Why?

There are some possible answers and thoughts at the end of the chapter.

Understanding why something is done in a particular way in a given situation allows us to understand the context of an action in the clinical setting. As shown in Activity 1.1, a developing understanding of the nature of nursing and what it means to nurse helps us to make sense of the world of work and the roles in which we find ourselves. The same is true of leadership and management, where actions taken out of context may appear to be wrong.

One of the enduring difficulties for student nurses can be to understand the provision of care beyond the individual. Often the context of nursing management and leadership is about achieving the best outcomes on a regular, recurring and equitable basis for the many. The need to achieve good outcomes for the many rather than the few may help us to understand the context of a management or leadership style we see before us. This view is one which can only develop if we are willing and able to question the leadership and management practices we see around us and are then willing and able to reflect on the answers we find.

Case study: The newly qualified nurse

Julius is a newly qualified staff nurse working on a busy cardiology ward. Julius is irritated by the apparent inactivity of the ward sister Deirdre, who spends vast amounts of time in the office doing what to him appears to be endless and pointless paperwork instead of providing patient care. Julius confronts Deirdre about the lack of time she spends on the ward and suggests much of the time she is doing noth-ing of value while she is 'hiding away' in her office.

Deirdre understands the point Julius is making and is wise enough to appreciate that his frustrations arise not out of malice towards her but as a result of his inexperience and lack of understanding of what it takes to keep a busy ward functioning smoothly. Deirdre takes Julius into her office and shows him some of the tasks she has to perform on a regular basis, which include writing the duty roster, completing staff appraisals, entering patient dependency scores on to a monitoring database, ordering stock and overseeing staff development planning.

Deirdre explains to Julius she too is frustrated by the lack of time she has to provide care on a daily basis: that, she explains, is after all why she came into nursing. But she also understands her role now is less about providing care and more about facilitating the delivery of care. Deirdre explains she achieves this through supporting the staff on the ward to improve, using appraisals and accessing appropriate education and development; rostering to allow for a good work–life balance; and managing the budget while ensuring the hospital administrators know what the needs of the ward are by recording the level of dependency of the patients and the stock requirements. She explains she sees her role as supporting the staff to care for the patients, and if she did not do the necessary tasks then there would be chaos.

Julius concedes he had not looked at things in this way and he needed to understand the wider context before criticising.

From this example we can see that leadership and management often involve the need to see the bigger picture – which may not always be evident to members of the team. In order to understand the challenges and benefits that accrue from good leadership, it is necessary to understand some-thing of the context of nursing leadership and management.

Clearly, from this example we can see that one of the necessary qualities of a good manager or leader is the ability to see the bigger picture and anticipate and plan what the team will be doing and how they will do it. Leadership and management are therefore as much a forward-looking activity as about managing what is happening in the here and now. One of the characteristics of good managers or leaders is understanding what it is they want to achieve and being able to communicate this, and perhaps effectively delegating associated tasks, to the team.

What we should remember at this stage is that one of the most important things that motivates us as nurses to achieve the goals we do is our values. Before we explore some more about the context of nursing leadership and management, we should stop for a moment to reflect on the values we have as humans, nurses, leaders or managers and see what impact they might have on leadership and management in nursing.

It is not at all easy to state exactly what values are. A cursory search on the internet for values of caring throws up scores of words, all of which may have relevance to nursing, but none of which explain what they are. Various descriptions include reference to best interests, moral duties, likes and preferences.

Concept summary: Human values

One of the widest-cited definitions of values, and one which has resonance with nurse leadership, is the definition by Schwartz (1994, page 20), who says that a value is *a belief pertaining to desirable end states or modes of conduct that transcends specific situations; guides selection or evaluation of behavior, people, and events; and is ordered by the importance relative to other values to form a system of value priorities.*

The notable elements of the definition by Schwartz are that values relate to:

- achieving a good outcome;
- something more important than individual situations;
- how we ought to behave;
- what we ought to look for in the behaviour of others;
- how events ought to be managed;
- ways in which we might prioritise how we use our time and effort.

In essence the suggestion here is that our values should be at the centre of everything we do, both as a guide to how we act as well as what it is we act upon. The additional issue for leaders and managers is of course that they need to role model these values to those they lead.

Evidently, within the case study above, Deirdre had not forgotten the values that took her into nursing in the first place. What had changed then for Deirdre as she moved from a clinical role to a more managerial post was simply the way in which these values were allowed to express themselves. In order to develop continually as nurses, leaders and managers, it is important not only that we question our values from time to time, but that we are also able to express what these values are and refine them in discussion with our colleagues.

Activity 1.2   *Decision making*

Take some time to think about the values you have as a nurse. Now think about how these values show themselves in the ways in which you act when in the clinical setting. Next time you are in practice, ask your team leader or ward manager what values s/he holds and how s/he thinks s/he expresses them in practice. Now compare the lists, looking for areas of overlap and areas of difference. What do you notice about the similarities and differences between your list of values and corresponding actions and the leader's values and actions?

There are some possible answers and thoughts at the end of the chapter.

What is clear about the values of practising nurses, ward managers and more senior nursing staff is they should, and to a great extent do, share similar values and goals. The role of the leader or manager should be to facilitate the team in the achievement of these goals. Evidently, where there are differences in the values and goals of the team and the team leader, then difficulties will arise. When nurses or nurse leaders forget what their values are, then they will lose sight of what it is they are trying to achieve.

Sometimes it is hard to know what exactly our values are or the limits to which they can be stretched. One method for understanding our values as potential leaders or managers is to ask ourselves hypothetical questions, the answers to which can be searching and difficult for us. The answers to these difficult questions enable us, however, to understand what sort of person we are and what motivates us as humans, nurses and managers. Understanding our own values and underlying motivations will then tell us something about what is likely to motivate and guide the actions of those that may be called upon to lead.

Scenario 1.1: Doing the right thing

Imagine you are working in a nursing home on nights. You are tired, having already worked six shifts in a row. One of the residents, Jane, who is in her late 80s, has been in the home for some time as a result of having had a stroke. Jane needs to be turned 2-hourly to avoid her developing pressure sores, but you and the nurse you are working with decide to turn her just occasionally. You justify this to yourselves by saying this avoids disturbing her sleep and it also protects your backs. At the end of the shift you turn her and record in her notes that you have done so 2-hourly throughout the night. She has not developed a pressure sore, so what is the harm?

Now consider this: you turn her at the end of the night and discover that a small area has broken down on her left hip. Is this your fault? If the matron asks if you have turned her 2-hourly, as stated in the care plan, what will you say? You could say you turned her 2-hourly – this would not change anything for Jane, but would make your life easier.

Alternatively you go to turn her at the end of the night shift only to discover that she has died some time during the night. She has been dead for a while judging from how cold she is and the blood that is pooling on the side she was lying on. You know you can just claim that you found her earlier in the night and prepare her body quickly before the day staff come in to work. Surely this will not change anything; no one will be hurt, will they?

Which, if any, of these scenarios are acceptable? Does the blame attached to any of them change because of the outcome? What does your choice of actions say about you? What values are being displayed here? How do they compare with the values you expressed in Activity 1.2?

There are some possible answers and thoughts at the end of the chapter.

Examining examples such as this enable us to see the bigger picture. They are also helpful for us in developing an increasing awareness of our own values as they relate to being led and managed and then, conversely, to us leading or managing. In part our values will be mirrored in the sort of person we are and how we see the world in general, but they will also shape the way in which the world sees us. Of course it might be equally bad if a nurse were to follow policy and procedure blindly, with no thought about the consequences. In this scenario, as in many leadership and management situations, deviating from what we know to be right (i.e. ignoring our values) can have dire consequences for those we care for.

Scenario 1.2: Being clear

You are working on a medical admissions unit and have asked a colleague, Emma, to go round and do the observations. She takes the temperature, pulse and blood pressure of every patient on the unit, as asked. About an hour later you ask if all the observations were OK. Emma replies that the woman in the first bed had a temperature of 39°C. You ask why she had not informed you of this immediately. She replies that it was her job to do all of the observations as you asked, and that is what she has done.

What does this scenario tell you about managing and leading people in the clinical setting? What does this tell you about the need to understand what we do and why? Is there a place for understanding values of care in this scenario?

There are some possible answers and thoughts at the end of the chapter.

By now you should have developed a fairly clear picture of the values that you believe underpin what you do as a student nurse or nurse. You may well also have some insight into the values of those around you and the impact that working among other nurses has on the development of your own value set. It is important to understand that, for leaders or managers to be effective, there is a requirement for there to be some degree of overlap between their values and the values of their team, and the team must be aware of this (Grivas and Puccio, 2012).

What happens when values are forgotten?

Hospitals, care homes, clinics and community teams are made up of collections of people working together to achieve a common task. This common task requires that the values of the individuals involved in the care align to some extent; otherwise they would be working in opposition to, rather than with, each other. One of the challenges of modern healthcare is that our values can get lost in amongst all of the tasks we have to undertake and our attention may be drawn to achieving goals and targets, rather than remembering the values which bring us into nursing in the first place.

When nurses, or indeed any care staff, forget the values that should be driving their work, this has an impact on the culture they work in and this culture ultimately impacts on the care they give.

The following extract is taken from the Francis *Report of the Mid Staffordshire NHS Foundation Trust Public Inquiry* (2013):

> *The negative aspects of culture in the system were identified as including:*
>
> - *a lack of openness to criticism;*
> - *a lack of consideration for patients;*
> - *defensiveness;*
> - *looking inwards, not outwards;*
> - *secrecy;*
> - *misplaced assumptions about the judgements and actions of others;*
> - *an acceptance of poor standards;*
> - *a failure to put the patient first in everything that is done.*
>
> *It cannot be suggested that all these characteristics are present everywhere in the system all of the time, far from it, but their existence anywhere means that there is an insufficiently shared positive culture.*
>
> (Francis, 2013, page 65)

What Francis (2013) is identifying here is not a list of issues with the organisation, but a list of issues which arise as a result of the collective values of the people in the organisation becoming secondary to other issues. If we take each of the bullet points in turn, we can see each one represents a *value* which is not being exercised:

- competence;
- compassion;
- thankfulness;
- mindfulness;
- openness;
- trust;
- principles;
- care.

Francis goes on to say that:

> *To change that, there needs to be a relentless focus on the patient's interests and the obligation to keep patients safe and protected from substandard care. This means that the patient must be first in everything that is done: there must be no tolerance of substandard care; frontline staff must be empowered with responsibility and freedom to act in this way under strong and stable leadership in stable organisations.*

To achieve this does not require radical reorganisation but re-emphasis of what is truly important:

- *Emphasis on and commitment to common values throughout the system by all within it.*

(Francis, 2013, page 66)

The Francis report has had a major impact on the way in which care is delivered in the UK, not because what happened at Mid Staffordshire was unique, because it probably isn't, but because it reminded care professionals and politicians alike that, once managers impose the wrong sorts of *values* and *targets* on care professionals, then values of care can easily be forgotten.

It is probably fair to say that, in order to become an effective leader or manager of people, we first must know ourselves and our values as well as having some insight into how others see us and how they interpret the way in which we display our values. Part of leadership or management is presentation of self to others and encouraging others to follow our lead by behaving in ways and displaying values that others admire and can identify with – creating a situation where others wish to follow. When you think about it, a leader without followers is just a person working alone!

How we see ourselves and others see us

To understand how we see ourselves and how this compares to how others see us, it is worth looking at the work of Joseph Luft and Harry Ingham, whose Johari window illustrates the point about what we know about ourselves and what others know about us.

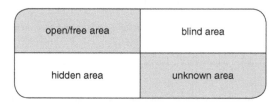

Figure 1.1: The Johari window

Source: Adapted from Luft and Ingham (1955), page 10.

What the Johari window allows us to see is how much of the perceptions and knowledge we have about ourselves is also seen and shared by others:

- The open/free area refers to what we know about ourselves and what is also known by other people – it is our public face.
- The blind area is the area of our personality we are blind to but which others can see – our blind spot.
- The hidden area is what we know about ourselves but we keep hidden from others, sometimes called the 'avoided self' or 'facade'.
- The unknown area refers to what is unknown both to ourselves and to others (which can be regarded as an area for potential development and self-exploration).

What is interesting about this model is it shows us there is great potential for us as individuals to lack understanding of ourselves as much as there is potential for other people not to understand us. To some extent we can manage the view others have of us as individuals by allowing them to see what we want them to see and by managing our behaviours at work and in our private lives. On the other hand, people are often aware of issues with our values and personality that we are sometimes aware of and sometimes not.

Being able to adapt who we are and how we behave at work is part of the process of socialising to be both a nurse and a member of society at large. By being aware of our values and acting upon them we allow ourselves the ability to become someone we want to become and potentially to develop the traits that will help us to develop as a person, a nurse and over time as a manager or leader.

Activity 1.3   *Communication*

In order to get some idea of how your view of yourself is similar to, or differs from, that of other people, undertake the following exercise which may tell you something about how you communicate with and are perceived by other people: Choose five words to describe what sort of person you believe yourself to be and write these down. Ask a number of people who you know to choose five words which describe what sort of person you are and write these down. Include fellow students, lecturers, mentors and other people you work with. Examine the lists for similarities and differences and assign the responses to the various boxes of the Johari window and consider what this says about how your perception of self concurs or contrasts with the views of others.

Since this is based on your own thoughts and reflections, there is no specimen answer at the end of the chapter.

Activity 1.3 will help you to see that sometimes people see good and sometimes bad things about us which we may or may not see for ourselves. The lesson for the would-be leader is to learn to change the negatives that we can change and to manage the areas of our personality that we cannot. You should also be prepared to take on board positive insights and use these to continue to improve your relationships with others.

What are the characteristics of a good leader or manager?

What makes a good leader or manager has been explored by many theorists and academics over the years. Some of the early theorists identified characteristics such as physical size, strength and 'presence' (Wright, 1996). Other characteristics and traits that have been favoured include intelligence, personality type such as extroversion, and **charisma** and other interpersonal skills.

Certainly it is true that being **charismatic** and intelligent helps with the processing of ideas and when communicating with others can help a leader. But, as we have seen above, there must be more to being a good nurse, good leader or good manager than these superficial qualities alone. Sometimes extreme examples allow us to see things that are perhaps not clear to us in the day-to-day process of being managed or led.

Activity 1.4   *Reflection*

Reflect on some of the well-known and successful leaders you know from history, perhaps Winston Churchill, Nelson Mandela, Martin Luther King or Florence Nightingale. What characteristics do they share that makes them great leaders? Why are they thought of as great individuals as well as successful leaders?

Next think about some of the other successful leaders from history, like Adolf Hitler, Napoleon Bonaparte, Joseph Stalin or Saddam Hussein. What characteristics made them successful leaders? Why are they thought of as immoral leaders?

There are some possible answers and thoughts at the end of the chapter.

Interestingly, from the examples of good leaders given above, none of them was particularly impressive physically, so their ability to lead and inspire has to be explained in some other way. Certainly this observation calls into question some of the early physical appearance theories of what makes a good leader. Clearly there may be issues relating to their charisma and intellect that attracted other people to them.

What we can see about the leaders in Activity 1.4, and what perhaps others know about some of them that they do not see for themselves, is the leaders we admire have a vision of something better for the people they lead. In the case of Mandela and Luther King, this was freedom from oppression and the achievement of equality of status and human rights. The pursuit of these values and the veracity with which they pursued them give us a clue as to one other quality we might admire in a leader: **integrity** (Frankel, 2008). In this sense integrity may be understood as acting in a manner that reflects the values, ethics and morals that an individual believes to be important.

Integrity alone is not enough, however. Hitler, Stalin and Saddam Hussein all perhaps believed in what they were doing; in that sense they had integrity. What is interesting about what they believed and what they set out to achieve was that it was often more about achieving power for themselves than it was about achieving what was right or something that benefits others.

What is missing therefore is an understanding about what this integrity and leadership should be aimed at achieving. Leaders and managers are the figureheads of teams and teams exist to get a job done (Ward, 2003). In nursing this job is about providing care for others in a manner that reflects the positive values we hold as humans and as nurses. For a nurse leader or manager, therefore, integrity of action means leading and managing in a manner that reflects the values of care which are part of what being a nurse is about and which you have identified for yourself in Activity 1.2.

Activity 1.5   *Reflection*

It is perhaps worth reflecting on the answers you gave to Activity 1.2 and comparing them to what you have learnt so far in this chapter. You should be able to see some commonalities between the ideas and therefore have some ideas of what being a good nurse leader or manager is all about.

Since this is based on your own observations there is no specimen answer at the end of the chapter.

So far in this chapter we have seen that being a good leader or manager in nursing is about the expression of the same values of care that being a good nurse requires. What changes when one moves from being a nurse to a nurse leader or manager is the way in which these values are expressed through what we do and how we behave towards others. The consistency of the values between nursing and nurse leadership/management demonstrates integrity. It is perhaps a sad fact that those nurse leaders and managers who we see losing sight of their values are the ones we least admire. The report into the failings at the Mid Staffordshire Hospital identified poor leadership coupled with clinical staff *accepting standards of care ... that should not have been tolerated* (Clews, 2010). The collective failing here was that clinically trained managers did not support their staff as well as they might have and the managers and leaders, as well as their staff, allowed the standards of care to slip below a level reflective of the true *values* of nursing.

One of the challenges of this book is for you to recognise and acknowledge the values that you have as a nursing student and to think about how you will continue to exercise these values throughout your nursing career.

Structures of nurse leadership

What we have not discussed so far are the structures that relate to the exercise of leadership and management. Clearly a manager occupies a formal role. The role of the manager is conferred upon the individual by an organisation and its staff are responsible to the manager by virtue of their contract of employment with the organisation – often called **legitimate power** (first identified by French and Raven in 1960). How these lines of responsibility are created and what they mean in practice should be clearer after the next activity.

Activity 1.6 *Reflection*

To understand the lines of responsibility that form part of a contract, look at the pro-gramme handbook for the programme you are on. There will be clear guidelines about some things you can and cannot do as a university student. There will be identified individ-uals to whom you would have to answer if you break these rules. This forms part of your contract with the university and ultimately with the Nursing and Midwifery Council (NMC) in relation to the fitness to practise criteria.

Alternatively, if you have a contract of employment you may notice it identifies the person to whom you are answerable, usually a line manager.

As this is based on your own observations there is no specimen answer at the end of the chapter.

Managerial power and responsibility, as you can see from Activity 1.6, are therefore formalised within the contract of employment or training. They are validated by the fact that we choose to submit to these contracts of our own free will, usually because they will confer some benefit on us (in the case of a job, through being paid and in the case of being a student nurse, in gaining a qualification). Similarly, as nurses we agree to be bound by *The Code* and other regulations pertaining to nursing (NMC, 2015).

Within most organisations there are a number of managers at different levels who have different responsibilities for different organisational activities. These managers report to a more senior manager who in turn reports to more senior management. Such structures are formalised and are usually created in order to allow for the overseeing of the functions of the organisation. Each tier within the system of management should be aware of their responsibilities and the limits of their powers in fulfilling the tasks associated with these roles. It is often helpful for novice nurses to have some idea of what the structure of the organisation they work in looks like.

In Chapter 8 we discuss a little about cultures of care and you may find it useful to look up Charles Handy's work (1994) on cultures in order to inform your thinking about the formal and informal management structures which can exist in health and social care.

Activity 1.7 *Evidence-based practice and research*

Try to find out something about the management structure in the hospital in which you are placed. There may be a diagram that shows the relative management positions (some-times called an organogram); then try to find out what the main responsibilities are of the people in the various roles you have identified. You might also like to do something similar for a ward or other practice area you work in so you can get an overview of who is respon-sible for what.

As this is based on your own observation there is no specimen answer at the end of the chapter.

So we can see that being a manager is a formalised position that is conferred by position within an organisation. Being a leader, on the other hand, may or may not be the result of position within a team or organisation. How can this be?

As we will see elsewhere in the book, leadership is in many instances one of the roles of a manager; think about the ward managers in the areas where you have worked who as well as managing the ward also lead the team. Think also about the areas where you have worked where individuals who occupy a junior role in a team exercise leadership. Sometimes then the leadership function is one of the roles of the manager, while on other occasions something else is at work.

How then do some non-managers function as leaders? Essentially there are three answers to this question. First, some leaders, such as team leaders at the ward level, are designated leaders because they are more experienced than the other staff or they hold a higher, non-management grade. They exercise the power of leadership also through virtue of the formal position they hold and the delegation of certain duties from their line manager. In this respect the power they exercise comes from the person who has delegated it to them – this is sometimes referred to as legitimate power. Legitimate power, within society and organisations, arises out of the fact that people vote for their leaders (in the societal sense) or they enter into contracts of work whereby they agree to be subject to the power of others within an organisation. The leadership roles within such arrangement are therefore legitimised by virtue of the fact that they represent a choice on the part of the people who are led by these elected, or contractual, leaders.

Second, other leaders exercise leadership in relation to specific projects or responsibilities within the team. For example, in many clinical areas there are link nurses with responsibility for areas such as diabetes care, wound management or infection control. Again their power to act as leaders is in part conferred by the position they are asked to play in the team and is delegated from the team manager. The other reason they are a leader in their particular area is because they have specialist knowledge of the practice, procedures and guidelines that relate to whatever it is they are responsible for. In this situation a good leader will share the information the team needs to know to get the job done – a bad leader will not! Clearly, then, one of the characteristics of a leader is information management and good communication.

Third, there are those people who lead by virtue of their character. These charismatic individuals are the sort of people others like and respond to. They are able to motivate others and to get the team to follow them by virtue of who they are. They have a compelling vision of what should be done and how, and have a conviction and surety about them which encourage others to follow their lead (Mahoney, 2001). They may not be in positions of formal power, but perhaps they have knowledge or good communication skills that single them out as people others like to follow.

Case study: The new nursing sister

Eileen is a newly appointed sister on the dialysis unit of a busy general hospital. Eileen is liked by all of the staff, but has rapidly built up a reputation for being quite disorganised. When she is in charge of the shift, things go wrong. She gets sidetracked by small details and disappears for long periods of time to sort out seemingly minor issues.

continued . . . •••

Karen is a healthcare assistant who has worked in the dialysis unit for many years. Karen is familiar with the routine and is able to cope with most situations that arise. Karen often takes charge of the unit, even when Eileen is there. She co-ordinates the workload, makes telephone calls and arranges transport. Karen uses her connections and the relationships she has built up over the years to get things done.

What we can see in this case study is that, even within an essentially quite hierarchical structure, leadership can be found at all levels of the team. In this example there is a real danger that Eileen will lose control of the unit and Karen might overstep her own competence, role and responsibilities. Clearly one of the issues that arises out of this scenario is accountability. Eileen as a registered nurse is accountable for what she does as well as the actions of her team, especially the untrained members. Karen as a care assistant is not accountable for her actions in the same way, but is responsible to her employer (actually, Eileen) for what she does.

In this scenario the power which Karen exercises is not strictly speaking legitimate. As with all members of the team, she has roles and responsibilities for which she may need to exercise the power given to her by virtue of her position. It may be that Karen has the power to order stores and perhaps organise transport, but these are subject to the need to recognise the roles and responsibilities of other members of the team, who may need support in developing the skills necessary for them to operate effectively within their identified role.

It may be argued therefore that the leadership that Karen exercises is in this instance a bad thing. Karen is perhaps motivated to get the immediate job done, but perhaps misses some of the bigger-picture issues, such as the quality of the dialysis, that she is not trained in and not in a position to understand. Because Karen takes over the day-to-day running of the unit, she is also both undermining Eileen and preventing her from developing into her new role. While in the short term this might appear to work, it is not a long-term solution.

Activity 1.8   *Reflection*

Take some time to think about the implications of this case study. What might this mean for the quality of nursing practice in the dialysis unit? What implications might this have for Eileen and for Karen in the long term? How are the other staff likely to feel about this situation?

There are some possible answers and thoughts at the end of the chapter.

So we have seen that leadership and management within nursing can be broken down into many levels, from the most senior member of the nursing team right through to the most junior, and the qualities that make a good leader can be present at all levels. We have also seen that some managers fail to lead and that some leaders do not really have the formal position or power to do so.

Leading and managing: the policy context

Nursing is not undertaken in a vacuum. What we do as nurses and what nurse managers and leaders do occurs within a healthcare context and is subject to policy, procedure and guidelines. If leadership or management is about leading or managing a team to achieve certain outcomes, and within healthcare these outcomes are derived from policy and guidelines, then there is a need for nurse leaders and managers not only to be aware of what the guidelines are but also to act on them and ensure their team acts on them too.

Historically the caring professions had a great deal of autonomy over the ways in which they worked. In the past they set the standards by which their work was to be measured and audited and decided on clinical and non-clinical priorities. More recently, most notably following the policies of the Thatcher government and subsequently New Labour, clinical priority setting and the standards for care have been determined more centrally through government policy via agencies such as the National Institute for Health and Care Excellence (NICE) or via nationally drawn-up structures for care, such as the National Service Frameworks. So part of the role of nurse leaders or managers will be having the ability to lead or manage their team through the change process to achieve the outcomes of care determined from outside the team (see Chapter 8).

As well as general policy and guidelines in the area of health, as nurses we are subject to policy and guidance from our professional body, the NMC. In order to understand the context of leadership and management in nursing from the point of view of the NMC, it is worth familiarising yourself with the standards of proficiency and Essential Skills Clusters identified at the start of each chapter and asking yourself how these apply within the context of each chapter. You may also wish to look at and reflect on how these ideas reflect the issues identified within other NMC documentation, including *The Code* (NMC, 2015). Most especially, this chapter has highlighted the need for nurse leaders to *be self-aware and recognise how their own values, principles and assumptions may affect their practice* (NMC, 2010), as expressed in Competency 4 of the 'Leadership, management and team working' domain of the competency framework, identified at the start of this chapter.

For example, in this chapter we have discussed some of the values that underpin nursing practice, as well as leadership and management characteristics of the nurse leader/manager which may contribute to our development as good leaders and managers. These characteristics translate well from both the code of professional conduct and the standards of proficiency identified at the start of the chapter. What they validate is perhaps the most important message of the chapter: in order to become a good leader or manager of nurses it is important to remain grounded in the values, beliefs and behaviours that guide professional nursing practice.

Chapter summary

Rather than launch straight into a discussion about the nature of leadership and management in nursing, this chapter has sought to identify some of the values, beliefs and behaviours that might be associated with becoming a good nurse leader or manager. These *continued* . . . .

characteristics have been compared and contrasted with some of the values that underpin being a good nurse. There is an explicit challenge within this chapter for you to identify and confront the values you have as a nurse, a nursing student, a team member and a leader.

In some part this challenge has been posed by reference to some of the shortcomings identified in the Francis report. While the failings at Mid-Staffordshire NHS Trust are useful as a benchmark of what can go wrong, they are exactly that, a benchmark. They should not be considered as merely a footnote in history, but should be seen as a salutary lesson in what could quite easily happen anywhere when nurses and other care professionals neglect their values.

An understanding of the context of care and of ourselves is an important first step on the road to becoming a competent leader of nurses; failure to understand what motivates us as individuals lays us open to external criticism. Furthermore, some of the skills and values we develop as nurses in clinical practice will translate well into leadership and management roles. It is never too soon for student nurses to think about what type of leader/ manager they want to be and to look around them for suitable role models to guide their development.

Activities: brief outline answers

Activity 1.1 Reflection

This reflection is not about understanding the rehabilitation of the elderly as such; it is about understanding context. As a new nurse you may consider asking people to undertake their own care as lazy nursing, because you consider nursing as a caring profession that does things for people. As you understand the nature of care better, you will see the same scenario in a different light, or context, as you understand that encouraging self-care is about helping people address their care deficits and achieve the activities of daily living for themselves.

Activity 1.2 Decision making

What you will notice is that the basic values of caring, moral behaviour, putting others before self, protection of rights, autonomy and dignity are common to both lists. What will be different is that the leader will attempt to achieve these aims through the way in which s/he leads. This will include acting as a role model and promoting the welfare of the team who in turn are expected to support these values one to one with patients and clients (Bondas, 2006). If you are still struggling to think about what your values are, try some of the words above or choose some from this list: accountability, accuracy, calm, committed, decisive, fair, honesty, integrity, justice, open, reliable, team worker or truthfulness.

Scenario 1.1 Doing the right thing

We hope you found none of these scenarios acceptable. On each occasion, regardless of the outcome, the choice being made was to avoid your duty to Jane to protect her from potential further physical harm. The values displayed here are self-regarding and not other-regarding and are against everything that is to be found in the nursing code of conduct. At best, the scenario demonstrates lies being told and at worst a dereliction of the duty of care, leading to harm to the patient. Some people might argue that, as no harm ensued, the first scenario might be all right, but the consequences that *could* accrue (as seen later in the scenario) show this to be wrong, regardless of any arguments about duty and outcomes.

Scenario 1.2 Being clear

This scenario suggests that as a manager or leader it is important not only to have team members who do what they are asked, but also that they understand the purpose of what they are doing. There is a clear need here for the nurse to understand that doing observations is not enough in itself; it is acting on what is found that is important. The values which should drive the undertaking of such tasks is **person-centred** care, which requires that nurses not only undertake a task, but that they think about what it means for the patient or client.

Activity 1.4 Reflection

Clearly one of the characteristics of good leaders is that people want to follow them. In many of the cases mentioned as potential positive role models, people choose to follow the leader because they believe in what the person is doing. This is also the case for some of the examples of negative leadership role models given, so what is the difference? Some people would not choose to follow the likes of Hitler or Hussein, and although many did, many more were forced to do so. Other people follow bad leaders because they generate a sense of belonging and solidarity, perhaps at a time when there is uncertainty in the world. The integrity and ethicality of the examples of bad leaders are questionable at best and evil at worst. So perhaps integrity and morality are two of the things that we admire in good leaders?

Activity 1.8 Reflection

While Karen does a good day-to-day job in making the dialysis unit function, there may be longer-term considerations to take into account. As we saw earlier in the chapter, one of the roles of a leader is operating within the bigger picture. This also resonates with the role of the trained nurse, who has to account not only for the day-to-day running of the dialysis unit but also for the long-term health of the patients. So while it may be all right for the leader to allow someone else to take charge of some of the activities of the team, it is better if s/he is selective about who takes over what tasks and what they do. The staff in a scenario where it is uncertain who the real leader is will be confused, and may even be slightly angry as they see someone without genuine authority taking control.

Further reading

Aldgate, J and Dimmock, B (2003) Managing to Care, in Henderson, J and Atkinson, D (eds) *Managing Care in Context*. London: Routledge.

This chapter explores the values of care as well as social inclusion.

Handy, C (1994) *Understanding Organisations* (4th edition). London: Penguin.

This is the classic text on organisational culture.

Scott, J, Gill, A and Crowhurst, K (2008) *Effective Management in Long-Term Care Organisations.* Exeter: Reflect Press.

See especially Chapter 4 on Leadership.

Useful websites

www.businessballs.com
An interesting and quirky leadership and management resources website.

www.kingsfund.org.uk/topics/leadership_and_management/index.html
Perhaps the leading UK healthcare think tank.

www.midstaffspublicinquiry.com/report
The Francis report: *Report of the Mid Staffordshire NHS Foundation Trust Public Inquiry.*

Leadership for Change

Barr, J. and Dowding, L.

Learning Outcomes

By the end of this chapter you will have had the opportunity to:

- Explore change theory
- Discuss the need for effective leadership throughout the change process
- Recognise effective change environments
- Debate the effects of change on individuals, groups and organisations
- Explore the value of Action Learning Sets in supporting change.

INTRODUCTION

This chapter attempts to draw together the various notions of leadership and examine their effects on leading for change. Leadership during periods of change can be extremely difficult so it is important to know just how the information in the preceding chapters and the theories of effective change management can be used together in order to work in an effective and harmonious environment. Well-handled change is seen to be for the benefit of all rather than something that is imposed upon the workforce. Organisational change is also a complex and well-researched area. This chapter will explain the process of change management and discuss the behaviours that might be seen in the organisation during change. Experience dictates that in many situations the process of change is not given enough attention to ensure that it is as successful and painless as possible. It may seem difficult, at times of change, to think about the future – particularly when there appears to be government legislation-induced change after change. Few periods of history can be thought of as transforming but currently we appear to be living through one of those periods, particularly in health care. We are facing two major conflicting challenges: control of health care costs *and* the provision of quality care to all patients and clients.

These two factors are fundamentally altering the health care delivery system and so impact on the ability to lead effectively during change.

DEFINING CHANGE

Although change appears constant and indeed a frequent event in health and health care, it is not always clear what it means. There are a number of definitions of change. The BNET Business dictionary states that change is 'the coordination of a structured period transition from situation A to situation B in order to achieve lasting change within an organization' (www.change-management-coach.com accessed 11 November 2014). However Clarke and Copcutt (1997: 2) noted more complexity to the concept:

Change is not a single process or group of processes: It ... does not exist at all. It is an ideal, a story made by everyone who is experiencing discontinuity. Viewed as a cause of events, by others as a consequence, it can be the disease, diagnosis and the cure.

Activity

What do the above definitions mean to you?

How could they relate to a recent personal change you have encountered?

The first could infer that change is about *moving* – like a house or a job move from one place to another. Or it could be more complex and depend on how you perceive it. A recent personal change involved the installation/movement of a new printer in my office. By the second definition, it involved buying a new printer with difficulty finding the ink cartridges (cause of events) and new printer cartridges being easily available and a scanning function as an added extra (consequence). There was a concern and indeed stress about learning how to use the printer and its connection to the Internet (disease). The benefit of taking time to read the manual and trying out various options means that there is an improved printing function but scanning and faxing is now possible – success (cure). From simple to complex definitions it appears that there will be some form of movement along a continuum which could be either linear (Figure 13.1) or cyclical (Figure 13.2).

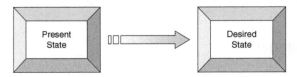

Figure 13.1 Linear continuum

However Freshwater (2014: 97) noted that 'change is not only inevitable and is also a fundamental aspect of being human'. She also alludes to the fact that change does not always equate to improvement and that the evidence and research for best practice for managing change appears to miss the *context* of how leaders facilitate a successful change and focus instead on the *process* of managing change.

LEADING CHANGE

There may be many examples of change in health care (see Table 13.1). Some involve very large projects such as changing NHS Trust structures and thus cultures

Figure 13.2 Cyclical process model. A combination of Lewin (1951) and Lippet et al. (1958)

Table 13.1 Some examples of changes in health care

- Advanced surgical, anaesthetic and medical treatments
- Cardio-pulmonary resuscitation techniques
- Rapid response treatment for patients with suspected stroke along with early discharge rehabilitation services
- Introduction of nursing led units in hospitals
- Innovation of wireless point of care systems. Clinical information systems are individualized in the electronic patient record (EPR) and the longitudinal electronic health record (EHR). The use of personal digital assistants (PDAs) and voice-over Internet protocol (VoIP) is developing.
- Diabetic, respiratory and cardiac care management by practice nurses
- Development of walk-in centres in the community
- SMS/ texting/ social media services to reduce rates of defaulted appointments or enhance health education
- How2trak software to improve wound care outcomes
- Online booking for better general practice access
- Development of skills such as Cognitive Behaviour Therapy (CBT), solution focused, promotional and motivational guidance therapies to enhance mental health of wellbeing in adults and children
- Setting up new local services to improve breast feeding rates, reduce post natal depression and address poverty and child protection issues through access to professional/ peer support.

and on the other side, others are quite small but all may have resonance with the health benefits for patients, clients and families. Ultimately these changes are about addressing *need* especially in an era of 'information revolution' and aligned health technology.

This array of examples are just a few in the changing world of health care innovations. If you get the opportunity to attend a professional conference, there are often a range of new ideas, research, health industry products and services that have been recently developed that you may want to consider in your own field of practice. As we develop professionally we are charged with the notion of improving care through innovation. MacPheem and Suryaprakash (2012) through project analysis research of 133 nurse leaders' year-long projects concluded that first-line nurse leaders were well able to successfully manage projects beyond their traditional scope of responsibilities. This highlights the nature of developing autonomy and responsibility in professional care.

From the plethora of published material on issues of change management, many models might seem relevant in the area of health and social care.

Ackerman (1997) identified three types of change:

- **Developmental change:** Planned or emergent incremental change focusing on the improvement of skills and processes
- **Transitional change:** Planned and more radical organisational change (based on the work of Lewin, 1951; Kanter, 1983)
- **Transformational change:** Radical organisational changes of structure, processes, culture and strategy based on learning and adaptation.

One widely recognised model of change, which is perhaps simplistic but well understood as in our first definition, is described by Lewin (1951), who suggests that there are three key stages to any change. These changes are:

1. **Unfreeze** or unlock from the existing level of behaviour
2. **Change** the behaviour or move to a new level
3. **Refreeze** the behaviour at the new level.

Lewin's three-stage model can be applied to almost all change situations in order to analyse the success and failure of the whole process. In 1958, Lippet et al. suggested a three-phase model to enhance Lewin's model:

- The **clarification** or diagnosis of the problem
- The **examination** of alternatives and establishing a plan of action for the change
- The **transformation** of intentions into actions to bring about change.

These two models jointly (Figure 13.2) create a useful cyclical process model that is applicable to the situation undergoing or requiring change. However, it should be noted that change in any health service is not always seen as being this simple.

Swansburg and Swansburg (1998) note other theorists, such as Havelock (1973) and Rogers (1983), who suggest more comprehensive staged models for change and innovation (Table 13.2).

Table 13.2   Rogers' (1983) vs Havelock's (1973) models of change

Rogers' (1983) Five Stage Diffusion of Innovation Model	Havelock's (1973) Six Stage Model
1 Awareness	1 Build Relationship
2 Interest	2 Diagnose Problem
3 Evaluation	3 Acquire Resources
4 Trial	4 Choose Solution
5 Adoption	5 Gain Acceptance
	6 Stabilisation and Self Renewal

 Activity

Do you have any preference for Rogers' or Havelock's models?

It appears that Havelock, despite being an earlier model, has integrated the importance of relationships and people into the model. This reflects a focus on whether people in the team will actually identify with a need for change, which reinforces the importance of the leader in a changing situation.

Global leadership for developing multinational industries involves great change. Global managers, for example in banking, pharmaceutical, retail or car industries, face the arduous task of catalysing and steering change efforts and aligning extremely large and far-flung multinational corporations and certainly do this amidst ethical concerns. Change interventions that work in one country do not always work in another so health leaders must be aware of cultural beliefs, values and expectations when suggesting changes in their own organisation.

However it must be said that global and even national research and development in health care delivery is important and may trigger innovative ideas for developing, rather than directly importing, in a different context.

 Activity

Have you read any recent clinical literature concerning your own specialism from abroad such as Europe, the USA, Australia or Asia?

You may have dismissed it as it was 'irrelevant or foreign'. Reflect on the relevant assumptions you held.

Time is always a problem for busy health care professionals working in practice and keeping up to date with literature and evidence. Bullen et al. (2014) note the challenge of conducting and integrating research into clinical practice and the difficulty of time constraints for practitioners engaging in research.

Having attended a few global and national conferences as well as procuring an RN licence abroad, the bigger picture is really helpful and I now appreciate there is much to learn from a broader global perspective. Health-related experience abroad helps us with the 'helicopter view of our own practice' and can proceed to plan for innovative changes. I remember being surprised with seeing whiteboards over patients' beds in the USA where nurses wrote and agreed the 'simple daily collaborative care plans/ goals' (this would follow a daily nursing health assessment). This felt 'patient agreed and centred' but was challenging for me against the backdrop of a reserved British and NHS culture. However I thought the alternative might be that UK patients/ families are often unaware of any informal/ formal daily assessment and plans for the day/ weeks. So now I question the notion of how we really involve patient and public communication in all health contexts. In retrospect, the USA and UK health cultures are so very different but I now believe a more open and transparent care partnership really is the way forward and opening myself to global evidence-based health care can advance medical and care innovation and change.

THE LEADER AS AN INSTRUMENT OF CHANGE

In previous chapters, we discussed the benefits of knowing about your leadership/ followership style (Chapter 1) and also your problem solving style (Chapter 2). Now we can take the perspective of the leader being an instrument of change. You, as a change leader, at any level, need to play to your strengths rather than your weaknesses/blind spots and use a reflective approach within your team when driving through change. It is important to remember that you will be seen as a role model and others will look to you for direction, motivation and commitment. The way you handle the process of change, the stress involved and the way you interact with others will determine the success or failure of the change project.

In order to ensure a successful change, then, the present situation must be considered and information gathered in order to set the direction for improvement. Galbraith's *star* model (2001) highlights the complexity of change within organisations, how change should 'fit' within a number of elements in the organisation and the interaction between all elements (see Jay Galbraith's article and model on his web page www.jaygalbraith.com/images/pdfs/StarModel.pdf). For example, changing the way tasks are carried out has implications for the organisational objectives, people, information, structures and rewards. Denison's (2009) model is maybe more advanced/ comprehensive, acknowledging the importance of culture and stability as well as the internal and external influences in complex change environments. Its elements of an internal and external focus as well as the features of:

- strategic mission/goals
- adaptability
- consistency and
- team involvement

are worthy of exploring to understand the relevance in your own analysis of any improvement, change or innovation you wish to consider.

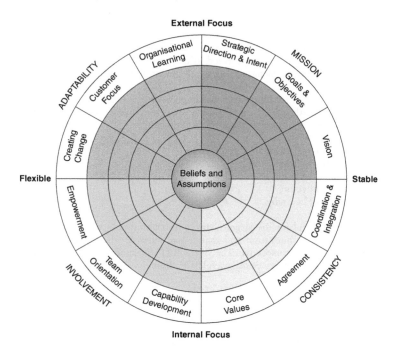

Figure 13.3 Denison's model of cultural change (2009)

 Activity

These models can be seen as very complex.

If you are new to your health care profession, do you agree?

(Continued)

(Continued)

What do you make of these for your own new leadership role?

If you have experience as a health care professional, what do you make of these for your own leadership role?

What action can you take to ensure you are considered a change leader?

It is useful to think of any new change in your clinical area and make notes about the wider aspects of change identified in these models; it may be that you would have liked more involvement or more development opportunities than have recently been promoted.

The NHS Institute for Innovation and Improvement (2009b) document relating to change in the health service noted five key areas for consideration for leaders when taking a team on an organisational or cultural change:

- Organisational Performance and Health
- The Discovery Process
- The Influence Model
- Change Architecture
- The Benefits Hierarchy.

This is really useful for the larger changes in health and is worth considering for smaller projects of innovation and change too. However the models above appear to have a top-down perspective. The 7-step RAPSIES model of change (Gopee and Galloway, 2009) may be a really useful 'step' framework for managing any change effectively.

The RAPSIES model focuses on the following steps:

- Recognising the need for an improvement in practice
- Analysing options for change-setting, identifying people involved
- Preparing for change – identifying change agent, the intended outcomes and education required
- Strategies for change process
- Implementing the change: piloting and timing
- Evaluation against intended outcomes
- Sustaining the change.

This change model gives more detail than Lewin's staged model and can be seen as a more democratic approach to change with a wide interpretation of where in the health industry this process may originate. So for instance a hospital porter who thinks there are too many patients waiting for hours on trolleys can provide a catalyst for change, as can a newly qualified health visitor who sees that there are conflicting health education messages for a 'back to sleep' policy from a paediatric orthopaedic department, or a health care assistant who is concerned that the speedy breakfast trolley routines in her ward do not allow enough time for more vulnerable older patients to be supported in helping them enjoy and eat their food.

RESPONSE TO CHANGE

Kramer (1974) identified a phenomenon described as the 'Reality Shock' that was seen to occur when a student nurse becomes a registered nurse. A conflict between the student nurse's expectations of the role and its reality in the work setting emerged. The four phases of role transition from student to professional identified in Chapter 11 are:

1. Honeymoon phase
2. Shock phase
3. Recovery phase
4. Resolution phase.

While Kramer's work related to a nursing scenario, these findings are well-known stages expected of any project change. It is natural that when a change is proposed there will be some reaction to the event. The point where the need for change becomes a desire to change is accepted as being pivotal and, therefore, the start of the movement process. If we take as an example the changes to moving and handling procedures, it was during the 1990s that the great risks of poor moving and handling practices in clinical care were identified. The RCN initiated change for professional groups amid little or no debate with external organisations. Due to the lack of involvement of care organisations, acceptance of change was not easy; there was no clear starting point and it is difficult to identify when the 'need for change' became a 'desire for change'.

Reactions to change are often surprising to change leaders because of the wide spectrum of emotions involved. Kubler-Ross (1970) identified ten potential reactions to bereavement. While her work examined the reactions to death and dying, the emotional features can be applied to all change – as those who experience the change are being drawn away from their comfort zone into an unknown area. The ten phases are highlighted in the resource on the companion website.

There are many reasons why resistance to change occurs, and leaders need to try and anticipate these and understand them as natural phenomena. Kotter and Schlesinger (1979) identified four key reasons:

- **Self interest:** People resist change if they perceive that they may lose out in some way. This could be as simple as loss of power or input in decision making. There are many individuals who simply resent being told what to do. Similarly, staff tend to think that their own approach is the best with sayings such as 'this is how it has always been done so why change' and 'if it ain't broke, don't fix it'.

- **Misunderstanding and lack of trust:** Strangely, efforts to create safer working systems can be negatively received and not trusted. It is vital that the leader engenders enthusiasm for the proposed change, letting all the team know what is happening at each stage in order to combat this element and take on board their individual issues into the change plan.
- **Low tolerance to change:** Some people are concerned with stability and security and find change daunting.
- **Different assessments or expectations:** There are often different perceptions of the change process held by the people involved and the costs of that change will be higher or lower for different groups. Indeed, the cost of the proposed change must be considered in influencing the outcome. The force-field analysis plays a large part in determining where change is needed and the cost of that change will lead to success. Conflict is seen when the benefits of a proposed change are biased towards one group's needs at the expense of another group. So if the change is seen to benefit only the organisational management structure but add further work for the workforce there is likely to be little cooperation with the process.

Trust me George... Leave it!

LEADING THE TEAM THROUGH CHANGE

Leaders need to assess the willingness of each individual to take on board change. There will be some people in the team who, inherently, do not like any sort of change and will demonstrate a low tolerance to any new initiatives. Within some areas of the health service there has been constant change over recent years and team members may exhibit signs of change fatigue in these rapidly developing areas due to constant patterns of change. However, there may be many levels of change makers and change resisters; within any team, there will be individuals who react to change in many different ways (Table 13.3).

This might seem quite a simplistic view and tends to categorise individual team members in relation to how they may react to change at one point in time rather than seeing individuals as changing as the process progresses.

 Activity

Think back to Chapter 2 (Leadership/Followership and MBTI® exercises) to see if you can spot any trends. Then ask yourself the following questions:

- Which behavioural pattern (below) do you most often adopt in response to change?
- Does your behaviour always fit this pattern or does it change depending on the situation or your maturity?

Table 13.3 Types of individuals (adapted from Rogers and Shoemaker, 1971)

Change (Progressivism) Innovator (Change Maker)	Proactive during the process of change, e.g. implements new policy or procedure
Early Adopter	Readily accepts the change, e.g. another professional adapts to the change
Early Majority	First group to follow early adopter, e.g. local team becomes involved in the change
Later Majority	Other groups follow suit, e.g. other teams introduce the policy
Laggards	A reticent group who tend to remain sceptical, although not openly hostile to change, e.g. colleagues who compare but do not take part
Rejecters (Change Resister) Status Quo (Traditionalism)	Openly oppose change, e.g. individuals resist becoming involved in the implementation of the policy

You will not be surprised to know that your attitude towards change depends on a number of factors; the situation you find yourself in has a great part to play together with whether you see the change as having a positive influence on your employment position. You might think of other factors that have influenced you in the past and made you behave like a laggard rather than an early adopter. It is now prudent to explore the effects of successful and unsuccessful change and the ways in which a leader can affect outcomes.

SUCCESSFUL vs UNSUCCESSFUL CHANGE

In health care provision, the need for change has never been greater, both in practice and management systems. The effective leader will recognise that change brings with it a number of feelings, including a sense of achievement, loss, pride and stress. As a leader, it is important that you understand the change development because leaders must be able to give a rationale for it and communicate an understandable plan to those who must manage the change and incorporate it into their lives (Malloch and Porter-O'Grady, 2005). Effective leaders will embrace change and lead healthcare delivery forward; they will exhibit exceptional planning skills and be flexible in adapting to the change they have directly initiated.

As previously discussed, the feelings generated when change is imminent are similar to those experienced during bereavement or loss (Table 13.2). Unplanned change may be accidental or change by drift (Marquis and Huston, 2006: 171) – this is particularly noticeable when the *change is imposed* and a selection of obstructive behaviours may be seen. By contrast, during a change that is expected, rehearsed and informed, the behaviours exhibited are more complementary and positive in their manner. Planned change occurs because of an intended effort by the change agent. As a leader, you will need to be that change agent and make efforts in planning change carefully.

It is clear that initiating and coordinating change requires well-developed leadership and management skills. Dye (2000) goes as far as to say that one of the most fundamental values that differentiates effective leaders from average ones is the desire to 'make a difference'.

UNPLANNED CHANGE

 Activity

Try to remember a time in your life that involved unnecessary or unplanned change.

Why did you think it was unnecessary?

Did it follow Lewin's or Lippet et al.'s model?

What could have been done to make the change more acceptable?

A colleague told me about her shift patterns at work, in a local GP practice, being changed overnight and without any consultation. When she spoke to her manager, she was told that her contract allowed this to happen and that there was no need for consultation. My colleague was not happy and felt that she had to find new employment as there was no way the employers were going to change their minds.

Following her resignation, channels of negotiation were opened and an agreement was reached. Clearly when this situation is related to Lewin's model one can see that there was no opportunity for 'unfreezing', whereby the situation is recognised as requiring change, but the managers went straight to the 'change' element with very little success. Had the situation been handled differently, with discussion and information being offered throughout, there may not have been as much resistance to the change, thereby leading to greater success.

All too often leaders of change have a plan but do not share it or encourage input from others. They might not see the importance of effective communication. For example, if the plan/change is seen as short term, the leader can become short-sighted; if it is someone else's idea and is not 'owned' by the leader, communication can be weak. Whatever the situation we must all recognise that change occurs and so we must be able to plan in order to manage that change. One example of this could be government deliberations related to the recent amalgamation of the small regional ambulance services into larger organisations in order to deliver better care to the patient (DH, 2005a). The thinking supporting this change was of increasing efficiency and cutting costs, due to fewer people being paid at the higher end of the salary scale. The White Paper noted the opportunity to build on the significant improvements of the previous few years and a statement was made to improve radically the services provided. It set out how ambulance services can be transformed from a service focusing primarily on resuscitation, trauma and acute care towards becoming a mobile health resource for the whole NHS. The object was to improve leadership – both clinical and managerial – so that the organisational structure, culture and style matched new models of care. Unfortunately, in terms of communication to the people involved 'at the rock face', it was not sufficiently detailed. Ambulance personnel perceived the real change issue as being the effect on job security during and after the change. As such, the change took place in an atmosphere of distrust and uncertainty, which lasted for many months. Figure 13.4 depicts the effects on people when change is not handled well and very few people know what is happening, why it is happening, or how long the change will take.

All change cannot be contained, directed or managed. Unplanned change will continue to happen in a haphazard way but planned change will be targeted and purposeful. When managers make decisions that appear to be unrelated to current work practices it can be unsettling for the workforce. The uncertainty of the whole process means that decisions may be based on unspoken, sometimes unconscious assumptions about the organisation, its environment and future (Mintzberg, 1989), so resistance may be high. The common mistakes made when change is difficult or unsuccessful are:

- Inappropriate time scales
- Unclear aims
- Inadequate resources
- Ignoring knock-on effects
- Contamination in trying to change too many things at once

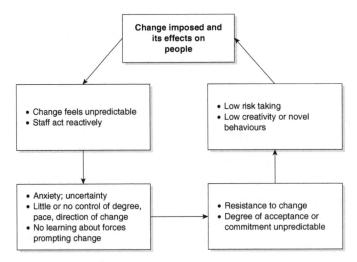

Figure 13.4   Effects of imposed change

- Hijacking – where someone who may wish to settle an old score tries to sabotage the new project
- Incorrect diagnosis – limited force-field analysis or knee-jerk reaction to solving the problem
- Lack of ownership.

PLANNED CHANGE

Planned change is well thought out, timely and necessary. The rhetoric of planned change features all the positive aspects of informing the workforce of what is happening and why. It is a reasoned and well-thought-out activity which will have a positive benefit for care delivery. In reality, the change might be thought to be well planned but there may be pockets of the workforce who have a less rosy view of it. Figure 13.5 depicts the effects on people when the change is handled well and everyone knows what is happening, why it is happening and how long the change will take.

Kotter and Schlesinger (1979) described a broader range of strategies a leader of change might consider in order to facilitate a more successful process. They are:

- Education and persuasion
- Participation and involvement
- Facilitation and support

- Negotiation and agreement
- Manipulation and co-option
- Implicit or explicit coercion
- Review and monitoring.

 Activity

Can you think of a well-planned change in your practice area? Jot down which elements within Figure 13.5 were successful.

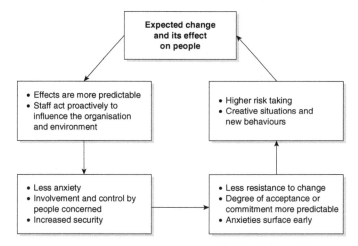

Figure 13.5 Effects of planned change

You might have thought of many instances where change was discussed and started well but hit difficulties, and the whole process became confused due to slippage or various interpretations of people's expectations. In hindsight you may have thought that those leading the change could have managed the change approach better. Bennis et al. (1985) identified three simple strategies to promote organisational or group change (see the resource on the companion website).

The diagram in Figure 13.6 depicts the notion that integrating all elements of change strategies is useful for successful change and no one strategy would achieve effective change alone.

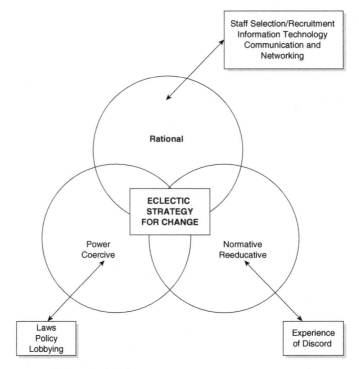

Figure 13.6   Strategies for change

EDUCATION AND PERSUASION

One of the most frequently used ways of minimising resistance to change is through educating people about the need for change. Education is vital during the 'unfreezing' stage of the change process. However, persuasion is required within the approach. There are a variety of approaches to education and persuasion that might be of help:

- The legal argument
- The ethical argument
- The financial argument
- The evidence argument
- Meeting professional standards.

PARTICIPATION AND INVOLVEMENT

It is important that staff, carers and those receiving care are involved in the decision-making process.

Facilitation and support

If negative feelings towards the change are exhibited then it is important to consider the empathetic and sympathetic approaches of facilitation. Training is usually seen as a good start to the support process, moving on to co-working and effective supervision during the change. Skilled facilitators should spend time preparing as well as understanding the factual content of the change.

Negotiation and agreement

As part of acceptance of the new methods and behaviours there may be issues for group agreement. In order to reach a consensus and agreement, it may be necessary to negotiate the way forward in small steps to allow the 'later majority, laggards and rejecters' to reach an acceptable outcome. However you reach the desired outcome you – as leader – must ensure that undue pressure is not placed on any single individual.

MANIPULATION AND CO-OPTION

If the change process is not working, it may be necessary to resort to a more subversive method in order to manipulate people to agree. Co-opting a hesitant member of staff to assist in the process may give them ownership and can be very effective in getting them 'on side'. Once this has been achieved they may bring others with them, so assisting in the smooth running of the process. Should you have a group member who is strongly opposed to the change, they may try to hijack the outcome and affect the dynamics of the group; the infiltration of a key supportive individual might assist in changing the views of that person.

IMPLICIT OR EXPLICIT COERCION

When all else fails, creating a power base where the change leader could offer some sort of reward for adhering to the change or punishment for resisting it can be resorted to. Some care organisations resort to considering disciplinary actions if the change is not implemented. This can only be considered as a last resort. It must be remembered that if punishment is the driving force behind the change then there is a very real possibility that, once these threats are removed, the resisting group will go back to their old ways.

REVIEW AND MONITORING

As with all changes there must be an evaluative period to conclude. The change should be measured and related to how well it has been accepted and adopted. The review needs to be ongoing in order to ensure that the old practices are not reverted to.

 Activity

Have you been involved in a change situation where there was resistance to a particular change?

Consider the way this resistance was overcome and make notes on the effect the change had on the group.

I can remember a time where we wanted to introduce 'pre-operative visiting' for all our patients so that they would know what to expect in the anaesthetic room. We did not want to tell the patients about the details of surgery in case of raising anxieties. At the time, it was felt that all patients would want to know what was going to happen to them in the anaesthetic; they were shown photographs of the anaesthetic environment, briefly told about the monitoring equipment to be used and any questions they wanted to ask were answered. Clearly, for one anxious patient this was too much information and he declined the operation. Following this episode the surgeon forbade the anaesthetic nursing staff from going near his patients. We had to write a script so that the surgeon could see what his patients were being told, but for a while we only went to see the patients if requested. The change had been implemented without full communication with all involved but, fortunately, a compromise was reached which served the needs of all concerned.

PROJECT MANAGEMENT

The activity of planning a project for change is a vital skill for experienced healthcare professional leaders. Project management can be defined as the discipline of planning, organising, securing and managing resources to bring about the achievement of objectives within a project. There are various models for project management, depending on the industry involved. Within health care the use of models ranging from the very simple (such as Assess, Plan, Implement and Evaluate) to quite complex ones (such as Prince2) is prevalent. In Prince2 there are clear procedures for roles and tight management of resources. The overall corporate management oversees the starting up, initiation, controlling of stages, managing boundaries, and project closure as separate entities.

In the early stages of your career, once qualified, you may be asked to lead out on a practice innovation or service improvement. You may well then link this request with change management and initially consider a simple approach to a project management activity. Buttrick (2005) noted the stages of project management are seen as:

- Initiating
- Planning
- Executing
- Monitoring
- Closing.

It is important, in all these stages, to communicate with a wide group of stakeholders in order for success to occur and become more externally as well as internally focused. Initially you will need to liaise and network with patients, colleagues and interested parties – in both an informal and a formal manner prior to perhaps writing a report proposing your ideas for the project to gain support from senior colleagues. These activities require a number of management tools, some of which may be new and some quite challenging. Iles and Sutherland (2001) provided a wide range of useful suggestions in supporting change in the NHS. One of the first useful activities is to examine the project issue using PEST (Political, Economic, Social and Technological) and SWOT (Strengths, Weaknesses, Opportunities and Threats) analyses with various stakeholders.

PEST ANALYSIS

Upton and Brooks (1995) note various perspectives related to change management which help in trying to see the need for change. These perspectives can be viewed as:

1. Very broad trends at a national and international level
2. Regional and localised changes that affect patterns of service delivery
3. The leader as an instrument of change.

The first two perspectives are very important in understanding why change may be necessary, but the third is vital if you are to lead change effectively. Without this understanding it would be very difficult for you as a leader or manager to ensure that what you are doing fits with prevailing trends in society and healthcare delivery.

POLITICAL CONTEXT

Recent policy changes concerning NHS Trusts and community-led services in a market health economy continue to focus on quality, performance standards and patient power. Public accountability, while still allowing for local decision making, is still on the agenda but a reduction in the bureaucracy of health service management is planned. All these changes are purported to squeeze more out of the NHS while devolving accountability and responsibility away from central government to a level closer to the patient.

ECONOMIC CONTEXT

Most of the developed world's governments are looking at ways in which they can contain health care expenditure by rationalising or prioritising treatments, setting ceilings on procedure costs and achieving cost improvements. There are attempts to integrate cost, quality and outcome in order to aid decision making by policymakers and planners.

SOCIAL CONTEXT

As the population lives longer, the cost of care is increasing for the vulnerable and chronically ill. This, alongside global mobility from countries with poorer health-care provision, is out of line with other demographic factors. There are also higher consumer expectations about the breadth and quality of services that are received. In addition, there is greater public sophistication in terms of understanding and choosing what is needed or wanted. All of these factors add to the overall cost of health and social care.

TECHNOLOGICAL CONTEXT

Discoveries in the fields of health care interventions, medicine and total health systems continue to reshape the NHS and look likely to accelerate. Of course, this aspect is harder to predict but potentially may have the greatest impact on health-care delivery. Overall, it requires a high degree of flexibility and ability to respond quickly and effectively to change within the service.

SWOT ANALYSIS

This tool was discussed in Chapter 2 for personal development. It was documented by Ansoff in the 1970s and 1980s; although the originator is uncertain, it is useful in all project management in its assistance in reviewing the internal environment of the local organisation.

Activity

Considering your own clinical team, populate the SWOT grid below.

Strengths	Weaknesses
Opportunities	Threats

You might have considered as strengths your team's commitment to high quality patient care and that you have a full complement of staff; under weaknesses you may identify occasional team conflict around duty rostering. Opportunity for clinical updates for both students and staff may be recorded and threats may come from the amalgamation of services across acute and primary care.

PLANNING FOR CHANGE

Once the broad view of the internal and external environments has been explored, the impact of the project needs to be seen in the context of the strength of the drivers for change. Lewin's (1951) force-field analysis is another useful tool to review the sustainability of any change envisaged.

Using a force-field analysis that includes both hard (quantitative) and soft (qualitative) factors, it is possible to depict how important the proposed change might be and to predict its success. An example of a part analysis might be seen when a new 12-hour working shift pattern is suggested (Figure 13.7).

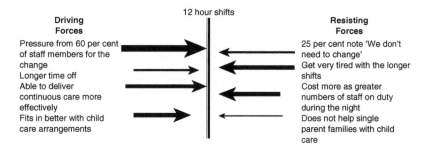

Figure 13.7   Force-field analysis for change related to implementing a 12-hour shift pattern

You can see from the strength of the arrows that some of the forces are much stronger than others, so that the overall need for change appears to be the stronger argument and it would, therefore, be useful to continue to plan for change. This change must be planned effectively and initially should be considered as a pilot project – with an evaluation date to see whether the change should continue.

 Activity

Think of a situation, within your clinical area, where a change may be necessary and draw up a force-field analysis of the need for that change.

You might have found this relatively easy. Did it give the results you expected? Did it highlight the need for the proposed change? Often the results of such an exercise demonstrate that the proposed change is not quite as strongly required as first thought. It also helps to identify the restraining factors, so that appropriate strategies might be considered, but it is important to gather together a project team if you can so that you get a good picture of the current situation. This will help the team develop a sense of ownership of the proposed change. You could ask some of the following questions to indicate how ready for change the workplace team is:

1. How ingrained are the various forces?
2. Which ones are the most open to reduction?
3. What influence can we use to help overcome difficulties or constraints?
4. Are there things we need to find out in order to get a clearer picture of the local influences?

It is therefore prudent to consider the following when driving through a change in the workplace: direction, timescales, communication, resources, making change real, and job security (Table 13.4).

The GANTT chart was developed by Henry Laurence Gantt in the 1910s and is used to illustrate a schedule of activity, usually against a timeline. We probably do not realise that we use them in everyday life, for example when planning for a holiday or shopping for Christmas. There are many examples of GANTT charts on the Internet; Google the term and surf around the wide variation offered – most work on an Excel application principle which may be the easiest method for starting.

ACTION LEARNING SETS

More and more, action learning sets are utilised to facilitate change in the health service, although they can be seen as taking valuable resources in a time-strapped health service environment (Malloch and Porter-O'Grady, 2005: 153). Action learning sets help individuals see the need for change and bring their own personal

Table 13.4 Considerations for driving through change

Direction	Everyone clearly understands what is happening. There is a sense of purpose.
Timescales	Clear and relevant – may be achieved by using a GANTT chart.
Communication	If ineffectual then there are clear grounds for rumour, innuendo and gossip. Gets rid of hidden agendas.
Consultation	Staff need to be informed and involved at every stage of the change.
Resources	Time, money, people, materials – where will they come from and how will they be paid for? Increasingly, employers rely on goodwill that may lead to employee resentment.
Making change real	Involve yourself and behave in ways consistent with the change you are trying to bring about.
Job security	During organisational mergers and reconfigurations, people need to know their place in the new structure. They will not commit to change if their personal place is not secured.

relationship into the change process. Action learning is seen in the context of learning and reflection, supported by colleagues, with the purpose of change. It is based on the following principles of team working:

- Meeting regularly
- Consistent membership
- Addressing members' problem tasks
- Sharing, support, questioning
- Group success
- Review
- Facilitation.

In order for action learning to succeed, there is a need to agree the following ground rules:

- Confidentiality
- Commitment and continuity of attendance
- Clarity of objectives
- Constructive challenge
- Work as a group of peers
- Recognise individual strengths/limitations
- The role of the facilitator is clearly defined.

Scenarios for change are set up and the facilitator assumes a questioning stance. The whole group engages with helping individuals face their particular change difficulty. The elements in Figure 13.8 could be potential frameworks in order to ensure all involved recognise the change issues and have ownership of that process.

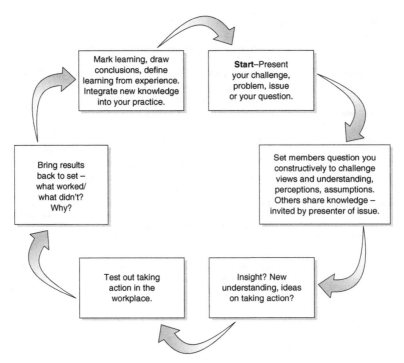

Figure 13.8 Action learning model

(*Source*: Revens, 2011)

Rayner et al. (2002) identify that action learning offers a unique opportunity to develop leadership skills in a safe, non-threatening situation. The ability of leaders or facilitators to analyse problems, gain personal confidence and identify solutions for change for the benefit of clinical effectiveness is paramount. Douglas and Machin (2004) emphasised the value of action learning sets for interdisciplinary collaboration in their grounded theory research in mental health.

The skills, knowledge and experience of the individuals whose responsibility it is to bring about change are varied and complex. It is vital that they consider the intricacies of people's response to change and how that might make the path to change difficult, full of barriers and pitfalls. Good preparation and planning of the process and involvement of interested parties at all stages helps to ensure appropriate support, encouragement and action, thus increasing the potential for successful change.

Summary of Key Points

This chapter has explored a variety of strategies that can lead to successful change. These are:

- **Explore change theory** A number of definitions, theories, models and perspectives have been utilised to reflect a breadth of theory underpinning the concept of change.
- **Discuss the need for effective leadership throughout the change process** The importance of leadership to shape change and lead people through the process of change was explored and there were a number of strategies proposed for effective leadership in this area.
- **Recognise effective change environments** Planned and unplanned change outcomes were discussed and the implications for success and difficulties were explored.
- **Debate the effects of change on individuals, groups and organisations** The varieties of effects of change on health care teams and individuals were debated and the impact on improving and changing care for patients and clients was highlighted.
- **Explore the value of Action Learning Sets in supporting change** This model of change was linked to the notion of team learning, problem solving and reflection using a facilitative approach.

FURTHER READING

Baulcomb, J.S. (2003) 'Management of change through force-field analysis', *Journal of Nursing Management*, 11: 275–80.

Butler, L. and Leach, N. (2011) *Action Learning for Change: A Practical Guide for Managers.* Cirencester: Management Books 2000 Ltd.

Davies, C., Finlay, L. and Bullman, A. (2000) *Changing Practice in Health and Social Care.* London: Sage/The Open University.

Gerrish, K. (2000) 'Still fumbling along? A comparative study of newly qualified nurses' perception of the transition from student to qualified nurse', *Journal of Advanced Nursing*, 32 (2): 473–80.

Gough, P. (2001) 'Changing culture and deprofessionalisation', *Nursing Management*, 7 (9): 8–9.

Paton, R. and McCalman, J. (2000) *Change Management: A Guide to Effective Implementation* (2nd edn). London: Sage.

Visit the companion website at https://study.sagepub.com/barr3e for more resources.

Managing Change and Innovation in Practice Settings

20

Gopee, N. and Galloway, J.

Change is a necessary feature of all forward-looking organisations. Health and social care organisations in particular are subject to ongoing change as an inevitable necessity, and for a number of unavoidable reasons, change is also ubiquitous. This chapter explores why change occurs in the work settings of care organisations and the DCM's role in managing change, including initiating, participating in and influencing change, and also evaluating its impact and sustaining the change.

Chapter objectives

On completion of this chapter you will be able to:

- identify various changes that impact on commissioning, delivery and outcomes of care;
- ascertain the reasons for change in health and social care, their impact in care settings and the significance of the management of change;
- explain in detail how to manage change systematically using a well-informed change management framework; and
- demonstrate how you have developed your skills in the management of change.

Changes in Treatment and Care

Changes in health and social care professionals' care interventions are often initiated by new evidence and are usually related to assuring or enhancing quality of care provision and delivery, as discussed in Chapter 5, or the need to ensure value for money and increase productivity. It is frequently also driven by specified outcomes for the NHS set by government reforms and directives, and local policies determined by care commissioners and care providers. Other reasons for change include new and more effective technology, research and rising consumer expectations.

Action point 6.1   Changes in the way health and social care is practised

Reflect on how care is currently delivered to patients and service users in your work-place, and identify aspects of care delivery that have changed recently, that is, over the last few weeks, a month, or even year.

Next, identify an aspect of practice in your work setting that you consider would benefit from change. This may be in relation to a research article that you have read recently or discussion with colleagues regarding perhaps a new way of resolving an issue, or an innovation that you came across at a study day or conference.

You should have been able to identify a few examples of changes or developments in the ways in which health or social care is provided or delivered in your practice setting. A number of examples of such changes are identified in Box 6.1.

Box 6.1   Examples of changes affecting care delivery

- Early warning score (EWS) systems for deteriorating patients
- Meals served on a colour-coded tray to identify patients who require support at meal times
- Cardio-pulmonary resuscitation (CPR) techniques
- Cognitive behaviour therapy for depressive illnesses and psychological problems
- Non-medical prescribing, e.g. nurse prescribing
- Increased health education by practice nurses to empower patients and enhance self-care
- Treatment of leg ulcers – using Doppler technique
- Health MOTs for people over 75
- Non-medical practitioners ordering X-rays and other diagnostic tests
- Needle-safe devices
- Zero tolerance of violent or aggressive behaviour by patients or their visitors

There are specific adaptations of 'early warning score'(EWS) mentioned in Box 6.1, and is at times referred to as 'modified early warning score' (MEWS). With regard to another two items in Box 6.1, for instance, the latest cardio-pulmonary resuscitation (CPR) guidelines published by the Resuscitation Council (2010) changed adult basic life support resuscitation from the previous protocol to continuous chest compressions, or 30 chest compressions to two rescue breaths. For needle safe devices, this is also a relatively recent development that is deliberately designed to sample blood safely, avoid needle stick injuries, prevent cross-infection and also provide extra comfort for both patients and professionals (Morton Medical Limited, 2004). Examples of recent changes in the organisation or management of care include:

- Assistive technology in health and social care.
- Single assessment process (SAP) and common assessment process (CAP).
- Virtual wards.
- Electronic records.
- Team midwifery and the development of the CSW role in midwifery.
- NHS Safety Thermometer.
- Introducing new shift patterns.
- Integrated care pathways (ICP).
- Care bundles.
- Outreach work.
- Quality assurance programmes, such as electronic patient satisfaction monitoring.
- Allowing parents to be present in the anaesthetic room.
- Intermediate care services.
- Walk-in centres.
- The modern matron role.
- Same-sex accommodation in in-patient settings.

With the use of assistive technology, for example, people with increasingly complex health and social care needs can be supported to have their needs met in their own home, where previously they may have required monitoring in an in-patient setting or to experience 24-hour care. Similarly, prior to the SAP, care practitioners in acute, community and social care sectors would individually conduct assessments to identify health or social needs of older people, rather than one care professional undertaking a generic assessment that can be used as a foundation assessment by all. This supports subsequent care planning so that it is more effective, efficient, co-ordinated, thorough and accurate, but without procedures being needlessly duplicated by different agencies.

Changes usually occur in response to a number of drivers or catalysts, which in addition to the reasons mentioned earlier in this chapter include evaluation of services, complaints and suggestions, local systematically implemented initiatives (e.g. those by NHS III 2008a, 2008b), and rising public expectations based on information from peers and the media or the Internet. At times, changes occur naturally in practice settings. However, implementers of change also need to consider when the time is right for the change to be introduced, taking into account other initiatives, other changes that are already being implemented, and additional staff members if and as required. Changes can be implemented at organisational level, or team or individual level in the care setting.

Change can also be differentiated from innovation in that a change occurs to something that is already established, and can mean developing the care activity by adding extra dimensions, substituting aspects of the activity, or even reverting to an older (but effective) mode of practice. 'Innovation' refers to the introduction of a new method of care delivery, or area of care provision that is relatively unprecedented.

Why Changes in Health and Social Care, and Why the Management of Change?

Change is essential for improvement and enhancement of health and social care services, and for the change to be successful it needs to be managed and implemented systematically (i.e. as a step-by-step plan of actions).

Why changes in health and social care?

One of the prominent reasons for the DCM requiring expertise in the management of change is that the manager's role includes change management as identified under the 'Caregiver and practice developer' role in Table 2.2, and in Mintzberg's (1990) management role theory as 'entrepreneurial roles' (also noted in Chapter 2), which in turn implies implementing tested ideas and innovating. Thus change is closely related to practice development, which is discussed shortly. Furthermore, changes in health and social care provision are firmly based on the expectations of the users of the service, as well as on prevailing socio-economic circumstances and policies.

With increasing focus on public health (i.e. the prevention of health problems and management of longer term health problems), another reason for change is the encouragement for nurses to develop as 'nurse entrepreneurs', whose venture is to initiate new care interventions that benefit specific groups of individuals in society, or patients or service users. Such enterprises are highlighted in journal articles, reports and guidelines such as by the RCN (2007) and Liefer (2005). Examples of such enterprises include offering teenage parents one-to-one support during and after pregnancy (Nursing Standard News, 2009), and encouraging reluctant communities to access diagnosis and management of longer-term conditions such as type 2 diabetes (Mooney, 2008).

Additionally, Drennan (2007) reports on a study that explored nurse, midwife and health visitor entrepreneurship in the United Kingdom, from which she devised a typology of entrepreneurs. In the first category of the typology, Drennan distinguishes between entrepreneurs and intrapreneurs, the latter focusing on innovation and change in practice pioneered by the organisation's own employees. The second category comprises 'infrastructure services' such as non-medical consultants, independent healthcare practitioners and inventors. In the third category are, for instance, primary care services such as non-medical services including complementary therapists and nurse–GP partners. Entrepreneurship is publicised and advocated in various DH documents such as *National Search for New Ideas to Improve the Lives of People with Dementia* (DH, 2011e).

Evidence-based Healthcare

One of the key triggers for changes in care delivery is evidence-based healthcare (EBHC), which is defined by one of its pioneers as an approach to decision-making in which the care practitioner uses the 'best evidence' available for making clinical decisions (Gray, 2001), and evidence-based practice (EBP). Thus without the availability of evidence, or the use of those that are available, practice risks becoming out of date, and therefore less safe, very quickly. There are five key elements of EBHC, namely:

1   Decisions are based on best evidence.
2   Nature and sources of evidence are determined by the health problem.
3   Best evidence integrates research and personal experience.
4   Evidence is translated into action so that it affects patients' or service users' health and wellbeing positively.
5   These actions are continually appraised.

There are differences between the overlapping terms EBHC, EBP and others such as evidence-based medicine (EBM). EBHC tends to refer to groups of patients and the management of longer-term conditions, for instance, whereas EBP refers to single care interventions. Other concepts such as EBM refer purely to medical practice, but are broader generic terms that have practice implications for the specific profession. Evidence-based social work, evidence-based management, evidence-based education and evidence-based assessment of competence are also well documented in the health and social care literature.

There are a number of possible sources of evidence that can support improvements in care. These include:

• Randomised controlled trials (RCT)
• Qualitative studies
• Personal experience
• Personal intuition
• Policy directives (from local sources/central/ local government legislation)

- Textbooks
- Own professional education
- Clinical guidelines
- The patient or service user/their family
- Colleagues/other professionals
- Trial and error
- Suppliers' information
- Journal articles
- Online references
- Unpublished evidence
- Overview of evidence by specific topic (i.e. critical appraisals).

The Cochrane Library and NHS Evidence, which are accessible via the Internet or library databases at the local university or NHS Trust, are usually the nearest means of accessing published sources of evidence. The evidence available can be categorised as grades or levels of evidence to identify the strength of evidence supporting the care intervention. In broad terms, five levels of evidence can be identified, namely (see Glossary for brief explanation of some of the following terminology):

- *Level 1:* very strong evidence based on a critical appraisal of several well-designed RCTs.
- *Level 2:* evidence based on at least one well-designed RCT.
- *Level 3:* evidence from several quantitative studies (e.g. experiments, action research, surveys etc.).
- *Level 4:* conclusions from one well-designed quantitative study or from qualitative studies (e.g. case studies, focus groups or individual interviews).
- *Level 5:* conclusions drawn by specialist and experts in the field and in authoritative organisations.

When applying evidence to practice, the patient or service user needs to be provided with the relevant information to enable them to make an informed choice. A systematic review of randomised controlled trials may represent the 'gold standard', but this option may not be the preferred choice for the patient.

Practice Development

Consider the developments in care provision that are currently occurring in your particular area of practice, and the changes that have been made recently, or can be made to specific care and treatments in your care setting, or by your team. Change and innovation in patient-related clinical practice is also known as 'clinical practice development'. This concept therefore refers to changing the way particular care interventions are performed, or for providing (or instituting) new healthcare services for patients. It has to do with improving and enhancing clinical practice where there is scope to do so.

The England Centre for Practice Development (2013) indicates that practice development is an internationally recognised and sustainable approach that aims to improve patient or service user experiences of care, transforming care and services so that they are person-centred, safe and effective, and ensuring that the best evidence and research informs everyday practice. Another helpful explanation of practice development is provided by Manley et al. (2008) who indicate that it is used for creating an environment that support the engagement of clinicians in evaluating and improving their practice. Later definitions of the term are less specific and refer to change in cultures and corporate strategies, which are no doubt components of effective practice development.

The focus of practice development is therefore on improving outcomes for patients and service users, and consequently has to do with changes in hands-on or direct patient or service user health or social care interventions for particular components of professional practice. Practice development is by no means a new phenomenon, as care professionals have always looked out for ways of delivering safer, less invasive and more effective care and treatment for patients and service users.

The DCM needs to take an analytical approach to the development of practice, which can be achieved in various ways. Based on an analysis of literature, focus group interviews with practice developers and individual interviews with care practitioners on practice development, Garbett and McCormack (2002) conclude that the purpose of practice development is to increase effectiveness in patient-centred care, and transform care and the culture and context within which it takes place. The attributes of practice development are that it needs to be systematic and rigorous, a continuous process, and founded on facilitation. The consequences of practice development include improved experiences of care in terms of their sensitivity to the needs of individuals and populations for users, and increased capacity for autonomous practice by professionals. The four main themes that emerged from the study were that (p. 92):

- it is a means of improving patient care;
- it transforms the contexts and cultures in which healthcare delivery takes place;
- it ensures that a systematic approach is employed to effect changes in practice; and
- various types of facilitation are required for change to take place.

Identifying the purposes, attributes and consequences of practice development constitutes an exercise that ensures a cautious and planned approach to change. Concluding from a four-year action research study related to a task-centred service to a patient-centred service, Titchen (2003) identified three generic principles of practice development which she suggested comprise a conceptual framework. These principles are:

- Changing the practice philosophy.
- Putting the process of change into practice.
- Investing in practice development.

McCormack et al. (2006) reported on a study that indicates that practice development comprises six crucial components, namely: policy and strategy, methodology and methods, roles and relationships, learning strategies, funding and evaluating effectiveness. How the DCM achieves such change will be discussed later in the chapter under 'How to manage change'. Furthermore, practice development can be undertaken at individual level, particularly by those who have autonomy in their day-to-day work; at unit or team level; or at organisational or supra-organisational levels. The Donabedian (1988) model of evaluation, which comprises considering and identifying the standard to be achieved, along with structure, process and outcome, is a systematic approach that can be adopted to monitor the effectiveness of the development.

In the Donabedian model, 'structure' refers to the equipment, staff and materials required for performing the care intervention; 'process' refers to the procedure or protocol that has been specifically established for particular care interventions, the training, and ongoing evaluation of the activity; and 'outcome' refers to the exact final product. The model was discussed in the context of quality assurance in Chapter 5.

In the context of practice development, 'structure' also refers to identifying the practice development function of care professionals, and may have been identified as part of annual IDPR. As to process or deployment, for some staff such as practice development nurses, this comprises the main focus of their role. However, each team member can be a practice developer, and this is documented in the *NHS KSF* (DH, 2004a) under the 'service improvement' domain (i.e. dimension).

There are several key publications on practice development and innovations from the RCN, DH and other organisations, including the RCN (2005b) *Maxi Nurses: Nurses Working in Advanced and Extended Roles Promoting and Developing Patient-centred Healthcare,* and the DH (2011f) *Implementing Innovation.*

Why 'Manage' Change?

Change is essential within health and social care to ensure that care is based on the best available evidence, that new technology is instituted and that use of the available resources are maximised. The components of care provision or delivery that needs to be changed can be implemented in any of the following ways:

- imposed;
- introduced after brief discussions;
- evolve gradually over time;

- self-directed, such as in lifestyle or behaviour change; or
- managed.

Wherever groups of individuals such as care professionals are affected by change, the change needs to be 'managed' if it is to be effectively implemented and is sustained.

Action point 6.2   Ways of making changes

Consider a recent change in your practice setting and think about the way the change was made, taking into account the five categories of change implementation identified above.

Change can have different effects on the different individuals the change will affect, such as:

- involvement and ownership;
- excitement;
- stress;
- increased individual responsibility; and
- improved patient care.

How to 'Manage' Change

The management of change involves taking a planned and systematic approach. The '7-step RAPSIES model for effective change management' (see Figure 6.1) is one such approach. This model is derived from the extensive literature on the topic and on our own experience as healthcare practitioners. The 7-step model comprises the essential components of the management of change, which are:

1 *Recognition* of the need for change, to solve a problem for instance, or to improve an element of practice.
2 *Analysis* of the available options related to the contemplated change, the environment or setting where change will be implemented, and the users of the change.
3 *Preparation* for the change, such as identifying an appropriately skilled change agent to lead the implementation of the change, education of the users of the change, defining intended outcomes and involving relevant colleagues.
4 *Strategies* for implementing the change (explained later in this chapter).

5 *Implementation* of the change, including piloting the change and timing of implementation.

6 *Evaluation* of the impact of the change against the intended outcomes.

7 *Sustaining* the change, i.e. ways of ensuring that the change endures and is mainstreamed.

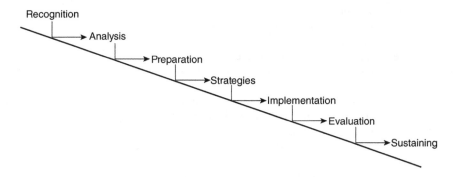

Figure 6.1   The 7-step RAPSIES model for effective change management

Recognising the need for change

Staff dissatisfaction with the way care is delivered, complaints received from patients or their relatives, and new research findings on how to improve care are some of the conduits that indicate the need for change. Several other reasons were identified earlier in this chapter under 'Why changes in health and social care?' One of the most significant attributes of a change is that it must improve or enhance the care provision experiences and outcomes for the benefit of patients or service users, and/or the organisation. More specifically, for instance, if changing to using a new research-tested care package, this should result in better care for the patient or service user (i.e. outcomes), and thereby benefit the organisation as well.

The change must also be compatible with the team's existing beliefs and values about health and social care delivery, that is, at a philosophical level, as well as pragmatic. How easily the change can be understood by patients and stakeholders must also be considered. The simplicity or the ease of using the change or innovation, and its 'trialability' (i.e. the possibility of piloting the innovation) must also be considered, as well as 'observability' (i.e. the change and its results must be explicit and tangible).

Analysis of the change

After identifying that a change is needed, the care practitioner must explore all options available before deciding on the best solution. For instance, in relation to the issue of ensuring that in-patients receive adequate nutrition, you may identify a number of changes to achieve this, such as:

- reducing other activities during meal times;
- implementing snack trolleys;
- staggering meal times;
- implementing volunteer feeders;
- implementing a colour-coded tray system (see Box 6.1);
- asking for feedback on the quality of meals;
- implementing protected meal times; and
- ensuring that assistance with eating is given to those who need it.

Several examples of real-life changes in health and social care delivery implemented by care professionals can be cited, such as using the most appropriate dressings on particular wounds, and implementing a redesigned sedation scoring system for critically ill patients in ICUs. More centrally advocated change includes personal budgeting for social care service users and the SAP mentioned earlier in this chapter. The DH (2006a) cites several other examples, such as peer-mentoring introduced by school nurses and the NHS 'Life Check' service. In response to Action point 6.1, you should have been able to identify a number of examples of changes in care delivery in your area of practice.

On deciding which specific change(s) is to be made, those involved need to consider the advantages and likely disadvantages of the change. This comprises an analysis of the specific change in more systematic ways, such as by force field or SWOT analyses (discussed shortly).

The users of the change

Analysis of the proposed change includes careful consideration of the users of the change. Planning includes 'selling' the change to the users, and exploring developmental needs as individuals or as a team. Based on research conducted some decades ago, Rogers and Shoemaker (1971) identified six categories of users of change, which were later also identified by Moore (2007) and which apply to most organisations at local level. These categories are:

1 *Innovators:* individuals in the team who get excited about new ideas and are keen to implement them.
2 *Early adopters:* individual team members who think about the new change over a few days and then adopt them.
3 *Early majority:* when a few team members adopt the new idea.
4 *Later majority:* when several members accept and adopt the new idea.
5 *Laggards:* individuals who tend to lag behind in adopting new ways of working.
6 *Rejecters:* individuals who are against new ideas or usually oppose them.

> ## Action point 6.3   The users of change in my practice area
>
> Consider your work colleagues and their response to a recent change that was implemented in your work setting. See if you can identify those who could fall into each of the categories identified by Rogers and Shoemaker. Consider various ways in which you could use the information about categories of users of change to operationalise the change management process.

With innovators, the change agent can, for instance, use their energy and allocate them responsibilities. The remaining categories of users comprise those who resist change either momentarily or longer term. Early adopters need recognition for their compliance with the change, whereas those who form the later majority as individuals who need more time to assimilate the new concept are given scope to try out before using the change. Laggards may need extra support and time to prevent disillusionment. As for rejecters, the change agent or the line manager will need to explore further to identify possible reasons for this. The employee may, for example, be privy to further knowledge, or has had previous experience in relation to the change, or be experiencing transient personal or domestic problems.

The setting or environment where the change is to be implemented

Another essential component of change management is the setting or environment where the change is to be implemented. The environment has to be 'ripe for change' for successful implementation. A practice environment that is conducive to change manifests:

- a progressive ethos where critical appraisal, creativity and openness are fostered;
- good channels of communication, i.e. two-way and effective communication that includes opportunities for feedback and evaluation;
- a cohesive team who work in partnership, with the patient or service user as the focus;
- team empowerment, i.e. the freedom to be innovative and creative within the wider organisation; and
- supportive leadership that actively promotes and supports a 'can do' approach.

From the critical analysis viewpoint, some of the factors that constitute barriers to research implementation or use also apply to implementing change, and include:

- Palfreyman et al.'s (2003) findings that nurses and physiotherapists have access to a wide variety of sources of knowledge, but both professions have problems overcoming the barrier of time.

- 'important research findings are not having the desired impact on practice' (West et al., 1999: 633);
- '... dissemination failings represent the single most significant factor in the research-practice gap' (Dickson, 1996: 5).

Other barriers to research implementation faced by care professionals can include:

- lack of critical appraisal and research knowledge and skills;
- lack of time to consider undertaking research;
- not having access to resources for conducting or appraising research;
- an organisational and managerial ethos and culture that do not value or encourage research;
- lack of power and financial control to implement new research findings;
- lack of valid research on specific components of practice; and
- lack of user-friendly reviews and guidelines.

McCaughan (2002) suggests that barriers to research implementation include:

- problems in interpreting and using research – it is seen as too complex, 'academic' and overly statistical;
- even healthcare practitioners who feel confident with research-based information experience a lack of organisational support;
- researchers and findings lack clinical credibility and fail to offer sufficient clinical direction in care delivery; and
- some care practitioners lack the skills and motivation to use research themselves.

> ## Action point 6.4   Relevance of barriers to research implementation in your practice setting
>
> Consider the above-mentioned barriers to research, and whether either of them apply to your practice setting. It should prove worthwhile discussing these barriers with a peer or work-setting colleague to ascertain their professional thoughts.

Preparation for Change

The change agent

The DCM's role in implementing change involves being both a change agent and a supporter of changes that are being implemented. Alternatively, the change agent could be a facilitator external to the organisation, or the team, or an employee within the organisation, the department or the work setting itself. The change agent is the person who is assigned to advocate, lead and implement the change, and might also be the initiator of the change. They need to be completely clear about the present state of readiness in the setting, and the potential future state after the change has been implemented. As Brookes (2011) reports, for example, the change agent can exercise 'appreciative leadership' and involve the entire team, so that each member feels ownership of the change that is needed.

In considering 'readiness for change', the change agent needs to consider how adequately staffed the care team is to accommodate the change or new mode of care intervention. Human resource issues therefore need to be addressed, but the change agent must also be cognisant of the components of change in the 7-step RAPSIES framework for effective change management, which of course includes sustaining the change after implementation. The change agent's key functions should include:

- 'selling' the change and promoting ownership by the care team;
- planning the change comprehensively;
- determining and deciding on relevant change strategies;
- identifying own and others' related development (or training) needs;
- monitoring and supporting change users throughout the process;
- evaluating the impact of the change;
- problem-solving to address any challenges that are experienced; and
- sustaining the change.

The characteristics of an effective change agent are also those of being an effective leader. Two leadership styles that are particularly relevant for managing change are transformational and transactional styles. The transactional style refers to the orderly breaking down of tasks, but the transformational style constitutes keeping a distance, and taking a strategic view of the whole. Table 3.1 identifies some of the main characteristics of the two styles of leadership.

The change agent's role thus incorporates dissemination of the evidence or knowledge base, on which change is being advocated and initiated, to all affected by the change. Scullion (2002) suggests that dissemination is a vital yet complex process which aims to ensure that key messages are conveyed to specific groups via a wide range of methods so that it results in measured reaction, impact or implementation. Methods of research dissemination include:

- Via professional associations
- Video/DVD/audio tape
- Written reports as feedback to respondents/research subjects
- Written executive summaries (most likely to be read if concise)
- Journal articles or editorials
- Journal clubs
- Conferences
- Poster presentation
- Newsletters
- Books, or chapters in books
- Inclusion in course curriculum
- Educational materials.

Social media can also be used; for example, internet forums, weblogs, social blogs, social networks and podcasts.

As for the users of the change, which can include your colleagues or patients, the key factors in the dissemination process include consideration of how ready they are to use the change, enabling them to become active sub-agents for the change rather than passive recipients, forming social networks, and choosing suitable strategies for that particular group of users.

Furthermore, change can evoke anxiety, and resistance to change can prevail because of:

- fear of the unknown;
- lack of confidence;
- lack of knowledge and skills to carry out the change;
- loss of influence and power; and
- resentment or perceived criticism of past practices.

For each of these components causing resistance to change, the DCM or change agent can take specific action to manage them. For 'fear of the unknown', this presents a degree of uncertainty in the user, in which case the change agent can, for instance, provide detailed and sufficient information to those who are resisting the change for them to become fully familiar with the proposed change. For lack of confidence, further information and support can be provided. For lack of knowledge and skills to carry out the change, organising workshops and study days might prove beneficial. For loss of influence and power, the key tasks can be made more explicit. For resentment or perceived criticism of past practices, the attributes of the change should be highlighted or emphasised as making progress towards further improvements in care.

In addition, people get accustomed to established practices as they feel comfortable and secure with them. They might also resist if they feel overburdened by too much change at a particular point in time, or if they feel the change is likely to reduce freedom or result in increased control of their movements. They might sense increase in workload while level of pay is unchanged, or feel more secure in using well-established ways and wish to retain the existing ways of practice. Therefore, the need for change should emerge through users' feeling that a bottom-up approach is being taken, including their active involvement in planning, implementation and evaluation of the process.

Strategies for implementing change

The discussion so far indicates that change needs to be managed, it needs to be planned thoroughly, and it needs to be participative to promote ownership. Various strategies are documented in the management literature that can be selected from according to their suitability for a particular change item. Strategies for effective organisational change can include:

- Plan-do-study-act (PDSA)
- Lewin's three-stage process

- Empirical-rational
- Power-coercive
- Normative-re-educative.

Plan-do-study-act

The PDSA cycle (NHS III, 2008a) (as illustrated in Figure 6.5) comprises a strategy for testing the impact of an identified change within the work setting. It allows testing to be undertaken on a small scale with the opportunity to refine it prior to making the change fully operational and subsequent wider application. The PDSA strategy involves a range of colleagues in trying out the change, and thereby also reduces the barriers to change and increases ownership of the change.

Action point 6.5   Implementing change

Think about a change that you would like to implement within your clinical practice. In order to support you to test the change, develop a PDSA cycle that addresses the following areas that have been adapted from the NHS III model:

Plan

- What you are hoping to achieve.
- What you think the outcome of the change will be.
- The support you consider you will need to be able to implement the change.
- The mechanisms you intend to use to test the impact of the change.

Do

- Implement the change in the identified area.
- Observe the change and document any problems that are encountered.
- Commence analysis of the data that you have collected.

Study

- Complete the data analysis.
- Compare the results achieved with those that you predicted in the planning phase.
- Summarise and reflect upon what you have learnt.

Act

- Using what you have learnt from the test, identify any modifications that you need to make.
- Prepare your plan of action for the next evaluation point.

Lewin's three-stage process of change

A programme of planned change and improved performance developed some years ago by K. Lewin (1951), but remains fully relevant today, involves a three-stage process entailing unfreezing, movement and refreezing.

- *Unfreezing:* reducing those forces that maintain behaviour in its present form, and recognition of the need for change and improvement to occur.
- *Movement:* the development of new attitudes or behaviours, and the implementation of the change.
- *Refreezing:* stabilising the change at a new level, and reinforcement through supporting mechanisms such as policies, resources and norms.

Systematic ways of unfreezing a set of circumstances include the well-known SWOT analysis, and also force field analysis, which entails the group together identifying the factors that are driving the change and those that are causing resistance. An example of a SWOT analysis for introducing flexible family friendly shifts in a care setting is presented in Figure 6.2.

Strengths and weaknesses are internal factors, while opportunities and threats are usually external to the individual or team. A SWOT analysis can be very subjective and therefore needs to be performed as a team whenever possible. Alternatively,

STRENGTHS	WEAKNESSES
• Happier staff • Better staff retention • Encourage recruitment • Staff morale • Maximum use of staff time • Gives individual staff more time at home • Not working too many shifts for long stretches • Less stress of travelling	• Difficult to accommodate everyone's requirements • Staff without school-age children might get less annual leave in summer • Lack of communication as they may not be present at handovers • Not feeling part of the team • Poor long-term continuity • Difficulty covering annual leave, sickness
OPPORTUNITIES	**THREATS**
• Extra day at home for study/education • Spend more time with family • Individual can pursue other interests • The organisation complies with *Improving Working Lives Standard* (DH, 2000d)	• Staff with no family might feel disadvantaged • Whether this can be legitimately explored at recruitment interviews • Tiredness, which can lead to unsafe patient care • Sickness rate can go up • Long-term staff might be against the changes • Fitting in with practical routine

Figure 6.2   SWOT analysis: Introducing flexible family friendly shifts

the change agent could facilitate the force field analysis, an example of which in relation to implementing an ICP is presented in Box 6.2.

Box 6.2 Force field analysis for introducing an integrated care pathway

Driving forces	Resisting forces
• Continuity of care needed	• Staff not knowledgeable about how ICPs work
• Consistent with government policy related to patient journeys	• Perceived criticism of current method of care delivery
• Greater patient satisfaction	• Extra paperwork
• More opportunity for health promotion	• Extra staff time required, and therefore costs
• More collaboration within MDT	• Social care and healthcare funding disjunction
• Enhances patient care	• More resources required in terms of staff time
• Increases cost-effectiveness through patient compliance	• Too many people disseminating information
• Learners get fuller picture of broader influences on personal health	• Funding
	• Patient information overload

The force field analysis in Box 6.2 has shown that many forces may be involved in driving or resisting change. According to Lewin's (1951) force field analysis theory, behaviour in any institutional setting is not static in nature, and instead comprises a dynamic balance of socio-psychological forces working in opposite directions within the institution. The force field analysis exercise can be undertaken by a team of staff or individually to identify the factors (i.e. people, resources and systems) that might facilitate or hinder change, as doing so 'unfreezes' the forces that maintain behaviour in its present form.

In attempting to change a situation to a new level, after unfreezing, three enabling actions are possible: (1) increase the driving forces by adding new ones or strengthening existing ones; (2) reduce or remove the resisting forces; or (3) translate one or more resisting forces into driving ones. If a change agent uses say only the first of these three actions, then change may occur, but it is often unstable and quickly reverts to the original condition. A combination of all three strategies is the most effectual.

Empirical-rational

The strategy referred to as 'empirical-rational' is based on the belief that people are guided by reason, that they are essentially rational, and that if they can be helped to understand the nature and reasons for the proposed change, then they are more likely to accept it. Thus, this strategy is based on empowerment through giving knowledge. Government health warnings are at times based on this strategy.

Power-coercive

The power-coercive strategy emphasises a different approach in that it is based on threats of sanctions by seniors, economic or status-wise, if the desired changes are not adopted, and where necessary the use of moral power, playing on feelings of guilt and shame are used.

The assumption is that those in control of the organisation will identify the need for change, and people with less power will always comply with their plans. If an empirical-rational approach does not prove as productive, then the power-coercive strategy might be used. It can include application of legitimate power to influence and secure compliance, and can incorporate legal considerations.

Normative-re-educative

Individuals, groups and organisations are seen as inherently active in ascertaining how similar they are in their practices and norms to other entities. This strategy includes suggesting that the proposed change is a normal practice in other similar settings, making reference to local socio-cultural value systems, norms and attitudes, and educating users in the value and benefits of the change. It incorporates the facility for personal growth and self-actualisation.

Combined strategies

Each of the latter three strategies is based on different assumptions about what makes people accept a component of change, or alter their behaviour and result in achievement of different degrees of success. The strategy used is chosen according to different situations, and requires that the individual or the group are capable of, and willing to change. It also takes into account the social, political and economic factors that influence the role of the health or social care practitioner.

However, a combined strategy can be used that harnesses and co-ordinates elements of the three above strategies, but to be effective it must encompass:

- rational (or validated) information;
- two-way communication and expertise in group processes;
- consensus on new norms and sanctions associated with a proposed change; and
- legitimate authority of the change agent, and the power to carry it through.

The combination could be staged in that one of the three strategies might be more appropriate at the very early stages of implementation of a particular change, and another at different stage.

Implementing the change

Action point 6.6   Implementing the change

Consider a change that you feel would be beneficial to implement in your work-place. Identify a comprehensive set of activities that would ensure that the change is successfully implemented and maintained. This can take the form of a detailed step-by-step plan.

The activities you have identified for successful implementation of change might include:

- plan the change thoroughly;
- attempt to create an environment conducive to change by encouraging a culture that encourages questioning, using initiative and a reflective-evaluative approach to care interventions;
- provide means for the acquisition of knowledge and skills, feedback and support;
- identify problems, e.g. resistance and barriers, and build ways to overcome them into your plan;
- provide a medium for staff to share experiences;
- provide supportive leadership by being involved throughout;
- provision for evaluation and feedback so that successes and difficulties can be shared and learned from;
- encourage active participation;
- ensure that there are good channels of communication; and
- ascertain opportunities for refinement based on evaluation.

Timing of implementation

The change agent also needs to identify the most suitable implementation date for the change. This ideally needs to be the time when the users are ready and the setting is 'ripe for change'. Times to avoid include periods when several staff are on annual leave, when there are staff vacancies or long-term sickness, or when other major managerial changes are imminent, or if there is organisational resistance to the change. Timing of implementation includes the point in the team's dynamics when there is openness and trust amongst staff, and morale is good.

Evaluating the change

After the change has been implemented its impact needs to be monitored both informally and in more structured ways. Informally, evaluation information can be obtained by general impressions and casual questioning. More structured ways of evaluation can involve the use of a framework, or model, of evaluation. It can be done formatively (i.e. at interim intervals rather than end stages), but summative evaluation also needs to be conducted at specific pre-determined points when the full impact of the change can be gauged.

Evaluation of the change can involve comparing outcomes to those anticipated before implementation of the change, with specific indicators such as length of hospital stay, reduction in costs and improved patient satisfaction.

Sustaining the change

After implementation, the change needs to be sustained through explicit recognition from more senior managers, and supported by the necessary resources, human and non-human. The PDSA (NHS III, 2008a) method can be used to test out progress on a small scale. The users of the change should be able to sense the benefits of the change after implementation.

A strategy for sustaining change should have been established at the very beginning of the implementation of the change. The term 'sustaining' is used to signify keeping the change in good health, that is, functioning, but more importantly, developing. This requires various forms of resources, the categories of which are discussed in Chapter 7 and include:

- appropriate human resources;
- appropriate financial resources;
- monitoring mechanisms, such as regular concurrent and retrospective audits (built-in evaluation/research);
- planned evaluation of the effects or impact of the change;
- continuing skill development in the context of new equipment and devices becoming available;
- disseminating the change to obtain external views;
- users retaining ownership of the change (active user participation);
- maintaining team spirit (as discussed in Chapter 10);
- leadership of senior staff in using the change; and
- effective communication.

At times, organisational resistance to implementing or sustaining change can be experienced, which is also referred to as 'barriers to change'. Some of the organisational barriers to change are:

- deficiency in more senior colleagues' understanding of the details of the change required in role, practices and relationships;
- lack of the knowledge and skills necessary to use the new practice;
- shortage of staff;
- lack of time;
- lack of support within the management hierarchy;

- failure of the leader to identify problems;
- lack of materials/equipment to practice the new method; and
- failure of the leader to adequately plan the management of the change.

Such resistance is less apparent in organisations that reflect the characteristics of an 'effective organisation' which Beckhard and Harris (1987) identified as including:

- having a strategic view;
- energising others lower in the system;
- having relatively open communication;
- rewarding collaboration;
- managing conflict, not suppressing it;
- valuing difference; and
- actively learning, through feedback.

The characteristics of an effective organisation should actively support change management. A change endeavour can succeed or fail depending on the various factors discussed above. However, if the components of the RAPSIES framework discussed in this chapter are fully considered, then the change should be achieved as desired.

An alternative to the RAPSIES framework for the management of change is the model of change proposed for the NHS (NHS Change Model website, 2013), which comprise seven elements:

1 Leadership for change
2 Spread of innovation
3 Improvement methodology
4 Rigorous delivery
5 Transparent measurement
6 System drivers
7 Engagement to mobilise.

See 'Further recommended reading' at the end of this chapter for more details on access to the NHS change model.

Guidelines for effective change management

The essential activities required for successful change management are:

- Ensure compatibility with existing values and practices.
- Ensure that users see advantages in the innovation over existing practices.
- Have detailed knowledge of various change strategies.
- Plan well in advance, and in detail.
- Analyse existing and proposed new structures.
- Examine adaptability to the innovation.
- Assess the readiness to change.
- Ensure effective communication at all stages.
- Institute education and training at key stages.

- Recognise early adopters' efforts explicitly.
- Assess your own knowledge continuously, and update and upskill as appropriate.
- Exercise leadership skills.
- Support the change during all stages of the process.
- Encourage active participation by intended users of the change.
- Build in evaluation/research.

CHAPTER SUMMARY

This chapter has focused broadly on the what, why, when and how to manage change, and on the DCM's role in the management of change and innovation in the practice setting, and having completed this chapter you will have explored:

- actual and potential instances of changes made in patient or service user care interventions, and in the management or organisation of care;
- why changes are necessary in health and social care and the importance of effective management of change;
- how to manage change, using the RAPSIES model for effective change management, which comprises recognising the need for the change, analysis of the available options, preparation for the change, identifying strategies for implementing the change, implementation of the change, evaluating its impact and sustaining the change; and
- analysis of issues related to the management of change in care settings, concluding with guidelines for effective change management.

RECOMMENDED FURTHER READING

- For details of hierarchy or levels of evidence in EBP, access and view the content of the following website for the Joanna Briggs Institute:

Joanna Briggs Institute (2012) *Welcome to the Joanna Briggs Institute*. Available from: www.joannabriggs.edu.au/.

- For details of the NHS's current perspective on a structured model of change, see:

Medical Directors' Bulletin (2012) *NHS Change Model Introductory Online Seminars*. Available from: www.changemodel.nhs.uk/pg/groups/29463/Online+seminars. (Accessed 3 April 2013).

- For a detailed account of leadership in successful management of change in a hospital ward, see article:

Brookes J (2011) 'Engaging staff in the change process'. *Nursing Management*, 18 (5): 16–19.

- For a discussion on change management see:

Kerridge J (2012) 'Leading change'. *Nursing Times*, 108 (4): 12–15; 108 (5): 23–25; and 108 (6): 23–25.

21

Guest Editorial: Integrated Services for Older People – The Key to Unlock our Health and Care Services and Improve the Quality of Care?

Oliver, D.

Integration – the new frontier?

Across the United Kingdom, there is growing interest from politicians, national and local service leaders and clinicians in integration, care co-ordination and partnership working (Curry and Ham, 2010; Goodwin et al., 2013b; Ham et al., 2011, 2013; NHS Confederation and Royal College of General Practitioners, 2013). Some specific policy levers and targeted funds and financial instruments have aimed to facilitate integration and make it the norm rather than the exception (Bennett and Humphries, 2013; Royal College of Nursing, 2014). There is a tacit assumption that a shift towards these models will be "win/win" – improving care for individual service users, whilst also saving services from the "triple threat" of population demographics, rising demand and financial austerity (Naylor et al., 2013). Influential health think tanks the King's Fund and Nuffield Trust (Goodwin et al., 2013a) and professional Bodies such as the Royal Colleges of Physicians (RCP, 2013), General Practitioners (RCGP, 2014) and Nursing (RCN, 2014) have focused increasing efforts on the cause of integration. Whilst my editorial focuses on the UK, other health systems facing similar challenges are increasingly embracing the same agenda (Goodwin et al., 2013a, 2013b, 2014; Ham 2011, Timmins and Ham, 2013).

I won't get drawn into endless, abstruse definitions of what we mean by integrated services. There is a body of literature for those with a niche interest in terminology or who like to close down discussion by saying "everyone's talking about it, but no-one can agree what it is". I am more concerned by how integration might help support people in need of health and social care and improve their experience and outcomes. We can return to definitions later. Let's start "bottom up" with people before worrying "top down" about structure and process.

Why older people are most likely to benefit from integration

In terms of *who* might benefit, many groups won't especially notice any difference; those usually well with episodic illness or injury, or undergoing elective procedures, and those with single or stable long-term conditions receiving all their support from one clinical team. Integration has more potential to help those with complex health and care needs, often using multiple services, dealing with several professionals and undergoing care transitions and hand-offs between agencies (NHS Future Forum, 2011). These *can* include children with chronic illness, young and working-age adults with mental health problems, learning difficulties or physical disability, the homeless, or those with multiple co-morbidities. However, by far the biggest group affected by disjointed care is older people with complex needs, and it is on this group that I have focused here and in a recent King's Fund paper I co-authored with colleagues: "Making Health and Care Systems fit for an Ageing Population" (Oliver et al., 2014).

Why ageing is a "game-changer" for health and care services

I want to step back at this point and consider how population ageing has created a pressing need for our service models to change radically to ensure that they meet the needs of the "increasingly older" people who now use them. This will help us focus on precisely what problems we are trying to fix.

When the NHS was founded in 1947, nearly half the population died before 65. This figure is now 14%, with the fastest growing section of the population the "oldest old" (Office for National Statistics, 2011). By 2030 there will be a projected 51% increase in the over 65 s and 100% increase in those over 85 (Office for National Statistics, 2013). Life expectancy at 65 – already around two decades in England – is projected to be 23 years for men and 26 years for women (House of Lords, 2013). Whilst many older people remain healthy, happy and independent well into old age, the rise in the overall numbers of older people is a "game-changer" for health and care services.

As Steven Dorrell MP recognised, when chair of the Parliamentary Health Select Committee:

> Systems designed to treat occasional episodes of care for normally healthy people are being used for people with complex and long-term conditions. The result is that they are often passed from silo to silo without the system having the ability to co-ordinate different providers. (Dorrell, 2013)

Most people over 75 have at least three long-term medical conditions (Barnett et al., 2012). Dementia already affects around 800,000 people in the UK, with the figure set to double over the next 20 years (Alzheimer's Society, 2007). Self-reported mobility problems grow with age, affecting most women over 80 (Melzer et al., 2012). In the face of acute illness or injury, older people are especially likely to lose mobility and functional independence quickly – often never to regain it without adequate rehabilitation. Although most older people are not disabled, most disability affects older people – and should not meekly be accepted as "because of your age" when there is often plenty which can be done to investigate and reverse it or make the disability easier to live with (Office for National Statistics, 2012; Oliver, 2008). Finally, older people are often reliant on family care-givers, many of whom are old and unwell themselves (House of Lords, 2013).

Multiple co-morbidities bring multiple medications, with 10% of people over 65 being on 10 or more prescribed drugs (Duerden et al., 2013). The importance of frailty – increasingly prevalent the older we become – cannot be overstated. People who are frail tend to have slow walking speed, weaker muscles and fatigue more easily. Because of poor functional reserve, they decompensate very quickly in the face of even "minor" illness and can present to services with falls, immobility, confusion or non-specific deterioration, and are often denied the kind of comprehensive assessment from which they can benefit for months to come. Frailty is predictive of poor life expectancy and should also be a "red flag" to initiate advance planning for the end of life (Clegg et al., 2013; National Council for Palliative Care, 2011).

Integrated care for older people as key to dealing with the efficiency challenge

Older people who live with one or more of these problems – especially those with multiple life-limiting long-term conditions – are in effect the "core customers" of modern health and care services; the group with the biggest activity, the biggest spend, the biggest variations and gaps in care and the highest chance of being in the wrong setting for their needs (Oliver et al., 2014). We cannot solve pressing system problems and financial challenges without getting care right for them. Look in acute hospitals, where two-thirds of bed days are now in over 75 s (Cornwell, 2012); in nursing and residential homes, where residents' average age is high and medical complexity higher (British Geriatrics Society, 2011); in intermediate care services, where patients' average age is 83 (NHS Benchmarking, 2013). See the criteria for social care needs in England and Wales classified as "substantial" and you can see that only those with the most complex needs get a look in. And despite an historical focus on end-of-life care for younger people with cancers, most end-of-life care ipso facto focuses on the oldest old.

Disjointed care for older people is still too common

There are also still huge variations in rates of hospital admission, bed occupancy or care home placement – even when adjusted for needs – with some (more joined-up?) health economies clearly working far more effectively to join up services (Audit Commission, 2011; Imison et al., 2012). And far too many older people are admitted to or stuck in bed-based facilities for want of adequate capacity or responsiveness outside hospitals or care homes (Edwards, 2014; NHS Benchmarking, 2013).

Whilst there are many excellent services for older people with complex co-morbidities and frailty, they repeatedly tell us that care can be disjointed and bewildering, with much information repeated or lost, with professionals not always talking to one another, with lack of care co-ordination by familiar clinicians, and systems of care which can be hard for professionals to navigate, let alone older people and their carers (Haggerty, 2012; Roland, 2013). Care transitions (e.g. admission to or discharge from hospital) can be especially unsettling (Age UK, 2012a, 2012b; Ellins et al., 2012). Older people are still not sufficiently involved in decisions about their own care, and often suffer from a lack of information. There remains evidence of widespread ageism and age discrimination (Centre for Policy on Ageing, 2009a, 2009b).

Moving towards constructive solutions

For integrated care to become the norm, we need far more collaboration between all agencies in a local area across all components of care. In our King's Fund paper (Oliver et al., 2014) we set these components out in one diagram with the patient at the centre, a "right–left" shift towards proactive prevention and wellbeing and integration binding the components together (Figure 1). The use of patient stories, such as "Sam's Story" (King's Fund, 2013) or "Mrs Andrews" (Health Service Journal, 2014) (both freely available on the internet) in conjunction with this schema can help focus the minds of frontline clinical staff and managers alike.

If all local agencies sign up to a shared vision and some shared standards, walk the whole care pathway for service users with complex needs, implement best practice in each component but crucially focus on information sharing, duplication, hand-offs, co-ordination and ensuring that the right capacity, workforce and responsiveness is in the right part of the system at the right time, and work in a genuine spirit of collaboration with a focus on sustainable changes in services, we can make services more joined-up. There are examples of this approach delivering change in several health systems (Ham and Walsh, 2013).

A genuine "bottom-up" focus on integrating around the patient's needs is more useful than starting the focus on structures or organograms or budgets – the approach that has led to services more focused on the interests of providers and professionals than the people using them. We also need to build in some outcome indicators of how well the *whole system* performs, rather than individual organisations and some patient-reported outcomes about how joined-up and responsive their care felt to them (Audit Commission, 2011; Bardsley et al., 2013; PIRU, 2014).

Redefining integration

So, back to definitions of integration: they are legion. But try these for size (Ham, 2011).

Macro Integration involves the creation of services for whole populations. This might involve full structural integration, with one organisation providing every service, or more

Figure 1. Ideas that change health care. Reproduced with permission from The King's Fund.
Source: Oliver D, Foot C and Humphries R (2014).

"virtual" integration with close collaboration between agencies. Examples include the US Veterans Administration or Kaiser Permanente (Curry and Ham, 2010; Ham, 2011) or Christchurch New Zealand (Timmins and Ham, 2013).

Meso Integration involves the creation of services for specific care groups or people with the same condition. Examples include the Torbay Model in the UK (Thistlethwaite, 2011), PRISMA in Canada and PACE in the USA (Goodwin et al., 2014).

Micro Integration entails more joined-up care for individuals and their families – in other words care co-ordination. Several examples of care co-ordination were set out in a recent King's Fund report (Goodwin et al., 2013b).

Because there are so many different approaches to integrating services and so many definitions, it is not appropriate to dictate "one size fits all" solutions. They must be tailored to local circumstances, though with due regard to what we have learned from the published evidence.

Ultimately, this is about people using services, and we must look at integration first and foremost through their lens. As National Voices set out in 2013, "integration" is fairly meaningless management-speak to most citizens. What they tell us they want is "person-centred co-ordinated care" based on knowledge of them as a person, of all their conditions and a good understanding of the system (National Voices, 2013). National Voices' "*I statements*" stand as a great example of really trying to put the person at the centre rather than simply mouthing platitudinous mission statements. We need to be brave enough to do this, whatever it means for professional or organisational interests.

As the practitioners most frequently in contact with patients, and as those often providing relational continuity and a good understanding of those individuals, and as expert "system navigators", nurses can and should be in the vanguard of the integration agenda.

References

Age UK (2012a) *Older people's experience of emergency hospital readmission*. London: Age UK. Available at: www.ageuk.org.uk/Documents/EN-GB/For-professionals/Research/Emergency_ readmission_older_peoples_experiences.pdf?dtrk=true (accessed 2 January 2014).

Age UK (2012b) *Right care, first time: Services supporting safe hospital discharge and preventing hospital admission and readmission*. London: Age UK. Available at: www.ageuk.org.uk/ Documents/EN-GB/For-professionals/Research/ID200060%20Right%20Care%20First%20Time%2028ppA4.pdf?dtrk=true (accessed 2 January 2014).

Alzheimer's Society (2007) *Dementia UK: The full report*. London: Alzheimer's Society. Available at: http://alzheimers.org.uk/site/scripts/download_info.php?fileID=2 (accessed 3 December 2013).

Audit Commission (2011) *Joining up health and social care: Improving value for money across the interface*. London: Audit Commission. Available at: http://archive.audit-commission.gov. uk/auditcommission/sitecollection documents/Downloads/vfmhscinterface.pdf (accessed 5 December 2013).

Barnett K, Mercer S, Norbury M, et al. (2012) Epidemiology of multimorbidity and implications for health care, research, and medical education: A cross-sectional study. *The Lancet* 380(9836): 37–43.

Bardsley M, Steventon A, Smith J, et al. (2013) *Evaluating integrated and community-based care. How do we know what works*. London: Nuffield Trust. Available at: http://www.nuffieldtrust.org.uk/sites/files/nuffield/publication/evaluation_summary_final.pdf.

Bennett L and Humphries R (2013) *Making best use of the better care fund. Spending to save?* London: King's Fund. Available at: http://www.kingsfund.org.uk/sites/files/kf/field/field_publication_file/making-best-use-of-the-better-care-fund-kingsfund-jan14.pdf.

British Geriatrics Society (2011) *Quest for quality – British Geriatrics Society joint working party inquiry into the quality of healthcare support for older people in care homes: A call for leadership, partnership and quality improvement*. London: British Geriatrics Society. Available at: www.bgs.org.uk/campaigns/carehomes/quest_quality_care_homes.pdf (accessed 20 January 2014).

Centre for Policy on Ageing (2009a) *Ageism and age discrimination in primary and community health care in the United Kingdom: A review from the literature*. London: Centre for Policy on Ageing.

Centre for Policy on Ageing (2009b) *Ageism and age discrimination in secondary health care in the United Kingdom: A review from the literature*. London: Centre for Policy on Ageing.

Clegg A, Young J, Iliffe S, et al. (2013) Frailty in elderly people. *The Lancet* 381(9868): 752–762.

Cornwell J (2012) *The care of frail older people with complex needs: Time for a revolution.* The Sir Roger Bannister Health Summit, held at Leeds Castle, Kent, November 2011. London: The King's Fund. Available at: www.kingsfund.org.uk/publications/care-frail-older-people-complex-needs-time-revolution).

Curry N and Ham C (2010) *Clinical and service integration: The route to improved outcomes.* London: The King's Fund. Available at: www.kingsfund.org.uk/publications/clinical-and- service-integration.

Dorrell S (2013) Quoted in: Health and Social Care, adjusting to changing patterns of need. *Ready for Ageing* report. London: House of Lords. Available at: http://www.publications.parliament.uk/pa/ld201213/ldselect/ldpublic/140/14016.htm (accessed 7 October 2014).

Duerden M, Avery T and Payne R (2013) *Polypharmacy and medicines optimisation. Making it safe and sound.* Available at: http://www.kingsfund.org.uk/sites/files/kf/field/field_publication_file/polypharmacy-and-medicines-optimisation-kingsfund-nov13.pdf.

Edwards N (2014) *Community Services. Key to transforming care.* London: King's Fund. Available at: http://www.kingsfund.org.uk/sites/files/kf/field/field_publication_file/community-services-nigel-edwards-feb14.pdf.

Ellins J, Glasby J, Tanner D, et al. (2012) *Understanding and improving transitions of older people: A user and carer centred approach.* Final report. Southampton: National Institute for Health Research Service Delivery and Organisation Programme.

Goodwin N, Dixon A, Anderson G, et al. (2014) *Providing integrated care for people with complex needs. Lessons from seven international case studies.* London: King's Fund. Available at: http://www.kingsfund.org.uk/sites/files/kf/field/field_publication_file/providing-integrated-care-for-older-people-with-complex-needs-kingsfund-jan14.pdf.

Goodwin N, Smith J, Davies A, et al. (2013a) *A report to the Department of Health and NHS Futures Forum 2013.* London: King's Fund and Nuffield Trust. Available at: http://www.kingsfund.org.uk/sites/files/kf/integrated-care-patients-populations-paper-nuffield-trust-kings-fund-january-2012.pdf.

Goodwin N, Sonola L, Thiel V, et al. (2013b) *Co-ordinated care for people with complex chronic conditions: Key lessons and markers for success.* London: The King's Fund. Available at: www.kingsfund.org.uk/publications/co-ordinated-care-people-complex-chronic-conditions (accessed 21 January 2014).

Haggerty J (2012) Ordering the chaos for patients with multimorbidity. *British Medical Journal* 345: e5915.

Ham C (2011) *Integrated care. What is it? Does it work? What does it mean for the NHS?* London: King's Fund. Available at: http://www.kingsfund.org.uk/sites/files/kf/field/field_publication_file/integrated-care-summary-chris-ham-sep11.pdf.

Ham C, Heenan D, Longley M, et al. (2013) *Integrated care in Northern Ireland, Scotland and Wales.* London: King's Fund. Available at: http://www.kingsfund.org.uk/sites/files/kf/field/field_publication_file/integrated-care-in-northern-ireland-scotland-and-wales-kingsfund-jul13.pdf.

Ham C, Imison C, Goodwin N, et al. (2011) *Where next for the NHS reforms? The case for integrated care.* London: The King's Fund. Available at: www.kingsfund.org.uk/publications/articles/where-next-nhs-reforms-case-integrated-care.

Ham C and Walsh N (2013) *Making integrated care happen at scale and pace: Lessons from experience.* London: The King's Fund. Available at: www.kingsfund.org.uk/publications/making-integrated-care-happen-scale-and-pace (accessed 23 January 2014).

Health Service Journal (2014) *Mrs Andrews' Story: Her failed care pathway.* Available at: http://www.youtube.com/watch?v=Fj_9HG_TWEM.

House of Lords (2013) *'Ready for ageing?' Select Committee on Public Service and Demographic Change.* Report of Session 2012–13. HL Paper 140. London: The Stationery Office Limited.

Imison C, Poteliakhoff E and Thompson J (2012) Older people and emergency bed use: Exploring variation. London: The King's Fund. Available at: www.kingsfund.org.uk/publications/older- people-and-emergency-bed-use.

King's Fund (2013) *Joined-up care: Sam's story.* Available at: http://www.kingsfund.org.uk/audio-video/joined-care-sams-story.

Melzer D, Tavakoly B, Winder R, et al. (2012) *Health care quality for an active later life: Improving quality of prevention and treatment through information: England 2005 to 2012.* A report from the Peninsula College of Medicine and Dentistry Ageing Research Group for Age UK. Exeter: Peninsula College of Medicine and Dentistry, University of Exeter. Available at: http://medicine.exeter.ac.uk/media/universityofexeter/medicalschool/pdfs/Health_Care_Quality_for_an_Active_Later_Life_UpdatedAug2013.pdf.

National Council for Palliative Care (2011) *Commissioning end of life care: Act & early to avoid A&E. Initial actions for new commissioners.* London: the National Council for Palliative Care/ National End of Life Care Programme. Available at: www.ncpc.org.uk/sites/default/files/ AandE.pdf.

National Voices (2013) *Integrated care: What do patients, service users and carers want?* Available at: www.nationalvoices.org.uk/sites/www.nationalvoices.org.uk/files/what_patients_ want_from_integration_national_voices_paper.pdf.

Naylor C, Imison C, Addicott R, et al. (2013)*Transforming our health care system. Ten priorities for commissioners.* London: King's Fund. Available at: http://www.kingsfund.org.uk/sites/files/kf/field/field_publication_file/10PrioritiesFinal2.pdf.

NHS Benchmarking (2013) *National audit of intermediate care report 2013.* Manchester: NHS Benchmarking Network. Available at: www.nhsbenchmarking.nhs.uk/National-Audit-of- Intermediate-Care/year-two.php.

NHS Confederation and Royal College of General Practitioners (2013) *Making integrated out-of-hospital care a reality.* London: The NHS Confederation. Available at: www.nhsconfed. org/Publications/Documents/Making-integrated-out-of-hospital-care-reality.pdf.

NHS Future Forum (2011) *Summary report on proposed changes to the NHS.* NHS Future Forum. Available at: www.gov.uk/government/uploads/system/uploads/attachment_data/ file/213748/dh_127540.pdf.

Office for National Statistics (2011) *Interim life tables, 2008–2010.* Newport: Office for National Statistics. Available at: www.ons.gov.uk/ons/publications/re-reference-tables.html?edition=tcm%3A77-223324.

Office for National Statistics (2012) *Family resources survey 2011/12.* Available at: https://www.gov.uk/government/statistics/family-resources-survey-201112 (accessed 7th November 2014).

Office for National Statistics (2013) *Population estimates total persons for England and Wales and regions, mid 1971 – mid 2012.* Newport: Office for National Statistics. Available at: www.ons.gov.uk/ons/rel/pop-estimate/population-estimates-for-uk–england-and-wales– scotland-and-northern-ireland/ mid-2001-to-mid-2010-revised/rft—mid-2001-to-mid-2010-population-estimates-analysis-tool.zip.

Oliver D (2008) '"Acopia" and "social admission" are not diagnoses: why older people deserve better'. *Journal of the Royal Society of Medicine* 101(4): 168–174.

Oliver D, Foot C and Humphries R (2014) *Making health and care systems fit for an ageing population.* London: King's Fund. Available at: http://www.canadiangeriatrics.ca/ default/index.cfm/linkservid/F5ABBC5A-B646-A0DD-9ED4D95D3408E694/showMeta/0/.

Policy research unit in Policy Innovation Research (PIRU) (2014). *Integrated care and support pioneers. Indicators for Integrated Care.* London.

Roland M (2013) Better management of patients with multimorbidity. *British Medical Journal* 346: f2510.

Royal College of General Practitioners (RCGP) (2014) *Coalition for collaborative care.* London: RCGP. Available at: http://www.rcgp.org.uk/news/2014/march/new-coalition-launched-on-long-term-conditions.aspx.

Royal College of Nursing (RCN) (2014) *Integrated health and social care in England: The 14 pioneer programmes.*

London: RCN. Available at: http://www.rcn.org.uk/__data/ assets/pdf_file/0009/584217/18.14_Integrated_Health_and_ Social_Care_in_England_The_14_Pioneer_Programmes_ A_guide_for_nursing_staff.pdf.

Royal College of Physicians (RCP) (2013) *Future hospital: Caring for medical patients. A report from the Future Hospital Commission to the Royal College of Physicians.* London: Royal College of Physicians. Available at: www.rcplondon.ac.uk/sites/default/files/future-hospital-commission- report.pdf.

Thistlethwaite P (2011) *Integrating health and social care in Torbay. Improving care for Mrs Smith.* London: King's Fund. Available at: http://www.kingsfund.org.uk/sites/files/ kf/integrating-health-social-care-torbay-case-study-kings-fund-march-2011.pdf.

Timmins N and Ham C (2013) *The quest for integrated health and social care. A case study in Canterbury New Zealand.* London: Kings Fund. Available at: http://www. kingsfund.org.uk/sites/files/kf/field/field_publication_file/ quest-integrated-care-new-zealand-timmins-ham-sept13.pdf.

David Oliver is a Consultant Physician in Geriatrics and General Medicine, the English Government's former National Clinical Director for Older People, President of the British Geriatrics Society, a Senior Visiting Fellow at the King's Fund leading on integrated services for older people, Professor of Medicine for Older People at City University and a specialist advisor to the NHS Emergency Care Support Team.

Delivering Health and Social Care for People with Long-Term Conditions: The Policy Context.

Hewison, A.

Overview

- The number of people with one or more long-term conditions is increasing
- This represents a significant policy challenge for service delivery and organization
- The NHS Social Care Model for long-term conditions in England has been influenced by US approaches and the reform process in the UK
- The policy process is complex and shapes the care people receive

Sixty percent of all deaths in the world are as a result of chronic or long-term conditions, and in Europe this figure rises to 86% (WHO, 2005). There are currently 15.4 million people in England with a Long-term Condition (LTC), and it is estimated that by 2025 there will be 42% more people aged 65 and over, who are therefore at greater risk of developing a LTC, living in England alone. This means the number of people with at least one LTC will rise to 18 million (DH, 2010a). People with LTCs account for a significant and growing proportion of health and social care resources and the costs of their treatment and care amount to nearly £7 in every £10 of health spending in England (DH, 2010a). In order to meet this increased demand for services, the management of LTCs is a key priority for the Department of

Health (DH), the NHS and social care services (DH, 2009a). Encouraging self-care for people with LTCs forms a foundation of this policy response (DH, 2009a). In the light of this situation the purpose of this chapter is to examine the policy shaping services for people with LTCs. Most health care systems in the developed world are designed primarily for treating acute, episodic illness (CHSRF, 2005), and so LTCs represent one of the most important health policy problems facing many countries (Singh, 2008). To address this challenge, changes to the organization and delivery of care for people with LTCs are being made, however there is no evidence to suggest that one policy approach is better than another in this area (Singh, 2008). Furthermore, the wider context the health and social care system is part of, influences the way such policy is developed. This will be demonstrated through examination of the policy response in England, as an example of how a range of factors combine to shape the policy framework in a given setting. First, though there is a need to present a working definition of policy as a starting point for the discussion.

Policy

Policy is not a specific, or concrete concept and so defining it is problematic (Crinson, 2009). Policies are on-going, dynamic, subject to change and involve a course of action or a web of decisions rather than arising from a single decision (Crinson, 2009; Ham and Hill, 1993). Policy making is complex because it can cross national borders, be made by individuals, organizations, agencies and governments and operate at regional, national and international levels (Earle, 2007). In response to this complexity analysts have suggested using a 'stages model' which characterizes policy as a process. An example is presented by Dunn (2004), who outlines eight stages, which are:

1 Agenda setting
2 Policy formulation
3 Policy adoption
4 Policy implementation
5 Policy assessment
6 Policy adaptation
7 Policy succession
8 Policy termination

The purpose of such models is to identify the different phases of the policy process and make it clearer. If policy analysis is concerned with understanding and explaining the substance of policy content, policy decisions and the way decisions are made (Barrett and Fudge, 1981), and it is not possible to encapsulate the nature of policy in a single definition, then breaking it down into a series of stages can help. For example the broad policy agenda is informed by the government's ideological approach. If it is committed to the discipline of the market as a means of governance, often associated with parties on the political 'right', its policies will be different from those on the 'left', which may favour a more collective orientation to societal problems. This also informs the identification of problems/issues. In the case of LTCs, is the demand for care an individual problem (it is each individual's responsibility to provide the means for their own care?) or a state problem (is it a collective responsibility to fund and provide care for anyone who needs it?). The consideration and selection of options for action then follow from the first two stages and so on. The 'stagist' model is helpful in presenting a broad picture of the process (Dorey, 2005); however policy is seldom developed in such a planned, ordered way, and is generally reactive and incremental (Lindblom, 1959, 1979). It is not a rational, objective, neutral activity devoid of values or the play of power (Hunter, 2003) and is often characterized by ambiguity of intent, unpredictability of response, and is complex and problematic (Bergen and While, 2005). Given this complexity, and the absence of a single agreed means of analysing it, an alternative approach is taken here using a model which focuses on the levels of policy making (Hudson and Lowe, 2004) to examine the context of service provision for people with LTCs.

- The macro-level encompasses the broad forces that shape policy such as globalization, the global market place, the rising number of people with LTCs internationally.
- The meso-level is the practice of policy making and the system-wide processes and changes necessary for implementation.
- The micro-level focuses down onto the engagement between consumers and agencies.

This provides a framework for thinking about policy which emphasizes the role of government, health and social care organizations, and individuals in shaping and implementing policy. It is consistent with recent work (Singh, 2008) which found that policy interventions in relation to LTCs generally fall into three categories, which mirror the policy levels identified by Hudson and Lowe (2004).

- System-wide or population health approaches (macro). These focus on developing national policy, structures and the resources needed for major change. They often incorporate an emphasis on disease prevention and health promotion and are designed to operate across settings and providers.
- Health delivery systems or selected components (meso). Health delivery systems use information systems, new roles, and organizational re-design to target the significant components of care. They aim to reduce duplication and improve health outcomes.
- The level of individuals (micro). Initiatives focused on individuals include behavioural change and simple case management. (Singh, 2008)

These interventions, operating at the different levels of policy, are not mutually exclusive and are often used together as part of an overall strategy designed to be appropriate to a specific context (Singh, 2008). This provides a comprehensive yet straightforward framework for examining English policy in the area of LTCs.

English policy for long-term conditions

System-wide approaches: Commissioning services for people with long-term conditions

The Labour government, which came to power in 1997, embarked on a programme of system reform and increased spending on the NHS. Between 2000 and 2007 health spending grew from 5.4% of national income in 1998/9 to 7.2% in 2005/6, and accounted for almost 40% of the increase in public expenditure as a share of national income (Chote, 2007). This was accompanied by widespread system reform aimed at introducing more competitive challenge, or contestability, to NHS providers to reduce waiting times and improve quality (Dixon, 2007). The main elements of this system level policy reform are summarized in Figure 11.1.

Central to the drive to bring about change in service provision and delivery is the commissioning process. In England commissioning is

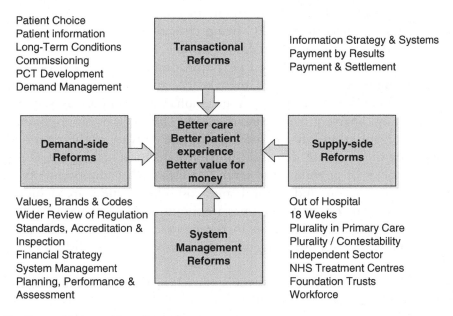

Figure 11.1   System-wide policy reform

Source: adapted from Prime Minister's Strategy Unit (2006)

undertaken by Primary Care Trusts (PCTs) and other public sector commissioners on the 'demand side' to ensure providers deliver the services needed by the local population. Currently PCTs have responsibility for the implementation of health policy and hold a budget for the primary and secondary care needs of their residents (between 200,000 and 1 million people). This has been developed recently into 'World Class Commissioning' which is a national programme to improve health outcomes, reduce health inequalities and increase quality of life (DH, 2010a). The commissioning cycle is made up of eight elements:

1   Assess needs
2   Review current service provision
3   Decide priorities
4   Design service
5   Shape structure of supply
6   Manage demand and ensure appropriate access to care
7   Clinical decision making
8   Managing performance

Each of these elements involves a wide range of activity, for example assessing needs includes measuring disease prevalence, demographics, deprivation levels, the socio-economic make-up and mortality rates of the population in the PCT area. This is followed by a review of current provision to determine which services are already available to meet the needs of people with LTCs and their suitability. These first two phases could result in a particular LTC being chosen as a priority, if a gap in service provision was discovered, for example. Priorities may also be set for improving the health of the LTC population by offering personalized care planning. Services should then be designed to meet the holistic needs of people with LTCs with an emphasis on supporting self-care, delivered by capable provider organizations. The PCT, or other commissioning organization, pay the provider for the delivery of these services. Managing the structure, demand and clinical decision making are all part of the process of providing the service to ensure that improvements are made year on year and clinical and cost effectiveness are achieved. Quality, performance and outcomes are monitored by assessment against metrics or standards written in to the contracts with providers which relate to national and local targets for the care of people with LTCs (DH, 2010a).

When considered in this way the approach seems clear and it might be anticipated that the policy challenge of organizing services to meet the needs of people with LTCs would be met. However, this is just one strand of policy which can conflict with others (de Silva and Fahey, 2008). For example, the focus of the NHS Health and Social Care Model is on prevention, supporting self-management and partnership working. However the 'Payment by Results' system, introduced to ensure providers work efficiently and economically, may inhibit a change to more community-based care, because it is not in the hospital's financial interest if more people are cared for in the community. The more in-patients treated the more income the hospital receives, a particular concern for 'Foundation Trusts' (de Silva and Fahey, 2008). In this way aspects of policy can conflict and hamper the development of new ways of working in one or more areas. Similar problems can also occur at the next level of policy activity.

Health delivery systems: The NHS and Social Care Long-term Conditions Model

The system structure which shapes the way services for people with LTCs are organized in England is the NHS and Social Care Long-term Conditions Model, which is based on system approaches used in the United States such as the Kaiser Permanente 'pyramid of care' and the Evercare model (Department of Health, 2004). Kaiser Permanente is a not-for-profit health maintenance organization in the United States which is funded through individual and corporate health insurance schemes and integrates prevention, treatment and care. It aims to maintain its members in good health and avoid inappropriate admissions to hospital by prioritizing the prevention of illness, and treating patients with common conditions. If an unplanned hospital admission occurs it is regarded as a failure in the system. People with LTCs receive structured care from multidisciplinary teams located in the community, based in facilities that are similar to the surgeries used by primary health care teams in the UK, although they are bigger as they house facilities for core diagnostic services and a wider range of staff (Ham, 2005). The Kaiser triangle is used to 'segment' the population of patients with long-term conditions into three groups reflecting their care needs (see Figure 11.2). Several 'Beacon Sites'[1] have been established in England and have resulted in improvements to the services provided for patients (Ham, 2010). The key elements of this system are summarized below:

- Level 3: Case management – requires the identification of the high intensity users of unplanned secondary care. Care for these patients is co-ordinated by a community matron or other professional(s) using a case management approach, to co-ordinate health and social care.
- Level 2: Disease-specific care management – this involves providing people who have a complex single need or multiple conditions with responsive, specialist

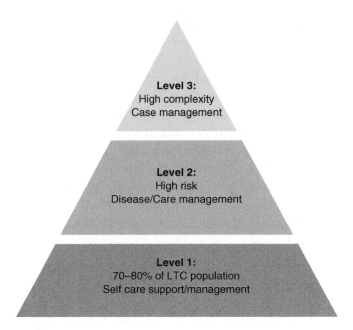

Figure 11.2   The Kaiser permanente pyramid of care

Source: DH (2005b)

services using multidisciplinary teams and disease-specific protocols and pathways, such as the National Service Frameworks (DH, 2005a).

- Level 1: Supported self-care – helping individuals and their carers to develop the knowledge, skills and confidence to care for themselves and their condition effectively (DH, 2005a, 2005b). This builds on an earlier Expert Patient initiative (DH, 2001) which sought to place patients' knowledge of their own conditions at the heart of care.

Central to this system of care is case management, a term used to describe a range of approaches that have been taken to improve the organization and co-ordination of services for people with LTCs. There is no single model of case management, and it exists in many forms in the NHS. However its core elements are: case finding or screening; assessment; care planning; implementation; monitoring and review. These activities can be undertaken by a single 'case manager' or as a series of separate, linked tasks by members of a multidisciplinary team (Hutt et al., 2004). As part of an integrated care model the purpose of case management is to ensure the delivery of co-ordinated care to meet the varied and differing needs of individual clients with LTCs. This service development was also informed by the Evercare model which was piloted in nine PCTs in April 2003 and case management subsequently became part of Government policy for supporting people with LTCs (Busse et al., 2010). Evercare is a model of care for frail older people, developed in the United States by a for-profit health insurance company, which incorporates nurse-led assessment and intensive case management.

Assessing the impact of this aspect of policy is difficult because there is no clear evidence to demonstrate that case management prevents admissions to acute care or reduces the use of emergency services (Hutt et al., 2004; Singh, 2005). This suggests that policy transfer (Hulme, 2005), applying policy pre-scriptions from one health system to another, is not always successful. Similarly an evaluation of the Evercare model pilot in England found that emergency admissions of people with LTCs were unlikely to be reduced by more than 1%, and if greater reductions were to be achieved it would require the appointment of between 20 and 24 Advanced Nurse Practitioners in each PCT (Boaden et al., 2005). With regard to the case manager role, which has been assigned to Community Matrons in the main, there was a commitment to appoint 3,000 by March 2007 to 'spearhead the case management drive' (DH, 2005b). Yet in 2006/7 58% of PCTs had not achieved their target to appoint the planned number of community matrons, and only 32% of 'very high-intensity users' were under their care (Boaden, 2008). Although they are popular with patients and improve the situation for individuals, the case management element of the policy is unlikely to reduce hospital admissions in the absence of a more radical system redesign (Boaden et al., 2006). This emphasizes the point that many health systems are still largely built around an acute, episodic model of care and changing the system to better meet the needs of people with complex LTCs is difficult. The health systems in different countries vary widely and each needs a solution that fits with its overall structure and system model (Nolte et al., 2008). The broad policy commitment is clear, in that everyone with one or more LTC(s) should be offered a personalized care plan, developed, agreed and regularly reviewed with a named lead professional to help manage their care (DH, 2008) with this process managed as part of the system. However if this is to be achieved better co-operation among health and social care organizations needs to be addressed as a priority if deep rooted vested interests and profes-sional scepticism are to be overcome (Busse et al., 2010). This requires good management and political support. A third strand of policy that needs to be adapted to specific national concerns operates at the micro level.

The individual focus: Personalized care planning

The Department of Health has issued guidance on how to incorporate self-care into the policy framework for LTCs (DH, 2009a, 2009b). Effective self-care involves providing appropriate information for individuals and their families, developing a supported process to enable people with LTCs to appraise their current lifestyle choices, think about their individual goals, and build the confidence to attain them. A number of health and social care professionals will be involved in this process, depending on the complexity of the individual's needs (DH, 2009a). Commissioners will require evidence from service providers that the services they 'buy':

- put the individual, their needs, choices, health and well-being at the centre of the process;
- focus on goal setting and clear outcomes;
- are planned, anticipatory and include contingency planning to manage crisis episodes better;
- ensure that people receive co-ordinated care packages, which reduce fragmentation between services;
- provide relevant, timely and accredited information to support client decision making;
- provide support so that people can self-care/self-manage their condition(s) and prevent deterioration;
- promote joined-up working between different professions and agencies, especially between health and social care. (DH, 2009b)

This should result in the collation of all the information about the individual into a single comprehensive paper or electronic care plan, which should also be accessible by the client and those who have a legitimate reason to use it, including out of hours and emergency/urgent care services (DH, 2009b). This micro level policy is designed to give individual patients more leverage in the system. If they learn more about their LTC(s) and the services they can access, it is anticipated that the role of clients as active service users will be enhanced and passive acceptance reduced. It is part of the system-wide policy whereby they become a driver for change as part of the 'demand side' dynamic. However a survey conducted on behalf of the Department of Health (Carluccio et al., 2009) presents a mixed picture of progress in the development of personalized self-care. Information was found to be central in helping people take a greater role in the treatment of their long-term condition with one in five reporting this to be the case. Yet nearly two thirds of the respondents (64%) were not aware of any available training courses that taught self-care skills, and only 4% had accessed a training course of this kind. Although people were generally satisfied with the information and support they received, two in five adults with a LTC had not approached any individual or organization for advice on self-care or information about their LTC (Carluccio et al., 2009). This suggests there is still some way to go before clients are fully engaged in directing their own care.

Recent additions to the policy mix, which have been described as two of the most exciting initiatives to date (Glasby and Duffy, 2007), may accelerate this process as part of the personalization agenda. Direct payments are cash payments made to disabled people between the ages of 18–65 years in lieu of directly provided services. The payment can then be used by the individual to purchase services from a voluntary or private agency (Glasby and Duffy, 2007). This is taken a stage further in the form of individual budgets which indicate how much individuals have to spend on their care, and ensure they have control over this funding (Glasby, 2008a). This has the potential to transform the relationship between the individual and the state from the traditional 'professional gift model', where the state uses the money it receives from taxation to provide services for clients, to a 'citizenship model', in which the individual is at the centre of the process and controls the resources to organize the care she/he wants (Glasby, 2008b). Individual budgets have been tested with 6,000 people since 2003 and have resulted in improvements in personal well-being and system efficiency (Glasby, 2008a) and these positive results could offer a framework for reforming the funding of long-term care more generally (Glasby, 2008a). The ultimate outcome of this would be that if providers are to introduce genuine personalization of services they would need to appeal to 'micro commissioners' (Dickinson and Glasby, 2009), individuals. This would constitute a significant change in the organization and delivery of health care, yet it is difficult to predict how policy for LTCs will develop in England because there is now a new government in office.

Next steps

The policy approach to the provision of care for people with LTC is to be reviewed. The Conservative and Liberal Democrat Coalition which came to power in May 2010 published a White Paper which included a number of proposals that will have a direct impact on policy in this area. One of the major changes outlined in the White Paper was in the commissioning process. The government plans to devolve power and responsibility for commissioning to consortia of General Practitioners (GPs) and their practice teams (DH, 2010b), which will result in PCTs being phased out by 2013. The intention is that by shifting responsibility for commissioning and budgets to groups of GP practices, services will be shaped around the needs and choices of patients and that following the passage of the Health Bill, the consortia will take on full responsibility for commissioning in 2012/13 (DH, 2010b). At the time of writing the precise details of how this new approach will work are yet to appear, for example: How many patients will each consortium be responsible for? How many GPs will be involved in each consortium? What will the management structure be?

And perhaps most importantly what governance arrangements will be put in place? Previous attempts to involve GPs more directly in managing budgets and commissioning services have produced mixed results (Curry et al., 2008; Glennerster et al., 1994; Smith, 2010) and so this new approach to commissioning will need to be managed carefully if it is to be successful.

Although 'choice in care for long-term conditions' as part of personalized care planning is to be available from 2011 (DH 2010b) the extent to which a focus will be maintained on the needs of people with LTCs is not entirely clear and could potentially become less of a priority if the consortia concentrate on commissioning services from secondary care (hospitals). Another significant change that is likely to have far reaching effects on the organization of care for people with LTCs is the establishment of a commission on the funding of long-term care and support which will report in July 2011 (DH, 2010b). The current financial strictures affecting health systems across the world (Newbold and Hyrkäs, 2010) are likely to result in reductions in services as governments seek to correct deficits. For example, the NHS in England will be required to save £15–20 billion in 2011–2014 (Ham, 2009). The review of funding of long-term care will, in all likelihood, lead to different arrangements and the imposition of financial limits and the rationalization of services. However the full picture will not be clear until the commission reports its findings and recommendations. This underlines the need to continually examine the policy context in England and elsewhere, if the organization and delivery of services for people with LTCs are to be understood.

Conclusion

Although there is a comprehensive range of models and guidance to indicate how services for people with LTCs should be organized this can in itself complicate matters further. For example in a document about commissioning personalized care for people with LTCs (DH, 2009b), direction is given to 28 other documents that must be consulted if the process is to be fully understood. When this is considered in the context of a new administration seeking to introduce fundamental reforms it becomes clear that although policy statements may emphasize the need to focus on clients and ensure high quality service delivery, these aspirations can be sidelined in the efforts to overhaul the system and make savings. In common with many other areas of health policy the management arrangements for people with LTCs are subject to frequent change. Reviewing policy using a model such as the one outlined here is necessary to track the origins and implications of such changes.

Summary

This chapter has shown how the macro, meso, micro approach to policy analysis can provide a useful framework for examining the organization of care for people with long-term conditions in England. It is clear that there is no single policy model for the management of the health and social care for people with long-term conditions and policy approaches have to be adapted to the context of different systems. The role of the new GP Commissioning Consortia in England will be crucial to service delivery in this area.

Note

1 Beacon sites are usually individual departments that are using innovative approaches to address problems or promote best practice in health and social care. The NHS Beacon programme was launched with 290 sites in 1999.

Further reading

Jones, K. and Netten, A. (2010) 'The costs of change: A case study of the process of implementing individual budgets across pilot local authorities in England', *Health & Social Care in the Community*, 18(10): 51–8.
Naylor, C. and Goodwin, N. (2010) *Building High Quality Commissioning – What Role Can External Organisations Play?* London: King's Fund.

References

Barrett, S. and Fudge, C. (1981) 'Examining the policy-action relationship', in S. Barrett and C. Fudge (eds), *Policy and Action: Essays on the Implementation of Public Policy*. London: Methuen. pp. 3–32.
Bergen, A. and While, A. (2005) 'Implementation deficit and street-level bureaucracy: Policy, practice and change in the development of community nursing issues', *Health and Social Care in the Community*, 13(1): 1–10.
Boaden, R. (2008) 'Can community matrons cut hospital admissions?', *Pulse*, 27 March [Online]. Available at: http://www.pulsetoday.co.uk/story.asp?storycode= 4118121 (accessed 4 August 2010).
Boaden, R., Dusheiko, M., Gravelle, H., Parker, S., Pickard, S., Roland, M., Sheaff, R. and Sargent, P. (2005) *Evercare Evaluation Interim Report: Implications for Supporting People with Long-term Conditions*. Manchester: National Primary Care Research Centre, University of Manchester.
Boaden, R., Dusheiko, M., Gravelle, H., Parker, S., Pickard, S., Roland, M., Sargent, P. and Sheaff, R. (2006) *Evercare Evaluation: Final Report*. Manchester: National Primary Care Research and Development Centre.

Busse, R., Blümel, M., Scheller-Kreinsen, D. and Zentner, A. (2010) *Tackling Chronic Disease in Europe: Strategies, Interventions and Challenges.* Denmark: World Health Organization, on behalf of the European Observatory on Health Systems and Policies.

Canadian Health Services Research Foundation (2005) 'Interdisciplinary teams in primary health care can effectively manage chronic illness', *Evidence Boost*, September, [Online] Available at: www.chsrfa.ca, 1-2 (accessed May 2006).

Carluccio, A., Carroll, P. and Worley, T. (2009) *Long-term Health Conditions 2009.* Research Study Conducted for the Department of Health. London: IpsosMORI/DH.

Chote, R. (2007) 'Health and the public spending squeeze. Funding prospects for the NHS', in J. Appleby (ed.), *Funding Health Care 2008 and Beyond. Report from the Leeds Castle Summit* . London: King's Fund. pp. 35–42.

Crinson, I. (2009) *Health Policy – A Critical Perspective.* London: Sage.

Curry, N., Godwin, N., Naylor, C. and Robertson, R. (2008) *Practice-based Commissioning: Replace, Reinvigorate or Abandon?* London: King's Fund.

De Silva, D. and Fahey, D. (2008) 'England', in E. Nolte, C. Knai and M. McKee (eds), *Managing Chronic Conditions Experience in Eight Countries.* World Health Organization, on behalf of the European Observatory on Health Systems and Policies. Denmark: WHO.

DH (2001) *The Expert Patient: A New Approach to Chronic Disease Management for the 21st century.* London: Department of Health.

DH (2004) *Annual Report.* London: The Stationery Office.

DH (2005a) *The National Service Framework for Long-Term Conditions.* London: Department of Health.

DH (2005b) *Supporting People with Long-term Conditions (4230).* London: Department of Health.

DH (2008) *High Quality Care for All NHS Next Stage Review-Final Report.* London: Department of Health.

DH (2009a) *Your Health, Your Way. A Guide to Long-term Conditions and Self Care.* London: Department of Health.

DH (2009b) *Supporting People with Long-term Conditions – Commissioning Personalised Care Planning.* London: Department of Health.

DH (2010a) *Improving the Health and Well-being of People with Long-term Conditions: World Class Services for People with Long-term Conditions – Information Tool for Commissioners.* London: Department of Health.

DH (2010b) *Equity and Excellence: Liberating the NHS.* London: Department of Health.

Dickinson, H. and Glasby, J (2009) *The Personalisation Agenda: Implications for the Third Sector.* Briefing paper 30. Birmingham: Third Sector Research Centre.

Dixon, J. (2007) 'Improving management of chronic illness in the National Health Service: Better incentives are the key', *Chronic Illness*, 3: 181–93.

Dorey, P. (2005) *Policy Making in Britain: An Introduction.* London: Sage Publications.

Dunn, W. N. (2004) *Public Policy Analysis – An Introduction*, 3rd edn. New Jersey: Pearson/Prentice Hall.

Earle, S. (2007) 'Promoting public health in a global context', in C.E. Lloyd, S. Handsley, J. Douglas, S. Earle and S. Spurr (eds), *Policy and Practice in Promoting Public Health.* London: Sage Publications. pp. 1–32.

Glasby, J. (2008a) *Individual Patient Budgets: Background and Frequently Asked Questions.* HSMC Policy Paper 1. Birmingham: Health Services Management Centre, University of Birmingham.

Glasby, J. (2008b) *'Who Cares?' Policy Proposals for the Reform of Long-Term Care.* Birmingham: Health Services Management Centre, University of Birmingham.

Glasby, J. and Duffy, S. (2007) *Our Health, Our Care, Our Say – What Could the NHS Learn from Individual Budgets and Direct Payments?* Joint HSMC and *in Control* discussion paper. Birmingham: Health Services Management Centre, University of Birmingham.

Glennerster, H., Matsaganis, M., Owens, P. and Hancock, S. (1994) *Implementing GP Fundholding: Wild Card or Winning Hand?* Buckingham: Open University Press.

Ham, C. (2005) 'Lost in translation? Health systems in the US and the UK', *Social Policy and Administration*, 39(2): 192–209.

Ham, C. (2009) *Health in a Cold Climate – Developing an Intelligent Response to Financial Challenges Facing the NHS.* Briefing Paper. London: The Nuffield Trust.

Ham, C. (2010) *Working Together for Health: Achievements and Challenges in the Kaiser NHS Beacon Sites Programme.* Birmingham: Health Services Management Centre, University of Birmingham.

Ham, C. and Hill, M. (1993) *The Policy Process in the Modern Capitalist State.* New York: Harvester Wheatsheaf.

Hudson, J. and Lowe, S. (2004) *Understanding the Policy Process.* Bristol: The Policy Press.

Hulme, R. (2005) 'Policy transfer and the internationalisation of social policy', *Social Policy & Society*, 4(4): 417–25.

Hunter, D.J. (2003) *Public Health Policy.* Cambridge: Polity.

Hutt, R., Rosen, R. and McCauley, J. (2004) *Case-Managing Long-Term Conditions: What Impact does it have in the Treatment of Older People?* London: King's Fund.

Lindblom, C E. (1959) 'The science of 'muddling through', *Public Administration Review*, 19: 78–88.

Lindblom, C. E. (1979) 'Still muddling, not yet through', *Public Administration Review*, 39: 517–25.

Newbold, D. and Hyrkäs, K. (2010) 'Managing in economic austerity', *Journal of Nursing Management*, 18(5): 495–500.

Nolte, E., McKee, M. and Knai, C. (2008) 'Managing chronic conditions: An introduction to the experience in eight countries', in E. Nolte, C. Knai and M. McKedd (eds), *Managing Chronic Conditions – Experience in Eight Countries.* World Health Organization, on behalf of the European Observatory on Health Systems and Policies. Denmark: WHO. pp. 1–14.

Prime Minister's Strategy Unit (2006) *The UK Government's Approach to Public Service Reform* [Online]. Available at: www.cabinetoffice.gov.uk/media/cabinetoffice/strategy/assess/sj_pamphlet.pdf (accessed 3 November 2008).

Singh, D. (2005) *Transforming Chronic Care: Evidence about Improving Care of People with Long-term Conditions.* Birmingham: Health Services Management Centre, University of Birmingham.

Singh, D. (2008) *How Can Chronic Disease Management Programmes Operate Across Care Settings?* Copenhagen: World Health Organization Europe.

Smith, J. (2010) *Giving GPs Budgets for Commissioning: What Needs to be Done?* London: The Nuffield Trust.

World Health Organization (2005) *Preventing Chronic Disease: A Vital Investment. WHO Global Report.* Geneva: WHO.

World Health Organization (n.d.) *Solving the Chronic Disease Problem.* www.who.int/chp/chronic_disease_report/media/Factsheet5.pdf (accessed 20 October 2010).

Defining and Exploring Clinical Skills and Simulation-based Education

Aldridge, M.

Studies have shown (Alinier et al., 2004; Lauder et al., 2008; Reilly and Spratt, 2007; Nursing and Midwifery Council (NMC), 2007) that the use of simulation in healthcare education curricula can have a positive impact upon learners' self-efficacy and self-confidence. Furthermore simulation allows learners to rehearse skills and enact scenarios that would be considered undesirable or unsafe to practise on real patients or clients for the first time (Broussard, 2008). Simulation can be a relatively resource-intensive learning and teaching methodology when compared with more traditional classroom-based didactic methods; however, there is an ever-increasing body of evidence which suggests simulation is not only valued by learners, but also is having a positive impact upon healthcare curricula and patient/client care enhancement.

FIDELITY OF SIMULATION

Fidelity is a widely discussed term when considering simulation and is described by Maran and Glavin (2003) in terms of engineering fidelity, in which the equipment reflects the true nature of the clinical setting, and psychological fidelity which refers to the authenticity the learner attributes to the setting, that is, their perceptions of its realism. Fidelity is an important consideration when designing and implementing simulation scenarios as it can impact upon the learning experience, both positively and negatively. Great care and effort could be placed in creating a technologically competent scenario using human patient simulators, however, if careful consideration has not been given to the fidelity of the actual scenario or expectations of the learners, then overall fidelity of the simulation may suffer.

NOMENCLATURE OF SIMULATION

The nomenclature and taxonomy of terms used within simulation are often debated, with some terms used interchangeably by different commentators. Very often the taxonomy of the fidelity of simulation is discussed in the terms of part-task training, low fidelity, medium fidelity and high fidelity simulation.

PART-TASK TRAINING

The term 'part-task devices' refers to equipment which allows the replication and rehearsal of a skill in isolation from the rest of an anatomical model. For example, intravenous therapy 'phantom arms' which allow venous cannulation and therapy, or 'phantom heads' which allow for dental training or the assessment of facial injuries.

These devices are useful as they are relatively cheap when compared with a full human patient simulator, have a reasonably good level of fidelity in replicating the real look and feel of the anatomical area in question, and provide skills rehearsal without risk to a real patient.

Roger Kneebone from Imperial College London has done some novel work on the use of 'hybrid models' which allow the adaptation of a part-task training device to be attached to a real person, thus allowing the rehearsal of both technical and non-technical skills simultaneously. This has been translated into a number of practice areas such as suturing, injection techniques, urinary catheterisation and female pelvic examination.

LOW FIDELITY SIMULATION

A low fidelity simulator may be just a static manikin or anatomical model, with no physiological signs or parameters, such as heart rate and blood pressure. However, this type of simulator may have some features such as an oral cavity or genitalia, which may allow the practice of some technical skills such as oral care or catheterisation. Another example may be the use of an orange to practise intramuscular injection techniques.

MEDIUM FIDELITY

Medium fidelity resources may include manikins which can replicate some physiological parameters or anatomical features. Examples of such devices are an electronic blood pressure training arm or a cannulation arm, which allow the learner to practise the skill with some degree of visual or tactile feedback.

HIGH FIDELITY SIMULATION

High fidelity resources include advanced physiological models and anatomical components which allow for the replication of medical and surgical conditions, often in the full context within which the situation would appear in the real-life setting. Examples may include advanced human patient simulators and advanced laparoscopic surgical trainers. Conversely, there may be no equipment used at all, and it may be the simulation of a communication scenario with a patient's/client's relative using a role player (Standardised Patient). Clearly the use of a human being to simulate a human interaction would give the highest degree of 'engineering fidelity', but the scenario and interaction would still require careful construction to ensure good 'psychological fidelity'.

TEACHING A CLINICAL SKILL

The teaching of clinical skills is sometimes – wrongly it must be stated – not given the same credence as other academic content in the curricula of undergraduate healthcare professionals. If we are to train competent, intelligent and enquiring healthcare professionals to fulfil a clinical role, then it is absolutely vital that they are equipped with both the academic and technical skills in order to carry out their role competently and confidently.

The system of 'master and apprentice' has often prevailed in the teaching of clinical skills in the past, though fortunately in recent years there has been a shift to recognise that learning will not necessarily happen just because a learner is exposed to a skill by a competent person in clinical practice, and indeed this is not considered a safe way to learn and rehearse the majority of clinical skills. A structured and curriculum-integrated approach should be taken to the teaching of clinical skills so that the theory and practice of a skill can be embedded in educational design and delivery.

Objective Structured Clinical Examinations (OSCEs) are now an established means of assessing a learner's ability to perform a clinical skill and are often included as a summative assessment somewhere in the majority of undergraduate healthcare curricula. OSCEs can be a reliable means of measuring a learner's understanding and performance of a clinical skill, though can be resource-intensive in the room, equipment and examiners required. Hence they need careful forethought and planning to run smoothly.

It is true that classroom-based didactic teaching requires a different skill set to that of the clinical skills laboratory setting, though this certainly should not infer any order of merit.

Peyton (1998) describes a widely used four-stage approach to teaching a skill:

1 Demonstration – Educator demonstrates the skill at normal speed without commentary
2 Deconstruction – The skill is broken down into its component parts while the educator gives commentary
3 Comprehension – The educator demonstrates the skill while the learner describes the steps
4 Performance – The learner demonstrates the skill while describing the steps.

The use of a detailed step-by-step lesson plan which explains each step in the skill and its rationale can be useful for both educator and learner to refer to, and will allow the learner to continue to rehearse or review the skill at a later time.

It is acknowledged (Hamilton, 2005; Oermann et al., 2010) that 'skills fade' or the degradation of retention of the ability to perform a clinical skill can occur as little as three months after the learning of a given skill. For this reason, repeated rehearsal and use of a skill would seem to be recommended in order to maintain competency. Repetition would appear to be vital in the teaching and learning of a skill as, in the educational setting, learners are frequently exposed to the teaching of a skill for as little as one hour, and then may not have the opportunity to revisit or rehearse that skill until they experience it on a 'real-life' patient in the clinical setting. Some educational delivery organisations have acknowledged the need to allow learners to practise clinical skills in their own time, in an area of low or remote supervision, thus allowing for repeated rehearsal and mastery of the psychomotor aspects of clinical skills.

There is a widespread belief that for skills- and simulation-based education to have its maximum impact it should be integrated into curricula, where possible, rather than being a stand-alone entity which may have limited value as a training event when delivered out of context to the curriculum as a whole.

PROBLEM-BASED LEARNING (PBL)

Problem-based learning offers the educator a means of providing simulation which requires very little resource. PBL is not appropriate for teaching technical skills; rather it allows the learner to exercise their cognitive, analytical and problem-solving skills by exploring a problem for themselves and determining appropriate solutions. Jones (2008: 213) lists one of the key benefits of PBL as: 'Increased motivation for the learner by focussing learning on real-life scenarios'.

Problem-based learning is often initiated by one or more 'trigger' sessions, which allow the educator to set the problem and feed-in information to learners about the complexity or nature of the problem, if necessary, at a later stage. Learners are then required to work alone or in groups to explore the problem and devise appropriate solutions. PBL can be used in both a formative and summative context, with learning objectives and assessment tasks set accordingly. As with other forms of simulation, the educator is required to act more as facilitator than teacher. Rather than imparting knowledge to the learner, the educator is required to manage the dynamics of the group, guide students in their reasoning and monitor the progress of learning. This type of facilitation deviates from the normal skill set of a didactic lecturer, and requires ground rules and training for the facilitator before expertise can be achieved.

PBL may also be combined with other modes of simulation, and some of the triggers used may be more hands-on simulations using role players (Standardised Patients) or human patient simulators.

THE USE OF ROLE-PLAY

Role-play can be described as a 'rehearsal for a future event', and when done in a controlled, structured and sensitive manner can be an immensely powerful learning tool. Role-play can be used to challenge and change attitudes of learners, involve a group in active learning, enhance critical thinking, and encourage synthesis and evaluation of information (Clark, 2008).

In the most basic form of role-play, it is possible to ask learners to take on the role of a particular patient or client and ask them to play this out with their colleagues. This may be suitable for short interactions, or to get learners to think outside of their own situations and ask them to consider how a patient or client would feel. However, downsides to this approach may be that learners feel uncomfortable with role-playing a particular role or do not have the prior experience to be able to put themselves in a given situation.

The use of professional role players, sometimes referred to as Standardised patients (SPs), is a concept that has been used in healthcare education, particularly in the undergraduate medical curriculum, for a number of years. SPs can be used in this setting to stage mock clinical assessments for history taking, clinical assessment and prescribing scenarios. They can also be used when sensitive situations need to be rehearsed, such as intimate examinations or the breaking of bad news. The use of SPs needs careful consideration and provision of appropriate training to function at this level, and in particular to give useful feedback to the learner. Suffice to say, a good actor does not necessarily make a good role player for healthcare education purposes.

It is essential that SPs are given some sort of preparation or training to fulfil their role, as they will often be required to re-tell comprehensive histories or symptoms which will convince the learner of a particular condition or situation. It is often desirable, and useful, for the SP to give feedback on the learner's performance following a scenario. For this reason, it is essential that SPs who are expected to give feedback are given some training on the use of feedback and debrief techniques. The feedback from a SP can be particularly rich and powerful as it gives the learner the perspective of a patient/client in a safe and low-risk environment.

EXPERT PATIENTS/CLIENTS/SERVICE USERS

The use of expert patients or service users can be helpful in relaying the perspective of the 'care receiver' to the 'care provider'. Personal experiences relayed by the service user of their experiences of healthcare can be rich and enlightening for the learner. However, careful consideration must be given to the psychological and emotional wellbeing of the service user. For instance, it would not be considered appropriate for a service user with mental health issues to play the role of a mental health service user in a simulation scenario, or a cancer patient to play the role of a person receiving the news about a diagnosis of cancer, due to the risk of distress this may cause to service users. The inclusion of service users as consultants in the design of curricula and the writing of simulation scenarios is becoming increasingly popular, as this can greatly increase the authenticity and fidelity of a scenario through the inclusion of first-hand experience. The inclusion of service users as stakeholders and consultants in education and care delivery should be welcomed, but requires careful management and organisation to ensure a coherent and safe approach to their involvement.

ELECTRONIC OR SCREEN-BASED SIMULATION

Electronic simulation programmes offer the advantage of the learner being able to learn away from the more formal setting of the clinical or skills laboratory. This method can allow for learning at the learner's own pace, with multiple attempts underpinned by the notion of self-directed learning. Depending upon the software platform and information technology (IT) infrastructure used, it could be possible for the student to access the resource through a web-based platform, allowing learners to use the resource wherever they have access to the Internet. One particular benefit of electronic simulations is that they can be done without the presence of an educator and can be used to free-up curriculum time by delivering educational content or preparing the student for practical face-to-face simulation. A downside of the use of screen-based simulation is the lack of fidelity and a disassociation a learner may feel between the simulation and the actual task; and this may be more the case with the generation that has grown up with video games and online resources that allow the user to be absorbed in an 'alternate reality'.

There is little evidence to suggest what is the best use of screen-based simulation, but it may be useful in the preparation of learners to exercise their cognitive abilities before practising the psychomotor domain in the skills lab or clinical practice setting.

HUMAN PATIENT SIMULATORS

A number of medium to high fidelity electronic human patient simulators exist and are available to educators, including: Laerdal Medical's 'SimMan'™ and 'SimBaby'™, METI's 'iSTAN'™ and Gaumard's 'HAL'™. These simulators are all designed to replicate the physiological observations, sounds, and in some cases, movements of a real human patient. The obvious advantage of this type of simulator is the high degree of fidelity offered to the user in their replication of a real patient, but without the risks of practising on live human patients. Such manikins can be programmed with pre-set scenarios which allow the facilitator to run a scenario with minimal set-up and intervention to the manikin's controls during the scenario. However, human patient simulators are also able to be used 'on the fly', whereby the facilitator can alter the manikin's vital signs and responses in real time, in response to the learner's actions or omissions as the scenario unfolds.

USE OF AUDIO VISUAL SYSTEMS

Various audio visual (AV) systems are available which will allow audio and video feeds to be recorded and/or broadcast simultaneously to another area. This can be particularly useful when large numbers of learners are involved, such as with undergraduate healthcare programmes, and can allow for large numbers of learners to participate in a scenario remotely. Such systems will also allow for 'event tagging' which allows the facilitator to highlight a particular incident during the recording of a scenario and then jump to that particular section later on during debrief while watching the video. The use of AV can be particularly useful to highlight behaviour or a performance which the learner was unaware of during the actual scenario.

If the use of AV systems is to be considered, it is highly advisable to involve an organisation's Information Technology (IT) department at the earliest opportunity so that they may assist with the consultation on the capabilities and limitations of an organisation's IT infrastructure before the purchase of any equipment. This will help to avoid issues of incompatibility of systems and equipment, and hopefully secure the buy-in of the IT department to maintain and support the equipment in the future. Ethical and legal consideration must also be given to the use, availability and storage of video images, in order to ensure that images are used appropriately and with the full consent of all parties involved.

GIVING FEEDBACK

It can certainly be argued that the debrief might be the most important part of any simulation exercise, as this is where the learner makes sense of what has happened during the simulation, and begins to explore and rationalise any learning that has taken place. Most importantly, the learner may have not yet noticed that a learning opportunity has taken place; therefore, it is essential that the facilitator is able to present such learning opportunities, with the assistance of AV playback perhaps, to the learner in a constructive and supportive manner.

DEBRIEF

Debrief should be:

- **Carried out as soon as practicable after the scenario ends** It is important to guide the debrief process to prevent candidates from deconstructing their own or their colleagues' performance without guidance
- **Structured** It is important that debrief has a structure to prevent it from becoming a rambling discussion or being hijacked by the agenda of a learner or their colleagues. A framework such as Kolb's (1984) experiential cycle of learning may be adapted to be used for simulated learning (see Figure 2.1)
- **Open and honest** Learners value an honest approach to debrief; 'sugar-coating' feedback or lying about a learner's performance in order to avoid hurting their feelings ultimately results in a poor learning experience. A less than honest debrief may also foster a false sense of security in a learner about their own performance
- **Constructive** It is important to be honest about a learner's feedback, but this must be done constructively and not become a character assassination of the learner. Inadequate and poor performance needs to be highlighted, but should be done in a manner which allows the candidate to frame this in a positive approach to improvement. Conversely, when a candidate displays good performance, this should be acknowledged and reflected upon so that lessons can be learnt for future practice.

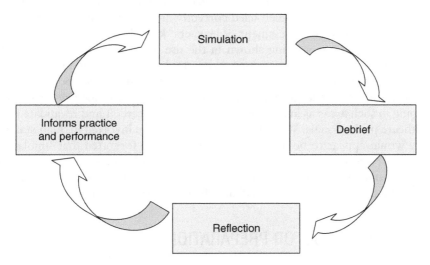

Figure 2.1

Adapted from Kolb's (1984) Cycle of Experiential Learning

- Debriefs must be diagnostic
- The organisation should create a supportive learning environment for debrief
- Team leaders and team members should be encouraged to be attentive of team work processes
- Team leaders should be educated on the art and science of leading team debriefs
- Ensure that team members feel comfortable during debriefs
- Focus on a few critical performance issues during the debrief process
- Describe specific teamwork interactions and processes that were involved in the team's performance
- Use objective indicators to support feedback
- Provide outcome feedback later and less frequently than process feedback
- Provide both individual and team-oriented feedback, but know when each is more appropriate
- Minimise the delay between task performance and feedback as much as possible
- Record conclusions made and goals set during the debrief to facilitate feedback in future debriefs

Figure 2.2

Salas et al., (2008) list a best evidence list of practices for successful debrief, reproduced here in Figure 2.2.

USING SIMULATION FOR ASSESSMENT

Simulation lends itself very well to formative assessment as it allows abundant opportunities to give detailed, directed and structured feedback on performance in a safe and supportive way. However, the use of simulation as a means of summative assessment is growing and, when used correctly and judiciously, can provide a reliable and robust means of assessment of learners' knowledge and performance.

An increasing interest is being shown in the use of simulation to accredit learners in 'high stakes' events, and has long been used in the testing and accreditation of professionals who are expected to perform Advanced Life Support (ALS) in the clinical environment. The growing use of simulation for competency assessment is developing in such areas as anaesthesia and surgery to accredit and revalidate the skills of healthcare professionals. While the assessment of skills involved in 'high-stakes' care delivery would appear to be desirable, it should not be forgotten that simulation has the potential to be a very powerful formative learning tool, and learners should be given every opportunity to rehearse skills in the simulation lab setting, accompanied by high-quality formative assessment and feedback, before exposure to summative assessment.

EDUCATOR/INSTRUCTOR PREPARATION

The creation and delivery of simulation sessions can at first appear a daunting undertaking to educators who have not used this method before. However, this need not be the case and careful preparation is often the key to allaying fears. If the expectation is for other educators to run a scenario they have not created then, at the very least, an instruction manual should be provided. This manual should provide:

- Learning aims and objectives
- Equipment and resources list
- A background to the simulation and context (scene-setter)
- A description of roles and cues to be used by Standardised Patients (if used)
- Prompts for learners and how to involve them in the simulation
- A description of settings for electronic manikins and human patient simulators, with instructions how to programme (if used)
- A step-by-step guide to how each scenario or step of the simulation unfolds
- A guide to debriefing the simulation, with key learning and discussion points
- A resource pack with any additional material, for example, relevant guidelines or notes and charts to be used.

McGaghie et al. (2010: 53) make the observation that 'Clinical experience is not a proxy for simulation instructor effectiveness.' This acknowledges that even the most accomplished and experienced clinicians, who intend to embark upon simulation-based educational delivery, require some sort of preparation in order for them to become effective teachers or instructors, and in order to capitalise upon their skills and experience in the classroom or skills and simulation lab. There appears to be a gap in the validation and accreditation of simulation instructors and facilitators. It has long been acknowledged in education that a Post Graduate Certificate in Education (PG Cert Ed) is an accepted and respected qualification to prepare some-one to teach in further and higher education, but no uniform comparable qualification exists in the preparation of simulation instructors/facilitators. There is a growing interest in the use of simulation for the accreditation and validation/revalidation of healthcare professionals and, if this is to be the case, there is then a strong argument for the creation of uniform programmes of preparation to ensure validity and reliability in this form of assessment and accreditation.

Familiarisation training, particularly when using electronic equipment and human patient simulators, is a valuable means of helping to allay fears and maximise the use of equipment. Facilitators may not feel comfortable using a particular piece of equipment simply because they are not familiar with its controls or functions.

Conversely, neophyte educators and instructors may also benefit from instruction in the pedagogical models of simulation, including: Lave and Wenger's (1990) situated cognition, Benner's (1984) 'novice to expert' model and Tanner's (2006) theory of clinical judgement. Reflective insights such as Kolb's model and Schon's (1983) 'Reflective Practitioner' have also been combined with pedagogical frameworks to create models for simulation.

It may be helpful to consider the component parts of healthcare education delivery as a cyclical model when designing simulation.

LEARNING OUTCOMES

Design of all learning and teaching experiences should begin with setting learning outcomes and using these as a 'peg' or framework upon which to 'hang' the rest of the content.

Assessment

The learning activities should be closely aligned with both the learning outcomes and the assessment methods (Biggs, 1999) to ensure that the learning has meaning, value and purpose.

Simulation activities

This may include part-task training, low and medium to high fidelity simulation opportunities.

Feedback

The inclusion of high-quality feedback in the form of: debriefs, informal feedback or more formal feedback, such as written feedback following an OSCE.

Opportunity for Skills Rehearsal

There should be an opportunity for learners to rehearse skills in their own time, with low or remote supervision, if deemed necessary, in order to combat skills fade and reinforce deeper learning.

Other Learning Activities

This may include Problem-based Learning (PBL), didactic delivery or screen-based electronic learning and can be used to deliver theoretical components, or support cognitive development.

Skills of the Educator/Facilitator

Do the educators or facilitators involved in the delivery and support of learning have the appropriate skills needed or is development required. How will you ensure parity, and validity and reliability of learning and teaching delivery among educators, i.e. core lesson plans or instructor manuals?

EVALUATING THE IMPACT OF SIMULATION

A commonly utilised framework for the evaluation of educational delivery upon pre-set outcomes is Kirkpatrick's (1979) Hierarchy of Evaluation (see Figure 2.4).

Kirkpatrick's model details the levels of evaluation from the reaction of the learner through to impact upon the learner's behaviour and its impact upon systems or processes.

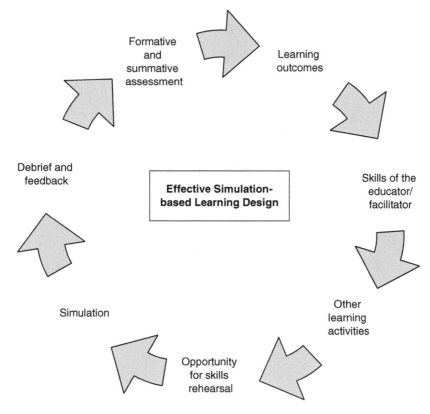

Figure 2.3

It is acknowledged that considerable difficulty exists in the measurement of outcomes of simulation-based educational delivery. It is relatively easy to measure a learner's self-efficacy pre- and post-simulation (Kirkpatrick levels one and two); however, it is more difficult to reliably measure the impact of simulation-based educational delivery on patient/client outcomes in the clinical area (Kirkpatrick levels three and four), often due to the multi-factorial nature of the clinical environment and patient/client situation. It could be said that it is difficult to measure the impact of any educational delivery upon patient/client outcome, though the stakes may be much higher for simulation as often significant resources and financial support are required to initiate and sustain simulation-based delivery, and some education and care providers may decide that sufficient evidence to support the cost–benefit ratio exists. Some authors (Phillips, 1996) have argued for the inclusion of a 'fifth level' to the Kirkpatrick model of evaluation, a 'Return on Investment' level, where the benefit to the organisation or outcome is measured in terms of the level of benefit it provides in relation to the resources invested. This may become increasingly important as the fiscal climate in healthcare and education demands a clearer cost–benefit ratio on an ever-decreasing availability of funding.

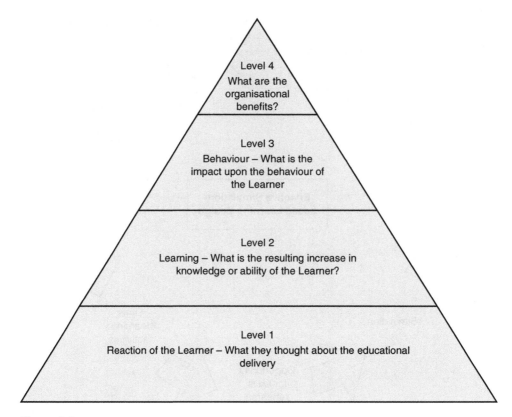

Figure 2.4

Source: Kirkpatrick (1979) Hierarchy of Evaluation

Clearly a more sustained and sophisticated effort is needed with the evaluation of simulation-based educational delivery to determine the best and most cost-effective ways of delivering benefit, both to the learners and to patients/clients.

CONCLUSION

Simulation can be an immensely powerful learning and teaching tool, but is in no way a 'magic bullet', which when fired in the direction of a course or curriculum, will instantly solve all issues. Simulation, like all other learning and teaching methodologies, must be used cautiously and judiciously when designing a learning experience. Consideration must be given to the learning styles and levels of the intended learners and the resources, time and expertise available to the educator.

This book may be particularly useful to both learner and educator, as it not only demonstrates a raft of clinical skills, procedures and a broad knowledge base, but also highlights how the learning and teaching methodologies involved in simulation can be used to enhance the learner experience.

USEFUL ORGANISATIONS AND NETWORKS FOR FURTHER INFORMATION

Association for Simulated Practice in Healthcare (ASpiH): http://www.aspih.org.uk/
Society in Europe for Simulation Applied to Medicine (SESAM): http://www.sesam-web.org/
Society for Simulation in Healthcare (SSiH): http://www.ssih.org

REFERENCES

Alinier, G., Hunt, W.B. and Gordon, R. (2004) *Nurse Education in Practice*, 4 (3): 200–7.

Benner, P. (1984) *From Novice to Expert: Excellence and Power in Clinical Nursing Practice.* Menlo Park: Addison-Wesley. pp. 13–34.

Biggs, J. (1999) *Teaching for Quality Learning at University.* Buckingham: SRHE and Open University Press.

Broussard, L. (2008) 'Simulation-based learning: how simulators help nurses improve clinical skills and preserve patient safety', *Nursing for Women's Health*, 12 (6): 521–4.

Clark, C. (2008) *Classroom Skills for Nurse Educators.* Boston, MA: Jones and Bartlett Publishers.

Hamilton, R. (2005) 'Nurses knowledge and skill retention following cardio pulmonary resuscitation training: a review of the literature', *Journal of Advanced Nursing*, 51 (3): 288–97.

Jones, W. (2008) 'Problem-based learning for simulation in healthcare', in R. Riley (ed.), *Manual of Simulation in Healthcare.* Oxford: Oxford University Press, pp. 213–226.

Kirkpatrick, D.L. (1979) 'Techniques for evaluating training programs', *Training and Development Journal*, 33 (6): 78–92.

Kolb, D.A. (1984) *Experiential Learning Experience as a Source of Learning and Development.* NJ: Prentice Hall.

Lauder, W., Holland, K., Roxburgh, M., Topping, K., Watson, R., Johnson, M. and Porter, M. (2008) 'Measuring competence, self-reported competence and self-efficacy in pre-registration students', *Nursing Standard*, 22 (20): 35–43.

Lave, J. and Wenger, E. (1990) *Situated Learning: Legitimate Peripheral Participation.* Cambridge: Cambridge University Press.

Maran, N.J. and Glavin, R.J. (2003) 'Background low- to high-fidelity simulation: a continuum of medical education', *Medical Education*, 37 (1): 22–8.

McGaghie, W., Issenberg, B., Petrusa, E. and Scalese, R. (2010) 'A critical review of simulation-based medical education research: 2003–2009', *Medical Education*, 44: 50–63.

Nursing and Midwifery Council (2007) Simulation and Practice Learning Project. Outcome of a Pilot Study to Test the Principles for Auditing Simulated Practice Learning Environments in the Pre-registration Nursing Programme.

Oermann, M., Kardong-Edgren, S., McColgan, J., Hurd, D., Haus, C., Snelson, C., Hallmark, B.F., Rogers, N., Kuerschner, D., Ha, Y., Tennant, M., Dowdy, S. and Lamar, J. (2010) 'Advantages and barriers to use of HeartCode BLS with voice advisory manikins for teaching nursing students', *International Journal of Nurse Education Scholarship*, 7 (1): Article 26.

Peyton, J. (1998) *Teaching and Learning in Medical Practice*. Rickmansworth: Manticore Europe Ltd.

Phillips, J. (1996) 'How much is the training worth?', *Training and Development*, 50 (4): 20–4.

Reilly, A. and Spratt, C. (2007) 'The perceptions of undergraduate student nurses of high-fidelity simulation-based learning: a case report from the University of Tasmania', *Nurse Education Today*, 27: 542–50.

Salas, E., Klein, C., King, H., Salisbury, M., Augenstein, J.S., Birnbach, D.J., Robinson, D.W. and Upshaw, C. (2008) 'Debriefing medical teams: 12 evidence-based best practices and tips', *Joint Commission Journal on Quality and Patient Safety*, 34: 518–27.

Schon, D. (1983) *The Reflective Practitioner: How Professionals Think in Action*. London: Temple Smith.

Tanner, C. (2006) 'The next transformation: clinical education', *Journal of Nursing Education*, 45: 99–100.

SECTION 3

Practice Learning

Making Sense of Clinical Placements

Price, B. and Harrington, A.

NMC Standards for Pre-registration Nursing Education

This chapter addresses the following competencies.

Domain 1: Professional values

1. All nurses must practise confidently according to *The Code: Professional standards of practice and behaviour for nurses and midwives* (Nursing and Midwifery Council, 2015) and within other recognised ethical and legal frameworks. They must be able to recognise and address ethical challenges relating to people's choices and decision-making about their care, and act within the law to help them and their families and carers find acceptable solutions.

8. All nurses must practise independently, recognising the limits of their competence and knowledge. They must reflect on these limits and seek advice from, or refer to, other professionals where necessary.

Domain 2: Communication and interpersonal skills

1. All nurses must build partnerships and therapeutic relationships through safe, effective and non-discriminatory communication. They must take account of individual differences, capabilities and needs.

2. All nurses must use a range of communication skills and technologies to support person centred care and enhance quality and safety. They must ensure people receive all the information they need in a language and manner that allows them to make informed choices and share decision making.

Chapter aims

After reading this chapter, you will be able to:

- summarise the nature of critical enquiry you need to engage in within clinical placements;
- detail what preparations will enable you to complete a successful clinical placement;
- discuss the part played by the student–mentor relationship in a satisfying and effective learning placement;

(Continued)

> *(Continued)*
>
> - explore the part placement learning plays in the service of more patient-centred care, that which respects the dignity and integrity of others;
> - understand the reflective and open approach you must use if feedback is to aid your studies.

Introduction

You are about to venture forth on your first clinical placement. What will it be like? What are the expectations associated with the placement? Will you make mistakes and can the staff tolerate that? Will there be someone there to support you? Irrespective of whether you are now a veteran of many such clinical placements or approaching your first one, the above questions and ones like them are likely to sound familiar. Learning within the clinical setting is exciting but potentially stressful, and it is helpful to understand why that is, and what you can do to counter the anxieties. Clinical placements are where you will have to develop your reflective reasoning abilities. There is little room for absolutist thinking here. The best care is usually nuanced and it is mediated by patient needs and circumstances prevailing. But you will need to think on your feet as you act and then protect some time too to look back and muse on what episodes of care teach you.

In this chapter, we explain what is different about learning in the clinical setting; what you should do when preparing to join a clinical placement; how you might work better with your mentor there; and what might be done to ensure that you do well in clinically based assessments. We pay particular attention to the skills of observation, questioning, interpreting and speculating as they apply here. Critical thinking and reflection have a particular resonance, because of the wealth and diversity of information you will encounter. These skills will play a central role in helping you to both enjoy and learn from the time you spend in the clinical area. We examine how an understanding of narratives and discourses here can help you to develop the sort of empathetic skills that are central to the work of nurses and our reputation with the public at large.

Why clinical learning is different

We asked Gina to make her key points about why clinical learning was different. Here are her observations:

> *What immediately impressed me was that this was a workplace and that learning had to be much more 'on the hoof'. That shouldn't have surprised me, but honestly, the impact of this change is bigger than you imagine. You forget how centre stage you are in the classroom, how much your learning means to the teaching staff. The clinical staff care, but learning has to fit in with the delivery of services. It's right and proper that the first concern of staff is the patients and the ways in which they experience care.*
>
> *The second thing I noted was that some of their teaching wasn't about the skill of nursing, it was about the etiquette of practice. I was being socialised into the team and being taught about where, how and*

when to ask questions. On reflection, that wasn't surprising, as clinical practice is a theatre, it's where the public witness what we do. The staff were anxious about whether I might damage their reputation.

The third thing I noticed was how difficult it was to obtain a rationale for what was being done. You suddenly realise how much trained staff carry in their heads. I felt like a child, always wanting someone to answer the question 'why?'! Clearly, the nurses couldn't always answer those questions, and especially in front of anxious patients. You had to wait for explanations.

The fourth thing I would say is that you face an information deluge. By that I mean you cannot stop to consider all the options, not as you might wish to anyway. It was the speed of thinking that blew me away and made me wonder whether I would ever learn here.

Gina offers an excellent summary of what makes learning in the clinical environment different. There is far less structure to the learning experience when compared to a well-run lecture. Students are required to seize the initiative and ask pertinent questions about what is happening. Clinical mentors are mindful not to overestimate students' confidence or ability, but they do not automatically remember to explain points that to them are second nature. Students might be supervised by a range of different people, each with their own way of supporting students (Hasson et al., 2013). There is, then, a need to choose when to ask the right questions, and Gina is right to infer that questions can seem impertinent if asked at the wrong moment. Learning the etiquette of enquiry is important, not only because it helps you to become part of the clinical team, but also because it enables the practitioners to carry on their work.

What Gina's account emphasises is the need to think in an inductive way: 'What is happening here?' Such inductive questions help you make sense of experiences, which is highlighted by Gina as she talks about the speed at which colleagues think. Clinical placements can overload you with information, and it is not necessarily presented in a coherent form (Cohen, 2013). You are confronted with a series of jigsaw pieces that you will need to fit together to create a picture. Some of those pieces you already have: they come from your past lectures, the theory of nursing and lessons on physiology, pharmacology and practical skills. Others will become available in placement – those connected with the patients, their diagnoses, their experiences (expressed as stories or narratives) and current treatments. This situation reflects the reality of practice for qualified staff as well. All must continue to make sense of events, and the challenges and needs that arise wherever patients are cared for.

Much of the higher-order reflective reasoning that you read about in Chapter 3 is associated with this sense-making ability. You have to reason contextually. That is, that you have to imagine and speculate about how patients feel, what they know or do not know and what they might most likely want from any care episode that you share. Some of this you learn from accumulating personal experience, what would assure or support you, but much more is learned from listening to what patients hope for. Notice what they say, how they say it and what they chose to focus upon. When they return again and again to the same topics, there are often unresolved concerns worrying them. As you work with patients, you will need to confront that patient's preferences, attitudes, beliefs and values may on occasion be different to yours. So you need to explore their preferences and hold in abeyance sometimes that which you believe to be best, what you would wish to happen to you. The highest level of reflective reasoning operates within the realms of beliefs and values, as well as dealing with the pragmatic circumstances of care delivery (see Table 3.2, pages 50–1).

Thus, to learn effectively in clinical placements you will need to be inquisitive, sensitive to others around you, analytical as you piece together disparate pieces of information, and diligent (Ailey et al., 2015). You will need to deal with a greater level of uncertainty than you may have been accustomed to previously, but you are also likely to be reassured as more experienced nurses describe their own learning curve. One nurse advised Gina:

> *One of the things you learn here is how to build up a picture of what is required by a patient. You learn to accept that you are always learning, always questioning your last ideas. You don't do that on your own; the team help you and expect you to share what you think as the process continues.*

To Gina's list of characteristics of clinical learning, we would add a fifth important point, that learning here is communal. Elsewhere, you may have learned in a more private and personal way. In the clinical arena, there is less scope for private deliberation. The team only learns how best to care for patients if its members share their incremental insights. This is ably illustrated in a number of processes that you will witness, including:

- 'teaching' rounds, where clinicians deliberate on care strategies;
- report handovers, where the team deliberate on the care delivered so far and where new priorities are identified, and on what the patient or relative is saying, which helps explain how they see the situation today and challenges head;
- case conferences, where individual patient care is discussed in some depth and next steps are contemplated.

Practice narratives and discourses

In Chapter 2, we introduced practice narratives – the accounts and discourses that are the focus for a great deal of placement-based learning. We now look at how these are connected to the development of empathy, which is vital in nursing (Atherton and Kyle, 2015). Look back to Table 3.2 (pages 50–1) and note just how much the development of empathy is high-order reflective thinking. To practise empathetically is to demonstrate, at a minimum, contextual level reflection and, at best, independent thinking. Empathetic thinking, understanding and respecting the concerns of others, in the face of your own personal values, demonstrates an extremely high level of professionalism. You will need to be supportive not only of patients and their relatives but also of professional colleagues. Because the clinical environment includes a great deal of uncertainty (what is wrong, what is happening, what might work best, what is safe?), it is especially important to listen hard to what is said and to try to ascertain what is meant. We can illustrate the importance of this by sharing a scenario with you. Imagine a situation where a patient (Mr Jones) has for some weeks suffered from a productive cough. The sputum produced now is bloodstained. The patient, a cigarette smoker in his mid-60s, has recently lost weight. His wife fusses around him while he waits for some tests to confirm the diagnosis.

Mr Jones remarks that the cough is a nuisance and he has lost sleep over it. His back aches and he struggles to inhale deeply. He admits that the cigarettes 'haven't helped'. Of course, the difficulty sleeping might simply be about waking as a result of the cough. But it could also be about anxiety and his fear of what the bloodstained sputum signifies. You will only understand the underlying narrative (his real concerns) if you piece together a collection of things that he has said. You will only learn about this patient's needs and worries if you enquire a little further: 'So how have you been feeling about this?'; 'We must wait for the tests, but I wondered how you prefer to deal with uncertainty?' Here and now, the questions have a particular function, to establish what worries the patient and demonstrate a proper concern for him as a person. You are unable to confirm what is wrong, nor can you pre-empt what senior colleagues will deduce or recommend. It must be enough to understand and, where appropriate, to report on the patient's concerns to others.

Mr Jones, though, is not the only person who is developing a narrative here – an explanatory story of what they think is happening. Mrs Jones and the doctor investigating his problem are also building narratives. Mrs Jones's fussing might simply express love and concern, but it could also relate to past knowledge of what bloodstained sputum could mean. Her father died of tuberculosis and he showed similar signs. You will only understand and support Mrs Jones if you are able to learn a little more about this narrative from what she hints at, and what she begins to signal through her care activities. 'My husband always tries to see the positive in everything, but I know that things don't always turn out so well,' she said, and this is an opportunity to gently enquire further.

The doctor's account of events can be described as scientific and investigative. He has begun a methodical series of investigations to help confirm one diagnosis and to exclude others. His accounts, especially before the patient, are measured and cautious; he does not wish to reach any premature conclusions. But if you have the opportunity to ask him, and talk about what he sees and hears, you might learn that his narrative is about the possibility of lung cancer. He may express all the same concerns that you feel. But you can only help manage communication and patient support before diagnosis (the discourse under way) if you hear what he says.

What is important, then, is that you listen with purpose and attend carefully. An understanding of the narratives will help you to ask appropriate questions at the appropriate times. You realise it is necessary to understand the doctor's deliberations before you venture into more extensive discussions with the patient. If you inadvertently lead the patient to premature conclusions, possibly the wrong ones, the work of the healthcare team may be more difficult. So you search for patterns of information. These tests (for cells within the sputum, a bronchoscopy and the detailed notes within the patient history taken) suggest the possibility of lung cancer. They alert you to the importance of understanding the patient's worries, without, at this stage, alarming him. The balance of listening and explaining is determined by your reading of the situation. Remember, just because your coping style is to have all the possible diagnoses spelled out from the outset, the patient's coping style might not be. Rational insight guides your thinking, how you see yourself as a person, but it might be very different for Mr Jones. Before a diagnosis is confirmed, listening and understanding are key. After a diagnosis, the emphasis may shift to explaining and reassuring. Where you clearly attend to the concerns of the patient or relative, listening hard and clarifying what worries them, you demonstrate compassion. It is not assumed that you will automatically and instantly resolve patients' difficulties, but you will establish a reputation for treating them as individuals.

Activity 6.1   *Reflection*

Look back to Gina's four points regarding what makes clinical learning different and draw upon any personal experience gained so far to illustrate these in action. For example, can you cite examples of where you think you were being socialised into the clinical team? Next, study the points above regarding accounts, narratives and discourses. Can you recall any clinical placement incidents that confirm the importance of attentive listening, identifying the narratives and the discourses that underpin what is said or done there?

Preparing for the placement

Preparation for your placement can significantly reduce the anxiety that you feel on your first days there. The more you can bring structure and order to the learning experience, working with your mentor, the more constructive the learning will seem. Table 6.1 suggests what might be done in advance of your placement.

Strategy	Benefit
Review the learning outcomes that have to be achieved during this placement and any assessment arrangements that apply.	You focus on what has to be achieved.
Research the work of the department, ward or practice by looking at any details on healthcare agency websites and by asking students who have had placements there before.	By asking some preliminary questions you won't have to ask quite so many on your placement. Interpreting what is going on will seem easier.
Revisit your portfolio to identify particular practice skills that you like wish to improve on, for example patient history taking.	You calmly discriminate what needs your attention. Explaining where you would particular guidance helps the mentor to plan their support.
Make personal contact with the clinical team, writing or emailing the nurse in charge.	You establish an immediate rapport if you show such personal organisation. You make your first argument: I am diligent and well prepared and I value this placement.
Try to establish in advance who your mentor will be.	Knowing this, and whether you might share the same shift, will increase your confidence and is one less thing to think about later. Successful mentors' reputations sometimes go before them.

Strategy	Benefit
Ascertain what sorts of illness, injury or other health challenge are confronted by patients in this clinical area. Make a note of what might worry them most and what might seem most sensitive as regards communication there. For example, if patients are suffering from cancer, the management of information pre-diagnosis is of great concern. Patients may be especially concerned about prognosis or the effects of treatment. Jot them down.	By anticipating what may be of greatest concern and require the most careful enquiry, you can demonstrate to your mentor at first interview that you have a due concern for both patients and colleagues. You start well.
Check when your first shift is and arrive in good time, correctly attired.	

Table 6.1: Getting ready for clinical placement study

Activity 6.2 — *Reflection*

Refer to your portfolio and check whether there are practice skills that you promised to focus on in your next clinical placement. If not, write in your portfolio three skills that you wish to develop further, adding a short rationale to each. Referring to these skills in your first conversation with your mentor will demonstrate your commitment and personal organisation. You are likely to get more from your mentor if you prove ready to seek information as well as to request it.

Observing, questioning, interpreting and speculating

Earlier, we referred to the importance of questioning within clinical placements and noted that questions often have to be reserved until later. It is worth anticipating what that will feel like, so that you can ask questions more strategically when you are in the placement. Figure 6.1 outlines what typically happens.

1. Observations and experience

Learning starts with experience, and clinical placements provide a constant stream of experience. It is difficult to decide what to focus on, what to consciously observe and what to think about and what to let slip by. You cannot observe everything, neither can you analyse the whole experience before you. It is normal that you process only a percentage of the information available. Your observation will become more purposeful if you do four things.

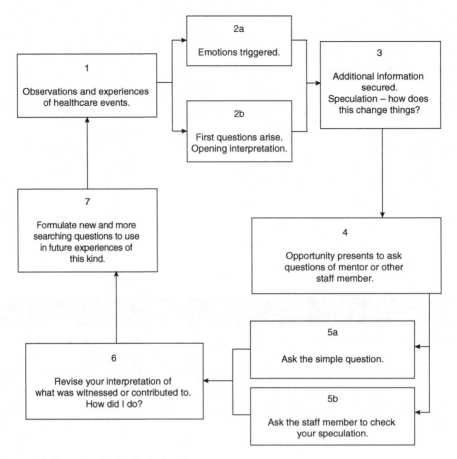

Figure 6.1: Learning in the clinical setting

- Note what seems most important to the patient. This usually means reading first and foremost what could entail risk for them and, after that, the events that may determine their experience of the quality of care. For example, the patient reports that they are allergic to penicillin. This needs noting down and reporting to others.

- Remember the learning outcomes that you need to achieve and the skills you wish to develop. It may help if you distil these into four or five priority interests. Lengthy lists of learning objectives are difficult to remember in the clinical area.

- Look for patterns of behaviour and sequences of events that seem to tell a story about the nature of nursing care. For example, patient admission to hospital is a storyline and one that involves several nursing skills.

- Relate those observations that interest you most to your previous teaching. Does this confirm what you learned in class? Does it modify your understanding or augment the information that you received there?

2. Questions and emotions

Two things happen simultaneously at this point. You will certainly experience a number of emotions associated with what you experience in practice. You might note excitement, admiration, encouragement, confusion, disappointment, cynicism or anxiety. Experience is 'in the raw' here and you are confronted with an insight into nursing that may or may not support your preconceptions. The goal here, then, is to acknowledge honest feelings but not to have them derail your learning. If you worry about, wonder at or even disapprove of something witnessed, allow for a moment that you might not yet have all the information to allow a full evaluation. Mentally save those feelings and formulate a question about them for later. For example, 'I noted that you were very firm with Mrs Brown's daughter this morning. She had been warned that her mother would be discharged this week. Does that approach work best?'

Alongside the first emotions will be some questions in your mind and some initial interpretations of what is going on. These will constitute your first ideas about what is happening. In the above example, you may have wondered, 'could the nurse have seemed more empathetic towards this relative?' or 'what is at stake here, rehabilitating the patient, freeing up a much needed bed or expecting of a relative a shared duty of care?' If you are alert, you will begin a tentative interpretation of the event: 'I suspect that this nurse has few choices. The need to attend to lots of patients places some limits on the extent to which she can personalise care.'

In the early stages of your course, you might notice a number of frustrations associated with nursing care and the organisation of services you meet during placement. Absolutist thinking (as summarised in Table 3.2 on pages 50–1) is characterised by set values and quick judgements. Something is right or it is wrong. It is good or it is bad. Care may be worthwhile or useless. It is extremely tempting to think in these ways while you are yet naive about the pragmatics of health care. While patient dignity and safety are critical in all circumstances, it is nonetheless true that care is often collectively managed in one institute or another. So priorities have to be identified and sometimes patients are supported with a holding care measure or explanation. It is well worth talking to your tutor about these emotional experiences, those relating to what you believe should happen and what seems more realistically to be the case. On the one extreme, you must of course be prepared to report malpractice but, on the other, you must manage a lifetime career in the profession where care prioritising is a skill in itself.

3. Additional information

It is likely that the stream of new information will continue coming your way. You need then to store your first thoughts and allow a new layer of thinking to develop. You are in the business of speculating. At this stage, there is no guarantee that your ideas are correct but speculation is still required. So, in our example, we may learn from the ward secretary that Mrs Brown's daughter works full time and that she has already lodged a request that her mother stay in hospital until the weekend. She was aware of the planned discharge but hoped to argue that she could support her mother better if she were available during her first days at home. The additional information probably demonstrates the daughter's concern to be an active carer but leaves doubts, too, about whether she trusts the other community care arrangements that have been put in place. You find yourself speculating further about systems and service, and about professional and lay care liaison. The nurse needs to work with a system but to advocate, where possible, the concerns of lay carers too.

4. Question opportunity

Opportunities to question arise later and in a variety of guises. It may be a one-to-one chat with the staff nurse during a coffee break or an opportunity for expression of concerns during a shift change. Nurses, doctors and others might invite questions after a ward round. The majority of such opportunities will be managed away from the audience of patients and lay carers. As we see below, there are two sorts of questions that could be asked but, irrespective of which you choose, it is necessary to demonstrate a respect for colleagues.

5. Asking your questions

Sometimes the complexity of things observed makes it difficult for you to pose anything other than a very simple question. 'What was problematic about the situation with Mrs Brown's daughter? I sensed a tension there.' Better by far, though, and with a trusted mentor, is to pose a question that invites them to check out your early speculation about events. 'I noticed the difficulty with Mrs Brown's daughter and started mulling over what that might be. I sensed that she wanted the discharge to work with her own arrangements; that she was really motivated to help with the transition home. But then again, she might have also been distrustful of the arrangements that we have made too. It isn't easy to find the compromise and we have to live with the discomforts of that … is that how you read it?'

6. Revising your interpretation

The answer you gain to your questions allow you to revise your interpretation of events. The interpretations may develop in several interesting ways and it is from this point that you can make some useful portfolio notes. For example, you might reinterpret your skill at reading practice episodes. Do I seem to be improving? You might re-examine your understanding of the mechanisms of hospital discharge and return to relevant policies.

7. Forming new questions

Having summed up your thoughts in the light of feedback, you are ready to observe practice with new insights. In our working example, you might consider in more detail how clinical colleagues work incrementally towards hospital discharge of a patient. How soon do they start preparing patients and carers for this? Do they always hear and understand what others are saying? In the end, are there economic and logistic tensions that inherently underlie such things?

Activity 6.3   *Critical thinking*

Study Figure 6.1 and consider whether the process of steps described there might assist you to be a more strategic learner in clinical practice. Why is it important to attend to what each step teaches us during the course of a placement?

Working with your mentor

Students are not always aware of what a mentor brings to clinical supervision, so let us start with that. Mentors are experienced practitioners, who are familiar with their area of care and its local policies and protocols, who have undertaken a short course in the principles of learning, teaching, support and assessment, and who are charged with guiding you during your clinical placement. They act as advocates of learning but they also have responsibilities to inculcate you into the team and its work (Price, 2012). They work assiduously to help you to master necessary skills and apply your knowledge, but retain responsibilities towards their patients, colleagues and the profession. Mentors share unique insights into practice wisdom – the practical ways of conducting nursing work (Price, 2013).

Successful work with your mentor will:

- help you to manage your anxieties about learning in the clinical setting;
- help you to develop an acceptable approach to enquiry in this setting;
- open doors to other expertise in the clinical setting (a mentor might introduce you to colleagues with specialist knowledge and highlight your enthusiasm as a student);
- give you thoughtful and honest weekly feedback, so that you are well prepared for assessments and end of placement reports;
- help you to address your own learning agenda as well as that required by the course.

Activity 6.4   *Communication*

Pause to think about how you can establish an early rapport with your mentor. Make a list of things that you could do and give a short rationale for each.

The working relationship with the mentor should be one of trust, purposeful work and mutual respect. Mentors expect students to arrive ready and eager to learn in the placement setting. Not all mentorship relationships are equally satisfying, however. It is possible that you will complete some placements where you feel that you did not achieve a good rapport with your mentor. You may still have passed the assessments and gained new insights, but it was much harder work than one where the mentor seemed enthusiastic, receptive to your enquiries and ready to gently challenge your assumptions. Search for, savour and celebrate the exceptional working relationships with mentors and acknowledge your own hard work with the less satisfying ones. Then ask some reflective questions. Could you have approached matters differently? Sometimes circumstances are against you both, for instance where staff sickness disrupts the continuity of your supervision.

As the working relationship develops, opportunities exist to deepen understanding between you and to begin to explore what it means to work as a nurse. Table 6.2 describes some of those opportunities and includes reflections from Gina on what does or does not seem to help.

Managing assessment

Reports are linked to clinical placements. They cover matters such as the development of your skills, the attitudes that you demonstrate in practice, your commitment to nursing care and the gains made in your knowledge there (Bennett and McGowan, 2014). In previous times,

Learning opportunity	Gina's notes
Evaluating your own performance, for example associated with a clinical procedure.	*It is a mentor's duty to give you honest feedback on your performance, but sometimes you get the best of this when you ask for their comments. You need to indicate that you're ready to hear constructive criticism.*
Sharing some doubts about your ability or understanding.	*You pay the mentor a compliment when you confide a doubt, and the best of them really appreciate this. I did so concerning my maths and the calculation of drugs. My reward was a series of mini teach-ins that boosted my confidence.*
Talking honestly about a team relationship that worries you.	*You won't get on with every member of the team. I think that it's good to try to resolve issues in the placement if possible. In one instance, the mentor was able to explain why a consultant seemed brusque and I felt reassured that I wasn't doing something wrong. Remember, though, you cannot expect the mentor to help you if the discussion remains completely secret. The mentor might need to represent your concerns elsewhere.*
Expressing some hopes and aspirations about future nursing work.	*I hadn't thought about this, but you're right! We need to keep dreaming. It helps us keep going when times seem tough. There were mentors who encouraged career aspirations.*
Securing recommended reading.	*Yes. I have even been loaned books and articles by a considerate mentor. But, remember, the library doesn't shut because you have gone on a placement.*
Celebrating your successes.	*The first person to congratulate me after I passed my first placement report was my mentor. It wasn't a perfect performance, but the mentor said to me, 'Do you realise how rare it is to achieve such warm comments from so many different professionals?'*
Appraising what needs to be done to meet objectives, to pass assessment.	*Definitely. The end report should never be a surprise and, if you're open with your mentor, you will get lots of warning about what needs improvement.*

Table 6.2: Mentorship-linked learning opportunities

assessment was formalised as a series of events and these events were linked to key tasks, such as the medicine round. Today, assessment is said to be 'continuous' and we need to consider the psychology of this process. The first thought that many students have is just how daunting it seems: 'During a clinical placement I am likely to make many mistakes, say a number of "wrong things" and inevitably alienate someone!'

There does need to be judgement on performance and this remains an issue for qualified nurses. Annual staff appraisals, complaints by patients and reviews by auditors are all part of professional life. Assessments that are made of your performance are mediated by an understanding of your stage of training and the learning objectives set; they comprise inputs from a number of staff members and take account of both the 'good days' and the 'bad days' of your time in placement (Price, 2012). The staff are interested in your learning and your response to guidance. While you might demonstrate shortfalls in skill or knowledge, these can often be compensated for by a willingness to receive instruction. What makes it very difficult for mentors and others to pass a student on their placement are shortfalls in skill and/or knowledge, combined with a refusal on the part of a student to change.

To help you to manage assessment, you need to be critical of your own performance and to search for gaps in your skill or knowledge. You will need to recognise misconceptions that are not serving you well. Such a personal audit of week-by-week performance will then enable you to seek the guidance of your mentor and, at the earliest possible point, to start correcting any short-falls and building on your successes. The following represent a series of week-by-week questions that might help you to evaluate your progress.

- What do you think was the best of my work this week and what still needed improvement? (Notice the search for both. It helps to receive praise as well as constructive criticism. Recognition of effort and attentiveness will stand you in good stead.)

- If you were to suggest one focus for improving my practice next week, what would it be and why? (Sometimes it is important to focus on a specific area and, if you can demonstrate a major improvement here, you will show your ability to reflect and develop.)

- How do you think it feels for a patient to be nursed by me? (This is a bold question, but patient experience is everything. An exploration of what represents quality there can be very useful.)

- I have written down three things that I think I am good at and three things where I think I could do better. Would you check whether I have made good choices? (Here you are using the 'check my speculation' approach, which is powerful because it shows your openness to change and reveals where you think there could be problems. At worst, the mentor will gently point out your misconceptions and you can refocus your efforts. At best, you are told honestly that you underestimate yourself in several regards.)

Assessments of your performance during a clinical placement will focus on your skills, the way in which you apply your knowledge and on your attitudes and values. The judgement of skills is usually well received by student nurses. They understand that the mentor, and others who contribute to the assessment of your performance, are themselves skilful. Receiving critique of your applied knowledge is also usually well received, at least, where the mentor and others have asked you pertinent questions. It seems fair to critique applied knowledge where you have had opportunity to reason aloud and to demonstrate why you think or proceed as you do. Assessment of attitudes and values however can sometimes be contentious and it often feels hurtful. This is because your attitudes and values are inferred by what you do, what you say and how you approach care and colleague relationships. When students struggle in this area of their learning, skilful coaching may need to follow in the next placement (Kelton, 2014).

Pause to reflect on how different the campus and the clinical environment are as places of learning. The robust enquiry and debate attitude that is so important on campus might seem aggressive in practice. Absolutist thinking, something that we have equated in Chapter 3 with lower levels of critical thinking and reflection, may in practice become stereotypes that have been applied to patients, relatives or professional colleagues. It is vital that nurses learn to explore and respect the concerns of others. If you label individuals ('she doesn't care about other patients, she thinks we're there just for her!') or groups ('trying to get doctors to listen to patients' worries is like drawing teeth'), this may indicate to assessors that you have not paused to consider all possible explanations of events encountered. Remember, transitional thinking is characterised by the consideration of different possibilities. We imagine that situations might not be as they first seem. This, at the absolute minimum, is what you should be aiming for.

One of the ways to demonstrate your positive attitudes and values relating to care is to seize opportunities to discuss care philosophy with your mentor and other senior staff. If you demonstrate an enquiring and respectful interest in what is being done, you are much more likely to convey favourable impressions to others. So, for example, you might reflect that a patient's struggles with alcohol addiction clearly make it harder for their liver to recover and that this distresses you too. You wish that patients could behave more rationally as regards using substances that carry risk. But then you acknowledge, too, that you have not really ever confronted addiction yourself. In expressing distress that the patient risks their health by excess intake of alcohol, you express compassion. In acknowledging that you do not understand addiction completely, you convey humility. Students are usually well evaluated where both compassion and humility are combined. To evaluate others as 'wrong', 'stupid', 'naive' is likely to convey an arrogant attitude.

Whatever you proclaim regarding your attitudes and values, though, remember that deeds speak at least as loud as words. Have you worn your uniform correctly? Have you been punctual? Have you shown a due degree of flexibility as regards what others need to do? Are you polite? How do others know that you are listening attentively to what they tell you, especially if it is something that seems unwelcome to you? The patterns of shifts that you complete as a student on placement are a foretaste of what work will feel like. For nurses to trust you as a colleague, they must feel sure that you will attend on time and work with interest in what the team is trying to achieve. Part of the contextual thinking that you learned about in Chapter 3 is associated with work and practice ethic, getting the job done in a professional, effective and efficient manner.

If you have received critical commentary as regards your attitudes or values, we recommend the following:

- Clarify what, specifically, the mentor is referring to, without challenging the assessment itself ('can you just help me with that point, I need to understand which colleagues I have seemed dismissive of?'). A mentor should be able to cite examples of where your behaviour has seemed problematic. Better still they can articulate the conditions under which this happened. Perhaps you seem more dismissive when under stress?

- Ask how the assessment was made. It is unusual for a mentor to reach this judgement by themselves, so ask whether they have conferred with others before reaching the judgement. A professional mentor will have conferred on such matters, realising how unsettling such an evaluation can seem. If the mentor relates how several different colleagues have noted the same problematic, it is highly unlikely this is simply a matter of opinion.

- Ask whether there was any counter behaviour which seemed especially good to offer a different impression of your attitudes and values. It is quite reasonable to ask for assurance that the balance of your behaviour has been considered too.

- Take the criticism away and think about it, before raising your concerns with the mentor or link tutor associated with the placement you are concluding. If you wish to raise points about these matters, write them down and acknowledge both strengths and weaknesses in your practice. Confronting mentors with the challenge 'you're all wrong' is unconvincing and suggests a lack of insight. It is better to explore a problem with the same humility and interest as you have been recommended here to approach the placement as a whole. A placement report may still record concerns about your attitudes and/or values, but these may be mediated too, by your willingness to explore behaviour afresh and identify some areas for improvement yourself.

Chapter summary

There are several key messages in this chapter. Learning in clinical practice is different, sometimes intense, and you must be an active and organised learner. You help shape the learning experience by working with your mentor and using the steps described in Figure 6.1. Learning in clinical practice need not seem chaotic, confusing or inaccessible if you think critically about what you encounter and continue to ask questions about what you experience and achieve. Part of your learning work is to accommodate the emotions that attend new experiences. Pausing to mull these over will enable you to ask sensible questions later on. It takes time to resolve emotional differences between what you think should be and what could be – between *my way* and *their way*.

A cycle of inquisitive questions will not by themselves guarantee learning. You will need to invite questions and challenges from others. You need to search out and carefully consider the feedback you receive. It can seem bruising to face a criticism about something you thought you were good at, but remember, contexts change and what worked in one place might not be appropriate in another. Nursing is a craft, an art and a profession that works within contexts. Mentors in particular do not give critical feedback lightly, mindful as they are of how vulnerable learners can feel. The feedback will usually be carefully considered and supported afterwards with a review of what might improve matters.

Forming a good working relationship with your mentor significantly increases your learning opportunities. In a trusting relationship there is scope to express doubts and to confront long-held fears. You may, like Gina, resolve a difficulty that liberates your learning throughout the rest of the course. Building a rapport with your mentor offers the prospect of a placement that not only teaches you a great deal, but provides you with a great deal of learning pleasure.

Further reading

Dinkin, S, Filner, B and Maxwell, L (2013) *The Exchange Strategy for Managing Conflict in Health Care.* Maidenhead: McGraw-Hill.

Clinical areas are sometimes places of conflict, those relating to values, resources and priorities. This text-book for conflict modellers and teachers offers much that can be used by students, mentors and link teachers as they review what seemed problematic as regards attitudes and values within the clinical arena.

Price, B (2012) Key principles in assessing students' practice-based learning. *Nursing Standard,* 26(49): 49–55.

This article explains just why the assessment of learning in practice is a sophisticated process and sets out principles for fair assessment of students.

Sharples, K (2011) *Successful Practice Learning for Nursing Students,* 2nd ed. Exeter: Learning Matters.

This volume provides further in-depth discussion of the process of learning within the clinical setting, and includes further material on working with a mentor and preparing for your placement.

Standing, M (2014) *Clinical Judgement and Decision Making for Nursing Students,* 2nd ed. London: Sage/ Learning Matters.

This valuable book leads the reader through different ways of thinking about clinical decision making and explains how an understanding of ethics, reflection and priorities can lead to better decision making.

Walsh, D (2014) *The Nurse Mentor's Handbook: Supporting students in clinical practice,* 2nd ed. Maidenhead: Open University Press/McGraw-Hill.

This book includes clear indication of excellent mentor practice but also that which is less helpful. If you encounter difficulties working with a mentor it may be helpful to draw on the principles of best practice as you explain your worries to the mentor or link tutor.

Useful websites

www.nmc-uk.org/code

Nursing and Midwifery Council: The Code: Professional standards of practice and behaviour for nurses and midwives (revised 2015).

Studying the revised and updated version of the NMC Code is vital. This document responds to many of the criticisms of nursing care that have arisen as healthcare provision struggles to meet the demands of an ageing and a growing population. While there seem a lot of nuanced responsibilities to address, many are clustered together around due concern for the patient, their information, collegiate working with others and sustaining live updates in your learning as a professional.

www.cetl.org.uk/learning/tutorials.html

City University/Barts and The London Hospital School of Medicine and Dentistry, Centre for Excellence in Teaching and Learning.

One of the best ways to develop and revise clinical skills is to watch video recordings of excellent practice. Although clinical skills may be practised slightly differently from institution to institution, it is still helpful to explore resources such as these to better analyse what may seem problematic while learning in practice.

 Additional Online Material
For examples of analytical essays and other useful material, please visit the companion website at **www.sagepub.co.uk/price_harrington**

Working with my Mentor

Sharples, K.

NMC Standards for Pre-registration Nursing Education

This chapter will address the following competencies:

Domain 1: Professional values

5. All nurses must fully understand the nurse's various roles, responsibilities and functions, and adapt their practice to meet the changing needs of people, groups, communities and populations.
8. All nurses must practice independently, recognising the limits of their competence and knowledge. They must reflect on these limits and seek advice from, or refer to, other professionals where necessary.

Domain 2: Communication and interpersonal skills

1. All nurses must build partnerships and therapeutic relationships through safe, effective and non-discriminatory communication. They must take account of individual differences, capabilities and needs.

Domain 4: Leadership, management and team working

3. All nurses must be self aware and recognise how their own values, principles and assumptions might affect their practice. They must maintain their own personal and professional development, learning from experience, through supervision, feedback, reflection and evaluation.

NMC Essential Skills Clusters

This chapter will address the following ESCs:

Cluster: Care, compassion and communication

7. People can trust the newly registered graduate nurse to protect and keep as confidential all information relating to them.

Cluster: Organisational aspects of care

10. People can trust the newly registered graduate nurse to deliver nursing interventions and evaluate their effectiveness against the agreed assessment and care plan.
19. People can trust the newly registered graduate nurse to work to prevent and resolve conflict and maintain a safe environment.

> ### Chapter aims
>
> The aim of this chapter is to clarify for you the role and responsibility of your mentor in terms of your practice learning experience and assessment of your competence.
>
> After reading this chapter you will be able to:
>
> - identify the accountability and responsibility of a mentor in relation to the NMC standards for mentorship;
> - understand the mentor's role in facilitating your learning;
> - explain the factors that mentors must consider when undertaking your assessment in practice and determining your competence;
> - recognise the requirements of the sign-off mentor role in relation to your practice support.

Introduction: learning in practice

In Chapter 2 we dealt with the primary expectations of you as an adult learner. However, it is also likely that you will have some expectations related to the type of support you should receive during your practice experience. Obviously, learning is a two-way process and, in many ways, your learning will be related to and directly affected by the quality of the learning environment in which you undertake your practice experience.

The aim of this chapter is to help you understand the nature of the practice environment, the role of your **mentor** and the factors related to practice support. We will start by considering your current understanding of how your role in practice fits with the mentor's role. Next, we will examine the standards the NMC expects of mentors and also the type and nature of support your university is required to provide for you in practice. The role of the mentor will then be looked at in some detail, as well as your mentor's accountability. The additional support mentors can access is then covered, and the chapter ends by looking at the role of sign-off mentors.

Expectations of practice learning

Before you can even begin to learn in practice, you will need to have a very clear understanding of what your role is in practice and how this fits with your mentor's role. The student grapevine is notorious for turning myths into what seem like facts, so for this reason it is very likely that you may have heard stories or information about practice learning that are untrue and therefore incorrect. If this is the case, your expectations of your mentor in relation to practice learning will also be incorrect. False assumptions tend to lead to false conclusions. If you attend your practice area with incorrect expectations and false assumptions, the consequence can be an unfulfilling and negative experience. The starting point, therefore, is to begin by looking at the real facts regarding practice experiences, and hopefully dispel once and for all some common myths along the way.

Activity 4.1	*Reflection*

No doubt you will have some beliefs about your practice experience and what you can expect from your mentor. Use the space below to finish the sentence about the expectations you have in relation to your mentor. List as many things as you can that you feel your mentor should provide for you during your practice experience.

I expect that, during my practice experience, my mentor will . . .

_____

_____

_____

_____

For the time being you don't have to do anything with this list. However, from time to time during this chapter you will be asked to come back and refer to your list to remind yourself of your expectations.

As this activity is for your own reflection, there is no outline answer at the end of the chapter.

NMC standards regarding practice support

The list you have made in Activity 4.1 will contain the support you expect to receive from your mentor. What you may not realise is that the NMC has already decided on the level of support mentors are required to provide for you. The NMC has set very clear guidelines regarding this support, and these guidelines are listed in the *Standards to Support Learning and Assessment in Practice* (NMC, 2008b). These standards were first published in August 2006 and came into force on 1 September 2007. In July 2008 the standards were updated, and these are the guidelines that your mentor is expected to follow. Importantly for you, one section of these NMC standards states that you must be provided with appropriate support from your university and also the practice area while you undertake practice experiences. Thus, while you may have your own personal expectations, it is actually the NMC that sets the criteria and expectations for your support and assessment during your learning experience.

University support

You will already be aware that practice learning equates to 50 per cent of your total training, so 2,300 hours of your pre-registration programme will be spent in practice. The NMC makes it very clear to your university that students should be supported in both academic and practice learning environments (NMC, 2010). In order to ensure that you are adequately supported in practice, your university is required to audit the practice learning environment to identify the number and nature of students that may be effectively supported (NMC, 2010). This is to ensure that the practice area where you undertake your experience is the right sort of environment for your learning needs. These reviews are carried out either annually or biannually and your university is required to submit these reviews to the NMC when quality inspections are undertaken. There are many factors that are taken into consideration when deciding on whether a practice area can and should support students during their practice experiences, and your university and the area will make these decisions in partnership.

The role of a mentor

Your day-to-day support during practice experiences is undertaken by a mentor. Therefore, it is very important that we now take the time to look at the specifics of a mentor's role and responsibility in far more detail, paying particular attention, in this section, to how your mentor should fulfil their role.

Who is a mentor?

Let us start by defining who a mentor is, based on the NMC definition:

> *An NMC mentor is a registrant who, following successful completion of an NMC approved mentor preparation programme, has achieved the knowledge, skills and competence required to meet the defined outcomes.*
> (NMC, 2008b, p19)

This means that your mentor must have completed and passed an NMC-approved mentorship course in order to gain a mentorship qualification. From this point on, a mentor is professionally bound to adhere to the *Standards to Support Learning and Assessment in Practice* (NMC, 2008b).

Mentor support

Once qualified, the NMC requires mentors to support learning in practice in a variety of different ways. These can be found in the above-mentioned standards (NMC, 2008b) and have been summarised as follows.

- To provide support and guidance to students when learning new skills or applying new knowledge.
- To act as a resource to the student to facilitate learning and professional growth.
- To directly manage a student's learning in practice to ensure public protection.
- To directly observe a student's practice, or use indirect observation where appropriate, in order to ensure that NMC-defined outcomes and competencies are met.

Therefore, as the name would suggest, your mentor's role according to the NMC standards is to support your learning and to support your assessment. We will look at each of these aspects in turn.

Support of learning in practice

The NMC makes it very clear that your mentor is required to coordinate appropriate learning experiences for you during your practice. This is quite a substantial role and involves both of you working together in partnership to ensure that you are provided with realistic and appropriate experiences. Both you and your mentor will need to have a very good understanding of your learning goals in order to choose and maximise the best range of learning experiences.

Activity 4.2   *Reflection*

Take the opportunity now to reflect on the list you created in Activity 4.1 regarding the expectations of your mentor.

- Are any of your expectations focused on the facilitation of your learning?
- Have you mentioned anything that suggests that your mentor will be supportive of your learning?
- Based on the notes you wrote for Activity 4.1, are your expectations accurate and realistic, regarding the *Standards to Support Learning and Assessment in Practice* (NMC, 2008b)?

As this activity is for your own reflection, there is no outline answer at the end of the chapter.

If your previous expectations of your mentor are very different from what you now understand about their role, take some time now to reflect on your answers to Activity 4.2. Consider why this may be the case. Have you relied on other students to advise you on the role of the mentor, or have you made assumptions based on your own feelings? Unless your source of information regarding the role of your mentor is from a reliable source, it is likely that the information you have will be incorrect. For factual information you could refer to either the *Standards to Support Learning and Assessment in Practice* (NMC, 2008b) or university information regarding your mentor's role. Very often this will be preprinted for you in your practice assessment document.

One of the more common misconceptions held by students is that your mentor will act as a teacher during your practice experience. If so, then take note that this is inaccurate and unrealistic. It is the type of myth that is assumed by students to be fact. However, the NMC makes it very clear that your mentor is not required to be your teacher. Some students find this a very difficult concept to grasp, and have an expectation that their mentor will allocate time to undertake 'teaching'. On the contrary, it is expected that, as an adult learner, you will be more inclined to engage with facilitation of learning experiences rather than relying on didactic teaching. We will have the opportunity to explore this further in Chapters 5 and 6, where we will discuss self-regulated learning and **experiential learning**. In the meantime, it is worth having a look at the accountability and responsibility of mentors within the *Standards to Support Learning and Assessment in Practice* (NMC, 2008b).

Accountability and responsibility of mentors

- *Organising and coordinating student learning activities in practice.*
- *Supervising students in learning situations and providing them with constructive feedback on their achievements.*
- *Setting and monitoring achievement of realistic learning objectives.*
- *Assessing total performance – including knowledge, skills, attitudes and behaviours.*
- *Providing evidence . . . of student achievement or lack of achievement.*
- *Liaising with others . . . to provide feedback, identify any concerns . . . and agree action as appropriate.*

(NMC, 2008b)

Facilitation of learning

It is very clear from this list that the NMC requires your mentor to be focused on the facilitation of your learning, rather than teaching. In fact, 'teaching' is not mentioned at all. This concept fits in very neatly with the notion of an adult learner that we dealt with in Chapter 2. Remember that, as an adult learner, it will be expected that you will take mutual responsibility for your learning, rather than expect it to be done for you. You will have an opportunity to discover ways in which you and your mentor will be engaging with learning experiences described in Chapter 6.

Case study

A mentor speaks about their experience of facilitating student learning.

I actually love mentoring students. It's really rewarding when you have a student who is just so keen to learn everything they can, and you're able to see them becoming more confident as they develop their skills with the patients. It keeps me on my toes as well, especially when we discuss a patient's care plan or treatment. The last student I mentored asked me something about a new procedure I'd never heard of and that was great; we ended up learning something new together.

That's why I find it so hard when a student just isn't interested in learning. Some students just seem to hang around, as if they're waiting for me to teach them something. We just have so many demands on our time now that it's not possible to do separate student teaching. If I could give students one piece of advice it would be to know what it is they want to learn and not expect their mentor to work it out for them. That's why my last student had such a great practice experience; he just knew what he wanted to do and it made all the difference. In the first week he asked if it would be OK for him to get his own patient caseload every day and for me to give him feedback at the end of the shift. I said to him 'brilliant – you go for it.' I really respected the fact that he came to me with what he wanted and didn't want to waste his time.

The main point is that you should attend your practice experience with a very clear understanding of what it is you would like to learn and the types of experiences you would like to engage with in order to fulfil your learning outcomes. The NMC then requires your mentor to coordinate and facilitate appropriate learning opportunities according to your individual needs.

Learning takes place through the feedback you receive. This means that the real driver of your learning is you. If you undertake a practice experience without a clear understanding of your learning objectives, your mentor will have nothing to facilitate. The risk is that, with no clear objectives, you may be seen as an extra pair of hands rather than as a learner (Johnson and Preston, 2001).

Case study

Elizabeth is undertaking a practice experience in a children's day-care unit. By the second week, several mentors have noticed that Elizabeth seems to lack motivation and, on a number of occasions, she has been late back from her lunch break. She has been offered opportunities to assess children coming into the unit and to help develop treatment plans, but she seems reluctant to involve herself and sits down regularly at the desk. When Elizabeth attends the daily planning meeting she does not ask to be allocated her own patients, and prefers to shadow her mentor throughout the shift. Elizabeth's mentor decides to question her regarding her motivation as she is clearly unhappy. Elizabeth explains that she is unhappy because she feels she is not learning anything on the practice experience.

Her mentor cannot understand this comment and reminds Elizabeth that she has been offered responsibility every day for her own patients: to help admit them into the unit, plan, manage and deliver care, and organise discharges throughout the day. 'Oh I know,' says Elizabeth, 'but I'm not learning – no one is teaching me anything.'

Support of assessment in practice

The second role that your mentor must fulfil during your practice experience is to assess your competence. When you arrive in practice you will already have been provided with a set of learning outcomes. It is your mentor's job to assess you on these outcomes during your practice experience. The learning opportunities that you engage with during your practice will provide your mentor with an opportunity to observe your practice and make a judgement about your competence. Your mentor is required by the NMC to assess your total performance in order to determine competence (NMC, 2008b).

Have a look at Figure 4.1. This represents the three aspects of competence that you will be assessed on for each of your learning outcomes. You will note that all aspects of competence are of equal importance, so your knowledge, for example, is no less or more important than your attitude or skill. It is very important that you understand that your competence will be judged not just on what you can do (skills; also known as psychomotor skills), but also on what you know (knowledge; also known as cognitive skills) and the way you act (attitude; also known as affective

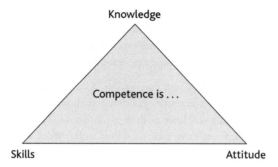

Figure 4.1: What is competence?

skills). Just as we discussed in Chapter 1, you must prove to your mentor that you are a 'knowledgeable doer'.

How competent do I need to be?

The competence level that you will be expected to meet has been set by the NMC and outlined within the *Standards for Pre-registration Nursing Education* (NMC, 2010). We first looked at the contents of this document when examining the design of your pre-registration curriculum in Chapter 1 and also in the Introduction to this book, so it may be worth referring back to these to refresh your memory. The fact is that all your learning outcomes will be related to the competency level expected of you at each stage of your nursing programme. It should come as no surprise, therefore, that both of these documents also contain information related to your practice assessment and the role of your mentor. In fact, no matter what stage of the programme you are on, your mentor will be required to assess you against NMC standards, whether this is to progress on your course or to qualify as a nurse.

Mentor accountability and responsibility

Your mentor is accountable and responsible to the NMC for all the assessment decisions they make about you. The following statement in the *Standards to Support Learning and Assessment in Practice* makes this very clear:

> *Mentors will have been prepared to assess student performance in practice and will be accountable for their decisions to pass, refer or fail a student.*
> (NMC, 2008b, p32)

The NMC provides each university with very clear guidelines on the structure and nature of your practice assessment. In turn, your university will provide you with a practice assessment document that is based on these guidelines. Your mentor is professionally obligated to follow this assessment process, as the NMC will hold them accountable for the assessment decision they make about you. The assessment process that your mentor is required to follow means that they must provide evidence of your achievement or lack of achievement during your practice experiences.

Feedback on competence

Typically, the evidence of your competence that your mentor must provide will be in the form of documented notes within your practice assessment document or practice portfolio, and verbal feedback throughout your practice learning experience. This is to ensure that you are kept well informed of your progress. However, the feedback is not just for your benefit. At the end of your practice experience, the NMC requires your mentor to document your progress within an 'ongoing achievement record'. This is to allow comments and feedback from your mentor to be passed on to your next practice area in order to enable your next mentor to make judgements on your progress (NMC, 2008b).

The feedback you receive, both written and verbal, is an essential aspect of your learning experience, so we will deal with this subject in far more depth later in this book. For the time being, it is important to understand that the provision of feedback is not optional, and the NMC requires your mentor to do this because it is fundamental to your learning. The documentation that your mentor provides within your assessment document also furnishes evidence that your assessment has been undertaken fairly, accurately and according to assessment guidelines. Without such documentation there is no proof that your assessment has met the required standards set by the NMC.

Additional practice support

If your mentor has concerns about your progress during a practice experience, the NMC requires them to seek help. Some students find this particular aspect of the mentor role very difficult to understand and this can lead to them feeling that they have been betrayed by their mentor. However, it is very important to understand that your mentor is not your friend, but your assessor. This is not to say that your mentor should not be friendly; but their role is functional and does not have the same features, functions or attributes as a friendship.

From the time your practice experience begins, your mentor is under significant pressure to make an accurate and objective assessment decision regarding your competence. They just cannot afford to get this wrong. If they require help in their mentoring role, the NMC makes it very clear that they should ask for it.

Scenario

Georgiana has just passed her driving test and decides to buy her first car. She spends a whole weekend looking through magazines, searching the internet and walking around car dealerships. By the end of the weekend she has some idea about the best car to buy, but decides to get some help from others before making her final decision. Her best friend, Dorothy, has driven a similar model before and is able to share her experiences. Her grandfather, Keith, is a retired mechanic and offers to go with Georgiana on another test drive. Her brother, Michael, has had recent experience buying his own car and gives her some advice regarding finance options. After making use of all this advice and support Georgiana is far more confident about her decision and becomes the proud owner of her first car.

The point of the above scenario is that, when important decisions need to be made, it is good practice to share your dilemma with someone else who can offer a different perspective and may be able to suggest alternatives that have not yet occurred to you. The value of someone else's opinion when faced with a difficult problem is often invaluable. The same can be said for mentors who are concerned about your progress.

Support for mentors

The support your mentor may access can include other mentors, practice teachers, practice facilitators or link tutors from your university. They may ask for assistance with the facilitation of your learning experiences, action planning or assessment strategies (NMC, 2008b). Your mentor can also ask that other members of the teaching and healthcare team contribute to your learning and assessment in practice; however, they alone will be accountable and responsible for undertaking the summative assessment of your learning outcomes (NMC, 2004). It is reasonable, therefore, to expect that a range of people may be involved with the facilitation of your learning, discussing your progress and assessment of your competence.

Activity 4.3   *Reflection*

Once again, reflect on the expectations you had of a mentor at the beginning of this chapter.

- Think about the expectations you had of your mentor in relation to assessment, learning and feedback.
- How have your expectations changed?

Based on what you have learned in this chapter, you may like to use the space below to summarise your new expectations.

By writing these down you will be able to clarify the expectations you have for your mentor and also what their expectations will be of you.

_____

_____

_____

_____

- Now that you have a clearer understanding of the role of your mentor during your practice experiences, how will this change your approach to your next practice event?
- How will you check that your expectations remain accurate, especially as you move through future practice experiences?

As this activity is for your own reflection, there is no outline answer at the end of the chapter.

Sign-off mentors

By now you should have a very clear understanding of your mentor's role in relation to your practice learning. However, in order to safeguard the health and well-being of the public, the NMC must be assured that, at the end of your programme, you have been assessed and signed off as capable of safe and effective practice (NMC, 2008). As a result, the NMC has decided that the mentor who makes the final decision regarding your competence for registration must fulfil additional criteria, and will be called a **sign-off mentor**.

How will the sign-off mentor role affect you?

It is very important to understand if and when the sign-off mentor role will affect you. If you began your pre-registration nurse training after 1 September 2007, you will need to be assessed on your final practice experience by a sign-off mentor. The practice period during which you will require a sign-off mentor will depend on the length of your course of study and the programme you are on, so you will be kept informed of this by your university. Needless to say, practice areas throughout the UK are constantly developing sign-off mentors in order to ensure that there are adequate mentors for all pre-registration nursing students on final practice experiences.

When you are being assessed during your final practice experience by a sign-off mentor, it is important to understand that the criteria for your assessment will not change, and neither will the criteria you will need to demonstrate in order to achieve competence. It will mean, however, that your mentor should be given protected time to provide feedback when undertaking their mentoring role, as this should be made possible under the mandatory time specification for sign-off mentors (Sharples, 2007b). Keep in mind, though, that, as the fundamental aspects of mentorship, facilitation of learning and assessment of competence remain unchanged, the sign-off mentor role will be an adjunct, rather than a change, to your final practice experience.

Chapter summary

The role of the mentor is very clearly defined within the *Standards to Support Learning and Assessment in Practice* (NMC, 2008b). In order to make the most of your learning opportunities during practice experiences, it is very important that you have clear and accurate expectations of your mentor. In this chapter we have looked at the role of the mentor in relation to both your learning experience and assessment of competence. The criterion for assessment of competence has been addressed, as has the professional obligation of a mentor in terms of written and verbal feedback. Additional support for mentors during a student's practice experience can promote objective assessment and, as such, is an NMC requirement to support learning and assessment.

Further reading

Elcock, K and Sharples, K (2011) *A Nurse's Survival Guide to Mentoring.* London: Elsevier.

This is a useful text that explains the role of the mentor and the mentoring process from the perspective of the mentor. It is a useful guide for understanding facilitation of learning from the perspective of the mentor.

Nursing and Midwifery Council (NMC) (2008) *Standards to Support Learning and Assessment in Practice: NMC standards for mentors, practice teachers and teachers.* London: NMC.

The NMC standard is quite a long document, but it does provide a comprehensive overview of the professional accountability and responsibility of mentors.

Useful websites

www.rcn.org.uk/search?queries_search_query=MENTOR+TOOLKIT

The RCN mentor toolkit can be downloaded from the RCN website. The toolkit offers tips and advice for mentors on facilitating your learning experiences during your practice learning experience.

The Reflective Practitioner

Howatson-Jones, L.

NMC Standards for Pre-registration Nursing Education

This chapter will address the following competencies:

Domain 1: Professional values
1. All nurses must practise confidently according to *The Code: Professional standards of practice and behaviour for nurses and midwives* (NMC, 2015), and within other recognised ethical and legal frameworks. They must be able to recognise and address ethical challenges relating to people's choices and decision-making about their care, and act within the law to help them and their families and carers find acceptable solutions.

Domain 3: Nursing practice and decision-making
4. All nurses must ascertain and respond to the physical, social and psychological needs of people, groups and communities. They must then plan, deliver and evaluate safe, competent, person-centred care in partnership with them, paying special attention to changing health needs during different life stages, including progressive illness and death, loss and bereavement.

NMC Essential Skills Clusters

This chapter will address the following ESCs:

Cluster: Care, compassion and communication
4. People can trust a newly qualified graduate nurse to engage with them and their family or carers within their cultural environments in an acceptant and anti-discriminatory manner free from harassment and exploitation.

By the first progression point:
3. Adopts a principled approach to care underpinned by the code (NMC, 2015).

5. People can trust the newly registered graduate nurse to engage with them in a warm, sensitive and compassionate way.

By the first progression point:
2. Takes into account people's physical and emotional responses when engaging with them.

continued . . .

Cluster: Organisational aspects of care

11. People can trust the newly registered graduate nurse to safeguard children and adults from vulnerable situations and support and protect them from harm.

By the first progression point:

2. Shares information with colleagues and seeks advice from appropriate sources where there is a concern or uncertainty.

Chapter aims

After reading this chapter you will be able to:

- define and identify morally active practice;
- recognise the fallibility of professional knowledge and developing practice;
- develop some strategies to manage knowledge deficits, near misses and mistakes in your practice;
- understand the need for reflecting on the complexity of decisions and consequences.

Example story

Debbie was in the third year of her nurse preparation programme. She was on a specialist placement with the **multiple sclerosis (MS)** nurse, Gill. Debbie was very interested in seeing how Gill worked with a caseload of her own patients, referring them to other health professionals as appropriate. This was a different view of nursing and one Debbie was not familiar with. She thought about what she had observed from seeing Gill working with a variety of patients with differing degrees of illness severity. Debbie was surprised that, at times, Gill acknowledged to patients that she was not sure what was causing their symptoms, but that working together they would be able to devise an appropriate plan. When Debbie asked about this, Gill highlighted that patients were the experts in terms of what they were experiencing and their coping strategies. MS is such a variable illness and more is being discovered about it all the time.

Gill related the example of **benign MS**, which had been assumed not to cause significant nerve damage, and therefore patients developed milder symptoms that were usually non-progressive, and often not taken seriously. However, recent research findings had suggested that far more significant damage was sustained within the first attack and could lie dormant until further illness and ageing activated damaged areas and potentially triggered progression. Gill used this example to explain to Debbie how important it was for the health practitioner to work with patients and constantly review their own assumptions of what was happening and what they were noticing. She also explained how it was most important to reflect on what they were doing and the aesthetics present within their practice.

Debbie realised that what she was experiencing was a reflective practitioner in action who was not afraid to acknowledge uncertainty, but who embraced it by reflecting with patients in a skilful way that drew out what concerned them the most, and worked imaginatively with possibilities. Supporting this was Gill's up-to-date knowledge base, caring and concern for her patients, and ability to interpret and review complex issues. Debbie realised Gill was the type of role model practitioner she aspired to emulate.

Introduction

The example above demonstrates the changing nature of knowledge, and why it's important to reflect on practice in order to be able to respond effectively to change and add to the evidence base. Gill is using her knowledge of MS, but also acknowledging the unique experience of the individual, to guide the advice and support she offers. The openness to work with change in practice is a fundamental feature of the reflective practitioner. If we accept that professionals are fallible and do not always get things right, we have a point from which to start to examine the effectiveness of practice by reflecting on what might be done differently. Equally, as clients are unique human beings, they may not always respond in expected ways and such issues need to be added to the body of evidence. Being open to change and reflecting on it allows the practitioner to learn and develop. It is important for students and novice practitioners to be able to acknowledge limitations within their knowledge as well as to take ownership of potential mistakes through reflection, in order to learn how to be accountable and reflective practitioners.

This chapter links with another book in the series, *Evidence-Based Practice in Nursing* (Ellis, 2013), and encourages students to cultivate a reflective approach to their daily experience, and integrate what they are learning with their practice. We begin by examining what morally active practice is.

Morally active practice

Morally active practice is defined as critically exercising decisions based on ethical and moral principles and being able to justify these (Brechin, 2000). The morally active practitioner recognises there are situations when some influences, such as evidence and policy, may take precedence over others, such as personal values and patient preference, which might not be reasonable. However, some ethical principles (such as equity) must be applied, so practitioners need to be aware of the consequences of their actions (Howatson-Jones, 2015a).

Our moral thinking is influenced by the cultures we have experienced and our own histories. Moral practice is informed by professional expectation and acceptability and concern for human beings with regard to the individual in that situation at that time.

It is important to be clear about our motives and the expected consequences of our actions, as well as being respectful about people's concerns and well-being. For example, you might have strong views about people smoking when they know it is harmful. This might translate into differing attitudes towards those presenting for treatment. Even if this is repressed, it may nevertheless still be active within your thinking and, therefore, reflecting. A more extreme example might be when faced with caring for someone who is an abuser, or a person who has inflicted some harm on themselves or others. Equity means that care should be provided immaterial of personal feelings or prejudices. However, reflecting on reactions to such situations is an important part of being able to deal with them, and of learning from the experience. Consider the following scenario and then answer the questions at the end.

Scenario: Greg's morally active care

Greg was a newly qualified nurse working on a busy medical ward during his preceptorship period. Many of the patients had complex health problems and Greg often left the ward feeling exhausted with the pace of work. Greg was particularly troubled about Gina, a 26-year-old patient with diabetes. Gina had been admitted to the ward twice in the last six weeks due to binge drinking which had affected her diabetes. Greg was strictly teetotal and found it difficult to understand why Gina was putting her health at risk in this way. Nevertheless, he set aside his background influences and tried to see things from Gina's perspective by conversing with her whenever he was undertaking nursing tasks. Greg's preceptor Ivan (who was aware he was teetotal) commented on this when they met to complete some of Greg's documentation.

Greg said he did sometimes feel uncomfortable around Gina because of her lifestyle, but through conversing with her he had developed some understanding of the reasons for her behaviour. He considered Gina's hospital admissions to be avoidable, but thought counselling might provide a route to help Gina develop coping strategies. Ivan explained what he had observed about Greg's communication style with Gina and asked Greg to write a reflective log about this situation to share at their next meeting. Ivan thought this might provide a useful start to a practice teaching session for student nurses.

Questions

- What is the NMC (2015) *Code* likely to have emphasised about this situation?
- What might Greg have focused upon in his reflection?
- What changes might Greg be thinking of making?

There are outline answers to these questions at the end of the chapter.

The morally active practitioner utilises a reflective rather than a judgemental approach to examine the outcomes of their actions and decisions. This is important when reflecting on actions that give rise to such hesitancy and for bringing everything into view. This also means using your whole self when thinking about practice, engaging feelings and being aware of intentions.

Activity 7.1   *Reflection*

Use the following questions to spend a little time reflecting on your own values and beliefs.

- What is important to you and why?
- What do you find difficult to bear and why?
- Have the answers to the above questions changed during the course of your life and, if so, why?
- How have these issues related to your practice?

There is an outline answer to this activity at the end of the chapter.

Professional experience is helpful for providing the skills necessary to develop, but it is also important to consider what we think about being a professional and how we interpret professionalism. For example, the fact that practitioners are able to negotiate freely the nursing environment, while patients and clients are not, puts you, as the practitioner, in a position of power. This needs to be considered with regard to how you approach your practice. Employing an authoritarian approach that places you firmly in control means that you may be cut off from learning other points of view, namely the patient's or others', which also inform practice and are useful for reflecting on. Equally, when you are just following instructions and policies you may appear to be professional, but if you omit reflection on your practice all you are doing is conforming to established behaviours. This is not the same as reflecting to ensure the effectiveness and development of practice. The following scenario will help illustrate this point.

Scenario: Pavlina's professional experience

Pavlina was in the second year of her nurse preparation programme working in a radiology department. Everything was new to her and she was worried about the radiation involved in imaging procedures. Her mentor, Gabriel, asked her to read the radiation protection guidelines in her first week. Pavlina reflected after reading these. She thought about how she had felt on her first day and wondered whether patients might have similar feelings and concerns about radiation. She considered the new knowledge she had gained from reading the guidelines and how this could inform her practice.

Pavlina observed a variety of diagnostic and interventional procedures, always making sure she was in position to reassure the patient. As the placement continued, she felt more confident to inform patients about what was happening. Gabriel involved her in setting up procedures and undertaking nursing observations. Pavlina learnt a lot during patient handovers to ward staff after interventional procedures as well. She was, however, concerned that these handovers took place in a public space.

Pavlina reflected with Gabriel at the end of her placement. Gabriel told her how impressed he was with the way she had translated her reading of the radiation protection guidelines into reassuring explanations for patients. He also praised Pavlina's hard work and dedication to her learning. Pavlina told continued . . . •••

Gabriel how much she had enjoyed the variety of learning opportunities available in this placement, but she also voiced concern about patient handovers occurring in public spaces and the way that the radiologists explained the procedure in the room and then asked the patient for their consent. Pavlina felt that this could be perceived as coercive as everyone was ready for the procedure to start. Gabriel reflected with Pavlina on these issues.

Questions

• What do you think Pavlina has learned about professionalism in this scenario?
• What else might she have learned about effective practice through reflection with Gabriel?
• What options for change might they have considered?

There are outline answers to these questions at the end of the chapter.

When reading the scenario above you may have immediately had some further questions and thoughts about what was happening. It is for this reason that Abrandt Dahlgren et al. (2004, p15) urge practitioners to reflect 'about' practice as well as 'on' or 'in' practice. Practical awareness can only develop when such reflective thinking occurs and helps nursing as a profession to move forward. Taking responsibility for your own learning through reflecting about the practice you are involved in is an important part of this process. We proceed now to examine how professionals might sometimes be fallible, and the role of reflection in managing this situation.

Practitioner fallibility and reflection

As a healthcare practitioner you are subjected to scrutiny from a number of directions. The NMC (2015) sets the standards for practice and regulates professional behaviour. The government legislates the policies with which healthcare is expected to comply (DH, 2009, 2015), and the Quality Assurance Agency (QAA, 2014) through the Code for Higher Education inspects the validity of teaching and assessment. With so many dictates for practice, it is hardly surprising that professionals sometimes get things wrong. Human error theory asserts that error is inevitable at some stage, but it is important to establish the reasons for flaws in judgement in order to address any problems (Armitage, 2009). Activity 7.2 will help you identify some issues that play a part in potential practitioner fallibility and, with this knowledge, to reflect on how you might avoid these issues.

Activity 7.2   *Critical thinking*

Think of a decision you made that you considered was a bad decision. Try to think of what might have interfered with your ability to make judgements and decisions by considering the following questions.

continued . . .

- What were the circumstances?
- What was the result?
- What do you think contributed to it being a bad decision?
- What did you do afterwards?
- What do you think about it now?

Using your previous answers, now consider how to make good decisions.

As this activity is based on your own experiences there are limited answers at the end of the chapter.

The decisions that professionals make usually require them to process information and use some level of intuition and cognitive aspects (Muir, 2004). Information processing refers to making sense of all the information available in terms of what is observed, heard, felt, smelt and read (Howatson-Jones, 2015b). Intuition refers to knowledge from experience being activated by the situation and inducing a response. Cognitive aspects relate to thinking about all of this and coming to a decision. During the process of deciding, choices are analysed in terms of their possible consequences, although sometimes we might not be wholly aware of this.

Social judgement theory suggests that the problem and informational cues link to the situation on which judgements are based. The ordering of importance of the cues determines how accurate the judgement is for the actual situation (Thompson and Dowding, 2002). Creativity through remaining flexible and responsive, using information-processing skills to understand emerging data, being clear about what you are aiming for, seeking guidance as appropriate, and knowing the extent and limits of your knowledge are all contributing factors to good decision making (Bohinc and Gradisar, 2003). By reading the following scenario and answering the question at the end you may be able to identify some issues relating to practitioner fallibility.

Scenario: Elsie's escapade

Rose was in the first year of her nurse preparation programme and working on a ward caring for older people. One of the patients, Elsie, was quite confused. On this particular day, Elsie was found to be missing from the ward and Rose joined her mentor, Mary, in searching for her. Elsie was eventually found by the main road sitting on the grass. Rose and Mary collected Elsie, putting her in a wheelchair and returning her to the ward. As Elsie was cold, Rose helped her into bed to warm up. Mary asked Rose to complete a set of observations of Elsie's temperature, pulse and blood pressure to check on her and for entering into the clinical incident form. Rose recorded these and noted that Elsie's temperature was a little low, but nothing else appeared abnormal. The doctor was also informed of Elsie's escapade, but as she appeared not to have suffered any effects he told Mary to just continue to keep an eye on her. The rest of the day was uneventful, although Elsie was restless and would call out every so often. She eventually went to sleep that night.

continued . . . •••

Rose was on the early shift the next morning. As soon as she came on duty she heard Elsie wailing. When she asked what the problem was, Mary told her that Elsie had woken up in pain. When the staff pulled her covers back they noticed that her left leg was externally rotated and shortened, a classic symptom of a fractured neck of femur. As Elsie had not been out of bed overnight (she had a urinary catheter) no one had noticed this deformity until Elsie woke in pain. Rose asked Mary how it was possible they had missed this.

Elderly bones are more fragile than younger ones because mineral density decreases with age, so even a relatively minor fall can lead to a fracture. Sometimes the muscles that encircle the hip go into rigid spasm and this can, temporarily, hold the hip in reasonable alignment. When the body relaxes, as happens in sleep, the muscles no longer maintain their hold and the deformity becomes apparent. It is unlikely that Elsie would have been able to walk on this leg, but as she returned to the ward by wheelchair this also was not obvious.

Questions

- What contributed to practitioner fallibility in this scenario?
- What should or could have been done differently?
- What might be learned from this situation?

There are outline answers to these questions at the end of the chapter.

While the registered practitioner is accountable for their actions and those they are supervising, nevertheless the student is responsible for ensuring that they notify changes or deficits that they have become aware of. Reflection itself may be fallible when based on inaccurate perceptions. Schön (1987) makes the point that, when understanding is not grounded in proper practice through careful examination and checking of knowing, inaccurate ideas about practice may perpetuate because the reflection itself is flawed. Reflecting with others, as discussed in Chapter 8, and analytical approaches, such as those explored in Chapter 11, can help to combat such fallibility. We proceed now to consider how to manage near misses and mistakes.

Managing deficits and near misses or mistakes

Fragmented inter-nurse and interprofessional relations can make managing deficits difficult and lead to lack of communication between groups, creating working processes conducive to errors.

Equally, anxiety can hold back progress as a person finds it difficult to make a decision for fear of getting it wrong and therefore relies on being told what to do by others. Without the confidence and knowledge to interrogate your practice, and that of others, poor practice and mistakes may be perpetuated as the following case study illustrates.

··

Case study: Rhian's experience of poor practice

Rhian was in the first year of her nurse preparation programme and on placement in a nursing home. She was keen to make a good impression and anxious to do things correctly. A number of the patients had continence problems but, during the day, through careful observation and trips to the toilet, the problem was dealt with in a dignified way. But Rhian had started to notice, when she was on an early shift, that some of these patients had many incontinence pads in their beds, and that these were making their skin sweat and were consequently sticking to them. When Rhian mentioned this to a care assistant, the care assistant told her not to interfere as this was the way things were done on the night shift. Rhian was not sure about this, but did not want to make a fuss and show herself up. She decided to talk to her mentor about it. When Rhian spoke to her mentor, Dave, he said that it was different at night because the patients could not get up as easily to go to the toilet and so the pads were necessary. Rhian relayed that there seemed to be rather a lot of them and they were always very wet. Dave said he would look into it. However, the weeks passed and Rhian did not see any change. She feared that perhaps she had been wrong to think this was not right. Rhian left her placement with the view that using a lot of incontinence pads at night was normal practice. Three months later, when reflecting after another placement, she realised that what she had seen in the first placement was wrong. She decided that if she was concerned about practice again she would challenge the practice and talk to her mentor, but she would also follow it up with a link tutor.

··

The case study has illustrated that, without reflection, practice and developing knowledge can be difficult. The Francis (2013) report highlighted the consequences of not following through concerns about practice. Completing Activity 7.3 explores what you might do in a similar situation.

Activity 7.3   *Critical thinking*

You are encouraged to look at your university and placement institution policies for raising concerns and then think about the following questions:

1. What factors would help you recognise a concern?
2. What might be barriers to raising a concern and how might you overcome them?
3. How could you consolidate your learning from thinking about these processes?

As this activity is based on your experiences there is a limited answer at the end of the chapter.

Like Rhian in the scenario you might have recognised a concern by the uneasy feelings you were left with. However, this is not concrete evidence and reflecting on the situation and analysing surrounding factors can help you to develop a better evidence base. Developing reflective ability is a transitional process that involves struggle, accepting the challenge, making connections, learning to reflect more deeply and sharing with others (Glaze, 2001). Rhian could have progressed from her struggle with understanding, to accepting the challenge to find out more herself. This might, in turn, have helped her to make different connections and learn.

Mistakes can be a form of 'shocking' learning through their abrupt nature, which also triggers an emotional response. Mistakes can leave you feeling emotionally upset and lower your self-esteem, unless this can be resolved and transformed into learning through reflection, supporting the regaining of self-confidence. This involves considering how action, or inaction, contributed to the error, thinking about the nature of the mistake and what it means to be a professional. Responses can be categorised as emotional, cognitive and behavioural as follows.

Emotional response

Stage 1   shock and grief;
Stage 2   defending by projecting blame.

Cognitive response

Stage 3   scrutinising own practice, acknowledging shortcomings;
Stage 4   scrutinising others' contributing practice to identify influences;
Stage 5   identifying the core problem and accepting responsibility;
Stage 6   checking core knowledge.

Behavioural response

Stage 7   reflecting on the error and behaviour and how to change;
Stage 8   identifying how to improve and regaining confidence.

It is important that emotional responses to difficult practice and errors are acknowledged at the start if you are to move forward to thinking about what needs to change. Consider the following scenario.

Scenario: Roger's near miss

Roger was in the final year of his nurse preparation programme working on a day surgery unit. The pace of work at the start of the day was quite fast with many people arriving and needing to be prepared for theatre. Often premedications were required and had to be given quickly. One of the patients had been ready for a while and Roger and his mentor, Sarah, went to get his premedication. They checked that it was prescribed and properly signed for by the doctor, that it had not already been given and that the patient had no allergies to the drug. They then checked the patient's name band and told him that the tablets they were giving him were his premedication. The patient's wife said that he had just been given tablets in the last ten minutes. When Sarah checked with the other staff she discovered that the patient had been given his premed previously, but that the nurse had forgotten to sign for it because she was busy. Due to the alertness of the patient's wife this had been a near miss. Sarah and Roger completed a critical incident form for this episode. Sarah reported the incident to the unit manager.

continued . . . . •

During a lull later in the morning Sarah and Roger reflected on this incident. Both of them felt quite shocked at the near miss and angry with the nurse who had not signed after giving the premedication. Roger discussed the merits of, in future, asking patients whether they had been given the premedication already, but Sarah pointed out that patients may not know what type of drugs they had already been given. Sarah highlighted that all professionals are fallible and that the only guard against this was to follow drug administration guidelines and to learn from such incidents. What they had both learned was to ensure that documentation was completed in a timely manner and to delegate tasks that might prevent this. Subsequent to this event Roger was very careful when checking any medication and also with his documentation.

Questions

- What learning did Roger take from this incident?
- In what ways are emotional, cognitive and behavioural responses evident in Sarah's and Roger's reflections?
- If you are an experienced practitioner how might the unit manager have dealt with this incident and the nurses involved?

There are outline answers to these questions at the end of the chapter.

Regaining confidence after a mistake requires support as well as guidance in order to be ready to identify where the point of departure from effective decision making comes. We proceed now to consider reflecting on complex decisions in order to assist with the process of identifying effectiveness.

Reflecting on complex decisions

Practice experiences incorporate perceptions and interpretations that require acting upon. The decisions you make may be simple or more complex and you are likely to use a variety of data to come to a judgement. Subjective experience relates to how a person experiences their situation and is usually relayed through description. Interpretation may add further subjective data. An objective view, on the other hand, makes use of data that can be measured and recorded, such as vital signs and test results, for example (Hinchliff et al., 2008). Within clinical practice, both of these views are relevant and indeed valuable.

However, what reflection adds is the possibility of looking for threads of meaning running through, and possibly between, the information produced from these approaches. An analysis of these threads of meaning as additional processes helps to surface issues such as power, including lack of it, and how these relate to the situation. It is meaning that is not immediately obvious, and reflection endeavours to draw this out in order to read situations more accurately and to develop decision making and the effectiveness of practice. Reading the following scenario and thinking about the question at the end will help you understand these processes further.

Scenario: Natasha's experience of under-age consent

Natasha was near the end of the second year of her nurse preparation programme and working in an A&E unit. On this particular shift, a 15-year-old girl – Milly – was brought in with a suspected **ectopic pregnancy**. *Milly was adamant that she did not want her mother to know. Natasha recorded her vital signs of temperature, pulse, respirations and blood pressure, and noted that Milly's pulse was elevated and her blood pressure was lower than was normal. Natasha started to develop a conversation with Milly while she undertook this task and asked her why she did not want her mother to know. Milly told Natasha that she had always felt judged by her mother, who did not like her friends and was always criticising her. The situation she was now in would only confirm to her mother that she was 'no good', as she put it. Milly said that she mostly stayed with friends and spent as little time at home as possible. Milly asked Natasha to call her boyfriend instead.*

After Milly had had an ultrasound scan, the obstetrician and gynaecological surgeon decided that she would need an operation. Milly was still adamant that she did not want her mother to know. Her boyfriend was not interested in staying, saying he would 'see her later'. Milly went to theatre without her mother knowing and with Natasha accompanying her. Natasha, only four years older, wondered about the sense of this.

Questions

- What are the main issues within this scenario?
- Who holds the power and in what way?
- What alternatives were available to the practitioners concerned?

There are outline answers to these questions at the end of the chapter.

Chapter summary

This chapter has illustrated a number of ways in which you can develop as a reflective practitioner. Through the examples and scenarios it has highlighted the importance of learning from mistakes and has offered opportunities for learning to challenge poor practice in ourselves and others. By continuing to use reflection to inform your practice, you will be able to recognise the connections between events and how you are progressing, as well as how issues such as power are important to the outcome of decisions. The importance of sharing your reflections in order to develop practice within the wider profession of nursing is continued in the next chapter, which looks at forms of reflecting with others.

Activities and scenarios: Brief outline answers

Activity 7.1: Reflection (page 99)

You might have identified that honesty from yourself and others is important to you so that both parties can be relied upon. You may also have found that doing as you would be done by is a central value for you, so that you can be trusted. You might have identified that you find unkindness difficult to bear because of the emotional distress it can cause. It is likely you will have become aware of changes in your values and beliefs when entering your teenage years and when embarking on working life, and possibly parenthood. You might even have noticed changes when entering your nursing preparation programme. Changes are likely to have resulted from greater life experience modifying and altering value responses, although core values will still remain. These issues might relate to your practice, in how you think about team working, and your attitudes to both patients and colleagues.

Activity 7.2: Critical thinking (pages 100–1)

Contributing factors that may have interfered with your decision making may range from tiredness and overwork to stress and lack of knowledge. Equally, not taking account of the patient's view may mean that interventions fail due to non-compliance. What you are likely to have tried to do afterwards was to rectify the decision and rebuild your self-esteem. However, without reflecting on the quality of the decision and the surrounding circumstances, not all the deficits might have been noticed, therefore only a partial solution may have been put in place. Equally, if you have not reflected you are likely to view the decision with shame and think less of yourself. Reflection helps to rebuild self-confidence and self-esteem. When considering how to make good decisions in response to your reflection you might have identified that including others in the decision-making processes could help to overcome stress and lack of knowledge. Equally, including the patient could also help to avoid non-compliance. You might also have thought about reflecting with others to develop your own decision-making skills.

Activity 7.3 Critical thinking (page 103)

Some factors that might alert you to a concern are:

* Feeling uneasy.
* Seeing actions and behaviours that are contrary to what you have been taught.
* Seeing negative effects for patients.
* Inaction by staff to address issues.

Barriers to raising concerns might be:

* Not wanting to draw attention to yourself.
* Not being sure of your evidence.
* Not knowing the process to follow.
* Any others that apply to you.

Consolidating your learning might involve reflecting on your experience and writing a critically reflective account (there is more information on this in Chapter 11).

Scenario: Greg's morally active care (page 98)

The *Code* makes it clear that practitioners should avoid making assumptions and treat people with dignity, respect and compassion. Greg might have focused in his reflection on how his background was influencing his prejudices about Gina. Depending on his knowledge base, he is likely to have explored potential reasons for her drinking and methods for coping with her diabetes and how this fits with information he has gained from talking with Gina. Greg might be thinking of how he developed his attitude and communication style to be more compassionate. It is likely that Greg would want to discuss ideas about this with Ivan at their next meeting to help them develop a practice learning session for student nurses.

Scenario: Pavlina's professional experience (pages 99–100)

Pavlina is likely to have learned that different professionals can work as a team. Pavlina may have also learned the importance of policy and guidelines for informing practice. Her reflection with Gabriel has highlighted that she has been able to translate her new knowledge into explanations to reassure patients. During their reflection they might have considered the power relations between different staff groups. They might also have considered whether consent was really informed when taken just before the procedure. The potential options for change that they might have thought about could include the following.

* The radiologists could visit inpatients on wards and give explanations and take consent in the morning. The attendance of outpatients for procedural appointments can be assumed to imply consent.

- Patient handover to ward staff could be undertaken in an office with checking of nursing observations and wound sites undertaken in the procedure room.

Pavlina is likely to have left this placement with a view of professionalism that is open to feedback and which is constantly reflecting to develop practice.

Scenario: Elsie's escapade (pages 101–2)

What contributed to practitioner fallibility in this scenario was an assumption that Elsie's behaviour was related solely to her confusion and that, because her observation recordings were normal, there was nothing wrong. It is easy to dismiss possible cues in such a way. What should have been done was to view the situation critically. This would have entailed asking a number of questions, such as:

- What might have contributed to Elsie ending up sitting on the grass?
- Is the way she is calling different from usual?
- What is triggering it?
- What calms her?

A thorough physical examination should have been carried out as there were no witnesses to how Elsie ended up sitting on the grass. If the nurses had started this, they might have been alerted by more signs, which would have given more impetus for the doctor to come and see Elsie as well. Other measurements, such as recording oxygen saturation and blood sugar, might also have been appropriate to ascertain why she had ended up sitting. It is likely the practitioners will have been asked to review and justify their decision-making processes via a clinical incident form and through statements. Students involved in such situations would also be required to provide written testaments.

What might be learned from this situation is the need for assertive decision making and leadership that reads the cues from situations accurately. Continual assessment that focuses on the patient and does not rely only on monitoring devices is an essential part of this process. Recognising that a situation has changed comes partly from experience, but also through being open-minded and having a reflective attitude that does not accept circumstances at face value.

Scenario: Roger's near miss (pages 104–5)

Roger learned that even with the correct checking procedures mistakes can still happen when there are earlier errors in a chain of events. He has learned to ensure that in his own practice documentation is carried out in a timely manner and the importance of delegation when the unit is busy.

Sarah and Roger both responded emotionally to the near miss with shock and anger aimed at the colleague who had put them in this position by not documenting correctly. When thinking about the incident they considered their options, although Roger's suggestion of asking the patient was viewed as not entirely reliable. It could also send a message that staff might not be competent. Sarah and Roger's behavioural responses were to ensure their own timely documentation when involved in drug administration.

The unit manager is likely to have undertaken some group reflection with the staff concerned, then developed this into refresher training for all staff to ensure such an incident did not happen again. By taking an educative rather than a punitive approach, the unit manager is much more likely to enable the staff concerned to regain self-esteem and develop good practice. Another option would be to introduce regular clinical supervision opportunities for staff to help them reflect on their own practice in a confidential environment.

Scenario: Natasha's experience of under-age consent (page 106)

The main issues are Milly's clinical condition, which is serious, her request for confidentiality, Milly's age, her mental competence and the rights of her mother. The clinical danger comes from the possibility of ectopic rupture, which can cause major haemorrhage and which requires operating on. Since the passing of the Gillick Law in 1985, doctors are required to assess the competency of under-age minors to make their own decisions. If Milly is deemed to be competent and fully understands the facts of the situation, she may be deemed competent by the doctor to make the decision and to be able to give consent. However, it is for the doctor to decide whether the complexity of the decision is in keeping with the limits of consent and Milly's competence.